A Companion to Early Twentieth-Century Britain

A COMPANION TO EARLY TWENTIETH-CENTURY BRITAIN

Edited by

Chris Wrigley

THE
HISTORICAL
ASSOCIATION

THE VOICE FOR HISTORY

Blackwell
Publishing

© 2003 by Blackwell Publishers Ltd
a Blackwell Publishing company

350 Main Street, Malden, MA 02148-5018, USA
108 Cowley Road, Oxford OX4 1JF, UK
550 Swanston Street, Carlton South, Melbourne, Victoria 3053, Australia
Kurfürstendamm 57, 10707 Berlin, Germany

The right of Chris Wrigley to be identified as the Author of the Editorial Material in this Work has
been asserted in accordance with the UK Copyright, Designs, and Patents Act 1988.

First published 2003 by Blackwell Publishers Ltd

Library of Congress Cataloging-in-Publication Data

A companion to early twentieth-century Britain / edited by Chris Wrigley.
    p. cm. – (Blackwell companions to British history; 3)
  Includes bibliographical references and index.
  ISBN 0-631-21790-8 (alk. paper)
    1. Great Britain – Civilization – 20th century – Handbooks, manuals, etc. 2. Great Britain –
History – Edward VII, 1901–1910 – Handbooks, manuals, etc. 3. Great Britain – History – George V,
1910–1936 – Handbooks, manuals, etc. 4. Great Britain – History – Edward VIII, 1936 –
Handbooks, manuals, etc. 5. Great Britain – History – George VI, 1936–1952 – Handbooks, manuals,
etc. 6. World War, 1914–1918 – Great Britain – Handbooks, manuals, etc. I. Wrigley,
Chris. II. Series.

DA566 C66 2003
941.082–dc21

                                                                                    2002071222

A catalogue record for this title is available from the British Library.

Set in 10 on 12 pt Galliard
by SNP Best-set Typesetter Ltd., Hong Kong
Printed and bound in the United Kingdom
by TJ International, Padstow, Cornwall

For further information on
Blackwell Publishing, visit our website:
http://www.blackwellpublishing.com

BLACKWELL COMPANIONS TO BRITISH HISTORY
Published in association with The Historical Association

This series provides sophisticated and authoritative overviews of the scholarship that has shaped our current understanding of British history. Each volume comprises up to forty concise essays written by individual scholars within their area of specialization. The aim of each contribution is to synthesize the current state of scholarship from a variety of historical perspectives and to provide a statement on where the field is heading. The essays are written in a clear, provocative and lively manner, designed for an international audience of scholars, students and general readers.

The *Blackwell Companions to British History* is a cornerstone of Blackwell's overarching Companions to History series, covering European, American and World history.

Published

A Companion to Britain in the Later Middle Ages
Edited by S. H. Rigby

A Companion to Stuart Britain
Edited by Barry Coward

A Companion to Eighteenth-Century Britain
Edited by H. T. Dickinson

A Companion to Early Twentieth-Century Britain
Edited by Chris Wrigley

In preparation

A Companion to Roman Britain
Edited by Malcolm Todd

A Companion to Britain in the Early Middle Ages
Edited by Pauline Stafford

A Companion to Tudor Britain
Edited by Robert Tittler and Norman Jones

A Companion to Nineteenth-Century Britain
Edited by Chris Williams

A Companion to Contemporary Britain
Edited by Paul Addison and Harriet Jones

The Historical Association is the voice for history. Since 1906 it has been bringing together people who share an interest in, and love for, the past. It aims to further the study of teaching of history at all levels. Membership is open to everyone: teacher and student, amateur and professional. Membership offers a range of journals, activities and other benefits. Full details are available from The Historical Association, 59a Kennington Park Road, London SE11 4JH, enquiry@history.org.uk, www.history.org.uk.

Contents

Contributors

Peter J. Beck is Professor of International History at Kingston University. His publications include *The Falkland Islands as an International Problem* (1988) and *Scoring for Britain: International Football and International Politics, 1900–1939* (1999). He edited *British Documents on Foreign Affairs. Reports and Papers from the Foreign Office Confidential Prints: The League of Nations 1918–1941*, vols 1–10 (1992–5). Currently he is a member of the editorial board of the *International Journal of the History of Sport*.

G. H. Bennett was formerly a Senior Lecturer at the University of Plymouth. He is the author of *British Foreign Policy during the Curzon Period, 1919–24* (Basingstoke, 1995).

Michael Bentley is Professor of Modern History at the University of St Andrews. He is well known as a commentator on late Victorian and early twentieth-century politics in Britain, and is the author of *Politics Without Democracy 1815–1914* (1984), *The Climax of Liberal Politics, 1868–1918* (1987) and a recent study of Conservative politics, *Lord Salisbury's World* (2001).

Sue Bowden is a Professor in the Department of Economics at the University of Sheffield.

D. George Boyce holds a personal chair in the Department of Politics and International Relations in the University of Wales, Swansea. He is a Fellow of the Royal Historical Society. His previous books include *Nationalism in Ireland* (3rd edition, 1995), *The Irish Question and British Politics* (1988) and *Decolonisation and the British Empire* (1999).

K. D. Brown is Professor of Economic and Social History and Pro-Vice-Chancellor at Queen's University, Belfast. He has written widely on aspects of modern British labour, religious and business history, and is currently working on a company history of the Liverpool toy manufacturer Meccano. He has also published on the economic history of modern Japan, following visits there under the auspices of the Japan Society for the Promotion of Science (1994) and then as a visiting professor at Osaka City University (1996). His most recent book, a comparative economic and social history of Britain and Japan since 1900, was published in 1998.

Steven Cherry is a Senior Lecturer in the Wellcome Unit for the History of Medicine and the School of History at the University of East Anglia, Norwich. His publications include *Medical Services and the Hospitals in Britain 1860–1939* (1996), *Mental Health Care in Modern England* (2003) and articles in *Medical History*, *Social History of Medicine*, *Population Studies* and *Economic History Review*.

Christine Collette was Reader in Class and Gender Studies at Edge Hill College of

Higher Education and is now a freelance historian. She serves on the executive committee of the Society for the Study of Labour History and is a member of the editorial panel of *Labour History Review*. Her previous books include (with Stephen Bird) *Jews, Labour and the Left* (2000), *The International Faith* (1998) and (with Fiona Montgomery) *The European Women's History Reader* (2002).

Peter Dewey is Reader in Economic History at Royal Holloway, University of London. He is Secretary of the British Agricultural History Society. He has published two books, *British Agriculture in the First World War* (1989) and *War and Progress: Britain 1914–1945* (1997).

Colin Divall is Head of the Institute of Railway Studies, a joint initiative of the National Railway Museum and the University of York, and Professor of Railway Studies at the University of York. He works on the history of transport, the history of technology in the nineteenth and twentieth centuries, and the public histories of both of these fields. His most recent books are (with Andrew Scott) *Making Histories in Transport Museums* (2001) and (with Sean F. Johnston) *Scaling Up: The Institution of Chemical Engineers and the Rise of a New Profession* (2000).

Clive Emsley is Professor of History at the Open University, where he also directs a research group on the comparative history of policing. He is currently serving a second term as President of the International Association for the History of Crime and Criminal Justice. He was awarded a D.Litt. by the Open University in 2000. His books include *Crime and Society in England 1750–1900* (2nd edition, 1996), *The English Police: A Political and Social History* (2nd edition, 1996) and *Gendarmes and the State in Nineteenth-century Europe* (1999).

David French holds a chair in History at University College London. He was educated at the University of York and King's College London. His most recent book, *Raising Churchill's Army: The British Army and the War against Germany, 1919–1945* (2000), was awarded

the Templer Medal of the Society for Army Historical Research. He is currently writing a book that will explore the significance of the regimental system in the development of the British army and its place in British society between 1870 and 2000.

I. G. C. Hutchison is Reader in History at the University of Stirling. A former editor of the *Scottish Historical Review*, he has published *A Political History of Scotland, 1832–1924: Parties, Elections, Issues* (1986), *The University and the State: The Case of Aberdeen, 1860–1963* (1992) and *Scottish Politics in the Twentieth Century* (2001).

Anne J. Kershen is Director of the Centre for the Study of Migration and a Senior Research Fellow in the Department of Politics at Queen Mary University of London. She is a Fellow of the Royal Society of Arts, a member of the Council of the Jewish Historical Society of England and Chair of the Social History and Exhibitions Committee of the Jewish Museum, London. She has published widely, her publications including *Food in the Migrant Experience* (2002), *Language, Labour and Migration* (2000), *A Question of Identity* (1998), *London the Promised Land? The Migrant Experience in a Capital City* (1997) and *Uniting the Tailors* (1995).

M. W. Kirby is Head of the Department of Economics and Professor of Economic History in the Management School at Lancaster University. He has published extensively in the areas of business history and the history of industrial policy. His history of operational research was due to be published in 2002.

Martin Kitchen is Professor of History at Simon Fraser University, Canada. Among his many books are *The British Empire and Commonwealth: A Short History*, and *British Policy Towards the Soviet Union, 1939–1945*. His most recent publications are *The German Offensives of 1918* and *Kaspar Hauser*.

Keith Laybourn is Professor of History at the University of Huddersfield. He also edits the *Annual Bulletin of Historical Literature* for the Historical Association. His recent books include *Women, Unemployment and*

Employment 1900–1951 (2002), *A Century of Labour* (2000), *Modern Britain since 1906* (1999), *Under the Red Flag* (with Dylan Murphy) (1999), *The Rise of Social Policy in Britain 1881–1951* (1997), *Britain on the Breadline* (1990, 1997), *British Social Policy and the Evolution of the Welfare State* (1995), *The Guild of Help and the Changing Face of Edwardian Philanthropy: The Guild of Help, Voluntary Work and the State, 1904–1919* (1994) and *The General Strike* (1993).

Roy Lowe is Research Professor of Education at the University of Wales, Swansea, and has recently stepped down as President of the History of Education Society of Great Britain. He was for six years Head of the Education Department at Swansea and was awarded an OBE for services to education in the 2002 New Year's Honours List. He has written and edited several books on aspects of the history of education in Britain and the United States, most notably *Education in the Post-war Years* (1988) and *Schooling and Social Change, 1964–1990* (1997). He is currently working on a major book on the eugenics movement and education during the twentieth century.

Arthur J. McIvor is a Reader in History at the University of Strathclyde. He is co-director of the Scottish Oral History Centre and a previous editor of the journal *Scottish Labour History*. He is currently working on the history of occupational health and safety in the UK since 1850. His previous books include *Organised Capital: Employers' Associations and Industrial Relations in Northern England, 1880–1939* (1996), *A History of Work in Britain, 1880–1950* (2001) and (with R. Johnston) *Lethal Work: A History of the Asbestos Tragedy in Scotland* (2000).

Helen Meller is Professor of Urban History at the University of Nottingham. Her research interests are in the social and cultural history of cities and she has published widely on themes related to leisure, women, citizenship, planning and philanthropy. Her previous books include *Leisure and the Changing City 1870–1914* (1976), and a major reassessment of the life and work of a maverick in the town planning movement, *Patrick Geddes: Social Evolutionist and City Planner* (1990). Current work is on the historical context of planning history and recent books include *Towns, Plans and Society in Modern Britain* (1997) and *European Cities 1890–1930s: History, Culture and the Built Environment* (2001). She was on the founding committee of the Women's History Network, and is a member of the executive committee of the International Planning History Society, the Urban History Group and the council of the Royal Historical Society.

R. Merfyn Jones is Professor of Welsh History and Pro-Vice-Chancellor at the University of Wales, Bangor. He was editor of *Llafur: The Journal of Welsh Labour History* (1980–95). Previous books include *The North Wales Quarrymen, 1872–1922* (1982) and *Cymru 2000: Hanes Cymru yn yr Ugeinfed Ganrif* (*History of Wales in the Twentieth Century*) (1999). He is a regular broadcaster on modern and contemporary Welsh history.

Stuart Mews is Reader in Religious Studies at the University of Gloucestershire, having previously taught the history and sociology of religion at Lancaster University. He is a former president of the Ecclesiastical History Society and editor of *Religion*. He has edited several books, including *Religion and National Identity, Modern Religious Rebels* and *Religion in Politics: A World View*. He held a Leverhulme Fellowship at the time of writing his contribution to this volume.

R. C. Michie has been a Professor at Durham University since 1974. Throughout his academic career he has specialized in financial history, especially the history of stock exchanges in Britain and abroad, on which he has written extensively. He has also researched and written on the history of the City of London over the years. More recently, he has embarked on a project to investigate the history of the London foreign exchange market in the twentieth century.

Andrew Miles is Senior Lecturer in Modern Social History at the University of

Birmingham. His previous publications include *Building European Society* (1993, edited with David Vincent), *The Remaking of the British Working Class* (1994, with Mike Savage), *Social Mobility in Nineteenth- and Early Twentieth-century England* (1999) and *HISCO – Historical International Standard Classification of Occupations* (2002, with Marco van Leeuwen and Ineke Maas). He is currently working on the history of the modern career.

Tim Rooth is Reader in Economic History at the University of Portsmouth. His main research interests have focused on British external economic policy in the twentieth century, and his previous publications include *British Protectionism and the International Economy: Overseas Commercial Policy in the 1930s* (1993). He is President of the British Association for Canadian Studies (2002–4).

G. R. Searle is Emeritus Professor in the School of History at the University of East Anglia, Norwich. His previous publications include *The Quest for National Efficiency* (1971), *Corruption in Modern British Politics, 1895–1930* (1987), *Entrepreneurial Politics in Mid-Victorian Britain* (1993), *Country Before Party, 1885–1987* (1995), *Morality and the Market in Victorian Britain* (1998) and *The Liberal Party: Triumph and Disintegration, 1886–1929* (1992; new edition, 2000).

Anthony Sutcliffe is a Special Professor in the Department of History, University of Nottingham. Recent publications in the history of the cinema and the history of art reflect his enthusiasm for visual and experiential approaches to reality. His latest book is *An Economic and Social History of Western Europe since 1945* (1996). He is currently working on an architectural history of London since Roman times.

Duncan Tanner teaches in the Department of History and Welsh History, University of Wales, Bangor, where he is Professor of History. Previous books include *Political Change and the Labour Party 1900–1918* (1990). He has contributed to and co-edited two overviews of the Labour party's history: *Labour's First Century* (2000) –

a thematic history of the party across Britain – and *The Labour Party in Wales 1900–2000* (2000). He is currently completing a book on Labour politics between the wars, and is about to start a major project on the history of Welsh devolution.

B. R. (Tom) Tomlinson is Dean of Arts and Humanities and Professor of Economic History at the School of Oriental and African Studies, University of London. He has written extensively on the economic, political, environmental and business history of the British Empire, and in particular on the history of colonial India, notably in *The Indian National Congress and the Raj, 1929–1942* (1976), *The Political Economy of the Raj, 1914–1947* (1979), *The Economy of Modern India, 1870–1960* (1993) and in *The Oxford History of the British Empire*, vols 3 and 4 (1999). His current research is on the development of Scottish business networks in Asia in the late eighteenth and early nineteenth centuries.

John K. Walton is Professor of Social History and Director of Research in History at the University of Central Lancashire, Preston. He was previously Professor of Modern Social History at the University of Lancaster. His research interests include the social and cultural history of seaside resorts and tourism, especially in Britain and Spain; regional history and regional identities with special reference to tourism and sport, especially in Lancashire, the English Lake District and the Basque country; and the social history of insanity in Victorian England. He held an Elcano Fellowship at the University of the Basque Country in 1995 to work on the social history of San Sebastián. Recent publications include *Blackpool* (1998), *The British Seaside: Holidays and Resorts in the Twentieth Century* (2000) and (edited, with F. J. Caspistegui) *Guerras danzadas: Futbol e identidades locales y regionales en Europa* (2001).

Philip Williamson is Professor of History at the University of Durham and a British Academy Research Reader, 2002–4. He is author of *National Crisis and National Government: British Politics, the Economy and Empire 1926–1932* (1992) and *Stanley*

Baldwin: Conservative Leadership and National Values (1999), and editor of *The Modernization of Conservative Politics: The Diaries and Letters of William Bridgeman* (1988).

Chris Wrigley is Head of the School of History and Art History and Professor of Modern British History at Nottingham University. He has been President of the Historical Association (1996–9), a Vice-President of the Royal Historical Society and Chair of the Society for the Study of Labour History. He was awarded an Honorary Litt.D. by the University of East Anglia in 1998. He was also editor of *The Historian* from 1993 to 1998. His previous books include *David Lloyd George and the British Labour Movement* (1976), *Arthur Henderson* (1990), *Lloyd George and the Challenge of Labour* (1990) and *Lloyd George* (1992).

Introduction

CHRIS WRIGLEY

While hindsight is a danger in writing the history of any period, it is a notable hazard for Britain in 1900–39. It is very easy to let knowledge of the great weakening of the British economy from midway in the Second World War, and the relegation of Britain from world power status soon after the end of that war, to affect later views of the first four decades of the twentieth century.

Britain remained a major player in international relations in the interwar years. With Germany and Russia weakened, she was a key European power. It was easy to see Britain, France and resurgent Germany as the proper focus for an explanation of the origins of the Second World War, as A. J. P. Taylor did in his famous book of that name in 1961.[1] Contemporaries, especially those based in Europe, were prone to underestimate the importance and power of the United States and Japan after the First World War.

The British Empire still had great meaning to many English, Scottish, Welsh and Irish people. There were many imperial families. It was not uncommon to have grandparents, parents, uncles and aunts and brothers and sisters who had all been employed in one part of the empire or another. This was so with the family of Bernard Montgomery, later field marshal. His grandfather had been lieutenant-governor of the Punjab, his father was born in Cawnpore and became bishop of Tasmania, an uncle was commissioner in Rawalpindi, another uncle was a commissioner in Kenya, his eldest brother was chief native commissioner in Kenya, another lived in Canada, another was rector of Ladysmith, South Africa, and his youngest brother served in the Indian army.[2] Many British families in 1900–39 had one or more close relatives in Australia, New Zealand, Canada, South Africa or elsewhere in the empire. These were often people who had settled there after retiring from the British armed forces or the Indian or colonial service.

Empire Day, 24 May (Queen Victoria's birthday), was a major annual occasion that attempted to remind people in Britain and throughout the empire of their good fortune in being part of one big international family. To encourage their interest, schoolchildren in many countries were given a half-day off school and often a small sum of money to spend. Empire Day broadcasting was given an initial boost by the Empire Exhibition at Wembley in 1924, with several broadcasts from the exhibition including the speech of George V (now a prime item in the BBC's archives). In 1925 Empire Day was marked by several broadcasts and by a two-page lead article in the *Radio Times* written by the earl of Meath, founder of the Empire Day Movement in 1903, heralding the radio as 'an Empire force'.[3] From 1932 families spread across the empire could think of each other as they listened to George V, and later George VI, broadcast a Christmas Day message. Before the royal broadcast each year there was a radio-link programme, with very bland discussions between the broadcasters in London and those in different parts of the empire.[4]

There was also a culture of empire, which suggested that it would continue beyond the lifetimes of all those alive in the 1930s. One aspect of this was a mystique of brave (usually upper-crust) men, very few women, who risked all to defend the empire against dastardly foreigners. John Buchan, 'Sapper', Dornford Yates and, for younger readers, W. E. Johns were among many immensely popular writers whose stories contributed to an awareness of empire and often portrayed it as a higher cause. John Buchan wrote of his dream of 'a world-wide brotherhood with the background of a common race and creed'. His son commented that while his father was 'respectful but rather vague' about 'the future of the black races', '[h]is concern seems always to have been with the white Anglo-Saxons, with Canadians, Australians, New Zealanders, the Dominions rather than the Colonies'.[5] There were many political apostles of empire, running from Joseph Chamberlain, Lord Milner and 'Imperial' Perks to Leo Amery and Lionel Curtis. For them it was a noble cause and, after 1917, a British alternative to Bolshevism.

British strength still rested heavily on the Royal Navy. Britain's ability to be a world power and to dominate all areas was increasingly questioned before 1900. The Anglo-Japanese Alliance of 1902 was an early example of Britain recognizing an imbalance in her commitments and resources and then finding an ally to bridge the gap. Yet, in spite of the pre-war *Dreadnought* panics, or perhaps because of them, Britain had a dominant position in home waters during the First World War. In the 1920s Britain continued to outbuild others, including the United States, in warships.[6] The limits of British naval power were displayed during the Second World War, not least with the sinking of the *Prince of Wales* and the *Repulse* in late 1941, and the strength of US naval power, notably in the Pacific.

The emergence of air power offered a relatively cheap and effective way of policing Britain's greatly increased global responsibilities after the First World War. Sir Arnold Wilson, after two years as acting high commissioner in Mesopotamia, reported in February 1921 that the RAF personnel there were 'better trained and more efficient than most military units' and that they relied 'almost exclusively' on machinery that was not seriously affected by the hot climate. Churchill hoped to withdraw two-thirds of British troops from the area and to save millions of pounds.[7] In such areas as Iraq, Aden, the Sudan and the North-west Frontier of India, imperial policing was carried out very cheaply compared to reliance on a military presence. As Charles Townshend has succinctly put it, 'the war that had given Britain these problems also brought it the means of coping with them. The development of the military aircraft created a weapon with the near-miraculous property of lengthening the arm of government whilst shortening its purse'.[8]

Yet air power in a hostile international environment threatened British confidence in her security by the 1930s. Naval supremacy was no protection against bomber aircraft. Stanley Baldwin, the Conservative party leader, expressed an exaggerated fear of air attacks when, on 10 November 1932, he told the House of Commons,

> I think it is well also for the man in the street to realise that there is no power on earth that can protect him from being bombed. Whatever people may tell him, the bomber will always get through. The only defence is offence, which means that you have to kill more women and children more quickly than the enemy if you want to save yourselves.[9]

Baldwin's fears of aerial bombing proving to be a knockout blow were shared by many of his ministerial colleagues. This view was shown to be too pessimistic during the Second World War.[10]

It is also easy to overstate the poorness of Britain's economic performance relative to other industrial nations. Indeed, as Barry Supple has observed, 'in some important historical circumstances national evolution is better characterised by the concept of "change" rather than "decline"'. Britain's early lead in industrialization made it certain that as others industrialized her share of world manufacturing output would drop, and nearly certain that her share of world trade in manufactures would fall. The record shows that this happened, with Britain's rate of growth being slower than many of her rivals. While aggregate national wealth rose, anxieties about Britain's economic performance in the twentieth century grew. British fears, as Barry Supple has argued, were raised by 'the loss, not so much of income or wealth, as of relative power and international standing as a leading industrial nation'. Such feelings were accentuated by others surpassing Britain, in spite of her success in two world wars.[11]

While the First World War broadly had an adverse impact on the British economy, it was not as severe as the Second World War. Then Britain sold assets and ran up debts on a far greater scale, with less subsequent recovery of her position relative to other industrialized countries. Within a few years of the end of the Second World War it was clear that Britain had fallen from the ranks of the first-rate economies and political powers, even if she benefited from the 'golden age' of the international economy.[12] In the interwar period, international economic conditions were less propitious, notably in 1921–2 and the early 1930s, than in the 1950s and 1960s, yet Britain was still a major power and a substantial economic force.

General living standards rose between 1900 and 1939. In this period the deaths of infants under 1 year per thousand live births dropped from 154 to 51 in England and Wales, from 128 to 69 in Scotland, and from 109 in Ireland to 71 in Northern Ireland and 66 in the Republic of Ireland. Estimates of average real incomes in a wide range of occupations suggest a rise of 18 per cent between 1920 and 1938. There was also a marked drop in the average number of persons per house between 1900 and 1939: from 5.4 to 3.5.[13] Such aggregate figures conceal continuing poverty and some vile housing conditions. Even during the near full employment of the First World War years there were those who experienced hardship: the elderly on fixed incomes or on pensions lagging behind inflation, women with dependants relying on soldiers' or sailors' pay, and those who were disabled, including ex-servicemen. There was also much suffering between the wars, especially in the areas of structural unemployment (south Wales, Belfast and the Lagan Valley, Clydeside, Tyneside, Lancashire and the north-east).

In contrast, the interwar years were generally good for the middle class who were in steady employment. After 1921 and especially in the 1930s, prices were relatively low and so real wages were strong. Houses and consumer goods were available at favourable prices for the middle class and skilled working class. There was also more disposable income for young people in work, with increased spending in the inter-war years on such entertainments as the cinema and dancing as well as on consumer goods (motorcycles, radios, magazines, clothes and cosmetics).[14]

The period 1900–39 had its fair share of political reverberations from the previous century. A significant instance was the issue of tariffs, which had wrecked the Conservative party in the 1840s and resurfaced in the 1880s. In 1903–32 it caused further problems for that party. This issue also affected the Liberal party. In 1903–6 and 1923 tariffs had united the party in defence of free trade, but too much dependence on free trade as a central creed left the party's ideological cupboard much depleted when free trade collapsed in the world depression of 1931–3.

With India, there were also sharp divisions of opinion within the Conservative party, most notably in the early 1930s. Then Churchill's resistance to political change set back his ministerial career by nearly a decade. Earlier, the debates in the House of Commons over the Amritsar massacre of 1919 had reactivated fears of a new 1857. Sir Edward Carson, in defending General Dyer, said he might have 'saved the most bloody outrage in that country, which might have deluged the place with the loss of thousands of lives, and may have saved the country from a mutiny to which the old mutiny in India would have appeared small'.[15]

The period also saw the culmination of the question of Britain's relationship with Ireland. Gladstone's crusade to achieve devolution of much power to Ireland having been thwarted in 1886 and 1893, the issue refused to be rubbed clean from British politics (as suggested by Lord Rosebery in a famous speech at Chesterfield in December 1901 in which he called for a 'clean slate' for the Liberal party). After a great deal of bloodshed in 1916–21, much of historic Ulster was separated from the remainder of Ireland under the Irish Treaty of December 1921, which led to the creation of the Irish Free State in December 1922. For the British it seemed, as A. J. P. Taylor could write in 1965, that '[t]he Irish question had been settled for good or ill'.[16] By the end of the 1960s it was clear that it had not been resolved nearly fifty years earlier.

Irish issues had highlighted the constitutional problems of the British parliament. While Disraeli had idealized the practices of the British constitution, the Home Rule conflict, after his death, had led to a House of Lords even more heavily weighted in favour of the Conservative party. Lord Salisbury and Arthur Balfour, his nephew and successor as prime minister, had seen the House of Lords as a bulwark against radical change. While the House of Lords had acted with impunity against Liberal measures passed by the House of Commons in 1892–5 and 1906–8, in 1909–10 the rejection of the budget led to the 1911 Parliament Act. This measure provided for the passage of money bills, certified as such by the speaker of the House of Commons, without the House of Lords' assent, and for the passage of other bills which had been passed in three successive sessions by the House of Commons.

Another constitutional issue, the lack of political rights for women, also came to a head in the period. By the start of the twentieth century there was substantial pressure from both well-to-do and working-class women for the right to vote in parliamentary elections. In the case of working women there was growing political self-confidence, with their strategy developing from petitions to an alliance with the

Labour Representation Committee and the Labour party.[17] Emmeline and Christabel Pankhurst, who formed the Women's Social and Political Union (WSPU) in October 1903, placed the issue centre stage in British politics with the WSPU's militant tactics. Women secured the vote on the same terms as men in two stages, in 1918 and 1928. Women's roles in the wartime economies (1914–18 and 1939–45) did not transform women's work opportunities or promotion prospects, neither did the feminist pressures and legislation of the 1960s. At the start of the twenty-first century the average wage gap between men and women in Britain was 35 per cent, putting Britain alongside Greece and the Netherlands as the countries with the worst pay gender gap in the European Union.

The essays that follow review many important themes of the period. Though extensive, the book is not intended to be an encyclopaedia and some aspects of the period are therefore not covered. Leading historians do, however, provide substantial introductions to Britain's history in the period between 1900 and 1939.

NOTES

1 A. J. P. Taylor, *The Origins of the Second World War* (London, 1961).
2 C. Allen, ed., *Tales from the Dark Continent: Images of British Colonial Africa in the Twentieth Century* (London, 1979), p. 34.
3 J. M. MacKenzie, ' "In touch with the infinite": the BBC and the Empire, 1923–53', in J. M. MacKenzie, ed., *Imperialism and Popular Culture* (Manchester, 1986).
4 P. Scannell and D. Cardiff, *A Social History of British Broadcasting* (Oxford, 1991), pp. 280–7.
5 W. Buchan, *John Buchan: A Memoir* (1982; London, 1985), pp. 112–13.
6 J. R. Ferris, ' "The greatest power on earth": Great Britain in the 1920s', *International History Review*, 12, 4 (1991); E. Goldstein, 'The evolution of British diplomatic strategy for the Washington Conference', *Diplomacy and Statecraft*, 4, 3 (1993).
7 M. Gilbert, *Winston S. Churchill*, vol. 4 (London, 1975), pp. 531–2 and 538.
8 C. Townshend, 'Civilization and "frightfulness": air control in the Middle East between the wars', in C. J. Wrigley, ed., *Warfare, Diplomacy and Politics: Essays in Honour of A. J. P. Taylor* (London, 1986), pp. 93–119.
9 K. Middlemas and J. Barnes, *Baldwin: A Biography* (London, 1969), p. 735.
10 U. Bialer, *The Shadow of the Bomber: The Fear of Air Attack and British Politics 1932–1939* (London, 1980), pp. 21–4.
11 B. Supple, 'Introduction: national performance in a personal perspective' and 'Fear of failing: economic history and the decline of Britain' (1994), in P. Clark and C. Trebilcock, eds, *Understanding Decline* (Cambridge, 1997).
12 A. Maddison, *Dynamic Forces in Capitalist Development: A Long-run Comparative View* (Oxford, 1991); C. Bean and N. Crafts, 'British economic growth since 1945: relative economic decline . . . and renaissance?', in N. Crafts and G. Toniolo, eds, *Economic Growth in Europe since 1945* (Cambridge, 1996); N. Crafts and T. C. Mills, 'Europe's golden age: an econometric investigation of changing trend rates of growth', in B. van Ark and N. Crafts, eds, *Quantitative Aspects of Post-war European Economic Growth* (Cambridge, 1996).
13 B. R. Mitchell, *British Historical Statistics* (Cambridge, 1988), pp. 58–9 and 172; B. B. Gilbert, *British Social Policy 1914–1939* (London, 1970), p. 201.
14 D. Fowler, *The First Teenagers: The Lifestyle of Young Wage-earners in Interwar Britain* (London, 1995).

15   131 H. C. Deb. 5s, c.1714; 8 July 1920.
16   A. J. P. Taylor, *English History 1914–1945* (Oxford, 1965), p. 236.
17   J. Liddington and J. Norris, *One Hand Tied Behind Us: The Rise of the Women's Suffrage Movement* (London, 1978); S. S. Holton, *Feminism and Democracy: Women's Suffrage and Reform Politics in Britain, 1900–1918* (Cambridge, 1986).

PART I

British Political Life

CHAPTER ONE

The Conservative Party, 1900–1939: From Crisis to Ascendancy

PHILIP WILLIAMSON

In recent years early twentieth-century Conservative politics has generated two large interpretative debates. Between 1903 and the outbreak of the First World War in 1914 a 'crisis of Conservatism' has been identified: fierce internal disputes and three successive general election defeats, which exposed the party's deepest commitments to attack. How is this crisis to be understood? In contrast, between the armistice in 1918 and the onset of the Second World War in 1939 the party secured a remarkable ascendancy. It obtained more votes than any other party at every general election, won three of the largest-ever House of Commons majorities, occupied government after five of the seven elections, and was in opposition for just thirty-six months in total. How was such dominance achieved?[1]

The historical literature on these subjects contains pitfalls for the unwary. The contrast between crisis and ascendancy can be exaggerated, if each condition is overstated and then 'overexplained' as the outcome of social, electoral or organizational structures. Amidst the pre-war crisis the party's popular support remained substantial: in the two 1910 general elections it won nearly as many votes as Liberals and Labour combined. From 1918 to 1930 its position was less secure than hindsight suggests: in most elections it obtained a considerably lower share of the national vote than it had during its pre-war defeats. The Edwardian party's divisions might seem ample proof of weakness, yet internal disputes of similar proportions occurred during the party's interwar dominance. An assumption that divisions within a party are automatically damaging should be resisted, for these bring defeat only if they affect the fundamental concerns of a decisive number of voters on polling day. Otherwise internal differences are a normal – and generally healthy – condition of any political party's life. This is not only because competitiveness is endemic among ambitious politicians. Conservatives were a complex association of different types of members supported by combinations of different types of voters, with various interests and various opinions, agreeing on some broad matters but otherwise with disparate, and often not wholly consistent, concerns. Contrary to many incautious generalizations, they cannot be understood in any straightforward economic or social terms as the party of property owners or the middle classes. Propertied and middle-class groups were also numerous – and their interests given high priority – within the Liberal party and among its supporters.[2] About half the total Conservative vote in parliamentary elections came from the labouring population, and in the 1930s more of the 'working class' voted Conservative than Labour.

Even the terms 'Conservative party' and 'Conservative government' can cause confusion, because they are commonly used as shorthand phrases which obscure significant aspects of the party's strategy and presentation. The party was usually allied with other groups, and normally described itself and the governments containing its leaders in broader terms than just 'Conservative'. From 1886, what some historians call the 'Conservative party' was actually a Unionist alliance between Conservative and Liberal Unionist parties, which from 1895 to 1905 formed a 'Unionist government'. In 1912 the two parties merged into the 'Unionist party'. From 1915 to 1922 Unionists were partners with Liberal and Labour groups in successive 'coalition governments'. In 1925 the party in England and Wales – though not in Scotland and Northern Ireland – reverted to the name 'Conservative', while retaining the term 'and Unionist'. From 1931 to 1940 Conservative and Unionist leaders joined new Liberal and Labour splinter groups in another coalition, the 'National government'. During its interwar ascendancy the Conservative party only twice won elections without declared national alliances, in 1922 and 1924, and even then it benefited from regional or local electoral pacts with Liberals. When genuinely fighting alone, at the 1923 and 1929 elections, it lost. Only in 1922–4 and 1924–9 were there strictly 'Conservative governments'.[3]

Nor are these the only reasons why examination of Conservatives alone is insufficient to explain the party's electoral performance. Just as success could be connected with political alliances, so could defeat – by cooperation among its opponents. Electoral support could depend not just on the Conservative party's own resources, but on contrasts established with competing parties or alliances. Each party's activities and appeal, and its success or failure, were shaped largely by dynamics generated by the party *system*, which in this period always contained at least three substantial parties and often more. Consequently political decisions – arguments, images, strategies, alliances and issues – were at least as important as economic, class or electoral structure and party organization in determining the Unionist and Conservative record.

The Edwardian Crisis

The Unionist alliance, since 1886 the strongest political force, increased its parliamentary majority at the September 1900 general election. Over the next five years the Unionist government undertook important diplomatic, defence, administrative, educational and social initiatives. In July 1902 the premiership passed smoothly from one member of the aristocratic and Conservative Cecil family to another, from Lord Salisbury to his nephew, Balfour. Yet from May 1903 the government was in difficulties, as cabinet disagreement over proposals from the Liberal Unionist Joseph Chamberlain for 'tariff reform' – duties on imported foreign commodities, with preference (reductions) for colonial imports – led to resignations and dismissals, splits within each alliance party (both Conservative and Liberal Unionist), the creation of rival Free Food and Tariff Reform Leagues, and widespread criticism of Balfour's leadership. After the cabinet finally resigned in December 1905, the new Liberal government called a general election in January 1906 which resulted in a Unionist col-

Table 1.1 General election results, 1895–1910

Year	Unionists				Liberal		Labour		Irish Nationalist
	% poll	MPs	(LU)[a]	[unoppo][b]	% poll	MPs	% poll	MPs	MPs[c]
1895	49.1	411	(71)	[132]	45.7	177	–	–	82
1900	50.3	402	(68)	[163]	45.0	183	1.3	2	82
1906	43.4	157	(25)	[13]	49.4	399	4.8	29	83
Jan. 1910	46.8	272	(32)	[19]	43.5	274	7.0	40	82
Dec. 1910	46.6	271	(36)	[72]	44.2	272	6.4	42	84

[a] Liberal Unionist MPs, included in overall Unionist total.
[b] Total of Unionist MPs unopposed by rival candidates.
[c] Most Irish Nationalist MPs were returned unopposed, so their percentage of the poll is meaningless.
Source: adapted from F. W. S. Craig, *British Electoral Facts 1832–1980* (Chichester, 1981).

lapse, to just 157 MPs, considerably fewer than half the Liberal numbers (table 1.1). Difficulties persisted in opposition, even after Chamberlain's withdrawal due to ill health in July. Prolonged doctrinal disputes, rumbling indiscipline and two further election defeats in 1910 constitute an extraordinary phase in Unionist-Conservative politics, contrary to a usually firm instinct for collective self-preservation and pragmatic pursuit of power. A pioneering Conservative party historian, Robert Blake, confessed to being 'baffled' by the Unionists' behaviour, which appeared almost like some 'political death wish'.[4] It has seemed consistent with further remarkable episodes before the outbreak of war in 1914: outright rebellions, Balfour's displacement, and challenges to established political conventions. Nevertheless, although recent interpretations posit a continuous Edwardian 'crisis of Conservatism', conceptually the period divides into two distinct phases, separated in 1910.

Understanding has turned chiefly on tariff reform, as the cause of internal rupture and chief reason for the scale of the 1906 election defeat. The issue is commonly presented as a clash between the two leading Unionist personalities, symbolizing different types of politics. Following the unexpectedly protracted and expensive Boer War of 1899–1902, Chamberlain, as colonial secretary the minister chiefly responsible, became a dangerously combustible figure: he wanted to restore imperial strength, he had lost influence, and he wished to re-establish his authority and reputation. As his tariff reform proposals attracted considerable interest and controversy, he resigned from the cabinet to campaign for their acceptance as the chief Unionist policy. In doing so, Chamberlain reverted to the techniques of his career as a Radical Liberal before 1886: those of a populist cause, a programme and an organization. This new, energetic, radical version of Unionist politics was attractive to many Conservatives and Liberal Unionists, dissatisfied with the older, cooler, mandarin style of the Cecilian leadership. Balfour's efforts to preserve a semblance of unity through sinuous compromises exasperated tariff reformers, free traders and neutrals alike, who all supplied ammunition for an historical verdict that he bore much responsibility for the Unionist collapse. Balfour is blamed for failing to provide clear leadership, perpetuating the divisions, demoralizing government supporters and alienating voters. In contrast, Chamberlain and the tariff reformers are presented as modernizing forces, creating a positive Unionist appeal attuned to the politics of a mass electorate.

Increasingly, a clash of personalities and styles has seemed an insufficient explanation, and wider interpretations have been sought. Tariff reform is now regarded as one reaction to a general anxiety, manifested in all political parties and intensified by the strains of the Boer War, about British 'relative decline': increased commercial and imperial competition from other nations; reduced economic, administrative and military effectiveness; greater demands on government finance; and realization of the chronic poverty, bad health and poor education among much of the labouring population. Tariff reform attracted commitment because it seemed the most definite Unionist contribution to what Geoffrey Searle has called 'the quest for national efficiency':[5] short-term party considerations were outweighed by deeper imperial and political imperatives. To this explanation has been added an emphasis on electoral and party pressures, particularly the delayed effects from the enfranchisement of most male labourers in 1884. According to Alan Sykes, tariff reform was politically seductive because it was flexible, offering multiple appeals and serving changing purposes. Chamberlain's own primary concern was imperial unity, but the programme was extended to embrace protection of domestic agriculture and industries, increased employment, higher wages and social reform, as he and his allies sought wider support from farmers, rural landlords, manufacturers and especially working-class voters. Paradoxically, the 1906 election defeat made the issue of tariff reform seem more compelling, because it now became a positive alternative to 'socialism', as represented by the Labour party's electoral advance and later by the Liberal government's collectivist social policies.[6] In the most comprehensive examination, Ewen Green argued that tariff reform offered solutions to three interrelated problems of political identity. First, Unionist credibility as champions of national and imperial power had suffered from the public anxiety about 'national efficiency'. Second, as the Unionists' social base expanded from the landed interest to 'property in general', tensions developed between traditional rural and newer urban propertied supporters. Third and most seriously, as a combination of property owners the Unionist alliance could suffer from any growth of class politics, which would distance it from the largely 'propertyless' electorate. The function of tariff reform was as 'an economics of political integration', offering a restructured party identity which might consolidate natural adherents and increase mass support.[7]

An identity crisis there certainly was, but questions arise over its definition. Green's account turns on a characterization of the 'Conservative party' as the 'party of property and Empire'. If this really had been so, its internal difficulties would have been fewer and its electoral performance quite different. The Unionist alliance existed to defend the constitutional union with Ireland, while the primary Conservative party purpose – accepted to greater or lesser degree by their Liberal Unionist partners – was to uphold established political institutions and the established churches. Around these fundamental principles further interests and anti-Liberal opinions had assembled since the 1880s, giving the Unionist alliance a broad-based electoral appeal which both bridged and bisected socio-economic distinctions in complex regional patterns. It had attracted many (but far from all) urban and suburban property owners, especially in southern England. Contrary to a common interpretation that its success depended on minimizing the mass vote by exploiting low electoral registration and turnouts, it also had substantial 'working-class' support from the cultures of public houses, mass sports, friendly societies, paternalistic employers and the established churches; from popular Protestant, anti-Catholic and anti-Irish feeling (notably in Lancashire and west Scotland); and from workers in defence bases and industries, all mobilized with the assistance of Conservative working men's clubs and the Primrose League. The Unionist leadership was not hostile to trade unions, and it had a record of social reform and promised more, including old-age pensions until postponed by the cost of the Boer War. The liberal traditions of Liberal Unionism remained signifi-cant in Scotland, the west midlands and south-west England, not just in the number of its own MPs (see table 1.1) but also in lubricating the appeal of their Conservative allies. The advantage of many Unionist MPs returned unopposed by rival candidates (as many as 163 at the 1900 election) arose not only from Liberal weakness, but often from Unionist popular strength. This broad-based support was held together by a widely accepted association of 'Unionism' with 'national' interests and imperial strength, contrasted with the Liberal party's supposed sectional concerns – Home Rule for Ireland, 'faddist' programmes, and puritanical nonconformist efforts to regulate and restrict 'the pleasures of the people', including alcohol consumption.[8]

In the early 1900s this position was reversed – the outcome not of Unionist actions alone but also of intelligent Liberal strategy, especially by injecting a moral charge into leading issues. Unionism was made to seem self-interested and unprincipled; the liberal claims of Liberal Unionism were tarnished; and the Liberal party secured the moral high ground, extended its electoral appeal, and was able to contest many more constituencies. The Unionist government's 1902 Education Act and 1904 Licensing Act were presented as merely partisan support for Anglican church schools and the brewing interest, enabling Liberals to tap an outraged political nonconformity able to provide considerable assistance in organization, funds and candidates. Government hesitation in nullifying hostile legal decisions on trade union rights (especially the 'Taff Vale' case) was exploited with the Liberal–Labour electoral pact of 1903, which assisted many Liberal candidates as well as giving the Labour party a vital boost. Irish Home Rule was relegated from an immediate aim to an unspecified future, which deflated electoral hostility towards Liberals in mainland Britain and removed a leading source of Unionist solidarity. The government's imperial policy was made to seem immoral as well as ramshackle and expensive, with accusations of 'Chinese slavery' (harsh treatment of indentured Chinese labourers) in South Africa reinforcing earlier charges of 'methods of barbarism' ('concentration camps' for Boer families). Above all, tariff reform was presented not just as economically injurious but also as socially, politically and morally offensive, by being relentlessly stereotyped as 'protection' in the sense of advantages given to the vested interests of employers by means of taxes on the food of the masses.

Among Unionists themselves, tariff reform was corrosive for several reasons. Unionist 'free fooders' criticized it on similar grounds to those of Liberals (and some, including Churchill, joined the Liberal party). Balfour and his supporters assumed that electorally it was not 'practical politics', because many labourers would place their immediate concerns as consumers before uncertain promises to them as pro-ducers. Still more damagingly, it substituted a new programme for the priorities that had defined the party system since 1886, disregarding the established Unionist iden-tity and the bases of a successful electoral combination. What to tariff reformers seemed a politics of integration was to Balfourites a politics of disintegration, jeop-ardizing the Unionist function of constitutional defence.

This was a cogent view, one that deserves greater historical respect in the light of Unionist vulnerability amidst the Liberal assault on established institutional arrangements after the first 1910 election. It also goes far towards explaining how, through all the criticism, Balfour so long remained an unchallengeable leader: his determination to preserve the widest Unionist interests, by resistance to activists who unwittingly narrowed the Unionist appeal and played into Liberal hands. The position could not be salvaged before the 1906 election, and afterwards pressures from well-organized Chamberlainite majorities among Unionist MPs and in the National Union obliged Balfour to concede successive versions of tariff reform. Nevertheless, the three years from 1906 to 1909 revealed the possibilities of his strategy of minimizing that issue as far as practicable, while maximizing matters of traditional difference between Unionists and Liberals. Tariff reform, originally a policy of radical change, was subordinated to the priorities of conservative defence. A campaign of selective opposition to the Liberal government was adopted on the public platform as well as by the Unionist majority in the House of Lords – resistance to legislation on nonconformist and radical issues, notably education, licensing and land tenure, but acceptance of less controversial trade union, old-age pensions and other social reform measures, towards which, indeed, many Unionists were sympathetic. Doubts were also raised about the government's commitment to upholding national interests in the world, especially the preservation of naval dominance over Germany. By these means the sectarian interests and sectionalism of Liberals and their allies were exposed, their divisions widened and Liberal ministers demoralized. A series of Unionist by-election victories in 1907–8 indicated a substantial electoral recovery, encouraged greater unity and promised an end to Unionist 'crisis'.

Liberal determination as much as Unionist miscalculation again explains why the eventual outcome was very different. The 1909 'people's budget' brought to a climax the issue of Unionist obstruction of Liberal legislation in the House of Lords – Lloyd George's 'peers *versus* the people' – but at first Unionist leaders considered the budget as not just a vindictive 'socialistic' attack upon landed property, but also an opportunity to force and win an early general election. Almost all Unionists, including earlier free traders, now acquiesced in tariff reform, but only in a further narrowing of its purpose to that of a tactical device and financial policy, offering indirect revenue from imports as the alternative to Lloyd George's increased direct taxes. As expected, the House of Lords' defeat of the budget did precipitate a general election, in January 1910, and while it did not produce a Unionist victory it seemed at first to have created serious problems for their rivals. A large proportion of the 'people' had supported 'the peers', costing the Liberal party its overall parliamentary majority and leaving Irish Nationalist MPs holding the balance of power between Liberals and Unionists (table 1.1). However, the now minority Liberal government arrived at a momentous solution, confirmed at a second election in December 1910, which began a new phase of severe Unionist difficulties.

Recent historical interest in the 1910 elections has concentrated chiefly on the extent to which a 'new Liberalism' captured an emerging 'working-class' consciousness and consolidated the Liberal pact with the Labour party. But this was not their major feature. Nor should the 'class alignment' be overstated. The Liberal government's measures were selective, seeking to retain its own substantial propertied support. While the higher Unionist vote did comprise increased numbers of taxpayers hostile to Liberal financial and social policies, it continued to include many labourers persuaded by Unionist criticisms of the Liberal cabinet and disliking Lloyd George's other new taxes, on popular consumption of alcohol and tobacco. The larger outcome of the two elections did not lie in a social democratic 'Progressive' Liberal–Labour alliance and shift towards class politics. Rather, the main features were a revival of the Radical Liberal–Irish Nationalist alliance of the 1880s and 1890s, and a reinstatement of constitutional issues. Constitutional politics were now conducted with a vengeance – because the Irish Nationalist condition for alliance was a Parliament Bill abolishing the House of Lords' powers of veto, with the effect of re-establishing Home Rule as an immediate and achievable policy. It also cleared the way for other longstanding radical aims, especially another visceral issue for many Unionists, inadequately emphasized in party histories – the nonconformist cause of disestablishment and disendowment of the Anglican Church of Wales.[9]

All this revived the Unionist identity crisis, because it reopened the question of primary purpose – constitutional defence or tariff reform? Forced by the 'Radical government' into a stark choice, the core Unionist identity was reaffirmed: even most tariff reformers ultimately placed the constitution before tariffs. But this reversion to fundamental priorities was even more painful and disruptive than the diversion from them had been after 1902, and it generated a remarkable change in Unionist political style.[10] Many who had reluctantly accepted tariff reform in the hope of defeating the Liberal government now concluded that it had failed and should be sacrificed for the greater cause. But Balfour's attempt before the December 1910 election to sidestep the issue by offering to submit tariff reform to a future public referendum infuriated the 'whole-hog' tariff reformers. Yet Balfour also lost the confidence of many Unionists on the constitutional issue, after another Liberal ministerial coup was revealed: the king's promise, if necessary, to create enough new Liberal peers to overcome Unionist opposition to the Parliament Bill in the House of Lords. Balfour argued that it was better to let the bill pass and rely on the Lords' residual power to delay legislation until a general election than to have Liberals obtain an immediate and enduring House of Lords majority which could endorse radical measures whenever it wished. But his advice was publicly rejected by members of his shadow cabinet and a large contingent of Unionist peers and MPs – the 'diehards' – who were exasperated with yet more compromise, to the extent of trying the high-risk tactic of outright defiance of the government. This in turn caused a further split, as other Unionist peers considered the risks so great that against their personal preferences they voted with the government to save the Parliament Bill.

The significance of these bitter Unionist divisions is not just that they finally forced Balfour's resignation from the leadership, in November 1911. They were manifestations of a more general eruption of Unionist discontent, sometimes characterized as a 'revolt from the right'. Though mobilized in numerous organizations, the shared features included intensified 'national efficiency' anxieties, expressed as ultra-patriotism, imperialism and xenophobia, versions of tariff reform, and desire for stronger armed forces. To these were added hostility towards the rising power of Germany, support for Irish Unionists and especially the Protestant Ulster loyalists, and a populist belief that 'the people' would support all these causes if only they had clear, firm and honest leadership. One group, the 'social-imperialists', were distinctive as doctrinaire Chamberlainites with a contempt for parliamentary politics and a technocratic belief in government by policy experts. But these were a tiny minority, and it is the larger and more diffuse body of Unionist dissidents that has raised inter- pretative problems. Gregory Phillips showed that while the 'diehard' peers wanted to preserve the hierarchical social order, they were not fossilized 'backwoodsmen' but men active in public life and often favouring 'national efficiency' military and social reforms. For Searle the impatience with conventional party politics, the extreme lan- guage and the advocacy of armed resistance against Germany and Irish Home Rule defined these dissentients as a 'radical right', rebelling against the political structure in a manner similar to the later fascists. In contrast, Sykes explained the dogmatism and intransigence in more limited terms: as reactions to exceptional circumstances, yet serving a conventional purpose – the restoration of traditional conservative prin- ciples. The well-known proliferation of political 'leagues' (including Navy, National Service, Budget Protest, Union Defence as well as Tariff Reform leagues) can also be interpreted in alternative ways: as repudiations of the party system; as a clash between 'old' and 'new' politics; or, less dramatically, as single-cause pressure groups that could be accommodated within, and gain new supporters for, the Unionist alliance.[11]

The disruptive potential of the right was gradually contained under Balfour's replacement, Bonar Law. On tariff reform and Ulster the new leader shared their per- spectives, but above all he shared their enmity towards Liberal ministers. The intem- perance of Unionist politics from 1910 arose less from structural tensions than from specific political acts: the prolongation and radicalization of Liberal government. Without these, Unionist anxiety and anger about national efficiency and policy would have been much less, or not arisen at all. Nor would the political system have been so criticized, for the real grievances were not with party politics as such but with Liberal success and a Unionist leadership unable to check it. The Unionist 'crisis' now consisted of a politics of frustration and desperation, given a still fiercer edge by conviction of Liberal iniquity. Ministers were considered to have sacrificed principle for office; to have surrendered national interests to the sectional ambitions of Irish Nationalists and nonconformists; to have introduced constitutional changes without an electoral mandate; and to have violated constitutional convention by coercing the king, crippling the Lords, and establishing single-chamber government. The minis- ters were also regarded as hypocritical and corrupt, provoking class envy against landed property owners while flattering the financial 'plutocracy', selling political honours and, with the Marconi scandal, indulging in insider share dealing.

Bonar Law voiced this sense of an illegitimate and amoral Radical coalition, in an abrasive style of opposition which went far towards restoring Unionist morale and confidence in the official leadership. Assisted by reform and unification of the party organizations after the 1910 election defeats and by the common cause of opposi- tion to the Irish Home Rule and Welsh Church bills from 1912, Unionism again seemed an effective force. A parliamentary war of obstruction exhausted Liberal min- isters and whips, while public defiance, including Law's ringing endorsement of the Ulster loyalists, tested cabinet resolve to the utmost. Quite how far he was prepared to take opposition – whether the party would depart from its normal commitment to law and order by supporting armed resistance in Ulster – remains debatable. It seems most likely that Law's strategy was less extreme than his rhetoric. He aimed to intimidate the Liberal cabinet into making concessions, accepting a partitioned Ireland that would exclude Ulster from Home Rule, and allowing more generous treatment of the Welsh church. Above all, he wanted to force a general election that would halt all its radical proposals, including Lloyd Georgian finance and his new campaign for land reform. The measure of the changed condition of Unionist politics came in the winter of 1912–13, when Law and his shadow cabinet proposed to restore tariff reform as party policy. This produced a backbench rebellion, because most Unionists had now finally grasped that tariff reform jeopardized constitutional defence; and when Law offered to resign, tariff reformers joined the movement to persuade him to remain party leader while setting the policy aside.

Edwardian Unionist politics can be epitomized as the rise and fall of tariff reform, connected with a burgeoning class politics. But this misrepresents their character and complexity. A more accurate understanding lies in a different symmetry: an eclipse and revival of conservative Unionism, turning on a constitutional politics which supplied a focus for further conservative interests and opinions. Although economic and social issues were becoming important in party politics, these did not yet define the distinctions between parties. Unionism continued to draw strength from issues cutting across perceptions of class, enabling it to rebuild a broad electoral appeal after the erosions suffered between 1903 and the 1906 election. The new aspect that constitutional politics had acquired was Unionist belligerence, creating a dangerous condition of mutual brinkmanship by the rival party leaders. But by July 1914 the Liberal cabinet had been forced into negotiation over Ulster and was itself divided over Lloyd George's latest budget, while a strong Unionist by-election performance, giving the party thirty more MPs than the Liberals, showed that it was restored to at least equal terms with the Radical alliance.

Interwar Ascendancy

Even if Unionists had won a general election in 1915, their dominance after 1918 could not have been predicted. So great was the change in Unionist fortunes that it has been explained as an outcome of that massive dislocation, the First World War. Some domestic effects of the war undoubtedly helped the Unionist position. The party's anti-Germanism and calls for stronger armed forces, its brand of patriotism and insistence on the value of the empire, even a version of tariff reform – protection of strategic industries – were all vindicated. Its unqualified commitment to the war effort, accepting drastic extensions of state power, matched the predominant public attitude and the demands of 'mass mobilization'. Its leaders agreed to a wartime electoral truce, and although protesting at the enactment of the Irish and Welsh bills in September 1914, the Liberal government's decision to suspend operation of these bills for the duration of the war enabled the constitutional issues separating the rival party leaderships to be set aside. This eased a Unionist return to government as junior partners in the Asquith coalition of May 1915, then as the main constituents of the Lloyd George coalition from December 1916. Most importantly, the Radical alliance disintegrated. The Liberal party split into Asquithian and Lloyd Georgian factions, which fought the first two post-war elections as rival groups. The Labour party decided in 1918 to break with Liberals and become a genuinely independent national party. The Irish Nationalist party collapsed after the Easter rising in 1916, and the MPs of its republican successor, Sinn Fein, refused to attend the Westminster parliament. At the December 1918 general election, Unionists became

Table 1.2   General election results, 1918–35 (main political groups only)

Year	Un/Cons		Un/Cons allies and others[a]		Liberal		Labour	
	% poll	MPs	% poll	MPs	% poll	MPs	% poll	MPs
1918	38.8	382	14.6	141	13.0	36	20.8	57
1922	38.5	344	[9.9	53]	18.9	62	29.7	142
1923	38.0	258	–	–	29.7	158	30.7	191
1924	46.8	412	1.2	7	17.8	40	33.3	151
1929	38.1	260	–	–	23.5	59	37.1	287
1931	55.0	470	12.2	84	[Cons allies]		30.9	52
1935	47.8	387	5.5	42	6.7	21	38.0	154
1945	36.2	197	3.4	13	9.0	12	48.0	393

[a] 1918 Chiefly Lloyd George Liberals (127 MPs).
   1922 Lloyd George Liberals, many elected through local pacts with Unionists (but rejoined Liberals in 1923).
   1924 'Constitutionalists': in addition, there were numerous local electoral pacts between Unionists and Liberals.
   1931 National (4 MPs), National Labour (13), National Liberal (35), Liberal (32, most of whom ceased to be government supporters in 1932).
   1935 National (1), National Labour (8) and National Liberal (33).
Source: adapted from F. W. S. Craig, *British Electoral Facts 1832–1980* (Chichester, 1981).

by far the largest parliamentary party, with nearly as many MPs as in 1900 (table 1.2).

Yet Bonar Law had not felt his party strong enough to fight alone. The election was won not by Unionists on their own but by the coalition government, with Lloyd George remaining as prime minister and with a continuing alliance between Unionists and his Liberal followers. Even four years later most Unionist leaders wanted to continue this coalition. The war had created problems as well as opportunities for the party – some potentially fatal to Unionist interests. It transformed the political agenda, creating new issues and priorities (as is often and rightly emphasized) without wholly replacing older controversies and values (less frequently emphasized). Mass mobilization, increased state reliance on labour and business, and promises of post-war social reconstruction all elevated economic and social questions into central policy concerns. With the Labour party adopting socialism as the aim of independent working-class politics, and underpinned by a stronger trade union movement, a new rival had emerged and challenged Unionism precisely and fundamentally on the new priorities. The challenge seemed especially formidable given two additional sources of unsettlement: the strains of readjustment to peace, with a vast demobilization which some Unionists feared might generate a revolutionary crisis similar to that suffered in Russia; and the 1918 electoral reform, almost trebling the size of the electorate from 7.7 million (in 1910) to over 21 million, of whom over 70 per cent had never voted before and around (a different) 75 per cent were working-class voters. Faced with an intensification of class politics, Unionist leaders feared that their 'Party on the old lines [would] have no future'[12] and sought safety in a peacetime coalition. Although this combination smothered the Labour electoral threat at the

1918 election, this was plainly only a temporary check. After severe industrial unrest, inflammatory socialist rhetoric and Labour by-election successes, in 1920 Unionist ministers even considered abandoning their party's separate existence by fusing with their Liberal coalition partners in a new anti-socialist party.

One effect of the war's political repercussions did endure – renewed problems of party identity, more profound than those before 1914 and displayed in more frequent internal disputes. Difficulties emerged even under the wartime coalitions. Unionists at all levels did not readily accept their leaders' judgement that new conditions required suppression of earlier commitments. Many disliked their willingness to compromise on Irish Home Rule after the Easter rising in 1916, and were appalled by the Irish Treaty of 1921. Some disliked a Welsh church compromise of 1918–19. Party activists complained at delays in a promised House of Lords reform, to redress the Parliament Act. Post-war pressures on imperial relationships created new areas of disagreement, over responses to nationalist agitations, especially in India. Tariff reform enthusiasts, encouraged by new justifications and new support for the issue generated by the Labour threat and, after 1920, by economic depression and rising unemployment, found the leadership as resistant to their full policy as it had been before 1910, except for a delirious period in late 1923. Above all, the transformed policy agenda and party system required a redefinition of Unionism – yet quite different versions were possible. How should the Labour movement be treated? What should be the relationship towards Liberals? Where should Unionists stand on the new socio-economic issues that now defined party differences? There were no agreed answers. Post-war economic problems and an enlargement of state activity generated considerable discontent in the Unionist electoral heartlands – with inflation in 1919–20, high taxes and rates, increased social expenditure, and what was regarded as excessive coalition government sensitivity towards the unemployed, the trade unions and the Labour party. Discontent was fomented by a new style of 'conservative' mass circulation newspapers, owned by 'press lords' (Northcliffe, Rothermere and Beaverbrook) whose pretensions to political power independent of the party system was a further legacy of the war. The newspapers read by most interwar Conservatives were usually critical of the Conservative party leadership.

The outcome in the early 1920s was a proliferation of business, middle-class, imperialist and taxpayers' associations as considerable as that of the pre-war leagues. Though aimed initially against the coalition government and especially Lloyd George, regarded as undermining Unionist and propertied interests, they increasingly turned against Unionist ministers for remaining loyal to the coalition. A Rothermere-inspired party, the Anti-Waste League, obtained significant support in 1921, and a revived diehard group of peers and MPs ominously claimed in early 1922 to be the true 'Conservative party'. Both sponsored 'independent' parliamentary candidates, in some constituencies capturing local Unionist associations and in others fighting against official Unionist candidates. Consciousness of this backbench and constituency discontent magnified points of difference among Unionist party officials and ministers, until the party was split right up to cabinet level.[13] At the Carlton Club meeting on 19 October 1922, Austen Chamberlain, the party leader since April 1921, argued that fighting the next general election under Lloyd George was the only sure way to resist socialism. Nevertheless, he was defeated by a large majority of MPs, 185 to 88. So intense was the disagreement that Chamberlain and other senior Unionist ex-ministers, the 'Chamberlainites', refused to serve in a Unionist government – the first in seventeen years – formed by Bonar Law, reluctantly returning from retirement to become prime minister.

The November 1922 general election seemed to vindicate the anti-coalitionist claim that the Unionist party could succeed on its own – and it did so despite its divided leadership. Yet reassertion of the party's independence by no means guaranteed its longer-term dominance. It won the election on a low national vote, just 38.5 per cent. It had not been truly independent, with Unionist–Lloyd George Liberal pacts in 159 constituencies. A large Labour electoral advance placed it on the brink of becoming a party of government. Not only was the Unionist leadership split; major issues concerning the party's stance and policies remained unresolved. Although the leadership did eventually reunite on an agreed strategy in 1924, wider cooperation remained fragile, as became obvious in another party crisis after election defeat in 1929. Again there were rebellions, newspaper-inspired electoral challenges – Beaverbrook's Empire Crusade and Rothermere's United Empire party – and attempts to remove the party leader. What should be asked is not just how Unionist-Conservative dominance was achieved, but also how the party was held together.

In considering the dominance John Ramsden, Martin Pugh and Stuart Ball emphasize a combination of new structures – the balance of parliamentary seats, the composition of the electorate and the party system – and the party's organizational responses, including use of the mass media.[14] The 1921 Irish Treaty confirmed Sinn Fein's secession and removed seventy to eighty anti-Unionist MPs from the House of Commons, leaving ten to twelve Ulster MPs as a Unionist asset. The 1918 electoral reform gave Unionists another thirty to forty safe seats, chiefly by a redistribution of constituencies in favour of suburban areas, bringing a total of some 180–200 constituencies described as 'middle class' or 'agricultural' that were normally Unionist. Ramsden goes so far as to state that this new pattern of seats made Unionists into 'the natural majority party'.[15] Moreover, the largest group enfranchised in 1918 were married or propertied women over thirty, and even after the female franchise was equalized with that of men at age twenty-one in 1928, at each interwar election a majority of women always voted Conservative. During the 1920s these electoral conditions were magnified by an effect of a full three-party system in most of Britain: a high number of three-cornered constituency contests, in which Labour and Liberal candidates could divide anti-Conservative opinion, and so enable Conservative candidates to win with only a minority of votes (table 1.3). These structural advantages were reaped by an organization superior to that of the other parties: the largest individual membership, better financed, more firmly established in more constituencies, with more professional agents. It established a training college for party workers and specialist organizations for new voters, especially women and the young.[16] It published huge amounts of propaganda material, and as early as 1924 employed commercial advertising agencies for election campaigns. It operated a covert newspaper agency, mastered the new medium of radio broadcasts, and was particularly innovative in the use of film.[17] By these various means, the party was more successful than its rivals in reaching and mobilizing members of the greatly enlarged electorate.

These structural and organizational features were certainly important, but without further analysis they are essentially descriptions, assuming rather than explaining Unionist-Conservative strength. Quantity and efficiency of propaganda and media

Table 1.3 Number of three-cornered constituency contests at general elections, 1900–35

1900	7	1918	211	1929	447
1906	45	1922	212	1931	99
Jan. 1910	46	1923	254	1935	146
Dec. 1910	16	1924	223		

Not all of these interwar contests were Conservative–Labour–Liberal fights. Some – normally fewer than forty – involved minor party (chiefly Communist) and independent candidates.
Source: adapted from F. W. S. Craig, *British Electoral Facts 1832–1980* (Chichester, 1981).

access are to little purpose without effective messages. Good organization and large membership were as much an outcome as a cause of party strength – and Unionist candidates could succeed even where there were organizational failings.[18] The reasons for mass female Conservatism are elusive, while any advantage from the changed pattern of parliamentary seats depends on the equation of 'middle class' with Conservative. Yet the middle classes comprised groups with diverse interests, some by no means 'natural' Unionist supporters and others unreliable, prone to abstention or defection to other parties or interest groups. Anti-Waste, the Empire Crusade and the 'United Empire' each caused difficulties for Conservative associations in some regions, while the Liberal party, after its reunification in 1923, remained a serious non-socialist alternative to Conservatism. The three-party electoral effect could as easily operate against Conservatives as in their favour, because in numerous constituencies Liberal intervention was more likely to divide the anti-Labour than the anti-Conservative vote. For this reason the Liberal party, though now weaker than Labour, was the chief electoral threat to the Conservative party. The two interwar Conservative defeats, at the 1923 and 1929 elections, were largely caused by Liberal revivals. Moreover, the high number of constituencies described by some historians as safely Conservative is obtained by a definition of 'middle class' which in some cases falls as low as 20 per cent of voters: the electorate in such constituencies must therefore have been up to 80 per cent 'working class'. Nor were those seats decisive, because the party had to win over 100 seats with even larger working-class compositions.[19] If class in an objective sense did account for Conservative party dominance, the paradoxical conclusion must be that this was less because of middle-class support than because 'it was the working class party *par excellence*'.[20]

More fundamental explanations lie in argument, ideology, political culture, strategy and policies. The party did not just organize support placed at its disposal by structural changes. As Conservatives themselves well knew, other aspects of those changes might have condemned them to persistent defeat but for the party's own exertions. It constructed support for itself and turned the new conditions to its own advantage by capturing previously anti-Unionist interests, identifying itself with widely shared values, evoking new opinions and creating difficulties for the rival parties. In assembling a new electoral base, even more socially diverse than that of 1900, the party had two strengths. Although contending versions of Conservatism jeopardized party unity, they also gave it an unusually broad spectrum of appeals, from diehard reaction to democratic reform, which could attract an exceptionally wide range of voters. These different appeals – and the different types of party members – were held together partly because its main opponents, the Labour party, aroused greater fears than Liberals had done before 1914, but mostly because Conservative leaders and propagandists exploited and generalized those fears in a peculiarly effective way. Anti-socialism was an instinctive Conservative position which now really could consolidate most propertied and business interests as never before, but it did not automatically appeal to large numbers of working-class, young, female and former Liberal-Radical voters. Here the immediate post-war problems of severe industrial unrest, inflation, high taxes and unemployment helped the party. McKibbin has shown that Conservatives projected stereotypes of male trade-unionized workers as disruptive, greedy and self-interested, in order to marginalize the Labour party as sectional and divisive. This effect reinforced a further ideological manipulation, exploiting simple economic assumptions about the importance of stable money and balanced budgets to stigmatize Labour policies as dangerous to the well-being of all classes. As most workers did not belong to trade unions and were liable to be discomforted by industrial disputes, and as most women were chiefly concerned with home, family and the domestic budget, this hostile representation of the Labour movement reached across objective class distinctions. Conservatives successfully defined themselves in contrast as the party of the 'public interest'.[21]

Yet on its own a negative and aggressive anti-Labour and anti-trade union appeal would have repelled a decisive range of voters – the moderate, liberal, socially concerned or idealistic; those craving social harmony and disliking political provocation; the voter in the many marginal constituencies of a three-party system. Conservative leaders normally understood that success required avoidance of a reputation as reactionary defenders of material self-interest, resisting the cruder instincts of party activists and offering a positive and accommodating appeal. However great their fears of potential mass working-class support for socialism, many Conservatives drew confidence from their pre-war experience of conservative working-class voters.[22] In ideology and presentation the crucial figure was Baldwin, who became party leader after Law retired with a fatal illness in May 1923. Although Baldwin on occasion employed brutal anti-Labour rhetoric – during general elections and the General Strike – he more commonly enunciated an inclusive public doctrine. His rhetoric embraced the new democracy and celebrated liberal political freedoms, while deploying the older politics of constitutional defence as the guarantee of stability and order. He matched industrial unrest with moving calls for industrial peace. He competed with Labour and Liberalism on the moral high ground, presenting an ethic of responsibility and service. Against the challenge of class politics, he cast appeals to a shared humanity, community, love of nature, history, Christian faith and patriotism.[23] While always subtly anti-socialist and Conservative, his messages and his tone usually seemed to be 'non-political', and as such it assisted a process by which Conservatism became identified with 'the public' and with national institutions, and Conservative values became embedded in the innumerable social and cultural associations of rural and suburban Britain.[24] Baldwin commanded unusual respect across party boundaries, and his claim upon shared values was so impressive that he could even embarrass and disarm Labour critics. But his most effective appeal was to many former or potential Liberals, enabling him to play a large part in tying together the disparate 'moral, industrial, agrarian, libertarian, Anglican and nonconformist bodies of resistance' to Labour.[25]

At an early stage, however, Baldwin stumbled badly. The large Labour party advance at the 1922 election and the persistence of high unemployment convinced him that Labour domination could soon become irresistible, unless pre-empted by a dramatic demonstration of Unionist good intentions towards the working population. He proposed not only to revive the most positive Unionist economic policy – tariff reform, now openly called 'protection' – but also to call an early general election on the issue. Yet as after 1903, so again arguments about production and work were overwhelmed by those about consumption and prices. Although the Chamberlainite Unionists supported the policy, free-trade critics created another, different, division among Unionists. Defence of free trade reunited the Asquith and Lloyd George Liberals and gave them a perfect cause on which to revive their party. Baldwin probably expected a Liberal recovery to neutralize and counteract the Labour challenge, but the general election in December 1923 produced an increase in both Labour and Liberal MPs, resulting in the loss of an overall Unionist majority (table 1.2).

This emphasized the strategic problem of a three-party system and began the first of two phases, in 1924 and 1931, of ruthless Unionist-Conservative actions against their opponents which resolved the problem in their favour, and which enabled the party's other strengths – in electoral structure, organization and ideology – to become effective. Given the aim of assembling an anti-Labour majority, the crucial issue was the allegiance of Liberal voters and 'moderates' or 'mugwumps' committed neither to Labour nor to Conservatives. There were two possible strategies, not necessarily exclusive. As table 1.2 indicates, one strategy – that of 1918, and preserved in constituency pacts in 1922 – was to attract these voters through an alliance with Liberal politicians. But after the 1923 election the reunited Liberal leadership decided to vote against the Unionist government and so allow a Labour government to be formed in January 1924. This ended the Chamberlainites' hope of a restored coalition, and so reunited the Unionist party and helped Baldwin to remain party leader. It also converted all Unionists to the alternative strategy – that of seeking to fragment and crush the Liberal party, while persuading Liberal politicians and Liberal voters to defect to Unionism. Accordingly, while in opposition to the Labour government Unionist leaders both made themselves more attractive to Liberals by dropping protection and offering social reform, and exploited the doubts of many Liberals at their leaders' decision to install 'socialists' in government. When the contrasting impacts of Baldwin's 'non-political' appeal and the party organization's relentless stoking of anti-socialist scares (culminating in exposure of the 'Zinoviev letter') were added, the effect was devastating: a defecting group of 'constitutionalist' Liberals (in Churchill's case, re-defecting), many local Liberal–Unionist election pacts, over 100 fewer Liberal candidates and a Liberal party collapse at the October 1924 general election, producing a huge Conservative victory.

Under Baldwin, with Churchill as chancellor of the exchequer and Neville Chamberlain as minister of health, the 1924–9 government maintained the politics and policies of Conservative accommodation towards Liberal opinion and what were thought to be the concerns of many working-class and female voters: industrial conciliation, minimization of protection, preservation of unemployment insurance, a large extension of the pensions system, public support for slum clearance and increased house-building, and improved facilities for maternal and child care. But the government could not overcome chronic economic difficulties and mass unemployment, nor wholly resist party pressures for stronger 'conservative' measures, especially, after the defeat of the General Strike, for anti-trade union legislation. Although most Conservatives expected Baldwin's remarkable personal reputation to secure further victory for them,[26] the party was defeated at the May 1929 general election, falling back to 38 per cent of the national poll.

Again, as at the 1923 election, this was largely an effect of a three-party system, with another Liberal revival magnifying a renewed Labour advance amidst the highest-ever number of three-cornered contests (tables 1.2 and 1.3). Even though the second Labour government was again in a parliamentary minority and the Liberal party was considerably smaller than in 1923–4, the effort to address the strategic problem was delayed for two years. The Conservatives were distracted by internal party disputes over tariffs, empire trade and India, during which Baldwin's efforts to remain sensitive towards 'moderate' and Liberal opinion nearly cost him his leadership, amidst tides of diehard, imperialist and protectionist criticism. The party-political problem was further complicated by the onset of deep economic depression from late 1929. At first it seemed that the Labour government's inability to cope with a mounting economic, unemployment and financial crisis and a broad shift of opinion towards protection and public expenditure cuts would restore Conservatives to government, assisted as in 1924 by Liberal defections – since a group of Liberal MPs led by Simon was now prepared to accept tariffs as an emergency measure.[27]

In the event, however, the second phase in the destruction of the three-party system took a different and far more dramatic form. The August 1931 sterling and budget crises fatally split the Labour cabinet, but the circumstances created a serious difficulty for Conservative leaders. Instead of winning the next election on the issue of protection, they might lose it if they formed a government imposing cuts in unemployment benefits, social services and public service salaries and wages, and were opposed by a united Labour party presenting Conservatives as the party of the rich and comfortable minority imposing increased hardship on the poor or hard-pressed masses. Fearing dangerous repercussions for Conservative interests from such an explicit form of class politics, the Conservative leaders instead chose what became a more successful and prolonged version of the 1918 strategy. They proposed a coalition under the existing prime minister, even though MacDonald was a socialist; they accepted alliance with the Liberal leaders, together with MacDonald's few remaining Labour supporters; and they improved upon 1918 by calling the result a 'National government'. This government was intended as a temporary emergency arrangement, but during September 1931 most of the Labour movement went into outright opposition, shifted sharply towards the socialist left and resorted to class arguments, while the government failed in its declared aim of defending the value of sterling and faced the prospect of political humiliation. In these circumstances, Conservative ministers agreed to maintain the atmosphere of 'national crisis' and to preserve the political security of the National government at a general election, rather than run any risk of defeat by their party fighting independently. The Conservatives, Liberals and 'National Labour' together arranged hundreds of electoral pacts – crucially reducing the number of three-cornered contests (table 1.3) – and mounted a fierce anti-Labour campaign under a 'National' cause. The October 1931 general election produced the largest election victory and the largest number of Conservative MPs of modern times.[28]

Here, in the party-political manoeuvres, the creation of a 'National' coalition and the massive anti-Labour electoral and ideological alliance of autumn 1931, lie the chief reasons for the Conservative party's interwar dominance, because the National government continued until 1940. So attractive was this government to Conservative leaders that they went to remarkable lengths to preserve it. When half the Liberal party and some National Labour ministers refused to accept Conservative insistence on the final introduction of protection in February 1932, an 'agreement to differ' allowed them to criticize the policy publicly yet remain in the government. When these ministers eventually did resign in September 1932, rather than form a purely Conservative government Baldwin persuaded MacDonald and the Simon Liberals to continue. Even after Baldwin succeeded MacDonald as prime minister in 1935, a National Labour and National Liberal presence was preserved. The National government was continued by Conservative ministers because it allowed them to pursue policies – of economic intervention, preservation of social policies and Indian reform – which, given attitudes in the Conservative heartlands, would have been difficult for a purely Conservative government to undertake. Above all, the National government enabled their version of Conservatism to command much Liberal and 'moderate' support, and so created an apparently impregnable barrier to socialism. At the next general election, in 1935, the main threat came not from the Labour party but from a possible alienation of 'liberal' peace opinion which disliked the government's programme of rearmament against the military threats of Germany and Italy, as likely to encourage an arms race that would cause, rather than prevent, another war. Yet Baldwin's political touch was now so sure that he had little difficulty making rearmament palatable as vital to the preservation of peace, by underpinning collective security, the League of Nations and defence of freedom against totalitarianism.[29] Only after the Munich crisis of September 1938 and under the less ideologically sensitive premiership of Neville Chamberlain did the government face effective pressure, as groups of Conservative, Liberal and Labour critics of his policies of 'appeasement' began to coalesce into a 'national' opposition. Nevertheless, the first opinion polls organized in Britain, dating from early 1939, indicate that the National government would have defeated the Labour party if an election had been held in 1940. A second total war, however, had the reverse political effect to that of the first, with Labour rather than Unionists reaping the benefits of not being the party in power at the outbreak of war. As in 1915–16, so in 1940 conditions of 'total war' produced a new coalition government, under Churchill's premiership but with Labour leaders as equal partners to the Conservatives – occupying positions from which they assisted a movement of the ideological and policy agenda towards collectivist economic and social policies, and towards the largest defeat of the Conservative party since 1906.

NOTES

1 The best party history is J. Ramsden, *The Age of Balfour and Baldwin 1902–1940* (London, 1978). Useful introductions are S. Ball, *The Conservative Party and British*

Politics 1902–1951 (London, 1995) and J. Ramsden, *The Appetite for Power: A History of the Conservative Party since 1830* (London, 1998).

2   See e.g. the table of socio-economic backgrounds of MPs in Ramsden, *Age of Balfour and Baldwin*, pp. 98–9.

3   The word 'Tory' was rarely used by Unionists or Conservatives themselves, certainly not in reference to the whole party: it properly described a particular constitutional or paternalistic tradition. The term was most commonly employed by opponents, with pejorative meanings – a use perpetuated by some historians. Unless given an accurate historical meaning, the word is best avoided.

4   R. Blake, *The Conservative Party from Peel to Churchill* (London, 1970), pp. 181–4.

5   G. R. Searle, *The Quest for National Efficiency* (Oxford, 1971).

6   A. Sykes, *Tariff Reform in British Politics 1903–1913* (Oxford, 1979).

7   E. H. H. Green, *The Crisis of Conservatism* (London, 1995).

8   J. Lawrence, 'Class and gender in the making of urban Toryism, 1880–1914', *English Historical Review*, 108 (1993), pp. 629–52; M. Pugh, *The Making of Modern British Politics 1867–1939* (2nd edition, London, 1993), chs 3–4; I. G. C. Hutchison, *A Political History of Scotland, 1832–1924: Parties, Elections, Issues* (Edinburgh, 1986), ch. 7.

9   See K. O. Morgan, *Wales in British Politics 1868–1922* (Cardiff, 1970) and G. I. T. Machin, *Politics and the Churches in Great Britain 1869–1921* (Oxford, 1987).

10 Indeed, the earliest historical conceptualizations of a 'crisis of Conservatism' placed it in 1910–14, with events since 1903 given only as context: see Searle and Sykes in note 11 below. In Green, *Crisis of Conservatism*, 'the crisis' reaches as far back as the 1880s.

11 G. D. Phillips, *The Diehards* (Cambridge, Mass., 1979); G. R. Searle, 'Critics of Edwardian society: the case of the radical right', in A. O'Day, ed., *The Edwardian Age: Conflict and Stability 1900–1914* (London, 1979), pp. 79–96; A. Sykes, 'The radical right and the crisis of Conservatism before the First World War', *Historical Journal*, 26 (1983), pp. 661–76; F. Coetzee, *For Party and Country* (Oxford, 1990).

12 Bonar Law in 1917, quoted in Ramsden, *Age of Balfour and Baldwin*, p. 118. For the ambiguous political effects of the war, see J. Turner, *British Politics and the Great War* (New Haven, Conn., 1992).

13 The classic account of these Unionist difficulties is M. Cowling, *The Impact of Labour 1920–1924* (Cambridge, 1971), chs 2–4, 6–9, 11.

14 Ramsden, *Age of Balfour and Baldwin*, pp. 121–3, chs 10–11; Pugh, *Making of Modern British Politics*, pp. 236–44, 249–52; M. Pugh, 'Popular Conservatism in Britain', *Journal of British Studies*, 27 (1988), pp. 254–82; Ball, *Conservative Party*, pp. 75–9, and see Ball, chs 5, 7, in A. Seldon and S. Ball, eds, *The Conservative Century* (Oxford, 1994).

15 Ramsden, *Appetite for Power*, p. 235; also Ramsden, *Age of Balfour and Baldwin*, p. 121.

16 See esp. N. McCrillis, *The British Conservative Party in the Age of Universal Suffrage* (Columbus, OH, 1998).

17 R. Cockett, 'The party, public and the media', in Seldon and Ball, *Conservative Century*, pp. 547–64; T. Hollins, 'The Conservative party and film propaganda between the wars', *English Historical Review*, 96 (1981), pp. 359–69.

18 I. G. C. Hutchison, 'Scottish Unionism between the two world wars', in C. Macdonald, ed., *Unionist Scotland 1800–1997* (Edinburgh, 1998), pp. 79–80. For a good review of the problems, see D. Jarvis, 'The shaping of the Conservative electoral hegemony 1918–39', in J. Lawrence and M. Taylor, eds, *Party, State and Society* (Aldershot, 1997), pp. 131–52.

19 Pugh, *Making of Modern British Politics*, p. 243; Ball, *Conservative Party*, pp. 77–8. The shared source for calculations of 'middle-class' seats is M. Kinnear, *The British Voter* (London, 1981), pp. 122–4.

20 R. McKibbin, *The Ideologies of Class* (Oxford, 1990), pp. 95, 287–8.

21 'Class and conventional wisdom: the Conservative party and the "public" in inter-war Britain', in McKibbin, *Ideologies*, pp. 259–93.

22 Cf. D. Jarvis, 'British Conservatism and class politics in the 1920s', *English Historical Review*, 111 (1996), pp. 59–84.

23 P. Williamson, 'The doctrinal politics of Stanley Baldwin', in M. Bentley, ed., *Public and Private Doctrine: Essays in British History presented to Maurice Cowling* (Cambridge, 1995), pp. 181–208, and more fully, Williamson, *Stanley Baldwin: Conservative Leadership and National Values* (Cambridge, 1999).

24 R. McKibbin, *Classes and Cultures: England 1918–1951* (Oxford, 1998), pp. 96–7, 529–30; Hutchison, 'Scottish Unionism between the wars', pp. 80–3.

25 Cowling, *Impact of Labour*, p. 421.

26 P. Williamson, 'Safety first: Baldwin, the Conservative party, and the 1929 general election', *Historical Journal*, 25 (1982), pp. 385–409.

27 S. Ball, *Baldwin and the Conservative Party: The Crisis of 1929–1931* (New Haven, Conn., 1988).

28 For the politics of August–October 1931 and the character of the National government, see P. Williamson, *National Crisis and National Government* (Cambridge, 1992), chs 9–12, 14.

29 M. Cowling, *The Impact of Hitler* (Cambridge, 1975), chs 1–3; P. Williamson, 'Christian Conservatives and the totalitarian challenge 1933–1940', *English Historical Review*, 115 (2000), pp. 607–42.

FURTHER READING

Ball, S., *Baldwin and the Conservative Party: The Crisis of 1929–1931* (New Haven, Conn., 1988).

Blewett, N., *The Peers, the Parties and the People: The General Elections of 1910* (London, 1972).

Cowling, M., *The Impact of Labour 1920–1924: The Beginning of Modern British Politics* (Cambridge, 1971).

Cowling, M., *The Impact of Hitler: British Politics and British Policy 1933–1940* (Cambridge, 1975).

Francis, M. and Zweiniger-Bargielowska, I., eds, *The Conservatives and British Society 1880–1990* (Cardiff, 1996).

Green, E. H. H., *The Crisis of Conservatism: The Politics, Economics and Ideology of the British Conservative Party, 1880–1914* (London, 1995).

Jarvis, D., 'British Conservatism and class politics in the 1920s', *English Historical Review*, 111 (1996).

Jarvis, D., 'The shaping of the Conservative electoral hegemony 1918–39', in J. Lawrence and M. Taylor, eds, *Party, State and Society: Electoral Behaviour in Britain since 1820* (Aldershot, 1997).

McCrillis, N., *The British Conservative Party in the Age of Universal Suffrage: Popular Conservatism, 1918–1929* (Columbus, OH, 1998).

Macdonald, C., ed., *Unionist Scotland 1800–1997* (Edinburgh, 1998), esp. ch. 5 by I. G. C. Hutchison.

McKibbin, R., *The Ideologies of Class: Social Relations in Britain 1880–1950* (Oxford, 1990), esp. ch. 9.

Morgan, K. O., *Consensus and Disunity: The Lloyd George Coalition Government 1918–1922* (Oxford, 1979).

Pugh, M., *The Making of Modern British Politics 1867–1939* (Oxford, 1982; 2nd edition, 1993).

Ramsden, J., *The Age of Balfour and Baldwin 1902–1940* (London, 1978).

Ramsden, J., *The Appetite for Power: A History of the Conservative Party since 1830* (London, 1998).

Seldon, A. and Ball, S., eds, *The Conservative Century: The Conservative Party since 1900* (Oxford, 1994).

Sykes, A., *Tariff Reform in British Politics 1903–1913* (Oxford, 1979).

Turner, J., *British Politics and the Great War: Coalition and Conflict 1915–1918* (New Haven, Conn., 1992).

Williamson, P., *National Crisis and National Government: British Politics, the Economy and Empire 1926–1932* (Cambridge, 1992).

Williamson, P., *Stanley Baldwin: Conservative Leadership and National Values* (Cambridge, 1999).

CHAPTER TWO

The Liberal Party, 1900–1939: Summit and Descent

MICHAEL BENTLEY

Few narratives of political change so boldly underline the sheer *unpredictability* of history than the story of the Liberal party's fortunes during the first half of the twentieth century. Could any observer of the Liberals' hammering in 1895 and their uncomfortable performance in the 'khaki' election of 1900 have foreseen that by 1906 they would return to power with a majority of momentous proportions? Could any of those witnessing the events of 1906 have had any clue that before the end of 1914 the Liberal state would be engulfed in world war? Would a Cassandra looking at the smashed state of the Liberals in 1918 have been justified in thinking that they would have nothing to contribute to the next two decades when, in fact, the calculations of the other parties so often turned on the need to capture their constituency? These years present great difficulty for historians, just as they bewildered contemporaries. Indeed, it is very arguable that understanding the removal of Liberalism from the centre of British politics constitutes one of the prime challenges facing historians who wish to come to terms with this volatile period. And for those coming to it for the first time, it will be important to grasp quickly that no simple solution to their questions is currently available. Partly this is because the Liberal party and what it claims to stand for – an ideology of liberalism – do not amount to the same thing, are often not to be found in the same place and have divergent histories. Partly it is because the process of democratization, with its own currents and tributaries, ran through its final moments in parallel with the Liberal difficulties that we shall be discussing here. Partly it is because the Liberal party cannot be understood in abstraction from the strategies and performances of the Labour and Conservative parties, despite the continuing determination of historians to present the Liberal story as one culled exclusively from Liberal sources. Partly it is because the entire trajectory of Liberal politics suffered critical distortion through the experience of the First World War and we have no way of knowing how it might have turned out without that formative force.

Analysing these contexts in a small space requires some heavy editing. This essay will not present a full narrative of the period. Instead it will concentrate on three perspectives that are intended to help those who need to acquire an overview of what an understanding of Liberal history demands from those who attempt it. First, we need to bring together some leading events in order to fix in the mind a basic curve of Liberal success and failure. Second, we need to identify and review some of the problems that this narrative suggests. Third, and crucially, we need to ditch any assumption that the history makes up an uncontested narrative and consider how it has been put together and argued about over the last thirty years. At the very least, a reader ought to take away from this essay the idea that the later years of the historic Liberal party remain, from the perspective of the twenty-first century, problematic and in flux.

The Events

The turn of the new century brought little for Liberals to celebrate. The Boer War had been unfolding – disappointingly – since the previous year; their new party leader, Sir Henry Campbell-Bannerman (1836–1908), had helped to pacify some of the personal antagonisms that had marked the senior reaches of the party since Lord Rosebery's humiliating ministry of 1894–5 and the electoral thrashing that had followed, but did not have the stuff of greatness in him; the wartime election set a seal on Liberal doom, leaving them with just 184 against 402 Conservatives and Unionists in the House of Commons. Peace in 1902 gave them better prospects and lessened the width of the division between Campbell-Bannerman's broadly anti-imperialist sector of the party and the Liberal imperialists, or 'Limps', who included among their number some of the party's best brains – Rosebery, Asquith, Grey, Haldane – and an important second tier of active politicians. Rosebery remained a thorn, it is true, until he overestimated his sharpness in 1905; he went thereafter into a limbo from which he never returned. The others for the moment shared the destiny of their leader, though not without wanting to be rid of him. Meanwhile, Liberal strength in the country seemed parlous. Not only was the Conservative government of Arthur James Balfour, who had succeeded his uncle, the 3rd marquis of Salisbury, in 1902, likely to take a great deal of beating, but the Liberals had also come to worry about the political arm of the labour movement, especially the Labour Representation Committee (LRC) of 1900, which had encountered some success in facing down Liberal candidates in by-elections. The so-called Lib–Lab pact of 1903 became one result of the latter anxiety. Liberals were luckier with the former difficulty for Balfour's government began to tear itself apart the moment it settled into office, with Joseph Chamberlain's campaign of tariff reform exposing the depth of free-trade and protectionist opinion among the Unionists.

Fighting the election that the Liberals were obliged to call once Balfour had surprisingly resigned at the end of 1905 revealed ominous signs in the negativity of the Liberal position: no ideas of their own, as Haldane said, just objections to everybody else's. But their pegging away against a range of Tory irritations – in South Africa, in educational policy, in Ireland and on a favourite Liberal theme, drink – made a powerful case when linked to their new weapon of opposing Chamberlain's 'food taxes'. The returns immediately proclaimed a landslide. In just a decade the Liberal party had turned a humiliation into the most spectacular result in living memory. They now had to deal with twenty-nine MPs sponsored by the LRC, who decided to call themselves the 'Labour Party', but they had 399 of their own with which to do so and the Conservatives had crashed to just 157. The balance of power had shifted remarkably.[1]

Campbell-Bannerman, whom the Liberal imperialists had failed to jettison, took office with one of the most talented cabinets in history behind him;[2] and, had not his health and his wife been against him, he might have gone on to become one of the century's more memorable political leaders. He surrendered office in 1908 to a far stronger man who did indeed go on to be associated with Liberal triumph and collapse in equal degrees. Herbert Henry Asquith (1852–1928), a career barrister with a smooth Oxford manner and an oppressive marriage, imported the Welsh devilry and political genius of David Lloyd George into the exchequer, balanced his administration between the thrusting 'New Liberal' and radical wings of the party, on the one side, and the Whiggish, aristocratic and moderate section, on the other, and continued 'C-B's' battle to make the Liberal party sound like the party of moderate common sense.[3]

The Liberal governments set out to do this between 1906 and the unforeseen disruption of war in 1914 by attempting a limited form of state welfarism of the kind Bismarck had undertaken in Germany, a long list of legislative provisions that included the infamous 'people's budget' introduced by Lloyd George in 1909, the introduction of old-age pensions the previous year, the setting up of labour exchanges to combat unemployment and a later, very unpopular, move towards a programme of contributory national insurance. They also had to cope, however, with rampant nationalism among the Great Powers, an aggressive arms race that had to be defended (not easy for Liberals) and funded (which was harder still), and the pressure of the Irish Nationalists for a resumption of the crusade to extract Home Rule for Ireland from the British government, the promise of William Gladstone in his later years (d. 1898) and official party policy since 1886. Nor was the new Labour party inactive. Although strongly attached to the Liberals by electoral agreement and their own financial weakness, Labour's sense of dependence on a party whose ideals, language and constituency differed manifestly from their own helped nurture grievance and potential revolt against the over-accommodating chairmanship of James Ramsay MacDonald (1886–1937). Even in parliament the Liberal administration struggled, despite its juggernaut majority, with the determination of the House of Lords to block all legislation that offended Conservative instincts. All these contexts compounded a continuing ambiguity within Liberalism about what the party was supposed to stand for, one that played some role in removing its majority altogether when Asquith's government found itself having to fight two general elections in 1910, one in order to marshal a popular mandate against the House of Lords' rejection of the budget, another to bring pressure on the king to create Liberal peers if the Second House's intransigence should continue.[4]

From the end of 1910 to the outbreak of war in August 1914, the Liberal and Tory parties faced each other across the swordlines in the House of Commons with virtually the same number of MPs on each side. Labour had climbed to forty-two but declined through by-election losses. The Irish held steady at just over eighty. From our perspective it appears a critical period with the developing threat of civil war in Ireland as the leaders of Ulster refused to submit to the government's attempts to impose a Home Rule Bill on them, with Labour's quiet strengthening of its national organization, with the so-called Great Unrest whose strikes in industrial and mining centres sometimes brought violence in their wake, with the drama of the suffragettes and the illiberal force-feeding that followed their imprisonment, with the kaiser's megalomania enlarged by spy stories and invasion literature intended to bring Britain to a state of nervous frenzy.[5]

The First World War created a climate in which Liberals needed constantly to talk about subjects uncomfortable to them – patriotism, xenophobia, censorship, state management of the economy and all human resources – while it simultaneously imposed constraints inhibiting politicians from batting 'all around the wicket' and forced a political discourse with which only the Conservative party felt at home. In the complex events and processes of those four years, three were to prove of decisive importance in Liberal history. The coming to power of Lloyd George in December 1916, following a constant undermining of Asquith since his decision to invite other parties into coalition in May 1915, not only split the Liberal cohort in parliament and the country but gave the Liberal party a wayward, powerful engine. Second, the return of the Tory party to centrality in British politics through the war rescued them from a potential marginality which their pre-war adventures in Ireland had seemed likely to confer on them and gave them the possibility of beginning the post-war period from a position of strength. Third, although Labour's taste of office in the war years proved fragmentary and transitory, their new confidence held out the promise of long-term challenge to Liberalism as the party of moderate progress, bolstered by a more effective constitution (1918) and the coming of universal manhood (plus limited female) suffrage in the Reform Act of 1918, and energized in the country by the uplift of Soviet example in Russia. Not all of this became apparent immediately. The general election held at the end of the war confirmed in lurid colour the plight of Asquithian Liberals: they came back with around thirty MPs (estimates vary). It concealed Labour's potential, partly because of the low turnout occasioned by the catastrophic 'flu epidemic, but also because the election's 'khaki' character enabled the other combatants to describe Labour as a pacifist party with a record of half-heartedness and subversion during the war. What it did not conceal was Lloyd George's triumphal pre-eminence as the man of the moment and the overwhelming strength of the Conservative party with whom Lloyd George had been working in coalition since 1916, and with whom he would remain in government until dropped by a party he could no longer control in October 1922.

Whatever one thinks of the state of the Liberal party after the election of 1918 – we shall review some of the possibilities shortly – it is clear in retrospect that the 1920s provided the last decade in which the plausibility of a Liberal revival as a party of government seemed even remotely conceivable until the party's reformation and re-emergence after the 1970s. They lacked major advantages.[6] Money began to run out, except for Lloyd George's own political fund, and became critical by 1924. Issues moved on: the pressing topics no longer encompassed the stamping grounds of pre-war years except for the threat and reality of civil war in Ireland and the reassertion of tariff reform by the Conservatives. Talent ran out, too. The great names in pre-war Liberalism retired or died during the 1920s, apart from Lloyd George himself, Churchill (who became a Conservative again), Sir John Simon and Herbert Samuel. Viscount Grey, Asquith's former foreign secretary, survived until 1933 but had taken little part in active politics for some years. The split of 1916 never healed, except for flurries of public reconciliation made necessary by Baldwin's calling a general election over the issue of protection in 1923. All the same, for a couple of years in 1923–4, and again for a few months in 1928–9, the Liberal party made itself felt in national politics, aided by a period of electoral instability that produced five polls in eleven years: 1918, 1922, 1923, 1924, 1929. Baldwin's gift-horse of 'tariffs' allowed Liberals a period of relevance and gave them their best electoral performance of the decade. Maybe they should have done more with it. A genuine three-party politics looked likely; but Asquith decided to hand the chalice of government to MacDonald and the Labour party in the hope, presumably, that they would make such a mess of governing that it would set them back considerably. They got their mess but Labour won a more important compensation in having shown itself capable of non-revolutionary administration. Asquith's last throw – he retired in 1926 – may therefore not have been his best. Lloyd George, meanwhile, read the runes to say that Liberalism was finished and that the future lay with the left. His own overtures to Labour came to nothing, however, and he threw himself and his money into a last major battle to impress the British public with a series of 'inquiries' and 'summer schools' that culminated in an important analytical study of Britain's problems, the so-called Yellow Book, entitled *Britain's Industrial Future* (1928). This became the basis of the Liberal message in their enormous and lengthy campaign at the forth-coming general election at the end of Baldwin's term of office (1924–9).

There would never be a better chance of revival, if any were possible. The Liberals had leadership, money, the best intellectual case by a great margin. Over the last decade, the 'New Liberalism' of the pre-war years had reformed into a persua-sive doctrine of state-led management, based to some extent on the still-evolving ideas of John Maynard Keynes. But 1929 brought disaster. Only fifty-nine Liberals returned to the new parliament, and even that small band contained serious divi-sions between those who followed Lloyd George, those who looked to a centrist Liberalism that distanced itself from the acrimony of the past few years, and the hard-line post-Asquithians who spoke the language of betrayed principle. Thereafter, the Liberal party operated as a group of fragments with only occasional eruptions of any significance, as when the complex politics behind the formation of a National gov-ernment in 1930–1 included some of them, or when Samuel took his fragment out of the National government when it turned to protection in 1932, or when Lloyd George, a self-parodic septuagenarian, tried to launch a 'New Deal' to resemble Roo-sevelt's in the United States.[7] The Liberal party remained important, not for its politi-cians or its programme, but for its *constituency*: those 5 million persons who between them held, as Churchill pointed out, the key to the future. Liberalism shrank as a political party while it expanded as a necessary element in all political rhetoric: Tories had to show how Liberal they were at heart, and Labour needed to reassure Liber-als in the country that they were the Liberal party's natural successors.

The Problems

'When and why did the decline of the Liberal Party become irreversible?' An exam-ination question from the 1960s will suffice to place the essential problem at the fore-front of the mind when we look back over this rather bland narrative, even if the question itself is not without assumptions of its own. Within this big question, however, lie more partial ones that affect particular phases of the chronology or sectors of the discussion; and once several of these come into play simultaneously, one's head begins to spin and argument seems confusing and contradictory. It may help to bear in mind two distinctions which help to focus and arrange the various arguments that have to be considered. The first separates those views that argue that the demise of the Liberal party took place before the First World War from those that see some potential for a political future during and after it. A further distinction puts on one side of the case arguments grounded in a view of 'internal collapse' and, on the other, views that imply that Liberalism perished through a form of 'external assault'. Many arguments involve both assertions; some fit more tidily into one or other of these distinctions; but keeping this framework of analysis in mind may help to identify points of difference and shades of emphasis.

One way of avoiding all these problems is to announce that the Liberal party was dead or dying before our period even began. This view points to fundamental changes in the nature of late Victorian society and the economy that underpinned it and contends that everything that happened after 1900 was part of a hopeless struggle against the facts of life. All the building bricks of a successful Liberalism – small-scale capitalism, thriving nonconformity, a booming economy and an absence of class warfare – had begun to crumble by the era of the so-called Great Depression of 1873–96. Worse still, mass unionism among the labour force and the emergence of a political wing committed to a working-class constituency took away the Liberals' natural constituency. Henceforth, Liberals would always find themselves trapped by these portents. Let us call this contention the writing-on-the-wall argument. The problems do not go away quite so easily, however. Liberal achievement at the election of 1906 has to be deleted from the wall as a monumental accident, a freak event that bucked the trend. The exciting programme of the Asquith administration has to be written off likewise as a desperate act of pandering to the left to win back support from the nascent Labour party. (Does a party with 399 seats normally feel compelled to pander to a party with 29?) The difficult years faced by the Liberals between 1910 and 1914 have to be made to sound difficult because of some deep inadequacy at the heart of Liberalism itself, rather than simply years that any political party would have found stressful without having one foot in the grave. Edwardian Liberalism has to be represented, not as a great moment in Liberal history, but as a final fling before extinction. Cabinet ministers enjoy their cocktails and garden parties while Rome quietly burns.

Whoever wrote the writing on the wall has a further problem, and a serious one. For the argument implies that although society and economic structures underwent change in late Victorian and Edwardian Britain, Liberalism did not. The entire interpretation stands on the assumption that Liberalism was a brittle ideology with no possibility of adaptation. Enter at this point the concept of a New Liberalism. This view insists that, on the contrary, the Liberal party responded to social and economic change, and did so with marked success. Beginning with the Liberal intelligentsia and gradually spreading down into the party and through its propaganda into the constituencies, Liberalism in this view became a powerful radical force with a coherent programme of welfarism and a deeply thought-through body of ideas associated with political thinkers of the calibre of John Hobson, L. T. Hobhouse, Henry Jones, Charles Masterman, Leo Chiozza Money and others. Far from being a fluke, the general election of 1906 showed the penetration of these new ideas and the influence of the 'social radicals' who embodied them. Instead of running away from a new situation of 'class politics' in Edwardian Britain, the Liberals had found an adaptation of surprising vitality. Far from waiting to expire, the Liberals could look forward to a long and active life if they reacted intelligently to events. They could persuade the still-limited electorate that they, and not Labour, held out the best hope of radical but not revolutionary change; and they could arrange to extend the franchise in the direction of a mass democracy when they were ready and on their own terms. Had it not been for the war . . .

Needless to say, this rhapsodic account also has its problems. This New Liberalism is easy to find among 'thinkers', but how many New Liberals do we find among politicians? Lloyd George and Churchill felt enthusiastic for a while, though both reverted to positions that were far from New Liberal. Other cabinet ministers showed no such enthusiasm, though some like to claim Asquith as a New Liberal. And *where* was this New Liberalism? There are signs of vitality in the north-west, fed by C. P. Scott's *Manchester Guardian*. Once across the Pennines into industrial Yorkshire, on the other hand, and Liberals start to look much Older. What about London? It may be that New Liberalism energized a fragment rather than the party or movement as a whole. Then there is the problem of the limited electorate and the issue (remarkably hard to pronounce on with any confidence) of what kind of person remained disfranchised before the war. We know that the proportion of adult males without the vote in this period may have been as high as 40 per cent. But which 40 per cent? If they comprised the very poor and disadvantaged, then they could be seen as potential Labour supporters, in which case the long-term prognosis for Labour looks good. If they were excluded because their social mobility made it impossible for them to fulfil residence qualifications, then many of them could be Liberals or Conservatives, which might help the New Liberal case.[8]

These knots – and there are many others – can be cut by standing back from the entire Edwardian period and declaring it marginal to our big question. Liberalism may have been healthy before the war; it may have been sick. What killed it, either way, was the war. This is the brutalist view. Liberals could cope with the difficulties that peacetime politics threw at them. They proved inadequate to the demands of total war under which they drowned, quite as surely as Lord Kitchener, before the end of 1916. Lloyd George survived. But he – the words are often spat out – was not a true Liberal at all but a careerist bully with not an idea between his ears and all his energies concentrated between his legs. The real strength of historic Liberalism finds its true expression, in this line of thinking, in the sad residue of Asquithians after the 1918 election. Here the problems lie in evaluating whether the war's specific environments – coalition, conscription and so on – attacked Liberalism in particular rather than all parties and in deciding whether the contemptuous view of Lloyd George, one that often had its origins in disappointed Asquithians, has any force. To question the first proposition, one turns to the complicated events of 1914–16 in order to show that Liberals did not feel any crucial challenge to their identity or policies but merely got themselves entangled in difficulties with the other two parties. To question the second is much easier. Lloyd George had his own doctrines about Liberalism and what it meant, assuredly, but that ought not to make him vulnerable to the charge that he had none at all. In 1918 he brought a programme of national reconstruction before the country and it contained strong Liberal elements, not least in its vision of a pacifistic foreign policy that would build a new international community along Wilsonian lines and in his brilliant 'solution' of the Irish difficulty in the partition of 1921.[9] In counter-response one can argue with some force that only Liberalism felt the full power of the war's demands because of the *nature* of traditional Liberalism and the aversion felt by all 'true' Liberals to violence and the tyranny of the state. As for Lloyd George, his 'Liberalism' can equally be described as a series of half-promises and sops necessary to retain some Liberal credibility while he simultaneously intrigued with the Tories to dispense with both parties and substitute a modern centre party with a broad appeal.[10]

Amid all this turbulence at the level of party politics, what of the -ism that Liberals supposed themselves to represent? Did it mean anything at all by 1918? It came in two forms during the 1920s. One praised what Asquith called 'Liberalism without prefix or suffix': the eternal verities of free trade, international pacification, generosity towards Ireland and the maintenance of freedom of action for the individual against the claims of an expanding Whitehall. The other, voiced by Lloyd George and his followers, dismissed such thinking as irrelevant to modern needs and tried to confront political realities – a Liberal party that contained a strong business element,[11] mass unionism with its threats of direct action, unemployment, urban deprivation, the need for progressive taxation – by constructing a Liberalism based on social research. In foreign policy the imperative lay in presenting the League of Nations as the hope for future peace, and Viscount Grey as its best embodiment. These ideas ultimately proved bigger than the party that lay claim to them and they were taken up in varying degrees by moderate Labour and by some Liberal Tories.[12] This latter point raises a major dimension. Between the wars Britain fell into a Conservative grasp with only the minority administrations of 1924 and 1929–31 to break the thrall. If a Liberal persuasion within that Toryism can be identified, then all was not lost with the Liberal message. The problem here, therefore, lies in deciding whether Liberal*ism* exercised an influence over the centre of the political spectrum between, say, 1922 and 1935 that the Liberal *party* could no longer sustain. Much depends on whether one thinks that ideas matter in British politics. The brutalists are likely to remain rooted in the mud of the Somme, with Liberal corpses all around them, envisaging a future in which only the hard-faced men of Baldwin's Britain are likely to survive.

Now, suppose we return to the big question. It has multiple answers which turn on the arguments, or combinations of arguments, that each of these sub-segments makes available and this complexity explains why no agreed formula has appeared in answer to it. For those attached to the writing-on-the-wall prescription., the decline of the Liberal party dates from well before 1900. For those impressed by electoral evidence, a case can be made for Edwardian Britain as the turning point. For labour historians cheering on the new Labour party, Liberal vitality had been severely sapped by 1914. For historians fascinated by New Liberalism, on the other hand, the rot cannot have set in before 1914. For wartime brutalists it cannot have avoided setting in by 1916. For those undeterred by three-party politics and enamoured of Lloyd George, one might go to 1924. For political theorists who see themselves above elections and personalities, 1929 or even 1935 look plausible. One way of placing these many orientations under a different light lies in asking questions about the historians who decided to argue them, and when and why they did so. The history of these constructions – their 'historiography' as professional historians call this kind of study – has special importance in these matters and sometimes throws its own illumination over why the subject has evolved in the confusing and contested patterns that we have been reviewing.

The Historiography

The story of Liberal *history* (as opposed to Liberal events) began in the 1930s when British Liberalism was still apparently alive and when, more to the point, so were many people who had participated in the political turmoil of the past three decades. An English expatriate historian of America, George Dangerfield, became drawn to the imaginative challenge of trying to make sense of the decline of Liberal power in modern Britain and he achieved his picture by drawing in the bold divisions of the canvas that seemed obvious to the eye of his generation. This meant seeing the Great War as a fundamental divide, separating a period of spacious civilization in Britain from the pinched and dark decade that followed the catastrophe. Yet although he felt the force of that argument, he looked deeper into Edwardian society, which many published memoirs were currently calling into public memory, and decided that the rot within Liberalism had begun long before the war in the social and economic shifts of the late Victorian period. These had left the traditional Liberal party without a base, for all its superficial success in 1906, and vulnerable to serious attack from without. He combined, therefore, the internal-collapse and external-assault perspectives in approaching his problem by seeing the two processes as sequential: Liberalism suffered internal erosion over a long period and then, from about 1910, three specific challenges revealed the vulnerability of Asquith's Liberal government and overwhelmed it *before* the Great War impinged. His external assaults came from the volatile trade union activity associated with the Great Unrest, from Ireland in the renewal of Home Rule agitation (and the threat of civil war if Ulster refused to accept it), and from the suffragettes who made a laughing stock of the government and showed them to be seriously illiberal in the force-feeding of women on hunger strike. All these contexts combined to bring about *The Strange Death of Liberal England* (1936). The performance was stunning as a literary event: imaginative, brilliant, perverse, stimulating, an historical novel which, once read, could never quite be forgotten. It became the starting point for all who followed.

Yet Dangerfield's account breathed its own time-bound atmosphere just as surely as Asquith and McKenna and Churchill and Lloyd George had been made to breathe theirs in his depiction. Dangerfield wrote amid a national crisis in unemployment and at a moment of great importance in the development of the left within the Labour party. He knew, as his Asquith had not, that 'Ireland' would persist and turn into actual civil war after 1921. He knew that women would win the vote in 1918 and 1928, establishing their permanent status in British electoral politics. Did he not take these environments from the 1930s and translate them back into the now distant pre-war world, making these three aspects overwhelming before their time? We all do it, of course. Sometimes it proves possible to curb this licentiousness by making it survive a close encounter with 'primary sources' – the period's letters, diaries and private artefacts. Dangerfield could not do that: the sources remained unopened to historical research in his day. He had to use his own period's published accounts and

with them came a gloss on the past fifty years from which Dangerfield had little hope
of distancing himself. Nor could he have foreseen that within a few years of his book's
appearance the whole of Europe would once more confirm that war – not labour or
Ireland or feminists but war – had the twentieth century by its throat. A post-Second
World War world would seek to place the Liberal party in contexts very different
from Dangerfield's.

It did so in two ways, both of which date from the 1960s – a decade whose special
characteristics were made relevant to the story. First, the emergence of a powerful
variant of labour history refocused attention on the working class and its development as the key element in Liberal trauma. Epitomized in the careful scholarship of
Henry Pelling and the coming together of specialist studies of particular sectors of
labour experience, this strand of argument wanted to say that Dangerfield had the
story straight in seeing the period before 1914 as pivotal, but that he had the cau-
sation muddled. The central threat to a continuing Liberal tradition in Britain lay in
the creation of a politics that turned on social class rather than vague uplifting principles of the kind Gladstone had deployed. Class, moreover, had turned against
Liberalism by making a new kind of working-class voter who attached himself – there
were still no women on the roll – to a vague but persistent 'labourism'.[13] It became
a writing-on-the-wall argument because it implied that, whatever the Liberals did,
the coming power of a new class would set the seal on its irrelevance. A second initiative had more immediate effect and radically altered the discussion. Again it found
its voice from across the sea, this time in the Australian scholar Trevor Wilson. At
one level Wilson's account of *The Downfall of the Liberal Party* (1966) simply offered
a fresh narrative that could, unlike Dangerfield's, take advantage of unpublished
sources. But it did more than that in fingering the First World War as the crucial
determining element in the Liberals' fortunes after 1900. Wilson conceded that the
party did not look in robust health by 1914; but it was unquestionably alive as a
governing force and by the 1930s, he argued, it was not. So the best guess had to
be that the events of the war and its aftermath killed historic Liberalism and left a
pathetic rump where once there had been a great political party.[14] Both of these interpretations spoke of external assault: from Labour in the one case, and war in the
other. But they rocked the argument differently around the fulcrum of 1914. Labour
was supposed to have done its damage before 1914, on the first hypothesis, and, on
the second, the war after 1914 killed Liberalism no matter what Labour had done
to it during peacetime.

A specific and important assumption that we have already noticed ran through
Dangerfield's view and the 1960s revisions of it. They all took the Liberal party to
be incapable of significant change. Everything else changed. The economy took
on a different aspect, society went through major transformations, nonconformity
dwindled, Labour turned itself into a threatening force, war exploded with its new
demands, unemployment and Hitler walked onto the stage; but Liberals stood still.
It was Peter Clarke who blew away this deeply unhistorical outlook at the beginning
of the 1970s – a decade of optimism for Social Democrats – by taking seriously the
ideas and politics of New Liberals and claiming that the Edwardian Liberal party not
only resigned itself to class politics but learned to thrive in their new situation.[15] What
happened at the polls in 1906 reflected real success, on this reading, and not just a
mysterious ignorance of the writing on the wall. Two implications seemed to follow.

The first undermined any certainties that the Liberals had gone under by 1914: they could swim. The second suggested that one should not simply assume that they could not have survived the First World War. If they could cope with a context in which one of their key ideas – their dislike of class politics – had come under pressure and provoked a Liberal transformation, why could they not adapt again and deal with a world that brought others among their ideals into question? This view has run into strong criticism through the 1980s and 1990s but it announced a very serious thought which everyone now has to consider. It is that the internal nature of Liberalism played as important a role in the story as Dangerfield said it did, but with the opposite result. One did not have to treat Liberalism as an ageing and sclerotic player, kicked around the field of politics by bigger and stronger opponents. It had a life of its own.

Responses to this initiative again have divided into two types. One of them returned to the Labour problem and saw it in a new light. The other reconsidered the inner nature of Liberalism and did something different with it.

Perhaps the most significant discussion of twentieth-century Liberalism has centred on the question of who could vote in the pre-1918 system and what the effect of universal suffrage might have been after 1928. Work on the Edwardian franchise cast real doubt on any confidence that Liberal politicians were dealing with a democratic franchise; and in 1976 three Oxford historians replaced that confidence with an assertion that the franchise remained profoundly undemocratic before 1918 and that the segments of male society excluded during that period *would have been potential Labour supporters*.[16] The vote turned on owning property, this argument ran; people excluded must have been excluded for failing to own it; people without property were likely to form the social base of a Labour constituency. Conclusion: Labour banged their heads against a glass ceiling until 1918 (so their poor performance before then was both understandable and excusable) and they would be bound to prove formidable once that ceiling was removed in the Reform Act. This is the writing-on-the-wall argument with its dates rubbed out and new ones substituted: it is now the post-war era when Labour's rise will become insurmountable and the doom of the Liberals inescapable. It could be joined up with an argument from other Labour historians that the war represented a crucial turning point in Labour fortunes and exposed the inadequacy of Liberalism in both its Asquithian and Lloyd Georgian varieties.[17] Against this drift in the literature we have witnessed a range of thoughtful and unsettling responses contesting an optimistic story of Labour's unfair repression before 1918. In particular a study by Duncan Tanner altered the landscape in 1990 by proclaiming that franchise exclusions had more to do with failure to meet residence requirements than property thresholds.[18] Those who could not vote were those who were geographically – and probably socially – mobile. And *they* would have voted Liberal or Conservative if anyone had let them vote at all. Rather than seeing Labour as working under peculiarly disadvantaged conditions before the First World War, it should be viewed as enjoying potentially its best years and failing to exploit them.

The second approach sat comfortably with the idea that we should be looking after 1914 for the critical events in the destruction of British Liberalism; but it turned back to the inner nature of Liberalism itself, as Dangerfield had done, and thought about the ideology as much as the practices of the Liberal party. It proved possible

to emerge from this discussion persuaded both that the Liberal party did not effectively survive the war and also that Liberalism remained an important force across all
parties. In 1977 the present writer's study of *The Liberal Mind* in this period
concluded that the war made Liberals contemplate actions which few Liberals could
honestly envisage and reminded them of ideological positions which many of them
had long forgotten. It made 1916 especially important in creating a type of Liberalism
recommended by Lloyd George and his allies which 'genuine' Liberals found abhor-
rent; and it suggested that the split in the party mimicked a still deeper one in the
way that Liberals thought about themselves.[19] Since then Michael Freeden has gone
further to propose that the -ism broke free from the party and became the central
justificatory theory for some Labour party positions.[20] In this way it becomes possible to see Liberalism as a sort of creeping mist occupying the centre ground of
politics in interwar Britain – no longer a viable political machine, for all Lloyd
George's antics, but nevertheless a significant contaminant in the language and policies of government and opposition.

Much of this historiographical debate took its tone and direction from the
tortured days of Harold Wilson's Labour party and the seeming inability of Labour,
especially under James Callaghan, to cope with a mass industrial society. Then came
Mrs Thatcher. The new issues raised by 1980s Conservatism threw historians, though
they often did not realize it at the time, into a rediscovery of Toryism as an historical problem and rescued Liberal historiography from the self-fascination into which
it had perhaps fallen. Since then it has been the history of Conservative politics in
this period that has come to the fore, reminding us that no party history can ever
make sense in its own terms and that British politics has to be studied as an interactive, cross-pollinating environment. That story is followed elsewhere in this volume.[21]
But it has had important implications in compelling Liberal historians to think harder
about the relationship between their subject and social change. Did the Edwardian
Liberals not see that their willingness to live with an Aliens Act that transparently
discriminated against individuals on the ground of race contradicted their doctrines
about freedom of movement and the dangers of state compulsion?[22] If the interwar
period became a Tory hegemony, it did so largely because of the kind of society that
Britain had become. Perhaps Liberals suffered, *per contra*, from those same changes.
If Tories benefited from their cultivation of women in the new electorate, perhaps
Liberals did not work hard enough in that area or failed to see the ambiguities of
the female electorate.[23] If suburbanization and the mushrooming of London became
a Tory advantage, did it make any Liberal recovery out of the question or invite a
form of *Poujadisme* on which the Liberals failed to capitalize? If unemployment ought
to have hurt the Tory party, why did the most intelligent programme of measures
against unemployment fail to revive the Liberal party in 1929? There remains much
to explain.

At almost a century's distance from these various aspects and problems of
Liberalism, we stand in danger of losing the human element which, for all his way-
wardness, Dangerfield so brilliantly portrayed. The crisis in modern Liberalism was
no trivial piece of political engineering – dismantling one contraption and bolting
together a different one. Entire lives endured and prospered under the protection
and *teaching* of Liberalism from John Stuart Mill and Matthew Arnold to New Liberal
thinkers such as Hobson and Hobhouse and revered newspaper editors such as C. P.

Scott, A. G. Gardiner and J. A. Spender. Liberals imbibed the message at school, drank it in daily with their tea and toast, felt the force and truth of it in chapel. To talk about the First World War 'challenging their principles' trivializes this thought-world and misses the point about what the war did to them. It made the unthinkable not only thinkable but unavoidable. Yet in agreeing to the necessity, Liberals lost all those ideals that made this or any fight worthwhile and sold the future that they had believed secure for their children. Some of them traced this abandonment back to the 'bastard' Liberalism of the welfare period before the war. All of them felt some discomfort at the loss of free trade, the coming of conscription and Lloyd George. High politics has its human side, too. Anyone giving public lectures on Liberalism as late as the 1980s would find an aged participant at the back of the room determined to shout that he or she remembered it all and that Lloyd George had killed the Liberal party. Perhaps it is not so disturbing a simplification. Viewed from one angle, Lloyd George understood many things better than his contemporaries but he never understood the doctrines and teachings of his own party; and there are few so insensitive as those who do not know what they are doing. Viewed from another, he saw more clearly than most the ways in which a modern Liberal party had to behave and brought a consistent sympathy for the underdog to the task of reformu-lating a Liberal message: there was always a Liberal trying to get out. Whether it would have made a jot of difference had the Welsh whirlwind blown itself out in the Labour party or in the renewed fusions of a centre-party project after 1924 has to remain moot. What we can say is that, by embodying in a politician of genius the elements of twentieth-century culture that the majority of Liberals most loathed, Lloyd George's presence after 1916 made it harder to find a future for their cher-ished outlook. Just as he outlived Asquith, he lived long enough to see all that Asquith's generation had taken themselves to represent dying around him in Baldwin's world while finding no plausible direction or role for himself. He discov-ered the poignant satisfaction of attending his own protracted funeral.

NOTES

1   For the 1906 election, see A. K. Russell, *Liberal Landslide: The General Election of 1906* (Newton Abbot, 1973).
2   Cf. G. L. Bernstein, 'Sir Henry Campbell-Bannerman and the Liberal imperialists', *Journal of British Studies*, 23 (1983), pp. 105–24. Bernstein sees the imperialists as second-rate politicians and Campbell-Bannerman as never seriously threatened.
3   The personalities of this government have attracted much attention. See, among many others, J. Wilson, *CB: A Life of Sir Henry Campbell-Bannerman* (London, 1973); S. Koss, *Asquith* (London, 1976); J. Grigg, *Lloyd George* (3 vols, London, 1973); J. Campbell, *The Goat in the Wilderness, 1922–31* (London, 1977); K. Robbins, *Sir Edward Grey: A Biography of Lord Grey of Falloden* (London, 1971); R. S. Churchill, *Winston S. Churchill*, vol. 2 (London, 1967); D. Dutton, *Simon: A Political Biography of Sir John Simon* (London, 1992).
4   The important context of the budget is analysed in B. K. Murray, *The People's Budget 1909/10: Lloyd George and Liberal Politics* (Oxford, 1980).
5   The literature addressing these crucial years is voluminous, but for particular problems instanced here see P. Jalland, *The Liberals and Ireland: The Ulster Question in British*

Politics to 1914 (Brighton, 1970); R. McKibbin, *The Evolution of the Labour Party, 1910–1924* (Oxford, 1974); F. Henderson, *The Labour Unrest: What it Is and What it Portends* (London, 1911); A. Rosen, *Rise Up Women! The Militant Campaign of the Women's Social and Political Union* (London, 1974). The material on spies and invasion threats is most conveniently surveyed in D. French, 'Spy fever in Britain, 1900–1915', *Historical Journal*, 21 (1978), pp. 355–70.

6 See K. O. Morgan, *Consensus and Disunity: The Lloyd George Coalition Government, 1918–1922* (Oxford, 1979); M. Cowling, *The Impact of Labour, 1920–1924: The Beginning of Modern British Politics* (Cambridge, 1971); M. Freeden, *Liberalism Divided: A Study in British Political Thought 1914–1939* (Oxford, 1986).

7 The National government's inception is explained in P. Williamson, *National Crisis and National Government: British Politics, the Economy and Empire 1926–1932* (Cambridge, 1992). For the New Deal, see S. Koss, 'Lloyd George and nonconformity: the last rally', *English Historical Review*, 89 (1974), pp. 77–108, and for the later years, D. Dutton, 'John Simon and the post-war Liberal party: an historical postscript', *Historical Journal*, 32 (1989), pp. 357–67.

8 I shall consider the literature dealing with this important debate later in this survey.

9 For a powerful presentation of this case, see Morgan, *Consensus and Disunity*, esp. pp. 1–25.

10 Cowling argues the 'fusionist' case in *Impact of Labour*, pp. 108–50.

11 Cf. G. R. Searle, 'The Edwardian Liberal party and business', *English Historical Review*, 118 (1983), pp. 28–60; J. Turner, ed., *Businessmen and Politics: Studies of Business Activity in British Politics, 1900–1945* (London, 1984).

12 I have considered this theme elsewhere: M. Bentley, 'Liberal politics and the Grey conspiracy of 1921', *Historical Journal*, 20 (1977), pp. 461–78; and 'Liberal Toryism in the twentieth century', *Transactions of the Royal Historical Society*, 6th series, 4 (1994), pp. 177–201.

13 Symptomatic of the labour historiography in this decade are R. Miliband, *Parliamentary Socialism: A Study in the Politics of Labour* (London, 1961); E. Hobsbawm, *Labouring Men: Studies in the History of Labour* (London, 1964); R. Harrison, *Before the Socialists: Studies in Labour and Politics 1861–1881* (London, 1965); H. Pelling, *Social Geography of British Elections, 1885–1910* (London, 1967) and *Popular Politics and Society in Late-Victorian Britain: Essays* (London, 1968). R. Gregory, *The Miners and British Politics, 1906–1914* (Oxford, 1968) posed questions about an ineluctable rise of labour in mining areas, and these were echoed in A. W. Purdue's revisiting of 'Jarrow politics, 1885–1914: the challenge to Liberal hegemony', *Northern History*, 18 (1982), pp. 182–98.

14 T. Wilson, *The Downfall of the Liberal Party, 1914–1935* (London, 1966). His metaphor has become part of the discourse: 'The Liberal party can be compared to an individual who, after a period of robust health and great exertion, experienced symptoms of illness (Ireland, Labour unrest, the suffragettes). Before a thorough diagnosis could be made, he was involved in an encounter with a rampant omnibus (the First World War), which mounted the pavement and ran him over. After lingering painfully, he expired' (p. 18).

15 P. Clarke, *Lancashire and the New Liberalism* (Cambridge, 1971), *Liberals and Social Democrats* (Cambridge, 1978). Cf. Clarke, 'The electoral position of the Liberal and Labour parties, 1910–1914', *English Historical Review*, 90 (1975), pp. 828–36.

16 H. C. G. Matthew, R. McKibbin and J. A. Kay, 'The franchise factor in the rise of the Labour party', *English Historical Review*, 91 (1976), pp. 723–53. Much of the 1970s arguments rested on material provided by N. Blewett, 'The franchise in the United Kingdom, 1885–1918', *Past and Present*, 32 (1965), pp. 27–56.

17 McKibbin, *Evolution of the Labour Party*; C. Wrigley, *David Lloyd George and the Labour Movement: Peace and War* (Hassocks, 1976) and *Lloyd George and the Challenge of*

Labour: The Post-war Coalition, 1918–1922 (Hemel Hempstead, 1990). Cf. J. Turner, *British Politics and the Great War: Coalition and Conflict 1915–1918* (New Haven, Conn., 1992).

18 See D. Tanner's important monograph on *Political Change and the Labour Party, 1900–1918* (Cambridge, 1990), esp. pp. 99–129.
19 M. Bentley, *The Liberal Mind 1914–1929* (Cambridge, 1977).
20 Freeden, *Liberalism Divided*.
21 See chapter 1.
22 See D. Feldman's interesting argument about the relationship between immigration strategies and the withering of Liberalism in his essay on 'The importance of being English: Jewish immigration and the decay of liberal England', in D. Feldman and G. Stedman Jones, eds, *Metropolis. London: Histories and Representations since 1800* (London, 1989), pp. 56–84.
23 M. Pugh, 'The limits of Liberalism: Liberals and women's suffrage, 1867–1914' and P. Thane, 'Women, Liberalism and citizenship, 1918–1930', both in E. F. Biagini, ed., *Citizenship and Community: Liberals, Radicals and Collective Identities in the British Isles, 1865–1931* (Cambridge, 1996). For the ambiguities, see C. Hirshfield, 'Fractured faith: Liberal party women and the suffrage issue in Britain, 1892–1914', *Gender and History*, 2 (1990), pp. 173–97.

FURTHER READING

Biagini, E. F., ed., *Citizenship and Community: Liberals, Radicals and Collective Identities in the British Isles, 1865–1931* (Cambridge, 1996).
Clarke, P., *Liberals and Social Democrats* (Cambridge, 1978).
Collini, S., *Liberalism and Sociology: L. T. Hobhouse and Political Argument in England, 1880–1914* (Cambridge, 1979).
Dangerfield, G., *The Strange Death of Liberal England* (London, 1936).
Freeden, M., *Liberalism Divided: A Study in British Political Thought 1914–1939* (Oxford, 1986).
Jalland, P., *The Liberals and Ireland: The Ulster Question in British Politics to 1914* (Brighton, 1970).
Morgan, K. O., *Consensus and Disunity: The Lloyd George Coalition Government, 1918–1922* (Oxford, 1979).
Murray, B. K., *The People's Budget 1909/10: Lloyd George and Liberal Politics* (Oxford, 1980).
Tanner, D., *Political Change and the Labour Party, 1900–1918* (Cambridge, 1990).
Turner, J., *British Politics and the Great War: Coalition and Conflict 1915–1918* (New Haven, Conn., 1992).
Wilson, T., *The Downfall of the Liberal Party, 1914–1935* (London, 1966).
Wrigley, C., *Lloyd George and the Challenge of Labour: The Post-war Coalition, 1918–1922* (Hemel Hempstead, 1990).

CHAPTER THREE

The Politics of the Labour Movement, 1900–1939

DUNCAN TANNER

The labour movement is generally assumed to comprise the Labour party, trade unions, cooperative organizations and the Communist party. If socialists have often argued that these organizations possessed broadly similar aims, notably the further-ance of working-class living standards, historians have regularly criticized their ability to act together and protect those interests. The Labour party has borne the brunt of this criticism, particularly in relation to the period between 1900 and 1939. Whilst many argue that it benefited electorally from social changes that created a sense of working-class identity, few have suggested that its political actions contributed greatly to this development. On the contrary, for many Labour was politically unimpressive. Dependent on its Liberal inheritance for ideas, Marxist critics argue that Labour failed to defend the interests of unions and workers – to act as the political arm of the labour movement – by implementing socialist ideas and resisting fascism. It was too anxious to become a 'party of the people' rather than the party of the working class. Yet those writing from very different perspectives suggest that Labour also failed to become an effective mechanism for advancing social democratic ideals aimed at the nation as a whole, rather than the working class. It failed to absorb new Keynesian economic ideas that might have helped the whole country to recover from the slump. It also failed to break the hold of a male-dominated trade union culture by creating a party more open to feminist ideas and women's interests. Indeed, for such critics Labour was too tied to the politics of the labour movement to become a party of general progress and reform.

More recently, historians have examined the politics of the Labour party from a different perspective, judging it comparatively (i.e., against the records of other parties) and with due regard to practical considerations and constraints. Such histo-rians identify the scale of the problems facing all democratic parties – the challenge created by nationalistic rivalries before 1914, and by the threat of war, worldwide economic slump and fascism thereafter. Very few parties coped with these problems successfully. Indeed, by the 1930s most European liberal, nationalist and conserva-tive parties had collapsed (and sometimes voluntarily conceded) to the fascist right. Nor had socialist parties stemmed the slide by attracting support from the moderate voters who swelled the ranks of the fascist parties as the economic slump progressed. Only in Australia and Sweden did the left offer a popular and workable remedy to the economic problems of the 1930s. Finally, it is increasingly recognized that there was no obvious socialist 'solution' that Labour blithely ignored, no weak evasion of obvious 'truths'. The 'solutions' offered by western European Communist parties were unworkable. The politics of workers' violence and association with Soviet Russia simply pushed people to the right. Alliance with such elements in defence of working-class interests was hardly a viable strategy. Many Labour party historians now prefer to ask whether Labour missed opportunities which it might reasonably have taken in pursuit of its own goals and aims – to examine what it wanted to achieve, how far it turned down good advice, evaded difficult decisions, failed to adapt and change. It is equally reasonable to examine how far the broader labour movement helped or hindered the party in this process of adaptation and change.

Social and Economic Change and its Impact on the Labour Movement

It was once commonly assumed that Labour expansion across the period from 1900 to 1939 stemmed inevitably from the rise of social class and expansion of trade union-ism.[1] This assumption has been actively contested in recent years. The pattern of the Labour party's advance in parliamentary elections is shown in table 3.1. At no point

Table 3.1 Parliamentary election results, 1900–35 (% of the vote)

Year	Labour	Liberal	Cons	Other[a]
1900	1.3	45.0	50.3	3.4
1906	4.8	49.4	43.4	2.4
1910–Jan.	7.0	43.5	46.8	2.7
1910–Dec.	6.4	44.2	46.6	2.8
1918	20.8	13.0	32.5	33.7
		(12.6)[b]	(6.2)[c]	
1922	29.7	18.9	38.5	12.9
		(9.9)[b]		
1923	30.7	29.7	38.0	1.6
1924	33.3	17.8	46.8	2.1
1929	37.1	23.5	38.1	1.3
1931	31.1	6.4	55.0	7.5
		(3.8)[d]		
1935	38.0	6.7	47.8	7.5
		(3.7)[d]		

[a] Largely nationalists, except when there were coalition governments (1918–22, 1931–9).
[b] Coalition Liberals extracted from 'Others' column.
[c] Conservatives, extracted from 'Others' column.
[d] National Liberals, extracted from 'Others' column.
Source: C. Rallings and M. Thrasher, *British Electoral Facts 1832–1999* (Aldershot, 2000).

Table 3.2 Labour electoral support and trade union membership (in millions)

Year	Election result	Trade union membership
1918	2.25	6.5
1922	4.24	5.6
1923	4.44	5.4
1924	5.49	5.4
1929	8.37	4.8
1931	6.65	4.6
1935	8.33	4.9

Sources: C. Rallings and M. Thrasher, *British Electoral Facts 1832–1999* (Aldershot, 2000); H. Pelling, *A History of British Trade Unionism* (2nd edition, Harmondsworth, 1971), pp. 281–2.

was Labour 'the party of the working class', since of the 70–80 per cent of the electorate belonging to this social group, substantially less than half could have voted for the Labour party. Even in 1935, after the Liberals had been almost eradicated as a rival and in the midst of an economic crisis, the 'natural' party of the working class obtained just 38 per cent of the vote. Recent and very detailed analysis of municipal election results for the period after 1935 suggests that whilst there may have been some temporary improvement in Labour support immediately after 1935, rearmament and the threat of war altered the position in the Conservatives' favour.[2]

Nor can the expansion of trade unionism explain the pattern of Labour support. There were clearly areas where it was a major influence – notably within the mining areas, which gradually became Labour strongholds. Male trade union members were probably more likely to vote Labour than non-unionists, especially women.[3] However, as table 3.2 shows, there is no simple correlation between the growth of Labour's electoral support and the rise and fall of trade union membership. Its major electoral breakthrough in 1929 came largely as a result of increased support in areas like the south-east and the midlands, where trade unions were neither numerous nor especially influential.[4] Equally, Labour's major success in the 1930s was in London, hardly an area of trade union strength, where it captured the London County Council for the first time in 1934 and was re-elected with an increased majority in 1937.

Recent historians place more emphasis on the role of a party's political actions in creating its electoral support. They do not suggest that voters clinically evaluate party programmes. However, they do suggest that the policies advanced and the message put forward have a significant impact on a party's image, on the way it is perceived. During the Edwardian period, the Liberals offered a radical alternative to Labour, which successfully limited and confined Labour's growth. Although there were weaknesses in the Liberals' appeal before 1914, it was the war that shattered the party and undermined its capacity to advance radical ideas. Labour's pre-war inability to replace the Liberals was not a consequence of an unfair electoral system, as some have argued, but a consequence of working-class voters opting to support the existing parties.[5] Even after the war, the Liberals' claim to be the party of sane reform, divorced of class interest, attracted working-class support and inhibited Labour's expansion.

Similarly, in the 1920s the Conservatives attracted a good deal of support from the less affluent by portraying themselves as the party of hardworking and decent people, and Labour as a narrow, selfish and 'Bolshevik' sect.[6] In the 1930s, the National government's various reforms lent credibility to a substantially similar appeal, and with even better results. Labour could never rely on class interest alone, nor on the assumed loyalty of the labour movement. Rather, it needed a political message to counter the political messages of its rivals – a message which showed that Labour was the real 'party of the people', with a credible programme that would improve the quality of their lives. The pursuit of such a programme was to dominate Labour politics in the 1920s and 1930s.

Labour's Political Values, 1900-1914

Historians have often claimed that before 1918 Labour stood for little more than the protection of trade union interests. This is understandable but only partially correct. When the party was formed in 1900 it admitted just one aim – that of electing working-class men to parliament who would remain independent of the Liberal party. Labour adopted no programme and explicitly refused to embrace socialism. The majority of trade unions only affiliated after the Taff Vale case of 1901 threatened to undermine their capacity to conduct industrial action. For many (but not all) trade unions, the Labour party was a pressure group that would represent trade union interests to the Liberals. Subsequently, Labour found it difficult to distance itself from a Liberal party that advanced ideas and policies which many Labour and trade union leaders, and many voters, heartily endorsed.[7] A tacit electoral alliance with the Liberals provided Labour with representation in parliament and an opportunity to try to build up its strength. Yet despite these areas of cooperation, Labour was always more than the party of the unions. Even moderate Labour leaders like MacDonald and Snowden did not agree with the underlying principles of Liberal policy, whilst more radical socialists had deeper reservations.[8] Such people developed their own ideas on the policies that Labour should pursue. Those ideas placed considerable emphasis on the role of the state in creating an effective economy, capable of sustaining both high wages (the party's first aim) and good public services, security and opportunities for all. These ideas were not well developed before 1914, even if they were evident in the party's discussion of the need for a national minimum wage in 1912-13.[9] The party lacked the manpower, the research basis and the desire to create a more well-defined programme. None the less, the raw views formed in this period had a significant influence on subsequent Labour politics. The people who led the party up to 1939 – initially MacDonald and Snowden, and then Henderson, Lansbury and Attlee – developed their values and ideas before the First World War. If expert advice and new circumstances challenged some of those ideas, the way in which Labour leaders perceived issues, and their broad political orientation, were never entirely undermined.

The Expansion of the Labour Party, 1900-1924

One of the early Labour party's main priorities was to establish itself as a political force. The Independent Labour party (ILP) – the socialist group that preceded the

Labour party and which most Labour leaders had first joined – affiliated to the Labour Representation Committee (as the Labour party was called before 1906) in 1900. This gave the new party an organizational base in parts of Britain, notably Lancashire and Yorkshire.[10] However, there was no central Labour organization in 1900, nor any constituency organization in most parts of the country. Ramsay MacDonald and Arthur Henderson devoted much of their early careers to creating this infrastructure. The Labour Representation Committee's first office was a bedroom, normally inhabited by MacDonald's young son. MacDonald wrote endlessly to local activists about the details of party procedures and strategy, whilst Henderson (once a Liberal election agent) worked to develop trade union support and establish a party machine.

The effort of the party's tiny staff of organizers and officials was prodigious, the results substantial. By 1914 there were 179 constituency organizations and 101 trade unions affiliated to the Labour party. The party fielded seventy-eight parliamentary candidates in January 1910, and was expanding on this when war broke out and interrupted the process in 1914. In the municipal election of 1913, Labour fielded nearly 500 candidates across England and Wales. Nearly 200 of them were successful.[11] Some local parties had their own newspapers, active organizations, a social programme and a paid election agent. Labour had its own national newspaper, the *Daily Citizen*, from 1913 and could draw on the intellectual talents of socialists from the ILP and the Fabian Society, who debated Labour policy in their journals the *Socialist Review* and *New Statesman*. This was a huge step forward. Yet compared to the Liberals and Conservatives the party was minute. It was only electorally and organizationally strong enough to fight around 90–100 seats, even by 1914. Large parts of the country had almost no Labour organization, whilst even in many industrial areas Labour attracted little support. For all the trade unions' formal commitment to Labour representation, they were unwilling to fund candidates or the party's newspaper to any substantial degree, whilst many local union members left organizational work to socialists from the ILP.[12] Although leaders of the Cooperative Society and some local cooperative branches supported Labour, the membership voted against direct affiliation to the Labour party in 1915. Although Labour was trying to build up its organizational strength, other sections of the labour movement did not respond with clear enthusiasm. Frustration crept in. Party members, especially those on the left, often felt organizational development was taking precedence over the need to create socialists through propaganda campaigns. Party leaders felt that attacks on its policies and approach were unrealistic and bitter. Some of the party's small intellectual wing felt isolated from the broader membership, and (in Beatrice Webb's case) expressed their views on the limited abilities of trade unionists in graphic language.[13]

The war changed some of this at least. Initially Labour's prospects seemed poor. The party was divided over Britain's entry into the war. There were socialists who saw it as a consequence of imperialism, pacifists who opposed it on principle, and people like MacDonald and Snowden who saw this particular war as the outcome of secret alliances and the arms race. However, the party as a whole supported the war effort. As a result, MacDonald and Snowden effectively withdrew from their prominent leadership roles. The remaining party figures put much effort into war-related concerns – recruiting, protecting the living standards of workers, campaigning for lower food prices and rents, securing better pensions for widows and disabled soldiers. Some Labour figures – notably Arthur Henderson – joined the coalition government in 1915. Yet it also became clear that divisions in the Liberal party, and the hostility of Liberal radicals to Liberal policy, would present a new opportunity for Labour when the war ended. Henderson left the coalition in 1917 and set about reconstructing and expanding the party. He pursued trade unions for additional funds. Some gave willingly, influenced by wartime industrial experiences that suggested the need for a strong Labour party. Others had to be persuaded. Considerable effort went into establishing new constituency associations. Whereas once constituency parties were told to wait until they were strong before fighting, Henderson saw an opportunity to strike whilst the Liberals were weak. Constituency parties were encouraged to select candidates even in seats where there was no evident chance of success.[14]

At the national level Labour created an organizational structure which began to resemble that of the other parties, although with just one national newspaper lending its support (the *Daily Herald*) and an income that never matched that of the Conservatives, its activities were more restricted. In the constituencies too some changes were merely cosmetic. Whilst some local parties started to develop a large individual membership between 1918 and 1924, and to organize more political campaigns, in many heavily unionized areas the party remained dependent on a small team of union officials, whilst in rural and middle-class areas it relied on a handful of committed and often middle-class activists. The position was particularly bad in Scotland and in Wales, where many Labour-held seats had fewer than 100 individual members.[15]

Programme and Politics, 1918–1924

Labour also drew up a full constitution and a party programme during the war. The constitution gave the trade unions power to determine which conference proposals became party policy, because trade union delegates voted on behalf of all members who paid the political levy. This was termed the 'block vote'. By contrast, constituency parties had much less influence, even though their members were more directly involved in party activity. Huge significance has been attached to one clause of the party's new constitution (Clause IV), which committed Labour to the nationalization of the means of production, distribution and exchange. This became the touchstone of the party's commitment to socialism. Hence when Gaitskell and then Blair tried to delete it in the 1950s and 1990s, the left reacted angrily. Yet it is important to note what Labour thought it was adopting when it introduced Clause IV, not how subsequent party members have redefined its meaning. Clause IV was drawn up by Sidney Webb, who was hardly on the left of the party.[16] It was accepted without comment by moderate party leaders such as Snowden and MacDonald and by the equally moderate trade unions. It has been suggested that trade unions did not need to oppose this, because the block vote gave them the power to determine policy. However, this misses the point. A larger role for the state, as proposed in Clause IV, was uncontroversial within the Labour party. Party members accepted that capitalism was inefficient and that state regulation was necessary to prevent excessive competition, which pushed down wages. Many unions thought that wartime regulation of key staple industries (like railways and mines) had brought order to chaos, whilst ensuring decent wages and conditions. MacDonald took exactly the same line. Clause

IV simply expressed the broad political values developed across much of the party before 1914. It was never meant as a political programme.[17]

The development of party policy in 1917–18 reflected this fact. Labour's first major policy statement, *Labour and the New Social Order*, stressed the state's role in policy but did not suggest wholesale nationalization. It advocated a national minimum standard of living, financed by redistributive taxation and improvements in industrial efficiency. These aims were to dominate Labour campaigning during the first part of the 1920s, particularly in the immediate post-war years when Labour ran its 'mines for the nation' campaign.[18]

Labour's commitment to social ownership as part of a practical and moderate socialist programme distinguished it from the Communist party, which despite seeking affiliation to the party in 1918 opposed Labour's main objectives. Accordingly, Labour and trade union leaders opposed its attempts to affiliate. Initially some Communists were also members of the Labour party, or were elected as trade union delegates and hence attended Labour meetings. Labour gradually adopted rules to prevent this, disaffiliating or disciplining constituency organizations in Wales, Scotland and London that refused to comply.[19]

Labour was more open to ex-Liberals. Many joined the party during and after the war, including a fair number of MPs. The party's new policy advisory committees were used to involve them in policy debates, although theirs was not the guiding hand on most committees (with the exception perhaps of the International committee, which looked at foreign and imperial policy). Rather, G. D. H. Cole and then Arthur Greenwood, the latter chosen by the Trades Union Congress (TUC), orchestrated proceedings. They used ex-Liberals for their specific expertise in areas such as imperial affairs and agriculture, where Labour's own experience was limited. Yet to see this Liberal influx as a moderating influence on Labour policy would be incorrect. On the contrary, many ex-Liberals aligned themselves with the left of the party, or advocated a more constructive policy than that advanced by the party leadership.

Labour also (half) opened its doors to women. Its new national and regional organizers were encouraged to extend individual membership to women. Labour women had their own conference and newspaper. Rather more ex-Liberals than women became MPs, although Labour was at least ahead of the other parties in this regard by the mid-1920s. Many women recruits, like the ex-Liberals, sought to advance a constructive reformism. Several prominent Labour women paid particular attention to education, health and housing, sometimes instead of feminist issues (such as birth control provision or equal pay), sometimes in conjunction with them.[20]

Despite Labour's evident desire to set a new democratic socialist agenda, it also wished to see off the Liberal challenge and absorb at least some of its support. Party organizers believed this was essential if it was to become a serious threat to the Conservatives' ascendancy. Thus Labour stressed its Liberal inheritance, identified even Liberal rural areas as an essential electoral target, and moderated some policies. The best example of this is the capital levy, a proposal to raise revenue through a one-off tax on war profits. There was always some division between those who wanted a capital levy in order to pay off the war debt (like the future Labour chancellor of the exchequer Philip Snowden) and those who saw it as a means of funding social reform. However, following allegations from Liberals that the capital levy prevented Labour capturing more Liberal votes in 1923, the idea was abandoned.[21]

The first ever Labour government was formed following the general election of December 1923. With a little less than 31 per cent of the vote, Labour was just 1 per cent ahead of the Liberals and 7 per cent behind the Conservatives (the single largest party with 258 MPs). However, with 191 seats, and the informal support of the 159 Liberals, Labour was able to form a minority government. Party leaders saw this as an opportunity to prove that the party could govern. They preached caution, which, given their dependence on Liberal support, was almost inevitable. The party's main legislative success was Wheatley's Housing Act, which extended state subsidies for building council houses and led to a major increase in public sector housing provision. More was spent on education and pensions, whilst royal commissions were established to prepare the foundations for changes in health insurance and schooling. The party attracted plaudits for its efforts to improve the performance of the League of Nations and restore international solvency.[22] The government fell – much to the disquiet of Philip Snowden – when some poor strategic decisions and presentational mistakes by MacDonald inflamed blatantly unreal, but politically shrewd, Conservative allegations that the party was sympathetic to Bolshevism. In the subsequent election many Liberals supported the Conservatives' anti-socialist campaign. The Conservatives swept back into office, but the Liberal vote collapsed and Labour was consequently confirmed as the main anti-Tory party.

The Labour Party and the Trade Unions, 1924–1929

The attitude of some trade union figures to the Labour party was clearly expressed by the general secretary of the TUC in November 1931. The Labour party was created by the trade union movement, he stated, 'to do those things in Parliament which the trade union movement found ineffectively performed by the two party system'.[23] Socialists saw things rather differently, whilst the party's leaders felt they had a broader mission. The 1924 Labour government's response to strikes in the docks and the London tramway system had drawn critical comment from union leaders. Bevin of the Transport Workers' Union subsequently argued that unions should not moderate their industrial demands just because a Labour government was in office. It was correctly noted that the first Labour cabinet – including friends of the unions like Arthur Henderson – had kept the TUC at arm's length. The lessons were clearly stated at the TUC conference in 1925:

> even with a complete Labour majority in the House, and with a Labour Government which was stable and secure, there would be a permanent difference in point of view between the Government on the one hand and the Trade Unions on the other . . . (which) arose from the fact that the Trade Unions had different functions to perform than the function of Government.[24]

The problems were exacerbated by strong characters on both sides. MacDonald and Snowden had no roots in the trade union movement, and disapproved of its attempts to influence the party. This distance was particularly evident during the General Strike. The TUC leadership did not want Labour leaders involved; the Labour leadership felt the strike was a mistake, however much they sympathized with the economic circumstances and opposed the managerial rigidities that had caused the dispute. At local level, Labour parties did what they could to help, especially with relief work. None the less, this was no partnership.

There was, however, a clear similarity of interest and policy in many areas. Labour and TUC leaders both wanted to develop clear, practical policies. They shared a similarly robust view of how to deal with those who advocated more extreme tactics or views, or who ignored party policy. They saw state regulation as the means of creating a platform for progress, based on more efficient industrial production. The Balfour committee on trade and industry, established by Labour in 1924 and containing a substantial number of trade union and Labour figures, produced a minority report which reflected this shared view. It proposed rationalization of industry to create larger and more competitive units, with nationalization where necessary, accompanied by welfare legislation and good pensions to address any unemployment and an increased school leaving age to reduce the labour supply.[25] With the defeat of the General Strike, trade union leaders increasingly looked to the political arena to achieve their policy aims. Labour was their natural ally.

Labour Policy and Politics, 1924–1929

After 1924 it was clear that Labour had to prepare itself to become a party of government – to prepare concrete, workable legislation and to find ways of funding it. This challenge had first presented itself in local government. Some councils were captured by Labour at the very first post-war municipal elections in 1919. As a result, Labour had to provide and administer schools, housing, transport, parks, social services and a variety of other amenities. There were some major successes in this respect – notably in Sheffield, which became Labour's municipal flagship. Labour regularly used municipal control to expand social provision and opportunities. It was often prompted to consider such ideas by its own women's sections. Party leaders discussed means of raising money to fund additional services through municipal banks or local taxation.[26] Thwarted by national controls over local government expenditure, Labour councillors in Poplar and Bedwellty made illegally high welfare payments to those in need, resulting in major conflicts with the Conservative government (which the latter inevitably won).

Control of local councils ultimately broadened Labour's experience, concerns and programme. Party policy committees also gave considerable attention to how the party might improve social services through central government legislation. They discussed improved health and maternity services and supported an altered – and longer – school life.[27] This was to embrace both nursery education and a reformed secondary education to at least the age of fifteen, and later sixteen. Nor should university education be confined to the wealthy. Party members argued that inequalities could only be addressed if those from poorer backgrounds were given educational opportunities. To support this, they called for family allowances and/or maintenance allowances for children who remained in school. Party financial experts examined the role of a 'super-tax' in funding these developments.

There were clear weaknesses in Labour's thinking. Labour rejected Keynes's radical economic ideas. It declined to support state provision of birth control advice or family allowances, the former because of traditionalist views on the family and morality, the latter because trade unions were concerned about the impact of family allowances on wages.[28] These weaknesses have attracted considerable attention: the party's strengths have been largely ignored. Much of the work done in opposition and in local government was reflected in the tone of the party's 1928 policy statement, *Labour and the Nation*. Trying to show the relevance of socialism to everyday life, Labour argued that socialism was neither a utopian creed nor 'a blind revolt against poverty and oppression'. Industrial civilization had only expanded because of a

> tentative, doctrineless socialism, which . . . has found tardy and imperfect recognition . . . in the development of Local Government and the expansion of municipal enterprise, in the growth of public expenditure upon social services, and in the provision of the financial resources by which such services may be maintained. (p. 6)

Under the Conservatives, the whole community had been betrayed. It was now time to establish the new social order 'in which the resources of the community shall be organised and administered with a single eye to securing for all its members the largest possible measure of economic welfare and personal freedom'. Labour's principles, and its principal aims, were an extension of those identified in 1918:

(i)   To secure to every member of the community the standards of life and employment which are necessary to a healthy, independent and self-respecting existence.

(ii) To convert industry, step by step, and with due regard to the special needs and varying circumstances of different occupations, from a sordid struggle for private gain into a co-operative undertaking, carried on for the service of the community, and amenable to its control.

(iii) To extend rapidly and widely those forms of social provision – education, public health, housing, pensions, the care of the sick, and maintenance during unemployment – in the absence of which the individual is the sport of economic chance and the slave of his environment.

(iv) To adjust taxation in such a way as to secure that due provision is made for the maintenance and improvement of the material apparatus of industry, and that surpluses created by social effort shall be applied by society for the good of all.

(v)   To establish peace, freedom and justice by removing from among the nations the root causes of international disputes, by conciliation and all-in arbitration, by renouncing war . . . by economic co-operation through the League of Nations, and by mutual agreements. (pp. 14–15)

This was not a detailed legislative programme, but it was a clear set of guidelines and directions.

The 1929 Election and the Second Labour Government

The 1929 election saw Labour make substantial headway. Its popular vote increased to 37 per cent. For the very first time it rivalled the Conservatives, who despite receiving slightly more votes returned 250 MPs compared to Labour's 287. Labour's attempt to develop a broader profile had evidently worked, for it captured around seventy seats – mostly outside the traditional Labour heartlands – for the first time. With the implicit support of fifty-nine Liberals, Labour formed its second minority government.

From the outset Labour faced difficulties. It was now the government of a major European and world power. Longstanding party members (like Arthur Henderson) and newer recruits (such as Norman Angel and Philip Noel-Baker) applied their considerable knowledge of imperial issues, reparations and the League of Nations. Labour contributed constructively to the Round Table Conference on Indian affairs and international debates over arms limitation and reparations. On the home front, it set about implementing parts of its programme. It tried to organize industrial rationalization in order to address longstanding problems in the coal and textile industries. It introduced more generous benefits through the 1930 National Insurance Act, and addressed the problem of slum housing for the first time through the 1930 Housing Act. It increased pensions and drew up a bill to raise the school leaving age, whilst an administrative order allowed local authorities to give free birth control advice.[29] This opportunity was taken up by some, largely Labour-controlled, local authorities in the 1930s.[30] There were certainly policy weaknesses, notably a reluctance to force the pace of industrial changes through state incentives and pressures, whilst the Liberals' opposition to state regulation also hindered change. However, the government's main problem stemmed from the fact that Labour's programme of gradual changes – a perfectly reasonable programme for a different occasion – was rendered obsolete by a mounting economic crisis which few parties in the world confronted successfully.

The flaws in Labour's policy, leadership and institutional structures were highlighted by the events of 1931. Faced with a crisis, Labour proved inflexible. Policy had to be altered. Either the party needed to adopt measures to maintain revenue and employment – from public works through to tariffs – or it needed to cut expenditure and balance its budget, as the Treasury experts, opposition leaders and international bankers wanted. Snowden, Labour's chancellor, wanted to make cuts but knew there would be substantial opposition from his cabinet colleagues. He allowed the budget deficit to grow, eventually appointing a committee of external experts (the May committee) to tell the party what he wanted them to hear – that it must cut expenditure or face an economic collapse. Predicting a deficit of £120 million, the May committee called for tax increases to raise around £25 million, and expenditure cuts of £96 million, to include a 20 per cent cut in unemployment benefit.[31]

In July–August 1931 there were many cabinet attempts to resolve the problem. However, by this time a resolution was almost impossible. MacDonald had allowed the position to deteriorate, failing to oppose his chancellor when the latter resisted suggestions for a new approach in 1930. By 1931 MacDonald was no longer willing to act decisively or diplomatically. Between 1930 and 1931 part of the Labour left abandoned the party's policy, and to MacDonald's disgust ridiculed and belittled him and the government at every opportunity. Nor was MacDonald sympathetic to trade union pressures not to make cuts. He and Snowden had long felt that trade unions tried to dictate Labour policy, thought only of their members, demanded rather than reasoned and were arrogant in their manner. Consequently, they had not involved the unions in policy discussions. Indeed, when a crisis meeting between the TUC and Labour party executives was called in July 1931, it was the first such meeting for seven months. However compliant and constructive individual unions may have been in 1929–30, by this time they were primarily concerned with making a stand on working-class incomes, and were unable and unwilling to see the problems through the government's eyes. They opposed all cuts in expenditure. Opinion on both sides had hardened. As a result, during crisis discussions the party ignored those Labour moderates who insisted there was a workable compromise, arguing that the need for such massive cuts was being exaggerated by Snowden and the opposition.[32] On 23 August a large section of the Labour cabinet refused to support a cut in unemployment benefit. Faced with a precipitate drop in the value of the pound and a mounting economic crisis, MacDonald reluctantly (and, he hoped, temporarily) abandoned the party and formed a National government with the Liberals and Conservatives. He was followed by a few ministers, including Snowden, and a handful of back-benchers and peers. No Labour leader had wanted this to happen, even though Labour figures subsequently created the myth that MacDonald had welcomed the crisis as a means of leaving the party. None the less, the impact was dramatic. In the 1931 election Labour was routed.

Reconstructing Labour Politics

The impact of the 1931 crisis on the Labour party has been extensively debated, with some identifying substantial changes after 1931 while others marked continuities. There was certainly an immediate shift to the left in the 1931 election. As a result of the party's failings there was a clear determination to ensure that the circumstances of 1931 were never repeated. This determination was made manifest in three ways.

First, there was an immediate proliferation of think-tanks and similar organizations. The most important of these were the New Fabian Research Bureau (a radical rival to the stagnant Fabian Society) and the Society for Socialist Information and Propaganda (SSIP). These organizations included existing Labour intellectuals such as Hugh Dalton and G. D. H. Cole, more recent converts from the older parties (such as Stafford Cripps and Charles Trevelyan), and a new generation of intellectuals, often Oxbridge-educated economists. This included Douglas Jay, Evan Durbin and a future leader of the Labour party, Hugh Gaitskell.[33]

Second, two trade union leaders – Walter Citrine and Ernest Bevin – took a personal interest in these developments, but also sought to put the unions back at the heart of the party. They revived the National Joint Council, which brought the TUC and the Labour executive together on a regular basis, rechristening it the National Council of Labour. They also encouraged the National Executive Committee to take a much stricter line with those who were unwilling to accept agreed conference decisions on policy or strategy.

Finally, there was a major increase in party membership and propaganda activity. The party had planned a major membership drive in 1931 for financial reasons. However, the 'hysterical' collapse of popular support in 1931 suggested that a large membership was important as a means of spreading Labour's message and countering the sensationalism of the Tory press. There was a series of nationwide membership/propaganda campaigns, such as the 'Million Members Campaign' in 1932 and the 'Victory for Socialism' campaign in 1934. The TUC funded a newspaper, the *New Clarion*. There were renewed attempts to increase sales of the party's other newspaper, the *Daily Herald*, whilst across the country – but especially in London – free localized Labour newspapers were produced and distributed. These aimed at representing and serving communities, whilst also showing how local and broader concerns were being addressed by the Labour party. In London almost every borough had a local Labour newspaper in the 1930s, funded by London's cooperative societies. The party's membership also grew, from 215,000 in 1928, when figures were first declared, to a pre-war peak of 450,000 in 1937. Around 40 per cent of party members were women. The constituencies with the largest membership were Romford in Essex and Woolwich in south London. Whilst these seats contained large council housing estates, membership was also increasing in more affluent areas across the south-east of England. None the less, membership levels – and activity rates – were uneven. Across industrial Britain there were seats where members, and especially women members, were seemingly unwanted. Nor did trade unions always rally to the cause, with parties in seats such as Newport or Sheffield reporting limited active support from local union branches and members.[34]

Internal Conflicts

The Labour party has always contained committed people of differing views, who have argued enthusiastically for the implementation of their particular programme or pet interest. Under MacDonald's leadership, sections of the party came to believe that party leaders were becoming too moderate; equally, MacDonald and others felt that a section of the rank and file engaged in negative and unreasonable criticism. Mutual suspicion intensified, even though the majority of the party sided with the leadership prior to the 1931 crisis.

In the 1930s internal conflicts grew in significance and became more frequent. For the left, the international capitalist crisis demonstrated the validity of socialist ideology. Unemployment had reached epidemic proportions, blighting people's lives. The state granted miserable incomes to the unemployed, but only after a humiliating means test. Fascism and nationalism were gaining strength across Europe, and expanding imperialistically into Africa and south-east Asia. Countries were rearming; peace seemed increasingly fragile. Surely, radicals argued, it was right to fight against these developments as forcefully as possible?

Internal division became especially pronounced because the international position helped attract new elements into the Labour party. These members were often unwilling to accept the leadership's hesitant response to changing international circumstances. Many of these new recruits were articulate, educated men and women, able and determined to express their views. Their desire to fight fascism was supported by existing party members, including many prominent ex-Liberals. This created an influential and powerful dissenting group within the party. Not surprisingly, such people formed their own organizations to try to influence both public opinion and the party itself.

One such organization was the constituencies movement. This was particularly strong in the home counties, where there were few Labour MPs and new recruits felt isolated from party decision making. The constituencies movement called for a reduction of the block vote and the creation of regional bodies, which would have more influence within the party. Such people also joined the Left Book Club in large numbers. Founded by Victor Gollancz, a radical publisher, its million members agreed to purchase a book a month, usually on a radical theme. Concern with imperial and foreign policy led to the formation of many other left-wing organizations, from the League Against Imperialism to the Aid Spain Movement. On the home front, the SSIP sought to develop socialist policies and campaign for their adoption by the party. Its supporters included Bevin, Cole and Stafford Cripps, a wealthy ex-Tory barrister and nephew of Beatrice Webb who was to become Labour's chancellor of the exchequer in 1947. SSIP was soon to be renamed the Socialist League and to lose its trade union support. Cripps also founded the famous radical Labour paper *Tribune* to call for changes in policy.[35]

The Socialist League demanded radical action. It argued that an incoming socialist government should suspend the constitution, take control of the military, implement a programme of nationalization, including control of the banking system, and increase taxation. It wanted Labour to oppose the policy of non-intervention in the Spanish civil war, rather than simply collect money and medical and other supplies for Spanish refugees, women and children. As the fascist threat increased, Cripps argued for an alliance with the Communist party against fascism abroad and at home (for Cripps the National government was a semi-fascist force). His 'Unity' movement soon grew into a Popular Front movement, calling for an alliance against fascism that would embrace Liberals and even dissident Tories.[36]

It is hardly surprising that socialists should wish to create an active, campaigning party. Several historians have condemned the party leadership for not embracing these ideas. The party leaders' actions – less commonly studied or explained than the left's ideas and politics – were based on several assumptions. They did not trust the Communist party. Since the Communist party had asked its members to undermine the Labour party and the trade union movement for much of the 1920s, and decried its leaders as 'social fascists', this is scarcely surprising. Whatever their individual views, Communists took their orders from the Soviet Union, which was hardly interested in sustaining western democracy. There was certainly evidence of a pro-Soviet bias within the Left Book Club.[37] Nor could Labour leaders see any value in an alliance with the minute British Communist party, arguing that it would alienate moderates and that individual Communists willing to renounce revolution could simply join the Labour party. Finally, Labour argued that the Socialist League was adopting unrealistic ideas, particularly in resisting domestic rearmament (because it feared the use which the National government would make of such resources). Whilst there was a non-Labour audience for pacifist propaganda in the mid-1930s (and a substantial pacifist element in the Labour party), the Socialist League's ideas seemed increasingly unrealistic to the electorate and to the party by 1937–8. A party that preached the danger of war and then declined to defend against it – as Cripps wanted – faced electoral suicide.

The party leadership fought back. The TUC in particular argued for tough action against the left. Labour proscribed membership of various pressure groups, expelling those who would not leave them or who ignored party policy. Stafford Cripps and Aneurin Bevan were expelled for a time. Labour also developed its own radical programme. Although moderate economists had argued for the adoption of Keynesian ideas, Labour's programme reflected the ideas of those who advocated a planned and controlled economy, especially Herbert Morrison and Hugh Dalton. As in the 1920s, nationalization and state control were prominent – but now, having learned the lessons of 1931, the programme paid more attention to the role of the banking system and to organized state planning. Dalton claimed Labour stood for a 'practical socialism'. The party's 1937 'Immediate programme' reflected his views fairly closely. Labour's hostility to tariffs and import restrictions (which forced up prices to consumers but helped farmers) was supported by the cooperative societies. The party's insistence on practical measures for increasing employment across Britain attracted support, even in left-wing strongholds across Wales and Scotland. Here dependence on a few heavy industries was a recognized weakness, and economic diversification a recognized aim.[38] A sound economy was the basis of prosperity; the free market had failed to provide it. Labour's practical programme of state aid was the solution.

Nor did the party leadership focus simply on economic policy. Its social programme – again little studied by historians – included a 'children's charter', better pensions, a major increase in maternity provision and health services generally, as well as investment in transport and education. Once again, this reflected what Labour was doing in municipal government – the London County Council under Morrison was a model in this respect.[39] Although this emphasis was supported by the growing number of women who were active within the party, there were other influences at work as well. Finally, Labour did not ignore foreign policy issues. Labour's leader Clement Attlee visited Spain and actively attacked the government on this issue within the House of Commons. Attlee was also quite amenable to radical ideas on decolonization, taking a particular interest in India and its governance. Although this was not an interest shared by many trade unions, or indeed by most activists, Labour was the 'natural' home for those who supported colonial development and independence.[40] If the party leadership was not as active in promoting independence as they wished, it was more progressive and realistic than the Communists or any other party.

Devising a programme of changes that the party would accept was difficult enough. Developing a programme that would satisfy the party, the public and the 'labour movement' was almost impossible. The cooperatives represented consumer interests, the unions the interests of producers. Both had to be reconciled to the needs of the country as a whole, and to the desire of Labour's socialists for policies which looked after the unorganized as much as the organized workers. Bringing the Communist party into an alliance was even more difficult (as socialists in France were to find out). Although many who visited the Soviet Union were impressed by its achievements, it supplied no blueprint for changing a western economic and democratic system, no ideas that might turn crumbling capitalist economies, rife with competitive nationalism, into a haven of international brotherhood and economic prosperity. The various elements of the 'labour movement' did not speak with one voice, or represent a single interest. Although leaders of the labour movement were closer by the end of the 1930s than they had been in the 1920s, many members of the labour movement continued to support other parties.

Conclusion

The period from 1900 to 1939 was a long learning process for the Labour party. After each new episode – each partial failure – it learned and adapted. In the process the party was transformed from a pressure group to a national organization, from a party consisting largely of male workers interested in domestic economic issues to a party that contained a substantial number of professionals, with a much broader range of expertise and concerns. None the less, its ideals and economic prescriptions remained broadly the same – unsurprisingly, since its leaders remained the same and the problems simply intensified. By 1939 it had developed ideas on economic, social and international issues which were to form the basis of its programme in 1945, even if some new elements and changes were introduced during and after the war.[41] Mistakes were certainly made during this period of growth and development. There were poor judgements from leaders who could not lead. There was shallow opposition from impatient followers, who declined to follow. There were persistent prejudices and institutional rigidities which handicapped attempts to counter inequalities, particularly racism in the empire and gender bias at home. But there were no easy solutions that Labour *wilfully* ignored, no *systematic* failure to unify an easily unified opposition to capitalism, no *persistent* denial of injustices that could easily have been altered. If other parties in world politics had acted as 'unsuccessfully' as this, then the 1930s may not have turned into the devil's decade.

NOTES

1   For example, K. Laybourn, *A Century of Labour: A History of the Labour Party 1900–2000* (Stroud, 2000), p. 148.
2   S. Davies and B. Morley, *County Borough Election Results in England and Wales 1919–1938: A Comparative Analysis* (2 vols, Aldershot, 1999, 2000).
3   D. Jarvis, 'British Conservatism and class politics in the 1920s', *English Historical Review*, 96 (1996), pp. 80–2.
4   D. Tanner, 'Class voting and radical politics: the Liberal and Labour parties, 1910–31', in J. Lawrence and M. Taylor, eds, *Party, State and Society: Electoral Behaviour in Britain since 1820* (Aldershot, 1997), pp. 120–1.
5   D. Tanner, *Political Change and the Labour Party 1900–18* (Cambridge, 1990), passim.
6   R. McKibbin, 'Class and conventional wisdom: the Conservative party and the "public" in inter-war Britain', in R. McKibbin, *The Ideologies of Class: Social Relations in Britain 1880–1950* (Oxford, 1990), pp. 259–93.
7   K. D. Brown, ed., *The First Labour Party 1906–14* (London, 1985), pp. 11–12.
8   F. Trentmann, 'Wealth versus welfare: the British left between free trade and national political economy before World War I', *Historical Research*, 70 (1997), pp. 74–93.
9   D. Tanner, 'The development of British socialism, 1900–1918, *Parliamentary History*, 16 (1997), pp. 59–61.
10 D. Howell, *British Workers and the Independent Labour Party 1888–1906* (Manchester, 1983), chs 8–9.
11 R. McKibbin, *The Evolution of the Labour Party, 1910–1924* (Oxford, 1974), p. 85.
12 Tanner, *Political Change*, pp. 321–5 and, e.g., pp. 172–5, 211–12, 244–5, 263–4, 274–5.
13 D. Tanner, 'Ideological debate in Edwardian Labour politics: radicalism, revisionism and socialism', in E. Biagini and A. Reid, eds, *Currents of Radicalism: Popular Radicalism, Organised Labour and Party Politics in Britain 1850–1914* (Cambridge, 1991), pp. 279–92.
14 A. Thorpe, *A History of the British Labour Party* (Basingstoke, 1997), ch. 2; Tanner, *Political Change*, pp. 396–404.
15 D. Tanner, 'The Labour party and its membership', in D. Tanner, P. Thane and N. Tiratsoo, eds, *Labour's First Century* (Cambridge, 2000), pp. 250–1.
16 J. Winter, *Socialism and the Challenge of War: Ideas and Politics in Britain, 1912–1928* (London, 1974), ch. 8.

17   N. Thompson, *Political Economy and the Labour Party: The Economics of Democratic Socialism, 1884–1995* (London, 1996), ch. 6.

18   D. Tanner, 'The Labour party and electoral politics in the coalfields 1910–47', in A. Campbell, N. Fishman and D. Howell, eds, *Miners, Unions and Politics* (Aldershot, 1996), pp. 79–80.

19   McKibbin, *Evolution of the Labour Party*, pp. 191–205.

20   M. Francis, 'Labour and gender', in D. Tanner, P. Thane and N. Tiratsoo, eds, *Labour's First Century* (Cambridge, 2000), pp. 203–4.

21   R. Whiting, 'The Labour party, capitalism and the National Debt, 1918–24', in P. Waller, ed., *Politics and Social Change in Modern Britain* (Oxford, 1987), pp. 140–59.

22   P. Thane, 'Labour and welfare', in D. Tanner, P. Thane and N. Tiratsoo, eds, *Labour's First Century* (Cambridge, 2000), pp. 90–2; H. Winkler, *Paths Not Taken: British Labour and International Policy in the 1920s* (Chapel Hill, NC, 1994), ch. 5.

23   R. Garner, 'Ideological impact of the trade unions on the Labour party 1918–31' (Department of Politics, University of Manchester, occasional paper, 1989), p. 8.

24   R. Lyman, *The First Labour Government, 1924* (London, 1957), p. 277.

25   *Final Report of the Committee on Trade and Industry* (London, 1929). For a more sceptical view, see A. Thorpe, 'The industrial meaning of "gradualism": the Labour party and industry, 1918–31', *Journal of British Studies*, 35 (1996), pp. 88–98.

26   M. Savage, *The Dynamics of Working-class Politics* (Cambridge, 1987), pp. 195–7; C. Williams, 'Labour and the challenge of local government, 1919–1939', in D. Tanner, C. Williams and D. Hopkin, eds, *The Labour Party in Wales 1900–2000* (Cardiff, 2000), pp. 140–58.

27   R. Barker, *Education and Politics 1900–1951: A Study of the Labour Party* (Oxford, 1972), pp. 54–61; J. Stewart, *'The Battle for Health': A Political History of the Socialist Medical Association, 1930–51* (Aldershot, 1999), ch. 3.

28   R. Skidelsky, *Politicians and the Slump: The Labour Government of 1929–1931* (Basingstoke, 1967), p. 60; P. Graves, *Labour Women: Women in British Working-class Politics 1918–1939* (Cambridge, 1994), pp. 80–108.

29   Thane, 'Labour and welfare', 94–5; N. Riddell, *Labour in Crisis: The Second Labour Government, 1929–31* (Manchester, 1999), pp. 142–3, 145–6, 157–8.

30   K. Fisher, '"Clearing up misconception": the campaign to set up birth control clinics in south Wales between the wars', *Welsh History Review*, 19 (1998), pp. 108–12, 124–5.

31   A. Thorpe, *The British General Election of 1931* (Oxford, 1991), ch. 4.

32   Ibid., pp. 75–7; Riddell, *Labour in Crisis*, pp. 87–90, 200–2.

33   P. Pugh, *Educate, Agitate, Organize: 100 Years of Fabian Socialism* (London, 1984), chs 16–17; E. Durbin, *New Jerusalems: The Labour Party and the Economics of Democratic Socialism* (London, 1985), ch. 4.

34   Tanner, 'Labour and its membership', pp. 252–6.

35   B. Pimlott, *Labour and the Left in the 1930s* (Cambridge, 1977), chs 12 and 16.

36   C. Bryant, *Stafford Cripps: The First Modern Chancellor* (London, 1997), chs 10–12.

37   R. Edwards, *Victor Gollancz: A Biography* (London, 1987), pp. 296–300.

38   D. Tanner, 'The pattern of Labour politics, 1918–1939', in D. Tanner, C. Williams and D. Hopkin, eds, *The Labour Party in Wales 1900–2000* (Cardiff, 2000), pp. 130–4.

39   L. Baston, 'Labour local government 1900–1999', in B. Brivati and R. Heffernan, eds, *The Labour Party: A Centenary History* (Basingstoke, 2000), pp. 456–8.

40   S. Howe, 'Labour and international affairs', in D. Tanner, P. Thane and N. Tiratsoo, eds, *Labour's First Century* (Cambridge, 2000), pp. 120–30.

41   S. Brooke, *Labour's War: The Labour Party during the Second World War* (Oxford, 1992), pp. 1–33, 269–70; M. Francis, *Ideas and Policies under Labour 1945–51* (Manchester, 1977), pp. 1–11.

FURTHER READING

Brown, K. D., ed., *The First Labour Party 1906–14* (London, 1985).

Durbin, E., *New Jerusalems: The Labour Party and the Economics of Democratic Socialism* (London, 1985).

Graves, P., *Labour Women: Women in British Working-class Politics 1918–1939* (Cambridge, 1994).

Howell, D., *British Workers and the Independent Labour Party 1888–1906* (Manchester, 1983).

Lyman, R., *The First Labour Government, 1924* (London, 1957).

McKibbin, R., *The Evolution of the Labour Party, 1910–1924* (Oxford, 1974).

Marquand, D., *Ramsay MacDonald* (London, 1977).

Pimlott, B., *Labour and the Left in the 1930s* (Cambridge, 1977).

Riddell, N., *Labour in Crisis: The Second Labour Government, 1929–31* (Manchester, 1999).

Savage, M., *The Dynamics of Working-class Politics* (Cambridge, 1987).

Tanner, D., *Political Change and the Labour Party 1900–18* (Cambridge, 1987).

Tanner, D., Thane, P. and Tiratsoo, N., eds, *Labour's First Century* (Cambridge, 2000).

Thorpe, A., *A History of the British Labour Party* (Basingstoke, 1997).

Winter, J., *Socialism and the Challenge of War: Ideas and Politics in Britain, 1912–1928* (London, 1974).

CHAPTER FOUR

The Politics of National Efficiency and of War, 1900–1918

G. R. SEARLE

During the Second Boer War (1899–1902) a new political catchphrase rose to prominence: 'National Efficiency'. The *Spectator* noted in 1902 that there was 'a universal outcry for efficiency in all the departments of society, in all aspects of life'; from every side the cry went out, 'Give us Efficiency, or we die'. Another seasoned journalist agreed that 'efficiency' had become the 'hardest worked vocable in politics'.[1]

In fact, 'National Efficiency' was not a phrase of totally new coinage,[2] nor were the anxieties which the phrase encapsulated altogether new. From the 1880s onwards, critics were warning that Britain risked losing her commercial supremacy: the slide would only be halted, they argued, if Britain made a greater investment in education, particularly in the area of technical and commercial instruction. The loss of markets to foreign rivals, especially the Americans and the Germans, raised further anxieties about possible national 'decline' and focused attention on the theme of 'competitiveness'. In short, even in the 1890s there were those who sensed that British power and influence in the world had already passed their zenith.

All the same, when Britain declared war against the Transvaal and the Orange Free State in October 1899, most of her citizens optimistically assumed that the world's greatest empire would quickly triumph over a race of 'backward' Boer farmers. In December such complacency gave way to alarm, even to a sense of crisis, when the British army suffered three separate military defeats within the space of a single week: at Stormberg, Magersfontein and Colenso. Dismay over this national humiliation turned to boiling anger with the revelation of the bungling that had led to the carnage at Spion Kop in January 1900.

The tide of war soon turned. But Lord Roberts's defeat of Cronje's forces at Paardeburg in mid-February 1900, leading to the occupation of Pretoria in June, lifted the gloom only momentarily. For the enemy, instead of gracefully surrendering, fell back on a campaign of guerilla harassment. Even with the support of over 30,000 volunteers from the white dominions (not including the South African forces), the British army had to wait until the summer of 1902 until it was in a position to impose a settlement on the Boers.

Nor after the Peace of Vereeniging (31 May) did memories of the national humiliation of 'Black Week' quickly fade. The damning Report of the Royal Commission into the causes and conduct of the war (the Elgin Report) came out in the autumn of 1903. But still the national inquest dragged on: an investigation into the corruption and mismanagement surrounding the disposal of war stores was only concluded in 1905.

Against this background, politicians, journalists and sundry self-appointed prophets warned that the empire would not survive the new century unless both government and people learned the 'lessons' of the South African War. Yet what were these lessons? It was easy to lampoon blundering soldiers such as General Sir Redvers Buller; yet were the military solely to blame? Some also pointed an accusatory finger at the war secretary, Lord Lansdowne. The Treasury and the cabinet, too, came in for condemnation. But others argued that what had gone wrong on the South African veldt was a manifestation of a much deeper national malaise.

Lord Rosebery, the former Liberal prime minister, summed up this viewpoint by calling on his countrymen to dedicate themselves to the quest for National Efficiency – a slogan that brought into sharp focus all the anxieties that had been building up over the previous decade and a half. Britain, it was alleged, was suffering from an over-reliance upon slap-dash methods and improvisation. One monthly magazine carried an article entitled 'A nation of amateurs':[3] it was a gibe which stuck.

National Efficiency contained within itself a number of somewhat different strands. One was 'technocratic': from this viewpoint, all branches of public life, including the practice of government, needed to be organized on scientific lines under the aegis of the relevant 'experts'. Another strand was managerial. The empire, it was said, should be 'put on a business footing' and administered by 'business methods'. There was even loose talk of importing businessmen into Westminster and Whitehall – an objective favoured by a new pressure group that emerged in 1900, the Administrative Reform Association.[4]

The rhetoric of 'National Efficiency' sometimes assumed a moderate, and sometimes an extreme, form. Thus, whereas all its advocates emphasized the importance of firm leadership, most wanted to find ways of harmonizing leadership with parliamentary control. But the movement also attracted demagogues such as the journalist Arnold White, who violently attacked not only the political parties ('Mandarins' and 'Old Gangs' were common targets), but also parliamentary institutions themselves.

All, however, could come together in disparaging the values of a sentimental humanitarianism. Social injustice and suffering might abound in the world, but the advocates of 'National Efficiency' identified waste and muddle as the principal enemies of the British state. Salvation accordingly lay in the application of scientific planning and the development of national 'brain-power'. The advocates of National Efficiency thought that all these qualities were present in contemporary Germany, for which they professed a somewhat indiscriminate enthusiasm – the Bismarckian system of social insurance and German technological universities inspiring particular admiration. In fact, as Germany increasingly emerged from 1902 onwards as a threat to Britain's global position, the British people were urged to adopt many features of German political life in the interests of national survival.

Obviously not all Edwardians chose to join in this modish cult. Many expressed exasperation at what they saw as its vacuousness: 'Efficiency as a watchword!', fumed the Liberal leader Henry Campbell-Bannerman, 'Who is against it?'[5] Yet, for all its shallowness – perhaps because of its shallowness – National Efficiency made a wide social appeal, attracting members from quite different occupational groups.

Many upwardly mobile white-collar workers, technicians and members of the lower professions responded sympathetically to the critique of hereditary privilege.[6] But 'efficiency' was also embraced by grandees such as Rosebery, who, welcoming its call for greater seriousness and higher professional standards, urged members of their own class to justify their wealth and privilege by demonstrating that they were more efficient than those they aspired to rule.

National Efficiency, then, was socially eclectic. It also drew people from right across the ideological spectrum. Admittedly, old-style Liberals intensely resented the attempt to 'Germanize' British public life, while class-conscious socialists, too, were predictably hostile. On the other hand, three political groupings were particularly associated with the movement. First, there were modernizing Conservatives and Unionists,[7] impatient with the caution shown by their leader, the prime minister Lord Salisbury. Second, there were Liberals who sought to bring Liberal values more into line with contemporary needs by emphasizing their commitment to empire – these were the so-called Liberal Imperialists, of whom Rosebery was, for a time, the acknowledged leader. The third group consisted of the leaders of the Fabian Society, notably Bernard Shaw, H. G. Wells, and Beatrice and Sidney Webb, who, though theoretically committed to socialism, had grown weary of the sterilities of the class struggle and now hankered after a scientifically ordered society run by experts – the expertise in question to be supplied in large measure by themselves. The advocates of National Efficiency thus formed an incongruous amalgam of middle-class technocrats, reform-minded aristocrats and Fabian social engineers.[8]

Despite belonging to different political groupings, these variegated people shared enough common ground to cooperate in the great project of national renewal. This can be seen in the composition of a small dining club created by Sidney Webb in November 1902. Called the 'Co-Efficients', its twelve founder members, each supposedly an expert within his allotted field, provide a microcosm of the wider movement for National Efficiency. Webb (municipal affairs), H. G. Wells (literature) and Bertrand Russell (philosophy and science) were prominent members of the Fabian Society. The Liberal Imperialist wing of the Liberal party supplied R. B. Haldane (law), Edward Grey (foreign affairs) and the geographer Halford Mackinder. And from Unionist ranks came Clinton Dawkins (banking), L. S. Amery (the army) and Leo Maxse (journalism) – all personal friends of Lord Milner, the British high commissioner in South Africa, another celebrated apostle of 'Efficiency'.

The three groups were linked together by an intricate network of personal friendships and professional contacts, in which the Co-Efficient dining club formed only one of several nodal points. The Liberal Imperialist Haldane, for example, had been best man at the Webbs' wedding, but he also kept in close touch with Milner, while working closely with his fellow Scot, Lord Rosebery.

In his memoirs Amery claims that the Co-Efficients aimed to function as a kind of 'General Staff' that could mastermind the construction of a new party of efficiency. Though nothing of the kind occurred, a serious attempt to escape from the constrictions of party was made at two points during the Edwardian period: between 1900 and 1902, and later in 1910.

During the first of these two phases public interest focused on Lord Rosebery, by now considerably detached from the Liberal party but increasingly identified with the creed of National Efficiency, the merits of which he trumpeted in a series of high-profile speeches. Between 1900 and 1902 Rosebery enjoyed considerable cross-party support, and there were many who hoped that, should Salisbury, the prematurely aged premier, retire from office before the war had ended, his place might be taken by Rosebery at the head of an emergency 'National government'.

However, in the late summer of 1900 Salisbury's ministry took advantage of divisions within the Liberal party by calling an early general election, from which it returned with a comfortable majority. Even though dissatisfaction over its performance had by no means abated, the administration was now reasonably secure.

What further stymied all attempts at engineering a 'National government' was the strained relationship between Rosebery and the ministry's most powerful member, the colonial secretary Joseph Chamberlain, widely praised for his allegedly 'businesslike' qualities. Essentially what kept the two men apart was that each had a different conception of what 'National government' might mean. Rosebery favoured some sort of cross-party grouping. But Chamberlain wanted to make a 'national' party out of the Conservative and Unionist party by imposing upon it his own 'constructive programme'; he certainly did not want to share power with his political opponents. Indeed, during the 1900 'khaki' election Chamberlain had deliberately set out to undermine Rosebery and the other Liberal Imperialists by impugning the patriotism of all Liberals. The indignant Liberal Imperialists retaliated by joining Lloyd George in his attacks on the Chamberlain family's allegedly corrupt business dealings (the Kynochs scandal). Haldane and Grey (though not Rosebery) sought instead to cultivate Milner and prise him away from the colonial secretary – a futile strategy since, in the last analysis, Milner knew that it would be folly to exchange Chamberlain's support for that of a poorly led opposition faction.

And so Salisbury stayed in office until the war ended, when he was replaced as head of the Unionist ministry by his nephew, Arthur Balfour, who sympathized with the need for educational reform in the interest of National Efficiency but obviously had nothing to gain from a wholesale party reorganization.

Then in May 1903 the restless Chamberlain broke free and launched his tariff reform campaign, before resigning as colonial secretary in September. This *démarche*, by reviving traditional party warfare, fragmented still further the ranks of the National Efficiency group (weakening the Co-Efficients in the process). For while Unionists such as Amery and Maxse embraced the gospel of imperial preference, Rosebery, Grey, Haldane and, even more fervently, Asquith rallied to the Liberal party's defence of free trade. This rescued the official Liberal leader Campbell-Bannerman, who went on to guide his largely reunited party into a smashing electoral victory in early 1906. Some informal cooperation between members of the old 'efficiency' grouping continued to take place across party lines, but comparatively little was heard of National Efficiency between 1904 and 1909.

Things changed after 1909 with the Unionist-dominated Upper House's rejection of Lloyd George's famous 'people's budget'. This precipitated a general election in January 1910, the result of which was that the Liberals lost their overall Commons majority and fell dependent on Labour and the Irish Nationalists. As the Liberals moved to reduce the powers of the House of Lords, the Irish successfully insisted that Home Rule be brought out of cold storage and put once more onto the Liberal government's legislative agenda. Such a threat to the Union drove the opposition into frenzied protests.

The resulting dispute shook the British political system at a time when leading politicians in both main parties had other grounds for apprehension. Since 1902 relations with Germany had deteriorated alarmingly, in the wake of an escalating naval arms race: in the January 1910 election the opposition claimed that Britain's margin of naval supremacy had been eroded as a result of Liberal pusillanimity and the government's misplaced desire for economy. Meanwhile there were signs of mounting industrial tension: in the course of 1910 the number of days lost in strikes rose to nearly 10,000. Admittedly, the Liberal government was already attempting to stabilize Britain's class-riven society by sponsoring welfare reforms: old-age pensions had been enacted in 1908, and a measure of health and unemployment insurance was also in the pipeline. But such efforts had seemingly done little or nothing to pacify the anger of the dispossessed, though they had thoroughly alarmed the Unionist opposition, which warned of creeping socialism and complained of ministerial demagoguery.

Faced by these seething social, national and party political tensions, cautious politicians on both sides of the House paused to reflect on the precariousness of the nation's plight. The death of Edward VII in May led to a 'truce of God', with Liberal and Unionist representatives agreeing to participate in a conference summoned by the speaker, aimed at trying to find a resolution of the constitutional impasse. However, this conference, which first assembled in mid-June 1910, broke up in November – much progress having been made, but not quite enough to bridge the gap between the two parties, principally the result of their conflicting Irish policies.

In the autumn of 1910, with the conference in recess, an ingenious attempt was made to surmount the crisis by setting up a 'National government', a coalition of responsible men from both main parties, the justification for which was essentially provided by a revival of the rhetoric of National Efficiency.

However, the cast of actors had changed since Boer War days. Joseph Chamberlain was still an MP, but he had been an invalid since suffering a severe stroke in July 1906. Rosebery, never the most reliable of leaders, had largely withdrawn into self-imposed isolation, emerging only to inveigh against the 'socialism' of old-age pensions, his former ambitious, if vague, programme of national reconstruction now largely forgotten. Haldane at the War Office and Grey at the Foreign Office were almost entirely immersed in the running of their respective departments, while Asquith, by instinct a centre-of-the-road Liberal, had been serving as prime minister since Campbell-Bannerman's retirement in the spring of 1908.

Into the breach left by these defections moved two recent recruits to the National Efficiency cause: Winston Churchill and David Lloyd George. Both ministers were still largely identified in the public mind with partisan Radical positions. But Churchill, a one-time Conservative who had crossed the floor of the House over the fiscal issue as recently as 1904, had never been – and was never to be – an orthodox party man. Moreover, although after 1906 he became deeply interested in social policy, being to the fore in framing a measure of labour exchanges and in drafting an unemployment insurance scheme, his motives were hardly those of a mainstream Radical. In 1908 he had, significantly, struck up a friendship with Sidney Webb, from whom he imbibed some key National Efficiency ideas. Then, as the crisis of 1909–11 deepened, Churchill's thoughts turned to the possibility of creating a National government – an ambition in which he was encouraged by his close personal friendship with the swashbuckling Conservative MP, F. E. Smith.

However, in this endeavour Churchill found himself playing second fiddle to Lloyd George, a recent convert (though an erratic one) to the ideology of National Efficiency. Despite his reputation as a Radical firebrand, Lloyd George, when president of the Board of Trade (1905–8), had impressed the businessmen with whom he came into contact with an approach that paid scant attention to party orthodoxies. Having met many of the great 'captains of industry', Lloyd George was saying in 1910 that he was confident that he could work with them.

In August 1910, while on vacation in north Wales, Lloyd George dictated a memorandum, outlining the case for a National government. The country, he declared, was being needlessly torn apart by party rivalries at a time when all men of intelligence and good will needed to pull together. Both parties had able men and both had 'duffers'. Why could not the former unite around a compromise programme that would by-pass the issues that divided them (for example, the tariff and Irish Home Rule, as well as the future of the House of Lords) and pool resources in the interests of national reconstruction?

In early October, as the delegates reconvened for another session of the constitutional conference, Lloyd George approached Balfour, the Unionist leader, whose interest he tried to engage.[9] By late October some twenty figures, drawn from both sides of the House, had been let into the secret. Indeed, one of the first to be informed was Churchill, who responded with enthusiasm. Lloyd George also enlisted the support of the flamboyant journalist J. L. Garvin (an intermittent attender at Co-Efficient club dinners), who gave the notion of a national settlement favourable publicity in his Sunday paper, the *Observer*.

However, the 'secret coalition' talks petered out by the end of October, just as the parallel discussions in the constitutional conference were reaching deadlock. Many reasons have been adduced for their failure. Fundamentally, the two sides could not agree on the future of Ireland. Lloyd George tentatively suggested that it might be possible to displace Home Rule by a wider measure of 'Home-Rule-All-Round' or federalism, which would also give the Scots and the Welsh (and perhaps the English) their own legislative assemblies. The backbencher F. E. Smith and the journalist Garvin saw here the germs of a constitutional settlement worth pursuing for its own sake. The shadow chancellor Austen Chamberlain (Joseph's son) also sympathized. But Balfour rejected the proffered compromise as politically dishonourable and administratively unworkable.

By the end of 1910 both parties had returned to battle stations, with Lloyd George and Churchill showing themselves second to none in the intensity of their partisan invective. Events now followed a predictable path. The Liberal government won a second qualified victory in the general election of December 1910, forced through the Parliament Act reducing the delaying powers of the House of Lords, and then raised the political temperature still further by introducing a new Home Rule Bill. Between 1913 and 1914 the country seemed to be in a state of bloodless civil war, as friction in Ireland between Nationalists and Unionists threatened to precipitate violence on mainland Britain, where each Irish group enjoyed fanatical support.

During this tense period both Lloyd George and, still more, Churchill sometimes looked back wistfully on the 'lost opportunity' of 1910. In November 1913 Churchill invited Austen Chamberlain aboard the Admiralty yacht and dangled before him the advantages of 'federalism'. Churchill's friend F. E. Smith had meanwhile approached Lloyd George to see whether compromise was possible between the two front benches, not only on Ireland, but also on House of Lords reform and the land question. To this Lloyd George had made encouraging noises.[10] But neither set of leaders dared shrug off their obligations to the Irish Nationalists and the Ulstermen, respectively. It would need a crisis more acute than the one being experienced between 1909 and 1914 to replace party government with the politics of 'National Efficiency'.

The failure to establish a 'National government' between the Second Boer War and the Great War did not, however, mean that the ideology of National Efficiency achieved nothing. For its advocates were able to fall back upon a second approach: that of attempting to 'permeate' the existing political system by urging on those who held power the case for institutional modernization and social reconstruction in the light of the 'lessons of the war'.

Many important reforms followed. True, few of these new legislative and administrative initiatives were caused, in any simple sense, by memories of what had earlier happened on the South African veldt: most of the changes commonly attributed to the war had in fact been debated throughout the 1890s, if not earlier.[11] But the war's legacy was to impress upon legislators and ministers the urgency of reform by making it seem a patriotic necessity – and this really did matter.

The need for a thorough overhaul of army and War Office needed little underlining. Indeed, even before the fighting had ended the war secretary St John Brodrick (appointed in September 1900) had rushed into the work of military reorganization. But Brodrick's failure to produce a viable reform scheme (his successor Arnold-Forster fared little better) left the way open for Haldane, who went to the War Office in December 1905 when the Liberals replaced the Unionists. Within three years Haldane had created a new, highly trained volunteer army equipped for overseas service, the British Expeditionary Force, and had also reorganized the various ramshackle home defence forces into the Territorial Army.

Reformers of the National Efficiency school of thought, such as Amery, *The Times*'s military correspondent, had long advocated that the army be furnished with a 'brain'. Haldane agreed that this was necessary. He accordingly established the Imperial General Staff (an innovation begun by Arnold-Forster), with a view to separating military policy formation from routine administration. The spirit of National Efficiency also underlay Haldane's decision to send some of his senior army officers to specially created army classes at the London School of Economics, where, it was hoped, they would gain in professional competence. It also explains his anxiety to raise the technical proficiency of the Army Medical Service, and his filling of the new Advisory Committee on Aeronautics with scientific experts, which met under the chairmanship of the distinguished physicist Lord Rayleigh, Balfour's brother-in-law.

Even before Haldane arrived at the War Office, the navy was undergoing a similar modernization – perhaps less as a result of the shock of the Boer War (in which the navy had acquitted itself quite adequately), but more because of the combined impact of German naval expansion and the explosive personality of Admiral 'Jackie' Fisher, who cited the war in support of schemes to which he had long been committed.

Fisher agreed with Haldane that in modern war bravery and gallantry would not be enough and that 'character' must, in future, be allied with 'intelligence'. Tragically Fisher neglected to establish a proper naval staff, but he sponsored the Selborne Education scheme for trainee naval officers, as well as ensuring that the British navy remained in the vanguard of technological progress, being quick to see the importance of the submarine and radio telegraphy. Fisher also masterminded the development of a revolutionary new weapons system with the launch in 1906 of the all-big-gun battleship, the *Dreadnought*.

Interservice rivalry had long dogged the activities of Britain's defence planners, and the advocates of National Efficiency had consistently urged the importance of establishing some body with oversight of all the empire's strategic needs. Balfour responded to this pressure by reorganizing the Committee of Imperial Defence (CID). In its final form (dating from 1904) the CID brought the heads of army and navy together, while also allowing senior service officers to sit around the table on a basis of equality with their ministerial superiors, under the presidency of the prime minister – an innovation that was possible because the CID, at least in theory, possessed only an advisory role and so did not challenge the cabinet's supremacy as a formulator of policy. Attached to the CID was a secretariat which under successive secretaries, George Clarke, Charles Ottley and Maurice Hankey, marked an important step in the professionalization of government. True, the CID did not fulfil all that its founders had intended for it, but that does not detract from its institutional importance.[12]

The desire to bring the careers of army and navy officers more into line with the learned professions presupposed, however, the existence of a sound educational substructure. As it happened, a bold attempt to bring order into England's chaotic educational provision was provided by the 1902 Education Act, passed just after the conclusion of the war – a measure which for the first time integrated the local administration of publicly funded schools with control over the largely church-maintained voluntary institutions, while at the same time creating local education authorities (LEAs), with responsibility for all grades of instruction, from elementary to higher levels. Balfour, the new prime minister, took responsibility for steering this controversial measure through the Commons, an endeavour in which he enjoyed the backing of Haldane, who broke ranks with his fellow Liberal MPs to do so; Sidney Webb, currently the chairman of London's Technical Education Board, also came out in support.

The 1902 Education Act, admittedly, amounted to very much more than an expression of National Efficiency. Indeed, it might never have been introduced at all had the leadership of the Conservative party not been anxious about the financial plight of the ailing Church of England schools. Moreover, what propelled the Unionist ministry into tackling the issue was a legal ruling, the Cockerton judgement, which had thrown London's technical education into total confusion. Yet Balfour was not being wholly disingenuous when, presenting the bill to parliament, he dilated on the importance of closing the educational gap between Britain and her major commercial rivals. Moreover, as a measure of organizational rationalization, the 1902 Act well reflected the imperatives of National Efficiency, in particular through its provision for the co-option of 'experts' on to the new LEAs – yet another means of reconciling democratic accountability with an input of professional experience.

Meanwhile various members of the National Efficiency group worked, in their different ways, to improve and enlarge Britain's university sector. In 1895 the Webbs had already created the London School of Economics (LSE), which aimed at providing advanced training in politics, economics and public administration of a kind that would benefit both civil servants and businessmen. After 1900, helped by Rosebery who accepted the presidency of the college, its facilities were further extended. Haldane, another good friend of the LSE, also played a key role in linking together individuals and agencies interested in giving London a great technological university; this resulted in the foundation of Imperial College – labelled the London Charlottenburg after the famous Technische Hochschule in Berlin – which first opened its doors to students in 1909.

At the same time provincial universities were being fashioned out of sundry colleges of further education and university colleges. In 1900 Chamberlain, motivated by commercial considerations as well as by civic pride, spearheaded the movement to gain a charter for Birmingham University, while Haldane acted as counsel in the legal action that led, between 1903 and 1905, to the break-up of the former Victoria University, out of which emerged separate universities in Liverpool, Manchester and Leeds. Many of these developments might have happened anyway, but the rhetoric of National Efficiency was helpful in propagating the notion that it would be unsafe, even unpatriotic, not to invest heavily in human capital in this way.

The British state also began to involve itself more directly in the funding of scientific research, something for which the group of scientific propagandists surrounding Norman Lockyer and his journal *Nature* had long been arguing. In 1900 the National Physical Laboratory was founded, broadly modelled on the Physikalisch-Technische Reichsanstalt in Germany, though much less generously funded.[13] In October 1905 Lockyer, hoping for more state support, created the British Science Guild, of which Haldane became the first president, which self-consciously set out to harness scientific knowledge to the wider cause of National Efficiency.[14]

Social thought and social policy were affected even more profoundly by such developments. Advocates of National Efficiency gave a powerful lift to social legislation by presenting it, not as a humanitarian enterprise, but as a hard-nosed way of making the most of the 'raw material' of the British population. How, it was asked, could the empire flourish if governments allowed conditions to exist that created weak, hollow-chested citizens incapable of ever being enlisted, if needed, in the defence of the *patria*? Viewed from this perspective, the promotion of the welfare of schoolchildren seemed nothing less than 'sound Imperialism'.

This emphasis on the human body tended to encourage the 'medicalization of welfare' by focusing attention, not so much on citizens and their entitlements, but rather on the improvement of the 'national physique'. Pride of place in this undertaking was accordingly seized by doctors, medical officers of health and other experts, who all played a particularly active part in the Edwardian cult of maternity and in the movement to provide needy schoolchildren with subsidized breakfasts and rudimentary medical treatment.

It is no coincidence that some who thought in this way also felt a measure of sympathy for eugenics, the 'science' of race improvement. In 1907 the Eugenics Education Society was established. It aimed to encourage those from healthy stocks to propagate more freely, while urging the state to intervene to discourage the 'multiplication of the unfit'. Sidney Webb, and still more Bernard Shaw and H. G. Wells, gave their blessing to this attempt to extend 'planning' from the environment to the improvement of the human stock. However, most mainstream advocates of National Efficiency attached more importance to social conditioning than they did to good 'germ plasm': in other words, they were primarily interested in rearing, not in breeding, a better human race.

How important were considerations of National Efficiency in the unfolding of the welfare reforms passed by the Liberal government between 1906 and 1914? The shock produced by the rejection of large numbers of would-be recruits during the Boer War led directly to the establishment of an Inter-Departmental Committee on Physical Deterioration, whose 1904 report helped pave the way for the Education (Provision of Meals) Act of 1906 and the institution of school medical inspection the following year. However, these measures were supported for other reasons than National Efficiency. For example, a genuine humanitarian concern for the plight of the poor and the desire to propitiate the infant Labour party also contributed to their adoption. No monocausal explanation of the Liberal reforms will suffice.

The minister most obviously influenced (albeit briefly) by National Efficiency arguments was Winston Churchill, who in February 1908 struck up an alliance with Sidney Webb, from whom he derived the notion of a National Minimum: a norm 'below which the individual, whether he likes it or not, [could not,] in the interests of the well-being of the whole, ever be allowed to fall'.[15] Churchill also became intensely interested in the German social welfare system. Writing to Asquith in December 1908, he beseeched the government to 'thrust a big slice of Bismarckianism over the whole underside of our industrial system'; Germany, he argued, was 'organized not only for war but for peace. We are organized for nothing except party politics'.[16] Churchill's own labour exchange scheme was presented to the public in just such a guise: as a device for 'organizing' the labour market and thereby promoting social stability and economic growth.

However, significantly, Churchill soon fell out with the Webbs over their scheme for breaking up the Poor Law, as elaborated in their Poor Law minority report – a scheme which, whatever its theoretical advantages, would have involved unpopular state intrusions into family life. The Liberal government could not afford to take so great an electoral risk. On the other hand, National Efficiency arguments did help the Liberal government by making it much more difficult for the opposition to dismiss all social legislation as misplaced sentimental philanthropy. The state itself, it now seemed, had an interest in developing the physical well-being of its people. This was to become almost universally accepted after 4 August 1914, when Britain found herself at war with Germany.

The National Efficiency group had long warned of the imminence of a crisis that would test the mettle of its people and the fabric of the state. The Great War provided just such an ordeal by battle. How would the political establishment react? In fact, even before the ultimatum to Germany had been delivered, Churchill, via F. E. Smith, had sounded out the opposition front bench to see whether they would be prepared to fill any vacancies caused by Liberal resignations; he received a dusty answer from the opposition leader Bonar Law, still smarting with anger at the Liberal ministry's recent conduct. Instead Asquith shored up his government by offering the War Office to Lord Kitchener. Significantly, Kitchener saw no immediate need for conscription, the one major issue whose implementation would have required the combined effort of the two political parties. Even Lloyd George accepted that the time was not yet ripe for a National government.

However, party politics were scarcely compatible with the waging of total warfare, and the Unionists soon found it difficult to sustain their policy of supplying 'patriotic' support from the backbenches. Similarly, some senior Liberal politicians started to reappraise their party's strategy of 'going it alone'. Then in May 1915 the Asquith ministry was rocked by two serious crises: the headstrong resignation of Fisher (recently reinstated as first sea lord), and the breaking of a news story about a serious shortage of shells at the western front. Fearing that they were losing the initiative to their restless followers, the two front benches rapidly coalesced to form the first coalition government. (Ironically its most senior victim was Winston Churchill, who was demoted from the Admiralty, at Conservative insistence, and given the meaningless post of chancellor of the Duchy of Lancaster, from which he resigned six months later to rejoin his regiment at the front.)

This development obviously took place for entirely pragmatic reasons. But the notion that, at a time of 'crisis', an appropriate response would be a suspension of party animosities was one with which the wider public had become familiar as a result of over a decade of propaganda from the advocates of 'National Efficiency'.

Yet those, such as Garvin, who had long espoused the establishment of a 'National government' were disappointed in the composition and performance of the Asquith coalition, which gave more the impression of being a combination of parties rather than an attempt to transcend party by enlisting the services of the best men for the job – something for which so tradition-bound a figure as Asquith had little stomach. Partly for this reason and partly because the war was continuing to go badly, the Asquith coalition disintegrated in the course of 1916; in December it gave way to a new coalition, this time headed by Lloyd George, though heavily reliant on Conservative party support.

The Lloyd George coalition pursued an agenda that accorded quite closely with what the pre-war National Efficiency group had earlier championed. Power was concentrated in the hands of a small war cabinet of five ministers, all but one of whom was freed from day-to-day departmental responsibilities – a marked contrast to the former regime, described by one minister as a 'system of governing by 22 gabblers round a table with an old procrastinator in the chair'.[17] The war cabinet was serviced by a secretariat (directed by the CID's secretary, Hankey), which prepared an agenda for its meetings and took a formal record of the decisions that it reached – an innovation that had been long discussed, but which Asquith had always opposed. In selecting members for his war cabinet Lloyd George also paid scant heed to considerations of party balance; Bonar Law, the Unionist leader, was necessarily included, but its other members were chosen for their personal fitness for office: Arthur Henderson, the Labour leader, because of his influence with organized manual workers, Lord Curzon because of his expertise in foreign and colonial affairs, and Milner because of his proficiency as a technocrat and bureaucrat. How unimportant party had become can be seen from the fact that the Liberal leader, Asquith, now sat on the backbenches.

The old slogan of 'business government', too, was now translated into action. Lloyd George, who had never had much time for civil service protocol, had already recruited businessmen in large numbers into administrative posts, and he now acted to give the ablest of them ministerial office. Thus a wholesale grocer, Lord Devonport, was made food controller (admittedly he had earlier been a Liberal MP), while a Glaswegian shipowner, Joseph Maclay, became director of shipping without holding a seat in either House of Parliament, and Eric Geddes, formerly a railway manager, reached the dizzy heights of first lord of the Admiralty. Not all these businessmen justified the confidence placed in them, but that is another story.

Meanwhile the country's dangerous dependence on Germany for such crucial war-related materials as synthetic dyestuffs and optical glass was boosting the 'endowment of science' movement by giving a new credibility to its claim that scientific 'brain-power' was as important as sea-power to national survival. In May 1916 the government responded by setting up the Neglect of Science Committee, and by the end of the year the Department of Scientific and Industrial Research (DSIR) had come into being.[18]

Another legacy of the Edwardian 'National Efficiency' movement was the unfolding of the government's programme of 'Reconstruction', a slogan which carried many of the same meanings as 'Efficiency'. In July 1917 the Committee on Reconstruction, set up earlier by Asquith, became upgraded into a full ministry, under Lloyd George's close ally Christopher Addison. Its objectives were ambitious if somewhat ill focused. In the short run the ministry was entrusted with the task of smoothing the transition from war to peace (through demobilization, for example), but at the same time it set itself the task of economic modernization and the promotion of social justice (the origins of the 1919 Housing Act and the 1920 Unemployment Insurance Act). At a more fundamental level, Reconstruction rested on the premise that it was desirable to negotiate an historic compromise between Conservatism and Liberalism, so that a creative synthesis could be established between imperialism and social reform – a major enterprise that required cooperation between the two older parties.

One historian has correctly observed that the Ministry of Reconstruction was intended to be 'a species of government-supported idea-factory for a postwar party that would evolve under the leadership of Lloyd George'.[19] No wonder, therefore, that Addison was at the centre of discussions in late 1917 and 1918 to set up a new 'national party', comprising, *inter alia*, progressive Conservatives and patriotic Liberals. This project remained at the talking-shop stage, but when the war suddenly ended in late 1918 only the Labour party withdrew from the Lloyd George coalition; the Conservatives and the 'National' wing of the Liberal party went on to fight the 'coupon' election in December as allies.

Moreover, scarcely had the election been won than renewed attempts were made to buttress the Lloyd George coalition by a 'fusion' of parties. Prominent among the politicians trying to prevent a return to adversarial party politics were many who, influenced by considerations of National Efficiency, had once worked for a national settlement in 1910. Their numbers included not only Lloyd George and Churchill (who had been brought back into government in July 1917), but also Austen Chamberlain and the lord chancellor, Lord Birkenhead (the former F. E. Smith) – plus Balfour, now free to consider the national interest unfettered by ties of party leadership. But in March 1920 these crucial negotiations foundered, the Reconstruction programme was shortly afterwards wound down, and the coalition itself eventually collapsed in the autumn of 1922.

After 1922 little more was heard of the slogan 'National Efficiency' – except in the pages of the 'Yellow Book' of 1928, which outlined the programme on which the Liberal party, under Lloyd George's leadership, fought the general election of the following year. 'National Efficiency' had perhaps been too closely bound up with a view of Germany as enemy and as model. In the 1920s Germany, for the time being, offered little of a threat, and it may be that its crushing defeat during the Great War made it no longer seem such a paragon of efficiency – it was American business organization that was now viewed as the model to be followed. On the other hand, the term 'Reconstruction' enjoyed a much longer lease of life – a Ministry of Reconstruction, for example, was created during the Second World War.

There are many reasons why National Efficiency failed to achieve its initial promise. For a start, it was a 'top-down', manipulative creed, which treated the poor and dispossessed at best with condescension, at worst with brutality. This was a risky strategy to deploy, even during the Edwardian years when the franchise was held by a mere 60 per cent or so of the adult male population. It made even less sense in the 1920s, when the political system became fully democratized. Little wonder if National Efficiency only became viable in times of war, when democratic and parliamentary restraints on the powers of the executive were temporarily in abeyance.

Significantly, National Efficiency advocates tended to view working-class demands with suspicion, making little or no effort to establish links with senior trade unionists or with organized labour. Indeed, during the Great War and afterwards the movement increasingly took on a 'counter-revolutionary' character; thus by 1920 'fusion' seemed quite as much animated by fear of socialism as by a positive enthusiasm for a broad programme of social reform uniting all people of good will. Fearing internal turmoil, the National Efficiency group hoped to transcend class by stressing the higher interests of nation and empire; but, whatever their progressive protestations, in doing this they cut themselves off from most manual workers. For example, in identifying themselves with National Efficiency, the Webbs for many years forfeited their influence over the rest of the socialist and labour movement.[20]

Nor did the National Efficiency advocates have much to say, as a group, about the 'waste' of talent and energy being caused by the denial to women of full economic and political rights. Before 1914 some prominent individuals, such as Haldane and Grey, personally pressed the case for equalizing the franchise. But others (notably the Chamberlains, father and son) adhered obstinately to traditional notions of 'separate spheres'. As for the Webbs, they did not think the political emancipation of women to be that important. The ideology of National Efficiency thus remained largely rooted in a male agenda.

There was a similar insensitivity to the importance of national feelings and loyalties, and a positive lack of sympathy for the aspirations of the Irish. In fact, members of the efficiency group came from all quarters of mainland Britain, not just from England: Liberal Imperialism was particularly strong in Scotland, the homeland of Rosebery and Haldane, while Lloyd George, of course, was Welsh. But although some members of the group, in a half-hearted sort of way, advocated 'Home-Rule-All-Round', this owed more to their desire to dispose of the irritating Irish question and to relieve congestion at Westminster, possibly with a view to the later federalization of the empire; its corollary, self-rule for Scotland and Wales, was seldom stressed.

These backward-looking impulses go far to explain the eventual collapse of the National Efficiency movement. Yet not all of the ideas that it generated fell on stony ground. On the contrary, what its promoters were essentially doing was to identify and validate that form of social organization thought by the sociologist Max Weber to be most characteristic of the modern world – 'bureaucracy', recently redefined as 'the tendency for ever larger spheres of social life and institutions to be brought under a unified and coherent system of rationalisation and administration'.[21]

National Efficiency has also bequeathed to posterity two powerful sets of political ideas. One is mistrust of party; this, coupled with the conviction that managerial competence matters more than ideology, has continued to exert a powerful influence. Long after the restoration of party government in 1922, the assumption that national salvation required leadership from statesmen prepared to put 'country before party' regularly resurfaced at moments of 'national crisis': for example, during the financial crisis of 1931, and again during the Second World War (when, appropriately, the focus of such feelings was Winston Churchill).

National Efficiency's second main legacy has been the insistence that nations need constantly to adapt to new challenges if they are to survive.[22] Central to this obsession with 'modernization' is the claim that science and technology furnish the means whereby people's energies, released from futile class conflict and the suffocating weight of tradition, can be concentrated on institutional reform and national renewal.

The final irony is that a movement which once sought to circumvent the obstructionism of the Labour movement has more recently been taken up by the Labour party for its own purposes. Thus, at the 1963 Scarborough conference Harold Wilson extolled 'planning', called for a union of science and socialism, and, in an unconscious echo of the Edwardian rhetoric of National Efficiency, warned of the danger of Britain remaining 'a nation of Gentlemen in a world of Players'. More daringly still, Tony Blair has converted New Labour itself into an instrument of modernization. The twentieth century opened with a movement that promised an escape from the tyranny of history by promulgating a cult of the 'modern' and the 'new'. By a neat symmetry, the dawn of the following century has seen a return to not dissimilar ideas.

NOTES

1 G. R. Searle, *The Quest for National Efficiency, 1899–1914: A Study in Politics and Political Thought* (Oxford, 1971), pp. 1, 3; reissued with a new introduction (London, 1990).
2 See Lord Reay's address of 1894, cited in M. Fry, *Patronage and Principle: A Political History of Modern Scotland* (Aberdeen, 1987), p. 114.
3 G. C. Brodrick, 'A nation of amateurs', *Nineteenth Century and After*, 48 (Oct. 1900), pp. 521–35.

4 It was a direct imitation of a body with the same name that had been founded in 1855, at the height of the Crimean War.

5 Campbell-Bannerman to Herbert Gladstone, 18 December 1901, in J. A. Spender, *The Life of the Right Hon. Sir Henry Campbell-Bannerman* (London, 1923), vol. 2, p. 14.

6 One historian has called National Efficiency 'the engineering ethic' (J. Rose, *The Edwardian Temperament 1895–1919* [Athens, OH, 1986], p. 119).

7 The party in office since 1895 was technically a coalition, comprising the Conservative party and the Liberal Unionist party, the latter being the breakaway grouping of Liberals who had rebelled against Gladstone's Home Rule commitment.

8 For the view of National Efficiency as a 'cohering ideology', see Searle, *National Efficiency* (1990 edition), pp. xiv–xxiv.

9 See Searle, *National Efficiency*, ch. 6.

10 G. R. Searle, *Country Before Party: Coalition and the Idea of 'National Government' in Modern Britain, 1885–1987* (Harlow, 1995), pp. 82–3.

11 G. R. Searle, 'National Efficiency and the "lessons" of the South African War', in D. Omissi and A. Thompson, eds, *The Impact of the South African War* (Basingstoke, 2002), pp. 194–211.

12 N. d'Ombrain, *War Machinery and High Policy: Defence Administration in Peacetime Britain 1902–1914* (Oxford, 1973).

13 Interestingly, its establishment had been agreed to in 1897, well before the outbreak of the South African War. See P. Alter, *The Reluctant Patron: Science and the State in Britain 1850–1920* (Oxford, 1987), pp. 138–48.

14 F. M. Turner, *Contesting Cultural Authority: Essays in Victorian Intellectual Life* (Cambridge, 1993), pp. 217–21; Alter, *Reluctant Patron*, pp. 92–6.

15 S. Webb, 'The necessary basis of society', *Contemporary Review*, 93 (1908), pp. 665–7.

16 Searle, *National Efficiency*, pp. 248–9.

17 Cited in D. French, *British Strategy and War Aims, 1914–1916* (London, 1986), p. 102.

18 However, the origins of the DSIR can be traced back to before the outbreak of the war. See R. Macleod and E. K. Andrews, 'The origins of the D.S.I.R.: reflections on ideas and men, 1915–1916', *Public Administration*, 48 (1970), pp. 23–48.

19 B. Gilbert, *British Social Policy, 1914–1939* (London, 1970), p. 9.

20 After 1912, frustrated at the government's refusal to implement the Poor Law Minority Report, the Webbs moved back once more into the mainstream of Labour politics. In 1924 Sidney served as a minister within the first Labour government, where one of his fellow ministers was his old friend Haldane, the only Liberal Imperialist to come to terms (belatedly) with class politics.

21 R. Cooter, in R. Cooter, M. Harrison and S. Sturdy, eds, *War, Medicine and Modernity* (Stroud, 1998), p. 6.

22 Expressed, earlier in the twentieth century, in the language of social Darwinism, with its invocation of the 'struggle for existence'.

FURTHER READING

Alter, P., *The Reluctant Patron: Science and the State in Britain 1850–1920* (Oxford, 1987).

Cooter, R., Harrison, M. and Sturdy, S., eds, *War, Medicine and Modernity* (Stroud, 1998).

Davenport-Hines, R. P. T., *Dudley Docker: The Life and Times of a Trade Warrior* (Cambridge, 1984).

Hall, S. and Schwarz, B., 'State and society, 1880–1930', in M. Langan and B. Schwarz, eds, *Crises in the British State 1880–1930* (London, 1985).

Lewis, J., *The Politics of Motherhood: Child and Maternal Welfare in England, 1900–1939* (London, 1980).

Matthew, H. C. G., *The Liberal Imperialists: The Ideas and Politics of a Post-Gladstonian Elite* (Oxford, 1973).

Morgan, K. O., *Consensus and Disunity: The Lloyd George Coalition Government 1918–1922* (Oxford, 1979).

Rose, J., *The Edwardian Temperament 1895–1919* (Athens, OH, 1986), ch. 4.

Scally, R. J., *The Origins of the Lloyd George Coalition: The Politics of Social Imperialism, 1900–1918* (Princeton, NJ, 1975).

Searle, G. R., *The Quest for National Efficiency, 1899–1914: A Study in Politics and Political Thought* (Oxford, 1971; reissued with a new introduction, London, 1990).

Searle, G. R., *Country Before Party: Coalition and the Idea of 'National Government' in Modern Britain, 1885–1987* (Harlow, 1995).

Semmel, B., *Imperialism and Social Reform* (London, 1960).

Sturdy, S. and Cooter, R., 'Science, scientific management, and the transformation of medicine in Britain c.1870–1950', *History of Science*, 36 (1998), pp. 421–66.

Turner, F. M., *Contesting Cultural Authority: Essays in Victorian Intellectual Life* (Cambridge, 1993).

Turner, J., *British Politics and the Great War: Coalition and Conflict 1915–1918* (London, 1992).

CHAPTER FIVE

Scottish Issues in British Politics, 1900–1939

I. G. C. HUTCHISON

I

In the period from 1900 to 1914, Scottish politics displayed a rather different pattern from that in England, inasmuch as in the former the Liberals were much stronger while Labour and the Conservatives were weaker. In the last pre-war election, December 1910, the Liberals held fifty-eight of the seventy Scottish seats, whereas in England they won only 187 out of 456.

The Liberal performance was the more impressive because the 1900 election was the worst for the party since 1832. The Scottish party was particularly wracked by the Liberal imperialists, who were strong in Scotland, as Lord Rosebery had long been the leading party figure in the country, and two of his senior lieutenants, Asquith and Haldane, were prominent Scottish MPs. The party organization was badly run down, with many constituencies lacking a formal structure. Additionally, the longstanding association with Irish Nationalists, who were proportionately more numerous in Scotland, had been fractured, as the Irish felt the Liberals were not pressing Irish Home Rule with sufficient vigour. One paradoxical consequence of this was that the doughtiest friend of Ulster Unionism, Bonar Law, entered parliament on the back of Irish Home Rule supporters.

The Liberal recovery was rapid and pervasive, with the launching of Chamberlain's tariff reform campaign in 1903 proving decisive. The economic case for protectionism had virtually no appeal in Scotland. The great heavy industries. which dominated the Scottish manufacturing sector, depended on full and free international trade, while Scottish agriculture felt under no threat. The Liberals were reunited, and the Liberal League in Scotland faded away earlier than in England. Moreover, the party gained converts: several influential Liberal Unionists, such as a Dundee jute baron and a Glasgow MP, switched back in protest at the new policy.

But the party was not content to rely on Unionist blunders, for the Liberals began to shift their policies from nineteenth-century issues like disestablishment, which were becoming of diminishing relevance. The merger of the two largest dissenting Presbyterian churches into the United Free Church (UFC) in 1900 was quite soon followed by the beginnings of moves by the UFC to merge with the state Church of Scotland, so that the disestablishment campaign had patently lost momentum by the early 1900s. Instead, collectivist social reform was espoused by a new generation of Scottish MPs, who entered the Commons in increasing numbers from 1906. The arrival of Winston Churchill as MP for Dundee in 1908 cemented this trend. The minimum wage and social insurance were taken up by social radicals like Arthur Ponsonby, A. MacCallum Scott and J. W. Pratt. The most salient issue was the land question, which was more central to Scotland than English politics: a Labour party enquiry in 1911 concluded that Labour would not prosper in Scotland while the Liberals kept the land question at the forefront. The crofters' war of the 1880s had been the most recent episode to propel landownership into debate, but earlier protests had marked Scottish politics in the middle of the nineteenth century. By taking an old issue and injecting it with a new content from 1910, the Liberals kept the initiative. Accordingly, the Scottish land legislation of 1911 was much more radical than its English counterpart. Lloyd George's land tax proposals were extremely popular in Scotland, as they provided a neat method of simultaneously reinvigorating declining rural areas and offering a solution to the urban housing crisis that outflanked Labour's municipalization scheme. The Liberal campaign throughout Scotland in 1914 to rally support for land reform was a huge triumph.[1]

The party was energized by the Young Scots, formed during the Boer War to champion Liberal values. This body achieved several goals. First, it injected dynamism into the party's organization: by the immediate pre-war years it had branches in most Scottish towns, and its membership far exceeded that of the Independent Labour party (ILP). Constituency work in general, and electioneering in particular, was taken up with great gusto, and Tories drew unflattering comparisons between the energy and calibre of their own younger activists and the Young Scots. Second, the Young Scots revivified the Liberal parliamentary party by bringing on several of the most impressive of the MPs entering the House from 1906 – most notably J. M. Hogge and J. W. Gulland, both of whom eventually became Liberal chief whip. Third, the association became a think-tank for applying New Liberal concepts in a Scottish context. The major breakthrough in this field was to take the call for Scottish Home Rule from its earlier identification with nineteenth-century national self-determination and rework it as a crucial element in the social regeneration of Scotland. The Young Scots contended with regularity in the half-dozen or so years before 1914 that the case for a Scottish parliament was essentially predicated on the need to deal urgently with the acute problems (e.g. emigration, rural depopulation, urban squalor) encountered in Scotland which the Imperial parliament had no time to address.[2]

There was hence a sort of Caledonian version of the Progressive Alliance, with Young Scots activists cooperating with the Fabians and the ILP. Indeed one Young Scot, Roland Muirhead, was happy to help finance the ILP's *Forward* in the pre-war era. This close network may have contributed to the transition after the Great War of many former Radicals from Liberal to Labour – for example John L. Kinloch, Rev. James Barr and A. MacCallum Scott.

The Liberals' stance on the question of women's suffrage underlined the forward-looking nature of the party. Despite the presence of Asquith and Churchill – the Liberal arch-enemies of votes for women – as Scottish MPs, the bulk of Scottish Liberals took a different tack. Many of the women leaders of the Scottish suffragists were prominent Liberals, and the Scottish Women's Liberal Federation grew increasingly committed to the cause. About three-quarters of the Scottish Liberal MPs backed the cause, as did numerous Liberal-run municipalities. Scottish Labour's somewhat uneasy relationship with the women's vote issue (and indeed with women in politics in general) enhanced the Liberals' position. The Liberals had a large and lively women's wing, whose membership more than doubled in the immediate pre-war decade, and which engaged wholeheartedly in electioneering and political education.

Liberal organization as a whole was markedly improved in the period. Under Lord Tweedmouth's direction in the early 1900s, the Scottish Liberal Association began to develop fully representative constituency associations, and the new breed of Liberal MPs took a close interest in building up local parties: MacCallum Scott in Glasgow Bridgeton is a prime example of this. Full-time agents were brought on and they were able to build up registration work, an activity in which the Unionists' vast superiority in the 1890s had won several seats for that party. As a result, the grassroots strength of the party remained highly effective down to the outbreak of war, and in terms of membership and subscription levels, there was little sign of any faltering, at either the national or constituency level.

The clearest indicator of the relative dominance of the Liberals in Scotland in contrast to England was the differing response to the challenge posed by Labour in the early 1900s. The English Liberals felt compelled to enter into a pact with the Labour Representation Committee (LRC) in 1903 in order to avert a full-frontal electoral collision. In Scotland, the Liberals firmly resisted any such deals, instead taking on Labour wherever that party chose to fight in 1906. As a result, Labour in England, with twenty-six MPs out of 456, secured a greater presence in the 1906 parliament than in Scotland, where only two of the seventy seats were won.

For the Tories, this period was one of intense disappointment and difficulty, after the 1900 election results marked the first time they had won a majority of seats since 1832. As already indicated, much of the source of the setbacks they endured was to be found in policy matters. The free fooders were well represented north of the border, and their impact was considerable. The Scottish secretary, Lord Balfour of Burleigh, left the cabinet over tariff reform. Elsewhere, lairds and businessmen alike refused to help the party in the 1906 and 1910 elections: in Greenock and Renfrewshire West, Sir Michael Shaw-Stewart of Ardgowan, the most influential Tory landowner in the area, declined to endorse the Tory candidates, with dire consequences. The land question, so significant in Scotland, also worked to the detriment of the party. The strenuous campaign by landowners of opposition to Sinclair's land legislation only reinforced the perception of the Tories as a reactionary, unpopular group.

An enduring major difficulty for the party had lain in establishing a secure urban base. In some places the Orange card had been tried, but this was fairly unproductive: on the one hand, association with what in Scotland was seen as a disorderly, violence-prone organization deterred solid, respectable middle-class voters from identifying with Toryism; but simultaneously the order could deliver very few parliamentary voters, as its support was largely drawn from the working classes who were severely disfranchised in Scotland.

The split in the Liberal party in 1886 had effectively given the Tories an urban ally, for Liberal Unionists tended to be exceptionally strong in industrial Lowland constituencies. The close links – cultural, economic, religious and demographic – with Ulster which obtained in the west of the country gave a distinct boost to Liberal Unionism in Scotland, which regularly outperformed the English movement in elections after 1886. But this strength of Liberal Unionism also posed a problem for the Tories. Unlike England, the two parties remained separate entities until the very eve of the Great War. Liberal Unionists insisted on retaining their separate identity over a quarter of a century – indeed, even in the early 1920s some could yet be found insisting that they were still not Tories. The retention of distinct parties and the ensuing tensions left the Unionist alliance always rather fragile in Scotland. Disputes over the right to nominate candidates in seats produced conflict long after this had been resolved in England. Even when the merger at last took place in 1911, the Scottish Liberal Unionists professed unhappiness at this act of *force majeure* by British party leaders.

In consequence of these divides on policy and party identity, Tory organization in Scotland was frequently less than perfect. In many seats, the party was completely in the hands of the landowning elite, with no broad base, so highlighting the profile of the party as aloof and out of touch. Candidates accordingly found it hard to get canvassers and election workers in sufficient numbers, while financial donations were restricted to a few wealthy people. In contrast to England, the Primrose League never established itself as a vehicle for mobilizing the ordinary man and woman in the street on behalf of Conservatism.

On the eve of the First World War, the position of the Unionists still looked rather unpromising: organization was being only slowly built up, and in terms of policy, the Liberals seemed in command: the land tax was very popular. Even the old hostility to Irish Home Rule, once a sure-fire recruiter for Unionism, seemed to have lost its allure. The displays of support for Ulster resistance were muted in Scotland. When Carson led a deputation of Ulster loyalists to Britain in 1912, the response in Glasgow was decidedly cool: only about 8,000 were reported to have attended a mass rally, whereas in Liverpool, the other traditional British mainstay of pro-Ulster opinion, an estimated 100,000 turned out.

Labour never established a secure footing in electoral terms before 1914, and this was for a variety of factors. First, support for the ILP – although probably one-sixth of the British total – remained highly evanescent. Many branches of the party lasted only a few years, even in areas where it might have been expected to flourish. Often the survival of a local party depended on one or two individuals whose withdrawal meant the collapse of the branch. Even allowing for the fact that the paid-up membership substantially underrepresented those actually participating in ILP activity, its support remained low compared to other parties: in Glasgow in 1913 there were perhaps 2,000 members and supporters, whereas the Glasgow Unionists had around 7,500 subscribers. In Glasgow just before the war, as a long-term member subsequently recalled, the party seemed at a low ebb, with little signs of popular enthusiasm for the cause.

In any event, the ILP was not an electioneering organization as such, and it did not engage in activities like registration work. Rather, it saw itself as a propagandist body. *Forward*, established in 1906, served as a proselytizing paper, widely read in the west of Scotland. Other activities included street-corner meetings, rallies in cinemas on Sundays, or beach meetings at Clyde resorts in summer. The ILP's message was straightforward and grafted easily on to radical sensibilities. There was little Marxist content, and rather an emphasis on ethical concerns, with issues like temperance, Scottish Home Rule and land reform prominent. But the movement went beyond Liberalism in its sense of working-class consciousness, and in its passionate concern for the plight of the poor.

Perhaps the major strength of the ILP was that it had established itself by 1914 as the dominant socialist body in Scotland. The British Socialist party (BSP) and the Socialist Labour party (SLP) by then were confined to a few strongholds, and were frequently isolated from the broad Labour movement because of their doctrinal purity. The ILP, however, had succeeded from its inception in establishing electoral alliances, for both parliamentary and local government contests, with trades councils, cooperative societies and other elements of the organized working class: Glasgow and Aberdeen were particularly noteworthy instances.

Trade unions in Scotland represented a smaller proportion of workers than in England, and many Scottish unions were numerically small and geographically restricted: in Clyde shipbuilding alone, there were around a hundred trade unions. Consequently, trade union support for Labour was less sustained. Additionally, with one or two notable exceptions, trade union leaders were not socialists, and indeed many were rather hostile to the ILP, so that in several localities relations between the socialists in the ILP and the less advanced trade unions were often strained. The three Labour MPs elected before 1914 were all trade unionists who steered well clear of socialist involvement in their campaigns.

Additionally, party organization was defective. Until 1908, Labour in Scotland operated under the auspices of the Scottish Workers Parliamentary Representation Committee (SWPRC), but this body proved less effective than the English LRC. There was virtually no effort to develop registration, to disseminate propaganda, or to help constituencies select candidates. The British-wide trade unions gave their money and support to the London-based LRC, starving the SWPRC of funds. After the Scottish body was merged with the Labour party, there was only a gradual build-up of organization: it was not until 1912 that a city-wide party structure was installed in Glasgow, and the formation of a Scottish Council was delayed until shortly before the First World War by squabbling between the union and the socialist wings.

Labour also struggled because before 1914 the Irish Nationalist vote, despite its overwhelmingly working-class composition, was normally given to the Liberals. This was not so much from any hostility to socialism on the part of the devoutly Catholic community; even though John Wheatley's Catholic Socialist Society did encounter priestly denunciation and had a very small membership, there was a good degree of broad sympathy for Labour. Indeed at sub-parliamentary elections, where the Irish National cause was not in play, Labour did attract Irish Nationalist backing, as in Glasgow in the 1890s. Although the imminence of Irish Home Rule from 1910 undoubtedly had an impact, there were not more than a couple of seats where the Irish Nationalist vote could be considered decisive.

A final obstacle for Labour was the highly restricted nature of the electorate. In urban seats, barely half of the working-class men were entitled to vote: even among the members of Glasgow trades council in 1910–11, a body of men who were highly activist and mostly representing the skilled trades, only 55 per cent were qualified to vote.[3] While such a large share of the class to whom the party's message was directed could not vote – a higher degree of exclusion than in England – Labour was unlikely to prosper, even though its message was primarily directed at the skilled worker.

II

It is, in general, accurate to say that the First World War was widely supported in Scotland, where the enrolment ratio was higher than in England. While there were signs of rising discontent towards the close of the conflict, support for anti-war opinions remained insubstantial, as we shall see. The end of war was greeted with pride, and the level of involvement in commemorating Armistice Day throughout the interwar years remained high.

For the Tories, the war offered a way out of the impasse in which they seemed to be trapped. Unionists were unequivocally in favour of the war and endorsed any methods applied to secure victory. Many, of course, served in the war, frequently as members of the officer class, making them feel closely identified with the war effort. The predominance of landed families in the officer corps assuredly helped restore the image of landowners in the eyes of the patriotic public. In the 1918 general election, no fewer than 46 per cent of Unionist candidates had some military title, against 10 per cent of Coalition candidates and 6 per cent of Independent Liberals – there was no Labour candidate. It is not coincidental that Asquith's Tory victor in East Fife was a colonel, whose wartime gallantry was emphasized in the campaign. On the home front, too, the Tories displayed unswerving loyalty to the war effort. While the Liberal party split over the war and allowed itself to be painted as not completely pro-war, the Scottish Unionist MPs showed no such proclivities.

Tories not of military service age channelled their war spirit into organizing recruiting campaigns and administering the war effort on the home front by serving on state tribunals and commissions. Moreover, with so much of the military materiel, such as warships and munitions, being produced in the Glasgow region, the businessmen running these concerns, who were overwhelmingly Tory, established their patriotic credentials. It is significant that several of these industrialists won seats in the 1918 election, mostly in seats around Glasgow – for example T. S. Adair, a manager in Beardmore's ordnance factory, and D. H. MacDonald, chairman of the Motherwell-based Brandon Bridge Building Co.

More so than the Liberals, the Tories maintained party organization in better shape during the war. For one thing, there were none of the internal debates and disputes that scarred numerous local Liberal associations, and funding of needy Tory constituencies was sustained throughout the war by agencies such as the Scottish Conservative Club. The Tory press was fully committed to the war effort, and the overwhelming backing given by the Presbyterian churches mightily assisted the Tories in the long run. Leading figures in the UFC, hitherto very closely identified with the Liberal party, gave wholehearted backing to the war. After 1918 its membership's support for the Liberals was never again so assured – and indeed by about 1924 it was widely regarded as lost.

The Liberals in Scotland suffered probably more than they did in England from divisions occasioned by the war. Some MPs opposed Britain's involvement from the start, while others grew increasingly disenchanted as the conflict continued, with the introduction of conscription a leading break-point. Lloyd George's seizure of the premiership in 1916, and the consequent move by Asquith into opposition, deepened the gulf in Scotland. This was in good part because, as he sat for a Scottish seat, Asquith exerted a strong pull on his fellow Scottish MPs. On the other hand, Churchill, still a prominent member of the coalition government and MP for Dundee, attracted several Scots, including MacCallum Scott, who acted as his wartime parliamentary private secretary. This underlined the rift in the pre-war Radical camp, as others, for example Hogge and Gulland, remained with Asquith, so that the party never regained its progressive drive after the war. It should also be noted that the more right-leaning Liberal MPs were also split between the two camps: P. A. Molteno followed Asquith, while Sir Henry Dalziel vehemently championed the coalition government.

These Westminster schisms had a doubly negative impact at the constituency level. First, anti-war MPs encountered fierce criticism from party activists, and a number – Ponsonby, Esslemont and Pringle – were in effect deselected. These tensions reinforced the demoralizing impact on the rank and file of the divisions at the top. Constituency officials stood down in numerous seats and were hard to replace, while ordinary members grew disaffected and withdrew from involvement. There was concern that younger people were not joining the party during the war. Subscriptions to local parties as far apart as Aberdeen and Stirling accordingly plummeted. All of this left the constituency organizations ill-equipped to shape up to the challenges of the post-war era; thus it was reported in 1922 that the Stirling Burgh Liberals had not met once since the end of the war, by which time what had formerly been one of the safest Liberal seats had fallen to Labour. Limited assistance was forthcoming from party headquarters, for a sharp downturn in subscriptions – over 600 individuals were said to have withdrawn financial support during the war, causing a 25 per cent fall in revenue – severely restricted resources. As a result, constituencies were left to fight the 1918 election with barely any central direction.

The events in Glasgow during and immediately after the war aroused great controversy then and subsequently. It may be safe to summarize the current state of scholarly debate on 'Red Clydeside' somewhat along these lines. Much of the unrest in the armaments factories had little more than a veneer of revolutionary socialism. The demands of the workers were essentially conservative, in that they sought guarantees that their pre-war skilled status would not be permanently destroyed despite the use of semi- and unskilled workers to carry out tasks previously the monopoly of the artisan elite. Once the state had grasped this point, and dealt ruthlessly with the shop-steward leaders of the Clyde workers, the danger seemed defused. On the other hand, it does appear that discontent, often laced with an explicit political angle, persisted after the collapse of the Clyde Workers' Committee defeat – indeed it may well have increased in the closing years or so of the war. Certainly, it seemed manifest in the forty hours' strike held in early 1919, although those involved in the direction of this episode have left conflicting interpretations as to just how revolutionary the agitation was intended to be. With the defeat of the January 1919 agitation, the appeal of the non-parliamentary road to socialism seemed bankrupt – the British state was too powerful and resolute – so many turned to the ballot box, boosting Labour greatly in the subsequent 1922 election.

In recent years, moreover, emphasis has tended to shift the focus of the significance of the war away from the factory floor and into the streets and closes of the city. The resistance to rent hikes imposed by landlords during the war, climaxing in the rent strikes campaign of 1914–15, was a seminal moment for Labour. These were particularly dramatic because working-class women provided much of the leadership, especially at the local level. Labour had not until then been very successful in engaging women in political activity, but now their politicization was rapid, and a number of these women played a prominent role in left-wing Glasgow politics between the wars. With the advent of female suffrage at the end of the war, the benefit in reaching this new force was a particular bonus. Equally weighty, however, was the overweening influence exercised within the rent strikes campaign by the ILP. The party had been marginalized in the shop-stewards movement, where the bulk of the leadership was identified with either the SLP or the BSP – with David Kirkwood virtually the sole ILPer. But in being intimately associated with the housing question, the ILP had identified itself with the major social issue in Scottish working-class politics. Further, by championing the case for jettisoning the free market in rented accommodation, the ILP, and through it the Labour party, had secured the primacy of their solution to the difficulty over the pre-war Liberal scheme of yoking housing improvements to the land tax.

These two processes (industrial unrest and the housing question) were mostly restricted to Glasgow, yet elsewhere, too, Labour was making progress, although in a more diverse pattern. In some places, such as Paisley, the party pulled together various working-class institutions to respond to the pressures of war. This trend presaged the growth in working-class unity that characterized post-war politics. The Workers' War Emergency Committee in Paisley served as a forum for the trades council, the local cooperative movement, trade unions and the Labour party to coordinate policy in defence of working-class interests on matters such as rationing, the allocation of food supplies and conscription.[4]

Whereas most of those prominently engaged in the 'Red Clydeside' phase were anti-war, many in the Labour movement were solidly and unreservedly committed to the war. This included many in the ILP, and a very large number of trade unionists. Scottish miners, for example, volunteered for war service in proportionately larger numbers than those in England and Wales. In Stirling, the miners withdrew from the town's trades council between 1915 and 1918 in protest at a decision to invite a member of the anti-war Union of Democratic Control to address the council. This patriotic image helped to make Labour acceptable to many after the war who might have shied away from voting for an unadulterated anti-war party.

III

For the Liberals, the interwar years offered no respite from the decline initiated during the war. By 1924, the party was effectively marginalized in most urban-industrial seats: after 1922, it held no seats in Glasgow, Lanarkshire and Ayrshire. Where it retained a toehold in central Scotland, it did so usually by courtesy of some sort of arrangement, overt or tacit, with the Conservatives. It was on this basis that Liberals were returned for Dundee, Greenock, Leith and Paisley. The party kept support more successfully in rural areas – notably the Highlands, the north-east and the Borders. The redistribution that accompanied the 1918 Franchise Act was highly detrimental to the Liberals, for seats were taken from Liberal-leaning regions and given to the very urban-industrial parts where the party was struggling.

Part of this Liberal decline occurred because the party's policies became either outmoded or were embraced by the other parties. Land reform, such a clarion call before 1914, now seemed irrelevant. The attempts to encourage rural regeneration by creating smallholdings were, on the whole, largely unsuccessful. The idea of using a land tax to finance social reform, especially housing improvement, was replaced by the concept of state-subsidized municipal house-building, Labour's preferred option – and endorsed by a Royal Commission in 1917. Free trade was a dwindling asset: in 1923, it still exercised much of the pull it had enjoyed in the pre-war tariff reform campaign, especially among the west of Scotland business community. However, the abandonment of free trade in the early 1930s evoked no serious protest in Scotland. Temperance and Scottish Home Rule were both taken over by Labour after the war.

The Liberals were severely wounded by the defection of many to other parties. The shift of Churchill, the erstwhile MP for Dundee, to the right drew many in Scotland to follow the same course. Labour gained too: Lord Haldane, Arthur Ponsonby and MacCallum Scott all joined in the early 1920s, while the ascension of Lloyd George to leadership of the reunited Liberals in 1926 precipitated a second, albeit minor, emigration – notably two MPs, W. W. Benn and A. M. Livingstone.

There were few new recruits to counterbalance this erosion, so the party's membership was both threadbare and elderly. Numerous constituencies had no organization to speak of for most of the interwar era. Financial problems were acute: for part of the 1930s the salary of the Scottish Liberals' secretary was several months in arrears. The party seemed dominated by a landed elite: Lord and Lady Aberdeen, Sir Donald Lamont and Archibald Sinclair did not appear terribly relevant to a Scotland plunged into a long-term industrial depression.

The party was also punished by voters for its wartime divisions, and for its leaders' record of opposition to female suffrage. With the Irish question removed from the political menu, the Liberals lost the support of the Irish Nationalist vote. The protracted and bitter division occasioned by the split between Lloyd George and Asquith after 1916 took a very acute form in Scotland. There was a proportionately higher number of contests between the two Liberal parties in the 1918 election in Scotland than took place in England, and this significantly deepened the schism. Asquith's candidacy at Paisley in 1920 precipitated a ferocious move by Lloyd George and his Scottish supporters to block the former's return. A sign of the slippage in support for the Liberals was the collapse of the Liberal press: in 1911 some fifty-nine newspapers were identified as pro-Liberal, but by 1938 there were a mere thirteen. Mergers in both Aberdeen and Dundee involved the swallowing of the Liberal dailies in these cities by their Tory rivals, while in Glasgow the Liberal standard-bearer, the *Daily Record*, was bought out by a pro-Conservative publishing concern. So desperate was the situation that in the mid-1930s the party entered into an arrangement with the ailing *Weekly Glasgow Herald* whereby, in return for party members subscribing in sizeable numbers to the paper, a page would be allocated for the party to use for propaganda. It is indicative of the Liberals' weakness that the scheme was aborted because not enough members could be persuaded to take out a subscription to the *Weekly Herald*.

As politics became ever more polarized along class lines, the position of the Liberals grew increasingly anomalous. In particular, middle-class apprehensions about the menace of socialism induced right-inclined Liberals to switch to the Tories:

Asquith's decision to let Labour form an administration in 1924 provoked a protest by seven leading businessmen in his own seat, and he was defeated at the next election. The crisis of 1931 marked a further stage in the absorption of Liberals into the Tory camp: the sense of national emergency and the belief that Labour's incompetence and hidebound ideology had created the problem influenced Liberals at all levels.

The Tories seized the window of opportunity for rehabilitation offered by the war, and consolidated their position with great skill, so that the interwar phase brought the level of electoral support for the Scottish Unionists much closer to that in England than hitherto. The main strategy, can be defined as attempting to secure and retain the support of former Liberals, which wider factors made achievable. The tilt in the press, already noted from the Liberal side, was considerable. Again, the eclipse of dissenting Presbyterianism, so long a major prop for Liberalism, boosted the Tories. While the main non-established Presbyterian body, the UFC, did not unite with the state Church of Scotland, the latter was clearly in the ascendant in the 1920s. The Kirk gave strong, if indirect, backing for the Tories. It deplored the impact of Catholic Irish immigration as a menace to Scottish society and values, calling for repatriation as the solution. The 1926 General Strike was roundly denounced, and there was little overt criticism of the prevailing economic and social conditions of the 1930s. Leftish ministers like George MacLeod, the founder of the Iona Community, were excluded from any influence. The dominant Church of Scotland figure for most of the interwar years, John White, was a committed Conservative. As late as the early 1950s, the appearance of a Church of Scotland clergyman on a Labour party platform could create a *frisson* of surprise and disapproval.

Because of the need to placate Liberals, the Tories turned their backs on the pre-war dalliance with the Orange order. The latter formally broke with the Unionists over the ceding of independence to Ireland, and the Tories made little sustained effort to woo the Orangemen back thereafter. In the late 1920s and early 1930s militant Protestant parties emerged to oppose the Tory-constructed Moderates in municipal politics in Edinburgh and Glasgow. The consequence was defeat for the Tories and their allies, but there was no bid either to outflank the extremists or to come to an accommodation. The Orange order became more of a social institution, offering the prospect of securing employment through membership, but its political clout was severely diminished: indeed, it is obvious that most lodge members voted Labour. In one or two seats, mostly in Glasgow and Lanarkshire, some closer links between the Tories and the Orangemen were indeed apparent, but these were local products rather than centrally driven.

Scottish Unionists were normally to the left of their English colleagues on policy matters between the wars. In 1922, for example, when the English Tories voted overwhelmingly to rupture the alliance with Lloyd George, in Scotland Bonar Law had very few supporters. In the elections of 1922 and 1924, pacts were arrived at between Liberals and Conservatives to maximize the anti-Labour vote. In order to cement this, the Tories eschewed any diehard tendencies. After the General Strike, there was scarcely any support for punitive measures against trade unions, and the party was strengthened in this stance by its postmortem on the 1929 setback. It was widely felt that the Tories had lost middle opinion in Scotland by being perceived as too harsh on the defeated trade unionists.

It was in social policy that the Tories' appeal to moderate progressive opinion was most apparent. Municipal house-building was stressed as the appropriate approach to redress the Scottish housing crisis – so the party boasted that most council houses were built under Tory administrations both at central and local government. So dismayed was the Scottish secretary of state, Walter Elliott, by what he saw as the dithering of local councils that he established the Scottish Special Housing Association in 1937, with the explicit object of increasing the stock of public sector housing. Protests by private landlords at the damage being inflicted on them by massive council house-building (61 per cent of houses in Scotland between the wars were built by the public sector against a mere 31 per cent in England) were brushed aside by the Tories in the 1930s. Likewise, the Tories called for better pensions, and also for public spending on infrastructure projects to tackle unemployment and economic inefficiency.

The party skilfully played to a sense of Scottishness by upgrading the status of the Scottish secretaryship to a secretaryship of state in 1926 (although the commensurate salary raise was postponed for some years). Just over ten years later, a Tory government presided over the installation in Edinburgh of the Scottish Office, moving the bulk of the hitherto London-based civil servants north of the border into the symbolically named St Andrew's House. These moves were in part designed to reduce the temptation to both ex-Liberals and some Tories to join the nascent Scottish Nationalist parties of the era.

Scottish Tory MPs included many of the most liberal Conservatives in Westminster. Prime among these was Walter Elliot, who had been highly sympathetic to socialism while an undergraduate. While a junior Scottish minister Elliot had introduced the supply of free school milk in the major cities, and in the 1930s as Scottish secretary he continually urged radical measures by the government to tackle the acute social problems in Scotland. His importunate stance earned him the dislike of the chancellor, Neville Chamberlain, who moved him to another position on assuming the premiership. Other leftish Tories included Noel Skelton, coiner of the most iconic phrase for forward Toryism, 'a property-owning democracy'. Robert Boothby, one of the earliest advocates of Keynesianism, called himself 'a liberal member for a liberal constituency' – and indeed the local Liberals declined to oppose him because they regarded him as one of their own. Most bizarre of all was the 'Red Duchess', Katharine Atholl, who championed the cause of the Republican side during the Spanish Civil War, a stance which involved her sharing platforms with Communists (an offence that would have brought immediate expulsion had she been in the Scottish Labour party).

Matched to this pursuit of the middle ground was highly efficient organization. More than Labour and the Liberals, the Tories successfully managed to harness two key groups – women and young people. The first woman MP in Scotland was a Tory, and between the wars there were more female Tory MPs than either Labour or Liberal. At the constituency level, women were encouraged to engage in political debate and to undertake electioneering work. Young people were also reached by the Tories, and by the 1930s these Young Tories were being elected as councillors. In general organization, the Tories were light years ahead of their rivals. Unlike Labour and the Liberals, cash continued to flow into their coffers, while professionally trained agents were employed in most seats. Membership of constituency associations was very high – in 1931 Glasgow boasted a total of 30,000 – and this was adroitly built up by social functions, particularly afternoon bridge and whist sessions.

After disappointing results in 1918, when only a scattered handful of gains were logged up, Labour made a dramatic advance in the three elections held between 1922 and 1924. While, as noticed earlier, events in Glasgow attracted the overwhelming bulk of attention, it must be borne in mind that the strides forward for the party were achieved on a broader geographical front; moreover, the 'leftness' of other Scottish Labour MPs was not always so evident.

By the contest of 1922, the mood among the Scottish working class had shifted from initial post-war euphoria. Unemployment rose steeply after the short-lived boom created by the peace evaporated; social provision remained inadequate; and living conditions showed infinitesimal improvement. Moreover, the threat of the abandonment of the rent controls imposed during the war stimulated a surge of support for Labour, the only party to announce its opposition to the return to market rents. Additional to these immediate discontents, longer social changes continued to work through to benefit Labour. Working-class homogeneity was promoted by the war. Wage differentials between skilled and unskilled were sharply cut back, so living standards were closer. The gradual spread of council housing meant more equal housing standards. A further unifying factor was that unemployment, mostly affecting unskilled workers before 1914, now hit the skilled with especial ferocity from 1920. The expansion of schooling consequent upon the 1918 Education Act arguably diminished the gap in life chances between working-class sectors, and even the emergence of mass leisure pursuits, such as attending football matches and going to the cinema or dance hall, standardized the social experiences of the entire working class.

Perhaps as important as all the foregoing was the spread of trade union membership after 1914. Whereas Scotland had been somewhat underorganized before the war, there was now a much closer alignment with England. Moreover, many of the small, localized Scottish unions were swallowed up in amalgamations, so that the sectional outlook was less evident. Equally significant was the adhesion to the Scottish Trades Union Congress (STUC) of several large British-based unions that had hitherto declined to commit themselves to it – pre-eminently the engineers. The STUC henceforward embodied the views of the huge preponderance of unionized workers – who were a broader swath of the entire working class – in Scotland.

Labour did especially well after 1918 in mining seats, so that by 1922–4 virtually all of the constituencies with a significant mining vote had been won. While it is clear that the ILP made converts among miners at the end of the war, other elements were involved. Many of the MPs chosen for coalfields seats were not out-and-out socialists; indeed, many had been ultra-patriotic during the war and showed no recantation afterwards. Labour's capture of Lanarkshire Bothwell at a by-election in early 1919 created consternation among the Tory and Liberal parties, whose leadership construed the result as a portent of the arrival of Labour as a serious challenger to the status quo. The successful Labour candidate was John Robertson, a leading official in the Lanarkshire miners' union. Robertson had been staunchly pro-war, earning the nickname 'Woodbine' because of his activities in raising funds to buy cigarettes for soldiers at the front. Duncan Graham, MP for Lanarkshire Hamilton, had denounced Ramsay MacDonald's anti-war stance, while Harry Murnin, MP for Stirling Burghs, was equally hostile to pacifistic tendencies. The attractions of maintaining the mines under state control, and the increasingly bitter industrial relations in the coalfields, particularly after a prolonged strike in 1921, won Labour massive recruits. Indeed, Robertson prominently stressed his commitment to public ownership of coal mining. The internecine warfare within the Scottish miners' union between Communists and moderates which characterized most of the interwar period served to keep most mining MPs on the Labour right – Jennie Lee, an ILP firebrand elected in 1929 for a Lanarkshire mining seat, testified to the hostility she encountered from other Scottish miners' MPs. In other non-mining areas, a similar sort of pragmatic pro-Labour trend seems to have operated – in Edinburgh, for example, where railway workers wanted to retain the wartime state control of their industry, and in Aberdeen, where the railway vote was also large.[5]

While Maxton, Wheatley and their 'Clydeside' associates enjoyed great publicity ('advertisement men', as a moderate ILP MP derisively dubbed them), their support within the Scottish ILP movement went into rapid decline from the mid-1920s. Now the dominant influences were Tom Johnston, always more moderate than he had appeared, or had allowed himself to appear, and Patrick Dollan. So, while Maxton gained control of the British ILP in the mid-1920s, his policies were steadily repudiated in the Scottish section: in 1928, the Scottish ILP conference opted for the more moderate minimum wage policy in lieu of the Maxton–Wheatley 'living wage' formula, and the ultra-radical Cook–Maxton manifesto elicited little backing in Scotland.

This move away from the left was reflected in the wider Labour movement, most notably in the STUC. Under William Elger, its secretary for nearly a quarter of a century from 1923, a policy of realism was systematically followed. The setback of the 1926 General Strike tended to confirm the eschewal of militancy among most trade unionists. Also, from the mid- to late 1920s, a group of Labour politicians and thinkers emerged who were less attracted by rhetoric, and more concerned to produce detailed practical policies that could be implemented by a Labour government. The experience of office in 1924, and even more so in 1929–31, doubtless encouraged this trend. Arthur Woodburn, who became secretary of the Scottish Labour party in the 1930s, epitomized this pragmatic orientation, as did Willie Graham, the Edinburgh Central MP until his untimely death in 1932. The mounting moderation in Labour may well have been accelerated by the party's growing gains in local government in the early 1930s – it won Glasgow for the first time in 1933. Councillors were preoccupied with immediate policy options rather than large social visions, and a marked new development in the 1930s was for municipal politicians to stand as parliamentary candidates.

A significant development in the 1930s was the demotion of Scottish Home Rule as a leading issue. After the First World War, the ILP effectively took over the advocacy of the case for self-government from the Liberals. Most of the Home Rule Bills introduced in the Commons in the 1920s were sponsored and supported by ILP MPs, In the 1930s, this changed: both the ILP secessionists and the bulk of the Labour party became increasingly committed to the argument that the only realistic approach to the profound economic and social crises was a centralized command structure, to a large extent based on the model of the Soviet Union. Commitment to the cause of a Scottish parliament then became the preserve of a tiny minority, some drawn from the right and others from the left of the political spectrum. Up until the outbreak of the Second World War, the Scottish Nationalists were characterized both by sectional infighting and by the utter indifference of the electorate to their programme.

Labour's travails in the 1930s were multiple in origin. The crisis of 1931 had devastating electoral consequences – it performed more poorly than in England, and so faced a massive task in rehabilitating itself in the eyes of the electorate. Additionally, the secession of the ILP in 1932, spearheaded by Maxton, had a more drastic impact in Scotland, whereas in England it was fairly inconsequential for Labour. These two factors conspired to weaken organizational strength in Scotland, which had always been far inferior to that in England. By the outbreak of war in 1939, however, most of the problems had been overcome, and a new sense of confidence could be heard in the party. Moderate policies, as noted earlier, had been initiated in the late 1920s, and now these were pushed ahead. The growing presence of Labour in municipal chambers as the governing party helped to bestow an impression of competence and common sense, transferring easily into electability for Westminster, a theme highlighted by the promotion of councillors as parliamentary candidates. The STUC heightened this moderation by adopting a consensual, not to say corporatist, approach on economic and industrial policy, joining employers in bodies such as the Scottish Council, designed to assist in the regeneration of the country's economy.

The menace posed by the breakaway ILP nevertheless turned out to be a paper tiger. Although impregnable in its fastness in the East End of Glasgow, outwith there the ILP had no major negative consequences for Labour. After an initial impetus at a by-election in 1933, the ILP polled poorly elsewhere. Labour pursued a policy of rigorous isolation against the ILP, as well as against the Communist party: any member of the Labour party cooperating politically with the other two faced expulsion, and this was executed repeatedly in the mid- and late 1930s.

Before 1932, grassroots constituency activists were not very numerous in Scottish Labour, and the average membership numbers were significantly below those in England and Wales. Despite the early involvement with women during the rents crisis, by the middle of the 1920s Labour seemed to have lost any serious commitment to build up its women's sections. After 1932, there was a resolute campaign to expand membership and to recruit women in particular. The STUC and the Scottish Cooperative movement joined forces with the party in these projects, and as the 1930s wore on levels of support did rise, although Scottish membership never attained the scale found south of the border. Nevertheless, the party felt strong enough to launch assaults on constituencies where hitherto it had never claimed more than a token presence, so that in rural seats like Dumfriesshire and Ross and Cromarty there was a serious assumption that Labour might capture them.

Thus by the outbreak of the Second World War, the pattern of electoral politics in Scotland was somewhat closer to the overall British format than had been the case before 1914. Nevertheless, the question of how effectively Westminster and Whitehall could deal with specifically Scottish issues and problems remained unresolved, and although the self-government case was in abeyance, this might be only a temporary quiescence.

NOTES

1   I. Packer, 'The land issue and the future of Scottish Liberalism in 1914', *Scottish Histori-cal Review*, 75 (1996), pp. 52–71.
2   R. J. Finlay, *A Partnership for Good? Scottish Politics and the Union since 1880* (Edinburgh, 1997), pp. 52–60.
3   J. J. Smyth, *Labour Politics in Glasgow, 1896–1936: Socialism, Suffrage and Sectarianism* (East Linton, 2001), pp. 10–17.
4   C. C. M. MacDonald, *The Radical Thread: Political Change in Scotland. Paisley Politics, 1885–1924* (East Linton, 2000), pp. 207–20.
5   J. Holford, *Reshaping Labour: Organisation, Work and Politics in Edinburgh during the Great War and After* (London, 1988), pp. 200–15.

FURTHER READING

Ball, S., 'Asquith's decline and the general election of 1918', *Scottish Historical Review*, 61 (1982), pp. 44–61.
Brown, G., *Maxton* (Edinburgh, 1986).
Donnachie, I., Harvie, C. and Wood, I., eds, *Forward! Labour Politics in Scotland 1888–1988* (Edinburgh, 1989).
Finlay, R. J., *A Partnership for Good? Scottish Politics and the Union since 1880* (Edinburgh, 1997).
Foster, J., 'Strike action and working-class politics on Clydeside, 1914–19', *International Review of Social History*, 35 (1990), pp. 33–70.
Fry, M., *Patronage and Principle: A Political History of Modern Scotland* (Aberdeen, 1987).
Holford, J., *Reshaping Labour: Organisation, Work and Politics in Edinburgh during the Great War and After* (London, 1988).
Hutchison, I. G. C., *A Political History of Scotland, 1832–1924: Parties, Elections, Issues* (Edinburgh, 1986).
Hutchison, I. G. C., *Scottish Politics in the Twentieth Century* (Basingstoke, 2001).
Knox, W. W., *Scottish Labour Leaders, 1918–39* (Edinburgh, 1984).
Knox, W. W., *James Maxton* (Manchester, 1986).
Knox, W. W. and Mackinlay, A., 'The re-making of Scottish labour in the 1930s', *Twentieth Century British History*, 6 (1995), pp. 134–53.
MacDonald, C. C. M., ed., *Unionist Scotland, 1800–1997* (East Linton, 1998).
MacDonald, C. C. M., *The Radical Thread: Political Change in Scotland. Paisley Politics, 1885–1924* (East Linton, 2000).
Mackinlay, A. and Morris, R. J., eds, *The ILP on Clydeside, 1888–1932* (Manchester, 1991).
MacLean, I., *The Legend of Red Clydeside* (2nd edition, Edinburgh, 1991).
Packer, I., 'The land issue and the future of Scottish Liberalism in 1914', *Scottish Historical Review*, 75 (1996), pp. 52–71.
Smyth, J. J., *Labour Politics in Glasgow, 1896–1936: Socialism, Suffrage and Sectarianism* (East Linton, 2001).
Walker, G., *Thomas Johnston* (Manchester, 1988).
Wood, I., *John Wheatley* (Manchester, 1990).

CHAPTER SIX

Wales and British Politics, 1900–1939

R. Merfyn Jones

In a number of significant ways the pattern of politics in Wales in the period 1900–39 was distinct from that in the rest of the United Kingdom. In the first place, the extraordinary contrast between the rapid economic growth that characterized Wales during the first twenty years of the century and the devastating depression that affected the second twenty years was not as apparent, nor so crucial, elsewhere. Second, despite consistently winning between 20 and 30 per cent of the vote, the Conservative party, such a dominant force elsewhere in Britain, was politically marginalized in Wales and only rarely succeeded in winning parliamentary representation outside Cardiff and Monmouth in the south-east of the country. In the general election of 1906, the Conservatives famously failed to win a single Welsh parliamentary seat. As the historian of the party in Wales during this period has concluded, 'The history of the Conservative Party in Wales has undeniably been one of consistent electoral failure throughout most of the Principality'.[1] As a result a third distinguishing feature was the fact that the predominant political currents in Wales were strongly and, at times, passionately anti-conservative, as witnessed as much in the Liberal rhetoric of David Lloyd George as in the socialist oratory of Aneurin Bevan. This anti-conservative terrain was contested not only by the Labour and Liberal parties. Other, smaller parties, notably the Communist party from 1921 and Plaid Genedlaethol Cymru (the Welsh Nationalist party) from 1925, also made an impact. And finally, as we shall see, the issues regarding Wales's status within the United Kingdom, and the survival of the Welsh language, continued to concern a wide spectrum of political actors.

Until 1922 the most dominant of the anti-conservative forces was the Liberal party, which won over 50 per cent of the vote in the elections of 1900, 1906 and the first general election of 1910, with the vote slipping to below half of the electorate only in the second election of that year. During these years they held between twenty-six and twenty-eight of the thirty-four Welsh constituencies. When Lib–Lab members are included, as they should be until 1908, the dominance of the party is even more remarkable, representing as it did thirty-two of the thirty-four Welsh seats in 1906, with only Keir Hardie and a lone Liberal Unionist outside the fold.[2] This success was based on a remarkably effective political coalition that united the tenant farmers of rural Wales with industrial workers in mines and steelworks and crossed class barriers to ally trade unionists such as William Abraham with small businessmen and shopkeepers, and even with coalowning magnates such as D. A. Thomas. Fundamental to the Liberal worldview was, on the one hand, a radical opposition to the traditional enemy identified as landlordism and Anglicanism and, on the other, an identification with Welsh culture and, in particular, with religious nonconformity. Despite the fact that Lloyd George had failed to construct a nationalist Liberal alliance in the 1890s, Liberalism remained permeated by these particularly Welsh sensibilities and the disestablishment of the Church of England in Wales, on the model of Irish disestablishment in 1871, remained a potent demand until finally implemented in 1920 following legislation in 1914 and 1919. Even though this victory occasioned relatively little political excitement, the measure itself did mark a significant repositioning of Wales within the British constitutional settlement.[3]

The most prominent advocate of Welsh Liberalism, and a figure who himself represented many of the characteristics of radical Welsh Liberalism, was, of course, David Lloyd George, the only Welsh politician ever to become prime minister. Elected for Caernarfon Boroughs in 1890, he became president of the Board of Trade in Campbell-Bannerman's 1905 cabinet before becoming Asquith's chancellor of the exchequer, 1908–15. During the First World War he was minister of munitions, 1915–16, and briefly secretary of war before becoming prime minister in 1916, a post he held until 1922.

The prominence of his political career, and the effectiveness of his reforming zeal, provide a major theme in modern British political history that has attracted considerable historical attention. Many historians, reflecting the view of contemporaries such as John Maynard Keynes, who described him as 'a goat-footed bard, a half-human visitor to our age from the hag-ridden magic and enchanted woods of Celtic antiquity', have rightly emphasized Lloyd George's Welshness and the intriguing impact this is held to have had on his policies and on his political style and personal character.[4] In his commitment to social reform as demonstrated in the Old-Age Pensions Act of 1908, and even more in the passion of his attacks on the House of Lords and on landlordism during the crisis that followed his 'people's budget' of 1909, he clearly drew on the rhetoric and intensity of Welsh Liberal nonconformity's long struggle against the perceived injustices perpetrated by what it characterized as an alien class. 'Who ordained', he challenged then, 'that a few should have the land of Britain as a perquisite? Who made ten thousand people owners of the soil, and the rest of us trespassers in the land of our birth? . . . The answers are charged with peril for the order of things the peers represent.'

His not altogether successful attempt to create a Welsh army during the First World War can also be seen not only as a recruitment ploy but as a further example of his continuing concern for maintaining the identity of Wales within the British state. During the treaty discussions at Versailles and later in the partition of Ireland in 1921, Lloyd George also brought to the table an understanding, born of his Welsh experience, not only of the plight of national minorities but also of Protestant fears. A Welsh speaker who brought into government other Welsh speakers such as Thomas Jones, assistant secretary to the cabinet and a ubiquitous figure in interwar Wales, he was himself conscious of what he described as the 'unconscious and only half conscious contempt with which the Englishman regarded the Welsh people'.[5]

Although born in Manchester, Lloyd George was brought up in Llanystumdwy, Caernarfonshire, in a thoroughly Welsh-speaking and nonconformist rural community. He later built his country home in Llanystumdwy and was to be buried there. As *The Life Story of Lloyd George*, a remarkable though hagiographical film about him made in 1918, emphasized, his childhood experiences were to fashion the man. A recent biographer has controversially yet perceptively noted that '[t]he cleavage in North Welsh county society between the landlord and the tenant and between the separate cultures that they represented . . . furnished Lloyd George with the one political issue he maintained throughout his life'.[6] It is a notable comment on the British parliamentary system that it was to this outsider that the British Empire turned in its hour of need in 1916.

The Liberal ascendancy in Wales coincided with a period of considerable economic success associated largely with the extraordinary growth of the south Wales coal industry and of iron and steel manufacture and tinplate. Coal mining recreated Wales in a number of ways. As people poured into the valleys of Glamorgan and Monmouthshire in the late nineteenth and early twentieth centuries, existing communities were expanded and new ones created.[7] The population of the Rhondda increased from 55,000 in 1881 to 167,000 in 1921 and the coastal ports also grew rapidly. Barry, on the south Glamorgan coast, hardly existed in 1890 but within twenty years it had a population of 34,000. The number of coal and other miners in Wales rose from 148,000 in 1901 to the astonishing total of 271,000 in 1921, making south Wales the largest, and the most strategically important, coalfield in Britain. By 1911, 27 per cent of the population of Glamorgan had been born outside Wales, the vast majority of them in England. The appalling explosion in Senghenydd in 1913 which killed 439 men further underlined the prominence and the lethal dangers of coal mining.

It has been convincingly argued that this early twentieth-century south Wales, based on coal, steel and tinplate, created a 'culturally distinctive human experience' which strained the cohesion of Liberal Wales.[8] At the turn of the century, however, the Liberal nonconformist coalition that sustained a constructed national cohesion in Wales still had some purchase. In the Rhondda in 1901, 64 per cent of the population still spoke Welsh, although that percentage was in sharp decline. The remarkable religious revival of 1904–5, which swept through industrial and rural Wales with equal intensity, upheld the power and appeal of nonconformity for another generation.

The portents of change, however, were only too apparent. While the parliamentary representatives of the coalfield might have been Liberals in 1906, they were also – Thomas Richards in West Monmouthshire, William Brace in Glamorgan South and William Abraham in the Rhondda – pre-eminently trade unionists and full-time officials of the South Wales Miners' Federation. And in Merthyr Tydfil and in Gower, Independent Labour party (ILP) members were returned to parliament.

Keir Hardie's victory in Merthyr Tydfil in 1900 was remarkable for a number of reasons, not least of which was the fact that the Scottish socialist expected to win in Preston, where he was also a candidate, rather than in Merthyr, from where he was largely absent during the campaign. His victory was a milestone in the history of the

Labour movement in Britain and was of great significance in the context of Welsh politics, but it did not signify a ground-breaking shift in Welsh electoral behaviour, for even in this radical, two-member constituency, where 68 per cent of the population spoke Welsh in 1901, Hardie came second to the Liberal candidate D. A. Thomas.

Hardie's victory was in part accounted for by his support for the miners in the south Wales lockout of 1898, which led to the formation of the South Wales Miners' Federation (SWMF), and the pivotal role of trade unionism in the politics of Wales became increasingly apparent during the first decade of the century. The 'Fed', as the SWMF was called, was an organization of enormous reach and authority in the coalfield.[9] When it affiliated to the Labour Representation Committee (LRC) in 1908 it shifted the balance of power irrevocably, although it was to take a further decade and franchise reform and boundary changes before that was translated into electoral success. Even in the 'coupon' election of 1918 Labour was to win ten seats; in 1922 it won eighteen, half the Welsh constituencies.

Increasingly, Wales came to be associated with industrial strife. At the start of the century there was an extraordinary conflict in Snowdonia in north Wales when, from October 1900, the 3,000 slate quarrymen at the giant Penrhyn quarries were locked out, to enormous press and political attention. But it was in south Wales that the most dramatic developments took place. In 1910–11 a violent strike in the Cambrian Combine suddenly catapulted the area, previously seen as a moderate district within the Miners' Federation of Great Britain (MFGB), to national and international attention as a centre of industrial militancy and political activism. In October 1910 police and troops clashed with striking miners at the Glamorgan colliery and rioting spread to the square in Tonypandy. In the ensuing political controversy the home secretary Winston Churchill came to be blamed by the miners for sending soldiers against them. Rioting in Llanelli in the following year, this time associated with the transport strike, led to the deaths of five men, two of them shot by troops.

Following the Cambrian dispute an Unofficial Reform Committee launched a campaign to reform the union and transform it into a weapon of revolutionary class struggle with the publication, early in 1912, of the pamphlet *The Miners' Next Step*. This publication attracted considerable attention and created great anxiety in some quarters as it was clearly informed by theories of revolutionary syndicalism and industrial unionism. These ideas were associated largely with one of the main authors, Noah Ablett, a miner who had played a central role in the Ruskin College student strike of 1909 and the subsequent establishment of the Marxist Central Labour College.[10]

The influence of these revolutionaries should not be overestimated, but neither should they be overlooked for, while the adherents of syndicalism in Wales might have been few, they were persuasive. Their emphasis on militant class struggle had a wide appeal in a coalfield that witnessed further major strike action in 1912 and 1915 before the traumatic set-piece battles of 1921 and 1926. This Welsh reputation for militancy was further enhanced by the fiery rhetoric of Arthur James Cook, from the Rhondda although born in Somerset, general secretary of the MFGB during the General Strike. As if to confirm the impression, the SWMF was one of only two major unions financially to sponsor the Central Labour College in London, and in 1921 it became one of the few unions in Britain seriously to consider affiliation to the Moscow-based Red International of Labour Unions.

In 1917 the government established a Commission of Inquiry into Industrial Unrest which produced a wide-ranging report on Wales that identified a number of factors held to be responsible for the militancy of the south Wales miners. The commission noted, amongst other possible causes, the chaotic spread of terraced settlement in the valleys, which lacked the social cohesion and municipal centres of towns, thus inhibiting social control. It noted also the impact of inward migration in weakening traditional constraints and creating a disproportionately large number of young males in the population. Culturally, the commission members pointed to the threat of cinema and music hall and they also identified the impact of adult education, particularly that brand associated with the Central Labour College and the Plebs League, which supplied local leaders with their 'advanced' socialist ideas and ambitions. Throughout the report there is a consciousness of the loss of vitality of the traditional Welsh Liberal world.[11]

Liberalism, however, was to survive in resilient fashion in post-First World War Wales, despite all the divisions and internal conflict occasioned by Lloyd George's war with Asquith and his subsequent role as prime minister of a formal coalition that was, in fact, largely dominated by the Conservatives. He fell from office, never to return, when the Conservative party withdrew its support for him at the Carlton Club in 1922.

Although, for Liberalism, the coalfield was largely lost by 1922, rural Wales continued to return Liberal members throughout the interwar period. The Liberal party remained the second largest party in Wales; in 1924 the Liberal vote in Wales, at 31 per cent, was almost twice as high as the Liberal share of the vote in England. Wales remained important for the survival of British Liberalism and in 1929 Clement Davies, a future leader of his party, described by one Liberal party historian as 'one of the unknown great men of modern times', was elected for Montgomeryshire. The Liberals also provided Wales with its only prominent female politician in this period when, in 1929, Megan Lloyd George was elected as member of parliament for Anglesey.[12]

By the time Labour's predominance was confirmed in 1922, Wales was already experiencing the depression that had descended on economic activity in the autumn of 1920, following the short post-war boom. Because of the country's dependence on those industries that were worst affected by the general economic downturn – the traditional heavy industries of coal and steel – Wales suffered disproportionately during the interwar depression and the return to the gold standard in 1925 rendered a bad situation even worse. Coal exports declined by half, and the number of coal miners also dropped dramatically by over half in the same period. Unemployment rates varied from area to area: throughout industrial south Wales in 1930 the overall percentage of the insured population out of work was 32 per cent, but this figure disguised the disaster in the real unemployment blackspots, such as Merthyr Tydfil, where 50 per cent were registered as unemployed. Even as conditions improved in the mid-1930s the statistics remained stubbornly and shockingly high. In 1935, 70 per cent of coal miners in the Merthyr and Dowlais area were unemployed, and in the upper stretches of the two Rhondda valleys there were 15,000 unemployed miners in 1935, a reduction of only 800 since 1931. Mass unemployment was endemic in these areas for a generation. Thousands of men spent years of their lives on the dole: in 1938 a quarter of all the unemployed people in Wales had been unemployed for over a year. In

Brynmawr, Monmouthshire, part of Aneurin Bevan's devastated constituency, 57 per cent of the unemployed miners had been idle for over two years and almost 30 per cent of those over forty years of age had been unemployed for over four years.

Government policy towards the stricken coalfield was depressingly clear – the transfer of people to more prosperous areas elsewhere. Emigration was thus the consequence of both economic necessity and government policy. It was estimated that 242,000 people had left south Wales by 1931 and the total population had declined by 70,000. This decimation cut into the human bone of communities across the coalfield: Rhondda lost 22 per cent of its population, Abertillery 29 per cent and Mountain Ash a further 22 per cent.

This devastating rate of emigration continued during the 1930s; it has been reliably calculated that between 1921 and 1938, 440,000 people left Wales, an enormous blow to a country whose population in 1931 was only 2.5 million. This was the highest rate of depopulation of any region in the United Kingdom, and tens of thousands of Welsh people found themselves in Slough, Coventry, Oxford and elsewhere in the midlands and south-east of England. As late as 1939, a report prepared by Political and Economic Planning advocated the closure of the town of Merthyr Tydfil and the removal of the population to a new location as it was not 'reasonable to ask the tax-payers of the rest of Britain indefinitely to pay hundreds of thousands of pounds a year in order to give large numbers of people the dubious pleasure and benefit of continuing to live at subsistence level'. It was the closure of steelworks and mines that had the greatest impact, but rural Wales was also in crisis following the price crash of the early 1920s. By 1930 the extent of cultivated land had fallen back to the levels of the 1860s. Only those areas that profited from the growth of mass tourism, such as the holiday resorts of the north Wales coast, enjoyed the impact of the boom affecting large parts of southern England.

The militant miner of popular perception now became a hunger marcher, and during this period the image of the south Wales miner as the archetypal proletarian gained wide currency. It was an image which films such as *The Citadel* (1938) helped to disseminate. The many published reports into the situation in the valleys and the intervention of social workers, Quaker settlements and others further confirmed the picture of Wales as an embattled proletarian bastion.

The gravity of the situation was real enough and presented a serious challenge to government policy. Recently published research has revealed the degree to which the crisis in south Wales led, by the late 1930s, to a highly significant shift in Whitehall thinking.[13] Population transfer and the untrammelled operation of the free market were replaced by a more interventionist approach in which publicly funded inducements were deployed to attract industry to the area, thus prefiguring the Keynesian approach of post-war governments. Intriguingly, the one politician who had consistently advocated such an approach with the publication of 'We Can Conquer Unemployment' in 1929, and his later 'new deal' programme and Council of Action of 1935, was Lloyd George. But his was a lone voice and Labour party policy was confused and unconvincing until reshaped by Hugh Dalton in the late 1930s. The change of policy came about largely through the pressure of Sir Wyndham Portal, who was appointed by the government to investigate the situation in south Wales in 1934. This led to the passing of the Special Areas (Development and Improvement) Act in the same year. Later, following the highly sensitive and significant visit of the king to Dowlais in 1936, when he reportedly commented that 'something must be done', the influential second Special Areas Act of 1937 was passed. This Act 'empowered the commissioner to clear sites, erect factories, promote trading estates and offer remission of rent, rates and income tax to any company'. Manufacturing industries were thus established in a number of locations, perhaps most importantly at the Treforest Trading Estate near Pontypridd, well before the Second World War so changed the economic landscape in Wales.

South Wales was not, of course, the only 'distressed' region; parts of Scotland and northern England were also seriously affected. But it is clear that the combination of the scale and gravity of the Welsh situation and the tenacity of Sir Wyndham Portal in influencing Treasury and Whitehall thinking did lead to a significant shift in government policy by the mid-1930s.

Another aspect of government policy on unemployment that was seriously affected by events in Wales was in 1935 when the setting up of the Unemployment Assistance Board (UAB) in January led to many of the unemployed experiencing drastically reduced benefits. Drawing on a tradition of direct action established during strikes and hunger marches, a wave of popular protest engulfed south Wales; it has been estimated that over 300,000 people demonstrated against the changes. In Merthyr stones were thrown at the UAB offices. The government relented and withdrew the new scales.

The wider political repercussions of the depression went deeper still in the political consciousness of large numbers of people in Wales. As late as 1969, Labour MP and former minister James Griffiths insisted that 'Wales has still to recover from the wounds of the thirties . . . the fears persist, the doubts remain and the wounds are unhealed'.[14] The depression further enhanced a widespread identification with, and loyalty to, the Labour party across industrial Wales, which was to last for generations. Even in the crisis of 1931, which proved so disastrous to the Labour party nationally, Labour in Wales remained conspicuously resilient: although the number of Labour members of parliament fell from twenty-five to fifteen in the elections of that year, the percentage of the vote remained steady. The Welsh members elected in 1931 constituted almost a third of the entire parliamentary Labour party. By 1935 Labour again won half of the Welsh constituencies and 45 per cent of the vote. Its grip on industrial south Wales was by then so absolute that in nine constituencies the Labour candidate stood unopposed, and in two further constituencies the only opposition came from the ILP and the Communist party, respectively. Support was not limited to the south of Wales; in 1935 the Labour party also regained Wrexham in north Wales, previously won in 1923 but lost in 1924, to be regained in 1929 and lost again in 1931.

At local authority level Labour power across large parts of Wales became entrenched as the party found itself in permanent occupation of town halls across industrial Wales. On Rhondda Urban Borough Council Labour became the largest party in 1915 and gained control in 1919. In the same year Labour gained control of Glamorgan County Council, which, representing a population of 1.25 million, was by some measure the largest and most powerful democratic body in Wales. By 1932, twenty-seven of the thirty-five councillors on the Rhondda Urban District Council were Labour and a similar pattern became familiar throughout the coalfield. This Labour dominance, coinciding as it did with a period in which employment opportunities were few and the attraction of work 'on the council' only too apparent, gave rise to charges of corruption and more general criticisms. One study published in 1938 complained of the 'degradation of local politics'.[15] However, the historian of politics in the Rhondda has concluded that the Labour party on the council, despite some incidence of corruption, 'had an interactive relationship with its community that provided it with an integrity capable of defying any individual malfeasance'.[16]

Many of the Labour MPs elected during the 1920s and 1930s were trade union officials whose parliamentary nomination was akin to a reward for loyal trade union service. Many were able and conscientious politicians and several achieved a degree of national recognition. Vernon Hartshorn was the only one to achieve high ministerial office in this period as postmaster general in the 1924 Labour government, and lord privy seal from 1929 to his death in 1931. Wales, however, did provide a constituency home for the Labour leader and prime minister Ramsay MacDonald in Aberavon from 1922 until 1929, as it had provided a constituency for Keir Hardie from 1900 to his death in 1915.

The one Welsh politician who had achieved considerable notoriety by 1939, and whose subsequent career was to be even more noteworthy, was Aneurin Bevan. Even the most critical of Bevan's biographers allows that he was recognized 'as one of the most gifted and creative political leaders of [the] century – the equal in potential, if not in achievement, of David Lloyd George and Winston Churchill'.[17] Born in the old iron town of Tredegar in 1897, the son of a miner, Bevan went to work underground on his thirteenth birthday in 1910 and his political apprenticeship was shaped by the turbulent industrial relations and politics of the period. By the time he was nineteen he was the youngest lodge chairman in the SWMF, and in 1919 his union sent him to complete his education at the Central Labour College, the Marxist finishing school for so many miners' leaders of this period.

On his return in 1921, he was unemployed and became fully engaged in the struggles of the mining communities in the lockouts of 1921 and 1926. He was also active in the local Workmen's Institute and its library as well as the Tredegar Medical Aid Society, later to be such an important model for the National Health Service he was to establish in 1948. In 1928 he was elected onto Monmouthshire County Council and then, following the unprecedented deselection of the sitting Labour member, Bevan was adopted as the Labour candidate for Ebbw Vale for the 1929 general election. He held the seat until his death.

Bevan's career until 1939 was largely spent as a rebel, much of the time against the leadership of his own party. He stood uncompromisingly on the left of the British political spectrum and represented that current within the Labour party in Wales and elsewhere which sought a socialist solution to the apparent failure of a collapsing capitalism. He mercilessly attacked the National government after 1931 for its policies towards the distressed areas. His attacks were voiced in parliament, in newspaper articles and on platforms across the country. Bevan became, and was long to remain, the British left's most prominent voice. Many of his contemporaries as Welsh members of parliament were more pragmatic and limited in their demands and did not share Bevan's more comprehensive root-and-branch approach. His critique of contemporary capitalism was detailed, perceptive and often devastating, but his espousal of left-wing causes found him regularly in trouble within his own party and the Labour whip was removed from him, and from Sir Stafford Cripps, in 1939. He had been briefly attracted by Oswald Mosley's 'New Party' before Mosley swung to the extreme right. Later he supported the idea of workers' 'freedom brigades', which seemed to many to smack of insurrectionism, and in the mid-1930s he argued for a popular front with the Communists, especially in support of the Spanish republic. In 1937 he established, and became editor of, *Tribune*, the most influential left-wing journal in Britain.

Bevan's consistent hostility to Welsh devolution and nationalism, and his emphasis on international working-class solidarity, both expressed his Marxism and reflected his own background not only as a miner, but also as the non-Welsh-speaking son of a Welsh-speaking father and a mother of English stock. His family was representative of the Monmouthshire coalfield of the period in its ethnic mix as well as in the younger generations' use of the English language. And yet Bevan was unmistakably Welsh in his accent, his commitment, and indeed in his very name. His most recent Welsh biographer has emphasized the huge complexity, range and power of Bevan's relationship with the culture and aspirations of industrial south Wales.[18]

Bevan, despite his advocacy at times of closer relationships with the Communists and his support for many Communist causes, was not seriously tempted to join the Communist party of Great Britain, in part at least because of his fierce commitment to parliament and the House of Commons. The Communist party did, however, establish a significant, if minority, presence within Welsh politics in the interwar period and was a persistent nuisance to the Labour party when not an actual threat. The South Wales Socialist Society, which grew out of the syndicalist fervour of the pre-war coalfield, was one of only a very small number of extreme left-wing organizations which united, with considerable difficulty, to form the Communist party of Great Britain in 1921. South Wales, along with the Scottish coalfields and the East End of London, came to be one of the few areas in which the party could claim to have a significant influence, and this further enhanced the area's reputation for socialist militancy.

According to an early historian of the party, 2,300 of the party's 7,377 members in 1927 were Welsh. The most prominent Communist leader in south Wales, the 'incorrigible rebel' Arthur Horner, seemed to confirm the influence of the party when he was elected president of the SWMF in 1936.[19] Other influential Communist leaders to emerge were the novelist Lewis Jones, the theoretician Idris Cox and the activist Will Paynter. The party was prominent in organizing the unemployed and crucial to the organization of the periodic hunger marches from 1922 onwards, and in supporting the Republicans in the Spanish Civil War both politically and by supplying volunteers for the International Brigades.[20] Confrontations with the police, unemployment benefit officials and bailiffs were common and imprisonment not infrequent. As a result the Communist party did build some real support, especially in its 'Little Moscow' of Maerdy in the Rhondda Fach valley, where its influence was extensive and visible. Electoral success, however, was harder to achieve, especially in the face of the unremitting hostility of most Labour leaders. The Communists fielded candidates in the Rhondda from 1929, but it was only in the parliamentary by-election in Rhondda East in 1933 that they mounted a reasonably successful challenge to Labour before 1945, with Horner gaining 11,228 votes compared to Labour's 14,127. Nevertheless, the historian of the Rhondda has concluded that '[n]o other party, be it Liberal, Conservative, or Plaid Cymru, was able to match the challenge that the Communists posed to Labour'.[21]

Outside of the Rhondda, however, where they elected four councillors in 1927 and seven in 1935, the Communist influence was far less visible and both J. R.

Campbell, who contested Ogmore in 1931, and Wal Hannington, leader of the National Unemployed Workers' Movement, who stood in Merthyr in a by-election in 1934, came bottom of the poll. Nevertheless, the presence of the Communists gave politics in Wales, particularly in the coalfield, a dramatic and volatile character which seemed to underline the widespread appeal of, and commitment to, socialism more generally.

The other party to emerge to challenge Labour and Liberal domination was Plaid Genedlaethol Cymru, the Nationalist party, which was to achieve very little electoral success in this period but whose establishment in 1925 is of considerable significance given subsequent developments in Wales. The party, which was launched at the National Eisteddfod at Pwllheli in 1925, was the result of a merger between two rather different groups. The secret Mudiad Cymreig (Welsh Movement) had been established in 1924 by a small group centred on Cardiff 'to save Wales from its present condition and to make it a Welsh Wales'. Another group, based in north Wales and meeting in Caernarfon, was initially called the Welsh Home Rule Army. It rapidly became clear that it was the southern group, and its intellectual members Saunders Lewis and Ambrose Bebb, who were to dominate the party's policies in its early years. Lewis became president at the party's first conference in 1926 and was to remain in that position until the war.[22] Lewis was an intriguing, controversial and far from typical figure in twentieth-century Wales; born into the middle-class Welsh community on Merseyside, he graduated from Liverpool University and served with distinction throughout the First World War. Deeply conservative on many issues, he was nevertheless capable of radical action. There were some left-wing elements within the Nationalist party, such as the miner-turned-economist D. J. Davies and, late in the 1930s, the small group associated with the Gwerin movement in Bangor (which desired a rapprochement between socialism and nationalism), but it was Lewis and his group who dominated the party.[23]

At the first conference, or summer school as the party characteristically called its annual meeting, in 1926, Lewis delivered a lecture entitled 'The principles of nationalism' which explored the philosophical and historical basis of his nationalism.[24] It was not an easy or comfortable message for an audience used to the Home Rule politics of the Liberal party and of nonconformity either to understand or to adopt. Lewis himself was always at pains to emphasize that his 'new nationalism' was in no way connected to the nineteenth-century Liberal tradition, which he castigated as being no more than 'the spare-time hobby of corpulent and successful men'. His redefinition of nationalism launched a long controversy regarding the influence on him and on other key intellectuals in the party, such as the historian Ambrose Bebb and the theologian J. E. Daniel, of conservative or neo-fascist French thinkers such as Maurice Barrès and, more controversially still, of the Action Française leader Charles Maurras.

Lewis's most startling conclusion was that Wales's misfortunes did not date back to the conquest of the country in 1282 and the end of independence, but rather to the period of Tudor government. He located the source of the evil in the Tudor period and in what he characterized as the nationalism of Henry VIII which had resulted in, on the one hand, the Acts of Union with Wales and, on the other, the Reformation and the break with Rome. Both developments had helped create a nation-state, which simultaneously oppressed Welsh culture and divorced Wales from its European inheritance. There are clear echoes of French right-wing thinking here, although Lewis was to deny any direct influence. Both analyses looked back admiringly at a medieval Europe before the advent of the centralized nation-state. That Europe was, of course, Catholic, and whatever spiritual journey led Lewis to convert to Catholicism in 1933, the political logic of such a move was certainly consistent with his overall analysis.

Within this context, it is not surprising that in later policy statements, such as the party's Ten Points of Policy published in 1934, a tension existed between some recognition of the problems of contemporary industrial Wales (in the call, for example, for a Welsh National Development Council) and a wish to return to a pre-modern world. In this vision 'agriculture should be the chief industry' and 'South Wales must be de-industrialised' for the sake of 'the moral health of Wales'. Lewis's apocalyptic vision of the coming struggle with Communism is also reminiscent of extreme right-wing European movements. In 1932, for example, he wrote: 'Five years ago I prophesied that what the political future held for Wales was a choice between Communism and Christian Nationalism . . . the day when these two forces and these two doctrines must come to grips with each other in Wales seems to me definitely nearer and I do not think it will be long delayed. Apart from these two, nothing else will count.'[25]

At the heart of Lewis's nationalism, as expressed in 1926 and constantly reaffirmed subsequently, was a passionate concern with the Welsh language and its associated culture. His definition of Welsh nationalism was essentially culturally constructed around the notion of a Welsh-language 'civilization'. His nationalism, he argued, was 'not a fight for Wales' independence but for Wales' civilization. A claim for freedom for Wales, not independence'.

At the heart of that civilization, he argued, lay the Welsh language, which in 1921 had declined to become the language of 37 per cent of the population. More alarmingly, for the first time the absolute number of Welsh speakers, which had previously continued to grow despite the decline as a percentage of the population, also showed a decline to 766,000. In response, Lewis insisted that 'Welsh should be made the sole medium of education from the elementary school to the university', and that Welsh should be Wales' only official language'. For, he argued, 'only thus will the chain of history and culture and civilized life be kept unbroken in this part of the world, linking us with the past and giving us nobility, tradition, stability and beneficial development'. In this schema non-Welsh speakers and English migrants would take their place in Welsh civilization via access to the language. This was not a racially constructed nationalism, still less a politically constructed one; this was essentially a cultural definition of nationalism and the Welsh language was seen as being central to that culture.

In this context Lewis insisted that 'every poet and writer and artist and scholar who enriches the literature and art of our country, is doing invaluable political work'. As a lecturer in the Welsh department of the newly established University College in Swansea, Lewis himself developed a reputation not only as a perceptive literary critic, but also as a pioneering and important dramatist in the Welsh language.

The first half of the twentieth century witnessed a remarkable golden age in Welsh writing. The publication in 1913 of John Morris-Jones's seminal work, *A Welsh Grammar: Historical and Comparative*, had a massive impact as it standardized and simplified the orthography and grammar of the language. The establishment of a

journal of scholarly literary criticism, *Y Llenor*, in 1922 was also both an encouragement to literary effort and an expression of the new vigour in the Welsh-speaking
intellectual world.

The period from the turn of the century to the Second World War produced Welsh
poetry of the highest quality and many of the leading figures in this literary renaissance identified themselves with the new Welsh Nationalist party. The outstanding
poet R. Williams Parry, who won the National Eisteddfod Chair in 1910, was a supporter, as was the leading Welsh-language prose writer Kate Roberts, who published
her important novel *Traed Mewn Cyffion* (*Feet in Chains*) in 1936. The themes that
dominated much of this literary output were insecurity and tragedy, both at the personal level and more generally, and the perceived threat to the existence of the Welsh
language was itself a source of insecurity and loss.

The nationalist political consciousness associated with much literary endeavour led
to some significant changes in the Eisteddfod. The National Eisteddfod, the centre-
piece of Welsh cultural life, was increasingly being criticized for its widespread use of
English. In 1937, however, a radical new constitution was adopted which established
a unified court for the Eisteddfod and also introduced a Welsh-language rule that
severely limited the use of English. Change was also achieved in the BBC and the
new medium of radio. Welsh was first heard on radio in 1923, and there were important developments in the 1930s following the appointment of the pioneering Welsh
broadcaster Sam Jones to the Bangor studios in 1935. In 1937, following considerable pressure, the BBC established its Welsh region.

The twentieth century also produced a remarkable generation of Welsh writers in
English, such as the poets R. S. Thomas (b. 1913), Dylan Thomas (b. 1914) and
Alun Lewis (b. 1915). The explicit nationalism of Welsh-language writers was, with
the marked exception of R. S. Thomas, largely absent from their work, but a number
of these writers dealt directly with aspects of contemporary Welsh life. Works such as
Idris Davies's famous poem of the 1926 General Strike, *The Angry Summer*, or
Richard Llewellyn's novel *How Green Was My Valley*, published in 1939, heightened
an awareness of the Welshness of the non-Welsh-speaking areas of Wales. This led
in 1937 to the establishment of the influential literary magazine *Wales*, edited by
Keidrych Rhys. This magazine and other publications gave the idea of an Anglo-
Welsh experience and literature, of writing in English that was nevertheless rooted
in Wales, a wide and influential currency.

The emphasis of the Nationalist party on the language and culture of Wales might
have created an impressive base of support amongst Welsh-speaking intellectuals and
writers, but its appeal to the electorate was minimal. The party first fought an election in the largely Welsh-speaking constituency of Caernarfonshire in 1929, but the
result was deeply disappointing as the candidate won only 609 votes and came bottom
of the poll. Further attempts in the same constituency in 1931 and 1935 succeeded
in increasing the vote to four figures but did not remove the party from the bottom
of the poll. Only amongst the graduates of the University of Wales seat was there
much support for the party, and Saunders Lewis polled a respectable 29 per cent of
the vote in that exceptional 'constituency' in 1931, although he was still soundly
defeated by the sitting Liberal member.

In the light of these disappointing electoral results Lewis sought other avenues to
further the cause and, in 1936, he was the central figure in one of the most remarkable events of interwar Welsh history, the arson attack on an RAF Bombing School.

After ten years of little political progress, and in the year of the 400th anniversary of the Act of Union, Lewis sought a dramatic gesture that he hoped would galvanize support for his party. The cause he chose was the campaign against the siting of an RAF base in the Llyn peninsula, a campaign that had attracted widespread support from local authorities and politicians in Wales. The campaigning and the petitioning were to little effect and the RAF, which had failed to establish the base at a number of English locations because of local objections, determined to proceed. On the night of 8 September 1936, Lewis and his co-conspirators set fire to the site and three of them, chosen for their respectable professions and high status in some circles, surrendered themselves to the police, while the rest of the group evaded arrest. The three – Lewis Valentine, a minister of religion, D. J. Williams, a writer and schoolteacher, and Lewis himself – were tried at Caernarfon. When the jury failed to reach a verdict the case was moved to the Old Bailey and they were sentenced to nine months' imprisonment, which they served in Wormwood Scrubs. Lewis was sacked from his University of Wales post.[26]

Lewis was partially successful in his strategy. Initially the crowds had been hostile, but as the trials proceeded the men won more support for their actions and on their release from prison there was a huge crowd to welcome them at the Pavilion in Caernarfon. This support was localized and appealed to a relatively thin stratum of public opinion. But nationalism had its heroes and 'The Three' were to be lionized by successive generations of nationalists. Lewis had also succeeded in establishing a link between unconstitutional direct action and the Nationalist party, which was to prove both an electoral embarrassment and an inspiration for activists for many years.

Lewis's final act before resigning the presidency of the party in 1939 was to lead it into opposition to the Second World War on the grounds that this was an 'English war'. Lewis had earlier expressed some sympathy for Hitler's aim to recreate a German homeland and some support for Franco in 1936. But his major target was what he termed the English government, which was, he claimed, 'to a great extent responsible for the . . . breakdown of peace in Europe'. The party adopted a neutral stance in April 1939, arguing that in the light of the government's 'inconsideration of the national rights of Wales' and the seizure by the armed forces 'of the Welsh coast and the immemorial homelands of the Welsh language and Welsh life', its members should not cooperate with the war effort in any way and should refuse military service on political, as opposed to pacifist, grounds.[27] As the striking success of the Peace Ballot of 1935 demonstrated, pacifism was a much more popular sentiment in Wales and, in fact, very few nationalists were to object to war service on political grounds.

Whatever the overall impact of the Nationalist party in this period, its very existence affected the political agenda and contributed to the debate concerning Wales's position in the United Kingdom. Apart from the disestablishment of the Church of England in Wales in 1920, there were few constitutional changes of significance in this period for the high point of Home Rule activity had come to an end before the turn of the century. But the issue was far from having disappeared. Many of the ambitions of the Liberal national project of the late nineteenth century came to fruition in the early twentieth. The Welsh department of the Board of Education was established in 1907. The University of Wales, the first genuinely national institution, had been created in 1893, but the magnificent university buildings in Bangor and Cardiff were not constructed until the first decade of the century. In 1905, the privy council authorized the establishment of a National Museum of Wales in Cardiff. The foundation stone was laid in 1912 and the building completed in 1927. At the same time, a National Library of Wales was established at Aberystwyth. These were all crucial building blocks in the creation of an institutional Wales.

Home Rule was not only a Liberal issue, it was also widely debated within the labour movement in Wales in the years 1910 to 1912, and Keir Hardie was to demand the establishment of a secretary of state for Wales on the Scottish model in 1910. After the war the issue was again widely discussed in a number of well-attended conferences, largely in response to the efforts of E. T. John, a Liberal MP until 1918 who stood as a Labour candidate in 1922 and 1923 and who was an ardent devolutionist and Pan-Celticist. This agitation led to some excited debate and to the preparation of a Government of Wales Bill by the Liberal MP Sir Robert J. Thomas in 1922.[28]

The onset of the depression, however, brought other priorities to the fore and few could envision any solution to the ruin of the Welsh economy other than by deploying the resources of the British state. What the crisis of the depression did succeed in bringing into sharp focus was the question of establishing a secretary of state for Wales. As the 1930s progressed a growing number of Welsh politicians became convinced that the creation of a politically powerful office at the centre of British politics could dramatically increase the influence that Wales so desperately needed. Bevan, and some others on both wings of the Labour party, saw this as a diversion from the task in hand, but others, including influential Labour figures such as D. R. Grenfell and James Griffiths, were determined to achieve change. Following a struggle of almost thirty years within the Labour party, Griffiths himself, the ex-president of the SWMF elected to parliament in 1936, became the first secretary of state for Wales in 1964, thus creating the crucial momentum for further devolution. Some Labour members supported a Liberal call for a secretary of state in 1937, and in 1938 Morgan Jones, the Labour member for Caerphilly, led a delegation representing the Welsh parliamentary party to lobby the prime minister, Neville Chamberlain. Chamberlain was to offer them little comfort, but it is significant that this issue, which was to engender so much political debate in the future, was firmly established as a priority for many Labour and Liberal politicians before 1939.

Despite the divisions between rural and industrial Wales, between Welsh-speaking and non-Welsh-speaking Wales, and between north and south Wales, which rapid economic growth and the subsequent depression had clearly exacerbated, there remained in this period and across a wide spectrum of political opinion some validity in the concept of Wales. It was the survival of this concept, despite the emergence of a distinctive south Wales region, and the terrible ravages of the depression, which enabled so much subsequent economic and political reconstruction to develop as it did. Politics in Wales between 1900 and 1939, therefore, both shared much with the rest of the United Kingdom and diverged from the general pattern in significant ways. Whether perceived from outside as the home of the archetypal miner or as a rural fastness, Wales, in this period, became further associated with radical thought and action.

NOTES

1 F. Aubel, 'The Conservatives in Wales, 1880–1935', in M. Francis and M. Zweiniger-Bargielowska, eds, *The Conservatives in British Society* (Cardiff, 1996), p. 96.

2   B. Jones, *Welsh Elections, 1885–1997* (Talybont, 1999).

3   K. O. Morgan, *Rebirth of a Nation: Wales, 1880–1980* (Oxford, 1981), pp. 137–42.

4   J. M. Keynes, *Essays in Biography* (London, 1961), pp. 35–6.

5   B. B. Gilbert, *David Lloyd George: A Political Life. The Architect of Change, 1863–1912* (London, 1987), p. 12.

6   Ibid., p. 20.

7   L. J. Williams, *Was Wales Industrialised? Essays in Modern Welsh History* (Llandysul, 1995).

8   D. Smith, *Aneurin Bevan and the World of South Wales* (Cardiff, 1993), p. 4.

9   H. Francis and D. Smith, *The Fed: A History of the South Wales Miners in the Twentieth Century* (London, 1980), p. 42.

10   D. Egan, 'A cult of their own: syndicalism and *The Miners' Next Step*', in A. Campbell, N. Fishman and D. Howell, eds, *Miners, Unions and Politics, 1910–47* (Aldershot, 1996).

11   Commission of Inquiry into Industrial Unrest, *Wales* (London, 1917), pp. 12–18.

12   R. Douglas, *The History of the Liberal Party 1895–1970* (London, 1971), p. 248.

13   T. Rowlands, *Something Must Be Done: South Wales versus Whitehall, 1921–51* (Merthyr Tydfil, 2000), p. 37.

14   J. Griffiths, *Pages from Memory* (London, 1969), p. 170.

15   H. Jennings, *Brynmawr: A Study of a Distressed Area* (London, 1938), p. 141.

16   C. Williams, *Democratic Rhondda: Politics and Society, 1885–1951* (Cardiff, 1996), p. 207.

17   J. Campbell, *Nye Bevan and the Mirage of British Socialism* (London, 1987), p. xi.

18   Smith, *Aneurin Bevan*, pp. 178–258.

19   A. Horner, *Incorrigible Rebel* (London, 1960), p. 147.

20   H. Francis, *Miners Against Fascism* (London, 1984), pp. 156–75.

21   Williams, *Democratic Rhondda*, pp. 156–7.

22   D. H. Davies, *The Welsh Nationalist Party 1925–45: A Call to Nationhood* (Cardiff, 1983), pp. 35–44.

23   B. Griffiths, *Saunders Lewis* (Cardiff, 1989).

24   S. Lewis, 'The principles of nationalism', in H. Pritchard Jones, ed., *Saunders Lewis: A Presentation of his Work* (Illinois, 1990), pp. 29–40.

25   *Welsh Nationalist*, January 1932.

26   D. Jenkins, *A Nation on Trial* (Cardiff, 1998).

27   *Welsh Nationalist*, May 1939.

28   R. M. Jones and I. Rh. Jones, 'Labour and the nation', in D. Tanner, C. Williams and D. Hopkin, eds, *The Labour Party in Wales, 1900–2000* (Cardiff, 2000), pp. 241–63.

FURTHER READING

Campbell, J., *Nye Bevan and the Mirage of British Socialism* (London, 1987).

Francis, H. and Smith, D., *The Fed: A History of the South Wales Miners in the Twentieth Century* (London, 1980).

Gilbert, B. B., *David Lloyd George: A Political Life. The Architect of Change, 1863–1912* (London, 1987).

Morgan, K. O., *Rebirth of a Nation: Wales, 1800–1980* (Oxford, 1981).

Rowlands, T., *Something Must Be Done: South Wales versus Whitehall, 1921–51* (Merthyr Tydfil, 2000).

Smith, D., *Aneurin Bevan and the World of South Wales* (Cardiff, 1993).

Williams, C., *Democratic Rhondda: Politics and Society, 1885–1951* (Cardiff, 1996).

Williams, L. J., *Was Wales Industrialised? Essays in Modern Welsh History* (Llandysul, 1995).

CHAPTER SEVEN

Ireland and British Politics, 1900–1939

D. GEORGE BOYCE

Few periods in modern Irish history have been as fortunate in the release of new sources as the first half of the twentieth century. Official government archives, as well as private archives, published and unpublished diaries and memoirs, provide historians with evidence with which to reappraise a turbulent era in Anglo-Irish relations. These years saw the crisis over the third Home Rule Bill bring the United Kingdom to the brink of civil war; the partition of Ireland and the secession of twenty-six counties; the gradual weakening of the link between the southern Irish state and the British Empire; and the increasingly divergent paths taken by Northern Ireland and the south before, during and after the Second World War. Not surprisingly, these events, controversial in themselves, have generated renewed, at times heated, debate. The Ulster Unionist rebellion against the imposition of Home Rule between 1912 and 1914 has been described by one modern historian as 'treason',[1] and the Dublin government's decision to declare for neutrality in 1939 still provokes controversy.[2] The historian is aware that perspectives not unrelated to contemporary issues, as well as fresh evidence, shape the interpretation of any topic, and especially this one.

From Home Rule to World War, 1900–1914

In 1900 Ireland was still an exclusively domestic British concern. There were 104 Irish MPs sitting in the House of Commons, and the Irish Parliamentary party, representing nationalist Ireland, was so much an integral part of the domestic political scene that few could imagine Westminster without its 'Irish nights'. The Irish Unionists too were permanent features of the House, closely tied to their Conservative and Unionist allies; the Nationalists still enjoyed their alliance with the Liberals: the legacy of the great divide over Irish Home Rule in 1886 continued as the fault-line of British as well as Irish politics. Yet by 1939 most of Ireland had experienced nearly twenty years of self-government and had defined a role for itself outside the United Kingdom. The six counties of Northern Ireland likewise enjoyed – if that is the word – a period of devolved government within the Kingdom, and were content to remain a permanent, but obscure, part of the British political scene. Britain, for her part, fought a low-intensity war to retain Ireland within the United Kingdom, and then struggled to hold the new Irish Free State to the imperial connection, while standing back from the troublesome northern state's business.

Ireland's transition from a bothersome, but integral, aspect of British political life to this curious hybrid could not have been foreseen at the start of the century. On 30 January 1900 the Irish Parliamentary party, which had suffered a series of splits following the fall of its greatest leader, Charles Stewart Parnell, in 1891, at last reunited under the leadership of John Redmond. In April of that same year Queen Victoria visited Ireland and issued orders for a new regiment, the Irish Guards, to be raised, as a mark of her appreciation of the bravery and dedication of Irish soldiers in the South African War. By then, Ireland had experienced what the Conservative and Unionist party believed she needed most: twenty years of resolute government. This involved a series of social and economic reforms that would, it was believed, deprive Irish nationalism of its driving power: the pursuit of the grievance. Historians have expressed a certain scepticism about this reform process, noting that legislation was haphazard and sometimes unenthusiastic, affected by more pressing needs of the Conservative party.[3] Nevertheless, the Conservatives could point to at least one great achievement, the final settlement of the land question, at least as regards landlord–tenant relations. Land purchase acts, culminating in the 1903 Land Bill, turned Ireland into a society of tenant proprietors. This bill provided £83 million to finance land purchase, with A. J. Balfour insisting that this was necessary to defuse nationalist sentiment. By 1906 some 85,000 purchase agreements were concluded.

There were signs, too, that the British political parties were distancing themselves from their respective Irish allies. In 1904 the Conservative government considered a scheme drawn up by Sir Anthony MacDonnell, under-secretary at Dublin Castle, and Lord Dunraven to extend the policy of cooperation (which had culminated in the 'round table' conference between landlords and tenants in 1903) to the administrative sphere, through what was called 'devolution'. This envisaged the creation of a central Irish Council endowed with local autonomy, but it was abandoned after strong Irish Unionist protests. In 1906–7 the Liberals, now firmly ensconced in power following their victory in the 1906 general election, introduced an Irish Councils Bill designed to increase participation in local government. But the Home Rule party were as indignant over this apostasy as Unionists had been over their similar experience, denouncing the scheme as a betrayal of the Liberal commitment to Irish self-government in the Gladstonian mould, with a full-blooded parliament and executive in Dublin. The two British political parties licked their wounds and muttered about the intransigence of their Irish allies; but, however resentful, they backed away from confrontation: an ominous portent of things to come.

There were new developments in Irish politics that were of future significance. The 'devolution' crisis of 1903–4 increased Irish Unionist concern about the fidelity of their British allies, and in 1905 the Ulster Unionist Council was formed, representing a popular body to coordinate northern loyalism. This institution did not have the patronage of any British politicians, and it was the first indication that Ulster Unionists were prepared, if need be, to reject the Westminster parliament as the primary focus of their allegiance. John Redmond's eyes were still firmly fixed on London, though he was troubled by agrarian disturbances at home, arising from disputes between farmers and large 'graziers', and by a recrudescence of cattle-driving, which Unionists exploited as evidence of the criminality that lay behind Irish nationalism. There were other, less familiar developments. In 1903 the journalist and economic thinker Arthur Griffith founded the National Council to protest against King Edward VII's visit to Ireland, and in 1905 Dungannon Clubs were founded to recall the great days of Irish republicanism in the 1790s. In 1907 these clubs and another separatist-minded organization, Cumann na nGaedheal (the Party of the Gaels), merged to form the Sinn Fein league, and almost a year later Griffith appropriated the term Sinn Fein to set the movement going, with the title of the movement representing the economic and cultural as well as political self-sufficiency that Griffith believed Ireland must acquire. Its first entry into the world of real politics in contesting the North Leitrim by-election of June 1907 turned out to be a defeat, but a reasonable performance, Sinn Fein winning 1,200 votes.[4] The movement thereafter declined, but it represented the after-effects both of the Gaelic revival impulse of the 1890s and the new mood in Europe generally that emphasized the unique qualities of distinct, historic nations.

All this was still marginal to the main question of the day, Home Rule. The British parties were more circumspect in their approach to this issue, and they had their own problems. The Conservatives were deeply split over the question of tariff reform, which was not only a matter of political economy but was central to the character and identity of the British state. The Liberals were not thus troubled, but their leader H. H. Asquith was worried about the large radical element in the party, and though this did not affect the Liberals' Irish policy, which was to continue with reform and above all the settling of the question of Irish university education, it was a nagging concern. Radicalism reared its head after 1909 in the dispute between the Liberal government and the House of Lords over its rejection of the 'people's budget', and this dispute gave Redmond his chance to move Home Rule up the agenda. In January 1910 the Liberals lost their overall majority in the House of Commons, and while they felt they could remain secure in the Home Rule party's support (and that of the new Labour MPs), they none the less had to comply with Redmond's claim for Home Rule to be the next great step forward. This was, in one sense, nothing more than the renewal of the Gladstonian tradition; but in reality the scene had shifted, for the Liberals were determined to remove the Lords' absolute veto on Commons legislation, and when they did so, then Home Rule must pass through the whole parliamentary process. The Parliament Act of 1911 was the prelude to the Home Rule Bill of April 1912, and the scene was set for the most dangerous conflict in British and Irish politics since the seventeenth century. The first act was the Ulster Unionists' signing of the Ulster Covenant on 28 September 1912, committing them to defeat the 'conspiracy' of Home Rule by all means that might be found necessary.

This crisis has attracted much debate, not least because some have seen it as the beginning of a return to violence in Irish politics. Others have pointed out that, had the Home Rulers and the Liberals recognized the genuine fears of Ulster Unionists at being placed under a Roman Catholic and nationalist Dublin parliament, then the confrontation might have been avoided. The respective leaders of nationalism and Unionism have been criticized, though on different grounds. Redmond is dismissed as out of touch, misleading the British government over the extent of Unionist determination to resist Home Rule. Yet Redmond had attended the bastion of Protestantism, Trinity College, Dublin, and it was here that he learned to appreciate 'the quality of Protestant Ireland'.[5] Sir Edward Carson, the Dublin-born leader of Ulster Unionist resistance, is open to the charge of leading a sectarian movement, but his origins were Liberal Unionist, and he declared in October 1912 that 'he would not be in this movement if he thought that in any way there was any single privilege taken from any man who differed from him in no matter what religion'.[6] Carson was determined to save all Ireland from Home Rule, and as he stood in the Belfast city hall on Ulster Day, contemporaries noted that he 'seemed oppressed with the responsibility of his act. His face was drawn, indeed haggard and ghastly pale'.[7]

If Redmond and Carson have attracted criticism, the same goes for Asquith and the Conservative leader after 1911, Andrew Bonar Law. Asquith seems weak and dilatory; but he faced the most perplexing dilemma confronting any Liberal, that of defying his own political tradition. Liberalism held that the constitution was, since the Great Reform Act of 1832, an inclusive one that could accommodate all individuals and groups. Now Asquith must contemplate coercing one group, the Ulster Protestants, or letting down another, the Irish Catholics. Even if he considered some exclusion of Ulster counties, this would leave Ulster Catholics stranded. Bonar Law appears to have the worst, if opposite, characteristics, those of intransigence and bigotry. But his case rested on the belief that Ulster Protestants were a different people from the majority, and that they were 'prepared to die for their convictions'.[8] Nevertheless, he was prepared to accept the verdict of the British electorate, if the Liberals would submit their Home Rule policy to a single-issue contest. Behind the scenes, talk of compromise was heard. Carson wrote to Law on 23 September 1913 that 'on the whole things are shaping towards a desire to settle on terms of leaving "Ulster" out'.[9] But it was hard for any British party leader to make the first move, if this seemed a sign of weakness, and by 1914 the government seemed to be moving towards a firmer line. In March the cabinet took what it claimed were precautionary moves. The British army would secure certain key installations, such as the railways, to forestall trouble. But this was accompanied by some belligerent language by members of the government, and the idea of a 'plot' against Ulster was born.[10] Any coercive intent was ended when fifty-seven out of seventy officers at the Curragh Camp in Ireland, led by major-general Sir Hubert Gough, declared that they would resign their commissions rather than permit themselves to be used to enforce Home Rule on Ulster Unionists. The government's retreat from confrontation was of vital importance. Had the army moved north and clashed with the Unionists' paramilitary force, the Ulster Volunteers (UVF), with military casualties, then British public opinion would almost certainly have rallied behind 'our boys'. The Unionists would have suffered a major propaganda as well as military reverse. The Curragh incident was swiftly followed by a successful gun-running operation on 24–5 April, at Larne, Bangor and Donaghadee; not only had the instrument of the lawful use of force broken in the government's hands, but now the UVF were well armed. Worse followed when in July the Irish Volunteers (IVF), founded in 1913 to defend Home Rule, followed the UVF example, only to be confronted by British troops. The result was the shooting dead of several civilians at Bachelor's Walk, Dublin.

By the summer of 1914, then, it seemed that the British parties had lost control, that parliament was irrelevant and the cabinet indecisive. Talks continued between government and opposition with the focus still on some special treatment of Ulster counties, but how many and for how long were still in dispute. There is no doubt that the outbreak of the European war, and Britain's participation in it, averted civil war at home. Yet the Home Rule party seemed to have won a victory of sorts when in September the Liberals, to the disgust of the Unionist opposition, placed the third Home Rule Bill on the statute book. Ireland was, in the eyes of most of her people, a nation once again. Indeed, some might say a real nation, united in the common cause of fighting for Britain in a just war, for Carson, though angry at the government's insistence on passing Home Rule, offered the UVF to the British army for service overseas, while Redmond, after calling for the UVF and the IVF to defend the shores of Ireland, urged the Irish Volunteers to go wherever the firing line extended. Ireland, it seemed, was united at last in a great common enterprise.

From World War to Partition, 1914–1923

This great enterprise has posed problems for historians and non-historians alike. Nationalist Ireland's participation in the war on the British side does not fit into the nationalist ideal, at least not as it was defined from the 1930s onwards, that stressed the long, essentially republican struggle for freedom. Unionists too have not been comfortable with the reflection that they did not possess a monopoly of loyalty in 1914, though fortunately for them nationalist Ireland rejected the Redmondite project of fighting for the rights of small nations on the British side. Above all, the Easter Rising of 1916, standing like a rock in the middle of the war, diverts both Unionist and nationalist Ireland into separate channels. It is difficult to shift the perspective away from the Rising, and of course this can go too far; the Rising was a seminal event in the making of modern Ireland. But it is tempting to see the war only as a preparation for the Rising, and certainly British official insensitivity (to put it no stronger) in refusing to create an 'Irish Brigade' in imitation of the 36th Ulster Division, which incorporated the UVF into the British army, raised nationalist concern. And the Home Rule Act was not to come into operation until the end of the war, which indicated that Britain had her own order of priorities, whatever might suit nationalist Ireland. Some historians, less than careful with the facts, have claimed that Carson's entry into the cabinet in May 1915 when the first coalition was formed was a snub to John Redmond; but Redmond too was offered a place in government, which he refused in line with Irish party policy since the days of Parnell.[11]

The Rising itself was the work of a handful of separatists, led by Tom Clarke, Patrick Pearse and James Connolly, mainly because they feared that Britain would emerge from the war as strong as ever, while Irish republicanism would be weak and disillusioned. The rebels hoped for German help, indeed at one stage were sure of it,[12] but when this failed they went ahead with their plans, turning what they hoped would spark off a popular uprising into a blood sacrifice that would encompass future generations within the republican ideal. There is debate over how much sympathy the rebels enjoyed, with some historians challenging the generally held opinion that the event was far from popular, but the evidence is inconclusive. The British reaction is as vital as the Irish, if not more so. British public opinion wanted to make the distinction between the handful of what they called (mistakenly) Sinn Feiners and the loyal Irish majority. The problem was that any government would have found it difficult to stay its hand after a rebellion in one of its capital cities in time of war. The military men on the spot believed that retribution was necessary. The govern-

ment seemed powerless to act, indeed was hardly in a position to act given the suddenness of the crisis, and the army executed sixteen ringleaders. All nationalist Ireland
protested, and one Home Rule MP warned that 'You raised the issue there after those
men were shot, the definite issue of English versus Irish'.[13] This was exactly the 'issue'
that the rebels hoped to raise, for it would arrest what they held was the terrible
failure of the last generation of nationalists, compromised by British politics. The
issue, of course, also polarized further Unionist and nationalist Ireland, but none of
the rebels seem even to have considered this possibility.

But the war worked its effect on British party attitudes to Ireland. Conservatives
and Liberals still did not love each other; they still bore the scars of the pre-1914
Irish fights. But the war came first, and from now on Irish issues must be seen in this
light. This prompted Asquith to authorize David Lloyd George, his minister for
munitions, to open negotiations with Carson and Redmond following the 1916
Rising to see if he could devise a settlement that would at least keep Ireland quiet.
Lloyd George offered a Home Rule parliament right away, subject to the exclusion
of six Ulster counties: Antrim, Armagh, Down, Fermanagh, Londonderry and
Tyrone, the final settlement to be decided upon after the war. He appears to have
allowed each of the Irish leaders to interpret the permanency or otherwise of partition as he preferred; but the real reason for the breakdown of the plan was the arousal
of the southern Irish Unionists who, supported by British Conservatives like Lord
Selborne, believed that the immediate implementation of Home Rule was a threat
to Ireland's political stability and a surrender to violence. Their opposition brought
to the surface what Lloyd George would have preferred to remain undisturbed, the
question of whether or not exclusion of Ulster counties was permanent or temporary, and the settlement plan foundered in July 1916.

One of the main objections of Conservative opponents of the Lloyd George plan
was that Ireland now posed a real security threat. Certainly the government behaved
as if it did. From April to November 1916 Ireland was placed under martial law, with
the civil authorities weakened by resignations from the Dublin Castle administration,
notably that of Augustine Birrell, the chief secretary. The Defence of the Realm Act
was deployed to curtail freedom of movement, association and publication. 'Special
Military Areas' were identified, where fairs, markets and sporting activities were
restricted. Meanwhile hundreds of 'Sinn Feiners' were interned in Great Britain,
where they learnt republican ways, and the whole thrust of British policy seemed to
be to treat Ireland as a potentially hostile country. This combination of failed concession in the 1916 negotiations, and repression during and after them, was typical
of the worst aspects of British rule in Ireland.

But the war still worked on the configurations of British as well as Irish politics. In
December 1916 Lloyd George became prime minister. Ireland was not in the forefront
of his mind, but the international situation was, and he hoped that the United States
might be enticed into the war on the allied side. America contained Irish Americans,
and it would be prudent to disarm any prejudice against the British cause. The United
States entered the war in April 1917. In May Lloyd George offered Redmond either
the 1916 settlement plan, or a convention in which Irish political and religious leaders
and other interested parties could work out Ireland's future, within the limits of
British and imperial needs. The convention first met in July 1917, and there was a
rapprochement between some southern Irish Unionists and John Redmond. But by

January 1918 it was clear that there could be no complete measure of agreement, with the Ulster Unionists and the Roman Catholic bishops finding themselves in oddly assorted opposition to the majority proposal for Irish self-government.

In March 1918, the month when John Redmond died, his Great War project was finally and fatally undermined. The German offensive on the western front almost broke the allied armies, and the British government turned once again to the vexed issues of conscription. This had always troubled Irish nationalists, even those who supported the British war effort. It had first been introduced in Great Britain in 1916, but so far Ireland had been exempted. Farmers' sons for their part had no desire to die in France when they could live in Ireland, and a mixture of self-interest and principle provoked nationalists to denounce the British determination to force conscription on Ireland. It was now that Arthur Griffith's hopes of dislodging the Irish Parliamentary party from the political scene took root. Sinn Fein had scored some notable by-election successes in 1917, but suffered three defeats between January and March 1918, in South Armagh, Waterford City and East Tyrone. The conscription crisis, followed by another bout of British repression based on the discovery of a not altogether convincing 'German plot', gave Sinn Fein its opportunity. In June 1918 it won East Cavan, though only narrowly. Its final breakthrough came in the United Kingdom general election of December 1918, when it achieved what its historian has called a 'respectable but not overwhelming victory', taking forty-eight out of eighty contested seats.[14] Sinn Fein could claim that it represented 'Ireland', provided it ignored the Unionist results in Ulster, and it sat in Dublin as 'Dáil Éireann' in January 1919. This was a strange moment. Dublin had just celebrated the return of its heroes from the Great War, with its streets festooned with Union flags. Sinn Fein rejected that war and those flags. On the very day that the Dáil met, Irish Volunteers (soon to style themselves the 'Irish Republican Army' or IRA) shot dead two policemen in Soloheadbeg, Co. Tipperary.

Ireland was now moving, with some foreboding, into several and vital years of civil strife that was to leave its mark upon her until the present day. As always, developments on both sides of the Irish Sea must be analysed. In Great Britain, the 1918 general election returned David Lloyd George to power as head of a coalition government of 322 Conservatives, 132 Liberals and twenty-two Labour supporters, along with fifty-two sympathetic Conservatives and sixteen Liberals who had not taken the 'coupon' (the agreement between the parties not to contest seats in opposition to each other). This gave the government a massive potential total of 554. But this overwhelmingly Conservative and Unionist phalanx was assembling in a parliament where the pre-war battles seemed suddenly far away and of reduced significance compared to the social, economic and diplomatic issues now confronting Britain. The coalition's election manifesto included the intention to resolve the Irish question, excluding anything that smacked of a separatist Ireland or the coercion of the Ulster Unionists.

The weakening of Unionism in Britain was paralleled in most of Ireland, where southern Unionism was fatally impaired in the war years. Ulster Unionists regrouped, but their determination in 1914 to resist Home Rule for the whole of Ireland was gone, and from 1916 they confined their political plans to defending the six 'excluded' counties, abandoning Cavan, Donegal and Monaghan. These developments gave the British government the chance to implement what it had sought in vain in 1914, a means of prising the Ulster Unionists out of the Irish question. One of the strongest supporters of Irish Unionism, Walter Long, now found himself chairing the government's Irish sub-committee, which reported in favour of a Home Rule parliament for Dublin and another for Belfast, with a Council of Ireland to act as a bridge between them, and perhaps even a means of reunification. Andrew Bonar Law chaired the committee meeting on 17 February 1920 that advocated a nine-county Northern Ireland state in the belief that a six-county state would be more likely to fasten partition for good, and would place the nationalist minority there in some difficulty. The Ulster Unionists made it clear to Walter Long when he consulted them that they would demand only six counties as an area they could hope to control. The government reluctantly conceded the point, conscious of the danger in alienating Unionists and nationalists at the same time.

Nationalists might have influenced this and other decisions now being made about the future political shape of Ireland; but Sinn Fein sat in Dublin and ignored the 'partition act'. Meanwhile the IRA, fearing that the politicians (by which it meant the Dáil) would outflank it and steal the spoils of its military efforts, increased its pressure on the British administration. The British government, faced with what is nowadays called a 'low-intensity war' of guerilla and terrorist acts, stumbled into a series of expedients that can hardly be dignified with the name of a security policy. It decided to fight a 'police war' and to reinforce the Royal Irish Constabulary with temporary constables, who were soon to gain notoriety as the 'Black and Tans'. Republicans liked to claim that these were the dregs of English society; but they included some 700 Irishmen, and most of the recruits, including the 10,000 non-Irish, were ex-army personnel who, while certainly battle-trained, were unlikely material for policing.

Recent research on the IRA has concentrated on the experience of ordinary members in local areas. This has uncovered what many knew about, but few wished to admit: that the IRA terrorized civilians, that most of its victims died without a weapon in their hands, and that many volunteers enjoyed the power that grew from the barrel of their guns, irrespective of the great cause of Irish freedom.[15] There were sectarian attacks on the Protestant minority, and indeed on anybody deemed by the IRA to be 'undesirable'. This campaign was met with a form of counter-terror by the Black and Tans, who were accused by responsible observers of random violence, shooting prisoners, setting fire to property, and drunkenness. The 'war' degenerated into a fight between two forces who seemed beyond political, let alone moral, control.

The behaviour of the crown forces aroused concern in influential sections of British public opinion, confronting for the first time the dilemmas of law enforcement in a morally ambiguous situation. There were accusations that the government was resorting to the very methods that Britain had condemned when the Germans had occupied Belgium in the Great War. In 1921 the British military effort began to show signs of improvement, with the more orthodox method of proclaiming martial law over much of the south and west of Ireland, and the more effective gathering of intelligence. But the question would not go away: how much coercion would the British public stand for, given that Ireland was going to get some form of self-government anyway? The IRA for its part was increasingly aware of the limits of its campaign. It had rendered ordinary law unworkable over some of the country, but it could not drive the British out. Both sides needed a truce, and when the British government was faced with some pessimistic reports by the military, it believed that the time had come to recover the initiative. The truce between the crown forces and the IRA of July 1921 put the best cards in British hands. Now that the British government was willing to talk, and then offered a generous measure of dominion status, British public opinion rallied behind the government. The British maintained and improved further their intelligence work during the truce. The IRA was now joined by many recruits, nicknamed the 'trucileers', who enjoyed their new-found status as war veterans. Michael Collins, who was the inspiration of the campaign, would have to work hard to organize his forces for a renewal of the war, which he did not believe could be won. The IRA was also divided by local jealousies, and Collins himself was not immune from such attacks.

After some preliminary sparring between Lloyd George and the president of Sinn Fein, Eamon de Valera, the two sides sat down to negotiate a treaty in October 1921. Lloyd George assembled a powerful team which knew what its last word was: dominion status with military safeguards. The Ulster question was his weak point. The Sinn Fein side was uncertain about what it would hold out for. Griffith was never wedded to pure republicanism, and saw nothing dishonourable in settling for dominion status. Collins, despite his republican credentials, was learning that statecraft and ideological conviction were not compatible. But the Irish had another difficulty: they had plenipotentiary status, yet were told not to sign any document without reference back to the Sinn Fein cabinet.[16] De Valera would have the last word.

The Ulster Unionists watched the London negotiations with suspicion, fearing that the British anxiety to achieve a settlement would jeopardize their insecure state. They were vindicated when the British were reluctant to transfer powers to them under the Government of Ireland Act of 1920, and alarmed when in November Lloyd George, having brought the Irish to the brink of accepting dominion status, now put pressure on the Northern Ireland government to exchange the rule of London for that of Dublin. The question was whether or not the Conservative party would support Ulster Unionism as they had in the old days. The answer was that it would not, but neither would it risk splitting the party, especially now that Bonar Law threatened to return to the fray should 'Ulster' be coerced. Lloyd George survived the crisis, because few Conservatives wanted to incur the odium of having destroyed the peace talks, and because the Irish were not sure if they wanted to 'break' on Ulster or not. Griffith was persuaded not to break on Ulster if Lloyd George would face down Conservative opposition.

This opened the way for a compromise on the lines first recommended (oddly enough) by Sir James Craig in 1919: a boundary commission to ascertain the wishes of the inhabitants about which state they would be in.[17] Now Lloyd George offered that, should Northern Ireland opt out of the settlement, then a commission would 'determine in accordance with the wishes of the inhabitants, so far as may be compatible with economic and geographical conditions, the boundaries between Northern Ireland and the rest of Ireland'.[18] This left an ambiguity over which should take precedence, wishes or conditions. Collins believed that wishes would prevail and thus 'save Tyrone and Fermanagh, parts of Derry, Armagh and Down'.[19] But he did not ask if wishes would triumph over conditions, and his reticence can be explained by his and Griffith's desire to leave the question to one side for the moment, until the greater gain of dominion status should be achieved.

Lloyd George, with a united cabinet, parliament and negotiating team behind him, now moved to the conclusion. On 5 December he told the by now exhausted and unhappy Irish delegation that it must sign the treaty as it stood or face immediate and terrible war. Griffith and Collins might have asked to refer back to de Valera. But they believed that what they were doing was right, in that it provided a 'stepping stone' to freedom.[20] Ireland gained the same status as Canada, but the Irish proximity to Great Britain and her vital role in wartime obliged her to accept British naval bases, the so-called 'treaty ports'.[21]

This settlement did not bring peace to Ireland; the divisions within Sinn Fein and the IRA precluded that. But equally important was the mutual suspicion that prevailed between the British government and its two states of Ireland, Northern Ireland and the Irish Free State. The Free State sought to 'republicanize' its constitution; the British responded by demanding that the letter of the treaty be adhered to, especially in the matter of the oath of allegiance to the crown as head of the empire. Lloyd George knew that the weak point in the British case was Ulster, the 'swamps of Lough Erne' as he put it,[22] and he knew that renewed coercion would soon pall with the British public and political parties. But his reluctance to commit his government too closely to defending Northern Ireland angered Sir James Craig, whose wife described the British as 'twisters'.[23] The outbreak of civil war in Ireland in June 1922 helped Northern Ireland achieve an uneasy peace. A year later the Free State defeated its enemies. The Irish question, it was hoped, would cease to trouble British party politics.

From Partition to Neutrality, 1923–1939

The Anglo-Irish Treaty left one important item of unfinished business, which was however quickly resolved, though not without rancour: the boundary commission. This was appointed in 1924, but without a Northern Ireland government representative, for Craig saw this as yet another danger to his state in reopening the territorial question. What he had he would hold. The report, leaked to the *Morning Post*, proposed the transfer of 183,290 acres and 31,319 people to the Free State (27,843 Catholics and 3,476 Protestants), and 49,242 acres and 7,594 people to Northern Ireland (2,764 Catholics and 4,830 Protestants).[24] Neither government found this acceptable, and the border remained where it was. Craig's continuing anxiety about his position was reflected in his abandoning proportional representation (PR), which the 1920 Government of Ireland Act included for the protection of minorities, first for local elections in September 1922, then for elections to the Northern Ireland parliament in April 1927. The British desire to distance themselves from these controversies is understandable, for if Craig were to resign over this issue, then London would once again be saddled with the direct rule of Northern Ireland. And there was the feeling too that Craig could be allowed to be master in his own house; as Sir William Joynson-Hicks put it when responding to Craig's proposal to eliminate PR for Northern Ireland elections, 'I "know my place" and don't propose to interfere'.[25]

But the British government had to interfere, or at least intervene, on another issue central to the working of Northern Ireland: finance. From the late 1920s the Northern Ireland government found itself unable to meet its obligations under the terms of the Government of Ireland Act. This Act fixed what was called the 'imperial contribution' (Northern Ireland's payment for common services such as defence) at £7.92 million. But Northern Ireland had long since passed the peak of her prosperity, and in 1925 a committee under Lord Colwyn recommended a fluctuating contribution, based on relative taxable capacity. This reduced the sum to a merely nominal £10,000 by 1934–5. Another financial problem became acute in a region with very high unemployment, which put intolerable strain on the unemployment insurance fund. In 1926, following negotiations between the Northern Ireland government and the British Treasury, it was agreed that the Treasury would assimilate the burden on the respective exchequers, keeping the two funds in a state of parity by the payment to Northern Ireland of a grant equivalent to three-quarters of the sum required to equalize per head of the total population the payments out of the two exchequers into their respective unemployment funds. This still proved insufficient, and in 1936 another agreement was drawn up resulting in a threefold increase in grant as against what would have been given under the old agreement: £722,000 as against £275,000. Some Labour MPs complained that the Northern Ireland government was being subsidized and that Britain was supporting a far from liberal regime, but, again, it was safer to leave well enough alone. The House of Commons ceased to debate Northern Ireland affairs, and the twelve Northern Ireland MPs (usually all Unionist) were content to sit quietly on the Conservative benches.

Both sides paid a price for this dispensation. Craig was able to govern his state as he saw fit, with little or no interference from London; but his own growing parochialism, and that of his followers, left his government in no good position, now or in the future, to understand the character of British politics; and it was on Britain that the state depended, in the last resort. London was able to slough off the Ulster Unionists (and by 1935 wind up its last obligations to the southern Irish Unionists by finally settling claims for compensation in the Troubles); but it was dissatisfied with upholding the Northern Ireland government financially, while not being able – or above all willing – to ask for better treatment of the Roman Catholic minority there.

Relations with the Free State proved equally troublesome at times, and occupied more time than the devolved government of Northern Ireland. This was because the Free State, in its search for freedom, was able to use the Commonwealth connection to move forward to the ultimate goal. The Commonwealth, which Lloyd George insisted the Free State must join, proved the very means of helping the Free State build up its credentials as a special, non-British nation. The Free State could rightly claim that it was only playing its part in extending the rights of all the Commonwealth members, and it made careful preparations for imperial conferences. There was indeed some wild talk in Ireland of moving towards Europe – perhaps making an alliance with France – but this was regarded by the Irish Foreign Affairs Department as doubtful, as the Irish people 'do not grasp the need of linking with the Continent'.[26]

The other British Dominions were themselves determined to assert their sovereignty, and supported the Free State's pursuit of 'absolute equality of status'.[27] The 1926 imperial conference, in which the Irish delegation played its part, resulted in what the head of the Irish Foreign Affairs Department, Joseph Walshe, called a 'new era in the history of the Saorstat and its sister states'.[28] The Dominions' right to make and sign treaties with foreign countries was of no immediate significance to the Irish, but it signalled that they were acquiring one of the most visible symbols of sovereignty. In 1930 the Irish delegation to the imperial conference again used the

Commonwealth link to its advantage, and the resultant Statute of Westminster of 1931 ensured that in future legislation by the British parliament would apply to the Dominions only at their request and with their consent. The British watched this anxiously, but acknowledged privately that 'there can be no compelling force short of civil war, which we tried once and are never likely to try again'.[29]

In October Desmond Fitzgerald wrote from London that

> The Free State is (or will be within a couple of years – without even a vestige of any form even to mar it) just a constitutional monarchy – with only that to make the difference between it and an Irish Republic. In the matter of independence and sovereignty there is no whittle of difference.[30]

This mood permeated the Foreign Affairs Department, which was opposed to any hardline policy on Anglo-Irish relations. But when de Valera's recently founded Fianna Fail party won office in 1932, the pace of change quickened. De Valera expressed as deep a commitment to the reunification of Ireland as he did to the republican goal, but his first target was the Commonwealth monarchical symbol, which would hardly endear him to Ulster Unionists. In 1932 the governor-general James MacNeill, who represented the British state in Ireland, found himself snubbed by Irish government ministers. The British took note of this; they had always feared that de Valera would come to power to attack the empire, and they set up an Irish Situation Committee to watch developments. The de Valera agenda included the oath of allegiance to the crown, the question of payment of land annuities (sums owing to the British exchequer under the land purchase schemes of the late nineteenth and early twentieth centuries) and the Ulster issue.

De Valera's determination not to pay to the British money for land purchase was based on the premise that the land belonged to the Irish 'people' (not the landlords) in the first place. This caused what was called the 'economic war' between Ireland and Britain, as each side placed duties on imports from the other. The Irish suffered more, but the British feared that de Valera had his eye on the Commonwealth question. In 1937 he drew up a new constitution for the state which, if it did not entirely remove the Free State (now renamed Eire) from the empire, certainly pushed it far beyond any previous bounds. Still the British prevaricated. The Commonwealth must not be aroused against the British government, so the government would treat the new Irish constitution, with all its republican trappings, as 'not affecting the fundamental alteration in the position of the Irish Free State, in future to be described under the new constitution as "Eire" or "Ireland", as a member of the British Commonwealth of Nations'.[31]

An observer might have well asked just what would affect this membership; but the problem was that while de Valera was single-minded in his pursuit of sovereign status, the British were obliged to take into account many other considerations. From 1937 European affairs were breaking in on British domestic politics and absorbing more time in parliamentary debates. The defence of the empire was still of first importance, but the prime minister Neville Chamberlain believed that in pursuing the policy of appeasement, Ireland came into the picture. Her proximity to Britain, her place in naval strategy, raised in acute form the question of the 'treaty ports'. De Valera was anxious to reclaim these, not only as part of the national territory, but in the knowledge that in any European war, British control of the ports must drag Ireland into the conflict.

In January 1938 negotiations began between the British and Irish governments, with the purpose of ending the economic war, the annuities dispute and any other outstanding Anglo-Irish business. De Valera and Chamberlain faced each other across the table: men of formidable political gifts, and with a complete mastery of their political parties. Chamberlain entered the negotiations determined to settle the outstanding problems in the light of his broader policy of appeasement. He believed that it was safer for the British to have an appeased, and therefore well-disposed, Ireland on her western flank, arguing that a 'free Ireland in terms of common risk could be for Great Britain only a friendly Ireland'.[32] He had evidence to support his claim. In March 1924 a party of British soldiers on leave from Cork harbour was fired at; one died of his wounds. The outrage was denounced by the Irish premier W. T. Cosgrave, but although it was an isolated incident, it emphasized the vulnerability of the British personnel in these installations. In 1934 a report from the British chief of staff claimed that 'in the face of a hostile mainland, our position is untenable'.[33] The Admiralty took comfort in the reflection that the convoy system and the improvement in anti-submarine techniques made the ports less vital. Chamberlain won his point, and the negotiations ended with the handing over of the ports, the first of these, Spike Island, being transferred without much ceremony in July 1938.

The Northern Ireland government watched these negotiations with suspicion. It was angry at the concessions on trade, for Eire was given freedom of entry for her goods into the United Kingdom, and was entitled to retain protective barriers against competition from Northern Ireland. Craig's government claimed that the Anglo-Irish Agreements proposed placing in the hands of the Eire government 'the means of bringing further economic pressure on Northern Ireland'.[34] These objections were brushed aside almost with contempt by the British, further evidence that, when it came to defining the British national interest, Northern Ireland took second place.

This was borne out after the outbreak of the Second World War in September 1939, although things were to change within a few years. De Valera was set upon maintaining Irish neutrality, though he appreciated the need for some degree of cooperation with the British. Irish neutrality has proved to be one of the most enduring of the many Anglo-Irish controversies, unlike Swedish or Swiss neutrality, which has not disturbed their relations with other states. De Valera's reasons for neutrality are easy to explain. Had he entered the war on the British side, even if that had been widely supported by the Irish public, he would have provided the chance for dissident republican troublemaking and serious internal turmoil. Historically, too, John Redmond's disastrous (as it turned out) support for the British in 1914 stood as a barrier against any Irish nationalist leader committing his country to the British side thereafter, except in the most extreme circumstances. De Valera was lucky to have to hand the excuse – for such it was – that a partitioned Ireland, which the 1938 negotiations had failed to modify in any way, debarred him from taking Ireland into the war. For the British, this issue proved divisive. On 5 September 1939 Winston Churchill asked the cabinet to appoint a committee to report on questions arising from the 'so-called neutrality of so-called Eire', describing de Valera's treatment of Britain as 'odious'.[35] Chamberlain's policy of leaving well enough alone stood against Churchillian indignation, but the mood passed, and the committee thus appointed concluded that a hostile Ireland was likely to be more dangerous to the war effort than Eire's position, unsatisfactory though this might be. In May 1940 the British took a different line, declaring willingness to reopen the partition question and reconsider Northern Ireland's position in the United Kingdom if de Valera would commit Ireland to the allied cause. De Valera refused to be tempted; he would have to make a definite move, but only with a vague reciprocal offer from the British. Sir James Craig's indignation at this scent of betrayal can be imagined.[36] It was clear that not even the greatest war in world history would move the dreary steeples of Dublin, let alone Fermanagh and Tyrone.

It would have been impossible in 1900 to even guess at the way in which the Irish–British relationship would turn out by 1939. The conflict of nationality in Ireland which reached such a dangerous level between 1912 and 1914 was one that British politicians found, to their astonishment, they could not manage or resolve in their normal parliamentary way. But the Great War is the event that marks out the difference between the Ireland of John Redmond and Sir Edward Carson, and that of Eamon de Valera and Sir James Craig. The war opened the way for a more intransigent Irish nationalism and an equally immovable Ulster Unionism. British politicians strove to control events in Ireland in ways that would prevent her posing a threat to British interests. To this end they wished to distance themselves from the Northern Ireland Unionists and their state, and to manoeuvre the southern Irish state into compliance with British strategic and economic interests (selfish or otherwise). These policies failed on both counts. Eire remained neutral in 1939, though leaning towards the British, as the Swedes leaned towards Germany. Northern Ireland participated, though without the enthusiasm of 1914–18, in the Second World War, and thus built up a debt to Britain (especially because of her naval facilities) that she was able to call in to protect her position in the United Kingdom when Eire finally left the Commonwealth in 1949. Between 1914 and 1939, international developments, and the expanding constitution of the British Empire, exercised a decisive influence on what, in 1900 and even in 1914, British politicians and parties of all shades of opinion regarded as a purely domestic political problem.

Yet there is a sense of make-believe about all this. From the foundation of the Irish Free State its citizens emigrated in large numbers to Great Britain: 35,000 a year left in the early years of the state's existence, dropping to 14,000 in the early 1930s, but rising again to 26,000 in 1937.[37] In the Second World War the state did not impede emigration to Britain for war work: in 1942, 51,711 Irish citizens departed, and about 30,000 southern Irishmen enlisted in the British army,[38] otherwise, as an Irish poet put it, Ireland would have experienced a '[n]eutrality we cannot afford'.[39] Many longed to return home; few did. This is, perhaps, the real and for many ordinary people the most enduring fact of the Anglo-Irish relationship, but not one that absorbed much of the politicians', diplomats' and gunmen's time in the first forty years of the twentieth century.

NOTES

1   M. Laffan, *The Resurrection of Ireland: The Sinn Fein Party, 1916–1923* (Cambridge, 1999), p. 7.

2 J. A. Murphy, 'Irish neutrality in historical perspective', in B. Girvin and G. Roberts, eds, *Ireland and the Second World War: Politics, Society and Remembrance* (Dublin, 2000), pp. 9–23.

3 A. Gailey, 'Failure and the making of the New Ireland', in D. G. Boyce, ed., *The Revolution in Ireland, 1879–1923* (London, 1988), ch. 2.

4 Laffan, *Resurrection of Ireland*, pp. 21–9.

5 P. Bew, *Ideology and the Irish Question: Ulster Unionism and Irish Nationalism, 1912–1916* (Oxford, 1994), p. 7.

6 Ibid., p. 41.

7 Ibid., p. 69.

8 A. M. Gollin, *The Observer and J. L. Garvin* (London, 1960), p. 389.

9 Bew, *Ideology and the Irish Question*, p. 99.

10 I. F. W. Beckett, *The Army and the Curragh Incident, 1914* (London, 1986), passim.

11 Bew, *Ideology and the Irish Question*, p. 138.

12 T. Hennessey, *Dividing Ireland: World War and Partition* (London, 1998), p. 131.

13 Ibid., p. 143.

14 Laffan, *Resurrection of Ireland*, p. 166.

15 J. Augustijn, *From Public Defiance to Guerilla Warfare: The Experience of Ordinary Volunteers in the Irish War of Independence, 1916–1921* (Dublin, 1996), passim; P. Hart, *The I.R.A. and its Enemies: Violence and Community in Cork, 1916–1923* (Oxford, 1998), passim.

16 Laffan, *Resurrection of Ireland*, p. 349.

17 Cabinet Conclusions, 15 December 1919, Public Record Office, London, Cab. 23/18.

18 N. Mansergh, *The Unresolved Question: The Anglo-Irish Settlement and its Undoing, 1912–1972* (London, 1991), p. 220.

19 Ibid., p. 221.

20 J. M. Regan, 'The politics of reaction: the dynamics of treatyite government and policy, 1922–23', *Irish Historical Studies*, 30 (Nov. 1997), pp. 542–63; p. 545.

21 The treaty ports were located at Queenstown (Cobh), Berehaven and Lough Swilly.

22 D. G. Boyce, *Englishmen and Irish Troubles: British Public Opinion and the Making of Irish Policy, 1918–1922* (London, 1972), pp. 174–5.

23 P. Buckland, *The Factory of Grievances: Devolved Government in Northern Ireland, 1921–1939* (Dublin, 1997), p. 86.

24 D. Keogh, *Twentieth-century Ireland: Nation and State* (Dublin, 1994), pp. 25–6.

25 Mansergh, *The Unresolved Question*, p. 257.

26 A. Nolan, 'Joseph Walshe and the management of Irish foreign policy, 1922–46: a study in diplomatic and administrative history' (Ph.D. dissertation, University College Cork, 1997), p. 18.

27 Mansergh, *The Unresolved Question*, p. 269.

28 Nolan, 'Joseph Walshe', p. 19.

29 D. G. Boyce, *Decolonisation and the British Empire, 1775–1997* (London, 1999), p. 81.

30 Keogh, *Twentieth-century Ireland*, p. 51.

31 Boyce, *Decolonisation*, p. 87.

32 Ibid.

33 C. J. O'Sullivan, 'Sentinel towers: the Irish treaty ports, 1914–1945' (Ph.D. dissertation, University College Cork, 1999), pp. 140–1.

34 Nolan, 'Joseph Walshe', p. 89.

35 Mansergh, *The Unresolved Question*, p. 311.

36 P. Canning, *British Policy towards Ireland, 1921–1947* (Oxford, 1985), pp. 266–87.

37 Keogh, *Twentieth-century Ireland*, pp. 88–9.

38 Ibid., pp. 122–3.

39 Ibid., pp. 136–7.

FURTHER READING

Bowman, J., *De Valera and the Ulster Question, 1917–73* (Oxford, 1982).

Boyce, D. G., *The Irish Question and British Politics, 1867–1996* (2nd edition, London, 1996).

Buckland, P., *Irish Unionism*, vol. 1, *The Anglo-Irish and the New Ireland, 1885–1922* (Dublin, 1972).

Buckland, P., *Irish Unionism*, vol. 2, *Ulster Unionism and the Origins of Northern Ireland, 1885–1922* (Dublin, 1973).

Buckland, P., *The Factory of Grievances: Devolved Government in Northern Ireland, 1921–1939* (Dublin, 1997).

Collins, P., ed., *Nationalism and Unionism: Conflict in Ireland, 1885–1921* (Belfast, 1994).

Dutton, D., *His Majesty's Loyal Opposition: The Unionist Party in Opposition, 1905–1915* (Liverpool, 1992).

Fitzpatrick, D., 'Militarism in Ireland, 1900–1922', in T. Bartlett and K. Jeffery, eds, *A Military History of Ireland* (Cambridge, 1996).

Harkness, D., *The Restless Dominion: The Irish Free State and the British Commonwealth of Nations, 1921–1931* (London, 1969).

Jackson, A., *The Ulster Party: Irish Unionists in the House of Commons, 1884–1911* (Oxford, 1989).

Jalland, P., *The Liberals and Ireland: The Ulster Question in British Politics to 1914* (Brighton, 1970).

Laffan, M., *The Partition of Ireland, 1911–25* (Dundalk, 1983).

Lawlor, S., *Britain and Ireland, 1914–1923* (Dublin, 1983).

McMahon, D., *Republicans and Imperialists: Anglo-Irish Relations in the 1930s* (London, 1984).

Mansergh, D., *Nationalism and Independence: Selected Papers by Nicholas Mansergh* (Cork, 1997).

Middlemas, K., ed., *Thomas Jones: Whitehall Diary*, vol. 3, *Ireland, 1918–1925* (Oxford, 1971).

O'Halloran, C., *Partition and the Limits of Irish Nationalism: An Ideology under Stress* (Dublin, 1987).

O'Halpin, E., *The Decline of the Union: British Government in Ireland, 1892–1920* (Dublin, 1987).

Pakenham, F. (Lord Longford), *Peace by Ordeal* (London, 1967).

Townshend, C., *The British Campaign in Ireland, 1919–1921* (Oxford, 1975).

Vaughan, W., ed., *New History of Ireland*, vol. 6, *Ireland under the Union, 2: 1870–1921* (Oxford, 1996).

Chapter Eight

Women and Politics, 1900–1939

Christine Collette

The wide extent of the activities covered by the title 'women and politics' in the early twentieth century has been uncovered by historians from the women's movement of its final decades. June Hannam wrote of women that:

> They engaged in general political and social reform campaigns as well as taking part in movements which focussed on their own oppression as a sex and sought to challenge inequalities in all areas of life. No clear cut distinction can be made between these two forms of political work.[1]

While fully reflecting this variety, the period 1900 to 1939 is of especial interest. It covers both the last great flowering of 'first-wave' (dating from the eighteenth century) feminism in the campaign for women's enfranchisement and the seeds of 'second-wave' (from the 1960s) feminism.

Indeed, the feminist chronology of the first, second and third (from the 1990s) 'waves' of activity is based on the recognition that while early feminists sought the education, financial independence and enfranchisement that would empower their full citizenship, success in winning the vote failed to meet expectations, necessitating renewed activity. The second wave, with its slogan 'the personal is political', was an inevitable outcome and its corollary was a broader view of past political engagement. Thus it is long since the years immediately following the suffrage campaign were seen as uneventful. However, prizing 'sisterhood', collaboration between women, second-wave feminists found it hard to deal with the numerous different groups and conflicting priorities of the period between the wars. The third, postmodern, phase is distinguished by a new appreciation that divergence is not necessarily weakness. Moreover, third-wave feminists have developed critiques of traditional theories of citizenship that typified men as rational/politically engaged/protectors of the polity and women as emotional carers. Interest in suffrage history has been reawakened, while women's campaign for inclusion in a patriarchal and imperialist state has been problematized. Encompassing these themes, this chapter will take a broad approach to 'women and politics', while including the suffrage campaign, which continues to attract fresh historical interest.[2]

Suffrage, 1900–1914

Reviewing some of the recent literature, Krista Cowman writes of suffrage history that its 'boundaries are continually expanded', the richness of material and analyses being reflected by distinct undergraduate history modules.[3] Moreover, for those coming new, or young, to the history of women, suffrage remains the one issue about which some knowledge may be assumed. The main outlines of the suffrage struggle from 1900 to 1914 are well known. Adherents of the large National Union of Women's Suffrage Societies (NUWSS) founded in 1897 numbered about 50,000 and, under Millicent Garrett Fawcett's leadership, followed a policy of civil disobedience, refusing to pay rates while lobbying for their cause. The much smaller Women's Social and Political Union (WSPU), which started in 1903, with about 5,000 members, was led by the dramatic figures of the Pankhurst family. The WSPU demanded a government reform bill and used aggressive tactics, opposing all Liberal candidates for parliament as representatives of an obdurate government, whatever their individual inclination. Breakaway groups from the autocratically run WSPU included the Women's Freedom League. WSPU tactics in particular, leading to imprisonment, and protests by hunger strikes, were successful in publicizing the cause. The government response included forcible feeding and the 1912 enactment of legislation to allow release and rearrest of hunger strikers (the so-called Cat and Mouse Act). The new alliance formed by NUWSS and the Labour party that year reversed WSPU tactics, setting up the Election Fighting Fund to return sympathetic Labour members to parliament. Private members' legislative initiatives, supported by NUWSS, included the 1910 Conciliation Bill, which promised well, having all-party support. However, women remained disfranchised at the outbreak of the First World War. The Speaker's Conference that met during the war to deal with problems including soldiers' omission from the electoral register added the grant of the vote to women to its recommendations. Women over thirty who were on local government registers or wives of registered men, and/or graduates of British universities, were duly enfranchised by the 1918 Representation of the People Act.

There are two major recent amendments to this history, the first on differences between the groups and their leaders, the second on their efficacy. First, it is now usually accepted that, despite their rival tactics and occasional hostilities, the NUWSS and WSPU did not form two discrete wings of a divided suffrage movement. Many women were members of both the NUWSS and WSPU, while some demonstrations were jointly run. In addition, the split between Sylvia Pankhurst, who formed the suffrage-socialist East London Federation, and her mother Emmeline and sister Christabel has been reassessed. In Sue Bruley's opinion, Sylvia Pankhurst's socialist-feminist orientation endeared her to second-wave feminists, who were impatient with Christabel Pankhurst's dictatorial style and espousal of the cause of sexual hygiene.[4] The issue of HIV/AIDS has changed attitudes towards sexual licence, while the assumptions of socialist feminism have been challenged in feminism's postmodern phase. The East London Federation and the Women's Freedom League were just two of the many groups that fell into neither the NUWSS nor the WSPU camps, while sometimes sharing members and activities. The complete picture of the suffrage scene was much more variegated than a traditional account of opposing NUWSS/WSPU camps allowed.

Moreover, the traditional adversarial model, concentrating on tactics, obscured the different motivations and the broader interests of the campaigners. Socialist women, for instance, wanted to be able to vote for welfare reforms that did not necessarily attract some of the more conservative participants. Not all groups privileged female suffrage; around half of eligible working men were missing from the registers. The People's Suffrage Association was concerned with disfranchised working men, as were, for instance, the East London Federation and the Lancashire and Cheshire Textile and Other Workers' Representation Committee. There was animosity between adult and woman suffragists; NUWSS rhetoric, nevertheless, was in favour of gender equality, while WSPU rhetoric emphasized gender difference. Smaller groups may be broadly divided by their members' profession, religion or geography and had their own agendas. The Jewish League for Woman Suffrage, for example, campaigned for representation rights for women in synagogues,[5] while the Lancashire and Cheshire group wanted to improve working conditions in the region. The South Wales Federation of Women's Suffrage Societies, while affiliated to the NUWSS, opposed the Election Fighting Fund because of the political geography of its region. Welsh Labour MPs in mining districts were less sympathetic to women's enfranchisement than Liberal MPs; moreover, the South Wales Federation made the reasonable point that the passage of a private member's bill demanded all-party support.[6]

Second, in assessing how effective suffrage campaigners were, Martin Pugh's influential 1974 opinion that the vote was won for women by men's espousal of the cause in the Speaker's Conference, rather than being a reward for women's war work or a result of suffrage campaigning, has been revised. The violence of the government's response lends weight to Pugh's opinion that aggressive campaigning undermined the suffrage cause, but feminist historians have critiqued this as a case of blaming the victim for her oppression. Further, feminists have shown that the government was moving towards an agreement by 1914; that there was an unremitting campaign by NUWSS during the war years; and that the government desired to escape renewed suffrage aggression after the war.[7] It should, however, be borne in mind that, as Martin Pugh has recently written, the principle of enfranchisement of all classes and both genders was won in the nineteenth century: 'But in essence the Edwardians were haggling over the details'.[8] Evidence for this is that, as local government councils and boards had been created, women had been enfranchised locally, although they did not win the right to sit on county councils or London borough councils and lost the right to serve on and be elected to school boards when these were transferred to local authority control in 1902.

Sandra Stanley Holton has distinguished four types of suffrage historiography, the constitutionalist or militant histories of contemporaries and subsequent masculinist and new-feminist histories. Constitutionalist historians tended to write from the NUWSS perspective, looking back to a tradition of democracy from Anglo-Saxon times, and were imbued with a sense of the superiority of the British 'race'. Militants, epitomized by Sylvia Pankhurst, wrote histories that emphasized the minutiae and the revolutionary ethos of the current struggle. Such histories were the basis for the traditional account of two opposed suffrage camps. Drawing on constitutionalist histories, later 'Liberal-masculinist' histories were sympathetic to women's claims of equality while maintaining a male perspective that viewed suffrage campaigning as a phenomenon. 'Sardonic-masculinist' historians were influenced by militant histories and treated aggressive militancy as a 'deviant, marginal and even dangerous aberration'. Finally, radical new-feminist historians drew from militant accounts an example of women's courage, valuing their networks of support and rhetoric of gender difference. Socialist new feminists dealt with labour movement links. Holton concludes: 'What all the varieties of new-feminist scholarship share is an appreciation of the suffrage campaign as a site of gender contestation'.[9]

War, 1914–1918

The outbreak of war had a complex impact on the relationship of women to the state. While imperialism had been little debated by suffragists, the experience of war demanded a consideration of foreign policy. Women's responses to the war varied from militarist to pacifist. The release of suffrage prisoners on the outbreak of war validated the support which the patriotic Pankhursts of the WSPU now gave to the government. Indeed, Emmeline Pankhurst's fervour led her to propose internment of aliens and to condemn men who failed to volunteer. The notorious white feather handed to the latter was a typical piece of Pankhurst flamboyance. Despite rallying supporters for a march demanding women's 'right to serve' in the war, and a relaunch as 'the Women's Party', the WSPU lost members. Ironically, while its extreme nationalism decimated the WSPU, pacifism and socialism adversely affected the East London Federation.

The NUWSS split over support for the war. Millicent Garrett Fawcett's opinion, that defending democracy against the belligerents was the prime task, was shared by some former activists whose husbands were in the trenches. Others favoured a negotiated peace, earning them the sobriquet 'peacettes', and resigned, three NUWSS members attending the 1915 Women's Peace Congress at The Hague. This conference gave rise to the International Committee of Women for Permanent Peace, and its British section, the Women's International League for Peace and Freedom. In Glasgow, two former suffragists launched the Women's Peace Crusade, which had a hundred branches by the end of the war. Some women joined the Union for Democratic Control (of foreign policy) or the No-Conscription Fellowship, whose titles are self-explanatory. Labour movement women had met internationally since 1907, when the International Women's Council and its British section were formed. Marion Phillips, later Labour party chief woman's officer, was secretary to this group. The international conference was postponed in 1914, but held the following year at Bern, with representatives from belligerent and allied countries; delegates demanded a speedy end to the war and a negotiated peace. As Marion Phillips wrote, 'Politically, women have a clean slate. They cannot bear any direct responsibility for the catastrophe that has overwhelmed Europe and drawn the world to disaster'.[10]

The introduction of conscription in Britain for the first time in 1916 redefined what it meant to be a citizen, explicitly making warrior status a criterion. Conscientious objectors were disfranchised. Compared to the latter, the women who joined the armed forces' support services, and those who were widowed, could claim to have paid the price of citizenship. These women's experiences, and the spectacle of women workers in industrial jobs that had belonged to men, undercut the argument of gender difference that had served to exclude women from parliamentary politics. However, the way in which women were reluctantly granted permission to enter these domains illuminated the fundamental continuing patriarchy of British politics.

Linda Grant de Pauw's Minerva Center was formed to investigate the history of women and war. De Pauw's opinion is that women may be discerned in four roles: the support role, which serves to emphasize traditional gender stereotypes; the quintessentially female victim role (sometimes adopted by female spies who use the stereotyping as cover for 'masculine' activity); the virago, clearly female but engaged in acts of male boldness; and the androgynous warrior, who challenges gender stereotyping.[11] Susan Grayzel's study of women who joined support services illustrates de Pauw's thesis and exemplifies the debate on gender ideology in the First World War. Grayzel shows that women's wish to mark their links to the armed forces by wearing uniform, preferably the new British khaki, was the subject of much controversy. Women were initially deemed unworthy to wear the national colour, because their sacrifice was unequal to the total commitment of life demanded of the soldier. While 3,372 women eventually registered as naval and military voters in 1918, the Act that enfranchised them did not use their war service as justification.[12] Louise Ryan's work on perceptions of women who protested against British imperialism by joining in the 1916 Irish rebellion gives examples of all four of de Pauw's types.[13] In the Irish Republican tradition, as in Britain, men were stereotyped as warriors and women as homemakers. Ryan shows that women were able to use their femininity to act as intelligence officers, and were widely reported as victims, but that their participation in fighting was ignored by the contemporary press.

Women working in war industries had to deal with the same gender stereotyping, that their sphere should be domestic and that their femininity should distance them from the products of war. In addition, by taking on men's jobs and claiming at least part of men's pay, they were challenging both industrial and familial patriarchy. Claire Culleton's history emphasizes the dangers faced by women war workers: explosions, industrial accidents, toxins, long hours and poor conditions. In addition, 'there were picket lines to cross, cross workers to pacify, pacifists to tolerate, intolerable war mongers to suffer and insufferable critics to sidestep on the way to the factories or the front'.[14] The Munitions of War Act of 1915 institutionalized perceptions of gender difference by specifying the temporary nature of the specific jobs that women were allowed to undertake. The 1919 Restoration of Pre-War Practices Act put a full stop to the greater part of this employment.

Although women were exploited and underrepresented, the experience of wartime work did have a political impact, in that many women joined trade unions for the first time. Marion Phillips, who served with other labour movement women (Margaret Bondfield, Susan Lawrence, Mrs Gasson) on the War Emergency Workers' National Committee, encouraged women to join trade unions, but also to demand equal pay. Women trade union leaders, notably Mary Macarthur, while championing women workers, also collaborated closely with labour movement men. Phillips and Macarthur both served on the Queen's Work for Women Fund, which became the Central Committee on Women's Training and Employment, and demanded that work be directed first to skilled women, for instance seamstresses working on uniforms, rather than allowing 'lady volunteers' accidentally to throw working women out of their jobs. Experience of industrial war work thus heightened women politicians' profile at national level, strengthened women's own organizations, and forged stronger links between men and women in class politics. From this empowering mix, a major organization developed, the Standing Joint Committee of Industrial

Women's Organizations (SJC), which was politically important for women in the interwar years.

The discussion above of women's war experiences adds a further sidelight to the contention that the vote was a 'reward' for women's war activities. They were not welcome in masculine spheres and changes in gender stereotypes were resisted. Some women strongly supported the war effort, but others opposed British foreign and imperial policy. The entry of women into the labour movement was no recommendation to the Conservative party, which ended the war in a position of strength relative to the pre-war years. However, women were able to build organizations that would enable them to maintain a post-war political presence.

Politics and Public Life, 1918–1939

Finding it difficult to attract new recruits when alternative groups such as Women's Institutes (formed 1915) competed for their attention, NUWSS reformed in 1919 as the National Union of Societies for Equal Citizenship (NUSEC), open to any group whose aims were 'real equality of status, liberties and opportunities'. Millicent Garrett Fawcett resigned due to this change in focus and was replaced by Eleanor Rathbone.[15] NUSEC and the Women's Freedom League, renamed the Women's Suffrage National Aid Corps, continued their campaigns for women's enfranchisement on equal terms with that of men.

However, NUSEC's ethos was not that of gender neutrality – which Eleanor Rathbone called 'me too' feminism, where women claimed male roles, rights and responsibilities – but an acknowledgement and equal valuation of different gender roles. Such an outlook has sometimes been called 'new' feminism, and Rathbone was forecasting some of the issues of present-day third-wave feminism when she spoke of the need to escape 'looking at our problems through men's eyes and discussing them in men's phraseology'.[16] Rathbone's great campaign for sizeable family allowances that would give women the choice of a domestic, child-rearing role sprang from this ethos. Ruth Lister, amongst present-day feminist writers on citizenship, has addressed this problem of whether women should claim gender-neutral citizenship, or a citizenship that reflected their caring role.[17] The Six Point Group (1921) and the Open Door Council (1926) gained members dissatisfied with Rathbone's iteration of gender difference, although the Six Point Group also addressed issues that concerned women as mothers, such as equal guardianship of children. NUSEC split in 1928, Rathbone's supporters forming the National Council for Equal Citizenship (NCEC) and the opposition forming the National Union of Townswomen's Guilds. NCEC membership fell, so that the 478 original branches had been reduced to ninety by 1929 and forty-eight by 1935.

There is much the same historiographical debate on post-war as on pre-war suffrage groups. Both the diversity of post-war groups and their ability to network are now recognized. Helen Jones, for instance, has argued that while groups had different priorities, their policies were similar and they shared members: 'the range of organisations in which women were involved . . . was a sign of flourishing thought among women and a means of them trying to order competing priorities'.[18] Concentrating on differences obscures the vitality of women's political involvement. Cheryl Law has written of the 'cross-fertilisation of ideas': 'A growing number of women's clubs, restaurants and other favoured locations made up a circuit of venues which came to be regularly used by feminist groups for meetings, press conferences and celebrations'.[19] The change was that suffrage became one item on the agenda of the diverse post-war women's groups. Before the war, most groups of women, however initiated, formed suffrage societies: after the war, groups maintained their original focus, while participating in suffrage demonstrations. The Electrical Association for Women (1924), which focused on the burgeoning electricity industry, was a case in point.[20]

Catriona Beaumont has argued that the full extent of women's political organization in the 1920s and 1930s is obscured by overemphasizing the role of the suffrage spin-off groups. A comprehensive account, in Beaumont's opinion, should include the activities of a broad range of organizations, including the Women's Institutes and Townswomen's Guilds, the National Council of Women (derived from the National Union of Women Workers, formed 1918) and, more controversially, the Mothers' Union (Anglican, 1885), the Young Women's Christian Association (1877) and the Catholic Women's League (1906), all of which had a very large membership. Beaumont maintains that, despite declaring that they were not feminist, these groups made a big contribution to women's political empowerment:

> Following the extension of political citizenship to women, feminist, working-class and mainstream women's organisations endeavoured to educate their members in citizenship and highlighted the social and economic rights that women now had as equal citizens. What is most significant . . . is the emphasis placed on the rights and duties of women citizens by women's organisations . . . which publicly and repeatedly denied having a feminist agenda.[21]

The breadth of this interest in citizenship augured well for the continued struggle for equal suffrage. Parliament set up an Equal Political Rights Committee and there was much press coverage. Neither should the incessant watchful campaigning of groups such as NUSEC be undervalued, nor the excellence of the generalship of the final assault, which saw Emmeline Pankhurst and Millicent Garrett Fawcett both on platforms at the end of a procession of forty women's groups.[22] There were only ten votes in opposition to the passage of the Representation of the People (Equal Franchise) Act, which finally fully enfranchised women in 1928.

An anomaly that had indicated that success would eventually reward the suffrage campaign had been the passage, in three weeks, of the 1918 Parliament (Qualification of Women) Bill by 274 votes to twenty-five, which made women eligible for nomination and election to parliament. The 1918 general election was contested by 1,623 candidates, of whom seventeen were women.[23] Suffrage campaigners were used to working across the political divide rather than taking party political identities, and few stood for election. Christabel Pankhurst was the most successful, failing to win a seat as a Conservative by a mere 775 votes. The Labour and Liberal parties nominated four candidates each and Sinn Fein two candidates. Mary Macarthur stood for the Labour party. One woman was elected, Sinn Fein's Constance Markiewicz. Conducting her campaign from Holloway jail, where she was held on suspicion of conspiring with the enemy against Britain, having received an amnesty for her part in the 1916 rebellion, Markiewicz refused to take her seat in protest at British imperialism.

Viscountess Astor was the first woman to take up her parliamentary seat, winning Plymouth at a by-election in 1919, caused by her husband's accession to the peerage. The first three women MPs in the House of Commons all replaced their husbands. In all, fifteen Conservative seats were won by women from 1918 to 1939, four Liberal, sixteen Labour (including Marion Phillips, 1929), one Independent (Eleanor Rathbone, elected 1929) and one Sinn Fein. These roughly fit with the periods of government of the respective parties, three Labour women MPs being elected for the first time in 1923, eight from 1929 to 1931, and eleven Conservative women MPs from 1931. The presence of women did not change the party political balance. The bills they introduced were broadly on social policy, including the bastardy laws, adoption, nursing home regulations, the Poor Law, expectant mothers and the death sentence, hire purchase and alcohol licensing.[24] Brian Harrison, after exhaustive review of the debating hours initiated by women MPs, concluded that the majority of these took place in the 1920s when Nancy Astor and Margaret Wintringham 'were struggling to alter the political priorities of a male assembly'.[25] Women MPs were usually much valued in their constituencies and had a heavy workload, with women correspondents and lobbyists nationally seeking their interest. As Marion Phillips's biographer has pointed out, women MPs in constituencies far from London, such as Phillips's Sunderland, faced great difficulties; they were salaried, but expenses and accommodation, secretarial, telephone and postage costs were not paid. An economist, Phillips was secretary to the Special Committee, which the Labour government formed to examine the issues of currency and exchange that caused its fall in 1931. The committee's advice was ignored and Phillips robustly opposed government economic policy.[26] Just four women MPs had been appointed to cabinet positions by 1939: Margaret Bondfield (Labour, parliamentary secretary, Ministry of Labour, 1924; minister of labour, 1929–31); the duchess of Atholl (Conservative, parliamentary secretary, Board of Education, 1924–9); Susan Lawrence (Labour, parliamentary secretary, Ministry of Health, 1929–31); and Florence Horsborough (Conservative, parliamentary secretary, Ministry of Health, 1939–45).

Astor continually recommended the appointment of women to public bodies and, in particular, wanted to expand the women's police service. Women had begun to get a toe-hold on public appointments before the war, notably in the factory and prisons inspectorates, the Board of Trade and labour exchanges, although they had not been allowed entry into civil service administrative grades. As shown above, the war had presented women with an opportunity for advancement in public life. They also served on reconstruction committees. However, as Helen Jones has shown, women remained tolerated in, rather than welcomed to, public life: 'Women remained the supplicants'.[27] Many women were dismissed from the civil service at the close of the war, as they were from industrial jobs, and were not allowed to compete in the selection procedure until 1925. The Council of Women Civil Servants was formed in 1920 to find ways through the glass ceiling, but some single women supported the continued operation of the marriage bar, thus maximizing their own opportunities. It was not until 1935 that the principle of equal pay was agreed. Women formed merely 15 per cent of local councillors in the 1930s and lost the right to serve on Poor Law boards when these were merged with local authorities in 1929.[28]

Still disadvantaged, but partially enfranchised and with a parliamentary presence, women had the options of either forming their own parliamentary party, or forging party political alliances. As we have seen, party political alliances were distasteful to former suffragists who had worked across the party divide and had relied on private members' bills winning all-party support for their cause. In addition, as Alberti has written, '[m]any feminists were unable to adopt the full programme of any party'.[29] The Six Point Group, for instance, never developed party links. Eleanor Rathbone, who had resigned from the NUWSS when it formed links with the Labour party before the war, remained firmly independent. However, while NUSEC and other groups in the women's network were, in a sense, women's parties, a parliamentary women's group was never seriously considered. Nancy Astor, who was generous to her female colleagues, identified a women's interest in political life and attempted to represent this with an all-party Consultative Committee of Women's Organizations. This had a fragile existence from 1922 to 1928, never attracting Labour women.[30] Similarly, the Women's party failed to win widespread support. More successful were the Women's Citizen's Associations, formed in a number of regions as agencies for various local women's groups, but these did not grow into a political party. Indeed, the class-conscious politics of the interwar years were reflected in adversarial debates in the House of Commons, in which women MPs vigorously participated. While NUSEC supported women from all parties in the 1922 general election, only two stood as Independent candidates. Law, however, has shown that closer inspection of the backgrounds of the thirty-three women who stood reveals the importance of the women's network; a mere eight women were without previous women's network affiliations.[31]

The potential benefits of an alliance were illustrated by the passage of the 1919 Sex Disqualification Removal Act. The Labour party, open to influence from the SJC, had promoted a wide-ranging bill, including equal franchise, but this was replaced by the government's own measure, limited to allowing women entry to the legal profession and the magistracy. Law is of the opinion that the frequent elections of the interwar years enhanced the value of women, useful as canvassers, to political parties.[32] All parties, of course, wanted to win the 8 million new votes. There remained practical difficulties: 'In all the political parties "glass ceilings" and "glass doors" prevented women occupying more than a confined space'.[33] Women were not selected for safe seats.

Second-wave feminist interest in instances of socialist feminism were revived by the election of a Labour government in 1997 with a record number of women MPs. While the attempt to find past instances of common purpose between Labour men, representing industrial areas, and middle-class feminists often presented difficulties, as the south Wales experience above suggested, women formed part of the Labour party community from its inception. The Women's Labour League was formed in 1906 and achieved the election of women to a diversity of local bodies. Marion Phillips served as its organizer from 1912. The League merged with the Labour party and formed the basis of its women's sections in 1918. These were popular, so that women formed half the Labour party membership by 1939. Meanwhile the SJC, representing Labour, Cooperative and trade union women, carried on its separate existence, lobbying the government on matters relating to women such as the marriage bar and equal pay, domestic service and protective legislation, and advising the Labour party on these issues. The SJC explicitly advised its affiliates to vote Labour, to beware of the Women's party in particular, but also of the Women's Citizens' Associations. The latter might have laudable aims, but the SJC stressed that working-class organizations could only work for working-class aims. Women Labour MPs did not prioritize gender issues; Harrison has estimated that 8 per cent of Ellen Wilkinson's House of Commons speeches were on such questions, 5 per cent of Margaret Bondfield's and 1 per cent of Susan Lawrence's.[34] Margaret Bondfield, Women's Labour League organizer in 1911, and president of the People's Suffrage Association, had come under fire from the League executive when she weakened a League suffrage resolution submitted to the Labour party conference. As minister of labour her reputation was severely damaged when, under pressure to find cuts during the economic crisis, she stopped unemployment benefits for married women who did not intend to return to paid work. Elsewhere on the left, while there was a women's section of the Communist party of Great Britain, women members resisted ghettoization in a group whose interests were perceived as subordinate to the main thrust of party policy. The large Cooperative Women's Guild, formed in 1884, was perhaps the nearest thing to a middle way between woman-centred and class-oriented politics. With close links to the labour movement, it retained a separate existence and its own style and ethos, representing the consumer and demanding women's rights in the domestic sphere.

Women were less well served in the older Liberal and Conservative parties. The Liberal Women's Federation (1886) and National Association (1892) joined to form the Women's National Liberal Federation. This had nearly 100,000 women members at the end of the war but kept a low profile, losing members in the 1920s. Liberal women's groups suffered the most from the firmly independent line of NUWSS/NUSEC, many of whose members were their natural constituents. The Open Door Council was also Liberal in outlook, but not affiliated to the party. Conservative women joined the Primrose League (1884), and the Conservative Women's Unionist Association was formed in 1918. Helen Jones argues that Conservatives remained covertly hostile to women, while welcoming their canvassing and social abilities.[35] Rather than being cast as estranged from, or opposed to, the mainstream women's network, party political women, on the right or left of the political spectrum, should be seen as an intrinsic part of women's experience and experiment with politics between the wars. Negotiation and compromise formed part of women's political practice from 1900 to 1939, and the contributions that could be made within the mainstream political parties were as worthwhile as those extraneous to party politics.

The Politics of Sexuality

The ways in which the women's network dealt with issues of sexuality indicate how women could work within and without party political alliances. There had been good reason to hope that women's alliance with the labour movement would be productive of feminist reforms to the politics of sexuality. The 'woman question' debated at the turn of the nineteenth century had coincided with an efflorescence of socialist societies and with the phenomenon of 'new life' socialism which had explored personal as well as community politics. The sexologist Havelock Ellis, himself a member of the Fellowship of the New Life, had insisted that women were sexual beings, even if his description of their sexuality was imbued with the patriarchal

notions of his time. Socialists and feminists in the Social Purity movement had successfully united over campaigns in the 1880s, such as raising the age of consent (to
sixteen) and repeal of the Contagious Diseases Acts, which had provided for the
forcible inspection and treatment of women suspected of soliciting men of the armed
forces in certain ports.

Feminists such as Stella Browne, inspired by Ellis's information, if not his patriarchal ideas, believed that sexual fulfilment was necessary for a complete life and argued
in the early twentieth century for contraception and abortion rights. However, there
were early indications that the brief period when such issues were debated relatively
freely in left-wing metropolitan circles would be followed by a period of greater
repression. Eugenicist ideas were lent weight by the 1904 Interdepartmental Committee on Physical Deterioration, which had been the response to poor performance
in the South African Wars. The Eugenics Society was founded in 1907 and its view
was that women, guardians of the future of the British 'race', should be both chaste
and fruitful. Some eugenicists held the employment of married women to be the
cause of both a decline in virility of the British 'race' and high infant mortality rates.
The Mental Deficiency Act of 1913 gave local authorities powers over pregnant
women who were homeless, destitute or 'immoral', in other words unmarried; many
were admitted to hospitals for the mentally ill, where some became long-term
residents. The prevalence of venereal disease was the cause of Christabel Pankhurst's
denunciation of male promiscuity and different standards of sexual morality for men
and women. For the NUWSS, Dr Louisa Martindale had expressed similar concerns.
The Social Purity movement was revived by the 1913 formation of the Association
of Moral and Social Hygiene.

The Labouchère amendment to the 1885 legislation which raised the age of
consent had outlawed homosexual acts in public. The gender stereotypification noted
as obtaining in the First World War increased cultural resistance to acceptance of
homosexuality. It also led to the passage of the notorious Clause 40D of the 1918
Defence of the Realm Act, which effectively reintroduced the Contagious Diseases
Acts, making it an offence for women to infect troops with venereal disease and
permitting their compulsory treatment. A government commission on venereal
disease had reported in 1916 and made available free treatment in specially designated clinics. Social Purity campaigners patrolled parks and military camps to prevent
immoral behaviour. The attractions of a uniform to impressionable young girls was
dubbed 'khaki fever'.[36] The National Council for Unmarried Mothers was formed in
1918, under the presidency of Jennie Baker, formerly of the Women's Labour
League.

The pro-natalist ethos pertaining at the end of the war led to a new appreciation
of married women's sexuality and the arrival of manuals such as Marie Stopes's
Married Love. However, far from allowing women in general greater freedom of
sexual expression, the new emphasis on married women's sexuality increased the perceived deviancy of lesbianism. There was an attempt in 1921 to criminalize lesbianism that received support in the House of Commons but was rejected by the House
of Lords.[37] The Obscene Publications legislation was used to repress Radclyffe Hall's
The Well of Loneliness (1928), which pleaded for acceptance of lesbianism. For
heterosexual women, NUSEC won a victory in its old style, the passage of a private
member's bill with all-party support, which resulted in the Matrimonial Causes Act

of 1923, making adultery the sole grounds of divorce for either spouse. Further grounds were added in the Matrimonial Causes Act of 1937, including a wife's right to divorce her husband for rape.

Stopes founded a birth control clinic, but contraception was controversial and its availability largely confined to middle- and upper-class women who had access to advice such as Stopes's. Prosecutions under the Obscene Publications Acts continued to face those, such as anarchists Rose Witcop and Guy Aldred, who published contraceptive advice. A long and ultimately unsuccessful campaign to extend the availability of contraceptive advice to working-class women was conducted by some labour movement women and condoned by Labour Women's Conferences in the 1920s. The SJC briefly debated the issue but took no substantive action and Labour women MPs, with the exception of Dorothy Jewson (MP for Norwich, 1923–4), were not supportive. The support of the Mineworkers' Union was won, but Labour governments declined to take action. The 1929 Labour government did issue a circular allowing advice to be given in circumstances where the health of the woman was at risk. Abortion remained illegal. Stella Browne, a founder member of the Communist party of Great Britain, resigned her membership because it failed to support her stance on abortion. She joined the Workers' Birth Control Group, which maintained links with the Communist party and in which Dora Russell was a leading figure, and continued to argue for women's right to seek abortion. NUSEC supported the Workers' Birth Control Group from 1927 and Eleanor Rathbone gave parliamentary support, aided by Nancy Astor. The Workers' Birth Control Group, together with the Birth Control International Information Centre, a lobbying committee for several women's organizations, reformed as the National Birth Control Association in 1931 and was renamed the Family Planning Association in 1939. The beginnings of some relaxation on the issue of abortion could be seen in 1929, when it became legal to abort if the mother's life was in danger. The Abortion Law Reform Association was formed in 1936 and had some success in lobbying for further reforms, a government committee being created to review the legislation in 1938. Stella Browne, giving evidence, admitted to having herself undergone an abortion.[38]

The campaigns on issues of sexuality illustrate both the breadth of the women's network and the way in which individuals and organizations overlapped. It was an Independent and a Conservative woman MP who gave sustained support to the promotion of birth control, but labour movement women who campaigned on this issue within a political party. The recognition that the issue was one of class as much as gender, as working-class women were those disadvantaged by lack of information, allowed women with Communist party links to ally with the non-party political NUSEC in forming what eventually became the Family Planning Association. However, it was a private member's bill, emanating from a Liberal MP and ideas of social justice, rather than class consciousness, which achieved parity in the divorce laws. The issue of social purity, which, while denouncing the double moral standard, appeared to go some way towards validating measures such as Clause 40D, is problematic for third-wave feminists who have preferred to emphasize women's right to express and discover their own sexuality. The politics of sexuality from 1900 to 1939, including the impact of eugenicism and experiences of lesbian feminism, remain to be fully explored in contrast with, for instance, the politics of women's suffrage.

The Politics of Work

As has been shown, the politics of work included the right to work, to equal pay and conditions, and the right to representation. The First World War did more to illustrate the difficulties women faced over these issues than to resolve them. Inevitably, labour movement women, through women's trade unions and the SJC, were at the forefront in demanding these rights, in wartime and post-war organizations. The Trades Union Congress (TUC) and the new, large, male-dominated general unions did little to help, but the SJC could contact women workers through its own vast network and conduct parliamentary lobbies in its own right. The SJC's extended campaign in the 1930s to provide representation for domestic workers was a case in point. The militancy of the female labour force has, as Sue Bruley writes, remained hidden; Bruley cites the case of the 1932 five-week strike of half a million cotton workers, 50 per cent of whom were women.[39]

Differing attitudes to the politics of work were the basis of one of the biggest controversies within the women's network: that of protective legislation. Labour women had worked for the passage of the 1909 Trades Boards Acts, which regulated pay and conditions in trades such as chainmaking and lacemaking, and women workers had engaged in industrial action to secure their wages under these Acts. Knowing the health and safety risks women of the working classes faced when dealing with dangerous materials such as wartime munitions or inflammable celluloid, abortifacients such as lead, and the risks of respiratory diseases and tenosynovitis in the garment trade, Labour women were firmly behind protection. NUSEC was originally opposed but split on the issue, some favouring protection where women in a trade demanded regulation, the majority agreeing that it was the trade that should be regulated rather than the woman. This sounded reasonable but begged the question that it was female trades where conditions were very poor and where the workers were the worst organized, partly because of the small workshops and homework that pertained, outside even the existing regulations. Other organizations such as the Open Door Council were strongly opposed to protection as restrictive of women's right to work and capacity to bargain.

This controversy has sometimes been understood as Labour women prioritizing class issues versus feminists prioritizing gender issues. It might rather be seen as a case of women with different experiences struggling to negotiate citizenship rights that would be meaningful to the women they represented. The difference lay in perceptions of the subjects of the rights. For Labour women the subjects were disadvantaged women who needed the right of protection from exploitation. For other women campaigners the subjects were enfranchised female citizens whose right to work, equal with that of men, had to be upheld. The relation of citizen to state in the context of a changing labour force was at issue. The Open Door Council aimed at gender-neutral citizenship but failed to deal with the problem of how to empower working-class women in the sweated workshops and new light industries of a capitalist economy. Labour women understood the difficulties of such women's position but failed to deal with the typification of women as vulnerable that was the obverse of protective legislation. Both sides lobbied Labour home secretaries and Labour women achieved a modicum of success, but women in protected trades remained disadvantaged in terms of pay and conditions.

Recent work has further emphasized the ways in which changes in the labour force affected perceptions of gender identity. It has long been accepted that women's growing employment in light industry, of which the celluloid trade was an example, together with widespread unemployment in the traditionally male sphere of heavy industry, broke down the gender segregation of the labour force. Labour women in the 1920s and 1930s also emphasized that the continued operation of the marriage bar meant that the industrial female labour force was a young one; older women were often restricted to homework or low-skilled jobs such as cleaning. Sally Alexander has shown how the growth of the new female labour force built on the experience of women taking over men's jobs in the First World War to profoundly affect working men, who feared that with the loss of their jobs they lost the basis of their masculine identity and its attendant privileges: 'Men's fears of not being wanted, of being displaced, of women taking men's jobs, ran through the memories of the twenties and thirties, and were confirmed by official statistics'. Trade unions, in opposing equal pay and birth control, sought to promote reactionary gender stereotypes. Unemployed men's losses included domestic powers, such as the freedom to decide how much of their income to contribute to household expenses. This was compounded by women taking on the role of negotiating with Poor Law authorities. However, despite their experience in negotiating with the authorities, gender stereotyping affected the participation of women in the unemployed workers' movement wherein, outside the textile areas, they remained underrepresented. Alexander argues that trade unions, civil servants and politicians, in dealing with unemployment, were also addressing what it meant to be a citizen, the relationship between the individual and the state and their respective rights and duties: 'They were searching for a more individual definition of citizenship'.[40]

Conclusion

The differing ideas of citizenship illustrated by the politics of work, and revealed also by perceptions of women as warriors, in Ireland, and attached to First World War troops as aides, mothers and wives, as nationalists, as members of an imperial state, accompanied women's struggle for equal enfranchisement with men, all part of the huge canvas on which women's politics from 1900 to 1939 were painted. By no means all of the issues which women addressed have been covered in this overview; women's international politics, for instance, included the struggle against fascism, which is represented elsewhere in this volume. However, the theme of citizenship was fundamental to women's political engagement from 1900 to 1939. As Sandra Stanley Holton's historiography of the suffrage movement has shown, the great commitment to the suffrage cause inspired enquiry into women's relationship to the state which extended both back in time and into the future. Enfranchisement was a prime goal: without the vote women were explicitly excluded from political participation. Once the vote was won, women continued their struggle for full civil, social and political emancipation, within personal relations, at work, and in public life. Some women fought out these issues within political parties and as representatives of the latter; others preferred to work outside the party political arena. These issues and their method of achievement continue to be controversial.

To describe women's collective political participation, the term 'women's network' has been used, illustrating both the variety of the different women's groups and their links. The term 'women's movement' would be equally accurate but has a special meaning for second-wave feminists, indicating the sisterhood which characterized the feminism of the 1970s and which failed to deal with difference. Seeking to apply this term anachronistically led to the misconception that the first women's 'movement' disappeared after 1918. The more recent terminology of 'waves' of feminist activity is a more useful historical tool, allowing the longevity of women's political participation to be appreciated. Equally, by implying that feminism is a historical construct that changes through time, and that women campaign for such goals and by such methods as seem appropriate in their own particular circumstances, the newer terminology prevents the historian from anachronistic value judgements, that one past group was 'more' or 'less' feminist than another. In the period 1900–39, women coped with competing priorities in a way that has only recently been fully appreciated. It is evident that women of different backgrounds and opposing party politics as well as those opposed to party politics managed to work together. They presented differing views of gender identity while challenging traditional and disempowering stereotypes. As Sue Bruley writes, the feminist challenge to historiography has been a big project:

> This enables us to view feminine identity as an historical construction which has been malleable and shifting over time, has been reworked and renegotiated, adapting to changing pressures and challenges.[41]

NOTES

1   J. Hannam, 'Women and politics', in J. Purvis, ed., *Women's History: Britain, 1850–1945* (London, 1995), p. 217.

2   J. Alberti, *Beyond Suffrage: Feminists in War and Peace* (London, 1989); R. Lister, *Citizenship: Feminist Perspectives* (London, 1997); J. J. Pettman, *Worlding Women* (London, 1996), pp. 37ff. This chapter does not cover women's international politics; see Collette, *The International Faith* (Andover, 1998). For Labour women see Collette, *For Labour and for Women: The Women's Labour League, 1906–1918* (Manchester, 1989) and 'Questions of gender', in B. Brivati and R. Heffernan, eds, *The Labour Party: A Centenary History* (London, 2000).

3   K. Cowman, 'Women's suffrage campaigns in Britain', *Women's History Review*, 9, no. 4 (2000), review of five recent books, p. 816.

4   S. Bruley, *Women in Britain since 1900* (London, 1999), pp. 27, 35.

5   C. Midgely, 'Ethnicity, race and empire', in Purvis, ed., *Women's History*, p. 252.

6   U. Masson, '"Political conditions in Wales are quite different . . .": party politics and votes for women in Wales, 1912–1915', *Women's History Review*, 9, no. 2 (2000), pp. 369–88, passim.

7   M. D. Pugh, 'Politicians and the women's vote, 1914–18', *History*, 59 (Oct. 1974); P. Summerfield, 'Women and war in the twentieth century', in Purvis, ed., *Women's History*, p. 318; Bruley, *Women in Britain*, p. 50; J. Purvis and S. S. Holton, eds, *Votes for Women* (London, 2000), p. 25.

8   M. D. Pugh, *Women and the Women's Movement in Britain* (London, 2000), p. 8.

9   S. S. Holton, 'The making of suffrage history', in Purvis and Holton, eds, *Votes for Women*, passim, pp. 22, 28.

10   M. G. Roberts, *A Woman of Vision: Marion Phillips MP* (Wrexham, 2000), p. 79.

11   L. G. de Pauw, keynote speech, Fourth Annual Holt History Conference, West Virginia University, October 2000.

12   S. R. Grayzel, ' "The outward and visible sign of her patriotism": women, uniforms and national service during the First World War', *Twentieth Century British History*, 8, no. 2 (1997).

13   L. Ryan, ' "Furies" and "die hards": women and Irish Republicanism in the early twentieth century', *Gender and History*, 11, no. 2 (July 1999).

14   C. Cullerton, *Working-class Culture, Women and Britain, 1914–1921* (London, 2000), p. 10.

15   Alberti, *Beyond Suffrage*, pp. 39–122, NUSEC aims cited p. 91.

16   Ibid., p. 164. See A. Nye, *Philosophia* (London, 1994), p. xv: 'If civilisation is male in its very constitutive structures, there is no medium for women's thoughts but men's thoughts; revised, corrected, but still categories, methods, arguments borrowed from men . . .'

17   Lister, *Citizenship*, passim.

18   H. Jones, *Women in British Public Life, 1914–1950: Gender, Power and Social Policy* (Harlow, 2000), p. 133.

19   C. Law, *Suffrage and Power: The Women's Movement 1918–1928* (London, 1997), p. 6.

20   Ibid., pp. 6–7.

21   C. Beaumont, 'Citizens not feminists: the boundary negotiated between citizenship and feminism in mainstream women's organisations in England, 1928–39', *Women's History Review*, 9, no. 2 (2000), passim, p. 411.

22   Alberti, *Beyond Suffrage*, p. 186.

23   Public Information Office, House of Commons, Fact Sheet No. 5, *Women in the House of Commons* (Oct. 1995), p. 3.

24   Ibid., pp. 7–9, appendix D, p. 20.

25   B. Harrison, *Prudent Revolutionaries: Portraits of British Feminists Between the Wars* (Oxford, 1987), p. 75. It is ironic that, to show respect to her husband, Margaret Wintringham reputedly refused to speak during her 1921 election campaign (Public Information Office, *Women in the House of Commons*, p. 4).

26   Roberts, *Woman of Vision*, pp. 156, 195.

27   Jones, *Women in British Public Life*, pp. 133–4.

28   Ibid., pp. 10–11, 134–5, 150–5; Bruley, *Women in Britain*, p. 85.

29   Alberti, *Beyond Suffrage*, p. 160.

30   Harrison, *Prudent Revolutionaries*, p. 80, noted three occasions when women MPs acted together: in November 1930 on feminist reforms of nationality law; in 1932, eleven (of fifteen) women MPs voted against withdrawal of unemployment benefit from married women; in 1936, all women who voted except the duchess of Atholl were in favour of equal pay.

31   Law, *Suffrage and Power*, p. 147.

32   Ibid., pp. 127–8.

33   Jones, *Women in British Public Life*, p. 135.

34   Harrison, *Prudent Revolutionaries*, p. 131.

35   Jones, *Women in British Public Life*, p. 136.

36   A. Wollacott, ' "Khaki fever" and its control: gender, class, age and sexual morality in the British homefront in the First World War', *Journal of Contemporary History*, 29, no. 2 (April 1994).

37   Bruley, *Women in Britain*, p. 78. Lesley Hall's opinion is that inclusion of indecency by females in the 1921 Criminal Law Amendment Bill was an attempt to wreck the bill.

38   L. A. Hall, *Sex, Gender and Social Change in Britain since 1880* (Basingstoke, 2000), pp. 129–30.

39   Bruley, *Women in Britain*, p. 65.

40   S. Alexander, 'Men's fears and women's work: responses to unemployment in London between the wars', *Gender and History*, 12, no. 2 (July 2000), passim, p. 403.

41   Bruley, *Women in Britain*, p. 1.

FURTHER READING

Alberti, J., *Eleanor Rathbone* (London, 1996).

Collette, C. and Bird, S., eds, *Jews, Labour and the Left* (Andover, 2000).

Graves, P., *Labour Women: Women in British Working-class Politics, 1918–1939* (Cambridge, 1994).

Holmes, J. and Urqhart, D., eds, *Coming into the Light: The Work, Politics and Religion of Women in Ulster, 1840–1940* (Belfast, 1994).

Hunt, K., 'Negotiating the boundaries of the domestic: British socialist women and the politics of consumption', *Women's History Review*, 9, no. 2 (2000).

Jeffreys, S., *The Spinster and her Enemies: Feminism and Sexuality, 1880–1939* (London, 1997).

John, A., *Our Mothers' Land: Chapters in Welsh Women's History, 1830–1939* (Cardiff, 1991).

Leneman, L., *A Guid Cause: The Women's Suffrage Movement in Scotland* (Aberdeen, 1991).

Oldfield, S., ed., *This Working Day World: Women's Lives and Culture in Britain, 1884–1945* (London, 1994).

Scott, G., *Feminism and the Politics of Working Women: The Women's Cooperative Guild, 1880s to the Second World War* (London, 1997).

PART II

Britain and the World

CHAPTER NINE

Immigrants, Sojourners and Refugees: Minority Groups in Britain, 1900–1939

ANNE J. KERSHEN

This chapter sets out to explore the diversity of Britain's minority groups during a period when Britain was perceived as fundamentally monocultural and when the notion of Britishness was the very essence of Englishness, the image of the Englishman (never the Englishwoman) being either that of a cricket-playing, liberal, white Christian, honourable gentleman or a plain-speaking, brave, warm-beer-drinking, God-fearing, working man. The concept of a multicultural Britain, incorporating multilingualism and religious plurality, was, even as late as the outbreak of the Second World War, still almost half a century away. In spite of this, within mainland Britain in the years between 1900 and 1939, there was an impressive variety of minority groups. In 1901 the Decennial Census recorded 0.7 per cent of the total population as alien; by 1931, as second-generation British-born began to outnumber their immigrant parents, this figure had dropped to 0.4 per cent. (The advent of war made it impossible to carry out the next Decennial Census and therefore we have no records for 1941. It is probable that with the arrival of refugees from Nazism and a small number of others in the 1930s, the percentage would have increased.) However, before we can embark on a more detailed examination of the nature of that kaleidoscope of minority groups, we need to understand the categories within which they fall and the ways in which the perception of those categories has altered in recent years.

At the outbreak of the Second World War the minority communities in Britain could be divided into three. First were those whose origins lay in the arrival and settlement of immigrants, the definition of immigrant in this context being understood as an individual who had taken a measured and rational appraisal of the benefits of moving from place of birth to 'elsewhere', in this case Britain. Within this category we can include, amongst others, eastern European Jews, who arrived in the late nineteenth and early twentieth centuries, and Germans and Italians, who settled in Britain from the middle of the nineteenth century. In the majority of cases the decision to move was based on economic rationality, which encouraged movement to a place where there were (or were *believed* to be) employment opportunities that would provide some form of financial security and future. As proposed by one of the earliest theorists of migration, the geographer E. G. Ravenstein, in the mid-1880s, these were the 'push-and-pull' factors, the 'push' being inadequate conditions at home, the 'pull' being the opportunity for improvement elsewhere. More recently, Steve Castles and Godula Kosack criticized the push and pull theory for its neo-classical values, for its being too dependent on rational choice, and for its being ahistorical and simplistic. Push and pull, they believe, ignores the operation of a capitalist society in which labour moves around to satisfy the aims and ambitions of the capitalist's needs, the Marxist view being that 'labour migration is a form of development aid given by poor countries to rich countries'.[1] Though we have little evidence as to what exactly the pre-Second World War immigrants included in their equation, a more balanced approach would be to suggest that the 'push and pull' theory is an ideal starting point from which to develop more complex theories that can accommodate the changes, vagaries and government restrictions of the postmodern world.

The second group embraces those who fall under the heading of sojourner or transient, people whose period away from home is intended to be temporary, either whilst they study, for example transient students, particularly those from Africa and India, who came to Britain in the early part of the twentieth century in order to improve their learning and prepare themselves for careers or political office in their home countries, or sojourners from the 'lower classes', who were determined to work long and hard in order to make enough money to return home as 'rich men of high status'. A sojourner, as defined by one commentator, is 'a person whose mental orientation is towards the home country . . . the full and final achievement of his objective . . . to be in his place of origin'.[2] In this latter category we can include sojourners from Asia and the Caribbean, who could be found living in Britain in the early years of the twentieth century. However, whilst nearly all the transient students returned home and fulfilled their ambitions – though some Indian and African doctors did remain in Britain, often having married British women – the sojourners who failed to make their fortunes all too frequently discovered that the reality did not live up to the dream and that the sojourn metamorphosed into permanent residency.

The third and final category is that of refugee. In 1933 the League of Nations defined refugee status as that of individuals who 'no longer enjoy the protection of their government'.[3] The term refugee itself was, until the late 1930s, perceived as historical rather than contemporary. Until the First World War, and at times even beyond it, the word refugee conjured up images of the Huguenots fleeing Catholic oppression in the seventeenth century rather than twentieth-century men, women and children escaping from the threat of war and invasion. It was in the interwar years that the reality of the desperate, and all too often unwelcome, presence of the refugee was forced home. Michael Marrus estimates that between 1918 and 1938, 4,000,000 people were forced to seek refuge. In Britain those seeking sanctuary from the Bolsheviks, the Nazis and the Spanish fascists, though all refugees, were identified in different ways. The 4,000 to 5,000 White Russians who arrived in 1918 were known, somewhat euphemistically, as émigrés, whilst refugees from Nazism who began arriving in Britain from the early 1930s were labelled 'alien immigrants' by certain government departments. In contrast, children brought to Britain from the Basque country during the Spanish Civil War, though acknowledged as refugees, were most frequently referred to as the 'Spanish children'.

In the past quarter of a century there has been a growing literature on the theme of refugees, and various attempts have been made to draw a line between the 'refugee' and the 'immigrant'. Danièle Joly and Robin Cohen, writing in 1989, suggested that '[i]mmigrants cherish the myth of return . . . for refugees the possibility of returning home is less feasible'.[4] However, it could be argued that refugees do cherish the myth of return, one to a land free from persecution and persecutors. For some the myth is maintained in the retention of culture and language – many Huguenots in the seventeenth and eighteenth centuries and refugees from Nazism in the 1930s clung to their language and their culture in their new-found homeland. At the beginning of the twenty-first century, as European nations tighten their controls on entry procedures, the dividing line has become blurred, and an increasing number of refugees are being reclassified as economic migrants.

The minority groups present in Britain during the first four decades of the twentieth century cover the spectrum of immigrant, sojourner, transient and refugee. Within this chapter one phrase – *ethnic minority* – has been intentionally omitted. It is a phrase that has come into usage only since the late 1960s, and would be out of place in the pre-1940s world. However, several of the groups that feature below would, under today's terminology, fit well into an ethnic category. Ethnic is currently defined as 'origin by birth or descent rather than nationality'. Whilst not always sharing the same nationality, some peoples, for example the Jews, share the same history, customs, codes, rituals, ceremonies and, of course, religion. Alternatively, as in the case of the citizens of the old Yugoslavia, people sharing the same nationality might well not be of the same ethnic origin. Therefore, in the context of this chapter, the Jews from eastern Europe and those from Germany may have carried different nationalities but in an ethnic sense would have been included under the same category, whilst German Jews and German Christian immigrants and refugees might be separated by ethnicity or linked by nationality. To avoid such complexity, writing of an era when the description was not applied, I have referred throughout to minority groups rather than *ethnic* minority groups, even though it could be argued that, in almost every example to be found below, the minority group was subordinate to the majority and in many instances was 'held in low esteem by the dominant society'.[5]

1900–1914: A Promised Land?

In 1901 the population of England, Wales and Scotland totalled 36,999,946. Of that number, 248,560 (225,933 in England and Wales) were, according to the Decennial Census, aliens. In terms of nationalities the alien groups included Germans, eastern Europeans (including Russians, Russian Poles and Romanians, almost 95 per cent of whom were Jewish), Italians, Chinese, Poles, Indians and Africans. In addition there were 631,629 Irish men and women resident (205,064 in Scotland). What had drawn these diverse nationalities to Britain, and how were they received?

With the exception of a small number of students, about 336 Indian and thirty African, predominantly studying law and medicine,[6] those coming from India and Africa, in common with the other minority groups mentioned above, had been drawn to Britain because of the economic opportunities they believed were to be found in her cities, towns and docks. There had been Indian seamen present in Britain since the eighteenth century. These men were mainly Lascars from the regions of Bengal and Sylhet – the latter today part of the nation-state of Bangladesh, which was established in 1971. Although the Lascar sailors would have classified themselves as transients, or at best sojourners, inevitably some became permanent residents, having cohabited with, or married, British women. Job opportunities in the docks also attracted African seamen, some of whom left their ships in favour of a shore life in the dockland areas of London, Cardiff and Liverpool. These small communities created a nucleus which would expand when soldiers from the West Indies and Africa stayed on after serving in the First World War.

The Chinese community was another minority group whose first point of settlement was the docklands. In 1901 it was estimated that over 61 per cent of the 767 members of the Chinese London community were seamen. During the next decade seamen who had formed lasting relationships settled permanently in Britain. Within ten years their economic epicentre had changed, and the now 1,319-strong Chinese community was actively engaged in the restaurant and laundry business. The first Chinese restaurant was opened in 1907, the first Chinese laundry having opened in Poplar in 1901; within thirty years there were 800 laundries in the capital alone. In spite of its small size and relative invisibility, the Chinese community was subject to racism. Chinese seamen were accused of being strikebreakers and of underselling their labour. On the moral front they were attacked for their propensity for gambling, opium smoking and seduction of young girls. The perceived sexual threat posed by those from minority groups was a constant; eastern European Jews were condemned as brothel owners and white slave traders, whilst in his novel *Sissero's Return*, Henry Nevinson highlighted the envy and dislike that surrounded the Negro who married an East End girl – white women with black partners were frequently abused in the streets. At the other end of the social scale, Indian students were portrayed as 'devious, sexual predators with designs on the unprotected female population of Britain'.[7] Racism extended to academic life. Oxford operated a covert colour bar and students looking for lodgings were all too frequently told, 'We don't take any blacks here'. After 1918, 'noticeably few Indian students . . . managed to secure any prizes or scholarships'.[8]

It was not only the personal and local which the alien threatened. During the closing decades of the nineteenth century British life became infused with notions of empire and racial superiority. Colin Holmes suggests that, following the unification of Germany in 1870, there was a discernible sense of xenophobia directed towards the German community, the second largest of Britain's minority groups (the largest being eastern European). The 1901 Decennial Census recorded the presence of 50,599 German men, women and children living in Britain. Seeking to avoid military conscription and the aftermath of political revolution, they had been drawn to London by the opportunities for clerical work, small-scale retailing and a variety of artisanal trades. By 1911 it was estimated that London's German community totalled 26,920. The industrial cities of the north too exercised their pull, and significant German communities were established in Manchester, Bradford and Liverpool. The Bradford community dated back to the 1840s and the arrival of textile merchants from Germany. At the close of the nineteenth century the city could boast of its 'Little Germany' quarter. Belfast, Dundee and Northampton also attracted German migrants who, in addition to the economic activities referred to above, worked in teaching, finance and hairdressing. Though the German immigrants integrated commercially, they retained a sense of *volk*, establishing their own social and political clubs, their own hospitals and churches. However low key and industrious, the

German community was still the subject of xenophobic responses, its members considered by certain elements of the host society as being 'unclean' and a threat to native job security.[9]

Germans were not the only ones accused of job stealing. Though Lucio Sponza suggests that 'most of the work they [the Italians] engaged in was not pursued by British labour',[10] Italian migrants in Britain were castigated by those who believed that their participation in the service trades – Italians worked as waiters, cooks, hairdressers and domestic servants – was unfair competition. It is clear that, by 1911, Italian immigrants in London were heavily engaged in the food and catering trades. In London alone there were 1,600 Italian waiters, 900 chefs, 1,400 bakers and confectioners and 500 café and restaurant owners. It was in the development of the ice-cream industry that the Italian migrants excelled. For example, in 1911 there were more than 1,000 Italian ice-cream shops in Scotland.

In common with so many migrants, Italians had been drawn to Britain by economic dreams. London was the beacon, and had been since the eighteenth century when the area around Clerkenwell became known as 'Little Italy'. Gradually the community spread to Holborn, Soho and King's Cross, where the Italian hospital and church were established. Italians also settled in south Wales where by 1921 there were 1,500 resident Italians, and by 1938 300 Italian-run cafés.[11] But though the Welsh fondly referred to 'our Italian friends', these migrants were not always regarded as such. There were those, such as a witness to the 1903 Royal Commission on Aliens, who reported that Italian ice creams were made in 'filthy conditions', and others who associated Italians with criminality and anarchism. At best, in the years before the First World War, the British attitude towards the Italian community could be described as ambivalent.

In addition to the minority European communities already noted, Britain provided a haven for Lithuanians and Poles seeking a future away from the land confiscation and Russification policies of the Tsar. By 1914 it was estimated that there were 11,000 Lithuanians resident in Britain, 7,000 living in Scotland, the majority working in the mines and the iron and steel works of Lanarkshire and Ayrshire. In common with so many other migrant labourers, they too were charged with undercutting, blacklegging, immorality and poor health.

The largest continental minority group resident in Britain before the First World War was the Jewish eastern European community, which in itself formed a part of the country's Jewish community. At the beginning of the twentieth century the Jewish community of Britain totalled approximately 250,000[12] and was composed of (1) a seemingly ever-increasing number of eastern European immigrants and (2) an established community of anglicized and British-born Jews whose roots in Britain could be traced back, in some cases, to the seventeenth century. This group itself could be subdivided into an upper class/aristocracy whose members held cabinet office and socialized with the Prince of Wales, an emergent middle class of liberal professionals, bankers and merchants, and a poorer artisan and working class. There was a clear geographic and socio-economic gulf between rich and poor, the more affluent London Jews being known as the 'West Enders', their poorer co-religionists inhabiting the overcrowded East End. There were smaller Jewish communities in a number of other towns and cities in Britain, including Belfast, Birmingham, Glasgow, Leeds, Liverpool, Manchester, Portsmouth and Sunderland.

The most popular form of economic activity carried out by the Jewish immigrant was tailoring. In Leeds, during the second half of the nineteenth century, what had been a small Leeds Jewish community expanded as a direct result of the recruitment of workshop hands from Russia-Poland by Leeds Jewish master-tailors responding to the needs of the city's burgeoning men's wholesale garment industry. In spite of the belief that foreign Jewish tailors were 'taking the jobs of Englishmen', Anne Kershen's research has shown that Jewish tailors in the Leeds subdivisional men's tailoring trade were doing jobs native-born tailors had refused. In London, the women's wholesale tailoring trade, which gave employment to thousands of English and foreign tailors, owed its origins to Morris Cohen, an immigrant from Russia.[13] Other eastern European immigrants worked as capmakers, shoe- and slippermakers and cabinet-makers. In Manchester, where the Jewish community's roots could be traced back to the eighteenth century, newer arrivals found work in the city's waterproof garment industry which, according to Manchester Jewish historian Bill Williams, was second only to the tailoring trade for Jewish commercial activity and employment.

The eastern European Jews came west in search of the *golde medinah* (the golden land). More than half of those who arrived in British ports were in fact in transit for America: it was estimated that of the 750,000 eastern Europeans who arrived in Britain between 1881 and 1911, only between 105,000 and 120,000 settled per-manently. The 1901 Census recorded the presence of 86,240 eastern Europeans in England and Wales and 10,373 in Scotland (of that total, perhaps 4,500 were non-Jews). This represented an increase of more than 55,000 on the previous Census. The concentrated visibility of these foreigners on the streets of East London gave rise to heightened anti-alienism. It was not only in London that tensions could run high. In 1911, in Tredegar, south Wales, there were riots over Jewish rackrenting and the overpricing of goods in Jewish shops. But London was the epicentre of anti-alienism and, in 1903, the government appointed an Aliens Commission to investi-gate the impact of the alien presence in response to demands from trade unionists and politicians such as Major William Eden Evans Gordon, member of parliament for Stepney and founder of the British Brothers League in 1901, for an end to pauper alien immigration. The findings of the Commission resulted in the construction and passage, under a Conservative government, of the 1905 Aliens Act. Though far less restrictive than the anti-alienists had hoped for – a watered-down interpretation of earlier versions – it was, however, the first such Act to be passed in Britain in peacetime and the starting point from which all subsequent Acts would evolve. The ever-open door to minorities was starting to close.

All the above minority groups have one characteristic in common: they were foreigners, outsiders whose roots lay in different nations and different cultures. The final minority community to be discussed in this section has a more oblique status. Acknowledged by Holmes as the largest immigrant minority in Britain,[14] until 1921/2, irrespective of whether they came from the north or south of the island, Irish immigrants held British citizenship. In spite of this, they were 'self-segregating' outsiders. As Lynn Hollen Lees has said, 'mobility did not produce geographic assimi-lation',[15] nor, according to Edward P. Thompson, did immigration produce a subject minority.[16] The Irish in mainland Britain frequented their own pubs and churches, read their own newspapers, followed their own politics and lived in Irish enclaves close to the docks in London, Cardiff and Liverpool. In short, they maintained their own subculture and, as such, if not perceived as alien in the same manner as the Jews, Lithuanians or Lascars, were still racially stereotyped as the Paddy, a heavy-drinking, disease-carrying Irish burden on the poor rates: 'intemperate, improvident, violent, totally ignorant of any notions of hygiene, mendacious and undependable'. In addition to criticism of their behaviour, the phenotypical characteristics of the Irish were used to add insult to injury. They were portrayed as 'ape-faced, small headed . . . unmistakable width of mouth, immense expanse of chin and forehead villainous low'.[17] The Irish worked longer and harder and for less wages than their English counterparts and were active and productive trade unionists. Even so, Holmes questions whether the Irish contribution to the British economy, as road and railway builders and domestic servants, may not have been exaggerated.[18] The Irish community in Britain was viewed as essentially working class. However, there was a small middle/professional class that included such literary luminaries as George Bernard Shaw and Oscar Wilde.

By 1901 the total number of Irish-born residents in Britain was, according to the Census, 631,631 (a reduction of 174,086 on the peak 1861 figure of 805,717). By 1911 the total had dropped still further to 550,030. Two factors account for this reduction in numbers: (1) the overwhelming pull of America at a time when the journey to the United States had reduced in price, and (2) the increasing number of mainland-born second-generation Irish. M. A. G. Ó Tuathaigh suggests that by the outbreak of the First World War, the Irish immigrant working man and woman had won a measure of grudging acceptance in British society.[19] Having gradually accustomed itself to city life, by the outbreak of war the Irish community in Britain was of an urban nature. This, together with a degree of interaction with the host community and the mass arrival of eastern Europeans, was instrumental in helping to destroy some of the myths. The following quotation is indicative of the fickle nature of racism:

> It used to be a street occupied by poor English and Irish people. In the afternoons you would see the steps inside cleaned and the women with their clean white aprons . . . now it is a seething mess of refuse and filth . . . they [the Jews] are such an unpleasant, indecent people.[20]

By the outbreak of the First World War the population of mainland Britain totalled 40,838,867, of which 0.75 per cent were 'foreigners' or 'not British-born'. The majority had been drawn by the dream of a promised land in which they and their children would find a better life. For many this was to be the case, only the achievement of that dream would take not months but years – years that would be coloured by discrimination, xenophobia and racism as the receiving society reacted with concern and, all too often, ignorance towards the presence of minority groups within British society.

1914–1939: British, Alien and Refugee

The outbreak of war in August 1914 did not put an end to the growth and diversity of minority groups in Britain. What changed were the push factors and freedom of entry. From 1914 onwards those wishing to enter Britain, immigrant, sojourner or refugee, had to conform to the requirements of the Aliens Acts passed in 1914 and 1919. The remaining twenty-five years of our period saw acceptance and rejection, discrimination and racism, integration and assimilation, become part of the way of life for minority groups in Britain.

In war

The outbreak of the First World War opened the door for the passage of an emergency Aliens Act which put an immediate end to the mass arrival of economic migrants. This new legislation 'finally swept away the vestiges of the traditional laissez-faire approach',[21] separating enemy alien from friendly alien and creating a benchmark for the treatment of members of Britain's minority communities.

If war put a stop to the arrival of immigrants who had made considered and rational decisions and choices about their pattern of migration, it brought to Britain's shores the first large-scale arrival of refugees for more than 230 years. Refugees are defined by Marrus, with more empathy than the League of Nations in the 1930s, as 'people obliged by war or persecution to leave their dwellings and seek refuge abroad'.[22] In the first year of the war 250,000 Belgians were offered refuge. Yet their experience, as a minority group living in Britain, albeit for a short time, has been marginalized by the majority of commentators. Perhaps, as Tony Kushner and Katherine Knox explain, this is because they were ephemeral, 'they disappeared as quickly as they had come'.[23] However, for the brief period of their stay on British soil, by 1915 more Belgians were leaving than arriving, they constituted a significant minority community and elicited a mixed response from the British people. The overall refugee body was urban, principally Flemish and essentially professional and white collar. Initially, they received a very warm welcome. Herbert Samuel, president of the Local Government Board, announced a programme of 'State hospitality to the Belgian refugees'. Government involvement was forthcoming for two reasons, first as an altruistic response to people who had been invaded by 'the Hun' and, second, as a means of control in order to avoid friction with British labour. The British government was determined that the Belgian presence should create the minimum of disruption that prevailing conditions allowed. A dispersal policy was adopted; women were found employment as domestic servants and men either took up military service or engaged in war work. In spite of this, as the hardships of war struck home, protesting British voices were heard. In response it was made abundantly clear that at the war's end the Belgian refugees in Britain would be repatriated as rapidly as possible. The 1921 Decennial Census provides clear evidence that the promise was kept; the presence of only 9,892 Belgians was recorded, the rest had gone home.

For some minorities war enhanced economic opportunity and 'pulled' a number of African and Indian seamen to Britain's shores. During the period 1914–18 the black and Asian population of Britain expanded as African and Lascar seamen either enlisted in the British navy or found employment in the merchant navy or munitions factories. In spite of their eagerness to fight for the mother country, Britain adopted a racist policy towards black and Asian servicemen; 'commissions for men of mixed blood were bitterly resented and at no point . . . were black troops allowed to engage in front line activity in the European theatre'.[24]

The main targets for vilification during the war years were Germans, Austrians and eastern European Jews. Immediately following the declaration of war all non-naturalized Germans were designated enemy aliens, though, as we shall see below, the general public took little note of the distinction made by the acquisition of British citizenship. Government policy was aimed primarily at removing enemy aliens who were perceived as a danger to the state and interning all German/Austrian males of military service age. Females, though not interned, were designated, together with the young, the sick and the elderly, for repatriation – unless they could persuade officials otherwise; between 1914 and 1919 some 23,571 Germans were repatriated.[25] Within a brief time the very sight or sound of anything German became unacceptable – roads with German names were renamed and the British royal family (albeit not until 1917 – the year of the Russian Revolution and the assassination of George V's cousin, the tsar) changed its title from House of Saxe-Coburg to that of Windsor. In the East End of London, particularly around Bethnal Green where there had been a German community for many decades, shops and businesses owned by Germans and Jews with German-sounding names were vandalized. Attacks on all things German continued throughout the war; in the first year violence flared in London, Crewe and Liverpool. Naturalized Germans sought to publicize their loyalty to their adopted homeland as those of German origin were expelled from British institutions. By the war's end, 'the German communities that had thrived throughout the Victorian and Edwardian years'[26] had been destroyed. Once lit the xenophobic flame spread. In spite of the fact that Chinese workers were helping the allied war effort in France,[27] Chinese seamen in Liverpool and other British ports were attacked.

The other main target was the eastern European Jews. Added to traditional anti-alien/anti-Semitic tensions were those created by the (non-naturalized) eastern European Jews' reluctance to volunteer. Not covered by the introduction of conscription in 1916, they saw no need to support an army that was fighting alongside Russian troops who had been their tormentors. The British public had little sympathy, choosing instead to believe the aliens were cowards and profiteers who benefited from the absence of British servicemen. In 1917, following the convention that demanded that eastern Europeans enlist either with the British or the Russian army (prior to the Revolution), tensions erupted into violence in the Leeds Leylands and in the East End of London where, in Bethnal Green, 5,000 people rioted. It should be stressed that, in contrast, British Jewry enlisted with pride and alacrity following the outbreak of war. Approximately 13.8 per cent of British Jewry served in the armed forces, compared with the national figure of 11.5 per cent.[28] Peace brought no lessening in anti-alienism and in 1919 there was little difficulty in passing a revised Aliens Act, which imposed far more stringent controls on alien entry and residence. No one could have foreseen that those to suffer most from the restrictions would be German Jews fleeing the nation they had fought for less than twenty years before.

In peace

Concerns over the threat of Bolshevism plus residual wartime xenophobia enabled the British government to pass a newly revised Aliens Act which, amongst other clauses, decreed that in order to enter the country, those unable to support themselves economically were required to obtain work permits. In response to new controls and the interwar depression, numbers of immigrants fell and, with a few noted exceptions, those seeking to enter Britain were refugees from Communism and fascism.

The peace did not produce 'a land fit for heroes', nor did it create a society free from xenophobia. Members of Britain's resident coloured and alien communities remained the objects of racist attacks and positive racism became a feature of British life. Only one year after the war had ended, the combination of unemployment and colour provided the touch paper for an outbreak of violence in Cardiff – a city which in 1911 was recorded as having the second highest number of foreign-born inhabitants after London. As the hardships and tensions increased, 'shots were fired and large mobs of whites began to attack blacks and their properties' in the area around the docks. Buildings were gutted and there was one fatality.[29] The clashes soon spread to the dockland areas of Liverpool and London; fortunately, in all three cities, as they had ignited, so the fires died down and peace was restored.

The working lives of the African, West Indian and Indian sailors in Britain were further jeopardized by the passage of the Special Restriction Order (or Coloured Seamen's Act) of 1925, which was a legislative reaction to the high level of unemployment in the docks. Black and Asian seamen were both target and tool. As a means of alleviating unemployment the government had agreed to subsidize merchant shipping if only British labour was employed. Black and Asian British nationals had to provide documentary evidence of their status and alien seamen were required to register at their local police station. By its very nature the Act was an iniquitous example of racial discrimination, victimizing many who had served Britain during the war, some of whom, though British-born, had been persuaded to register as alien in order to retain, or obtain, jobs at lower than the generally accepted rates of pay. Many of these men had no official proof of their British nationality and, as a result, were made redundant. Sporadic outbreaks of violence followed. Eventually, as a result of the work of Harold Moody, founder of the League of Coloured Peoples – one of a number of communal organizations founded by members of Britain's minority groups – the Act was withdrawn. However, in 1935, in the tail of the depression, the employment of British seamen was again prioritized. These were not the only examples of interwar 'institutional racism'. 'Hospitals would not employ' black nurses,[30] Jewish doctors found it very difficult to move up the medical ladder, and it was not until the threat of war became a reality in the late 1930s that agreement was reached to ensure that no colour bar would operate within the British armed forces. In addition under the darkening clouds of war, the armed forces confirmed that commissions *would* be available for black citizens and that, unlike the American paradigm, there would be no colour segregation.

In spite of Asian seamen suffering the effects of the depression, the Indian community did enjoy a level of expansion. During the 1920s, small numbers of Sikhs and Muslims arrived in Britain from the region of the Punjab. Initially they travelled all over Britain as pedlars and hawkers, much in the way the Jews had done 100 years before. According to Roger Ballard, 'by the end of the 1930s, small colonies of Punjabi peddlers . . . could be found in almost every British city'.[31] The interwar Indian community in Britain was essentially working class, the majority employed in the shipping industry. However, there was a minority middle class that included professionals, businessmen and even a Parsee Communist member of parliament for Battersea between 1922 and 1929.

Though blacks and Indians were subjected to both formal and informal discrimination, in the years directly following the First World War it was foreign Jews that were the prime target of government controls. Fears of the alien Jewish presence had been a powerful force in the passage of the 1919 Aliens Act. The repercussions of the Act changed the geography of London Jewry as, in the early 1920s, London County Council introduced its own discriminatory code for the 'alien' community. It would no longer provide them with jobs or homes, no longer rent them council accommodation or award them or their children scholarships to secondary schools. These restrictions, reversed in the 1930s, helped push Jewish East Enders out to the London suburbs. Encouraged by the boom in house-building, the availability of affordable mortgages and the development of the underground railway system, fledgling Jewish communities were established to the north, north-east and north-west of the capital, in suburbs such as Golders Green, Hendon, Willesden and Ilford. This movement to the suburbs was further aided by Hitler's blitzkrieg on the East End, his intention being to raze the docks and eliminate the Jewish community at one and the same time.

The coming to power of the Nazi regime in 1933 should have been a signal for the mass emigration of Germany's Jewish population, but, in reality, there was no 'automatic, progressive exodus'.[32] In the early years some perspicacious German Jews immigrated to Britain with sufficient funds to establish their own businesses. However, by 1938, German restrictions meant that Jews could take little, if any, capital or valuable items with them. In the aftermath of *Kristallnacht*, nearly all Jewish refugees needed work permits in order to gain entry and certain of the professions, particularly medicine and law, operated very tight controls. Some German Jewish academics were accepted, but it was mainly as gardeners, chauffeurs, domestic servants and odd job men that those adults who did find their way to Britain gained entry. As the war became imminent, Britain adopted a more tolerant approach to the plight of the German and Austrian Jews and a final attempt was made to rescue Jewish children whose parents had no hope of escape. Under the auspices of the Refugee Children's Movement, the *Kindertransport*, 9,354 children were brought to England. In all it is estimated that 56,000 Germans (50,000 Jews and 6,000 non-Jews) entered Britain in the years between 1933 and 1939. Though they augmented the Jewish community in Britain, in background and culture they were a different people and chose to retain their difference, and indeed their separation, from previous Jewish immigrants. The East End did not beckon and the newer Jewish settlers made their homes in the north-west of London. Very soon the suburbs of Golders Green and Hampstead became known by some as 'the German Consul in England'.

But if the victims of fascism and Nazism separated themselves from East End Jewry, the advocates of fascism did not. In a show of muscle and ideology, on 4 October 1936 Oswald Mosley attempted to make the East End of London his by marching his black-shirted supporters in phalanxes through its streets. The fascists were stopped by the combined forces of the Communists and Jews who determined that Mosley's men would not pass. The mythologized Battle of Cable Street that followed was one between the opponents of fascism and the police. Mosley and his men, somewhat shamefacedly, were turned back. At the end of that day it was made clear that whatever antipathies existed in Britain, the extremes of fascism would not prevail.

European fascism reached out to Britain in a variety of ways. Mussolini spotlighted the Italian expatriate community as one which, due to its commercial success, could be of benefit to the cause. By the 1930s the Italian community in Britain numbered some 22,000, many of whom ran small and successful businesses – cafés, restaurants, ice-cream factories and outlets. In 1933 the Association of Italian Ice-Cream Vendors boasted a national membership of 4,200.[33] Cheap Italian meals and 'luscious whips' provided an escape from the poverty of the depression. The largest Italian immigrant community remained in London, although by 1931 the Decennial Census for Scotland could record the presence of 4,842 Italians, the majority resident in Glasgow. But it was London that shone as a beacon of Italian success. According to Robin Palmer, in the interwar period 'London offered perhaps the most favourable environment for Italian migrants' and it was there that Mussolini's missionaries set out to 'fete and fund', supporting a variety of communal institutions as well as helping to establish an Italian School at Hyde Park Gate.

But the unacceptable face of fascism was omnipresent and, in 1937, it persuaded the British government to take in 3,826 Basque children who were caught up in the horrors of the Spanish Civil War. As with the reception of the Belgian refugees over twenty years earlier, the children were met with general sympathy. It was a short-lived community; by 1943 there were only some 411 refugees remaining in Britain. Augmented by the arrival of political, intellectual and professional exiles, they formed the nucleus of the small expatriate Spanish community that is to be found in Britain today.

Throughout the thirty-nine years covered by this chapter the Irish remained the largest immigrant group in Britain. By 1921 the total Irish population had reduced to 523,767 – 159,020 of that number resident in Scotland where, it has been suggested, Irish upward mobility was far more evident than elsewhere on the mainland. In common with so many other groups, the Irish community of Britain did not remain unaffected by the First World War. As Irish males enlisted and carried out vital government duties, their womenfolk were amongst the 1,500,000 females who took over the jobs of serving men. The fight for Irish Home Rule, at its height from 1916 to 1921, ran parallel with the war and the first few years of peace. As other minority groups became increasingly involved in local and national politics, Irish political energies were directed increasingly towards self-determination. In December 1922 the Irish Free State was created and subsequently there was to be a clear division between the 'aliens' from the Free State and the Northern Irish British citizens. In the years that followed the number of Irish migrants was low. Those who came between 1926 and 1936 were either Protestants, leaving the now Catholic Free State, or women seeking employment as their economic status deteriorated. Even here Irish cultural separatism was the pattern, though in later years there was an unavoidable process of integration, if not total assimilation. As David Fitzpatrick has said, by the interwar years, the Irish occupied '[a] curious middle place'.[34]

Conclusion

In the years between 1900 and 1939 Britain's minority groups covered a spectrum of culture, creed and colour, their geographic roots covering the globe from eastern Europe to Africa and from the Caribbean to Asia. With the few exceptions highlighted above, reasons for leaving 'home' and settling 'away' were economically based. For some permanent settlement had been part of the rationalization procedure, for others it came by default. For all but the fortunate few, the process of settlement, integration and assimilation was a tough rite of passage, marked by economic hardships and xenophobic/racist responses from state and society. Few, if any, groups escaped the more general accusations of job stealing and home stealing, whilst those considered sexually threatening and power seeking were more particularly selected. Racism and discrimination seem to have played a part in the history of all of those referred to above, and yet the majority stayed to make their homes in Britain. Why? To paraphrase the title of Holmes's book, was Britain a tolerant country? Clearly, there were examples of gross intolerance. As the economic cycle ebbed and flowed, the needs of the indigenous society were prioritized. As war threatened and was in full force, the (sometimes perceived rather than real) enemy was identified and outlawed, as, far more irrationally, were those whose skin colour and religion differed from those of the mainstream. In that sense it can be argued that Britain was (and continues to be) intolerant. And yet, for many incomers, most especially refugees from Nazism, Britain was seen as a haven and, certainly in the years under examination in this chapter, one of the more tolerant countries in the civilized world. As stated at the outset, Britain is now a multicultural society. The roots of that society were being grounded in the first thirty-nine years of the twentieth century. With the benefit of hindsight, we must acknowledge the significance of those years and the contributions made to Britain by the diverse members of the minority groups resident during that time.

NOTES

1   S. Castles and G. Kosack, eds, *Immigrant Workers and Class Structure in Western Europe* (Oxford, 1985), p. 7.
2   Quoted by J. Watson, ed., *Between Two Cultures: Migrants and Minorities in Britain* (Oxford, 1977), p. 5.
3   T. Kushner and K. Knox, *Refugees in an Age of Genocide* (Ilford, 1999), p. 5.
4   D. Joly and R. Cohen, eds, *Reluctant Hosts: Europe and its Refugees* (Aldershot, 1989), p. 6.
5   R. Cohen and H. S. Bains, *Multi-racist Britain* (Basingstoke, 1988), pp. 26–7.
6   S. Lahiri, *Indian Visitors in Britain 1880–1930* (Ilford, 2000), p. 7.
7   Ibid., p. 89.
8   Ibid., pp. 54–5.
9   See M. Ellis and P. Panayi, 'German minorities in World War One', *Ethnic and Racial Studies*, 17, no. 2 (1994), p. 246.
10 L. Sponza, 'Italians in London', in N. Merriman, ed., *The Peopling of London* (London, 1993), p. 133.
11 N. Evans, 'Immigrants and minorities in Wales 1840–1990', in C. Holmes, ed., *Migration in European History* (Cheltenham, 1996), p. 297.
12 It is impossible to provide an accurate figure as collation was dependent on the Decennial Census, which was not always correctly completed (due to language problems and a dislike of officialdom). In addition the eastern European community was transient and numbers fluctuated.
13 See A. J. Kershen, *Uniting the Tailors* (Ilford, 1995).
14 C. Holmes, *John Bull's Island* (Basingstoke, 1988), p. 20.
15 L. H. Lees, *Exiles of Erin: Irish Migrants in Victorian London* (Manchester, 1979), p. 63.

16 E. P. Thompson, *The Making of the English Working Class* (1963; 2nd edn, London, 1968), p. 480.

17 M. A. G. Ó Tuathaigh, 'The Irish in nineteenth-century Britain: problems of integration', in Holmes, ed., *Migration in European History*, p. 64.

18 Holmes, *John Bull's Island*, p. 38.

19 Ó Tuathaigh, 'Irish in nineteenth-century Britain', p. 75.

20 D. Fitzpatrick, 'A curious middle: the Irish in Britain 1871–1921', in R. Swift and S. Gilley, eds, *The Irish in Britain 1815–1939* (London, 1989), p. 45.

21 Holmes, *John Bull's Island*, p. 95.

22 M. Marrus, *The Unwanted* (Oxford, 1985), p. 3.

23 Kushner and Knox, *Refugees in an Age of Genocide*, p. 49.

24 J. Walvin, *Passage to Britain: Immigration in British History and Politics* (Harmondsworth, 1984), p. 77.

25 Holmes, *John Bull's Island*, p. 96.

26 Ellis and Panayi, 'German minorities', p. 252.

27 P. Bailey, 'From Shandong to the Somme: Chinese indentured labour in France during World War One', in A. J. Kershen, ed., *Language, Labour and Migration* (Aldershot, 2000), pp. 179–96.

28 V. Lipman, *A History of the Jews in Britain since 1858* (Leicester, 1990), p. 140.

29 Walvin, *Passage to Britain*, p. 78.

30 Ibid., p. 80.

31 R. Ballard and C. Ballard, 'The Sikhs: the development of South Asian settlement in Britain', in Watson, ed., *Between Two Cultures*, p. 28.

32 Holmes, *John Bull's Island*, p. 118.

33 R. Palmer, 'The Italians: patterns of migration to London', in Watson, ed., *Between Two Cultures*, p. 254.

34 Fitzpatrick, 'Curious middle', p. 46.

FURTHER READING

Alderman, G., *Modern British Jewry* (Oxford, 1992).

Castles, S. and Kosack, G., eds, *Immigrant Minorities and Class Structure in Western Europe* (Oxford, 1985).

Cohen, R. and Bains, H. S., *Multi-racist Britain* (Basingstoke, 1988).

Ellis, M. and Panayi, P., 'German minorities in World War One', *Ethnic and Racial Studies*, 17, no. 2 (1994).

Evans, N., 'Immigrants and minorities in Wales 1840–1990', in C. Holmes, ed., *Migration in European History* (Cheltenham, 1996), pp. 293–314.

Holmes, C., *Anti-Semitism in British Society 1876–1939* (London, 1979).

Holmes, C., *John Bull's Island* (Basingstoke, 1988).

Holmes, C., ed., *Migration in European History* (2 vols, Cheltenham, 1996).

Joly, D. and Cohen, R., eds, *Reluctant Hosts: Europe and its Refugees* (Aldershot, 1989).

Kershen, A. J., *Uniting the Tailors* (Ilford, 1995).

Kershen, A. J., ed., *London the Promised Land? The Migrant Experience in a Capital City* (Aldershot, 1997).

Kershen, A. J., ed., *Language, Labour and Migration* (Aldershot, 2000).

Kushner, T. and Knox, K., *Refugees in an Age of Genocide* (Ilford, 1999).

Lahiri, S., *Indian Visitors in Britain 1880–1930* (Ilford, 2000).

Lees, L. H., *Exiles of Erin: Irish Migrants in Victorian London* (Manchester, 1979).

Lipman, V., *A History of the Jews in Britain since 1858* (Leicester, 1990).

Lunn, K., ed., *Hosts, Immigrants and Minorities* (Folkestone, 1980).

Marrus, M., *The Unwanted* (Oxford, 1985).

Merriman, N., ed., *The Peopling of London* (London, 1993).

Ó Tuathaigh, M. A. G., 'The Irish in nineteenth-century Britain: problems of integration', in C. Holmes, ed., *Migration in European History* (Cheltenham, 1996), pp. 51–75.

Palmer, R., 'The Italians: patterns of migration to London', in J. Watson, ed., *Between Two Cultures: Migrants and Minorities in Britain* (Oxford, 1977), pp. 245–56.

Panayi, P., *The Enemy in Our Midst: Germans in Britain during the First World War* (Oxford, 1991).

Sponza, L., 'Italians in London', in N. Merriman, ed., *The Peopling of London* (London, 1993), pp. 129–37.

Swift, R. and Gilley, S., eds, *The Irish in Britain 1815–1939* (London, 1989).

Walvin, J., *Black and White: The Negro and English Society 1555–1945* (London, 1973).

Walvin, J., *Passage to Britain: Immigration in British History and Politics* (Harmondsworth, 1984).

Watson, J., ed., *Between Two Cultures: Migrants and Minorities in Britain* (Oxford, 1977).

CHAPTER TEN

British Foreign Policy, 1900–1939

G. H. BENNETT

Introduction

Academic and public views about British foreign policy in the period 1900 to 1939 are marked by a particularly bleak consensus that what happened should not have happened and that the failure of the policy makers was pivotal to Great Britain's decline as the pre-eminent power in the world. To misquote Lady Bracknell, to have one world war in the first half of the twentieth century was unfortunate: to have two perhaps smacked of carelessness. The debate about British foreign policy in the period 1900 to 1939, not unnaturally, has been coloured by those two wars.

In the popular imagination the First World War, whose origins are still hotly contested, remains a war which could perhaps have been prevented by a clear declaration by the foreign secretary, Sir Edward Grey, that Britain would fight to preserve the balance of power on the continent. The debate about British foreign policy in the interwar period has been marked by the possibility that the Second World War could also have been avoided, but in addition it has had the moral dimension of whether or not the policy of appeasement, so closely identified with Neville Chamberlain, was the best way to secure peace. In 1940 there was a call for the retirement of 'the guilty men' who had failed to prevent the war. This helped to set the tone for the historical debate over the next half century.[1] That the word 'appeasement' remains politically loaded, constituting a serious charge against any individual or state in the conduct of its external affairs, shows the continuing significance of British foreign policy in the period 1939 to 1945.

Background

At the end of the nineteenth century Britain remained pre-eminent, militarily, politically and economically. British manufactures dominated world markets, and the Royal Navy patrolled the ocean highways carrying British goods around the world. The British Empire covered one quarter of the world's total land surface. Victorian society appeared confident of Britain's place in the world to the point of jingoism and racism. And yet there was a range of threats to Britain's pre-eminence emerging. Their interlinking nature posed a grave challenge to Britain's security and prosperity. The first major problem was industrial. Britain had been the first nation to experience an industrial revolution and by the late nineteenth century her competitors, adopting newer machinery and processes, were making serious inroads into Britain's dominance of the world market for manufactured goods. The second problem was military: Britain's empire may well have been the world's largest, but it was scattered around the globe and required considerable military resources in order to defend it. The Royal Navy and British army had to be prepared to defend the British Empire from Europe to the Caribbean, Central Africa, Central Asia and the Pacific. The army was small and would rely on the use of troops from the empire in the event of any large-scale conflagration in Asia or Europe. Yet herein lay a third problem – a growing restiveness throughout the empire. Although in 1914 King George V would declare war on behalf of the whole British Empire, the white Dominions (Canada, Australia, New Zealand and South Africa) were increasingly reluctant to entrust their futures blindly to the government in London. The first Boer War from 1880 to 1881 had led to self-government in South Africa, but fears for the independence of Transvaal, and other grievances, caused a second conflict to erupt in 1899. During the war, which lasted until signature of the Treaty of Vereeniging in 1902, serious deficiencies in the British military were highlighted, even though the Boers were eventually defeated. In other parts of the empire, called on to supply troops and money for the struggle, the conflict underlined growing nationalist calls for self-government or outright independence from Britain.

Added to such difficulties new factors were also coming into play in Britain: an increasingly democratic political system, the rise of the Labour party, and the work of economists such as J. A. Hobson meant that the status quo about British politics and Britain's external policies was increasingly called into question. The rationale for British imperialism, and the aggressive foreign policy necessary to defend the empire, was under serious scrutiny, at least by a small number of individuals. The majority were only too happy to wave off the troops as they departed for South Africa, happy in the knowledge that the British Empire was the greatest instrument for human improvement created by man in God's universe. But as the military suffered a series of disasters the words of those who favoured a more insular, more enlightened approach to Britain's world role became more potent. 'Victories' such as the relief of Mafeking were received with hysterical celebration in small towns throughout Britain. The lessons of the war were obvious for the makers of British external policy – British military power was an impressive facade on a building whose foundations were inadequate to support the weight of the imposing edifice above it. The alternatives facing the British government were stark, but in 1902 they were less than clear and it was certainly impossible to make a choice between them. Either the bases of British power needed to be strengthened, or British foreign and imperial policy had to be more realistic in recognizing that Britain could no longer play the kind of global role that she had in the mid-nineteenth century. In typically British style some refused to think that a choice had to be made, while the majority thought that somehow providence would ensure that British foreign policy could simply muddle through.

In part, the dilemmas facing the policy makers in the period before 1914 were hidden by two developments. The first of these came about in 1906 with the election of a radical Liberal government with a large majority. The country was convulsed by a series of domestic political struggles involving issues such as the 'people's budget', the power of the House of Lords and Home Rule for Ireland. The country was plunged into two general elections in 1910, and only the death of Edward VII in the same year gave some respite from the political tensions gripping the country as the fight between the Liberal and Conservative parties became increasingly heated. Civil war threatened in Ireland, and some thought also in England as the growing number of industrial disputes pointed to the growth of socialism. The Conservative party seemed ready to push its opposition to radical Liberal legislation beyond the bounds of the constitution. When war came in 1914, some greeted it with a sense of relief. So bitter were the struggles that in July 1914, as Europe stood on the brink of war, British newspapers still gave over most of their columns to the domestic challenges facing Great Britain. The distractions of domestic politics meant that the foreign policy challenges facing the nation were not clearly perceived outside the Foreign Office and a close circle involving prime minister Henry Asquith and his foreign secretary Sir Edward Grey. Indeed, Grey was only too happy to make sure that Foreign Office business and intelligence were restricted to a small coterie. A cabinet engaged in bitter political warfare with the opposition was rarely given the opportunity to discuss the direction of foreign policy. The idea of democratically accountable foreign policy was being raised on the left wing of British politics, but at cabinet level an attitude of secrecy prevailed.

The Drift towards War

The second development which helped to conceal the dilemmas facing the policy makers was the increasingly erratic behaviour of Germany. At the turn of the century thinking within the Foreign Office and military circles still viewed France as Britain's most likely opponent in any conflagration on the European continent. As recently as 1898 during the Fashoda crisis Anglo-French rivalry in the scramble for Africa had almost led to war between the two countries. The signing of an Anglo-French entente cordiale in 1904 was an attempt to prevent imperial squabbles similarly imperilling peace between the two nations. It was an attempt to establish a *modus vivendi* between the longstanding rivals, rather than a symbol of heartfelt friendship. Germany, meanwhile, was felt to be an old friend, especially because of the links between the British and German monarchies. It was not forgotten that in 1815 Blücher's Prussian cavalry had helped to turn the tide at Waterloo and end another episode in France's quest to dominate Europe. However, things changed very rapidly.

In 1905 Britain suddenly found itself confronted with a crisis over Morocco. Germany had decided to challenge French imperial ambitions in Africa and Morocco became the flashpoint for a crisis. The question was whether Britain should support France, and thus uphold the spirit of the entente, support Germany, or stay neutral. Britain chose to support France, and this did not waver even as Britain was plunged into a general election in early 1906 which saw the Liberals returned to power. The line of policy established during the first Moroccan crisis, opposition to Germany's quest for a world role, would be sustained through the conference of Algeciras in 1906 and throughout later events. While hoping that Anglo-German friendship could be preserved, the British government was increasingly concerned at the unpredictability of German foreign policy and the rapid development of the German navy. Under the Liberal government Britain entered into a naval arms race with Germany, and from 1906 onwards there was a succession of diplomatic crises that confronted Britain. In 1908 Austria-Hungary annexed Bosnia-Herzegovina, giving rise to the prospect of a Balkan war involving Russia, Austria-Hungary and the smaller powers of the region. In 1912 and 1913 the smaller powers of the region did indeed go to war, leading to a further loss of stability there. Throughout, Britain worked for peace in Europe, acting as a moderating influence on the other European powers.

Herbert Henry Asquith, prime minister from 1908 to 1916, was concerned that in working for peace Britain should not commit itself to any particular course of action, and that the entente should not become a military alliance. He was especially concerned because Europe was dividing into two camps, the entente (a diplomatic grouping of Britain, France and Russia) and the Triple Alliance of Germany, Austria-Hungary and Italy. In 1911, at the height of a fresh crisis over Morocco, as Germany tried to lever imperial concessions out of France, Asquith became increasingly worried that Britain was once again being sucked into a dangerous situation. European relations seemed like a quagmire from which there could be no escape without a diplomatic retreat by the powers of the entente or Triple Alliance. The diplomatic groupings seemed ever more firmly polarized, and the ties between likely allies ever closer. Despite Asquith's desire to preserve his government's diplomatic room for manoeuvre in the event of a major crisis, and his concern that the entente should not metamorphose into an alliance under the pressure formed by the expansive nature of German foreign policy, British foreign policy drifted inexorably in this direction.

On 28 July 1914 Archduke Franz Ferdinand, heir to the throne of Austria-Hungary, was assassinated by a Serbian terrorist while visiting Sarajevo, the capital of Bosnia-Herzegovina. This set in chain a series of events that would lead to the mobilization of the forces of Austria-Hungary against those of Serbia, Russian mobilization against Austria-Hungary, German mobilization against Russia, and French mobilization against Germany. Britain was the last major power to declare its intentions in what was rapidly emerging as a major European war. After toying with the options, on 3 August, Britain declared war on Germany. Those options, and the reasons for the declaration of war, were set before the House of Commons by Sir Edward Grey. German violation of Belgian sovereignty was chosen as the narrowly defined reason for Britain's intervention. Britain had undertaken to maintain Belgian independence in a treaty of 1839. That treaty, violated by the presence of German troops on Belgian soil, offered an easily explainable and demonstrable *casus belli* for the British government. Britain's decision to go to war did not have to be sold to the public in the rather abstract terms of preserving the balance of power in Europe. Nor was there a need to inflame Germanophile and Francophobe opinion by declaring war against the 'beastly Hun' in the interests of Britain's longtime friend, France. Instead Britain would intervene for the sake of 'poor little Belgium'.

Despite the very active debate about the origins of the First World War which has raged since 1914, to which Grey contributed with his decision that the British documents on the origin of the war should be published, historians have concluded that Britain was largely blameless for the outbreak of war in 1914. If all the powers bore some responsibility then Britain's share was the least. There has been a considerable amount of research done on British foreign policy in this critical period, from comprehensive studies such as that by Zara Steiner through to the micro-histories formed by biographies of senior civil servants such as Eyre Crowe. There is a consensus that British foreign policy in the period 1900 to 1914 was well managed, flexible but firm. Britain's interests were protected and German militarism was contained in a prudent way. Britain sought peace, but by 1914 she had no choice but to go to war, or see a continent dominated by Germany.

Foreign Policy during the First World War

Naturally, British foreign policy did not come to a complete standstill during the First World War. Neutral opinion, especially that in the United States, had to be assiduously courted. The government made the most propaganda out of incidents such as the loss of American life with the sinking of the *Lusitania* in 1915. Where possible, as with Italy in 1915, negotiations had to be conducted so as to ensure that the remaining neutrals joined the war on the side of the entente powers. Negotiating inter-allied loans, supplies of war materials and other agreements added a further dimension to the conduct of British foreign policy during the war. Most important of all, the agreements made, and the promises given or implied, were to lead to long-lasting complications in the post-war period. For example, during the course of the war over a dozen different agreements, promises and declarations were made about the future of the Middle East. Britain was a party to most of these commitments and after the war it would be realized that, to some extent, they conflicted in detail if not in spirit. The McMahon–Hussein correspondence was a spectacular case in point. In return for staging and maintaining an Arab revolt against Turkish rule in the southern provinces of the Ottoman Empire, McMahon, the British high commissioner in Egypt, promised Hussein, the sherif of Mecca, that Britain would support the emergence of an Arab state. Not only did McMahon's territorial promises conflict with those of the Anglo-French Sykes–Picot Treaty of 1916, but later on differences were discovered between McMahon's original letters and their Arabic translations. Foreign policy was now being made by the Foreign Office, by diplomats, by politicians and by soldiers on remote battlefields. Confusion was the inevitable consequence.

In addition, the policy-making process was evolving in a haphazard manner as the old tried and tested methods broke down. One example of this came with the replacement of Asquith as prime minister in 1916 as his methods were not felt to be appropriate to a war that had escalated beyond all expectations. Asquith's successor, Lloyd George, was prepared to be innovative in the development of government policy and its attendant mechanisms, and more ruthless in his conduct of the war. The development of a cabinet secretariat to improve the conduct of the business of government, and a prime minister's secretariat (often referred to as the 'Garden suburb' because of the collection of huts in the garden of No. 10 Downing Street where it was based) challenged the traditional structures of policy making. The 'Garden suburb', staffed by able young men such as Philip Kerr, constituted an alternative source of advice to the prime minister on domestic and foreign policy. Lloyd George was also ready to use Kerr and others as personal emissaries and fact finders, rather than the staff of the diplomatic service.

In particular the 'Garden suburb', after the entry of the United States into the war in 1917, began to turn its attention to how Britain might shape a post-war world to fit her own desiderata. As Erik Goldstein has shown, the Foreign Office was also busy preparing for peace, but by 1918 the war was proceeding so unexpectedly that the policy makers could not keep up. The German armistice in November 1918 came as a shock to many who had thought that the war would last for at least another year, and by the end of 1918 British troops were scattered across Europe and Asia creating further potential complications. In particular, the presence of British troops in the Caucasus and Trans-Caspian regions, as well as in North Russia, held the potential for a conflict with Bolshevik Russia, born in November 1917 in the ashes of the Russian Empire. The existence of rival anti-Bolshevik armies, vying for British support, added a further complication, especially as the rest of eastern Europe dissolved into revolution against the old empires. This would lead to the emergence of new states and regimes such as the Baltic States, Poland, Czechoslovakia and Yugoslavia. The diplomatic map of Europe changed significantly, and it would take some time for the Foreign Office to catch up with a rapidly changing and fragmenting scene. In preparing for peace the policy makers simply could not keep up with a situation that continued to evolve rapidly throughout 1918.

Aftermath of the First World War

The war came to an unexpected end with the German armistice of November 1918. As the British team assembled at Paris in preparation for the peace conference in January 1919, there was a certain degree of confusion, but also optimism. The policy makers hoped that they could remake the world according to British desiderata and that American power would shore up the Pax Britannica, so that the dilemmas of rationalizing resources and commitments could be avoided. The competing demands of the other allied powers were largely overlooked, but they, and the difficulties of trying to remake the map of the world after a major conflict, were to produce profoundly disappointing results. The Treaty of Versailles imposed on Germany, and the other treaties imposed on the other defeated nations, Hungary, Austria and Bulgaria, created a Europe beset by the problem of reparations and territorial squabbles, in which some nations were armed for war and some were not. The post-war settlement created both stability, in that German power was weakened at least for a time, and instability, in that new nation-states such as Poland had territorial squabbles with all its neighbours. But at least the post-war settlement created a basis from which to work.

Within the British government there was a keen awareness of the imperfections of what had been 'settled' at Paris, and from it a mood of revisionism spread quite widely. John Maynard Keynes's attack on *The Economic Consequences of the Peace* (London, 1919), which questioned the economic wisdom of burdening Germany with heavy reparations payments, was one of the more learned expressions of this revisionism. Austen Chamberlain, the chancellor of the exchequer, advised his sister in December 1919: 'You must get Keynes' book . . . I wish that I could say that I differ seriously from Keynes' examination of Germany's ability to pay . . . There is only too much truth in Keynes' gloomy picture'.[2] Inter-allied conferences were held routinely after the First World War to discuss the settlement, its ongoing implementation and continued operation. Britain and France remained relatively close until early 1922, with Lloyd George fully recognizing French concerns about a revival of

German power. Lloyd George knew that to alleviate some of the burdens on Germany, especially the burden of reparations, which was held to be ultimately damaging to the British economy in depressing Germany's ability to trade with Britain, he would have to address the issue of French insecurity. Since 1919 the possibility of a military alliance, or unilateral British guarantee to aid France in the event of foreign attack, had been repeatedly raised as a means to convince the French to allow the modification of the peace treaty. Great obstacles lay in the way of the issuing of such a guarantee: it would entail the country in extra expense to maintain a continental expeditionary force; the Dominions were not keen for the mother country to enter into any obligations that might catapult them into another continental war; some questioned whether a unilateral guarantee might make the French feel that they could antagonize Germany whenever and however they liked; others wondered whether a guarantee to protect French security might mean that Britain would have to go to war in the event of an attack on one of France's alliance partners in eastern Europe. The question of an alliance raised grave doubts, but such was Lloyd George's political dominance that he was able to drive ahead with the issue. Standing at the head of a Conservative-dominated coalition government elected in 1918, he had little to fear from the official opposition, the rump Liberal party headed by H. H. Asquith. He was dominant in cabinet, and enjoyed a considerable measure of freedom in his handling of European affairs, which led contemporaries and subsequent historians to suppose that the Foreign Office and foreign secretary, Lord Curzon, were in 'eclipse'. However, in early 1922 Lloyd George's foreign policy was blown off course. In turn he was hit by a minor revolt within the coalition about the possibility of an early election, the collapse of the moderate French government headed by Aristide Briand and the coming to power of the right-wing nationalist Raymond Poincaré, and the collapse of the European economic conference at Genoa in April as the political pariahs of Europe, Germany and Bolshevik Russia, shocked the world with the signature of the Rapallo Treaty. By the middle of 1922 British foreign policy under Lloyd George seemed markedly to have failed. The failure of British foreign policy in turn weakened the bonds holding the coalition together, which in turn weakened the government's ability to pursue bold policy initiatives.

In late September the government began to fall apart as Britain faced the possibility of a war in Turkey. Since 1919 Lloyd George had given his backing to Greece, which had longstanding territorial ambitions in Asia Minor. Those ambitions were opposed by a Turkish national movement under Mustapha Kemal. He recognized that the old Turkish Empire could not be revived, but was determined to maintain the territorial integrity of the Turkish homelands. This brought him into conflict with Allied plans for the region enshrined in the draft Treaty of Sèvres, and with Greek expansionism. In early September the Greek army in Anatolia suffered a crushing defeat as the Turkish army carried all before it. The only factor preventing a complete victory for the forces of Turkish nationalism were contingents of the British army stationed around Constantinople and in a zone around the Straits linking the Mediterranean to the Black Sea. The neutrality of the Straits had long been held to be a vital national interest to Britain, and when Turkish forces began to menace the British position at Chanak, there was a possibility that a war might ensue.

In the midst of the crisis the features that marked British foreign policy in the interwar peiod were highlighted. A majority of the British public, after the horrendous losses during the First World War, did not want to fight the Turks at any price. While the policy makers might regard the neutrality of the Straits as a vital national interest, for the majority of the public this notion was rather too abstract. Demonstrations were held and the press questioned the policy that had led to such a terrifying possibility that Britain might have to fight the Turks yet again. Even within the military there was a strong sense that 'the bones of a single British grenadier' were not worth the price of opposing Turkish nationalism, or indeed of intervening in any territorial squabble in Asia Minor, the Middle East or eastern Europe that did not directly affect Britain.

In the search for reinforcements, needed because British military power had contracted sharply after the end of the First World War, the Lloyd George cabinet turned to the empire. The French and Italian governments had shown their belief in interallied solidarity by conducting separate negotiations with Kemal. On 15 September the secretary of state for the colonies, Winston Churchill, drew up an appeal to the colonies for military support. Forgetting the difference in time zones, and ever wanting to curry favour with the press, the appeal was published in the Canadian and Australian press before it had been properly received by the respective governments. Canada refused to send troops and the Australian and South African responses were only slightly less emphatic. The government could at least take comfort in that in the hour of need New Zealand and Newfoundland were ready to rally to the colours. The centrifugal forces at work within the British Empire were highlighted for all to see. Britain could no longer count on the Dominions for their unquestioned support, and yet for political reasons the fiction of the empire had to be maintained. In 1926 the Dominions would be accorded equal status with Britain, and in 1931 parliament passed the Statute of Westminster making them independent in their foreign policy. However, Britain retained the obligation of having to defend these independent outposts of empire. A neo-pacifist electorate, a shrunken and increasingly outdated military, and an empire that required defending but whose support was not automatic, as well as an economy that continued to decline, formed a less than satisfactory basis from which to develop and execute a successful foreign policy.

In the event, war at Chanak was avoided not by the policy makers but because of the actions of the senior military commander at Chanak. General Harington declined to present to the Turks an ultimatum drawn up by the cabinet calling for them to vacate the neutral zone. Harington feared that to present it would mean war. He delayed long enough, as the political temperature in London escalated, for the Turks to reach their own decision to vacate the neutral zone and seek peace by negotiation. In the aftermath of the First World War foreign policy had become an issue in domestic politics in a way not experienced since the days of Gladstone and Disraeli. Moreover, foreign policy did not merely provide rhetorical tools for statesmen to wrap themselves in the flag of nationalism. After the horrors of the western front the British electorate was only too well aware that foreign policy was the vital issue – on its outcome could depend the lives of millions. Such sentiments helped to propel the break-up of the coalition government. Incompetence, misfortune, interparty squabbles and personal jealousies between the different groupings within the coalition were one thing, but the existence of a group within the cabinet seemingly ready to plunge the nation into war was something different again. Lloyd George, Churchill and Lord Birkenhead seemed eager for war, possibly, some thought, as a means to call a khaki election to shore up the coalition. On 19 October the majority of the Conservative party decided to leave the coalition. Some, like the foreign secretary Lord Curzon, together with junior ministers such as Stanley Baldwin had already abandoned the coalition. They were at the heart of the Conservative government led by Bonar Law that took office in early November after a general election. What was truly signifi-cant was that foreign policy was becoming a driving force of Westminster politics.

During the mid- to late 1920s British foreign policy entered a period of compar-ative calm. War did not threaten, although Britain remained concerned about events on the continent. In particular, in January 1923 Franco-Belgian forces occupied Germany's industrial heartland, the Ruhr, after Germany had defaulted on repara-tion payments. The split between the entente powers which had become manifest at Chanak widened considerably. It was obvious that Britain could not support an action which many felt was driving Germany towards bankruptcy, nor could she address French concerns over her security while they were engaged in hostile operations against one of her neighbours. At the same time the cabinet became alarmed at the development of the French air arm. The French seemed bent on continental domi-nation and at Westminster some began to wonder whether Britain had 'backed the wrong horse'. Lord Curzon, who remained foreign secretary, tried to convince the French that they were in the wrong, while simultaneously preserving the facade of Anglo-French unity. At the same time he was desperately trying to keep the French in line while he negotiated peace with the Turks, in what became the Treaty of Lausanne – the only post-war settlement to stand the test of time. His failure to back France to the hilt was attacked at the Conservative party conference in late 1923. When, after the short interlude of the first Labour government from January to October 1924, Stanley Baldwin came to form his second administration, Curzon was not returned to the Foreign Office.

The Late 1920s

The first Labour government's contribution to the annals of British foreign policy was on the face of it remarkably minor, but it was pivotal. Ramsay MacDonald took the bold step of recognizing Soviet Russia, and while they were in power for only a matter of months MacDonald did try to propel things forward in the search for European stability. MacDonald wanted to work with the League of Nations, which had come into existence in 1919 to help oversee the peace settlement. However, during the Lloyd George premiership the statesmen preferred to keep the key decisions at the inter-allied level, and the Conservative party was largely antipathetic towards the new supra-national body. MacDonald believed in international cooperation and sought a means to strengthen it, and enhance European security. On 2 October 1924 the members of the League voted for the Geneva protocol to make arbitration of disputes compulsory for member nations. It was a step forward, although the incom-ing Conservative government refused to ratify it, partly because the Dominions opposed it. However, the Labour government's greatest contribution to the evolu-tion of British foreign policy in this period concerned its going. The minority Labour government that came to power in January would inevitably prove short-lived, and by October 1924 the country faced yet another general election. In the run-up to it, on 10 October the Foreign Office received a letter purportedly from Grigori

Zinoviev, the head of the Communist International in Moscow. The letter, to the head of the British Communist party, urged members to step up their campaign to stir up insurrection. Ramsay MacDonald, in the midst of the election campaign, underrated the potential significance of the letter until on 25 October a copy of it was reproduced by the *Daily Mail* with an appropriate editorial to the effect that the Labour party was in league with the Bolsheviks. The election campaign was electrified by the issue, and Stanley Baldwin and the Conservatives were returned with a large majority.

On coming to power for a second time Baldwin realized that he would have to take the initiative on European affairs. MacDonald's negotiation of the Geneva protocol placed the government in an awkward position. Baldwin wanted to reject it, but felt morally obliged to put something in its place. European relations could not simply be left to smoulder. In an attempt to signal a break with the past he appointed the Francophile Austen Chamberlain as foreign secretary. Chamberlain reacted eagerly when a basis for progress on European relations was suggested by Gustav Stresemann, Germany's foreign minister. Stresemann suggested that Germany could give some form of unilateral guarantee of her borders in order to appease French concerns. Chamberlain acted as a mediator between the Germans and the French and helped to negotiate what became known as the Locarno Pact, signed at Locarno in October 1925. Germany unilaterally guaranteed her border with France and Germany – in effect forgoing the revival of any claim on Alsace and Lorraine – and promised to change her borders in the east only through peaceful means. Locarno formed a guarantee that Germany would behave herself in future. Britain and Italy acted as guarantors of the pact. For Britain the Locarno Pact represented a masterstroke. It provided a basis for an improvement in Franco-German relations, with Germany being allowed to enter the League of Nations in 1926. France became less hostile towards Germany, paving the way for limited revision of the Versailles settlement. Reparation obligations were scaled down to the point when in the early 1930s, under the impact of the depression, they were entirely abandoned, and the timetable for allied withdrawals from the Rhine bridgeheads was speeded up. Meanwhile the cost to Britain was minimal. Locarno meant very little in the way of military obligations that would incur extra spending. The Dominions were exempted from its clauses so that they were happy. The French felt more secure and the Germans felt that the British had given their tacit acceptance to the peaceful revision of Germany's borders in the east at some point in the future. Finally, in concrete terms Locarno meant nothing – in the final analysis, if Locarno was breached Britain was compelled to do nothing that she might not want to do. Austen Chamberlain received the Nobel Peace prize for his efforts, but his cleverness in resolving a whole series of difficulties facing Britain's European policy went far beyond such awards.

If Locarno meant that the winds were set fair for British foreign policy in the late 1920s, then by the end of the decade the outlook was altogether different. The worldwide depression arising from the Wall Street Crash of October 1929 gave rise to conditions that proved increasingly problematic for the makers of British foreign policy. On the one hand Britain's capacity to take a lead in world affairs was prejudiced by economic weakness. Foreign policy decisions had to be taken with at least one eye on the economic consequences. Britain did not have the money or the industrial capacity to make good the deficiencies in her military establishment that had grown since the end of the First World War, and the introduction of a Ten-Year Rule which postulated that Britain would not have to fight a major European war for at least ten years in the future. On the other hand, the economic conditions helped put an end to Weimar democracy in Germany, make various European powers embark on a policy of autarky and think about territorial expansion, and destroy the illusion of hope that had been formed by Locarno. The world was suddenly a more dangerous place and instead of international cooperation under the League of Nations, the new international ethos smacked of Darwinian survival of the fittest.

The first major event of the new era for British policy makers came in September 1931 with Japan's seizure of the Chinese province of Manchuria. Japanese expansionism came almost at the same moment that Britain was being forced off the gold standard. As Japan's hold on the province tightened, in October Britain found itself in the midst of a general election that would see the election of a National government. Dissaffection within the Royal Navy, as government cutbacks led to a worsening in the conditions of service, provided yet another reason why, in a moment of crisis, Britain did not act decisively on the international stage. The League of Nations was left to provide a smokescreen to cover the paralysis of British foreign policy. The most policy makers could do was relent the fact that in 1922 Britain had allowed the Anglo-Japanese alliance to lapse in deference to the concerns of an isolationist United States of America. Japan was censured for her actions, leading to her withdrawal from the League of Nations, but economic or military sanctions were never seriously considered. In both economic and military terms, Britain was too weak to meet the challenge in East Asia.

Appeasement

The Manchurian crisis of 1931 has often been cited as the first major instance of the policy of appeasement that characterized Britain's external relations in the 1930s. Since 1939 appeasement – granting concessions to a dissatisfied power – has been seen in a very negative light. Indeed, some of the historians writing in the 1950s and 1960s regarded the policy of appeasement as one of the major factors contributing to the outbreak of war in 1939. They lamented the fact that in crises such as that over Manchuria in 1931, Britain's policy makers did not take a more resolute line. They reasoned that by granting concessions Britain only encouraged the demands of those nations inclined towards expansionism. So powerful was this impression that after the Second World War political scientists coined the phrase 'Munich syndrome' to suggest that post-war policy makers, in trying to learn the lessons of the past, were firmly against granting concessions to dissatisfied or aggressive nations. By the 1970s historians such as W. R. Rock were trying to show that it was time to re-evaluate the much-maligned policy. He wrote: 'It was not a coward's creed or a silly treacherous notion advanced alone by stupid men. Rather, its principal tenet of concessions through strength was a noble concept rooted in the moral and religious traditions of the English'.[3]

By the 1980s biographical studies of Neville Chamberlain, prime minister from 1937 to 1940 and the man most closely associated with the policy of appeasement, were suggesting that Chamberlain fully appreciated the dangers of Hitler and

Mussolini. He followed appeasement because he hoped that it would work, and in any case Britain needed time to rearm. In effect, appeasement was a policy of strategic retreat. More recently the work of R. A. C. Parker has focused attention on the fact that Chamberlain did have alternative choices other than to appease or go to war. Parker argues that through seeking closer ties to France and other European nations, Chamberlain could have 'tried to build a barrier to Hitler's expansion. After March 1939 British attempts to do so were either half-hearted or too late'.[4] The debate about what might be described as high appeasement under Neville Chamberlain remains ongoing.

The debate about British foreign policy in the period from 1933 to the advent of Neville Chamberlain in 1937 is much less vibrant. From 1931 until 1935 Ramsay MacDonald presided as prime minister. Under his leadership British foreign policy after the Manchurian crisis was marked by a series of contradictions. An attempted Nazi coup d'état in Austria in 1934, and Hitler's repudiation of most of the military clauses of the Treaty of Versailles in March 1935, led to the so-called Stresa front of April 1935 as Britain, France and Italy met at a conference to discuss and oppose Hitler's intentions. However, Britain immediately thereafter concluded a naval agreement with Germany tacitly accepting German naval rearmament while restricting its scope. In trying to secure peace in Europe, British statesmen had privately abandoned internationalism as the best way to secure British interests. Unfortunately in public they remained committed to international action through the League of Nations.

By late 1935 the dilemmas and contradictions facing the policy makers were simply overwhelming. Since December 1934 a crisis had been looming over Abyssinia – a member of the League of Nations and the only state in Africa under black leadership. Italy had harboured designs of territorial expansion at Abyssinia's expense since the late nineteenth century, and after a border incident at Wal Wal between Abyssinian and Italian troops on 23 November 1934 Mussolini was ready to press ahead with his plans. He knew by the time of the Stresa conference in April 1935 that the British and the French were almost wholly dependent on him to provide the decisive force to contain Hitler. It was the threat of Italian troops that had persuaded Hitler not to send in German troops to support the rising of Austrian Nazis in 1934. At Stresa, Ramsay MacDonald failed to make the right warning noises to Mussolini which he took as a sign that Britain would not oppose an assault on Abyssinia. As British forces noted an Italian military build-up in Italian Somaliland and Eritrea, the policy makers struggled with what policy to pursue. Italy was vital to the anti-Hitler coalition that had been formed at Stresa, but Abyssinia was a member of the League of Nations and Britain was pledged to oppose any attack on a member of the League. Britain faced a choice of realpolitik, and continued Italian goodwill, or idealism, and maintenance of the principles of the League. In the event the policy makers tried to have it both ways after a lengthy debate in which Robert Vansittart, the permanent head of the Foreign Office, came out firmly on the side of realpolitik. In June 1935 Antony Eden, Britain's minister for League Affairs, was dispatched to see Mussolini to try to arrange an exchange of territory in Africa between the British Empire, Italy and Abyssinia that might satisfy Italian aspirations. Eden came back empty-handed and in October 1935 Italian forces crossed over into Abyssinia. At that moment Britain was in the grip of a general election campaign in which the National government, now headed by Stanley Baldwin, was publicly committed to the League. As the fighting worsened the National government was returned to office. Economic sanctions were implemented although these had little impact on the Italian war machine. Indeed, deliveries of fuel were not embargoed and Britain allowed Italy to carry on using the Suez canal for the resupply of her troops in Africa. However, by December 1935, as the League planned to introduce further sanctions on Italy, the British government was convinced that it had to act. On 7 December the foreign secretary Sir Samuel Hoare arrived in Paris and held a series of conversations with Pierre Laval, the French foreign minister. Together they drew up what would be called the Hoare–Laval plan, which would place two-thirds of Abyssinia directly or indirectly under Italian control. They hoped that Abyssinia and the League would accept the plan, which would allow Britain and France to escape the policy dilemmas that had faced them for over a year. However, before the plan could be presented to the relevant parties it was leaked to the press and in a storm of public opinion Hoare was forced to resign. Internationalism and realpolitik had collided with spectacular results.

From this point on Italy drifted into the German camp and British foreign policy also appeared to drift. In March 1936 German troops occupied the demilitarized Rhineland in contravention of the treaties of Versailles and Locarno. Britain consulted the other interested powers, but no action was taken. In the same year the Spanish Civil War broke out and Britain was happy to participate in a policy of non-interference. By 1937, as Neville Chamberlain replaced Baldwin at No. 10 Downing Street, it was clear that Hitler's intentions must turn, sooner rather than later, to the territorial clauses of Versailles. Chamberlain was determined to preserve European peace. He and most of the statesmen of his generation were haunted by the casualty lists of the First World War. Chamberlain took the lead in trying to appease Hitler, although his optimism was taken by some as astonishing naivety. The prime minister's overoptimistic assessment of the international scene led to a breach between Chamberlain and Eden, who had replaced Hoare at the Foreign Office. On 20 February 1938 Eden resigned, but the political storm over his going proved short-lived.

One month later, in March 1938, Germany secured union with Austria, further inflaming the division between the appeasers and their opponents. More seriously, trouble also loomed over Czechoslovakia, where a vocal German minority demanded incorporation within greater Germany. With Hitler threatening war, Neville Chamberlain took the lead in trying to avert conflict. Inventing the idea of shuttle diplomacy, in 1938 Chamberlain flew backwards and forwards to Germany to talk to Hitler about his demands. However, it took a last-ditch conference at Munich in early September to avert war, which threatened to embroil France, Britain and possibly Russia as well as Germany and Czechoslovakia. Under the terms of the Munich agreement the Czech border regions containing the German minority were to be given over to Germany. At Munich Chamberlain also sought a separate agreement with Hitler that was embodied in a note saying that the agreement was symbolic of the desire of the German and British peoples never to go to war again. Chamberlain came back to Britain to proclaim that the note meant 'peace in our time', but the anti-appeasers took it as 'peace in our time' at the expense of the Czechoslovak Republic.

During the Czech crisis government contingency planning for war, which most expected, reached new heights. Rearmament gathered pace and many of the fighter aircraft that were to save Britain in 1940 were built in the twelve months after Munich. Within six months Munich was discredited as Hitler secured the break-up of the rest of Czechoslovakia in March 1939. Following this Britain, rather half-heartedly, opened talks with the Russians about containing Hitler, but Stalin was convinced that Britain would not stand up to Hitler and concluded his own Nazi–Soviet agreement with Germany in August 1939. In that same month, in an attempt to stop German expansionism, Britain gave a guarantee of Polish independence. After the Munich conference Hitler was determined to incorporate lands in western Poland that were ethnically German. Chamberlain's gamble did not pay off and on 1 September German troops invaded Poland. On 3 September, in line with the guarantee, Britain declared war on Germany. Neville Chamberlain's policy of appeasement, in part forced on him by the attitude of the British public, by the state of the British economy and the slowness of the drive to rearm, had seemingly ended in failure.

Conclusion

British foreign policy in the period 1900 to 1939 had not been characterized by its success. Britain had sought to avoid two world wars. Perhaps Neville Chamberlain in 1938 was motivated by thoughts that Grey might have done more in 1914 to have avoided war. As Parker has suggested, there were perhaps alternative policies that might have been pursued by the British government and Foreign Office, but at the time the choices that were made seemed wholly rational and based on the best possible analysis. The Foreign Office in 1939 was a markedly different department from that which it had been in 1900. The nature of foreign policy had also changed. The pace of communication and the speed at which wars could break out quickened dramatically between 1900 and 1939. The advent of shuttle diplomacy at the height of the Munich crisis was a reflection of this. More important, in 1900 foreign policy was the preserve of a narrow elite. In the interwar period foreign policy became perhaps the decisive issue in British politics: Chanak played a major role in bringing down Lloyd George, Hoare and Eden resigned dramatically and Neville Chamberlain staked his political reputation on appeasement. By 1939 everyone in Westminster and beyond had an interest in foreign policy. British foreign policy had moved from an age of aristocracy to an age of democracy. However, it was no more successful for the transition. Grey may have blundered in 1914, but in the late 1930s it was the British people's unwillingness to face the threat of war that left Neville Chamberlain little choice but to appease.

NOTES

1   Cato, *Guilty Men* (Harmondsworth, 1998), p. 123.
2   Austen Chamberlain to Ida Chamberlain, 21 December 1919, Austen Chamberlain papers, Birmingham University Library AC5/1/46.
3   W. R. Rock, *British Appeasement in the 1930s* (London, 1977), p. 87.
4   R. A. C. Parker, *Chamberlain and Appeasement: British Policy and the Coming of the Second World War* (Basingstoke, 1993), p. 347.

FURTHER READING

Bartlett, C. J., *British Foreign Policy in the Twentieth Century* (Basingstoke, 1989).

Bennett, G. H., *British Foreign Policy during the Curzon Period, 1919–24* (Basingstoke, 1995).

Cato, *Guilty Men* (Harmondsworth, 1998).

Charmley, J., *Chamberlain and the Lost Peace* (London, 1989).

Crowe, S. and Corp, E., *Our Ablest Public Servant: Sir Eyre Crowe 1864–1925* (Newton Abbot, 1993).

Dockrill, M. L., *Peace without Promise: Britain and the Peace Conferences 1919–23* (London, 1981).

Documents on British Foreign Policy 1919–1939 (3rd series, London, 1947–86).

Doerr, P. W., *British Foreign Policy, 1919–1939* (New York, 1998).

Goldstein, E., *Winning the Peace: British Diplomatic Strategy, Peace Planning, and the Paris Peace Conference, 1916–1920* (Oxford, 1991).

Gooch, G. P. and Temperley, H., *British Documents on the Origins of the War 1898–1914* (11 vols, London, 1926–1928).

Grayson, R. S., *Austen Chamberlain and the Commitment to Europe: British Foreign Policy 1924–29* (London, 1997).

Nish, I., *Anglo-Japanese Alienation 1919–1952: Papers of the Anglo-Japanese Conference on the History of the Second World War* (Cambridge, 1987).

Northedge, F. S., *The Troubled Giant: Britain among the Great Powers 1916–1939* (London, 1966).

Orde, A., *Great Britain and International Security 1920–1926* (London, 1978).

Orde, A., *British Policy and European Reconstruction after the First World War* (Cambridge, 1990).

Parker, R. A. C., *Chamberlain and Appeasement: British Policy and the Coming of the Second World War* (Basingstoke, 1993).

Reynolds, D., *Britannia Overrules: British Policy and World Power in the Twentieth Century* (London, 1981).

Rock, W. R., *British Appeasement in the 1930s* (London, 1977).

Steiner, Z. S., *The Foreign Office and Foreign Policy, 1898–1914* (Cambridge, 1969).

CHAPTER ELEVEN

The British Armed Forces, 1900–1939

DAVID FRENCH

Introduction

In the second half of the nineteenth century the functions of the Royal Navy were to police the empire, to keep open the sea-lanes linking its scattered parts and to deter any of the other Great Powers from interfering in its affairs or menacing its security. It achieved these goals with a remarkable degree of success. Despite some 'panics' in the 1880s and 1890s, the navy maintained its ability to deter naval threats from other European powers and simultaneously managed to offer the army significant support as it strove to maintain order along the frontiers of the empire. Britain's worldwide empire needed soldiers, not only to garrison its colonies and the overseas bases upon which the navy depended for its coal supplies, but also to deter a hostile force from landing in Britain itself. That was a task that most naval theorists, who adhered to the 'blue-water' school of strategy, thought could be fulfilled if enough soldiers were retained at home to repulse an enemy force of a few thousand men. The army might also be called upon to give aid to the civil power in Britain, to garrison distant colonies, of which India was far and away the most important, to wage colonial wars and to be ready to mount amphibious operations against an enemy's littoral in cooperation with the fleet. In the 1870s and 1880s two successive Liberal secretaries of state for war, Edward Cardwell and Hugh Childers, implemented reform programmes intended to make the army's officer corps more professional, to solve the perennial problem of recruiting by establishing close links between particular localities and regiments, and to create an Army Reserve so that the regular army could be rapidly expanded in a major emergency.

At a time when no major European power was seriously attempting to build a fleet to rival the Royal Navy or to establish its hegemony over western Europe, this policy served Britain well. It enabled the government to combine economy with security. But it began to crumble in the late 1880s and it collapsed completely in the first four decades of the twentieth century. In the 1880s, first the French and Italians, and then the Russians, embarked on major fleet-building programmes. As a consequence

British defence costs began to escalate, especially when in 1889 the Unionist government of Lord Salisbury passed the Naval Defence Act and insisted that Britain had to maintain a fleet of battleships that was the equal of the world's next two largest fleets. The Two-Power Standard was soon widely accepted as a symbol of British maritime superiority and as the ultimate guarantee of the security of its empire.

But increasing defence estimates did not signify that the British people felt any more secure. The application of industrial technology to armaments meant that the weapons employed by the army and navy became obsolescent ever more rapidly as rival powers introduced new weapons that could shoot further or sail faster. Nothing contributed so much to the growing sense of insecurity felt by public and politicians alike as their fear that, unless Britain adopted the most modern technology, its empire would be overthrown. But as each fresh generation of weapons was more expensive than the one it superseded, the Treasury only avoided a fiscal crisis in the late 1890s thanks to a lucky growth in prosperity and revenues.

In October 1899 the British went to war against the Boer Republics of the Transvaal and the Orange Free State. It was widely expected that the two small southern African republics could not long resist the power of the British Empire. In fact the war did not end until May 1902, and by then it had cost the British over £300 million and the lives of 22,000. The cost and duration of the war shattered any remaining complacency the British might have felt about the security that their army and navy afforded them. It ushered in a prolonged re-examination of British defence policy and highlighted the major constraint within which successive British governments were compelled to operate when devising their defence policies. Throughout the period from 1899 to 1939 British governments made policy within a liberal political culture, with its roots in the late eighteenth century. It was, therefore, impossible for them to give absolute priority to defence over all other goals. They accepted that Britain needed armed forces both to protect its interests and to project British power beyond its own frontiers. But, because of the armed forces' potential to sap the nation's wealth, they regarded them as being at best a necessary evil. The effect of this was most apparent in the case of the army. Except during the direst national emergency, such as faced Britain between 1916 and 1918, conscription was politically impossible. The regular army, therefore, had to rely on volunteers. But low pay, and the chance of spending long periods of service in India far from friends and family, meant that it was held in such low public esteem that it was forced to recruit most of its rank and file from amongst the unemployed. The fundamental assumption that underpinned British defence policy in this period was that defence spending was akin to an insurance policy, something which a prudent householder always purchased, but for which he was reluctant to pay more than was absolutely necessary.[1]

Between 1902 and 1939 the British pursued a combination of six policies to keep their defence premiums as low as possible. They tried to appease potential enemies; they threatened them with armed retaliation; they tried to reduce Britain's defence costs through arms limitation agreements; they sought to share their defence burdens by cooperating with other powers; they tried to maximize the effectiveness of their armed forces by employing high-technology weapons that they hoped would give them a decisive advantage; and they tried to use intelligence gathering and analysis as a way of multiplying the effectiveness of their armed forces.

The Armed Forces and Appeasement

Between 1902 and 1907, the Unionist and Liberal governments frankly acknowledged the impossibility of defending their empire and its maritime communications
without outside assistance. They therefore embarked on a determined and successful policy of using diplomacy to reduce the number of Britain's potential enemies.
Britain's decision to withdraw her forces from the western hemisphere, the Anglo-
French entente of 1904 and the Anglo-Russian agreement of 1907 marked the successful appeasement of all but one of her major rivals. But, despite three attempts to
reach a naval arms limitation agreement with Germany – at the Second Hague conference in 1907 and in bilateral negotiations in 1909–11 and in 1912 – the Liberal
government could not appease the Germans. In Britain there was a cross-party consensus that Britain had to possess a fleet large enough to defeat any possible rival.
The British therefore asked the Germans to accept a fixed ratio of battleships at a
time when the Royal Navy had a clear numerical superiority.[2]

The German response – a reduction in the pace of their building programme –
and the price they insisted upon – a British promise that they would remain neutral
if a European war broke out – only served to persuade some British policy makers
that Germany intended to establish its hegemony over Europe. Britain did not go to
war against Germany in 1914 because the two powers were colonial and economic
rivals or because they had antagonistic political cultures, although these factors hardly
made for close friendship. (If such things made good relations impossible, the Anglo-
Russian agreement of 1907 would never have been signed.) The paramount factor
in persuading British policy makers that Germany presented a possibly fatal danger
to them was the fact that the German fleet represented a growing menace to British
national security.[3] By contrast, French colonial ambitions in North Africa or Russian
ambitions in Persia only challenged Britain at the periphery of its empire. Germany's
political and naval ambitions demonstrated a fundamental fact for the British. Securing command of the seas was not an alternative to maintaining a European balance
of power. They were interdependent, for if Germany succeeded in subjugating its
continental neighbours it would be able to employ the shipbuilding resources of
western Europe to overwhelm the Royal Navy and blockade and bankrupt Britain
into subjugation without even the need to mount an invasion.[4]

In that event Britain could not be saved by a conscript army, despite the insistence
of right-wing pressure groups like the National Service League. If Britain had permitted Germany to outbuild the Royal Navy or to conquer and remain in permanent occupation of France and the Low Countries, Britain's security would have been
under permanent threat, its peacetime defence estimates would have reached unsus-
tainable heights and its status as an independent power permanently compromised.
These were not the fears of men suffering from paranoid delusions. The war aims of
the German naval high command were indeed designed to win for Germany a better
position from which to conduct a naval war against Britain.[5]

The horrendous casualties that the British suffered during the First World War,
including 900,000 dead, mean that it is tempting to see the war as a conflict in which
there were no winners and to number the British amongst the defeated powers.
Nothing could be further from the truth. Britain emerged from the First World
War as one of the victor powers and for the next twenty years it remained one of the

dominant players in the international system. Indeed, given its enhanced prestige and the collapse of the German, Ottoman, Russian and Austro-Hungarian empires, the decision of the United States to retreat into isolation, and France's concentration on forestalling a resurgent Germany, Britain was the only world power in the interwar period.[6] But after 1935–6 its position was again challenged by a number of antagonists, Japan in the Far East, Italy in the Mediterranean and Germany in Europe. This time appeasement failed. Unlike Russia, France and the United States before 1914, the fascist powers were not willing to be bought off with small concessions. On the contrary, they sought to create a new world order in which compromise between their ambitions and Britain's continued enjoyment of its status as an independent great power was impossible.[7] In September 1939 the Chamberlain government reluctantly concluded that it had no option other than to go to war to defend that position.

Deterrence

The diplomacy of appeasement, therefore, provided the essential framework within which British defence planners and the armed services operated. But the British rarely practised appeasement pure and simple. They habitually preferred instead to threaten potential aggressors with armed retaliation to make them more willing to compromise. Deterrence was thus a major feature of British defence policy long before the invention of nuclear weapons. Before 1914 the Admiralty and politicians of all hues were convinced that the possibility that the Royal Navy would be able to strangle Germany's overseas trade would dissuade the German government from aggression on the continent.[8] In 1921 the Lloyd George government announced that work would begin on a naval base at Singapore in the belief that the threat that the British would be able to base a large fleet in the Far East would deter the Japanese. Between 1921 and 1925 successive governments embarked on the creation of the Home Defence Air Force to deter the French from trying to use their own air force to blackmail the British into supporting some of the more objectionable aspects of their foreign policy.[9]

But the 1930s were the heyday of deterrence. In 1934 Neville Chamberlain, championing existing Royal Air Force doctrine, used his position as the chancellor of the exchequer in Ramsay MacDonald's National government successfully to insist that Britain could best contribute to the peace of Europe by creating an air force that was large enough to deter Hitler.[10] Three years later he was equally insistent that nothing was better calculated to deter a potential aggressor than Britain's evident political and social stability. And in the spring of 1939, following the German occupation of Prague, Chamberlain's government offered security guarantees to Poland, Greece and Romania in the hope that they would persuade Hitler to eschew, or at least postpone, further aggression.[11]

Most of these attempts at deterrence failed. Only the creation of the Home Defence Air Force was a success, and that was more apparent than real. The Royal Air Force had become the world's first independent air force in April 1918. The threat of the French 'air menace' was largely a myth created by the chief of air staff Sir Hugh Trenchard to defend its continued independence at a time when both the army and navy wanted to regain control over air power. The *Dreadnought* deterrent, the Singapore deterrent, the bomber deterrent and the diplomatic deterrent of the spring of 1939 all failed to forestall the wars they were designed to prevent. Some of them failed because the technologies upon which they rested did not remain a British monopoly for very long; others failed because they lacked military credibility. Between 1905/6 and 1908/9, the launching of HMS *Dreadnought* did disrupt the German fleet-building programme, but by 1908/9 the Germans were themselves building their own *Dreadnoughts*. Sometimes they failed because Britain palpably lacked the military means to make them effective. The Munich crisis in September 1938 showed all too clearly that the RAF did not have the capability to retaliate in kind against German cities if the Luftwaffe bombed London. The diplomatic guarantees of the spring of 1939 failed because the British lacked the wherewithal and the political will to furnish the Polish government with direct military assistance. In December 1941 the Singapore naval base failed to deter the Japanese because the Admiralty did not possess enough battleships and aircraft carriers to send to the Far East.

But there was also a common reason why these attempts at deterrence failed. At the same time that the British were trying to use military means to deter their potential enemies, they were also sending them political signals suggesting that they lacked the will to use the very deterrent they set such great store by. Before 1914 the Liberal government refused to transform its agreements with France and Russia into the kinds of binding politico-military alliances that would have sent a clear message to Germany. Sir Edward Grey, the foreign secretary, knew that if he sought continental allies he would face serious opposition from a powerful faction on the Liberal backbenches. Radical Liberals deplored the very notion of Britain having close relations with the autocratic tsarist regime, and, although they welcomed close relations with France, they shunned continental alliances as a manifestation of that 'gigantic system of outdoor relief for the aristocracy of Great Britain' which Richard Cobden had so memorably condemned in 1858.[12] Grey also continued to entertain the hope that he would be able to negotiate an entente with Germany similar to the one that his predecessor had negotiated with France. It was, therefore, hardly surprising that in August 1914 the kaiser could still believe that Britain might be willing to remain aloof from a European war.[13] In the 1930s the British sent a series of signals to the Germans that undermined the credibility of the various deterrents they tried to pursue. Chamberlain's insistence that it was against international law to bomb civilians hardly carried with it the threat that the German homeland would be devastated by British air attacks. The way in which the British stood by passively when Hitler denounced the disarmament clauses of the Treaty of Versailles, reoccupied the Rhineland, took over Austria and Czechoslovakia, and finally refused to give substance to the Polish guarantee by pursuing an alliance with Stalin, encouraged him to believe that Chamberlain might also stand aside when he attacked Poland.

Arms Limitation

In peacetime appeasement and deterrence often proceeded hand-in-hand with a third policy. British governments sought arms limitation agreements both in an attempt to reduce the need to compete with foreign rivals and because important domestic constituencies believed that money spent on weapons could be better spent on social programmes. The 1909 'people's budget' was successful in raising considerable amounts of extra revenue. But between 1912 and 1914 the Admiralty sought a 'naval holiday' in the *Dreadnought*-building 'race' with Germany in part because the same Liberals who deplored the very idea of Britain becoming involved in European balance-of-power politics also wished to divert defence spending towards domestic social programmes.[14]

In 1922, anxious to avoid the expense of a naval race with the United States that it believed it could not afford, Britain was one of the signatories of the Washington Naval Treaty. In the 1920s the Washington agreement was a good bargain because it enabled the Royal Navy to retain its position as the world's most powerful fleet. It was only in the next decade, following the signing of the London Naval Treaty in 1930, that the British departed from the principle of seeking arms limitation agreements to enhance their security. Until 1930 the Royal Navy retained the ability to confront two enemies simultaneously. But, by agreeing to prolong the moratorium on capital shipbuilding until 1936 and to place a limit on cruiser tonnage, the MacDonald government threw away that advantage.[15]

The Washington Treaty also highlighted one of the principles that usually under-lined Britain's quest for arms limitation agreements, the determination of British governments to use them as a way of enhancing their security. It was no accident that Winston Churchill, then first lord of the Admiralty, made his call for a 'naval holiday' at a time when the 'status quo' at sea still rested in Britain's favour. The experience of the First World War encouraged the British to travel further along this path, for it had demonstrated how exposed their maritime communications were to submarine attack and how vulnerable their cities were to air bombardment. Throughout the 1920s they tried to minimize the first threat by negotiating an international agreement abolishing submarines. When they failed they opted instead for agreements limiting their size and range.[16] The widespread phobia shared by politicians and public that the next war would begin with massive air raids that would deliver a 'knock-out' blow impelled British governments to search for some form of international air disarmament agreement designed to limit aircraft production, abolish bomber aircraft, or prohibit the bombing of civilian centres in wartime.[17] Their failure to secure such an agreement was a powerful influence shaping British rearmament policy in the 1930s. It was a major factor that persuaded the Baldwin and Chamberlain administrations to concentrate resources on building up the RAF at the expense of preparing an army that could fight alongside the French on the continent.[18]

Allies and Burden Sharing

The British were never able to construct a defence policy in an international vacuum, and nor did they ever attempt to do so. Indeed, one frequent response of British policy makers when they felt threatened was to try to share their defence burdens with other powers. In this period Britain entered into three kinds of burden-sharing relationships. Outside Europe, it repeatedly tried to persuade India and the Dominions to bear a heavier share of the cost of imperial defence. It met with only mixed success. In peacetime the imperial government was rarely able to persuade the Dominions to make any significant contribution to imperial defence, as opposed to their own local defence.[19] And, after 1918, London's freedom to use the Indian army, which had formerly been a major imperial military asset, was reduced by the determination of the British administration in Delhi not to alienate Indian taxpayers by insisting that they pay for the use of Indian troops outside India. However, during the First World War both India and the Dominions did contribute significantly to the empire's land forces. Indian soldiers played a major role in defeating the Turks in campaigns in Mesopotamia and Palestine. Australian and New Zealand troops formed a large part of the allied force that failed to take the Gallipoli Peninsula in 1915. They were then posted to the western front where, together with the Canadian Corps, they took part in every major British offensive between 1916 and 1918.[20]

In Europe, both before 1914 and between 1919 and 1939, the British preferred to establish loosely defined ententes with European powers rather than binding alliances. The reasons why Edwardian governments preferred this policy have already been examined. In the interwar period the knowledge that Britain's commitment to France and Russia had produced the holocaust of the western front seemed a good reason for eschewing further formal continental entanglements. Until the mid-1930s British statesmen hoped that by working through the League of Nations they could establish a concert of powers that would be willing to resolve international problems peacefully. However, policy makers knew that in another war against Germany they would have to rely upon the French; but close relations with France were impeded by the fact that in the 1920s French intransigence seemingly made it impossible to appease Germany, whilst in the 1930s they feared that France might prove to be a weak reed upon which to rest their policy. British policy towards its other potential European ally, Soviet Russia, did not even approach the lukewarm nature of the pre-1914 relationship with the tsarist regime. The USSR was the object of bitter distrust amongst the Conservative politicians who dominated the National government in the 1930s, and although some diplomats in 1935–6 toyed with an 'Eastern Locarno' in which Britain might join the USSR and France to deter the Germans, it was never pursued. The foreign secretary, Sir John Simon, feared that it would provoke German suspicions that her neighbours were attempting to encircle her just as they had done between 1907 and 1914 and Hitler might therefore mount a pre-emptive strike.[21]

Although a policy of ententes might leave British policy makers with the illusion that they retained a 'free hand' to shape their policy according to British needs, the disadvantages of their policy were apparent even in peacetime. Britain's loose commitment to its putative friends only encouraged its enemies to question the worth of cooperating with Britain. In both France and Russia before 1914 there were some politicians who doubted the value of their country's relationship with Britain and there were others who would have preferred a rapprochement with Germany. It was therefore not surprising that during the First World War the British quickly transformed these loose arrangements into more formal military alliances, if only to prevent the possibility that their pre-war arrangements might disintegrate. It was then that the British discovered the real cost of burden sharing. In 1914 the British hoped for the time being to be able to stand aside from the continental land war. In the meantime, Lord Kitchener called for volunteers to create his New Armies and was overwhelmed by the number of men ready to enlist. He hoped that by 1917, when his troops were ready, the armies of all of the other belligerents would have fought each other to a standstill. Britain would then intervene decisively and impose its war aims on both its allies and its enemies. But the early successes of the Central Powers, and the unwillingness of the French and Russians to permit Britain to fight to the last French or Russian soldier, quickly demonstrated the danger of this policy. By the winter of 1914–15, a British observer in Paris was reporting that 'the cry "perfidious Albion"' could be heard. In February 1916 the head of Wellington House, the organization responsible for disseminating British propaganda in allied and neutral countries, warned the cabinet of 'an undercurrent of uneasiness found manifesting itself in France and, to a lesser extent, Russia, as to whether the efforts and sacrifices being made by England were comparable to those of the Allies or commensurate with the importance of the struggle'.[22] One reason why the British army fought the battles of the Somme in 1916 and Third Ypres in 1917 was to demonstrate to their allies the reality of their commitment to the common cause. Within weeks of the Munich agreement in 1938 the British found themselves subject to similar pressure, and had perforce to react in the same way. Bereft of the support of the Czech army, the French did not think that promises of British air and naval assistance in a future war with Germany were enough. The French demanded a major British effort on land and, in the spring of 1939, the Chamberlain government was compelled to reverse its policy of opting out of planning to send troops to the continent in the event of war.[23]

Intelligence

British defence policy makers pursued two other policies, the development of a highly successful intelligence system and the adoption of high-technology weapons, to make the most effective use of their limited resources. Before 1914 Britain possessed only an embryonic intelligence community. It consisted of the intelligence departments of the two services, a small counter-intelligence force to check the activities of Irish seditionists and the handful of German spies in Britain, and an even smaller secret service charged with reporting German preparations to launch a surprise invasion of Britain. It also possessed a rudimentary capability to read the wireless and cable communications of other powers. It was not coincidental that the growth of the modern British intelligence community accompanied the growing use of wireless communications in warfare.[24] During the First World War these services burgeoned, acquiring the capability to read German naval and military ciphers almost as a matter of routine and employing nearly 6,000 agents in occupied territory to report on German troop movements. The still-underdeveloped state of the literature on the strategic impact of British intelligence during the First World War makes it difficult to estimate the overall significance of the material these agencies supplied. Research is currently being undertaken on the impact of operational intelligence on Haig's conduct of operations on the western front. But it is already apparent that information supplied by the code-breakers of 'Room 40' was of the greatest use to the Admiralty because it regularly warned them when the German High Seas fleet was about to sortie into the North Sea.[25]

At the end of the First World War the intelligence services experienced the same rundown of manpower and resources that the armed services as a whole experienced. However, despite the fact that for much of the interwar period, the former were deprived of both sufficient money and personnel, they did succeed in keeping in being a nucleus of professional code-breakers who were to provide the foundation for the highly successful signals intelligence service established at Bletchley Park during the Second World War. In the interwar period the code-breakers of the Government Code and Cipher School honed their skills by attempting to read, with varying degrees of success, the secret diplomatic and military codes of the United States, France, Turkey, Italy, Germany, the USSR and Japan. However, technical successes in gathering information were not always translated into an accurate perception of the capabilities of a potential enemy. The British, for example, undoubtedly under-estimated the strength of the Japanese economy and military in the 1930s and failed to realize that they would not be overawed by the Anglo-Saxon powers. And even when British intelligence agencies did develop an accurate assessment of enemy capa-bilities, as was the case when the War Office analysed German tank doctrine in the late 1930s, that knowledge could not always be put to practical use. For it was a harsh truism of intelligence that even the best information was useless unless the side receiving it had the capability to react to it in good time.[26]

High Technology

It was natural that Britain, the world's first industrial nation, should opt to use the products of industrialization to defend itself. The British repeatedly adopted high-technology weapons in order to multiply the effectiveness of the forces at their dis-posal and employed mechanical devices in an effort to minimize their manpower losses. At sea, in 1905 Sir John Fisher hoped that the *Dreadnought* and *Invincible* classes of battleship and armoured cruisers would so disrupt the naval building pro-grammes of Britain's potential enemies that Britain's maritime superiority would be frozen in aspic.[27] In August 1917 General J. C. Smuts, who had been charged by the Lloyd George government with discovering how to maximize Britain's war effort in the air, recommended that Britain should establish the world's first independent air force in order to fight the air battle far behind the Rhine. The new force would bring intense and war-winning pressure on German industry at a time when the British Expeditionary Force was still floundering in the mud of Flanders.[28]

On land the British either pioneered or rapidly developed two other innovations. Although the British did not invent poison gas, by 1918 it had become a major weapon in their armoury.[29] In September 1916, the British were the first nation to deploy tanks on the battlefield and they maintained their lead in tank technology and tactics until the early 1930s. However, the practical impact of tanks on the battle-fields of 1916–18 should not be exaggerated. Not only did they require enormous logistical support to get them to their start-line, but they were highly vulnerable to enemy artillery fire and dangerously prone to breaking down or to asphyxiating their crews within a few hours of the start of a battle. The oft-cited success of the Tank Corps on the opening day of the Cambrai offensive in November 1917 owed more to developments in artillery techniques than it did to the massed advance of nearly four hundred tanks.[30]

The fact that the British were able to deploy so many tanks on the opening day of Cambrai demonstrated that they were committed not just to employing high-technology weapons, but to employing them in the greatest possible numbers. In the winter of 1914–15 David Lloyd George, the chancellor of the exchequer, was so horrified at the losses that the British army was already suffering on the western front that he mobilized most of the British engineering industry to supply the army with the largest possible quantities of heavy artillery and machine guns.[31] In December 1917, the government opted to pursue the same policy on a grand scale and to maximize its dwindling manpower resources by increasing the production of the newest high-technology weapons such as tanks, aircraft, gas and smoke. By doing so it hoped to increase the British Expeditionary Force's firepower without the need to provide Haig with the hundreds of thousands of drafts he requested.[32]

This commitment to the mass production of high-technology weapons paid dividends in the final 'Hundred days' campaign on the western front. Although the British Expeditionary Force had lost heavily during the Germans' spring offensive, the Ministry of Munitions had no difficulty in resupplying it. The Germans, by contrast, found themselves at a fatal disadvantage because German industry was unable to make good their equipment losses in the closing stages of the war.

The appalling losses that the British Expeditionary Force had suffered in 1916–17 were partly caused by allied pressure that forced the British into prematurely committing Kitchener's New Armies to a series of costly offensives. But they were also caused by the clumsy manner in which the British high command in France used the weapons Lloyd George had given them. However, by 1918, through a system of trial and very many costly errors, the British Expeditionary Force had evolved an operational doctrine that enabled its commanders to orchestrate all of their weapons systems in such a way that they could cooperate to maximize their combat effectiveness on the battlefield.[33] Under the weight of the heavy losses that they suffered the morale of the British army sagged, but unlike the Russian, French and German armies, it never collapsed. There was plenty of war weariness in the ranks of the British Expeditionary Force in 1917–18, but very little defeatism. That the troops endured for so long was the result of a combination of factors. At a mundane but essential level the army's logistics system kept them supplied with food, shelter and medical attention. Half of the troops who served in the army were volunteers, not conscripts. They were in the trenches because they thought that the war was being fought over issues that were worth fighting for. And finally, the British army imposed a draconian disciplinary regime on anyone who stepped out of line. Over 300 British soldiers were executed for purely military offences such as desertion or cowardice between 1914 and 1918.[34]

Financial exigencies encouraged post-1918 governments to continue to rely on high-technology weapons in place of expensive and hard-to-recruit manpower. In accepting the 'Ten-Year Rule' in August 1919, the Lloyd George cabinet also accepted that defence estimates could be trimmed if air power and other mechanical devices were substituted for more expensive infantry battalions to police the empire.[35] In the 1920s the British army was in the forefront of tank development. In 1927 it established the first completely mechanized combat brigade in any army. In the second half of the 1930s it became the first all-motorized army in the world.[36] The RAF demonstrated the potential of air power when they imposed a system of 'control without occupation' on Iraq in the early 1920s. Trenchard claimed that the RAF could suppress the revolt threatening British rule in Iraq without great expense if most of the army's infantry battalions were recalled and if the RAF deployed a small number of squadrons to police the region from the air. Air policing on the periphery of the empire worked with reasonable success against scattered rural populations, although its effectiveness was reduced when its targets recognized that there were some passive measures that they could take to defend themselves. In this case Trenchard's reliance on air power was justified, for the cost of the Iraq garrison fell from £20 million in 1921–2 to only £2.3 million in 1924–5.[37]

But technology by itself did not always provide a complete solution to Britain's problems. After 1918 the General Staff sought to maintain a small, professional and well-equipped mechanized and motorized army, able to win victories quickly and cheaply by substituting technology for manpower. But its doctrine was poorly suited to exploit the advantages of such an organization to the utmost. Although it did develop a combined-arms doctrine, it remained committed to an autocratic command and control system that inhibited subordinate commanders from exercising their initiative and seizing the fleeting opportunities offered to them on the battlefield. The overriding importance of avoiding undue casualties encouraged the General Staff to place the necessity of consolidating gains won on the battlefield before the need to exploit success, and it developed organizational structures that sacrificed firepower to mobility and divorced commanders from the weapons they needed to give them the fire-support they required. The result was an arthritic command and control system that could not keep pace with the speed of the German blitzkrieg in 1940.[38]

Furthermore, in the late 1930s the British failed to keep pace with the numerical expansion of the German army, so that in May 1940 the British Expeditionary Force found itself without a single fully equipped armoured division with which to face the German panzers. This failure was not caused by the British army's blimpish attachment to its horses. It was the product of the budgetary constraints within which the army operated in the 1930s, the multiplicity of tasks that it was expected to fulfil and the government's refusal to prepare for a continental commitment until it was too late. The army's two main missions, policing the empire and contributing to the defence of the British Isles against air attack, did not call for large numbers of tanks. In the eyes of the politicians who determined national policy for most of the 1930s, preparing armoured divisions to fight in France came a poor third to these priorities.

Conclusion

There were several constants that determined the parameters within which British defence policy and its armed forces developed between 1899 and 1939. The need to garrison a worldwide empire was a continuous concern. Britain's dependence on imported foodstuffs and raw materials persisted throughout this period and ensured that defence planners had to give the highest priority to securing Britain's maritime communications. Britain's vulnerability to direct attack also remained constant, although the nature of the threat it confronted did change. By the 1930s fear of air bombardment had replaced the Edwardians' fear of seaborne invasion. But both threats ensured that the British had to maintain a constant and lively interest in resisting German attempts to fix her hegemony over Europe. The conviction of British policy makers that defence spending was only a form of insurance policy also remained constant. For a satiated power, avoidance of war, through a combination of appeasement and deterrence, was thus a habitual policy option. The size of the insurance premium the British were willing to pay to defend themselves varied with the immediacy of the threats that confronted them. But the wish to reduce them to the lowest possible level frequently persuaded the British to adopt new technologies as force multipliers in the hope of reducing the financial and human costs of defence.

If the British had a secret weapon in their armoury, it was not a particular weapon. It was the highly developed political skills of their leaders. In every instance when they were confronted by a major threat, they attempted, although not always successfully, to share the burden of confronting it with other powers. As one American military planner ruefully admitted after attending an Anglo-American strategic planning conference in 1941, 'One point which stood out in the British papers was adherence to the long-established policy of adroitly organizing other peoples to do the fighting necessary to sustain a mighty empire'.[39]

NOTES

1   D. Edgerton, 'Liberal militarism and the British state', *New Left Review*, 185 (1991), pp. 139–69.

2   R. Williams, *Defending the Empire: The Conservative Party and British Defence Policy 1899–1915* (New Haven, Conn., 1991); B. Semmel, *Liberalism and Naval Strategy: Ideology, Interest and Sea Power during the Pax Britannica* (London, 1986), pp. 99–118; D. J. Bettez, 'Unfulfilled initiative: disarmament negotiations and the Hague Peace Conference of 1899 and 1907', *Journal of the Royal United Services Institute*, 133, no. 3 (1988), p. 61.

3   P. M. Kennedy, *The Rise of the Anglo-German Antagonism 1860–1914* (London, 1980).

4   M. Howard, *The Continental Commitment: The Dilemma of British Defence Policy in the Era of the Two World Wars* (London, 1972), p. 52; A. Offer, *The First World War: An Agrarian Interpretation* (Oxford, 1989), pp. 217–32.

5   H. Herwig, 'Admirals versus generals: the war aims of the Imperial German Navy, 1914–18', *Central European History*, 5, no. 3 (1972), pp. 208–33.

6   A. Clayton, *The British Empire as Superpower, 1919–1939* (London, 1986); J. Ferris, '"The greatest power on earth": Great Britain in the 1920s', *International History Review*, 13, no. 4 (1991), pp. 726–50.

7   R. A. C. Parker, *Chamberlain and Appeasement: British Policy and the Coming of the Second World War* (London, 1993); P. Lowe, *Great Britain and the Origins of the Pacific War: A Study of British Policy in East Asia, 1937–41* (Oxford, 1977); M. J. Cohen and M. Kolinsky, eds, *Britain and the Middle East in the 1930s: Security Problems, 1935–39* (London, 1992).

8   K. Neilson, '"The British Empire floats on the British Navy": British naval policy, belligerent rights, and disarmament, 1902–1909', in B. J. C. McKercher, ed., *Arms Limitation and Disarmament: Restraints on War, 1899–1939* (Westport, Conn., 1992), pp. 21–41; H. Weinroth, 'Left-wing opposition to naval armaments in Britain before 1914', *Journal of Contemporary History*, 6, no. 4 (1971), p. 97.

9   J. Neidpath, *The Singapore Naval Base and the Defence of Britain's Eastern Empire, 1919–1941* (Oxford, 1981), p. 46; J. Ferris, 'The theory of a "French air menace", Anglo-French relations and the British Home Defence Air Force Programmes of 1921–25', *Journal of Strategic Studies*, 10, no. 1 (1987), pp. 62–83.

10 M. Smith, *British Air Strategy between the Wars* (Oxford, 1984), pp. 109–72; R. J. Overy, 'Air power and the origins of deterrence theory before 1939', *Journal of Strategic Studies*, 15, no. 1 (1992), p. 75; P. S. Melinger, 'Trenchard and "morale bombing": the evolu-

tion of RAF doctrine before World War II', *Journal of Military History*, 60, no. 2 (1996), pp. 243–70.

11 A. Prazmowska, *Britain, Poland, the Eastern Front, 1939* (Cambridge, 1987).

12 M. Howard, *War and the Liberal Conscience* (London, 1978), pp. 43–4; H. S. Weinroth, 'British radicals and the balance of power, 1902–1914', *Historical Journal*, 16, no. 4 (1970), pp. 653–82.

13 S. M. Lynn-Jones, 'Detente and deterrence: Anglo-German relations, 1911–1914', *International Security*, 11, no. 2 (1986), p. 144.

14 J. H. Maurer, 'Churchill's naval holiday: arms control and the Anglo-German naval race, 1912–1914', *Journal of Strategic Studies*, 15, no. 1 (1992), pp. 102–27.

15 J. Ferris, *Men, Money and Diplomacy: The Evolution of British Strategic Policy 1919–26* (Ithaca, NY, 1989), pp. 98–101, 181.

16 D. Henry, 'British submarine policy, 1918–1939', in B. McL. Ranft, ed., *Technical Change and British Naval Policy, 1860–1939* (London, 1977), pp. 80–4, 95–7; A. J. Marder, M. Jacobsen and J. Horsfield, *Old Friends, New Enemies: The Royal Navy and the Imperial Japanese Navy*, vol. 2, *The Pacific War, 1942–1945* (Oxford, 1990), pp. 217–18.

17 U. Bialer, *The Shadow of the Bomber: The Fear of Air Attack and British Politics 1932–1939* (London, 1980).

18 Smith, *British Air Strategy*, pp. 140–97; N. H. Gibbs, *Grand Strategy* (London, 1976), vol. 1, pp. 93–490.

19 D. C. Gordon, *The Dominion Partnership in Imperial Defence 1870–1914* (Baltimore, 1965); R. F. Holland, *Britain and the Commonwealth Alliance 1918–1939* (London, 1981), pp. 167–205.

20 K. Jeffery, 'The eastern arc of empire: a strategic view 1850–1950', *Journal of Strategic Studies*, 5, no. 2 (1982), pp. 531–45; F. W. Perry, *The Commonwealth Armies: Manpower and Organization in the Two World Wars* (Manchester, 1988).

21 M. Cowling, *The Impact of Hitler: British Politics and British Policy 1933–1940* (Cambridge, 1975), pp. 265–6; J. Charmley, *Chamberlain and the Lost Peace* (London, 1989), p. 67.

22 K. Neilson, ' "Joy-rides"? British intelligence and propaganda in Russia, 1914–1917,' *Historical Journal*, 24 (1981), p. 890; D. French, *British Strategy and War Aims, 1914–1916* (London, 1986), pp. 9–12.

23 B. Bond, *British Military Policy between the Two World Wars* (Oxford, 1980), pp. 244–336.

24 C. Andrew, *Secret Service: The Making of the British Intelligence Community* (London, 1985), pp. 1–85; T. G. Fergusson, *British Military Intelligence, 1870–1914* (London, 1984); B. Porter, *Plots and Paranoia: A History of Political Espionage in Britain, 1790–1988* (London, 1989), pp. 101–20; N. Hiley, 'The failure of British espionage against Germany, 1908–1914', *Historical Journal*, 26, no. 4 (1983), pp. 867–89; J. Ferris, 'Before "Room 40": the British Empire and signals intelligence, 1898–1914', *Journal of Strategic Studies*, 12, no. 4 (1989), pp. 431–57.

25 P. Beesly, *Room 40: British Naval Intelligence 1914–1918* (London, 1982); J. Ferris, *The British Army and Signals Intelligence during the First World War* (London, 1992); D. French, 'Sir John French's secret service in France, 1914–1915', *Journal of Strategic Studies*, 7, no. 4 (1984), pp. 423–40.

26 See W. Wark, *The Ultimate Enemy: British Intelligence and Nazi Germany, 1933–1939* (Ithaca, NY, 1985); A. G. Denniston, 'The Government Code and Cipher School between the wars', *Intelligence and National Security*, 1, no. 1 (1986), pp. 48–70; J. Ferris, 'Whitehall's Black Chamber: British cryptology and the Government Code and Cipher School, 1919–1929', *Intelligence and National Security*, 2, no. 1 (1987), pp.

54–91; R. Denniston, 'Diplomatic eavesdropping, 1922–44', *Intelligence and National Security*, 10, no. 3 (1995), pp. 423–48; A. Best, 'Constructing an image: British intelligence and Whitehall's perception of Japan, 1931–39', *Intelligence and National Security*, 11, no. 3 (1996), pp. 403–23; T. Harrison-Place, 'British perceptions of the tactics of the German army, 1938–40', *Intelligence and National Security*, 9, no. 3 (1994), pp. 495–519.

27 J. T. Sumida, *In Defence of Naval Supremacy: Finance, Technology, and British Naval Policy 1889–1914* (London, 1989), pp. 37–61.

28 M. Cooper, *The Birth of Independent Air Power: British Air Policy in the First World War* (London, 1986), pp. 100–3.

29 A. Palazzo, *Seeking Victory on the Western Front: The British Army and Chemical Warfare in World War One* (Lincoln, Nebr., 2000).

30 R. H. Larson, *The British Army and the Theory of Armoured Warfare 1918–40* (Newark, NJ, 1984); P. Harris, *Men, Ideas and Tanks: British Military Thought and Armoured Forces, 1903–1939* (Manchester, 1995); D. J. Childs, *A Peripheral Weapon? The Production and Employment of British Tanks in the First World War* (Westport, Conn., 1999).

31 R. J. Q. Adams, *Arms and the Wizard: Lloyd George and the Ministry of Munitions 1915–1916* (London, 1978).

32 T. Travers, *How the War Was Won: Command and Technology in the British Army on the Western Front 1917–1918* (London, 1992), pp. 32–49; T. Travers, 'Could the tanks of 1918 have been war-winners for the British Expeditionary Force?', *Journal of Contemporary History*, 27 (1992), pp. 389–405.

33 T. Travers, *The Killing Ground: The British Army, the Western Front and the Emergence of Modern Warfare, 1900–1918* (London, 1987); S. Bidwell and D. Graham, *Firepower: British Army Weapons and Theories of War 1904–1945* (London, 1982), pp. 61–148; R. Prior and T. Wilson, *Command on the Western Front: The Military Career of Sir Henry Wilson 1914–1918* (Oxford, 1992); P. Griffith, *Battle Tactics of the Western Front: The British Army's Art of Attack, 1916–18* (London, 1994).

34 G. Oram, *Worthless Men: Race, Eugenics and the Death Penalty in the British Army during the First World War* (London, 1998); J. G. Fuller, *Troop Morale and Popular Culture in the British and Dominion Armies 1914–1918* (Oxford, 1991).

35 J. Ferris, 'Treasury control, the Ten-Year Rule and British service policies 1919–1924', *Historical Journal*, 30, no. 4 (1987), pp. 853–83.

36 H. Winton, *To Change an Army: General Sir John Burnett-Stuart and British Armoured Doctrine, 1927–1938* (London, 1988).

37 D. E. Omissi, *Air Power and Colonial Control: The Royal Air Force, 1919–1939* (Manchester, 1990).

38 D. French, *Raising Churchill's Army: The British Army and the War against Germany, 1919–1945* (Oxford, 2000), pp. 12–47.

39 Albert C. Wedemeyer quoted in J. Gooch, ' "Hidden in the Rock": American military perceptions of Great Britain 1919–1940', in L. Freedman, P. Hayes and R. O'Neill, eds, *War, Strategy and International Politics: Essays in Honour of Sir Michael Howard* (Oxford, 1992), p. 155.

FURTHER READING

Andrew, C., *Secret Service: The Making of the British Intelligence Community* (London, 1985).
Bond, B., *British Military Policy between the Two World Wars* (Oxford, 1980).
Clayton, A., *The British Empire as Superpower, 1919–1939* (London, 1986).

Ferris, J., *Men, Money and Diplomacy: The Evolution of British Strategic Policy 1919–26* (Ithaca, NY, 1989).

French, D., *British Strategy and War Aims, 1914–1916* (London, 1986).

French, D., *Raising Churchill's Army: The British Army and the War against Germany, 1919–1945* (Oxford, 2000).

Holland, R. F., *Britain and the Commonwealth Alliance 1918–1939* (London, 1981).

Howard, M., *The Continental Commitment: The Dilemma of British Defence Policy in the Era of the Two World Wars* (London, 1972).

Kennedy, P. M., *The Rise of the Anglo-German Antagonism 1860–1914* (London, 1980).

Neidpath, J., *The Singapore Naval Base and the Defence of Britain's Eastern Empire, 1919–1941* (Oxford, 1981).

Offer, A., *The First World War: An Agrarian Interpretation* (Oxford, 1989).

Omissi, D. E., *Air Power and Colonial Control: The Royal Air Force, 1919–1939* (Manchester, 1990).

Parker, R. A. C., *Chamberlain and Appeasement: British Policy and the Coming of the Second World War* (London, 1993).

Perry, F. W., *The Commonwealth Armies: Manpower and Organization in the Two World Wars* (Manchester, 1988).

Smith, M., *British Air Strategy between the Wars* (Oxford, 1984).

Sumida, J. T., *In Defence of Naval Supremacy: Finance, Technology, and British Naval Policy 1889–1914* (London, 1989).

Travers, T., *The Killing Ground: The British Army, the Western Front and the Emergence of Modern Warfare, 1900–1918* (London, 1987).

Travers, T., *How the War Was Won: Command and Technology in the British Army on the Western Front 1917–1918* (London, 1992).

Williams, R., *Defending the Empire: The Conservative Party and British Defence Policy 1899–1915* (New Haven, Conn., 1991).

Chapter Twelve

The Empire, 1900–1939

Martin Kitchen

When Queen-Empress Victoria died in 1901, the British Empire stretched over more than a quarter of the world's surface. It comprised about 400 million people, with 41.5 million living in the British Isles, and 294 million in the Indian Empire.[1] Although British rule took on different forms throughout this vast empire, there were two basic approaches. The white settler colonies of Canada and Newfoundland, the Cape and Natal, Australia and New Zealand were largely self-governing in domestic affairs, with parliaments based on the Westminster model. They were subordinate to the British parliament and had no say in foreign affairs. Other settler colonies in the West Indies and Africa were given no such freedom, and the future of the Orange Free State and the Transvaal, which had been taken from the Boers, was still undecided. In 1910 they were joined with the Cape and Natal to form the Union of South Africa. Colonies without large settler populations were administered directly by a handful of white administrators without consultation with the colonized.[2]

The empire stretched from the poverty-stricken sugar plantations in the West Indies to the strategically important Mediterranean bases in Gibraltar, Malta and Cyprus, which in turn protected British interests in Egypt, the Sudan, Uganda, Kenya and Somaliland. Across the Persian Gulf were Aden and the Gulf States, which were also seen as essential to the defence of the route to India via the Suez canal, at the end of which was Ceylon with its naval base at Trincomalee.

Along with the settler colonies and possessions deemed essential to the defence of India were colonies that were exploited for purely commercial reasons. These included the former slave-trading colonies in West Africa, and Rhodesia and Nyasaland, which were ruled by Cecil Rhodes's British South Africa Company until 1923.

India, the jewel in the crown, was a case apart. Queen Victoria had been made empress of India in 1876, and her viceroy ruled the Raj as an absolute monarch, assisted by a handful of British administrators. On the eve of the Second World War India, whose population had risen to 353 million, was ruled by a mere 1,261 covenanted members of the Indian civil service.[3]

The coronation of Edward VII in 1902 was a splendid affair for which Elgar wrote the music for that stirring paean to British might: 'Land of Hope and Glory'. It seemed a perfect mirror of Edwardian self-confidence in the lines

> Wider still and wider, shall thy bounds be set;
> God who made thee mighty, make thee mightier yet.

The lyricist, the Cambridge English don A. C. Benson, was in no sense an imperialist and was somewhat alarmed that his 'occasional' piece became an ersatz national anthem, much favoured by boorish flag wavers and xenophobes.

Outwardly so splendid, the foundations of the empire were beginning to crumble. The Boer War was a shattering blow to British self-confidence, and an inspiration for those within the empire, from Ireland to India, who were seeking national independence. The country that once had been the workshop of the world had now been overtaken by Imperial Germany as Europe's leading industrial nation. Some keen observers noted that Britain was in a state of slow but relentless economic decline. Germany dared to challenge the proposition that Britannia ruled the waves, and a cripplingly expensive naval race had begun.[4]

Some even went so far as to ask the question whether the empire would still be around at the end of the new century. J. L. Garvin, soon to become editor of the *Observer* and to write the biography of Joseph Chamberlain, was hardly alone in thinking that it would not.[5] The liberal sociologist and journalist L. T. Hobhouse argued that the Boer War had shown how preposterous was the claim that Englishmen had a God-given right and obligation to rule the world.[6]

Others, most notably Joseph Chamberlain, recognized the symptoms of decline, but felt that the empire could provide the antidote. The proposed solution was 'imperial preference', hastily renamed 'tariff reform', whereby a tariff wall would be erected around the empire to protect it from foreign competition. The resulting prosperity would help finance generous social policies at home. It sounded convincing to many, but it was soon pointed out that since only one-third of British trade was with the empire, it was at best a risky proposition, and none of the political parties wished to abandon their belief in the virtues of free trade. Even Chamberlain was well aware of the seriousness of the situation, and in 1902 wistfully misquoted Matthew Arnold: 'the weary Titan staggers under the too vast orb of its fate'.

Chamberlain's Tariff Reform League found many recruits in Conservative ranks, but the party was badly split and suffered a crushing defeat in the 1906 election. Later in that year Chamberlain suffered a stroke that ended his political career. While the free-trading liberals enjoyed an overwhelming majority in the House of Commons, Chamberlain's grandiose scheme gathered dust in the archives.

Although Chamberlain's proposals for reform gained only limited support, there was widespread agreement that something had to be done to stop the conspicuous decline of British power and prestige. Recruiting offices for the war in South Africa sent alarming reports about the appalling physical condition of the nation's youth. As elsewhere in Europe, there was much wild talk about improving the racial stock. Numerous drastic remedies were put forward to stop the rot. They ranged from eugenics to compulsory circumcision, from welfare reform to an overhaul of the armed services, from scouting to religious revival. Questions were also asked about

Britain's imperial mission. Sir Charles Dilke, one of the more distinguished of Britain's long list of political might-have-beens, drew a clear distinction between what he called 'the true as against the bastard imperialism', the former being the right to self-government which had been remembered in Canada, but forgotten in South Africa.[7] One of the great imperial pro-consuls, Lord Cromer, complained that the empire had ceased to be 'philanthropic' and had become 'commercial'. Other critics of the empire, such as J. A. Hobson and E. D. Morel, were far more radical in their attacks, but as Lord Cromer remarked in 1913: 'Few, if any, pronounced anti-imperialists exist, but a wide divergence of opinion prevails as to the method of giving effect to imperial policy'.[8]

A number of prominent Liberals had been strongly opposed to the Boer War and had been denounced as anti-imperialist Little Englanders. But they were proud of the imperialist traditions of their party, and the 'Liberal imperialism' of Herbert Asquith and Sir Edward Grey was sufficiently fervent to silence the doubts of Conservative imperialists about the policies of the new government. Only John Morley's appointment to the India Office occasioned some concern.

There were, however, considerable differences between Conservative and Liberal imperialism. Liberals had no time for proconsuls such as Joseph Chamberlain's disciple Sir Alfred Milner, governor of the Cape Colony, whose racism, contempt for democracy and denunciation of the Commons as 'rabble' they found distasteful, and whose 'kindergarten' produced such unashamed imperialists as Leopold Amery, who remained faithful to Milner's creed of tariff reform and the 'unity of the British race'.[9] Nor did Liberals have any sympathy for Lord Curzon's grandiose schemes for turning the Persian Gulf into a British lake, and to seize control of Tibet, Afghanistan and southern Persia.[10]

The Liberals had no grand scheme for the empire; they simply hoped to muddle through as best they could. Thus the Imperial Conferences of 1907, 1909 and 1911 were magnificent affairs which gave some indication of where the empire was heading, but nothing fundamental was changed. John Morley summed up this attitude succinctly: 'I can answer for today; I can do pretty well tomorrow; the day after tomorrow I leave to providence'. Morley's radicalism had worn very thin by this time. He was prepared to make some concessions where necessary, rejected the approach of Curzon and the Conservatives who made the maintenance of order their first priority, but refused even to consider political reform. Morley believed that it was essential to stay 'cool and sceptical about *political* change, whether in India or other places'.

The viceroy, Lord Minto, saw things very differently. Advised by intransigents in the Indian civil service, he warned of another Indian mutiny if law and order were not rigorously maintained. Morley was appalled and urged restraint. There followed a cycle of violence and repression until the Morley–Minto reforms of 1909 bought temporary relief. More Indians were brought into government as a sop to the moderates in Congress around Gopal Krishna Gokhale, but this was not intended as the first step towards democracy. This policy of 'order plus reforms' was dressed up as heading in the direction of eventual self-government, but contained the warning that this would not be 'in their own day'. The Press Act of 1910 made it clear that order took priority over reform.

'Muddling through' in India was at best an attempt to choose the lesser evil, but hardliners in the Indian civil service faced intransigents in Congress, and it was all too easy to fall back on the old policy of divide and rule, playing off Hindus against Muslims, moderates against radicals, princes against middle-class intellectuals. Coercion was needed in India to maintain the army and to keep the market open for British goods, but a degree of cooperation was essential, and this required consideration of the conflicting claims of castes, religions and the myriad states and communities. The realization that the task was virtually impossible tried the patience of all but the most dedicated colonial administrator. That tempers were shorter in Delhi than they were in Whitehall was an additional problem.

In the Indian princely states, as in much of the rest of the empire, the British exercised 'indirect rule'. The states administered themselves under British paramountcy.[11] A similar system existed in Malaya where British officials 'advised' the sultans. The problem arose that in most cases the residents had no government to which they could offer advice, so they ended up running the administration, referring to the sultan only on matters of Islamic law and custom.[12] Variations of this system were found in many parts of Africa and the Middle East, but it was in Northern Nigeria that it took on an almost paradigmatic form.

Frederick (later Baron) Lugard, who was high commissioner of the Northern Nigerian Protectorate from 1900 to 1906, and governor general of Nigeria from 1912 to 1918, was fortunate in having in Margery Perham an admiring disciple and biographer, who credited him with perfecting indirect rule and thus creating an enlightened, humane and benign form of colonial rule.[13] Unlike the French or the Portuguese with their policy of assimilation, or the racial segregation of southern Africa, indirect rule respected native customs and traditions and encouraged development. The policy was cheap, the natives were appeased, the empire peaceful, and thus it provided an ideal form of rule in countries whose climate was inhospitable to white settlers.

Or so went the Lugard myth, the product of self-advertisement, plus the dogged efforts of his well-connected journalist wife and his protégée Margery Perham. He was in fact a poor, some even claimed incompetent, administrator with an autocratic temperament, who saw eye to eye with autocratic and incompetent Nigerian emirs. Lugard's indirect rule amounted to virtually no rule at all. It was more often than not the result of expedience, indolence, sometimes of desperation, never a deliberate policy. Economic development, education and health went by the board. Local despots were supported, and no effort was made to secure a role for educated Africans, or to prepare for self-government.[14] In the long run many of the white settler colonies had far better records in health, economic development and education; but that still amounted to precious little.

Indirect rule was enthusiastically supported by the academic establishment. Sir Henry Maine hymned the praises of self-governing, self-regulating and self-sufficient village communities in his classic study *Ancient Law*.[15] The theme was taken up by Lewis Morgan, who in turn inspired Friedrich Engels to make some wild speculations about the origins of the family, private property and the state, which in turn became a canonic text for those engaging in the daunting effort to reconcile Marxism with feminism.[16] Bronislaw Malinowski did for indirect rule in Africa what Maine had done for divide and rule in India.[17] For Malinowski indirect rule was the implementation of his functional anthropology, which taught that the delicate checks and balances of primitive society should not be tampered with, and that change should be minimal and slow. Margery Perham sat at Malinowski's feet and spread the gospel of his 'functional ideas' to colonial officials and African intellectuals.

African society was to be left to its own devices and develop at its own pace. Malinowski's legacy was on the whole harmful. Functional anthropology's emphasis on the virtues of the village community and local custom was echoed by the proponents of African socialism. To claim that one-party rule was rooted in traditional African society was an easy and tempting step to take. Indirect rule gave Africans little or no experience in administration or politics. The authority of backward, corrupt and despotic rulers was bolstered, and societies were frozen into a traditional mould.

Both Liberals and Conservatives paid lip service to the desirability of bringing progress and prosperity to the empire, but they had reluctantly to admit that this would not be possible without the intervention of capitalists and a degree of disruption to traditional societies. The Colonial Office had a snobbish dislike for people in 'trade' which was reinforced by the anti-capitalist thrust of the desire to preserve the village community, and by the precepts of functional anthropology. But capitalists wanted monopolies to offset the considerable risks involved, and offers of substantial investment in return for the grant of a monopoly were often hard to resist. The liberal conscience could easily be assuaged by the thought that something might trickle down to benefit the colonized.

A more attractive alternative was to encourage local peasants to sell their crops to native merchants, who in turn sold them to European factors. This helped the peasantry without seriously disrupting traditional society and was thus an appropriate economic form for indirect rule. The system worked well in West Africa, so well in fact that Sir Charles Lever attempted to set up a large-scale palm-oil operation in the region in 1907. British officials denied his request, so Sir Charles set up shop in the more congenial atmosphere of the Congo. Bovril was given similarly short shrift when the company requested ranching rights in Bechuanaland in 1919.

The situation in Egypt was something of an oddity. It was never called a colony, and it was supposed to be handed back to the 'natives' once the finances were in order. Egyptian nationalism was inspired by the example of the revolutionary Turks, fuelled by British insensitivity to matters of race and religion, and hardened by the savage repression of dissent and determination to hang on to the Suez canal for as long as possible. Cromer's heavy-handed approach towards the nationalists was conditioned by his refusal to do business with 'extremists'. He announced that conciliation was out of the question, 'save on terms which in India and Ireland spell political suicide, and in Egypt would involve a relapse into all the misgovernment and disorder of the past'.[18] Concessions made by his successor, Eldon Gorst, were too little too late, and simply encouraged the nationalist Wafd party. Gorst responded with a dose of Cromerian repression. He was replaced by Kitchener, who offered further concessions but made sure that he kept his powder dry.

Egypt was not the only part of the empire where there was violent resistance to British rule. The Zulu uprising in Natal from 1906 to 1908 resulted in 3,500 African deaths. This was a province, described by Winston Churchill as the 'hooligan of the British Empire', with the most disgraceful record of racial discrimination. It was here that Gandhi began his campaign on behalf of the large Indian population, which suffered appalling humiliations and indignities. There were revolts in Kenya, Nigeria and British Guiana, assassinations in India, and some Boers continued the struggle against the British; but, on the whole, the empire was remarkably peaceful in the years before the First World War. Compared to the brutality of the Germans against the Hereros and the Maji-Maji, the British Empire seemed positively benign. Critics blamed any resistance to British rule on the insensitivity of Milner and his 'kindergarten' and pointed to Milner's German origins as the source of his Bismarckian, Prussian and militaristic policies.

On the whole the empire was reasonably tolerant, and therefore reasonably tolerable. The relatively small minority who found British rule intolerable could easily be dealt with by a handful of soldiers and policemen. On the other hand, most people secretly agreed with Milner that the empire was at best a mess, and at worst a tyranny, and were critical of Liberal drift. The Great War provided a convenient excuse to shelve some of the more pressing problems, and the eagerness with which the empire rallied to the cause silenced many doubts as to its future. But the Great War also caused a profound change in the empire. Pressing issues could not be shelved for ever. It did not collapse like the German, Russian, Austro-Hungarian and Turkish empires, but the Second British Empire was fundamentally restructured in a series of reforms between 1917 and 1926, so that by the outbreak of the Second World War hardly anything remained of the old empire.

The Dominions of Canada, Australia and New Zealand enthusiastically supported the war, and French Canadians voted for the government to ensure a unanimous vote. Their support was largely rhetorical. Although 35 per cent of the population was French Canadian, they made up only 5 per cent of the Canadian Expeditionary Force.[19] In South Africa many Afrikaners remembered the kaiser's support for their cause, and seeing no reason to fight for the detested British, rose in revolt. Two Boer generals, the prime minister Louis Botha and the minister of defence Jan Christian Smuts, their eyes fixed on the prosperous colony of German South-West Africa, promptly crushed the uprising and agreed to the 'great and urgent imperial service' demanded of them.

It was not only the Dominions that sent volunteers: 1,440,437 Indians fought in the war and 62,056 were killed; 59,000 men from British East and West Africa enlisted, of whom almost 3,000 lost their lives; 857,000 came from the 'White Empire', of whom 141,000 were killed; 8,000 West Indians, 1,000 Mauritians and 100 Fijians served in non-combatant units. More than 2.5 million men from the empire fought for Britain and it is thus hardly surprising that old-style imperialists were convinced that the empire was heading for a glorious future.

The imperialists had been on the outside since 1906, but were welcomed back into Asquith's and Lloyd George's governments. By 1917 Curzon, Balfour, Milner and Smuts were in the wartime cabinet. Curzon and Milner were in Lloyd George's inner cabinet, and Curzon chaired a committee on 'Territorial Desiderata' which cast a rapacious eye on the Middle East and East Africa for territory to serve for the defence of India. Other imperialists such as Lionel Curtis, Philip Kerr, Leopold Amery and John Buchan who bemoaned an empire in decay, and believed in white racial superiority tempered with a degree of benevolence towards the lesser breeds, were close to the prime minister.

Of course the empire could not be strengthened, and Curzon's ambitions could not be realized, unless the war was won. The war could not be won without the empire, and concessions had to be made to ensure its continued support. Colonial garrisons were stripped of troops to plug the gaps on the western front. A mere 15,000 British troops were left in an India where Congress and the Muslim League had temporarily settled their differences, and the nationalist movement was on the march. Britain also depended on the good will and support of the United States, and had to swallow some high-minded denunciations of the evils of British imperialism. The Bolshevik revolution was an inspiration to revolutionaries and anti-imperialists, and the new regime in Russia supported movements of national liberation as far as its limited resources permitted. Imperialists might dream of an empire imbued with the spirit of August 1914, and forged anew in the crucible of war, but they expediently afforded concessions that were to have quite the reverse effect.

Ireland was more a British than an imperial problem, but the Irish nationalists' struggle was an inspiration to Indians and Egyptians, just as the Boers had provided role models to the Irish. The miserable record of the British in Ireland did much to discredit the imperial mission.[20] The passing of the Home Rule Act shortly after the war began did little to appease the Irish. Those who were most strongly in favour of Home Rule volunteered and went off to war. By 1916 there were almost 100,000 volunteers, very few of them from the six predominantly Unionist counties of Ulster. But by this time enthusiasm for the British cause had waned, and when conscription was introduced in 1916 it was not deemed prudent to apply it to Ireland. The Easter Rising in Dublin in 1916, although its extent was carefully played down by the British, had a powerful impact throughout the empire. Irish Catholics from the United States to Australia were appalled at the harshness of the treatment meted out on the rebels and began to question the British cause.[21] Others felt that the Easter Rising was proof of Irish seditiousness, a feeling that was reinforced when Roger Casement tried to raise an Irish brigade among Irish prisoners of war in Germany. In an increasingly poisoned atmosphere, few remembered the 49,400 Irish who died in the Great War.[22]

The year 1916 was also a turning point in India. Congress was now under the control of a radical, Bal Gangadhar Tilak, who was aided and abetted by a dynamic Irishwoman, Annie Besant, a high priestess in Madame Blavatsky's Theosophical movement and a fervent Indian nationalist. The situation got even more tense when the Indian government ordered her arrest. Edwin Montagu, appointed secretary of state for India in 1916, who had a healthy dislike for the arrogance of the traditional Raj, decided that concessions had to be made. In the following year he announced to a shocked House of Commons that he favoured responsible government in India. The lines were now clearly drawn between those who asked how the secretary of state could make such far-reaching concessions when India was stabbing Britain in the back, and those who insisted it was impossible not to do so when Indians were fighting and dying in large numbers for the common cause. Lord Curzon saw the writing on the wall. 'In the course of the war', he announced sourly, but not without justification, 'forces have been let loose, ideas have found vent, aspirations have been formulated, which were either dormant before or which in a short space of time have reached an almost incredible development.'[23]

In the following year Montagu travelled to India, had talks with Indian leaders, and worked out the details of an ambitious reform programme with the viceroy Lord Chelmsford. The resulting Montagu–Chelmsford Report, which was published in August 1918 and enacted in 1919, proposed a step-by-step approach to dominion-hood. The first step was 'dyarchy', whereby Indians were made responsible for education, public health and agriculture, while the British remained firmly in control of financial policy, internal security and defence. Dyarchy was not applied to Burma, although it was part of the Raj, and resentment at this unequal treatment spurred the nationalist movement.

In 1914 the British responded to the Ottomans' support for the Central Powers by declaring Egypt to be a protectorate, and annexed Cyprus. Vague promises were made that self-government would be granted to Egypt once the fighting was over. Egyptian nationalists were singularly unimpressed. In the following year the British, French and Russians began to discuss how the Ottoman Empire could be carved up between them. The Sykes–Picot agreement of April 1916 was the first step towards settling the rival claims of the British and French in the region, due consideration being paid to Russian ambitions in eastern Anatolia. The local inhabitants were not consulted.

Both Sykes and Picot knew that Sherif Hussein had requested British support for an Arab revolt against the Turks in the Hejaz.[24] Any help against the Turks was welcome, but the Arabs were not going to rid themselves of Turkish rule only to be subjected to domination by the British and the French. The British were therefore constrained to make a series of highly ambiguous declarations, loaded with provisos, contradictions and reservations, in order to appease the Arabs.

The best known of these declarations was made not to the Arabs but to the Jews. The Balfour Declaration of November 1917 was also typically vague; it promised that the British government would support 'the establishment in Palestine of a national home for the Jewish people'. Zionists thought it was a firm commitment, imperialists thought this meant another British colony in Palestine, Balfour and Lloyd George were honest enough to admit that it was simply propaganda. T. E. Lawrence (Lawrence of Arabia) admitted that he had made a series of promises to the Arabs which he knew he could not possibly fulfil. The situation was further complicated by Arab reactions to the Declaration and by the fact that the sherif's repudiation of the caliph, whom 80 million Indian Muslims regarded as their spiritual leader, was liable to have disastrous consequences.[25] The government of India protested vigorously, but to no effect. It was relieved that the caliph's call for a jihad against the infidel British fell mostly on deaf ears.

The Dominions were also determined to seize the opportunity afforded by the war to become sovereign states under the British crown. The appalling number of casualties suffered by the Anzacs in the badly bungled Gallipoli campaign caused much bitterness and intensified national consciousness in Australia and New Zealand. Pride in the Canadians' remarkable success at Vimy Ridge, and the South Africans' gallant defence of Delville Wood, did much to strengthen national self-confidence in both countries.[26]

Sir Robert Borden, the prime minister of Canada, and General Smuts agreed that the imperial constitution should be modified so as to reflect the obvious fact that the Dominions were no longer subject provinces of Great Britain but fully sovereign nations. At the Imperial War Conference of 1917 it was agreed that a conference should take place after the war to recognize the Dominions as sovereign nations that shared certain common interests and assumptions, and owed allegiance to the British crown. The Dominions and India were granted dual status at the peace conference.

As part of the British Empire delegation they were given access to all-important documents and served on all the significant committees and commissions. They were also given the status of smaller allied powers, which were not always privy to the deliberations of the Big Four. The Dominions were accepted as full members of the League of Nations, as was India, even though the League's covenant required that member states be self-governing. Australia, New Zealand and South Africa were given mandated territories from the spoils of the German Empire.

When Britain was the workshop of the world, an undisputed superpower providing vast quantities of cheap capital and the largest market for primary products, the empire was an impressive development agency, acknowledged as such by a wide range of commentators from Karl Marx to the most avid of Tory imperialists. The empire had expanded as a result of the Great War and now included Palestine, Transjordan, Iraq, Tanganyika, Togoland, Cameroons and New Guinea, but Britain was a shadow of her former self. The Dominions had become to all intents and purposes fully sovereign, India and Ireland were clearly headed for independence, and the rest was a vast colonial slum, exploited in a desperate attempt to offset Britain's relentless decline. The empire was falling apart, and none of the ambitious schemes for 'trusteeship' or 'partnership' could alter this fact. The Imperial Conferences merely acknowledged what had already happened and were unable to come up with any inspiring vision for the future.

That Britain's hold over the empire was precarious was highlighted in 1919 in the massacre in the Jallianwalla Bagh at Amritsar in the Punjab. A violent clash between Hindu, Muslim and Sikh fundamentalists got out of hand, the local police were unable to control the situation, a Hindu mob murdered five people, and a woman missionary came within an inch of losing her life. An army brigade under General Dyer ordered the unarmed crowd to disperse, warning that if they did not do so they would be fired upon. The crowd refused, the troops opened fire, and 379 people were killed. General Dyer ordered six men to be flogged, and forced all those who passed the spot where the missionary had been attacked to crawl.

The Amritsar massacre triggered off a fierce debate in India and in Britain. The Sikhs and the British community in India hailed Dyer as a hero, as did the majority of Conservative MPs in Britain. The viceroy's council ordered Dyer to leave the army, a decision that was upheld by the cabinet. Montagu condemned the massacre as an act of 'terrorism, racial humiliation and frightfulness'. Churchill also spoke of 'frightfulness' and announced that such violent measures were 'not a remedy known in the British pharmacopœia'. The Army Council and the majority of the British people felt that Dyer had been wronged.

The Amritsar massacre in April happened at the same time as serious clashes between Arabs and Jews in Palestine.[27] In May Britain was at war with Afghanistan, and there was a serious threat of war with Turkey. In May there was a full-scale revolt in Iraq, and an uprising in Persia was likely.[28] On the other side of the globe there were disturbances in British Honduras and Trinidad.[29] Closer to home a group of Sinn Fein MPs, who had refused to take their seats in Westminster, established their own assembly, the Dáil Éireann, and in a direct act of defiance proclaimed a republic. At the same time the Irish Republican Army (IRA) fired the opening shots in their guerilla war, while Sinn Fein's leader Eamon de Valera travelled across the United States collecting millions of dollars for the republican cause.[30]

The combined forces of the British army, the Royal Irish Constabulary, the para-military police force known as the Black and Tans, and the Auxiliary Division ('Auxis') were unable to stop the IRA. They answered terror with terror, thus strengthening support for the republicans. After a series of delicate negotiations between Lloyd George and de Valera the Irish Free State was formed, but since it did not include the six counties of Ulster, this solution was unacceptable to many, and the violence continued until 1923.[31] Ireland became a reluctant Dominion, republicans refusing to owe allegiance to the crown. On becoming prime minister in 1932 de Valera promptly set about cutting all ties with the Commonwealth, but it was not until 1949 that Ireland formally seceded. Ironically, an independent India joined the Commonwealth in the same year.[32]

The British government initially underestimated popular support for Sinn Fein and the IRA, but Edwin Montagu issued a timely warning that should such a movement arise in India it could only be dealt with by the use of force. The Amritsar massacre had shown that this would be counterproductive. Meanwhile leadership of Congress passed to Gandhi, who promptly began his *satyagraha* campaign of passive resistance and non-cooperation.[33] It needed more than the Mahatma to end violence in India. There were frequent outbreaks of violence, such as the clash between Hindus and Muslims in Madras in 1921, in which 500 people died, or the attack by Gandhi's followers on a police station in Chauri-Chaura in the United Provinces, where twenty-two policemen were brutally murdered. The British remembered Amritsar and were reluctant to intervene. Gandhi was charged with complicity in the Chauri-Chaura incident and jailed, but the young judge, C. N. Broomfield, when passing judgement referred to Gandhi as a 'great patriot and a great leader' and spoke of his 'noble and even saintly life'.[34]

The British bought time in India by continuing to make concessions to the nation-alists along the lines of the Montagu–Chelmsford Report, but they were never enough, and British morale was undermined as they came to realize that the days of the Raj were numbered. Gandhi had lost all his illusions about the benevolence of the British after the Amritsar massacre. He denounced the British government in India as 'satanic', and insisted that paying taxes amounted to subsidizing atrocities.

The new secretary of state for India, Lord Birkenhead, disingenuously argued that dyarchy equalled responsible government, and seemed unable to understand why the Indians were not satisfied. Fearing that Labour would win the next election, he set up the Statutory Commission in 1927 in order to forestall any far-reaching con-cessions. The Commission, under the chairmanship of Sir John Simon, travelled throughout India for six months. Congress considered it an insult and refused to cooperate, and wherever it went it was greeted by demonstrations and riots.[35] Before the Simon Commission published its report, the viceroy Lord Irwin (later Lord Halifax) made the dramatic announcement that India would be given full Dominion status. Gandhi trusted Halifax, but the young radicals in Congress, Jawaharlal Nehru and Subhas Chandra Bose, rejected the offer out of hand and demanded full inde-pendence.[36] Gandhi, fearful of being overtaken by the radicals, began his dramatic salt marches. Once again Gandhi's non-violent protest turned extremely violent. Gandhi was arrested, soon to be released by Irwin, and invited to talks in Edwin Lutyens's viceregal palace in New Delhi, a building then still under construction that was to dwarf Versailles. Churchill was as disgusted by Irwin's appeasement of Gandhi as he was to be of his appeasement of Hitler, and protested against 'the nauseating and humiliating spectacle of this one-time Inner Temple lawyer, now turned seditious fakir, striding half naked up the steps of the Viceroy's palace to parley on equal terms with the representative of the King Emperor'. Many Indian nationalists found the spectacle equally nauseating, and denounced Gandhi for talking to the enemy.

The Conservative prime minister Baldwin and his Labour successor Ramsay MacDonald agreed with Halifax that further concessions would have to be made to Congress. Three round table conferences were held, this time with Indian representatives, but while Gandhi was in London, wooing the crowds in the East End but failing to impress those in power, the truce in India broke down. The new viceroy, Lord Willingdon, decided to take a firm stand against civil disobedience and on his return Gandhi was once again arrested.

The British government's proposals for limited reform were enshrined in the Government of India Act of 1935, which Gandhi grudgingly accepted. The Indian provinces were now given responsible government, the governors being mere representatives of the crown but with emergency powers at their disposal under section 93. At the provincial level the reforms were relatively successful, but the proposed federal solution was a disaster. The princely states, most of which banned Congress, were overrepresented in the bicameral federal legislature, and the delegates were appointed rather than elected. Defence, foreign affairs, the protection of minorities and tariffs were still the province of the viceroy.

The princes rejected these proposals on the grounds that it would result in the country falling into the hands of Congress extremists. Consequently the central government remained firmly in the hands of the viceroy and his council. In the provinces the major problem was that the Muslims were largely excluded, since proportional representation was rejected in favour of the British constituency system. This strengthened Mohammed Ali Jinnah's conviction that the British Raj would eventually be replaced by a Hindu Raj, and that Congress was a Hindu party. Jinnah was certainly no religious fanatic. He enjoyed his whiskey and was married to a Parsee, but he was an immensely proud man who felt insulted by Gandhi and Nehru, who expected him to crawl back into the Congress fold when his Muslim League was trounced in the provincial elections of 1937. The tragic result was the partition of India, and one of the most terrible mass slaughters in recorded history.[37]

Although there had been considerable irritation in the Dominions over the failure of the consultative process during the war, most Dominion leaders agreed with the Australian prime minister Billy Hughes when he argued at the Imperial Conference in 1921 that since the Dominions were in all important respects independent nations, there was nothing much to discuss. Only Smuts, who was under pressure from secessionists, disagreed. The most serious area of dispute was in foreign policy. There was no mechanism for forming a common imperial policy. Britain wanted freedom of action, the Dominions were reluctant to share the burden of a system of imperial defence.[38] Thus Australia was keen to renew the Anglo-Japanese alliance in 1921, but Canada, ever mindful of the wishes of its neighbour to the south, adamantly opposed the idea. At the height of the Chanak crisis in 1922 Australia and New Zealand pledged support, but the Canadian prime minister Mackenzie King announced that the issue would first have to be debated in parliament.[39]

At the Imperial Conference in 1923 the Dominions were given the right to have their own diplomatic representation abroad, and to make treaties independently. The Canadian–American Halibut Treaty of 1923 was thus of greater significance than an agreement over a mere fish.[40] The British reserved the right to deal with European affairs without consulting the Dominions. The 'Balfour Report' of the Imperial Conference in 1926 went one step further in defining the Dominions as 'autonomous communities . . . equal in status, in no way subordinate one to another in any aspect of their domestic or external affairs, though united in common allegiance to the Crown, and freely associated as members of the British Commonwealth of Nations'.

In one important respect the Dominions were not fully sovereign. They were still subject to British statutes, but with the Statute of Westminster of 1931 the Dominions were no longer bound by any past or future British act, and the British parliament could not invalidate those of the Dominions. The only requirement for membership of the British Commonwealth of Nations, as the Dominion club was renamed in 1926, was allegiance to the crown. The statute thus gave legal status to the Balfour definition and was generally accepted. The Commonwealth was now an exclusive club within the empire, and membership was free. It offered many advantages, and demanded no obligations. All independent nations within the empire were happy to join, Burma being the one exception, and the Irish Republic left the Commonwealth in 1949.[41]

The Commonwealth was, from the start, more of an economic than a political organization. In 1931 Britain was forced to abandon the gold standard and sterling became the monetary standard throughout the empire, with the exception of Canada and Newfoundland.[42] The 'Ottawa Agreements' that emerged from an acrimonious economic conference in 1932 established the principle of imperial preference.[43]

Defence was also an important matter of concern to the Commonwealth, and it was as difficult to reach a consensus in this issue as it was over economics. Canada and Ireland were anxious not to make any commitments that might result in their becoming involved in a European war. South Africa was also concerned to preserve its independence. Thus there was considerable disagreement about the abandonment of sanctions against Italy in 1936, and the appeasement of Hitler. The British government frequently found it useful to cite a mythical 'Dominion opinion' as an excuse for a particular action or, more often, for inaction.

It is hardly surprising that the Dominions found it difficult to agree on any one particular issue. Canada and South Africa were rich countries, with significant minorities which harboured deep resentments against the British. Their trading links with Britain were a matter of choice rather than necessity. By contrast Australia, New Zealand and the Irish Free State needed British capital and British markets, and felt that the link with Britain was essential for economic survival, particularly during the depression.

With the Dominions independent, and British influence in India waning, many felt that the empire's future lay in tropical Africa. In Kenya Lord Delamere was the colourful and penurious champion of a white Dominion in East Africa, but his views on the superiority of the white race, although shared by many Conservatives, did not fit well with current notions of 'trusteeship' enshrined in the Devonshire Declaration of 1923, which stated that 'His Majesty's Government regard themselves as exercising a trust on behalf of the African population, and they are unable to delegate or share this trust, the object of which may be defined as the protection and advancement of the native races'.[44]

Delamere's vision of the Great White Dominion of Kenya, Uganda, Tanganyika, the Rhodesias and Nyasaland was shared by Amery, who became colonial secretary in 1925 and imagined that the white settlers would act as responsible trustees for the Africans. The worthy Fabian Sidney Webb (Lord Passfield), who was appointed colonial secretary in the 1929 Labour government, reversed this policy and reaffirmed the Devonshire Declaration.

Indirect rule, which depended on cooperation with the tribal authorities, was roundly condemned by the 'Afro-Saxons': the educated African urban elites. They pointed out that trusteeship had done nothing to improve the condition of the vast majority of Africans, even in areas where the economy was booming. There were no social services, sanitation was deplorable, health care rudimentary, housing totally inadequate. Hardly any children went to school, and the few existing schools were pitifully substandard. The total amount of money spent on the colonies was derisory, and with the onset of the depression it was reduced to a trickle.[45] Here was powerful ammunition for African nationalists, but for the moment their numbers were few, their influence minimal.

On the eve of the Second World War the empire was falling apart. The Dominions were independent nations, India was soon to become a sovereign state, other colonies in Africa, Asia and the Caribbean were to follow suit. But it seemed quite different at the time. The popular Dutch American historian Hendrik Willem van Loon was almost alone in suggesting that '[w]hat until a few years ago constituted the heart of a mighty Empire, will rapidly transform itself into an over-populated island lying somewhere off the Danish coast'. The British imagined that they were still a world power. Even radical socialists believed that the end of empire, for which they professed to yearn, would, like the proletarian revolution, come about in the distant future.[46] The case for appeasing Hitler was strengthened by the argument that the empire and Commonwealth had more to fear from Japan. Thus the staggering sum of £60 million was spent, and wasted, on improving the defences of Singapore. This illusion of power might now seem ridiculous, but it was the source of tremendous pride and strength that helped to sustain the nation in the darkest days of the coming war.

NOTES

1 The official population figure for India in 1900 was 294,361,056. Even without affording undue confidence to such precise figures, this meant that India alone had five times the population of the French colonial empire. For an overview: J. M. Brown and W. R. Louis, eds, *The Oxford History of the British Empire*, vol. 4, *The Twentieth Century* (Oxford, 1999); M. Beloff, *Imperial Sunset*, vol. 1, *Britain's Liberal Empire, 1847–1921* (London, 1969), vol. 2, *Dream of Commonwealth, 1921–42* (London, 1989).

2 B. Porter, 'The Edwardians and their empire', in D. Read, ed., *Edwardian England* (London, 1982); J. Eddy and D. Schreuder, eds, *The Rise of Colonial Nationalism: Australia, New Zealand, Canada, and South Africa First Assert their Nationalities, 1880–1914* (Sydney, 1988).

3   D. C. Potter, *India's Political Administrators, 1919–1983* (Oxford, 1986), ch. 1. Of these 367 were Indians. 'Covenanted' meant that they accepted a salary and a pension from the crown, rather than charging fees for their services. This peculiar terminology came from the East India Company.

4   That Britain was also lagging behind in technology was spectacularly demonstrated in the loss of the *Titanic* on its much-publicized maiden voyage in 1912, and was further underlined by the poor performance of the fleet at Jutland, which prompted Beatty to exclaim: 'There's something wrong with my bloody ships today!' In 1930 the huge airship R101 crashed, also on its maiden voyage.

5   Garvin contributed an article to this effect in C. S. Goldman, ed., *The Empire and the Century: A Series of Essays on Imperial Problems and Possibilities by Various Writers* (London, 1905).

6   L. T. Hobhouse, *Liberalism* (London, 1911).

7   C. Dilke, *The British Empire* (London, 1899); S. Gwynn and G. M. Tuckwell, *The Life of the Rt. Hon. Sir Charles Dilke* (2 vols, London, 1918). The Liberal prime minister Campbell-Bannerman once spoke of 'the vulgar and bastard imperialism of irritation and provocation and aggression . . . of grabbing everything even if we have no use for it ourselves'.

8   B. Porter, *The Lion's Share: A Short History of British Imperialism, 1850–1900* (London, 1975), p. 194. On the general theme: A. P. Thornton, *The Imperial Idea and its Enemies: A Study in British Power* (London, 1959). On Cromer see A. L. al-Sayyid-Marsot, *Egypt and Cromer* (London, 1968).

9   For Milner see A. M. Gollin, *Proconsul in Politics: A Study of Lord Milner in Opposition and in Power* (London, 1963).

10 For Curzon in India see S. Gopal, *British Policy in India, 1885–1905* (Cambridge, 1965).

11 R. Jeffrey, ed., *People, Princes and Paramount Power: Society and Politics in the Indian Princely States* (Delhi, 1978); T. C. Coen, *The Indian Political Service: A Study in Indirect Rule* (London, 1971).

12 S. Smith, *British Relations with the Malay Rulers from Decentralization to Malayan Independence, 1930–1957* (Kuala Lumpur, 1995).

13 M. Perham, *Lugard* (2 vols, London, 1956–60). See also her other works: *Native Administration in Nigeria* (London, 1937) and *The Colonial Reckoning: The End of Imperial Rule in Africa in the Light of British Experience* (2 vols, London, 1962); also A. Smith and M. Bull, *Margery Perham and British Rule in Africa* (London, 1991). Lugard's *The Dual Mandate in British Tropical Africa* (London, 1922) was widely read and greatly admired.

14 I. F. Nicholson, *The Administration of Nigeria: Men, Methods and Myths* (Oxford, 1969); J. E. Flint, 'Frederick Lugard: the making of an autocrat, 1858–1943', in L. H. Gann and P. Duignan, eds, *African Proconsuls: European Governors in Africa* (New York, 1978).

15 H. Maine, *Ancient Law: Its Connection with the Early History of Society and its Relation to Modern Ideas* (1861; Boston, 1963) and *Village Communities in the East and West* (London, 1895).

16 L. Morgan, *Ancient Society* (1878; Cambridge, Mass., 1964).

17 B. Malinowski, 'Practical anthropology', *Africa*, 2 (1929); G. Pandey, *The Construction of Communalism in Colonial North India* (Delhi, 1990); G. Stocking, ed., *Colonial Situations: Essays in the Contextualization of Ethnographic Knowledge* (Madison, Wis., 1984).

18 This speech was made on 28 October 1907 and quoted in R. Haym, 'The British Empire in the Edwardian era', in J. M. Brown and W. R. Louis, eds, *The Oxford History of the British Empire*, vol. 4, *The Twentieth Century* (Oxford, 1999).

19 R. C. Brown and R. Cook, *Canada, 1896–1921: A Nation Transformed* (Toronto, 1974).

20 K. Robinson, *The Dilemmas of Trusteeship* (London, 1965); F. Pakenham (Lord Long-ford), *Peace by Ordeal* (London, 1967).

21 There were sixteen executions and more than 3,500 arrests. C. Townshend, 'The suppression of the Easter Rising', *Bullán*, 1 (1994).

22 T. Denman, *Ireland's Unknown Soldiers: The 16th (Irish) Division in the Great War* (Dublin, 1992).

23 A. Rumbold, *Watershed in India, 1914–1918* (London, 1979).

24 The Grand Sherif Hussein of Mecca claimed direct descent from the Prophet.

25 The sultan of Turkey until 1919 was *ex officio* 'Caliph of the Faithful'.

26 C. E. W. Bean, *Official History of Australia in the War*, vols 1–6 (Sydney, 1933); N. G. Garson, 'South Africa and World War One', *Journal of Imperial and Commonwealth History*, 8, no. 1 (1979); D. Morton, 'Junior but sovereign allies: the transformation of the Canadian Expeditionary Force, 1914–18', *Journal of Imperial and Commonwealth History*, 8, no. 1 (1979); Sir C. Lucas, *The Empire at War*, vols 1–4 (London, 1926).

27 B. Wasserstein, *The British in Palestine: The Mandatory Government and the Arab–Jewish Conflict* (Oxford, 1991).

28 M. E. Yapp, *The Near East since the First World War* (London, 1991).

29 K. Singh, *Race and Class: Struggles in a Colonial State, Trinidad, 1917–1945* (Mona, 1994); A. Spackman, ed., *Constitutional Development of the West Indies, 1922–1968: A Selection from the Major Documents* (Barbados, 1975).

30 C. Townshend, *The British Campaign in Ireland, 1919–1921* (Oxford, 1975); K. Jeffery, *The British Army and the Crisis of Empire, 1918–1922* (Manchester, 1984).

31 Ulster originally consisted of nine counties, three of which had Catholic majorities.

32 D. W. Harkness, *The Restless Dominion: The Irish Free State and the British Commonwealth of Nations, 1921–31* (London, 1969).

33 J. M. Brown, *Gandhi: Prisoner of Hope* (New Haven, Conn., 1989).

34 Gandhi spent less than two years in jail in Poona. He used the opportunity to catch up with his reading, learn Tamil and have his appendix removed.

35 There was not a single Indian on the Commission.

36 S. Gopal, *Jawaharlal Nehru: A Biography*, vol. 1 (London, 1975).

37 T. G. Fraser, *Partition in Ireland, India and Palestine* (London, 1984); A. Jalal, *The Sole Spokesman: Jinnah, the Muslim League and the Demand for Pakistan* (Cambridge, 1985); R. J. Moore, *The Crisis of Indian Unity, 1917–1940* (Oxford, 1974).

38 Then, as now, Canada was among the countries with the lowest per capita expenditure on defence. In 1934 the Royal Canadian Air Force consisted of one Hawker Audax biplane on loan from the RAF.

39 Mustapha Kemal Atatürk, having expelled the Greeks from Asia Minor, was determined to force the British to abandon their stronghold at Chanak (Cannakale) on the south side of the Dardanelles. The British reached an agreement, and violence was avoided.

40 The Americans prudently checked with London to make sure that their neighbours were not stepping out of line.

41 The Commonwealth was a constitutional curiosity which left a number of questions open for learned debate. Was the crown divisible? Could the same man be king of England and king of Canada? Could he give his consent to contradictory acts? Could he declare war on himself? If all partners were equal, could a member be expelled?

42 C. R. Shenk, *Britain and the Sterling Area: From Devaluation to Convertibility in the 1950s* (London, 1994); P. J. Cain and A. G. Hopkins, *British Imperialism: Crisis and Deconstruction 1914–1990* (London, 1993).

43 I. M. Drummond, *Imperial Economic Policy, 1917–1939: Studies in Expansion and Protection* (London, 1974).

44 B. Berman and J. Lonsdale, *Unhappy Valley: Conflict in Kenya and Africa* (London, 1992).

45 The colonies were expected to be self-supporting, and in 1930 a mere £3 million was spent on them.

46 S. Howe, *Anticolonialism in British Politics: The Left and the End of Empire, 1918–1964* (Oxford, 1993); B. Porter, 'Fabians, imperialists and the international order', in B. Pimlott, ed., *Fabian Essays in Socialist Thought* (London, 1984).

CHAPTER THIRTEEN

The British Economy and the Empire, 1900–1939

B. R. TOMLINSON

The history of a distinct British imperial economy began in the closing years of the nineteenth century. From the 1890s to the 1930s powerful interest groups and important policy makers identified Britain's imperial possessions as an economic asset that could rescue her producers and consumers from the threats posed by national industrial decline and foreign competition. The concept of an imperial economy centred on Britain, but encompassing all the major colonies of settlement and of conquest, reached its peak at the Imperial Economic Conference at Ottawa in August 1932, and played a crucial part in policy making for the rest of that decade. Constructing an economic purpose and rationale for the empire based on a neo-mercantilist cost–benefit analysis had serious implications for contemporary thinking about Britain's links to her overseas possessions. Such an analysis has also been used by modern historians to assess the contribution of the empire to British economic history. The subject is therefore one that repays further study – both for what it can tell us about the material concerns and political ambitions that strengthened the structures of British imperialism in the twentieth century, and for the lessons it can teach about the economic realities that undermined and eventually destroyed them.[1]

Britain had ceased to be the only 'industrial nation' in the second half of the nineteenth century. Her share of world industrial production was around 20 per cent in 1900, then fell to about 14 per cent by 1913. Despite this relative decline, however, Britain remained one of the three largest industrial economies in the world (along with the United States and Germany) and was the largest single exporter of industrial goods, providing 33 per cent of the world total of industrial exports in 1899 and 30 per cent in 1913; Germany, her nearest rival, supplied 22 per cent of world industrial exports in 1899 and 27 per cent in 1913.[2] The British economy remained wealthy, but produced a much smaller percentage of the manufactures it consumed than in the past, and was more dependent on both exports and imports of manufactured goods than any of its main competitors. Britain now bought more manufactures from the most advanced European economies (Germany, Belgium, France and Switzerland) than she sold to them, but, overall, she still exported more than twice the value of manufactures to the world as a whole than she imported. British textiles and engineering manufacturers retained their world market share quite well in the 1900s, although the markets for these commodities were increasingly found within the 'semi-industrial' economies of Asia and Latin America, rather than in the richer markets of continental western Europe and North America. The only serious threat to British manufacturers' ability to find export markets, or even to supply domestic consumption, came in metal manufactures, notably iron and steel. This is the one industry where there is also clear evidence for entrepreneurial failure, and an unwillingness to invest in new technology, before 1913.

The British economy had consumed substantial amounts of imported goods throughout the nineteenth century. Industry required raw materials – especially raw cotton and iron ore – while the industrial cities needed imported foodstuffs, especially as British agricultural output declined from the middle decades of the nineteenth century onwards. Thus the British economy consistently imported more goods than it exported – even in the boom decades before her industrial leadership came under challenge. Balance of payments statistics for the nineteenth century are not very sophisticated, but the data we have show clearly that the visible trade deficit (excess of imports over exports of goods) was made good by a large surplus in invisible trade (income earned by shipping, insurance and other services to trade) and a large income from investments made by British residents abroad. Thus the British current balance of payments had a large surplus throughout the late nineteenth and early twentieth centuries, and this was used to finance a substantial amount of capital exports in the form of new investments overseas. Between 1861 and 1913 almost £3,000 million's worth of capital was invested overseas from Britain – the vast bulk of it to the expanding economies of North and South America and Australasia where European settlers were producing the food and raw materials that were so essential to the British industrialists, workers and other consumers. Even with these substantial sums moving abroad, however, the British economy gained an average of over £20 million a year between 1875 and 1913 from overseas investment income – the excess of income from past overseas investment over expenditure on new investments.

The importance of income from services and overseas underlines the point that Britain was far from being a solely industrial economy even in the Victorian age. The importance of the service sector was reflected in the relative population and relative wealth of different parts of the country – with London and the south-east of England (where many of the service industries were located) becoming clearly the richest and most populous region in Britain during the second half of the nineteenth century. This division of economic activity between 'North' and 'South' was noted by some contemporaries, and has been expanded and developed as a major explanatory tool by historians who stress that the strength of the service sector – especially in overseas finance and investments – meant that British economic and imperial policy in the nineteenth century was dominated by the interests of 'gentlemanly capitalism' based around the City of London, rather than the industrial capitalism of the great staple industries.[3]

The late nineteenth century was an imperial age, during which the boundaries of the British and other European empires expanded considerably – especially in Africa. However, as many contemporaries and historians have pointed out, these newly colonized territories (with the possible exception of the goldfields of Transvaal, for which the Second South African War was fought in 1899–1902) were not central to the economic performance of the British economy at this time. For trade and investment, the long-established areas of imperial control and influence were more significant – especially the Indian subcontinent and the colonies of settlement in Canada and Australasia, plus the other areas of European settlement in Latin America where Britain had established an 'informal empire' of influence by the 1860s. Almost 60 per cent of the British capital invested overseas between 1865 and 1913 went outside the empire (to Europe, the United States and Latin America); India and South Africa were the only colonies of conquest that had received substantial amounts – 12 per cent of the total. In trade, also, Britain acted internationally rather than imperially. While India was the largest single export market for British goods in 1913 (because of the large exports of Lancashire cotton textiles to the subcontinent), the data on the relative size of British export markets show that the empire as a whole took only 35 per cent of British exports in 1909–13; data on exports by commodity show that cotton textiles and iron and steel relied heavily on empire markets by 1913, but other trade was more diversified. All in all, the British economy (like the rest of western Europe) was still largely internationalized in 1913; it was this feature, by contrast with the much more nationalistic and competitive attitude of the 1920s and 1930s, that gave the late Victorian and Edwardian periods the retrospective aura of a golden age.

Contemporary discussion of the problems of Britain's relative industrial decline became complicated by domestic political considerations after 1900, when Joseph Chamberlain – then a member of Arthur Balfour's Conservative government – raised the issue of 'tariff reform' as a solution to Britain's problems. In Chamberlain's hands, the proposal to impose a tariff on imports to Britain of food, raw materials and manufactured goods had several aims – to provide finance for a modest scheme of old-age pensions, to provide the means to retaliate against foreign countries which had imposed import duties on British goods, to prevent the 'dumping' of foreign manufactures in the British market, and to give the basis for closer ties of imperial economic union (on the basis of empire free trade) that would eventually lead to an imperial political federation. Assisted by academic advisers such as W. A. S. Hewins (the founding director of the London School of Economics) and William Ashley (the first Professor of Commerce at Birmingham University), Chamberlain's campaign focused attention on the apparent costs of free trade in weakening Britain's ability to bargain for increased markets in continental Europe and the United States, in damaging industry and reducing industrial employment for the sake of finance, and draining resources from industrial investment at home through exports of capital. The tariff reform campaign was always as much about politics (and about Chamberlain's political ambitions to build a populist right-wing movement to counter the rise of socialism) as about economics, but proved electorally disastrous for the Conservatives in the 1906 general election, when the Liberal landslide was caused partly by the fears of many industrialists and trade unionists that an import tariff would lead to dearer food for the working class. This setback, plus Chamberlain's stroke in 1906, effectively ended the first phase of the campaign, although the issues surrounding it rose to the surface again in 1910 and during the 1920s, coming to dominate the political landscape in the 1930s.

By 1900, if not before, the era of the 'imperialism of free trade' had come to an end. British policy makers were increasingly concerned to justify their imperial possessions as potential or actual economic assets – 'underdeveloped estates', in Chamberlain's phrase – that could bring a direct return to the domestic economy more directly and more certainly than could independent territories. Viewed from the periphery, too, notions of collective imperial identity were important as a means of ensuring access to the British market for goods and capital. Colonial governments in Canada, Australia and New Zealand advocated schemes of imperial preference in the 1890s and 1900s – arguing that any future British tariffs on food and raw materials should give privileged access to their exports over those from other suppliers. In return, they were prepared to offer lower tariff rates to British exports in their domestic markets. But there were limits to their generosity here. Canada and Australia were largely urbanized economies that were developing substantial domestic manufacturing industries of their own by 1913. While Dominion governments were prepared to allow preferences for British manufactures that would give these an advantage over other imports, they were not prepared to sacrifice their own developing industries to the interest of British exporters. Thus preferences were given by raising tariff levels and allowing British goods a small discount, but ensuring that domestic production was provided with the assured profits it needed to expand despite its higher costs.[4]

The First World War brought about unprecedented imperial cooperation, especially between Britain and the Dominions, that influenced the thinking of the Lloyd George government about post-war reconstruction. Faced with a major strategic and supply crisis in 1917, London was prepared to offer significant political and economic concessions to the Dominions and India to shore up the war effort in the short term, and to envisage a much closer form of inter-imperial cooperation once the war had been won. In the closing months of the war the idea of a more formal federal structure for the government of the empire surfaced briefly, but its implications were too radical even for apocalyptic times. An imperial federation required Britain to commit herself to an imperial economic future – with a tariff that could give imperial preference, and with a joint management of sterling that would compromise London's ability to recapture its global role as the centre of the international financial system. Wartime concerns with the 'economics of siege' seemed irrelevant as the pre-war patterns of the international economy re-established themselves after 1919, despite the advocacy of closer links with British settlers overseas in schemes of emigration and trade by a vociferous group of 'imperial visionaries' led by Lord Milner, Leopold Amery and Phillip Cunliffe-Lister.[5] Tariffs again seemed to have been decisively rejected by the electorate when the Conservative government was defeated in the general election of 1924 that was fought on the issue of taxes on food. The British government signalled its commitment to an international rather than an imperial economic future when sterling returned to the gold standard at its pre-war parity of $4.86 in 1925. However, protectionism still retained powerful supporters among industrialists, some bankers and trade unionists, and a large section of the Conservative party, and would resurface when the policy of free trade ran into difficulties at the end of the decade.

By 1925 the British establishment had reasserted its faith in the ability of the economy to compete as an industrial and financial power on the world stage. Unfortunately, this faith was already misplaced, and this became increasingly obvious over the next few years. British industry was uncompetitive in many markets by the mid-1920s; even to maintain its position wage costs would have had to 'adjust' downwards considerably in the absence of technical innovation or productivity gains. In practice, the return to gold at the pre-war parity, which overvalued sterling by at least 10 per cent, made Britain's exports still harder to sell abroad and left her domestic market for manufactures exposed to competition from imported goods. Unemployment in the staple industries of coal, steel, textiles and transport equipment (especially shipbuilding and locomotives) became a major political issue for the rest of the decade. With a decline in Britain's dominance of world shipping, insurance and the financing of trade, the invisible balance of payments surplus was reduced at a time when the visible deficit was increasing.[6] Sterling was still in demand as a currency for transactions by foreign countries, and as a convenient and apparently safe asset for the currency reserves of overseas banks and private investors, but London's position was challenged by the rise of rival international capital markets in Paris and New York. By the late 1920s, Britain's ability to maintain her balance of payments in the face of an increased visible deficit and a decreased invisible surplus was only maintained by flows of short-term capital coming to London from continental Europe. So long as faith in the stability of the gold standard remained, foreign banks and governments were prepared to hold sterling, but that confidence could only be secured by a fierce defence of the exchange rate requiring restrictive monetary policies and high interest rates. Once confidence weakened, the sale of sterling would force down its price and damage the Bank of England's ability to hold the exchange rate and maintain the gold standard.

During 1930 and 1931 the shaky foundations on which the case for reviving the British economy's international role was based were swiftly dismantled. World trade contracted following the slump in the American economy in the summer of 1929, exacerbated by the Wall Street crash of October and the subsequent rise in tariffs. British exports declined as a result, since many of her remaining markets were in countries (such as India, Australia and Argentina) that exported heavily to the United States. The fall in exports caused a further slump in domestic economic activity and exacerbated the social and political problem of mass unemployment. A decline in British imports meant that the visible balance of trade deficit did not increase significantly, but Britain's invisible earnings, especially from shipping, fell sharply as world trade contracted. The difficulties faced by many primary producing countries led them to draw down the currency reserves that they held in London, and the banking crisis in Germany and Austria that broke in the summer of 1931 put further pressure on sterling. In July and August 1931 about £350 million was withdrawn from London by foreign holders of short-term sterling assets. The Bank of England now decided that it could no longer meet demands for foreign exchange and gold at the existing exchange rate, and on 21 September announced that sterling was leaving the gold standard, remaining convertible into foreign currencies, but at a rate to be fixed by supply and demand. The National government, which had taken office in early September to face the growing crisis, contained a number of prominent supporters of protection and imperial preference, headed by Joseph Chamberlain's younger son Neville, who used the continued balance of payments difficulties to make the case for a decisive break with the discredited policies of economic internationalism. The result was the UK Import Duties Act of April 1932, which imposed a 10 per cent *ad valorem* duty on all imports to Britain (except for a free list of food and raw materials from the colonial empire), subject to negotiations with the Dominions and

India over a scheme of mutual imperial preference to be held at the Imperial Economic Conference in Ottawa in August 1932. Imports from the Dominions and India were exempted from the import tariffs for six months from April 1932 to concentrate the minds of their negotiators at Ottawa.[7]

The opening of the Ottawa Conference represented the triumph of the ideas of protection, preference and inter-imperial economic cooperation that had been an important part of political culture in Britain and her Dominions since 1900; its results, and subsequent events, demonstrated how far political ambition diverged from economic reality even in those parts of the globe in which British control and influence remained powerful. Neither the British nor the Dominions governments arrived at Ottawa with a coherent vision of an imperial economic future. The negotiations revealed that each government was anxious to protect its own special interests, and would only make concessions to others if these were not put in jeopardy. The result of the conference was a series of bilateral agreements, dominated by agreements between each Dominion and Britain for free entry to the British market for specific items of food and raw materials, in return for preferential access to Dominion markets for specific items of British manufactures. India also attended the Ottawa Conference, but the two most important items of British trade there – cotton manufactures and iron and steel – were already granted small elements of preference, and so were subject to a different timetable for negotiation and renegotiation.

As in the 1900s and 1920s, Dominion governments depended on import tariffs on manufactured goods to raise revenue and to provide protection for their growing domestic industrial sectors. They were prepared to offer concessions to British manufactures only if these did not limit the market for domestically produced goods. The Ottawa Conference endorsed the 'domestic competition' principle – that tariffs should be set to provide the minimum level of protection needed for domestic industry, and that British goods should be offered preferences that would enable them to compete with domestic manufactures. But, in practice, this principle was never defined rigorously and was dropped in later revisions of the Ottawa system in 1937–8. Over the course of the 1930s British industry maintained its share of imports into the Dominions, but lost substantial amounts of business to import substitution – competition from Canadian, Australian and South African factory production that used the protection given by higher tariffs to replace imported manufactures in the domestic market. Between 1929 and 1937, for example, 85 per cent of Britain's loss of market share in Australia, South Africa and New Zealand was the result of import substitution – the same percentage as in the other industrializing economies around the globe with which Britain had no special arrangements for imperial preference.[8] Where British imports gained market share at the expense of foreign competitors, as in imports of motor cars to Australia in the early 1930s, this was the result of the depressed nature of the market and the temporary suspension of demand for more desirable, but more expensive, American cars. This retreat from the rhetoric of inter-imperial collaboration was not only on the Dominion side. Britain, too, had domestic interests to protect, and was never prepared to sacrifice the interests of her farmers to the requirements of Dominion producers. British wheat farmers were subsidized from 1932 onwards by a levy on the milling of imported grain, while beef and butter producers were offered price insurance and direct subsidy schemes.[9]

The immediate crisis of the Great Depression and the gold standard's abandonment of sterling had been weathered by 1933. While the United States and some continental European countries, notably France, remained in considerable economic difficulty, the British economy was recovering to its 1929 levels of production and consumption, and had re-established a favourable international balance of payments that supported sterling at its new level without difficulty. After 1934 the British authorities intervened frequently in the foreign exchange markets, but to keep the value of sterling down to their new target rate. Policy makers in London now began to think about reconstructing the international economic system once again, although this was to be an international system suitably modified to minimize the strains on British recovery. To secure this, British external economic policy had to be modified to provide for renewed or improved relations with economies outside the empire – first with important suppliers of primary produce in Latin America and northern Europe, and then with the major industrial economies of the United States and continental Europe. The Dominions, too, were aware from 1933 onwards that they could not rely entirely on the British market for their exports. Other links had to be renewed to achieve recovery – especially those between Canada and the United States, and between Australia and Japan. The result was a series of agreements between Britain and important suppliers of agricultural produce such as Argentina and Denmark negotiated in 1933–8 that gave these countries some assured access to the British domestic market at the expense of Dominion producers. The Anglo-American Trade Agreement of 1938 gave US exporters of agricultural products significant concessions in the British market. Dominion governments consented to this in the hope that it would lead to a lowering of US tariffs that might enable them to increase their exports. The trade agreement between Australia and Japan in 1936 allowed an agreed quota for Japanese textile imports in return for an agreed quota for Australian wool exports. The British government's attitude to Japanese competition in cotton textiles, by contrast, was much less flexible. Following the failure of trade talks in 1934, London imposed quotas on Japanese exports to the colonial empire that tried to limit these to their average levels of 1927–31.[10]

The history of India's imperial economic relations with Britain provides some interesting parallels with the case of the Dominions. Formal British political control was much more fully established in India, but the underlying economic structures that determined the course of bilateral relations were a more powerful force in practice. British policy in India during the late nineteenth century had provided a free-trade regime that removed tariff barriers to British exports, especially exports of cotton textiles from Lancashire. During and after the First World War, however, these possible advantages for metropolitan interests were sacrificed to the more fundamental need to retain political support for colonial rule. In 1916 the government of India was allowed to impose an import tariff on British cottons of 7.5 per cent in return for a contribution of £100 million for the purchase of British War Bonds. After 1919 the enactment of a new scheme of constitutional reform (the Montagu–Chelmsford reforms) gave increased political and financial autonomy to provincial administrations with significant Indian participation, and reduced the fiscal resources of central government to two main heads – import tariffs and income tax. The result was a rapid rise in import duties which contributed to the sharp decline in Lancashire's exports to what had been by far her largest single export market before 1913.

In the 1920s the government of India faced the twin imperatives of maintaining its fiscal base and meeting nationalist demands for greater autonomy amounting to home rule. Revenue duties on imports continued to provide the bulk of the central government's income, and also met local demands for the protection of local industries, especially cotton textiles and iron and steel. Preferences were offered to British goods, and protective tariffs had to be approved by a system of Tariff Boards that were sensitive to the demands of British exporters; despite these advantages British industry, in particular Lancashire textiles, lost ground steadily throughout the decade. Changes in the rules for the purchase of government equipment in the early 1920s encouraged local manufacture and assembly, while the preferences given to British goods were not large enough to enable them to compete with Belgian steel or Japanese cloth. India attended the Ottawa Conference, but British access to the Indian market for textiles and steel was negotiated separately in a series of trade agreements concluded in 1934 and 1936. The result of these arrangements was to provide British imports with some level of preference, but only in collaboration with the Bombay textile industry, and at the price of a scheme for guaranteed purchases of Indian raw cotton by Britain to minimize the effect of possible Japanese retaliation. Paradoxically, British exporters lost a greater amount of their market share in India, a territory still formally ruled by the British crown, than they did in the Dominions, which had their own elected governments with complete political sovereignty.[11]

By the end of the 1930s it had become clear that the opportunities of closer imperial cooperation in trade that had opened up at Ottawa were extremely limited. The British market was not large enough to allow Dominion and Indian farmers to produce their way out of depression, even if they had been given unrestricted access to it for their produce. The Dominion and Indian markets for manufactures were not large enough to provide assured employment in the British staple industries, and again British producers could not eliminate their competitors there (especially from domestic industry) in the name of imperial solidarity. The share of empire countries in British exports and imports increased during the 1930s, but the amounts involved were not large. One calculation has suggested that the increase in British imports from the empire that can be directly attributed to the effect of imperially oriented trade policies was about £46 million in 1933 and £98 million in 1938 – 7.2 per cent and 10.3 per cent of total British imports respectively. British exports gained even less – perhaps £13 million (3.5 per cent of total British exports) in 1933 and £28 million (5.4 per cent) in 1937.[12] Perhaps the most serious effect of the imperial trade agreements of the 1930s was not economic but political. The rhetoric of British imperial collaboration convinced powerful outsiders – notably the governments of the United States, Germany, Italy and Japan – that the British Empire was the foundation of British economic power in the world, and would have to be dismantled before their own ambitions to hegemony could be realized.

The attempt to reorient inter-imperial trade in the 1930s absorbed so much of the British government's time in the 1930s to so little effect that some historians have been tempted to see another logic to events, with other interests than those of British manufacturers or industrial workers shaping British policy.[13] Here the defence of sterling and the support of the City of London's role in international finance have been placed centre stage. It is clear that sterling policy formed an important part of the British government's plans for economic recovery after the traumas of 1929–31.

When sterling went off the gold standard in 1931 it quickly devalued by 30 per cent (from £1 = $4.86 to £1 = $3.40), and by the summer of 1932 had stabilized at about £1 = $3.60. Economic difficulties elsewhere, especially in the United States (which suffered a wave of bank failures in 1932 and 1933, culminating in the dollar being taken off the gold standard following a run on the gold reserves) and in France (which clung on to the gold-standard franc until 1936 despite serious domestic depression and capital flight to London), enabled sterling to retain its attractions as an international asset, and allowed the British government to keep the floating currency stable without jeopardizing the cheap money policy designed to boost the domestic economy. Monetary policy was not discussed very fully at Ottawa, since London was not prepared to concede any of its right to manage the currency in the British national interest. One concern was the repayment of sterling debts by Dominion, colonial and foreign governments, since it was thought that any major debt crisis would jeopardize international confidence in sterling. These concerns had some implications for imperial policy, and led to London's refusal to allow the government of India to devalue the rupee in 1931, to strong opposition to what were seen as 'irresponsible' expansionary policies in Australia at the height of the slump, and to the establishment of Reserve Banks in Canada, New Zealand and India by which the Bank of England could attempt (without much success) to steer policy along 'sound' lines. However, such concerns had implications for extra-imperial relations also, and one powerful argument for allowing foreign countries access to the British market (especially the primary producers with whom trade agreements were concluded in 1934–8) was to enable them to earn an export surplus to meet capital payments. Other examples of informal financial diplomacy in the 1930s – such as British relations with China – reinforce the point that the strength of sterling, and the interests of British investors and merchant bankers, could not be secured solely within an imperial setting.

The history of British economic relations with the Dominions and India in the first three decades of the twentieth century shows that economic logic had moved a long way beyond the political rhetoric in which policies of imperial solidarity were expressed. Britain's failure to rescue her staple export industries by securing access to imperial markets was not a failure of political power or the simple result of obstruction in the periphery to protect growing local industries. That failure was also one of economic logic. The British Empire did not make sense as a closed economic system, and all attempts to make it so merely made this essential flaw more obvious. However close their political relations (and these were not always smooth or harmonious), the mother country and her daughters overseas could not prosper on the basis of self-sufficiency. Triangular relations in international trade and finance, involving third countries in other parts of the globe, had been the main foundation of the economic growth of the imperial family during the nineteenth century, and remained so, even in the darkest days of international economic cooperation in the 1930s.

There was a similar contradiction in the attempts by successive British governments to rely on the potential economic strengths of the colonial empire to bolster her domestic economy and maintain the consumption and welfare of her citizens. While the profile of British power was much higher in colonial territories, this did not mean that the resources of these areas could, for long, be pre-empted to meet the needs of the British economy. In order to rule in Asia and Africa, British colonial governments had to raise taxation and maintain a measure of political acquiescence for the fiscal and monetary systems that accompanied colonial rule. This meant that there were limits on their actions, especially on their ability to favour metropolitan interests over colonial ones.

For most of our period, Britain's colonial possessions in Africa were largely ignored in the search for new markets. African colonies were seen as poor and backward, lacking infrastructure and resources that could create mass markets even for the simplest consumer goods. Lancashire cotton manufacturers turned to West Africa in the 1930s to seek protected markets to replace those lost to Indian and Japanese competition elsewhere, but the opportunities were limited. Despite this, however, sub-Saharan Africa became considerably more important to British trade during the 1930s than ever before. The region had taken 10 per cent of British exports and provided 5 per cent of British imports in 1925; by 1937 these figures were 17 per cent for exports and 7 per cent for imports: by 1937 sub-Saharan Africa bought almost as many British exports as the whole of Asia, having bought less than half the Asian amount in 1925. This region was the only area of the world with which Britain secured a balance of trade surplus throughout the period, and was one of only three in which British exports in 1937 had regained their 1925 level at current prices (the others were Scandinavia and the West Indies).[14] However, while British exporters came to rely more heavily on sales to non-industrialized tropical countries, Britain's share of the total market for manufactures in these countries continued to fall in the 1930s, although more slowly than before.[15]

The increased importance of African markets to British exporters was also reflected in the gradual evolution of thinking about colonial development during the 1920s and 1930s, marked by the Colonial Development Act of 1929 and the Colonial Development and Welfare Act of 1940. The first of these measures was designed to encourage British capital investment in the dependent empire to boost domestic employment, and to ease the burden of debt repayment on the colonies. This was done by a British government guarantee of interest payments, but with the money to meet this coming out of colonial budgets. Thus the rigours of financial orthodoxy necessary to maintain an export surplus from which remittances could be made became London's main concern in African development during the 1930s. As a result, public investment was largely confined to the construction of railways and port facilities; parsimony and retrenchment capped developmental expenditure tightly. The problems of social disorder in the West Indies in 1936–8, and a growing awareness in Whitehall that colonialism needed to be justified (to the Americans, as well as to the colonized) in terms of social and economic progress that might lead in the distant future to political advance, resulted in further thinking encapsulated in the 1940 Act. This set out, for the first time in British imperial history, a modest agenda for economic development in a modern sense, stressing social welfare and the need for long-term investment, and including a small budget for research on agricultural improvement.[16]

British administrators were anxious to encourage greater international trade, and increased production of exportable crops, minerals and other raw materials where they could. The spread of cash-crop agriculture and wage labour, and the creation of an export surplus that provided foreign exchange to make remittances to London to cover returns on public investment, and the costs of government services and military defence, provided a crucial underpinning for colonial regimes. Only where colonial regimes were also faced with the problem of sustaining the lifestyles of European settlers in a tropical environment – as in parts of East Africa and South-East Asia – were direct restrictions put on the ability of local producers to take advantage of market opportunities. The apparent willingness of Asian and African peasants to produce cash crops for the international market, or to provide labour for mines and plantations, was applauded. But this could only be encouraged so long as it did not disrupt the foundation institutions of native society, and did not compromise the local allies on which imperial rule had come to depend. Thus the command of labour for export production in Africa had to be moderated when it was seen to be undermining the power of local chiefs to gain the consent of their subjects, while the spread of agricultural capitalism in India which might jeopardize the position of landlords and peasant brotherhoods was limited by legislation to prevent the transfer of land from rural to urban interests.

British colonial administrations in the first three decades of the twentieth century were not 'developmental states' in the modern sense of the word. From 1900 to 1939 imperial rule was essentially a conservative force in Asia and Africa, concerned to preserve pre-capitalist social and economic systems (especially in peasant agriculture based on communitarian institutions of management), and to protect their subjects from the exploitation of rural capitalists, traders and industrialists based either in the colonies themselves or in Britain. Many members of the imperial services were recruited from a stratum of British society that was instinctively anti-industrial, or even anti-capitalist; the paternalist ideology of colonial rule was anxious to prevent their subjects from abandoning the essential differences – cultural, sociological, technological and behavioural – that seemed to set them apart from the spirit of the West, and that justified colonialism's insistence that they were not yet fit to manage their own affairs in a hostile world. The resources and markets of conquered territories were made available to the 'modern' forces of the international economy, but only provided that this process did not disrupt the 'traditional' society on which the justification and institutional structures of colonialism depended.

The dangers of increased market integration were clearly demonstrated by the impact of the Great Depression on colonial economies after 1929. With the export prices of primary products collapsing, many local producers could no longer maintain their incomes, and domestic credit networks (both for production and for consumption loans) were damaged by the withdrawal of liquidity from overseas. The result was a series of peasant revolts, expressed in India through the civil disobedience movement that was launched by the Congress party against British rule in 1930–1 and 1932–4, and in West Africa through a series of labour strikes and producer 'hold-ups' – withdrawing produce from the market in protest against the failure of colonial governments, and their allies in native society, to secure the prices of export crops. Without the liquidity and profits provided by the export trades, dominant groups of local landlords and rural capitalists could not secure the resources they needed to maintain their influence. As a result, the political economy of the Asian and African countryside became transformed, as peasants concentrated on self-sufficiency, labour migrated into the growing cities, and domestic industries bought up local raw materials to manufacture products for home consumption, in a process that has been described as 'export substitution'.[17]

By the 1930s the relationship between the British economy and the dependent empire had also reached an impasse. Colonial territories could only provide resources for Britain if capitalism were allowed to develop there, but the very development of such capitalism – with the political, social and economic changes that resulted from it – represented the most serious threat to the continuation of colonial control. The political economy of colonialism that had developed before the First World War, and that underpinned the political and economic actions of colonial administrations everywhere, depended on an open economy in which trade and export-oriented production could provide employment and government revenue. But such 'modern' activity had to be moderated so that it did not disrupt the lives of colonial subjects too much, and destroy the authority of the 'traditional' leaders of society on which British rule depended. Urban Africans, and those working in mines and on plantations, were caricatured by their colonial rulers as 'detribalized', and therefore beyond the control of established native authority. The rising Indian middle class of professionals and white-collar workers were consistently derided in the discourse of the Raj as 'babus', imperfect amalgamations of Indian and British culture, because they could not be trusted to defer to colonial authority as the imperial idea of Indian tradition demanded, while Indian factory workers were thought to provide easy pickings for Communist agitators. It was no coincidence that these groups provided the core support for early nationalist movements against colonial rule. The shift in external economic relations away from an international economy to a more imperial focus in the 1930s and 1940s sharpened the confrontation between the 'modern' sectors of local economies and societies and their colonial rulers. In India, the political battle between imperial purpose and national development had been lost by 1939. In Africa it was to be fought out in the hot-house conditions of the much more serious crisis of British reconstruction after 1945.

The idea of a British imperial economy was created to justify political action that could counter the threat to the continued wealth and welfare of British consumers posed by international competition and economic uncertainty in the first three decades of the twentieth century. Such ideas, which stressed the complementarity of the economies of 'Greater Britain'[18] and the potential of its united strength, had a powerful emotional impact, but they were based on a fatal misunderstanding of the real nature of Britain's economic relations with her empire, and with the rest of the world. They lacked an economic logic even in the depths of the Great Depression, and by 1939 their impracticability had been further exposed. The problems of war and post-war reconstruction gave them a further spurious life in the 1940s and early 1950s, but by 1960, at the latest, it was clear that Britain had lost all hope of using the resources of the Dominions and other colonial or ex-colonial territories as an asset that could make good the failings of her domestic economy. Yet the notion of Britain (or, increasingly, of England) as an economy with a unique heritage of global links that sets her apart from her neighbours in continental Europe has not disappeared from political rhetoric – it surfaced again in the debates over joining the European Economic Community in the 1960s and 1970s, and has mutated into the Euroscepticism of the present day.

NOTES

1   The exact constitutional position and appropriate terminology for the different parts of
    the 'British Empire' were complicated in the period 1900–39, and changed considerably
    during its length. To simplify matters, the term 'Dominions' is used here to designate
    those colonies of settlement – Canada, Australia, New Zealand and South Africa – that
    were granted complete sovereignty *de facto* in 1926 and *de jure* by the Statute of
    Westminster in 1931, when they collectively formed the British Commonwealth of
    Nations with the United Kingdom. 'India' is used to designate the areas of mainland
    South Asia that were administered by the India Office (present-day India, Pakistan,
    Bangladesh and Myanmar). The phrase 'colonial empire' is used to designate Britain's
    other colonies and possessions in Asia, Africa, the Caribbean and the Pacific that were
    administered by the Colonial Office.
2   The summary data on British trade, investment and balance of payments before 1914 is
    taken from S. Pollard, *Britain's Prime and Britain's Decline: The British Economy,
    1870–1914* (London, 1989); A. Maizels, *Industrial Growth and World Trade: An
    Empirical Study of Trends in Production, Consumption and Trade in Manufactures
    from 1899–1959* (Cambridge, 1963); P. J. Cain and A. G. Hopkins, *British Imperialism:
    Innovation and Expansion, 1688–1914* (London, 1993); L. E. Davis and R. A.
    Huttenback, *Mammon and the Pursuit of Empire: The Political Economy of British
    Imperialism, 1860–1912* (Cambridge, 1987).
3   See Cain and Hopkins, *British Imperialism: Innovation and Expansion*, especially chs 6
    and 7.
4   On the effect of tariffs and imperial preference on British trade before 1914, see S. B.
    Saul, *Studies in British Overseas Trade, 1870–1914* (Liverpool, 1960), chs 6 and 7.
5   W. K. Hancock coined the phrase 'economics of siege' in his *Survey of British Common-
    wealth Affairs*, vol. 2, *Problems of Economic Policy, 1918–1939, Part 1* (Oxford, 1940),
    pp. 94–110; the term 'imperial visionaries' is used in I. M. Drummond, *British Economic
    Policy and the Empire, 1919–1939* (London, 1972), ch. 2.
6   This discussion of the sterling problem in the 1920s is based on D. E. Moggridge, *British
    Monetary Policy 1924–1931: The Norman Conquest of $4.86* (Cambridge, 1972), esp.
    pp. 117–28, 139–40 and appendix 2.
7   On the making of the Import Duties Act and the 'political economy of protection' in
    the 1920s, see T. Rooth, *British Protectionism and the International Economy: Overseas
    Commercial Policy in the 1930s* (Cambridge, 1993), ch. 2.
8   Maizels, *Industrial Growth and World Trade*, tables 8.13 and 8.14. By 1937 British
    exports provided less than 30 per cent of the manufactured goods consumed in New
    Zealand and South Africa, less than 15 per cent of the manufactured goods consumed in
    India and Australia, and less than 5 per cent of the manufactured goods consumed in
    Canada. See Maizels, *Industrial Growth and World Trade*, tables A24, A27, A28, A29,
    A30 and E5.
9   On the Ottawa negotiations and the problems of 'imperial self-insufficiency' (Hancock's
    phrase), see Hancock, *Survey of British Commonwealth Affairs*, pp. 230–66, and Drum-
    mond, *British Economic Policy and the Empire*, ch. 3.
10 For the problems of negotiating with the Japanese, see Rooth, *British Protectionism*,
    pp. 181–8, and Hancock, *Survey of British Commonwealth Affairs*, pp. 253–5.
11 B. R. Tomlinson, 'Imperial power and foreign trade: Britain and India, 1900–1970', in
    P. Mathias and J. A. Davis, eds, *The Nature of Industrialization: International Trade and
    Economic Growth: From the Eighteenth Century to the Present Day* (Oxford, 1996),
    pp. 154–5.

12 Drummond, *British Economic Policy and the Empire*, pp. 102–3.
13 For a discussion of Britain's informal financial imperialism in the 1930s, see P. J. Cain and A. G. Hopkins, *British Imperialism: Crisis and Deconstruction, 1914–1990* (London, 1993), chs 5, 6, 8, 10.
14 B. R. Mitchell (with P. Deane), *Abstract of British Historical Statistics* (Cambridge, 1962), pp. 309–27. These percentages have been calculated from trade data in current prices.
15 Maizels, *Industrial Growth and World Trade*, table A2.
16 On the making of the Colonial Development and Welfare Act, see J. M. Lee, *Colonial Development and Good Government: A Study of the Ideas Expressed by the British Official Classes in Planning Decolonization 1939–1964* (Oxford, 1967), chs 2–3.
17 G. Clarence-Smith, 'The effects of the Great Depression on industrialisation in Equatorial and Central Africa', in I. Brown, ed., *The Economies of Africa and Asia in the Inter-war Depression* (London, 1989), p. 196.
18 This favourite phrase of late Victorian advocates of imperial unity had been popularized by Sir Charles Dilke – a Liberal advocate of a strong imperially based foreign policy, especially in Egypt – in the 1880s.

FURTHER READING

Brown, I., ed., *The Economies of Africa and Asia in the Inter-war Depression* (London, 1989).
Brown, J. M. and Louis, W. R., eds, *The Oxford History of the British Empire*, vol. 4, *The Twentieth Century* (Oxford, 1999).
Cain, P. J. and Hopkins, A. G., *British Imperialism: Crisis and Deconstruction, 1914–1990* (London, 1993).
Cain, P. J. and Hopkins, A. G., *British Imperialism: Innovation and Expansion, 1688–1914* (London, 1993).
Cooper, F., *Decolonization and African Society: The Labor Question in French and British Africa* (Cambridge, 1996).
Court, W. H. B., *British Economic History, 1870–1914: Commentary and Documents* (Cambridge, 1965).
Drummond, I. M., *British Economic Policy and the Empire, 1919–1939* (London, 1972).
Hancock, W. K., *Survey of British Commonwealth Affairs*, vol. 2, *Problems of Economic Policy, 1918–1939, Part 1* (London, 1940).
Hewins, W. A. S., *Apologia of an Imperialist* (London, 1929).
Rooth, T., *British Protectionism and the International Economy: Overseas Commercial Policy in the 1930s* (Cambridge, 1992).
Porter, A. (with Low, A.), *The Oxford History of the British Empire*, vol. 3, *The Nineteenth Century* (Oxford, 1999).
Saul, S. B., *Studies in British Overseas Trade, 1870–1914* (Liverpool, 1960).
Swinton, Lord (Sir Phillip Cunliffe-Lister), *I Remember* (London, 1949).
Tomlinson, B. R., *The Political Economy of the Raj, 1914–47: The Economics of Decolonisation in India* (London, 1979).
Walker, E. A., *The British Empire: Its Structure and Spirit* (London, 1943).

CHAPTER FOURTEEN

Britain in the International Economy, 1900–1939

TIM ROOTH

Britain was heavily and increasingly engaged in the international economy in the era before the First World War. Policy and institutions played a crucial role in sustaining this internationalism, notably through continued adherence to the gold standard and to free trade. The gold standard, which fixed a gold value for sterling and obliged the Bank of England to maintain that value, established a pre-eminent objective to which other aspects of government economic policy had to be subordinated. While the gold standard was supposedly automatic in operation and therefore free of political pressures, so free trade also ensured that no group could bargain for political privileges. It therefore followed that British producers had to face competition in both home and overseas markets, and, under the liberal agenda, these competitive pressures were supposed to ensure British industry remained efficient. These pressures were reinforced by the distinctive character of Britain's industrial structure, dominated as it was by small and medium-sized firms that made it difficult for firms to collude in fixing prices. The contribution of the state to an efficient economic system was to restrict its expenditure, keep taxation low and balance its budget.

Britain and the International Economy before 1914

Already heavily dependent on the international economy at the turn of the century, Britain had become even more fully engaged by the First World War: while in 1900 exports and imports of goods and services had accounted for 48.8 per cent of GNP, by 1913 they were worth 58.6 per cent. British visible exports continued to be almost totally dominated by manufactured goods, despite the increasing importance of coal. By 1913 as much as 45 per cent of manufactured output was exported (the comparable German figure was 31 per cent and the United States only 5 per cent). For some industries, notably cotton textiles, this dependence was extreme: in 1913, 85 per cent of piece goods were exported.

Overseas capital exports also became even more important before the war. British overseas investment had never followed a smooth pattern of steady accumulation; UK savings rates were low, and investment tended to alternate between decades of relatively high home investment and low overseas issues with decades of heavy capital exports and light home investment. The decade or so before the war witnessed unprecedented capital exports. By 1914 the total stock of British overseas investment had probably reached somewhere in the region of £4,000 million, as much as 160 per cent of GNP and probably generating an annual income *flow* of as much as 9 per cent of national income. British internationalism was reinforced by heavy emigration. High levels of capital export were accompanied by a revival of emigration during the 'Edwardian' era. This reached unprecedented levels between 1900 and 1914, with emigration from England and Wales peaking in 1912 and that from Scotland a year earlier.[1]

Clearly the international economy was of huge importance to Britain – and Britain had been and continued to be vital to the growth and smooth operation of the international economy. That industrialization had first occurred in a small country with a relatively narrow resource base had had profound implications for the shape and growth of the international economy. The diverse and fast-growing demands generated by British industrialization and population growth had outstripped domestic resources and spilled over into the international economy. The revolutions in transport and the existence of sparsely populated regions of recent European settlement, mainly in the Americas and Australasia, meant that these demands could be met and the Malthusian spectre banished. The adoption of free trade speeded the growth of imports. These demands stamped their imprint on the international economy as Britain came to dominate world imports of raw cotton, wool, timber, wheat, tea, dairy products and meat. Sterling became as ubiquitous in international payments as British shipping on world sea-lanes.

British capital had played a vital role in opening up land and resources overseas, going predominantly to finance railways, mines, plantations and the urban infrastructure of the land-abundant regions of recent European settlement. By the First World War the UK accounted for perhaps 44 per cent of foreign investment of the leading capital exporting countries.

British free trade supported capital exports and was central to the system of multilateral trade and payments. If overseas investments were to be serviced the borrowers had to earn sterling. This they did both by exporting to the UK and increasingly by selling directly to third countries, especially the United States and the industrial countries of continental western Europe. These countries in turn ran payments surpluses with the UK.[2] Open access to the British market smoothed the international payments system.

The international economy was stable in that the core industrial countries, although certainly not crisis free before 1914, never experienced a slump remotely as deep as that of the 1930s. The system was also stable in the sense that the major industrial countries achieved a long period of exchange rate stability before the First World War. The further we get from that era the more remarkable it seems. To contemporaries the explanation was simple: it was due to the gold standard, regarded as automatic and 'knave-proof'. Later commentators have been less convinced, tending instead to emphasize the international economic environment in which the gold standard operated. From the 1890s increased gold production eased pressure on international liquidity.[3] It was also important that the distribution of gold was reasonably equitable: as later experience was to demonstrate, gold hogging could wreck the system. But gold holdings were concentrated in the main centres, the five great European powers holding nearly half by 1914, the United States 22 per cent, thus leaving the rest of the world with less than 30 per cent. The willingness of Britain to reinvest its current account surpluses was therefore vital. Gold was also supplemented by holdings of those key currencies used heavily in international transactions; although gold reserves increased sharply before 1914, currency reserves rose even faster, probably accounting for nearly 20 per cent of international reserves by 1914. Sterling was the most important, but the use of francs and marks was outpacing sterling before the war. This highlights the role of the Bank of England in economizing on gold, for these holdings of sterling were, of course, short-term liabilities from the British perspective. London held surprisingly modest quantities of gold (perhaps £35–40 million before the war compared with about £120 million held by the Bank of France and not much less by Russia). One result was the very active use of bank rate to protect these reserves, so that between January 1904 and December 1914 the Bank of England changed bank rate forty-nine times as against the eight times of the Bank of France.

Yet for gold and short-term capital flows to be so responsive there had to be confidence in sterling. London's overwhelmingly strong long-term asset position contributed to this and the persistence of current account surpluses must have helped too. But Eichengreen is no doubt correct to emphasize not only the credibility of the unwavering commitment of British policy makers to gold convertibility, but the willingness of other nations to give assistance in times of exceptional distress: 'the commitment to the gold standard was international'.[4]

The International Challenge

British ascendancy of the international economy was severely threatened in the late nineteenth century. The fiercest challenge came from the United States and Germany, both formidable industrial powers. UK industrial output was exceeded by the United States in the early 1880s and by Germany around 1905. As early as the 1880s there had been widespread concern about the foreign competition, and this reached a new intensity during the anxious debate over the 'Condition of England' at the turn of the century.[5] The challenge of new competitors manifested itself in several unwelcome ways. Finished manufactures were increasingly important in Britain's total imports, rising from 15.8 per cent in the 1880s to an average of 24.6 per cent between 1901 and 1911; Britain experienced a higher degree of import penetration than other large industrial countries. Even more dramatic was Britain's falling share of world exports, illustrated in table 14.1. British exporters were losing the battle for world markets, and did disastrously in the 1890s.[6] Problems with exports combined with the sharply rising import bill to weaken the balance of payments surplus, particularly in the late 1890s and the first years of the twentieth century.

The emergence of major rivals and the intensification of competition stimulated a powerful challenge to the liberal orthodoxy, and broke the consensus between the main political parties. If Britain was to meet a challenge that was both economic and political/strategic and was to remain a great power in the coming century, positive policies were needed. Industrial modernization was imperative – if British industry was to withstand foreign competition in the newer and more dynamic sectors it

Table 14.1 UK share of world exports of manufactured goods, selected years 1880–1913 (per cent)

1880	41.4
1890	40.7
1899	32.5
1913	29.9

Source: S. B. Saul, 'The export economy', *Yorkshire Bulletin of Economic and Social Research*, 17, no. 1 (1965), p. 12.

needed tariff protection. In the vision of the Chamberlainites a positive policy of imperial economic integration was the key to Britain's survival as a great power; imperial preference was one element in developing and harnessing the resources of the empire. But import duties would also serve a third function – they would broaden the sources of revenue to finance social reform. Issues of public finance came to dominate the political debate of Edwardian Britain.

The tariff reform movement captured the Tory party but not the country, and was overwhelmingly defeated when the Liberals triumphed in the election of 1906. Internal contradictions in the campaign contributed to its defeat, but perhaps the main factor was the strength, pervasiveness and persistence of the free-trade gospel. This was not the end of the matter. Naval rivalry led to increased defence spending and programmes of social reform put further pressure on government budgets. The Tories continued to advocate tariffs as the means to raise revenue. Liberal governments, with this route closed, were forced to resort to income tax (and as a result drove some businessmen, including many in the City, into the tariff reform movement).[7] Global rivalry was threatening the liberal agenda, undermining free trade and forcing the minimalist state to extend its role.

Pre-war Boom

Yet in the decade or so before the outbreak of war some of the economic pressures resulting from intensified international competition appeared to ease. Between 1901/5 and 1913 the volume of UK manufactured exports expanded by 3.6 per cent per annum. This was not as fast as US or German export growth, but it was a better performance than France, Belgium or Switzerland managed to achieve, and enabled Britain to remain the premier exporter of manufactured goods by the eve of the First World War.[8] Several factors account for this. World trade as a whole was expanding rapidly, especially in the decade or so before the First World War. Primary producers, benefiting from rising prices after the mid-1890s, were particularly prominent in the process. Britain, which was heavily dependent on the semi-industrialized countries, was remarkably well placed to take advantage of these trends. Moreover, UK capital exports, running at unprecedentedly high levels before the First World War, reinforced the process of growth and acted as a direct stimulant to British exports.

The balance of payments strengthened. After declining between the late 1890s and the first years of the twentieth century, the current account surplus grew sharply in the decade or so before the war, despite increasing competition. After 1903 the rapid expansion of exports outpaced the growth of imports and caused the trade gap to narrow. Invisible income was buoyant; rising shipping receipts made a notable contribution, but the most important source was interest and dividends from overseas investments, which doubled between 1900 and 1913. By the eve of war the invisible surplus was paying for more than 40 per cent of UK imports, and ensuring that Britain financed its huge capital outflow without balance of payments strain.

By 1914 the policies and institutions of the liberal agenda stood largely intact. There had been, it is true, some expansion of the role of the state and a resort to a graduated and differentiated income tax for revenue. But Liberal internationalism was alive and well. Britain had stuck to free trade despite formidable protectionist pressures, and the gold standard had survived a crisis in 1907 that had demonstrated considerable international cooperation. Sterling remained strong, buttressed by increasing current account surpluses in the decade before the war but also by huge overseas assets. Nor was there any sign of an imperial bias in Britain's trade and payments. Despite the vast extent of the British Empire, the majority of UK imports, exports and overseas investments came from or went to non-empire countries. British trade and payments were cosmopolitan.

There were, however, weaknesses and potential dangers in Britain's international economic position. The great burst of exports in the decade before the war had been concentrated on a narrow base: textiles, iron and steel, and coal accounted for 70 per cent of visible exports. As with any export economy with a restricted range of products, Britain was vulnerable to unfavourable shifts in demand, to the development of substitutes and to the emergence of new competitors. Before 1914 there had been intimations of failing competitiveness, but in the immediate pre-war years these had been masked by the boom in international trade.

Post-war Boom and Bust

The price of Britain's high exposure to the international economy was paid between the wars. At first this was far from clear, for in the months following the ceasefire a frenzied but short-lived boom boosted exports. But following the collapse of the boom in April 1920 some of the graver international economic consequences of the war began to be revealed. British exporters suffered on several fronts. The diversion of British production to the war effort had encouraged importing countries to find alternative supplies either by expanding their own production or by importing from elsewhere, especially from the United States and Japan. In eastern and central Europe revolution, war and the subsequent peace treaties caused widespread destruction and prolonged dislocation.[9] The international monetary system had been and continued to be undermined by huge distortions of international monetary relationships associated with widely differing but often spectacular levels of inflation. Not least of the international repercussions of the war was the boost given to the economic ascendancy of the United States as trader and financier. American policies were poorly matched to its transformed international economic and political status.[10]

While earlier writing suggested that the purely domestic impact of the war on the British economy was not seriously adverse, recent research has increasingly seen British economic performance over the transwar period as peculiarly poor. Indeed the problems of international competitiveness faced by Britain in the 1920s stemmed much more from the events of the war and immediate post-war years than from the overvaluation of sterling in 1925. Although Churchill's action in returning to the gold standard in 1925 had immense symbolic significance and may well have condemned Britain to a further retreat in international markets in the later 1920s, the real damage was done earlier.

The hectic boom, social ferment and industrial unrest of 1919/20 left their imprint on the British economy for the remainder of the decade. One legacy was the reduction of working hours, averaging 13 per cent, without any compensating fall in money wages. This helped open up a price/cost gap between British exporters and their competitors that was never closed. Although UK prices fell rapidly in the subsequent depression of 1920–2, these were matched by a similar fall in American prices. A sharp appreciation of sterling, caused partly by a rise in bank rate to 7 per cent, compounded the problems of British exporters. Broadberry estimates that sterling rose more rapidly between 1920 and 1921 than between 1924 and 1925, and, measured against a basket of currencies, was higher in real terms in 1921 than after the restoration of the gold standard in 1925. This argument is reinforced by the calculations of Greasley and Oxley, who point to a deterioration in international competitiveness of 36 per cent that put British exporters at a formidable disadvantage once the post-war supply shortages eased and international competition resumed. They conclude that 'the force of the macroeconomic shock surrounding the First World War exerted a powerfully depressive influence on British industry throughout the interwar years'.[11] Low levels of profit over the transwar period, particularly during the slump, contributed to weak capital formation and exceptionally poor rates of economic growth between 1913 and 1929.

The post-war boom and slump also removed much of the impetus from the wartime 'modernization' movement. Drawing on its pre-war antecedents this had posed a major challenge to liberal orthodoxy. To meet the threat to British industry from Germany and the United States, the movement aimed to reorganize and rationalize industry and to overhaul the machinery of government. Closer economic integration of the empire remained an essential part of the programme. The movement, however, lost momentum. The suddenness and completeness of Germany's collapse in 1918 allayed the anxieties of those who had anticipated bitter commercial rivalry after the war.[12] The boom encouraged the scrapping of wartime controls and agencies, and the ensuing slump encouraged major cuts in government spending that undermined the reconstruction programme.[13]

Taking the International Option

The British monetary authorities had determined their course of action as early as 1918 when the Cunliffe Committee produced its first interim report. The tightening of monetary policy in 1919 and subsequent fiscal retrenchment were essential if the Bank of England was to regain control of the money markets and British price levels were to be brought into some approximation with those of the United States. The government moved as soon as Lloyd George gauged that the political ferment of 1919 had cooled sufficiently to allow spending cuts. This represented the reassertion of liberal orthodoxy. Yet the British economic structure was shifting and in some key respects the UK's relationship with the international economy was undergoing change.

By the 1920s Britain had become distinctly less cosmopolitan than on the eve of the First World War. One measure of this was exposure to the international economy: while in 1913 trade in goods and services accounted for 58.6 per cent of GNP, by 1929 it represented only 47.6 per cent. Dependence on exports had declined and the home market became correspondingly more important. Significantly, when British producers sold overseas, they had become far more dependent on imperial markets. While between 1910 and 1913, 35.8 per cent of exports had been sold to the empire, by 1927 that share had risen to 43.1 per cent. Although most sectors of British industry increased their dependence on empire markets, this appears to have been particularly true for some of the newer and more expansive sectors of world trade, including capital goods, especially electrical engineering products and the motor industry. In contrast to the nineteenth-century staples, capable of competing in global markets, the newer industries relied more heavily on the crutch of imperial preferences and other privileges in empire markets.

UK capital also increasingly favoured imperial outlets. New issues on the London market are not a totally accurate guide to the distribution of British investment, but they none the less strongly suggest the dominance of imperial lending, with £497 million going to the empire while foreign issues totalled only £280 million. One cause of this shift was the periodic restrictions on foreign lending, and these, together with the liquidation of dollar stocks during the war, contributed to the reorientation in the pattern of British overseas investment holdings.

Industry too was moving away from its characteristically disaggregated structure to one in which giant corporations played a far more prominent role. Whereas in 1907 the 100 largest companies accounted for 15 per cent of net manufacturing output, by 1924 this had risen to 21 per cent, and, by 1930, to 26 per cent. Within twenty years Britain moved from having one of the least concentrated industrial sectors among major economies to a level comparable to the United States.[14] This owed little to the organic growth of companies and a great deal to a wave of mergers, especially in 1919/20. Not only was collusion among firms facilitated, but individual companies could exert greater political pressure.

British economic policy also reflected the wavering commitment to internationalism. The greatest challenge came to free trade: the first protectionist inroads had been made by the McKenna duties of 1915 (although introduced mainly to raise war revenue and to save on shipping). Further duties were added in 1921, and in 1923 Conservative leader Stanley Baldwin unsuccessfully fought an election on a protectionist manifesto. When the Conservatives returned to power in 1924 they were pledged to eschew protection, and although the McKenna duties (repealed by Labour) were rapidly reinstated and some modest extensions made to other duties, they essentially honoured these promises. Churchill, a free trader and the surprise appointment as chancellor of the exchequer, was in a pivotal position to ensure the government kept to its word. He was soon involved in the controversial decision to return to the gold standard. Together with the disavowal of protectionism, the restoration of the gold standard with sterling at its pre-war parity level of £3.17.10$\frac{1}{2}$d. per ounce ($4.86 to the pound) can be taken as the assertion of the international option.

The return to gold has been represented as the triumph of City interests over industry. Certainly by the 1920s London had come to dominate Britain more thoroughly than at any time in modern history.[15] Within the City the power of the cosmopolitan merchant banks was virtually undiminished. For these interests it was axiomatic that Britain should return to gold at its pre-war parity, for unless it did so London had little hope of regaining its position as an international financial centre. In late 1924 sterling began to appreciate, partly because abnormal sales of Australian wheat to continental Europe after bad harvests in 1924 bolstered sterling reserves, but helped also by the return of a Conservative government thought likely to restore the gold standard. Since sterling rose from just under $4.50 in October to more than $4.70 in December, and soon crept up to $4.79, there was little further to go. If the pound was to be stabilized at an overvalued level it was industry that was likely to suffer because of intensified competition in export markets and at home. Yet the case against was clouded by the argument that since unemployment was heavily concentrated in the export industries, only the reconstruction of the international economy with stable exchange rates would revive international investment and trade that was essential to the recovery of the old export staple industries. The advocates of return marshalled their case cogently and deployed their arguments with clarity.[16]

Failure of the International Option

The government had turned its back decisively against state-induced modernization schemes and had taken the international option.[17] Key tests of the international option were to be the ability of British business to compete effectively in export markets, and, intimately linked, balance of payments performance and the unemployment record. All failed dismally and contributed, by the end of the decade, to growing disillusion with the liberal agenda.

British exports did badly notwithstanding the expansiveness of the international economy during the late 1920s. By 1929 British exports were still well below the values of 1924. In longer perspective the performance is even more dismal. Maizels calculates that between 1913 and 1929 the volume of international trade in manufactured goods grew by 37.5 per cent, yet British exports did so disastrously that by 1929 they had failed to regain their pre-war volume. This represented a dramatic retreat in world markets: the British share of manufactured exports fell from 30.2 per cent in 1913 to 20.4 per cent in 1929. How damaging was the return to gold at the old parity? The lack of consensus about the degree of overvaluation makes a precise answer impossible. Keynes's contemporary estimate was that sterling was 10 per cent overvalued against the US dollar, but subsequent estimates of the extent of overvaluation have ranged from zero to 14 per cent against the dollar but from 20 per cent to 25 per cent against a basket of foreign currencies. It would be absurd, however, to suggest that Britain's economic problems were simply the result of the wrong exchange rate. The UK suffered badly from the effects of import substitution. India, for example, was determined to build up its own manufactured textile capacity once it was free to impose tariffs. There was excess world capacity in steel and shipbuilding. New power sources depressed coal exports. The UK was overcommitted to products stagnating or declining in world trade and only thinly represented in the fast-growing sectors. Yet British prices do appear to have been substantially out of alignment with those of its competitors. Table 14.2 presents the evidence of Maizels. As suggested above, British exchange rates had appreciated at the beginning of the

Table 14.2 Unit values of exports of manufactures from the
UK and France and from their competitors (in terms of $US),
1913–1929 (1899 = 100)

Exporting countries	1913	1929
United Kingdom		
1 Exports	125	189
2 Exports from competing countries	111	149
3 1 as percentage of 2	113	127
France		
4 Exports	112	143
5 Exports from competing countries	115	162
6 4 as percentage of 5	97	88

Source: A. Maizels, *Industrial Growth and World Trade: An Empirical Study of Trends in Production, Consumption and Trade in Manufactures from 1899–1959* (Cambridge, 1963), p. 205.

1920s, and exporters had therefore lived with a high pound virtually throughout the decade, and not merely after 1925. But British experience after 1925 makes a sorry contrast to the rapid growth of the French economy, almost certainly benefiting from an undervalued currency.

Whatever weight is attached to the exchange rate or other factors, the dreadful British export record had profound consequences for other aspects of economic performance and policy. Failure to compete internationally helped to keep more than a million out of work, put pressure on the government's budgetary position, contributed to weakness in the balance of payments and ensured unprecedentedly stringent monetary policy.

A successful assault on British costs and prices would have alleviated the problems of overvaluation. But this failed in the most spectacular manner when attempts to cut miners' wages provoked the General Strike in 1926. Although government (and employers) appeared to triumph, they were subsequently nervous of pursuing a vigorous policy of wage reduction, and real wages rose modestly in the late 1920s. Poor export performance, together with import penetration, exacerbated unemployment in the old staple industries. This in turn imposed a heavy fiscal burden on government; deflation reduced government tax receipts and unemployment incurred extra expenditure, compounding Churchill's difficulties with his budgets in the late 1920s.[18] Moreover, defending sterling at its new rate obliged the Bank of England to maintain a tight monetary policy: real interest rates were exceptionally high in the early 1920s, and they remained at historically high levels throughout the period 1920–31. These high rates have been blamed for suppressing investment, especially in the interest-sensitive sectors such as housing, and may indeed have led to a dip in output in 1928.[19]

Lack of competitiveness was manifested in the weakness of Britain's overseas accounts, which themselves formed an integral part of the unstable international financial system of the late 1920s. The visible import deficit had widened both absolutely and relatively since the 1900–13 period. The large overvaluation of

1920–2 encouraged foreign firms to penetrate the UK market on a permanent basis.[20] As early as 1924 import volume was already above 1913 levels at a time when exports were still 25 per cent below their pre-war level. The merchandise deficit, which had averaged £87 million in 1910–13, stood at £296 million by 1925–9. A relative decline in the invisible surplus compounded weakness. In the Edwardian era this had run at twice the deficit on merchandise trade, but between 1925 and 1929 the surplus on invisibles was only 17 per cent above the visible trade deficit. London could not restore its pre-war international financial pre-eminence on this basis. Despite the intermittent use of controls on foreign issues on the London capital market, British long-term lending was well above the level warranted by the current account surplus, and the difference had to be financed by short-term borrowing. By 1929 London's short-term liabilities were considerably in excess of £275 million while reserves were only £146 million. This placed a premium on the maintenance of confidence in sterling.

Quite evidently the economic system was failing to generate prosperity or to reduce unemployment. There was growing restlessness over the operation of the market mechanism.[21] As many businessmen came to regard the competitive economic system as synonymous with waste and inefficiency, the rationalization of industry appeared increasingly necessary. By the eve of the slump deepening disillusion with the efficacy of the market mechanism was apparent, not least through a growing clamour for protection. Several major industries, including steel, engineering and woollens, campaigned for tariffs, and by 1929 the traditionally free-trade cotton industry was wavering too.

The World Slump

Britain was vulnerable to an international slump both because of its overall exposure to world trade and because of its particular patterns of trade and finance. Intimate trading and financial links with primary producers exposed the UK to the problems many had been facing in the late 1920s. Employment in the export-sensitive industries began to decline in March 1929, and had been preceded by a fall in exports to the low-income per capita primary producers as early as 1928.[22]

Yet it was the slump in the United States that was the catalyst for a global depression of unprecedented severity. It was transmitted from the United States to the rest of the world through two main channels, the curtailment of American foreign lending and the decline of US imports. From 1924 capital outflows had successfully masked the fault-lines of the international financial system, particularly by offsetting the US current account surplus. Nobody knows with any precision the magnitude of the decline of American overseas lending, but it set in during 1928 and was substantial.[23] Then, in late 1929, as the depression began to bite, American imports contracted, the beginning of a process that saw them fall from $4.4 billion in 1929 to $1.3 billion by 1932. The principal driving force in this decline was the collapse of US incomes and spending, but the resort to yet higher tariffs in the notorious Hawley-Smoot Act of 1930 encouraged the fall and stimulated worldwide retaliation.

The problems of the primary producers, already struggling, deepened. Weakening demand led to a meltdown in prices: these had been falling in the late 1920s, but in the single year of 1930 the export revenues of Asia, Africa, South America,

Oceania and Canada fell on average by a further 25 per cent. This happened at a time when international borrowing, which might have given breathing space for the balance of payments adjustment, was becoming virtually impossible. The UK, highly exposed to primary producers, was peculiarly vulnerable to their problems. British exports fell from £729 million in 1929 to £391 million by 1931. By some measures the decline in exports more than accounted for the British slump.[24]

The slump transformed the position of Britain in the international economy. Crises in 1931 drove the UK off the gold standard and shortly afterwards led to the abandonment of free trade. A financial crisis began in Austria when the leading bank, Credit Anstalt, which had been borrowing abroad short term and lending long term to industry at home, failed. The crisis spread to Hungary before attention switched to Germany where banks had followed the same practices as in Austria and where international accounts, burdened by reparations and exposed by the cessation of international lending, were vulnerable. Creditors began to protect themselves by withdrawing funds, precipitating a financial crisis in July when Germany froze foreign credits, including £70 million of British funds. Within two days the crisis had spread to London. London was vulnerable on several counts. As suggested above, it was embroiled in the problems of the primary producers. Between 1928 and 1931 the total deficit of the Rest of the Sterling Area probably amounted to over £450 million. Although the evidence is not decisive, it appears likely that the sterling area countries ran down their sterling balances in 1929–31.[25] If so this was unhelpful but by no means the worst of the problem. By 1931 Britain was experiencing its own balance of payments problems. Shipping income had been badly hit by the slump in international trade, and income from overseas investments fell even more dramatically between 1929 and 1931. The surplus on invisibles dropped from £319 million in 1930 to £219 million in 1931, and at that level it was insufficient to cover a widening deficit on merchandise trade. To compound matters, because in the late 1920s London had been lending long and borrowing short to finance capital outflows, reserves were slim and short-term liabilities rising. Along with Germany, Hungary and Austria, Britain was one of four European short-term debtors: significantly, all four suffered the most intense financial crises in the summer of 1931.[26]

At the heart of the problem was not so much an overall shortage of international liquidity as a gross maldistribution of gold reserves. The Americans were partly to blame: by the end of 1924 the US gold stock was over three times larger than in 1914 and represented 46 per cent of total world gold reserves. Although the United States imported a further $316 million of gold between 1925 and 1929, in the later stages of the emerging crisis France was the main culprit, its central bank gold holdings rising by nearly $1,445 million between 1928 and the end of 1931. This placed a near intolerable pressure on other countries in the system.

Even before World War I the gold standard depended critically on the maintenance of credibility and on international cooperation. Although the monetary policies of the United States and France probably condemned the gold standard system of the late 1920s to breakdown, the handling of the crisis by the British government turned probability to certainty. The publication of the Macmillan Committee report on 13 July 1931, just as the German banks were closing, revealed that foreigners held £407 million in deposits and short-term bills in London and also drew attention to the inadequacy of UK gold reserves. On 31 July the May Committee report produced estimates of the government's likely budget deficit for the financial year 1931/2. The committee suggested some modest tax increases but the thrust of their recommendations was for economies in public expenditure, by far the greatest savings to come from reducing 'dole' payments to the unemployed. In effect this became the condition for getting foreign credits. Anathema to many members of the Labour cabinet, the latter were unable to agree to Chancellor Snowden's recommendations and the government resigned.

Britain's Retreat from Internationalism

Notwithstanding the economies made by the National government that succeeded the Labour administration, and the credits accordingly raised in New York and Paris, within a month the pound was driven off the gold standard. Thus fell one of the great symbols of Britain's nineteenth-century international economic ascendancy. The other symbol, free trade, or at least its remnants, quickly followed. In November an emergency measure, the Abnormal Importations Act, imposed duties of up to 100 per cent. More considered legislation, the Import Duties Act, followed in March 1932. Although the new duties on most manufactured goods were initially set at only 10 per cent, these were almost immediately doubled on the recommendations of the Import Duties Advisory Committee, and further duty increases followed. Imperial produce was provisionally exempted.

The motivation for protection has been debated. Some have linked it to the gold standard departure, suggesting it was largely a technical device to counter the inflationary pressures that might have resulted if a deteriorating trade deficit had driven the unpegged pound into a tail spin.[27] Treasury documents provide some evidence for this view, although, as Peden observes, it is difficult to know when Treasury officials wrote from conviction and when to order.[28] What is not in doubt is that the new chancellor, Neville Chamberlain, was a convinced protectionist and a powerful minister. By 1931 there was massive and widespread pressure for the introduction of protection and imperial preference. This has encouraged other writers to argue that protection was introduced largely on political grounds although dressed up as a technical necessity to make it more palatable to free-trade Liberal and Labour members of the coalition government.[29]

Closer imperial economic integration had been an important component of the protectionist campaign. The opportunities for reciprocal preferences were explored at the Imperial Economic Conference held in Ottawa during the summer of 1932. Ironically, the circumstances that brought Commonwealth members together at Ottawa – the slump – were precisely those that were guaranteed to produce a fractious meeting and limited results. Britain agreed to continue free entry, widened some preferential margins, but hedged its concessions with various qualifications about the duration of the agricultural guarantees.[30] In return, many of the Dominions conceded wider preferential margins but often by raising the foreign tariff rather than liberalizing access for UK goods.

British exporters achieved little from the agreements: the obstacles, which were formidable, have been discussed elsewhere.[31] Although the agreements provided an opportunity for British exporters both to increase their share of empire markets and to raise their sales from the low levels of 1931, this was a limited achievement in the light of the shrinkage of exports that had occurred after 1929. The collapse of food and raw materials prices impoverished producers and created havoc with their balance of payments. Export earnings had been hit by the price falls. This was bad enough, but was compounded because several of the Dominions had been heavy borrowers in the 1920s, using the inflows on capital account to finance current account deficits. Since new capital flows had mostly dried up, these current account deficits now had to be turned into surpluses in the face of sharply reduced export income. Servicing existing debts imposed a massive drain on income. In this context the British market was the salvation of the Dominions during the 1930s – by extending imperial preference and mostly avoiding any restrictions, the basis was laid for a spectacular increase in the volume of imports and for increased earnings. Yet much of the Dominions' balance of payments adjustment was secured by drastic cuts of their imports. Debts were honoured and the flow of interest payments into London sustained. But while bondholders and the city gained, UK exporters bore much of the cost. Exporters gained more from a series of treaties the British government was able to make with the lightly indebted North European countries.[32]

These agreements revealed some of the tensions and ambivalence in British international economic policy in the 1930s. Although the most-favoured-nation clause was widely abused, it was never officially abandoned. British industry was furious at what it regarded as the weak-kneed policies of the government, its refusal to use Britain's potential bargaining power to extract maximum concessions from trading partners. Liberal traditions lived on in Whitehall, not least in the Board of Trade and in the person of its president, Walter Runciman. This is reflected in agricultural policy where most measures were designed to keep the British food market relatively open and the cost of living low. Quotas were often generous (that on foreign bacon was a notable exception) and tariffs on non-imperial supplies much lower than the Dominions would have liked. Yet open markets and low costs had to be reconciled with the desperate plight of British farmers, and after a series of experiments Whitehall was driven to the use of exchequer subsidies as the principal support for UK agriculture.

International efforts attacking the depression achieved nothing. The most conspicuous effort was the World Economic and Monetary Conference held in London in 1933, but this proved a spectacular failure. The United States is generally blamed for scuttling the conference: the Americans not only refused to discuss war debts, regarded by the Europeans as of outstanding importance and an integral part of any international settlement, but then devalued the dollar on the eve of the conference and refused to stabilize it. Yet they were not alone in subordinating international to national interests.[33] In preparatory discussions the British steadfastly refused to give undertakings about stabilizing sterling, only discovering an interest in exchange rate stability after the United States devalued. The Ottawa agreements were ruled out of contention and the British delegation made it clear that the UK tariff was inviolable.

How successful was British international policy during the 1930s in helping economic recovery? If it is judged by export performance, the conclusion must be that it failed. There is, it is true, some evidence at the turning point of the cycle, in late 1932, that increased exports made a contribution to the start of recovery. Exchange depreciation had clearly given UK exporters a competitive advantage, and trade treaties and preparations for them saw Britain raise its share of its trading partners' imports. Overall, the long-run tendency of Britain to lose its share of world trade was checked and temporarily reversed. But this could not be sustained. The intensification of competition, and particularly the erosion of exchange rate advantages, saw the UK retreating once more. But this time it was not Britain's share of world trade that mattered so much as the depressed level of international trade in the 1930s: by 1937, the best year of the recovery, world exports of manufactures were still 17 per cent below their 1929 level. British exports were still more than one-fifth below their 1929 volume.

Competitive export weaknesses were one source of balance of payments problems. The current account had moved sharply into deficit in 1931, and there it remained for the rest of the decade, albeit on a more modest scale than in 1931. Devaluation and protection had little impact on food and raw material prices, partly because many suppliers devalued with sterling and partly because protection touched food and raw materials only lightly. Although manufactured imports declined sharply, they had accounted for less than 30 per cent of total British imports in 1930. The strength of British economic recovery stimulated imports, and the merchandise trade gap widened in volume terms, and, measured in current prices, increased as a proportion of total trade from under 20 per cent in the late 1920s to 26 per cent by 1936/8. To make matters worse, net invisible earnings, which had dropped sharply during the slump, remained depressed for the remainder of the decade. Though earnings from shipping and financial services were part of the problem, it was compounded by the fall in investment income, hit by a combination of defaults, conversion operations to lower rates of interest, and reduced earnings from equity and direct investments.[34] In the decade after 1930 there was only one year, 1935, when the invisible surplus was sufficient to cover the deficit on visible trade. External solvency was achieved only because Britain ceased exporting capital. Capital embargoes helped, but there were relatively few attractive opportunities for investment, not least because many creditworthy governments were not only wary of burdening themselves with more debt but were actively repaying it. Britain almost certainly experienced an inflow of long-term capital during the 1930s.

British economic expansion in the recovery rested heavily on import substitution for industrialization, and on a set of industries that, by UK standards, depended very little on export markets. The UK became markedly disengaged from the international economy in the 1930s, exports plus imports of goods and services falling from 47.6 per cent of GNP in 1929 to 35.3 per cent by 1937. In the opinion of several authorities, recovery owed a great deal to the measures taken in 1931/2, notably the suspension of the gold standard and, more controversially, tariff protection. Suspending the gold standard shifted the priorities in economic policy making. Preservation of the standard was no longer the overriding objective of the monetary authorities. The Treasury saw *controlled* depreciation of sterling as a desirable step. Once tariffs were in place, capital exports restricted, and the Exchange Equalization Account established to intervene in currency markets, the authorities felt confident that sterling was safe. The easing of British monetary policy as bank rate was rapidly reduced from 6.5 per cent at the beginning of 1932 to 2 per cent by June helped create favourable monetary conditions for expansion. Currency depreciation together with tariffs led to a sharp contraction of manufactured imports. Between 1924 and 1931 the manufacturing sector's propensity to import had risen from 9.9 per cent to 12 per cent, but in 1932 it dropped to 8 per cent and stayed around that level for the remainder of the decade.[35] Earlier critical assessments of protection have tended in more recent years to become offset by a more favourable view of its impact on economic recovery. Available evidence now suggests that in the distorted and highly protectionist world trading system of the 1930s, protection in Britain may have been a suitable second-best strategy. Studies by Foreman-Peck, Hatton and by Kitson and Solomou indicate that protectionism had a favourable macroeconomic impact.[36] Tariffs and currency depreciation also encouraged inward investment in manufacturing, the long-term effects of which benefited British industry.[37]

It would be misleading, however, to suggest that by the late 1930s British industry had been revitalized or that renewed competition was welcomed. Business had typically responded to the excess capacity of the interwar years by seeking cartel agreements that looked to preserve rather than to eliminate excess capacity. The government, which saw the restoration of pre-depression price levels as vital for economic recovery, enthusiastically supported the formation of cartels. Industry greatly treasured the protection it had won by the 1930s, and fiercely resisted any moves that might weaken it. There were few indications that protection and imperial preferences were regretted, let alone active proposals to liberalize trade and payments. Some did recognize the pressures imposed on Germany by the breakdown of the multilateral payments system and particularly Britain's role therein. But ultimately the government responded to what was perceived as the threat of intensified German competition by encouraging industry to enter cartel arrangements.[38] Nor did the Anglo-American trade agreement of November 1938 signal the rebirth of the Cobdenite spirit. True, it did incorporate some reduction of imperial preferences for products in which the United States was interested, but the major driving force behind British participation was political/strategic necessity, and the negotiations were characterized by a spirit of illiberalism and the pursuit of narrow national advantage.[39]

Conclusion

Between the turn of the twentieth century and the Second World War Britain's international economic position and its role in the international economy were transformed. Economic liberalism and cosmopolitanism were dead. Free traders lost their battle, although vestiges of the old faith lived on in Whitehall. The gold standard was abandoned. Both free trade and the gold standard had been associated with Britain's ascendancy of the international economy, ostensibly keeping business efficient by ensuring it was open to international competition and making certain that state finance was conducted within a framework governed by the need to maintain a fixed exchange rate. By the 1920s the relatively small scale and disaggregated structure of British industry had given way to much greater concentration of ownership and production, a development that predated the demise of free trade. Adoption of full protection in 1931/2 had accelerated Britain's disengagement from the international economy. The essentially domestically based economic recovery in the 1930s confirmed and strengthened this tendency and was reinforced because London ceased, for the time being, to export capital. Before 1914 Britain's engagement in the international economy transcended the boundaries of empire. In the 1930s the economic links of empire tightened, encouraged by mutual imperial preferences and reinforced by the emergence of a sterling bloc. Born out of economic crisis, however, this failed to deliver the economic salvation that the Chamberlainites had hoped.

NOTES

1   D. Baines, *Migration in a Mature Economy* (Cambridge, 1985), pp. 59–61.

2   The best study of the fast-changing and complex system of multilateral settlements is by S. B. Saul, *Studies in British Overseas Trade, 1870–1914* (Liverpool, 1960).

3   This paragraph is based mainly on I. M. Drummond, *The Gold Standard and the International Monetary System 1900–1939* (Basingstoke, 1987); J. Foreman-Peck, *A History of the World Economy: International Economic Relations since 1850* (2nd edition, Hemel Hempstead, 1995), ch. 9; and P. H. Lindert, *Key Currencies and Gold 1900–1913* (Princeton Studies in International Finance, No. 24, 1969).

4   B. Eichengreen, 'The gold standard since Alec Ford', in S. N. Broadberry and N. F. R. Crafts, eds, *Britain in the International Economy* (Cambridge, 1992).

5   S. Newton and G. Porter, *Modernization Frustrated: The Politics of Industrial Decline in Britain since 1900* (London, 1988), ch. 1.

6   A. Maizels, *Industrial Growth and World Trade: An Empirical Study of Trends in Production, Consumption and Trade in Manufactures from 1899–1959* (Cambridge, 1963), pp. 136, 200; S. B. Saul, 'The export economy', *Yorkshire Bulletin of Economic and Social Research*, 17, no. 1 (1965), pp. 13–15.

7   A. Howe, *Free Trade and Liberal England 1846–1946* (Oxford, 1997), ch. 7; A. Marrison, *British Business and Protection* (Oxford, 1996), ch. 3.

8   S. Pollard, *Britain's Prime and Britain's Decline: The British Economy 1870–1914* (London, 1989).

9   D. H. Aldcroft, *From Versailles to Wall Street 1919–1929* (Harmondsworth, 1987).

10 D. H. Aldcroft, 'The disintegration of Europe 1918–1945', in D. H. Aldcroft and A. Sutcliffe, *Europe in the International Economy 1500 to 2000* (Cheltenham, 1999), esp. pp. 129–32.

11 D. Greasley and L. Oxley, 'Discontinuities in competitiveness: the impact of the First World War on British industry', *Economic History Review*, 49 (1996), pp. 98–9. See also S. N. Broadberry, 'The emergence of mass unemployment: explaining macroeconomic trends in Britain during the trans-World War I period', *Economic History Review*, 2nd series, 43 (1990); J. A. Dowie, '1919 is in need of attention', *Economic History Review*, 2nd series, 28 (1975); A. J. Arnold, 'Profitability and capital accumulation in British industry during the transwar period, 1913–1924', *Economic History Review*, 52 (1999).

12 R. P. T. Davenport-Hines, *Dudley Docker: The Life and Times of a Trade Warrior* (Cambridge, 1984), p. 132.

13 Newton and Porter, *Modernization Frustrated*; G. C. Peden, *The Treasury and British Public Policy, 1906–1959* (Oxford, 2000).

14 L. Hannah, *The Rise of the Corporate Economy* (2nd edition, London, 1983), pp. 180, 91.

15 R. W. D. Boyce, 'Creating the myth of public consensus: public opinion and Britain's return to the gold standard in 1925', in P. L. Cottrell and D. E. Moggridge, eds, *Money and Power: Essays in Honour of L. S. Pressnell* (London, 1988).

16 Ibid.

17 Newton and Porter, *Modernization Frustrated*, ch. 2; R. W. D. Boyce, *British Capitalism at the Crossroads 1919–1932: A Study in Politics, Economics and International Relations* (Cambridge, 1987).

18 Peden, *Treasury*, pp. 205–12.

19 S. Solomou, *Themes in Macroeconomic History: The UK Economy, 1919–1939* (Cambridge, 1996), p. 45; S. Solomou and M. Weale, 'UK national income: the implications of balanced estimates', *Economic History Review* (1996), p. 105.

20 Solomou, *Themes in Macroeconomic History*, p. 47.

21 Hannah, *Corporate Economy*, p. 29.

22 D. C. Corner, 'Exports and the British trade cycle: 1929', *Manchester School*, 26 (1956).

23 H. Fleisig, 'The US and the non-European periphery during the early years of the Great Depression', in H. van der Wee, ed., *The Great Depression Revisited* (The Hague, 1972).

24 C. Dow, *Major Recessions: Britain and the World, 1920–1995* (Oxford, 1998) estimates that the fall in exports (mainly to primary producers) accounts for the total fall in GDP between 1929 and 1932.

25 D. Williams, 'London and the 1931 financial crisis', *Economic History Review*, 15 (1962/3) and L. S. Pressnell, '1925: the burden of sterling', *Economic History Review*, 2nd series, 31 (1978) both conclude this was probable.

26 B. Eichengreen, *Golden Fetters: The Gold Standard and the Great Depression, 1919–1939* (New York, 1992), p. 264. But Eichengreen emphasizes that the British experience was different from the others because of the strength of the banking and financial system (p. 279).

27 E.g. B. Eichengreen, *Sterling and the Tariff, 1929–32* (Princeton Studies in International Finance, No. 48, 1981), pp. 7–14.

28 Peden, *Treasury*, p. 261.

29 S. H. Beer, *Modern British Politics* (London, 1980), p. 288; T. Rooth, *British Protectionism and the International Economy: Overseas Commercial Policy in the 1930s* (Cambridge, 1993), ch. 2.

30 I. M. Drummond, *Imperial Economic Policy, 1917–1939: Studies in Expansion and Protection* (London, 1974).

31 Ibid.; Rooth, *British Protectionism*, ch. 3.

32 Although this is less true of the Argentine agreement, which was mainly concerned with debt payments; Rooth, *British Protectionism*, chs 5–7 and 9.

33 P. Clavin, 'The World Economic Conference 1933: the failure of British internationalism', *Journal of European Economic History*, 20 (1991).

34 A. Cairncross and B. Eichengreen, *Sterling in Decline: The Devaluations of 1931, 1949 and 1967* (Oxford, 1983), pp. 90–4.

35 M. Kitson and S. Solomou, *Protectionism and Economic Revival: The British Inter-war Economy* (Cambridge, 1990), p. 43.

36 J. Foreman-Peck, 'The British tariff and industrial protection in the 1930s: an alternative model', *Economic History Review*, 2nd series, 34 (1981); T. J. Hatton, 'Perspectives on the economic recovery of the 1930s', *Royal Bank of Scotland Review*, 158 (1988); Kitson and Solomou, *Protectionism*.

37 P. Scott and T. Rooth, 'Protectionism and the growth of overseas multinational enterprise in interwar Britain', *Journal of Industrial History*, 3, no. 2 (2000).

38 S. Newton, *Profits of Peace: The Political Economy of Anglo-German Appeasement* (Oxford, 1996).

39 I. M. Drummond and N. Hillmer, *Negotiating Freer Trade: The United Kingdom, the United States, Canada and the Trade Agreements of 1938* (Waterloo, Ontario, 1989); Rooth, *British Protectionism*, ch. 10.

CHAPTER FIFTEEN

The State and the Economy, 1900–1939

M. W. KIRBY

Introduction

Up to the 1970s historians of British economic policy could claim that the twentieth century had witnessed an immense expansion in the role of the state with a notable divide in the extent and depth of intervention across the Second World War. Thus, under the heading of macroeconomic policy all governments, both Labour and Conservative, had come to accept responsibility for the level of employment, the stability of prices, balance of payments equilibrium and the rate of economic growth. These policy objectives were to be achieved through the application of fiscal and monetary instruments under the guise of demand management. As for microeconomic policy, the post-war decades witnessed substantial measures of intervention in the 'real' economy aimed at removing inefficiencies in the allocation of resources in order to enhance overall growth prospects. Thus, under the heading of supply-side management, governments by the 1970s had engaged in substantial measures of industrial restructuring, including the creation of a large nationalized public utility sector as well as statutory measures for the regulation of monopoly and competition. Indicative planning in the 1960s was followed by the 'industrial strategy' experiment of the 1970s, both of these initiatives resulting in important institutional reforms at the level of central government. In fact, the whole of the period from 1945 to 1979 can be characterized by an ongoing, if uneven, commitment to interventionist supply-side policies.[1] In all of these respects, early historical accounts of the post-war policy record offered a 'Whiggish' interpretation rooted in the assumption that there had been a linear progression in the development of a 'managed' economy from the publication of Keynes's *General Theory* in 1936, through the 1944 White Paper on *Employment Policy after the War* to the 'Keynesian' demand management era of the 1950s and 1960s.[2] As a counter to this view it is only necessary to point to the fundamental change in the course and direction of economic policy following the Conservative election victory in 1979. The new government was deeply antipathetic to the trend of previous policies in the belief that demand management had resulted in a rising trend in government expenditure as a proportion of total output, thereby

stimulating inflation to the detriment of industrial competitiveness. Supply-side measures, moreover, had either been ineffectual or had contributed to inefficiency by
undermining market disciplines at the level of individual households, firms and industries. The policy implications of this retreat from the managed economy were twofold
– first to 'roll back the frontiers of the state' in economic affairs, and second to
enhance the role of market forces in order to encourage allocative efficiency. In
practice, this entailed the introduction of a medium-term financial strategy aimed at
reining back the growth of public expenditure and reducing inflationary pressure via
lower interest rates, thereby creating a macroeconomic environment conducive to
the efficient functioning of the market economy. The subsidies payable to nationalized industries were reduced and this served as a prelude to an ongoing programme
of privatization of state-owned industries and firms as well as the reduction or elimination of financial support for specific industrial sectors and regions. Although the
state continued to exercise a powerful influence on the economy in terms of the
absolute amount of public expenditure, the whole of the 1980s was marked by a
weakening of governmental control of the economy as an entire range of customary
demand and supply-side policy instruments was downgraded or discarded.[3] Indeed,
as one distinguished observer of the direction of policy concluded, by the late 1980s
the range of instruments had narrowed to the point where, as in the period to 1913,
variations in bank rate were the major determinant of economic policy.[4]

In a chapter devoted to the developing relationship between the state and the
economy in the first four decades of the twentieth century the purpose of these introductory remarks is to place the period in a long-term perspective. This is an important aid to historical understanding in so far as a naive interpretation might
conclude that the evidence of growing interpenetration between the state and industry and the debate on macroeconomic policy stimulated by John Maynard Keynes
underscored an inevitable progression towards the post-war managed economy which
was to remain intact for the indefinite future. The searing effects of mass unemployment in the later interwar period may have helped to place 'economic management'
on the political agenda, but it is salutary to remember that contemporary policy debate
was dominated by the economics of imperial integration rather than the notion of a
Keynesian-inspired fiscal thrust as a solution to the unemployment problem.[5]
Similarly, with respect to state–industry relations, interwar governments were certainly
more interventionist than their pre-1914 counterparts, whilst some groups of industrialists were becoming accustomed to and dependent upon state direction and
support. But this is to miss the point that whilst the principle of laissez-faire in the
peacetime industrial economy had been breached substantially by the end of the 1930s,
interwar governments were very far from subscribing to the notion of an active and
generalized industrial policy.[6] In order to provide a coherent framework for analysing
the evolution of economic policy, the chapter is divided into four chronological
sections, each of them demarcating distinctive phases in the policy record and/or
consideration of the future role of the state in economic affairs. Thus, the next section,
covering the period from 1900 to 1914, deals with the Victorian inheritance rooted
in the three institutional pillars of the gold standard, free trade and balanced budgets.
The subsequent section analyses the stresses and strains on this 'anti-collectivist' legacy
posed by the First World War and its immediate aftermath. This serves as a prelude to
the penultimate section, which describes the attempt to return to 'normalcy' in the

1920s focusing on the institution of the gold standard. The final substantive section examines the course and direction of economic and industrial policy in the 1930s following the abandonment of the gold standard and the departure from free trade.

The Victorian Legacy

If the modern concept of macroeconomic policy is applied to the pre-1914 period it is fair to say that the aim of monetary and fiscal policy was 'to provide a stable environment in which capitalism could flourish'.[7] Reliance on market forces as the arbiter of resource allocation was paramount, and this was fully reflected in the economic ideology of the day and prevailing policy assumptions. The latter were rooted in three institutions – the gold standard, free trade and balanced budgets.[8] The gold standard was the overarching determinant of monetary policy as a means of settling international indebtedness. By 1900 the world's leading trading nations had adopted the standard, which rested on several 'rules of the game'. These included a commitment to a fixed rate of exchange, the free convertibility of the domestic currency into gold, and the linking of the domestic money supply to the movement of gold in and out of the country. According to the prevailing theory of the gold standard, in the event of sustained balance of payments deficit a country would experience an outflow of gold which, in reducing the volume of currency in circulation, would result in a fall in the level of internal prices, a movement that would eventually produce external equilibrium. This was, in effect, a theory of 'painless' and automatic balance of payments adjustment which, in underpinning stable international monetary relations, acted as a powerful stimulus to the growth of the international economy.[9] It is now accepted that the 'classical' economic analysis of the gold standard was a gross oversimplification in that it is far more accurate to describe it as a 'sterling' standard. To the extent that 'sterling operated on equal terms with gold',[10] the British currency was the principal medium of international exchange with gold only being transferred between countries as a balancing item. Given this role, it was vital that sterling should not only be in liberal supply, but that it should also be a currency of unshakeable strength. Before 1914, these conditions were fulfilled as a result of the distinctive structure of Britain's balance of payments. Theoretically, the fact that the balance on current account was in continual surplus could have given rise to a serious adjustment problem elsewhere in the international economy. For the core members of the system, enjoying good access to the London capital market, this was not, however, necessary because of the sustained export of capital from Britain at the same time as the country remained committed to a policy of free trade. As the world's leading lender, the annual net outflow of funds from London more or less matched the current account surplus, thereby relieving borrowing countries of much of the adjustment problem inherent in the classical theory.[11] That said, the gold standard 'pillar' was less robust than appears at first sight. Peripheral members of the system, for example, were certainly subject to problems of adjustment if they were distanced from London and departures from the gold standard at this level were a frequent occurrence before 1914. There were also emergent sources of weakness in Britain's own position as arbiter of the system. In particular, the rise of the United States as an influential force in the international economy had adverse consequences for Britain's balance of payments position in that the emergence of a substantial bilateral trade deficit heralded the arrival of a 'dollar gap' which was covered, in large measure, by a substantial surplus with India. The favourable Indian balance, however, was dominated by low-grade cotton piece goods which were vulnerable both to indigenous competition and Japanese import penetration. Any further erosion, let alone collapse, of the balance of trade would have potentially serious consequences for Britain's ability to sustain the gold standard.

The commitment to free trade fulfilled a triple function. In the first instance, the entry of foreign goods into the country free of tariffs helped to stimulate competition and efficiency in domestic industry. Second, it permitted borrowing countries to service their international debts by exporting to Britain, and third, it fulfilled a critical role in the developing network of worldwide multilateral settlement and hence the growth of the international economy after 1890. As one authority has commented, without access to the British market, 'both Industrial Europe and the United States would have been forced either greatly to adapt their internal economies and seek new sources of supply . . . or intensify world competition in manufactured goods. Probably the growth of world trade would have slackened and international friction would have increased'.[12] Free trade was obviously attractive to the cosmopolitan financial interests of the City of London. It was also of vital relevance to those industries such as cotton textiles, shipbuilding and coal mining that were dependent for their prosperity on overseas markets. But even in the face of these powerful vested interests, the pre-1914 period had witnessed a fundamental political attack on its rationale in the face of a rising tide of manufactured imports. Beginning with the 'fair trade' movement in the 1880s, the case for tariff reform reached its apotheosis in Joseph Chamberlain's campaign for imperial preference launched from within the Conservative party after 1903. Whilst Chamberlain's motives were politically complex, in economic terms his programme was designed to sustain domestic industry and employment and to use the British general tariff as a 'retaliatory battering ram' to enter protected markets in industrial Europe and the United States.[13] Although protectionism was rejected decisively in the general election of 1906, the fact remains that by the end of the first decade of the twentieth century the Conservative party had been won over to the cause of tariff reform.

As the third supporting pillar of the Victorian policy legacy, the budget was hardly significant as an influence on the economy given the relatively small share of national product that passed through the government's hands. The defining principles, however, were to cast a long shadow forwards into the twentieth century as the level of public expenditure began to mount. The principles themselves had emerged in the early part of the nineteenth century in response to concerns about the size of the national debt and the need to attain and then preserve free trade. The budgetary implications were clear – that reduction of the debt required 'some balance of income over expenditure', and free trade that government income and expenditure 'should balance at the lowest possible figure'. Defined in this way, budgetary policy in its Gladstonian guise was to result in an ingrained tradition of 'strict public parsimony'.[14] By 1914, however, the Victorian legacy had been modified to the extent that a rising trend in social and defence expenditures meant that fiscal rectitude in the Gladstonian sense was no longer seriously pursued. The principle of progressive taxation had also been accepted, although budget surpluses to reduce the national debt remained as an important policy objective.

To refer to public policy in the context of the 'real' economy in the decades before 1914 may appear a contradiction in view of the entrenched belief, grounded in prevailing economic doctrine, in the virtues of the free market. There were, however, two areas of state intervention which are worthy of mention in this context, the first relating to the regulation of railways and the second the evolution of policy with respect to the labour market. In the latter half of the twentieth century a continuing preoccupation with the control of monopoly and the maintenance of competitive industrial structures has been at the forefront of industrial policy in reaction to the inexorable trend towards concentration in business observable after 1914. It is salutary to remember, however, that these twentieth-century concerns were fully reflected in the previous century in the debate on monopoly and collusion in the railway sector. As early as the 1830s critics of the industry had noted its inherent structural tendency towards natural monopoly, reinforced by the potential for consumer exploitation that followed in the wake of successive bursts of company amalgamation. By the 1870s, the sector as a whole was in dispute with commercial users principally over the issue of differential rates. As oligopolies, railway companies could engage in price discrimination between customers, a practice that could bring economic benefits if it facilitated effective competition in product markets. To the trading lobby, however, the companies were exploitative monopolies, a charge that was successfully pressed in parliament and led to the passing of the Railway and Canal Traffic Act of 1894. Under this, the Railway and Canal Commission (created in 1888) was empowered to limit charges to the levels of 1892, unless the companies could prove that costs had risen. Dissatisfaction with railway charges continued after 1900, not least as a result of further concentration. In 1914, the Liberal government reacted to these concerns by establishing a Royal Commission to investigate the future organization of the railways, including the prospects for nationalization. Its deliberations ceased, however, on the outbreak of war.[15]

In the final quarter of the nineteenth century unemployment was viewed as a social problem in the context of increasing concerns with pauperism arising from casual employment. In this respect, the Board of Trade emerged as an important gatherer of statistics on the labour market. Following the passing of the Industrial Conciliation Act in 1896, it effectively replaced the Home Office as the principal agency of government responsible for industrial relations. Both of these roles were augmented considerably by the formation, under Board auspices, of the Trade Boards and Labour Exchanges in 1909. In this setting the Board aspired to the status of a 'key ministry' in the general context of the Liberal government's social reform programme after 1906. As a result of these developments the problem of unemployment was firmly established as an issue of governmental concern before the First World War, although the point had yet to be accepted that it was linked in any way to the level of aggregate economic activity.[16]

The Impact of War

At the outset of the First World War the general expectation was that the conflict would be of short duration and hence the need for state intervention could be confined to a few specific areas such as the foreign exchanges and the requisition of transport and war supplies. The lesson that the state would have to play a far more active role in the economy was learnt first in the munitions industry, where the 'Great Shell Scandal' of 1915, arising from the scarcity of ordnance at the front, revealed the limitations of the existing controls administered by a cabinet committee. The Ministry of Munitions was established in June 1915, headed by Lloyd George, and the Munitions of War Act which was passed two months after his appointment marked the beginnings of 'a considerable extension of the Government's powers of economic control over large sections of industry'.[17] In this respect, the ministry not only provided financial subsidies to engineering firms to expand productive capacity, but also established state-owned munitions factories and shipyards equipped with electric power and best-practice production techniques. Standardization and mass production were encouraged by the introduction of automatic and semi-automatic machinery at the same time as contracting firms were encouraged to amalgamate their interests and to engage in concerted research and development programmes. Time and motion studies were implemented extensively, especially in controlled establishments, while welfare provision for employees received the attention of the ministry's Welfare and Health section.[18]

The impetus to industrial modernization released by the Ministry of Munitions was seized upon by the Ministry of Reconstruction, established in August 1917 as the critical element in rebuilding 'the national life on a better and more durable foundation' once the war had ended. Although the new ministry's remit embraced social reconstruction in conformity with Lloyd George's undertaking to create 'a land fit for heroes', its economic aims were equally far reaching in that it wished to see the improvements in business organization and efficiency achieved in the munitions industries perpetuated into the peacetime economy. The principal consideration underlying the desire for an 'expanded state' was to secure the competitive advantage of British industry in the expectation that the pre-war export penetration of German industry would be resumed.[19] At the time of the ministry's formation this prospect appeared all the more likely in view of the distinct possibility that the war would end in a stalemate peace, leaving the sinews of German economic and industrial power intact.

It was Germany's sudden military collapse in the closing stages of the war which effectively removed 'the strongest, least vulnerable justification for the expanded state; it removed the prop which would have sustained the programme of state-initiated economic development'.[20] The Allied victory in 1918 was not, however, the only significant factor in undermining reconstructionist hopes of state-sponsored industrial modernization. Although physical destruction was minimal, the victors proceeded during the course of 1919 to impose a 'Carthaginian' peace settlement that appeared to wreak havoc on the German economy. The loss of key raw materials and the surrender of colonies as well as a considerable proportion of the merchant marine could be viewed as crippling blows to the material and commercial base of German industry. This was certainly the view of Keynes and it takes no account of the reparations settlement imposed on the defeated powers to the detriment of their internal and external financial stability.[21]

This is not, of course, to suggest that the German defeat was the sole cause of the demise of the expanded state. Governmental concern at the inflationary consequences of public expenditure had already been evident in 1917–18, and in the wake of the Armistice the chorus of complaint about staffing levels in new ministries and the domestic spending of the War Office began to mount, reaching a peak in the summer of 1919. All of this was compounded by Treasury worries about the vastly increased floating debt. In these circumstances, the government acted to increase the power of the Treasury in Whitehall by designating the permanent secretary as head of the home civil service. This move was followed, in December 1919, by an official announcement of the government's intention to cease borrowing and to rein back public expenditure, a policy which reached its zenith in 1922 in the form of the 'Geddes Axe'.[22]

All of the above influences on the side of fiscal policy were powerfully reinforced by considerations of monetary policy with particular reference to the gold standard. For all practical purposes Britain was off the gold standard during the war, although the sterling–dollar parity was maintained within striking distance of the pre-war exchange rate of $4.86 to the pound. Official departure from the standard was announced in April 1919 when inflationary pressures rendered it impossible to sustain the pre-war parity. Even before then, an official Committee on Currency and Foreign Exchanges had been appointed to 'report upon the steps required to bring about the restoration of normal conditions in due course'.[23] What this meant in practice was that the primary aim of post-war monetary policy should be to return to the gold standard at the pre-war parity as soon as circumstances permitted.[24] The committee, chaired by the retiring governor of the Bank of England, Lord Cunliffe, adopted an idealized view of the pre-war standard as that 'keystone of . . . economic interdependence which had provided the foundation for Britain's progress'.[25] In this respect, restoration of the gold standard held out the prospect of restraining domestic credit expansion as well as borrowing from the United States to sustain public expenditure. In short, the gold standard was the best guarantee against an uncontrollable inflation. In accepting the Cunliffe recommendations, the Bank of England raised bank rate to 6 per cent in November 1919 and to the penal level of 7 per cent in April 1920. The rate remained at this level for almost a year, but it was only one of several factors which had a severe deflationary impact on the economy. These included a restrictive budget in April 1920, cuts in public expenditure in the run-up to the Geddes Axe and the collapse of export markets at the end of the year, a factor which played a major role in boosting unemployment to unprecedented levels for the foreseeable future.[26]

The Return to 'Normalcy': The State and the Economy in the 1920s

With the benefit of hindsight it is clear that the guiding principles of macroeconomic policy in the 1920s were based upon a particular view of the operation of the pre-war international economy and Britain's position within it. The rallying cries of 'back to 1913' and the return to 'normalcy' were thus symptomatic of an unshaken faith in the virtues of the inherited liberal economic order both at home and abroad. Nowhere was this more true than in the case of the gold standard as the overarching concern of monetary policy. The interim report of the Cunliffe Committee had concluded that '[u]nless the machinery which long experience has shown to be the only effective remedy for an adverse balance of trade and an undue growth of credit is once more brought into play, there will be a grave danger of a progressive credit expansion which will result in a foreign drain of gold menacing the convertibility of our note issue and so jeopardising the international trade position of this country'.[27] As a statement in support of Britain's membership of the gold standard, this has the great merit of underlining the political and economic underpinnings of monetary policy in the aftermath of a war that had left Britain with a vastly increased national debt and inflated cost and price levels to match. In so far as the 'rules of the game' were non-discretionary, adherence to the gold standard provided an essential bulwark against an undue expansion of credit – and hence inflation – on the part of vote-seeking politicians.[28] Britain's return to gold would also help to restore the international financial system and multilateral trade to the benefit of industry and employment in a country more deeply penetrated by foreign trade than any other comparable economy.[29] There remains the issue of the parity and it is this factor, more than any other, which focuses attention on Britain's financial relationship with the United States. In the discussions that preceded the return to gold in April 1925, the overwhelming weight of official opinion was in favour of the readoption of the pre-war sterling–dollar parity. The generally accepted interpretation of this consensus is that it was rooted in a combination of moral and political judgements involving considerations of financial probity and, more especially, Britain's international financial prestige *vis-à-vis* the United States.[30] As the governor of the Bank of England stated, failure to return at the pre-war parity would result in a serious diminution of London's status as the world's premier financial centre in favour of New York: the country's invisible earnings would decline, thereby circumscribing Britain's ability to regain its former role in the international economy.[31] The problem confronting the authorities in returning to gold at the pre-war parity was the relative inflation of the British price level. Unless the price levels were equalized, the domestic economy would need to be subject to continuing deflation leading to higher unemployment. In a celebrated intervention following the restoration of the gold standard, Keynes claimed that sterling was overvalued by 10 per cent in relation to the dollar, thereby rendering British exports uncompetitive and encouraging import penetration of the home market. In this context, Keynes portrayed the coal-mining industry as the first victim of a soulless 'economic Juggernaut', representing 'in the flesh the "fundamental adjustments" engineered by the Treasury and the Bank of England to satisfy the impatience of the City fathers'.[32] Coal mining was, of course, a leading exporting industry which, at the time of the return to gold, was already experiencing severe financial difficulties in response to the precipitate collapse of its overseas markets. It is true that wages had been reduced substantially in 1921, but only after a lengthy and bitterly fought dispute. This experience was ignored by the authorities in 1925, as was the fact that the general deflation of the economy in the early 1920s had been assisted by cost of living-related wage reductions in a number of industries.[33] These agreements had subsequently met with increasing trade union resistance. Even in coal mining, despite the defeat of 1921, the structure of district wage rates was governed by a national agreement rendering it extremely difficult to reduce wages in particular coalfields without provoking considerable labour unrest. It is well known that the General Strike and miners' lockout of 1926 were fought unsuccessfully over this precise issue of wage reductions in the industry's hard-pressed exporting districts.[34]

The issue of the true extent of sterling's overvaluation has been the subject of ongoing academic debate with estimates within the range 10–20 per cent.[35] Whilst accepting that even the lower bound estimate represented a real handicap to exporters, the temptation must be resisted of ascribing the problems of British industry to an overvalued currency. In the first instance, account must be taken of the market distribution of British exports and relative price structures. Since nearly half of British trade was conducted with countries within the sterling system, re-adoption of the pre-war parity would have 'had absolutely no effect on the price-competitiveness of British goods in this theatre'.[36] In addition, there is substantial evidence in support of the fact that the overseas demand for many of the products of the staple export industries was profoundly price-inelastic. In the case of coal mining, it has already been noted that the onset of the industry's difficulties predated the return to gold and were intimately linked with short-term movements in the European coal market compounded by longer-term developments in fuel technology. So too in the case of cotton textiles, a lower exchange rate could hardly compensate for the industry's long-term structural problems in the context of Indian and Japanese competition.[37] Finally, there is considerable evidence to suggest that the devaluation of sterling would have been fully matched by competitive exchange rate movements elsewhere, thereby neutralizing any advantage to British industry and commerce.[38]

The significance of the return to gold lies in the fact that '[i]n the history of the idea of "conscious and deliberate management" of the economy, . . . [it] was a backward step'.[39] It was not only a 'policy error'; it also acted to constrain the content of economic policy with particular regard to the level of employment. Return, moreover, did not produce the effects anticipated by its supporters. There was, in fact, continuous pressure on the exchange rate which, ironically, necessitated discretionary management on the part of the Bank of England. With the government and employers unwilling to put further downwards pressure on wages in the aftermath of the General Strike, this meant that interest rates had to be maintained at a level high enough to sustain an inward flow of short-term capital from abroad. In this respect, London was in direct competition with New York at a time of unprecedented fluidity in the international capital market. As the Wall Street boom got under way after 1928, bank rate was increased successively in order to sustain London's competitiveness. Ultimately, the volatility of international capital would react with a critical weakening in the balance of payments to force Britain to abandon the gold standard in September 1931.

Fiscal policy in the 1920s was dominated by two concerns – the avoidance of inflation in the context of the gold standard and the need to reduce the vastly increased national debt. As noted already, the Treasury reverted as soon as possible after 1919 to the pre-war norm of strict economy in public expenditure. While substantial relief was obtained from a considerable reduction in defence expenditure, this was offset to a large extent by rising expenditure on social services, including relief for the unemployed. For the advocates of fiscal orthodoxy the latter was especially disturbing because it represented 'a dangerously open-ended commitment on the part of the state'.[40] The same applied to contracyclical public works as a means of reducing unemployment. The Unemployment Grants Committee had been formed as a coordinating body for the implementation of such works during the post-war depression. Although its establishment immediately preceded the 'Geddes Axe', the relief-work policy remained intact as a political palliative and also because 70 per cent of the total cost was borne by local authorities.[41] In the later 1920s, however, with the emergence of the 'hard core' million unemployed, the Treasury became increasingly hostile to public works in the belief that their contribution to a reduction in the level of unemployment was far less important than achieving a reduction in the costs of production in British industry. With wage cuts ruled out after the General Strike, government hopes for the unemployed were vested in the restructuring of industry under the guise of 'rationalization', reinforced after 1927 by a scheme of assisted labour mobility under the auspices of the Industrial Transference Board.[42]

The debate on fiscal policy in the later 1920s centred on this very issue of state-sponsored public works projects. In the general election campaign of 1929, the Liberal party, heavily influenced by Keynes, incorporated proposals for a large-scale programme of loan-financed public expenditure on housing, roads, electricity, telephones and agriculture in its election manifesto. This document, bearing the ambitious title *We Can Conquer Unemployment*, called forth the full weight of fiscal orthodoxy on the part of the Conservative government. This took the form of a White Paper coordinated by the Ministry of Labour on behalf of the Treasury.[43] The essential core of the 'Treasury view' was well summarized as follows in Winston Churchill's budget speech as chancellor of the exchequer in 1929:

> It is orthodox Treasury dogma, steadfastly held, that whatever might be the political or social advantages very little additional employment can, in fact, and as a general rule, be created by state borrowing and expenditure.[44]

The economic basis of the 'Treasury view' was grounded in the belief that there was a finite level of savings in the economy. Hence the borrowing requirements of a state-financed public works programme would push up interest rates and lead inevitably to a reduction in private investment. These 'crowding out' effects would be accompanied by inflation and a deterioration in the balance of payments, thereby endangering adherence to the gold standard. Thus, the Liberal programme would accentuate the difficulties currently affecting exporting industries. It was completely at variance with the real need of the industrial economy – the revival of the export trade through cost reductions and rationalization.[45]

In view of the Treasury's commitment to 'sound money and sound budgets' in the face of mass unemployment, it is tempting to erect a scathing denunciation of interwar fiscal policy, with Keynes and his supporters cast in the role of enlightened heroes and leading civil servants within the Treasury as intellectually bankrupt villains. There are, however, several reasons why such a view should not be pressed. As well as being conspicuously lacking in political influence beyond the Liberal party, Keynes's ideas were in a continuous process of evolution and until the publication of his *General Theory* in 1936 they lacked the detailed theoretical framework necessary to convert academic and ultimately Treasury opinion.[46] Second, it is important to note that the Treasury view was multifaceted, embracing political and administrative considerations as well as the purely economic. Thus, the 1929 Liberal election manifesto was condemned by the permanent secretary to the Treasury as necessitating 'the substitution of autocracy for Parliamentary Government'. Even if 'a Mussolini regime' with a considerable bureaucracy at its disposal 'could be proved to be desirable for the "war" against unemployment . . . the Country would [not] stand for it'.[47] Less subjective value judgements were applied to the issue of 'confidence'. Given the overwhelming conservatism of the capital market, how could the government float a substantial debt without provoking a crisis of confidence that, ultimately, might lead to a forced departure from the gold standard?[48] In effect, therefore, the bias of the capital market in favour of economic orthodoxy augmented that of the Treasury in determining the goals of fiscal policy. There were, in addition, a number of practical and administrative constraints that were articulated with increasing force within Whitehall after 1929. In this respect, the lead was taken by the Ministries of Transport and Labour. In the former case, critical attention was focused on road building as the main public works project within the Liberal proposals. This was viewed as naive in the extreme because it failed to comprehend the dynamics of the labour market and also because it 'ignored or underplayed the crucial requirements for adequate planning machinery, effective central co-ordination of spending agencies (especially local authorities which undertook the greater part of public investment) and pre-prepared unemployment plans. The British administrative system, in particular the relations between central and local government, was quite unsuitable without major and politically highly contentious reforms'.[49] As for the Ministry of Labour, the Liberal plan to employ nearly 400,000 men on road building and land drainage was condemned because it failed to take account of the immobility of the unemployed and also because the relevant programmes 'would simply create a problem of "demobilisation" at the end of the period'.[50]

In concluding this section it is appropriate to comment briefly on governmental attitudes to the industrial economy. Following the demise of the wartime expanded state, it is fair to say that by the middle of the decade government–industry relations had reverted in most respects to their pre-war pattern of regulation, notably with regard to company law and statutory obligations in the area of employee safety. The principal exception was the Safeguarding of Industries Act of 1921, which endowed a small number of strategically important 'key' industries with a degree of tariff protection. The issue of a general tariff was raised explicitly by the Conservative party in the 1923 general election when the Baldwin government espoused the protectionist case as a solution to the unemployment problem. The Conservative defeat and the evident divisions between industrialists themselves merely served to reinforce the arms-length nature of government–industry relations. On returning to office in 1924, the Conservatives, having promised not to introduce a general tariff without consulting the electorate, were obliged to concentrate their energies on the revival of British exports by resurrecting the pre-1914 international economic infrastructure. The return to gold, however, did not pave the way for an export revival, and with wage cuts ruled out as the route to cost competitiveness after the General Strike, the search began for a less painful means of achieving cost reductions. It was in this setting that the 'rationalization' movement came to prominence in the later 1920s. Rationalization was synonymous with the process of amalgamation in British industry as a means of achieving economies of scale by the closure of loss-making capacity. Its advocates conceded that the immediate effect would be to increase unemployment, but in the longer term, as industrial efficiency improved in response to technical and commercial economies, lost export markets would be regained and rationalized industries would begin to recruit more workers. The idea that rationalization was part of a structuralist solution to the unemployment problem had some appeal for Conservative ministers within the Board of Trade and the Ministry of Labour after

1926. However, they were not prepared to force the pace of amalgamation by compulsory measures, relying instead on the banking sector to exercise coercive power on debt-ridden companies. The banks as proxy rationalizers, however, proved to be a broken reed, unwilling to foreclose on loans in the belief that enforced liquidations would lead to disputes over priority of claims.[51] Even the Bank of England, which was favourably disposed towards rationalization on account of its deep involvement in the affairs of particular firms, was not prepared to act as a 'cat's paw' for government. In this respect, it is ironic that the Bank's most ambitious forays into the business of rationalization were occasioned by the fear that the post-1929 Labour government might embark on a programme of nationalization for the iron and steel and cotton industries. With the exception of the coal-mining industry, however, the government was as reluctant as its Conservative predecessor to intervene directly in the internal affairs of the boardroom.[52]

The 1930s: Change and Continuity

Following Britain's forced departure from the gold standard in September 1931, monetary policy was released from the constraints imposed by the need to maintain a fixed exchange rate. The principal developments here were the management of sterling by means of the Exchange Equalization Account and the inauguration of a cheap money policy.[53] It was sterling's rapid depreciation in the final months of 1931 which led to detailed discussions by the authorities as to the most appropriate exchange rate to aim for. The Bank of England, ever mindful of the spectre of inflation, favoured a relatively high rate of stabilization and was therefore reluctant to permit too rapid a fall in bank rate. The Treasury, on the other hand, was intent on promoting economic recovery and also on safeguarding the government's budgetary position. It therefore desired cheap money (that is, bank rate held to less than 3 per cent) in order to stimulate a mild internal reflation and also as a means of reducing the cost of servicing the national debt. A low exchange rate was preferred, again to stimulate reflation and as an aid to the recovery of exports. It was the view of the Treasury that ultimately prevailed.[54]

The cheap money policy was facilitated in part by the Exchange Equalization Account, established in April 1932. Its main functions were to stabilize the exchange rate and to insulate the domestic economy from gold and capital flows. As operated by the Bank of England, with Treasury advice and consent, the account utilized its holdings of Treasury bills to offset the purchase and sale of sterling assets by owners of funds moving in and out of London. By these means, the exchange rate was controlled successfully throughout the remainder of the 1930s.[55] The strength of sterling was reinforced further by the emergence after 1931 of the 'sterling bloc' consisting of all those countries enjoying close commercial connections with Britain. For the overseas members of the empire, in particular, there were distinct economic advantages in retaining the bulk of their foreign reserves in sterling and in maintaining their exchange rates steady in relation to sterling.

Only a few days after the establishment of the Exchange Equalization Account bank rate was reduced to 3 per cent. By the end of June 1932 it had fallen to 2 per cent, where it remained until August 1939. On 30 June, the government announced its plans for the conversion of 5 per cent war loan to 3.5 per cent as the second stage of its cheap money policy. The loan issue was an outstanding success, resulting in a considerable fall in the cost of servicing the national debt. Further conversion operations followed so that by 1938 the cost of servicing the debt as a proportion of total government expenditure had fallen to 13.4 per cent from a figure of 24.7 per cent in 1932. It might be thought that a movement favoured so long by the Treasury would have helped to loosen the reins of fiscal policy. This was not, however, the case in so far as considerations of monetary policy dictated a continuing commitment to fiscal orthodoxy. With the Treasury and the Bank of England committed to cheap money as an aid to economic recovery, the successful management of sterling and the maintenance of confidence in the currency were viewed as being incompatible with 'an activist fiscal policy'.[56]

Economic historians have long debated the overall impact of fiscal policy in the 1930s. The consensus is that the annual budget remained 'neutral, and even deflationary into the second half of the 1930s' before imparting a reflationary impulse in the later 1930s as a result of loan-financed rearmament expenditures.[57] Certainly, for the greater part of the decade the Treasury adhered to the stance articulated by Churchill in 1929 – that loan-financed public works were irrelevant to the reduction of unemployment.[58] It is true that in 1937, at a time of approaching recession, the Treasury authorized local authority financing of rephased public works, but this was very far from the central fiscal thrust advocated by Keynes and his fellow expansionists.[59] In any event, economic historians are now in general agreement that a loan-financed public works programme on a scale sufficient to approach 'full employment' in the labour market would have had profoundly adverse balance of payments and exchange rate effects leading to a crisis of confidence in the government of the day.[60]

There remains the issue of industrial policy in the 1930s. This can be linked directly to the enactment of a general tariff under the Import Duties Act of 1932. Under the Act individual industries could apply to the Import Duties Advisory Committee for enhanced protection in the face of foreign 'dumping'. This was granted to the iron and steel industry on condition that a national authority would be created to preside over major structural reforms. However, the resulting British Iron and Steel Federation was determined to adopt a defensive posture behind the tariff wall buttressed by the suppression of internal competition. As the industry's most recent historian has concluded, 'the final scheme was not one of reorganisation but solely of price maintenance' and until 1939 'the state sponsored a cartel over which it had little control'.[61] So too in the case of coal mining, the operation of the 1930 Coal Mines Act was dominated by the cartel structure imposed upon the industry rather than a drive for compulsory amalgamations. The state remained committed, in theory, to structural reform, but in the face of boardroom intransigence was obliged to accept the industry's view that amalgamations could only be secured by 'natural market forces'.[62] For the Conservative-dominated National government of the 1930s, therefore, radical state-sponsored programmes were ruled out by the desire to avoid direct involvement in industrial affairs for fear of falling into a policy morass that could lead to the undermining of private managerial prerogatives.[63] It has been argued that from the standpoint of the Treasury there was a consistent theme to economic policy in the 1930s to the extent that it was committed to a controlled price inflation as an aid to industrial recovery: a combination of rising prices – and hence profitability – together with the confidence engendered by fiscal orthodoxy and cheap money would raise investor confidence to the benefit of overall economic activity.[64] This is a plausible and attractive thesis, but one which has yet to be confirmed by research. In the current state of knowledge, it is only safe to assume that state–industry relations were based upon a mixture of ad hoc considerations that acted to preclude the formulation of a set of coherent and consistent industrial policy instruments.

Conclusion

Viewed as a distinctive era in the evolution of economic policy the first four decades of the twentieth century may be seen as a sustained period of transition. From a general position of laissez-faire on the eve of the First World War, it is possible to point to numerous examples of the encroachment of government on industrial affairs. It is only necessary to point to the enforced amalgamation of the railway companies in 1922, the establishment of the Central Electricity Board in 1926, the London Passenger Transport Board in 1933 and the British Overseas Airways Corporation in 1939, and the state-imposed cartelization of coal mining and agriculture after 1930. Most if not all these developments may have been '*ad hoc* and somewhat unrelated responses to immediate difficulties',[65] but they pointed, in a very real sense, to the development of the post-1945 'mixed economy' characterized by an ever-increasing interpenetration between government and industry irrespective of the political party in power. As for macroeconomic affairs, there were definite limits to state direction for the greater part of the period to 1939 as a result of the Victorian legacy of the gold standard and fiscal rectitude. After 1931, however, it is possible to discern a movement towards conscious economic management with particular reference to the exchange rate and the balance of payments. It is a point well taken, however, that confidence in the management of the exchange rate necessitated a continuing commitment to fiscal orthodoxy.[66] Rearmament in the later 1930s may have necessitated public borrowing, but the Treasury was determined that this should set no precedents for 'the war on unemployment'.

NOTES

1 M. W. Kirby, 'Supply side management', in N. F. R. Crafts and N. Woodward, eds, *The British Economy since 1945* (Oxford, 1991), pp. 236–57.

2 J. C. R. Dow, *The Management of the British Economy 1945–1960* (Cambridge, 1965); F. T. Blackaby, ed., *British Economic Policy 1960–1974* (Cambridge, 1978); J. F. Wright, *Britain in the Age of Economic Management: An Economic History since 1939* (Oxford, 1979).

3 Kirby, 'Supply side management'; A. Cairncross, *The British Economy since 1945: Economic Policy and Performance, 1945–1990* (Oxford, 1992).

4 Cairncross, *British Economy since 1945*, p. 236.

5 I. M. Drummond, *Imperial Economic Policy 1917–1939: Studies in Expansion and Protection* (London, 1974), p. 426; J. Tomlinson, *Public Policy and the Economy since 1900* (Oxford, 1990), pp. 132–3.

6 M. W. Kirby, 'Industrial policy', in S. Glynn and A. Booth, eds, *The Road to Full Employment* (London, 1987), pp. 125–39.

7   G. Peden, *British Economic and Social Policy: Lloyd George to Margaret Thatcher* (2nd edition, Oxford, 1991), p. 6.

8   D. N. Winch, *Economics and Policy: A Historical Study* (London, 1972), pp. 33–70; Tomlinson, *Public Policy*, pp. 14–41.

9   I. M. Drummond, *The Gold Standard and the International Monetary System, 1900–1939* (London, 1987), pp. 9–26; B. Eichengreen, ed., *The Gold Standard in Theory and History* (London, 1985).

10   W. M. Scammell, 'The working of the gold standard', *Yorkshire Bulletin of Economic and Social Research*, 17 (1965), p. 33.

11   M. de Cecco, *Money and Empire* (Oxford, 1974); Eichengreen, *Gold Standard*, p. 42.

12   S. B. Saul, *Studies in British Overseas Trade, 1870–1914* (Liverpool, 1960), p. 63.

13   B. Semmel, *Imperialism and Social Reform* (New York, 1968).

14   H. Roseveare, *The Treasury: The Evolution of a British Institution* (London, 1969), p. 143.

15   M. W. Kirby, 'Railway development and the role of the state', in R. Ambler, ed., *The History and Practice of Britain's Railways: A New Research Agenda* (Aldershot, 1999), pp. 21–35.

16   Tomlinson, *Public Policy*, p. 32.

17   S. Pollard, *The Development of the British Economy 1914–1990* (4th edition, London, 1992), pp. 44–5.

18   C. Wrigley, 'The Ministry of Munitions: an innovatory department', in K. Burk, ed., *War and the State: The Transformation of British Government, 1914–1919* (London, 1982), pp. 32–56.

19   M. W. Kirby and M. B. Rose, 'Productivity and competitive failure: British government policy and industry, 1914–19', in G. Jones and M. W. Kirby, eds, *Competitiveness and the State: Government and Business in Twentieth-century Britain* (Manchester, 1991), p. 25.

20   P. Cline, 'Winding down the war economy', in Burk, ed., *War and the State*, p. 149.

21   J. M. Keynes, *The Economic Consequences of the Peace* (New York, 1920).

22   Peden, *British Economic and Social Policy*, pp. 51–2.

23   Cmd 9182, Committee on Currency and Foreign Exchanges After the War, *First Interim Report* (1918).

24   S. Howson, *Domestic Monetary Management in Britain 1919–1938* (Cambridge, 1975), pp. 14–23.

25   Winch, *Economics and Policy*, p. 83.

26   Howson, *Domestic Monetary Management*, p. 24.

27   Cmd 9182 (1918).

28   Peden, *British Economic and Social Policy*, p. 63.

29   M. W. Kirby, *The Decline of British Economic Power since 1870* (London, 1981), pp. 36–41; Winch, *Economics and Policy*, p. 92.

30   D. E. Moggridge, *British Monetary Policy 1924–1931: The Norman Conquest of $4.86* (Cambridge, 1972), pp. 84–6, 111; Winch, *Economics and Policy*, p. 94.

31   Moggridge, *British Monetary Policy*, p. 90.

32   J. M. Keynes, *The Economic Consequences of Mr Churchill* (London, 1925).

33   Moggridge, *British Monetary Policy*, pp. 92, 110.

34   M. W. Kirby, *The British Coalmining Industry, 1870–1946: A Political and Economic History* (London, 1977), pp. 66–107; B. Supple, *The History of the British Coal Industry*, vol. 4, *1913–46: The Political Economy of Decline* (Oxford, 1987), pp. 238–55.

35   D. E. Moggridge, *The Return to Gold 1925: The Formulation of Economic Policy and its Critics* (Cambridge, 1969); N. H. Dimsdale, 'British monetary policy and the exchange rate 1920–1938', *Oxford Economic Papers*, 33 (1981), pp. 306–49; J. Redmond, 'An

indicator of the effective exchange rate of the pound in the nineteen-thirties', *Economic History Review*, 33 (1980), pp. 83–91.

36 B. W. E. Alford, *Britain in the World Economy since 1880* (London, 1996), p. 132.

37 Kirby, *The British Coalmining Industry*, pp. 77–8; M. W. Kirby, 'The Lancashire cotton industry in the inter-war years: a study in industrial organisation', *Business History*, 16 (1974), pp. 145–59; N. F. R. Crafts and M. Thomas, 'Comparative advantage in U.K. manufacturing trade 1910–1935', *Economic Journal*, 96 (1986), pp. 629–45.

38 R. S. Sayers, 'The return to gold, 1925', in S. Pollard, ed., *The Gold Standard and Employment Policies between the Wars* (London, 1970), pp. 321–4; Alford, *Britain in the World Economy*, p. 133.

39 Winch, *Economics and Policy*, p. 99.

40 Ibid., p. 106.

41 R. Lowe, *Adjusting to Democracy: The Role of the Ministry of Labour in British Politics 1916–1939* (Oxford, 1986), pp. 204–5.

42 Kirby, *Decline of British Economic Power*, p. 50.

43 Cmd 3331, *Memoranda on Certain Proposals Relating to Unemployment* (1929).

44 Cited in Winch, *Economics and Policy*, p. 118.

45 P. Clarke, *The Keynesian Revolution in the Making 1924–1936* (Oxford, 1988), pp. 54–69; W. R. Garside, *British Unemployment 1919–1939: A Study in Public Policy* (Cambridge, 1990), pp. 327–36.

46 Clarke, *Keynesian Revolution*.

47 Cited in Kirby, *Decline of British Economic Power*, p. 51.

48 Garside, *British Unemployment*, pp. 331–2.

49 R. Middleton, 'Treasury policy on unemployment', in S. Glynn and A. Booth, eds, *The Road to Full Employment* (London, 1987), p. 113.

50 Ministry of Labour, 1929, cited in Garside, *British Unemployment*, p. 335.

51 S. Tolliday, 'Steel and rationalization policies, 1918–1950', in B. Elbaum and W. Lazonick, eds, *The Decline of the British Economy* (Oxford, 1986), pp. 94–5.

52 Kirby, 'Industrial policy', p. 133.

53 Howson, *Domestic Monetary Management*, pp. 88–95; S. Howson, *Sterling's Managed Float: The Operation of the Exchange Equalisation Account 1931–1939* (Princeton Studies in International Finance, No. 46, 1980); S. Howson, 'The management of sterling 1932–1939', *Journal of Economic History*, 40 (1980), pp. 53–60.

54 Howson, *Domestic Monetary Management*, pp. 88–95.

55 Howson, 'Management of sterling'.

56 Tomlinson, *Public Policy*, p. 132.

57 B. Eichengreen, 'The origins and nature of the great slump revisited', *Economic History Review*, 45 (1994), pp. 311–12.

58 G. Peden, *Keynes, the Treasury and Economic Policy* (London, 1988).

59 Tomlinson, *Public Policy*, p. 115.

60 S. Glynn and P. Howells, 'Unemployment in the 1930s: the Keynesian solution reconsidered', *Australian Economic History Review*, 20 (1980), pp. 28–45; S. Broadberry, *The British Economy between the Wars: A Macroeconomic Survey* (Oxford, 1986); T. Hatton, 'The outlines of a Keynesian solution', in Glynn and Booth, eds, *Road to Full Employment*, pp. 82–94.

61 S. Tolliday, 'Tariffs and steel, 1916–1934: the politics of industrial decline', in J. Turner, ed., *Businessmen and Politics: Studies of Business Activity in British Politics* (London, 1984), pp. 69, 74.

62 Kirby, *British Coalmining Industry*.

63 Kirby, 'Industrial policy', p. 134.

64 A. Booth, 'Britain in the 1930s: a managed economy?', *Economic History Review*, 40 (1987), pp. 499–522.

65 B. W. E. Alford, *Depression and Recovery? British Economic Growth 1918–1939* (London, 1972), p. 65.

66 Tomlinson, *Public Policy*, pp. 131–2.

FURTHER READING

Alford, B. W. E., *Britain in the World Economy since 1880* (London, 1996).

Booth, A., 'Britain in the 1930s: a managed economy?', *Economic History Review*, 40 (1987), pp. 499–522.

Broadberry, S., *The British Economy between the Wars: A Macroeconomic Survey* (Oxford, 1986).

Clarke, P., *The Keynesian Revolution in the Making 1924–1936* (Oxford, 1988).

Drummond, I. M., *Imperial Economic Policy 1917–1939: Studies in Expansion and Protection* (London, 1974).

Eichengreen, B., *Golden Fetters: The Gold Standard and the Great Depression, 1919–1939* (Oxford, 1992).

Garside, W. R., *British Unemployment 1919–1939: A Study in Public Policy* (Cambridge, 1990).

Glynn, S. and Booth, A., eds, *The Road to Full Employment* (London, 1987).

Howson, S., *Domestic Monetary Management in Britain 1919–1938* (Cambridge, 1975).

Lowe, R., *Adjusting to Democracy: The Role of the Ministry of Labour in British Politics 1916–1939* (Oxford, 1986).

Peden, G., *British Economic and Social Policy: Lloyd George to Margaret Thatcher* (2nd edition, Oxford, 1991).

Peden, G. C., *The Treasury and British Public Policy, 1906–1959* (Oxford, 2000).

Pollard, S., *The Development of the British Economy 1914–1990* (4th edition, London, 1992).

Tomlinson, J., *Public Policy and the Economy since 1900* (Oxford, 1990).

Winch, D. N., *Economics and Policy: A Historical Study* (London, 1972).

Part III

Social and Economic Developments

CHAPTER SIXTEEN

The City of London and British Banking, 1900–1939

R. C. MICHIE

Financial history is probably the least popular of any recognized branch of history. While areas like military, cultural or political history can produce bestselling books and sustained media interest, financial history remains largely ignored and forlorn. Among the few aspects of financial history that impinge on the consciousness of the nation are events like the South Sea Bubble and the Wall Street crash or famous financiers like Nathan Rothschild and J. P. Morgan. As the more modern of these are American, it is obvious that little is known about Britain's own recent financial history. More importantly, there exists little or no understanding of the underlying financial and monetary forces that led to speculative booms and crashes or how financiers amassed large fortunes. The froth of fraud, the rise and fall of financiers, and the drama of money-making dominate what popular historical literature there is on financial history, while the largely unread academic literature focuses on the development of banks and stock exchanges or the relative merits of different financial and monetary systems. As a consequence, a large gulf exists between the perception most people have of Britain's financial history and the views of those who have researched the subject over the years. The problem is that, unlike many other branches of history, financial history does require some basic understanding of the technicalities of the subject, such as the need of banks to balance liabilities and assets if they are to survive and the relationship of the stock exchange to both the capital and money markets. Otherwise, much financial activity appears inexplicable and thus easy to dismiss as either inadequate or positively harmful.

This is an unfortunate state of affairs at the best of times for it leads to a poor understanding of what had really taken place and why, as most historians relied for their interpretation on views derived from the conclusions of politicians, media commentators, civil servants or the general public, all of whom had a limited grasp of the situation. However, probably no period of modern British history more requires an intimate knowledge of unfolding financial circumstances than the years between 1900 and 1939. In this period the financial system has been given a centre-stage role for it is seen to have made a major contribution to both Britain's long-term decline and the enduring mass unemployment of the interwar years. Either jointly or separately the City of London, with its concentration of financial markets and institutions, or the entire British banking system are accused of failing to support the development of emerging new industries like chemicals, motor vehicles and electrical goods so that Britain was left with an increasingly antiquated industrial structure even before the First World War. When that industrial structure then faced severe difficulties in the aftermath of that war, the financial system is further accused of not providing the funds needed to support, restructure and modernize long-established sectors like textiles, shipbuilding and steel. In contrast, the German financial system, in particular, is cast in a much more favourable light, being seen to have nurtured new industries, like chemicals and electricals, and provided general support to manufacturing, when it was in difficulty between the wars.

The First World War appears to have been a turning point in this critical perception of the British financial system. Prior to that war there appeared to be general satisfaction with the British financial system, which was felt to be superior to that of any other country, being free of the spectacular collapses to be found around the world. In the same way that the British Empire was bringing civilization to the world, so British banks and bankers were providing a model which others would do well to copy. Among its admirers was the economist J. M. Keynes, who noted in 1914: 'I believe our banking system, and indeed the whole intricate organism of the City, to be one of the best and most characteristic creations of that part of the genius and virtue of our nation which has found its outlet in "business"'.[1]

By 1913, there were an estimated 10,000 British bankers operating outside Britain, especially in Asia, Africa, Australasia and Latin America. The First World War, and the economic problems that followed it, shattered that sense of superiority as British banking came to be judged not on financial criteria such as stability and probity but on how well it supported domestic industry. Here it was considered to be lacking, especially in comparison with Germany, which Britain had so recently defeated in war. A. W. Kirkaldy, writing in 1921, expressed a view that was by then widely shared when he said: 'The German banking system, with its tentacles stretching into every important trade, particularly of a developmental character, has much for commendation from a national standpoint. To it has been largely due the extraordinary development of the trade, manufactures, and business of Germany in recent pre-war years'.[2] Whereas German banks were perceived as having funded the development of such crucial war industries as steel and chemicals, and then supported manufacturing during the difficult post-war years, it was felt that British banks had failed to do the same, with detrimental consequences for the British economy.

This view was given official endorsement during the interwar years in various government inquiries, none more so than the Committee on Finance and Industry, which reported in 1931. It concluded that 'the relations between the British financial world and British industry, as distinct from British commerce, have never been so close as between German finance and German industry and American finance and American industry'.[3] Out of this report came the term the 'Macmillan Gap', named after the chairman of the committee, Lord Macmillan. Though referring specifically to the lack of provision within the financial system for the needs of medium-sized businesses, it came to epitomize the gulf between finance and industry in Britain. With many industrialists facing difficult trading conditions between the wars, resulting in low profitability or persistent losses, it was only natural that they would blame banks for refusing to provide them with the funds to keep going or to invest in the new equipment that might make them more competitive, so providing ample evidence that the financial system was failing to deliver. Conversely, few understood the predicament that banks were in, faced with the necessity of balancing the interests of their depositors, whose money it was they were lending, and those of the industrialists who came to them for loans. Depositors expected their money to be both safe and immediately available, as well as paying them a high rate of interest, while borrowers looked for a loan that could not be quickly recalled, paid a low rate of interest and was granted regardless of the prospects of repayment. The consequence was that the accepted orthodoxy which emerged from the interwar years was that the banks had failed business, and this was the view that was taken up by generations of post-Second World War historians, who based their judgements not on a detailed examination of what banks actually did but on the criticisms made of them by contemporaries.

One of the major reasons given for the gulf that was felt to exist between banks and industry after 1900 was the organizational change that was taking place within the British banking system. In the middle of the nineteenth century, there existed numerous separate banks based in and operating from towns and cities throughout the country. There were also separate banking systems serving Scotland and Ireland. By the end of the century, many of these separate banks had disappeared, being replaced by London-based banks operating nationwide branch networks. In 1900 these London-based banks already controlled two-thirds of the deposits placed with commercial banks in England and Wales, while managing almost 60 per cent of the branches, and their influence continued to grow inexorably. In 1913 they handled 79 per cent of deposits and operated 77 per cent of the branches. The final consolidation came during the First World War when five London-based banks – London City and Midland, Lloyds, Barclays, City and Westminster, National and Provincial – came to dominate banking in England and Wales. The London-based banks had 89 per cent of deposits and 88 per cent of branches in 1920/1. Unlike the nineteenth century, when the financial needs of local manufacturing firms were served by banks that were owned and run by members of the same community, the twentieth century saw that replaced by a financial system in which the power now rested with head offices in the City of London. These were seen to be far removed from the needs and concerns of most manufacturing industries, like cotton textiles in Lancashire, woollen textiles in Yorkshire, shipbuilding in the north-east or coal mining in south Wales, for they were now served by branches run by career bankers rather than by those who identified with the region and its problems. Such a view was reinforced after the First World War by an awareness that it was precisely these industries that were depressed, leading to an obvious connection between their suffering and the lack of locally accountable banking. Forgotten, when making that connection, was the equally depressed state of the Scottish economy, with its reliance on depressed sectors like coal, shipbuilding and heavy industry, and the fact that its banking system remained locally based rather than run from London head offices. Also ignored was the fact that the number of branches continued to grow, not contract, in England and Wales, reaching 2.6 per 10,000 people in 1937 compared to 1.83 in 1913 and 1.52 in 1900. This indicated both a continued commitment by these London-based banks to all the areas in which they operated and an intensification of competition between them for available business, rather than consolidation being the product of a desire to exploit monopoly positions in local markets by closing branches.

This commitment was only to be expected given the origins of these London-based banks and the way they had been formed. The process of consolidation, which had led to the domination of British banking by a few London-based companies, had been achieved in a variety of ways and was not simply the result of expansion and take-over emanating from London. The two largest banks at the time – Midland and Lloyds – both originated in Birmingham and developed a London base by acquiring banks there as they expanded nationwide. Lloyds, for example, took over some fifty banks between 1865 and 1914. Therefore, though these banks were increasingly run from London, because of its greater importance and convenience as a financial and administrative centre, they retained strong regional connections. Similarly, though Barclays was a London-based bank, it had first expanded into other parts of the country by merging with a number of Quaker banks with which it had long been associated, and consequently it also had very strong regional roots. The National and Provincial bank was very similar for it had been created as a national banking operation. Thus, of the five main London-based banks, only the City and Westminster had grown into a national bank from a London base, and thus might have lacked an understanding of the financial requirements of northern manufacturing. In addition, each of these banks adopted different management structures, with some devolving a great deal of authority to regional head offices or to the individual branch manager, while others maintained strong central control. As a greater knowledge has been obtained of the way these banks evolved and were structured, it is no longer possible to accept the judgement, made by many contemporaries and then followed by historians, that the increasing control of British banking from London meant a poorer service for the north and for manufacturing. That judgement requires a careful analysis of what banks did with the money entrusted to them and the relationships they had with their business customers. It is this type of research that has been undertaken over the last few years by scholars such as Forrest Capie, Mike Collins and Duncan Ross, and this has helped transform our understanding of British banking between 1900 and 1939.

From that research it is clear that British banks had perfected a way of operation before 1914 that allowed them to make maximum use of the short-term deposits placed with them by savers across Britain, and to do so in a way that was both safe and remunerative for all concerned. Although there was a preference for loans of short-term duration, measured in months not years, longer-term loans were made when the need arose. An estimated 13 per cent of loans made to industrial firms, for example, were for over three years, reflecting conditions in industries like shipbuilding. It took a long time to build and sell a ship compared to the situation in an industry like textiles, and so banks adjusted their lending policies accordingly, knowing that if they did not a competitor would take the business away from them. Also, it is clear that banks knew their customers well, both in terms of the business they were in and from the operation of their individual accounts, so allowing them to make accurate assessments of the risks they ran when making loans. The losses on loans before 1914 were a mere 0.2 per cent of the amount lent. Similarly, around one-third of loans were based on no more than the personal guarantee of repayment by the borrower, rather than the existence of collateral in the form of goods or securities, indicating that the relationship between a bank and its business customers was a close and continuous one. Nevertheless, banks did not lend all the money placed with them to business customers for that would have neither always been possible, as the demand for credit rose and fell with the seasons and from year to year, nor advisable because of the risks involved. A bank had always to be in a position to supply cash, as depositors made withdrawals, and provide the credit its regular customers required. A failure to repay deposits would immediately create doubts that the bank was in financial difficulties. In turn, this would cause a panic as other depositors tried to get all their money out before the bank collapsed and they lost their savings. Such an event would destroy the bank for it was in no position to repay depositors in full, as the money had been lent out and could not be immediately recalled. However, if a bank kept enough cash to meet every possible eventuality that would reduce the interest it paid to its depositors, as cash produced no returns, as well as limiting the amount of lending it could undertake. The result would be to drive both depositors and customers to banks that offered a better rate of interest and had more money to lend. Instead, banks structured their lending so that there were always loans maturing and others that could be called in at short notice. Thus banks lent around 60 per cent of their available funds directly to customers, with the rest being kept in the form of cash or placed into easily saleable assets, very short-term loans or investments, and so were in a position to meet any withdrawal or request for credit.

As a result of this careful management of deposits and loans, British banking became highly stable in the years before 1914, avoiding the crises and collapses common elsewhere, especially the United States. The great strength of the branch banking system was that funds could be easily and quickly moved to where they were required, so providing defence against a local crisis that would destroy any single bank. It also meant that less needed to be kept as cash, for each branch could draw on a central pool of funds to meet sudden withdrawals or requests for credit. Instead, these nationwide banks could make greater use of the money placed with them by lending it out to local businesses or employing it in very short-term loans in the London money market. Certainly, there is no evidence that these banks were failing to provide their customers with the finance they required before the First World War, judging from the detailed research carried out into the needs of British industry, such as brewing and steel, by Katherine Watson. Obviously, new businesses in new fields had difficulty in persuading banks to provide both the amount and type of finance they wanted, but comparative work indicates that this was true of all countries at all times. Lending to the unknown for the untested involved far greater risk than the provision of funds to established customers with a proven record of success, or to established businesses operating in traditional areas, as the failure rate among new firms testified. Nevertheless, there remains a residual doubt, even after all the research, that British banks could have done more to help the establishment of new industries before 1914 by providing entrepreneurs with longer-term loans. However, among informed historians there is a growing consensus that banks were operating effectively before the First World War, and that any deficiencies in the financial system must lie elsewhere.

However, the First World War created a major shock for the banking system, exposed as it was to panic withdrawals by depositors worried by its stability in the face of a major European conflict. Traditionally banks had relied upon their ability to recall the short-term loans they had made to the discount market, and to members of the Stock Exchange, in order to meet any increase in withdrawals by their customers. The crisis created by the threat of a major war made this impossible, since those holding bills of exchange or stocks and bonds could not sell them and so repay their borrowings, as had been the case in the past. With the enormous uncertainty that war brought, no financial institution or investor was willing to commit funds that might be needed to meet some unexpected eventuality, whereas in the past the retrenchment of one was compensated for by the expansion of another. The closure of the Stock Exchange, for example, signalled to all the fact that those holding securities no longer had a market where they could be sold and so borrowed funds repaid. Faced with the prospect of a financial panic that could have brought down the entire banking system, and so inflict widespread damage on the economy, the Treasury, Bank of England and the commercial banks were forced to devise a scheme that would meet the public's demand for cash. The result was a large increase in the issue of notes and a general expansion of credit, which satisfied the immediate demand and averted a serious crisis. This close cooperation between the Treasury, the Bank of England and the banks was then continued during the war as it was essential not only to avert subsequent financial crises but also to ensure that the government obtained the funds necessary to finance the continuing war effort. By 1919, lending by banks to their individual and business customers had fallen to about half its pre-war level, or 32 per cent of the funds available, as government absorbed more and more of the nation's savings. The government's short-term borrowings rose from £16 million on 1 August 1914 to £1,500 million on 9 November 1918 and much of this came directly from the banks. In addition, banks lent to their customers so that they could buy the long-term bonds issued by the government, such as the 1917 War Loan that raised £1,000 million.

During the First World War, the British banking system had to respond to the needs of the British government rather than operate within a commercial environment where each bank had to compete for business. The result was to create a climate of cooperation, under the authority of the Bank of England, that contributed to the successful mobilization of funds for the war effort but reduced the incentive to compete actively for depositors and borrowers. At the same time the monopolization of credit by the government during the war left a legacy of unsatisfied demand from business. The result was a lending boom once hostilities ceased and government borrowing began to fall, fostered by the inevitable restocking boom which encouraged firms to borrow to expand production. Lloyds Bank almost doubled its advances between 1918 and 1920 as it responded to the needs of its business customers. When this boom collapsed the banks found themselves having to support overcapitalized firms in uncompetitive industries like steel, shipbuilding and textiles in the hope that improved economic conditions would allow the loans to be repaid. Generally, banks adopted a supportive attitude to their business customers, many of whom were longstanding clients, in the belief that prosperity would return and the current difficulties being experienced were temporary. Advances to customers by British banks continued to rise, for example growing from 48 per cent of total funds in 1923/4 to 52 per cent in 1928/30, despite the continuing problems experienced in traditional British industries.

However, advances did eventually collapse in the early 1930s in the face of the world economic depression, which had a devastating effect on the export markets for major sectors of British manufacturing. Even by 1936/8, bank advances had risen to only 41 per cent of available funds, or considerably below previous levels. This reduction in lending to manufacturing, in particular, has helped support a view that banks were uninterested in the plight of their industrial customers and were unwilling to provide them with the funds necessary to survive the depressed market conditions of the 1930s. It is also clear that the commercial banks operated a cartel among themselves at that time, which prevented competition for business through lower interest rates. This cartel was fostered by the Bank of England, as it made it easier for it to exert control, and was a product of the spirit of cooperation that had developed during the war. Nevertheless, recent research has established that banks did remain keen to lend whenever there was any prospect that the borrower could service the loan and repay when it became due. Instead, the problem was a lack of demand. The continuing depressed state of many industries both reduced their need for credit to finance production, let alone expansion, while expanding firms were able to tap alternative sources of funds, such as reinvested profits or the disposal of holdings of government debt acquired during the war. It was also increasingly cheap and easy to make small issues of securities to investors, as was the case with Morris Motors and Pye Radio, especially if the business was in a growth sector.

Nevertheless, the criticism remains that if banks had been more interventionist then British industry would have had many fewer problems. It is suggested that banks should have provided their industrial customers with both permanent funds and greater direction. As this did happen in the case of the Bank of England, which remained a public company until nationalized in 1946, it has been possible to evaluate the contribution that both bank funding and intervention had for those sectors of industry that were in difficulty during the interwar years. Prior to the First World War the Bank of England confined its activities to carrying out the government's banking business, such as receiving and paying out money and managing the national debt, and playing an important role in the London money market as lender of last resort. As such it had no direct connection with the finance of British industry. In contrast, faced with the weakness of important sectors of the British economy in the 1920s, which had serious consequences for the entire financial system because of outstanding commercial bank loans, the Bank of England followed a more interventionist stance. In 1927/8, it was involved in the reorganization of firms in the steel and armaments industry, which led to the setting up of the Securities Management Trust and National Shipbuilding Security in 1929, followed by the Bankers' Industrial Development Company in 1930. In retrospect these interventions are regarded as misconceived, partial, insufficient and incomplete and appear to have achieved little. The problems faced by certain sections of British industry were beyond the power of bankers to solve, even the Bank of England itself, for no amount or variety of funding could make firms in sectors like cotton textiles and shipbuilding successful when the markets they served had collapsed. When these prospects improved, as was the case with the steel industry with a growing demand from the motor car industry, firms began to prosper whereas without any recovery, as in cotton textiles, the businesses continued to struggle. Bank of England intervention may even have made the problems worse by delaying necessary reconstruction through the support given to the weakest firms.

These difficulties faced by British industry were to the disadvantage of the banks themselves for it reduced the demand for the credit facilities they provided and for which they charged interest. With a weak demand for loans, banks were forced to employ their funds in less remunerative investments, particularly government debt. By 1936/8 bank holdings of UK government securities stood at 28 per cent of funds compared to 19 per cent in 1923/5. Furthermore, the low rate of interest paid by the government on its debt during the 1930s undermined the ability of banks to compete for funds from savers. This was then exploited by the building societies, which employed the deposits they received to lend to those purchasing their own homes. The assets of building societies rose from £80 million in 1920 to £700 million in 1939 as a result. Although banks can be blamed for some lack of dynamism in the interwar years, it is now difficult to accept that this had any major effect on the performance of the British economy. The growing importance of the building society movement, in response to the need for housing finance, indicates that where funds were inadequate the financial sector, if not banking, was well able to respond. It also suggests that this was an opportunity being neglected by banks because they continued to focus on the provision of credit for industry and commerce, rather than respond to the new opportunities developing in the domestic housing market, but this is not the criticism that has been traditionally levelled at banks. Elsewhere, banks did exhibit dynamic behaviour during the interwar years, expanding into such areas as foreign exchange dealing and trade credit. Also, despite opposition from the Bank of England, a number of the largest domestic banks not only extended their operations to Scotland, as with Lloyds' acquisition of the National Bank of Scotland in 1918, but also overseas. During the nineteenth century there had developed a group of British banks which, though based in London, conducted almost all their business abroad, particularly in the empire and Latin America. In 1913 there were thirty-one of these banks and, collectively, they controlled 1,387 branches and had assets of £366 million. These banks were completely separate from the domestic British banks. As most of their business was conducted abroad, they did well during the First World War as economies like Australia and Argentina prospered. Consequently, with domestic consolidation already accomplished, the logical next step for the largest British banks was overseas expansion, and this was most easily achieved through the acquisition of one or more of the British overseas banks. Lloyds proceeded, in the 1920s, to build up a banking operation in Latin America while Barclays chose Africa. Unfortunately, the world depression of the 1930s hit both international trade and economies in Africa and Latin America particularly badly, so greatly reducing the value of these overseas operations. The Midland bank, which had confined its operations to Britain, as a result emerged as the most successful British bank of the interwar years. Nevertheless, with 2,315 branches overseas in 1938, and assets of £767 million, overseas banking remained a major success for British banking, as its international presence was far greater than that of any other country at that time.

In addition, it is now clear that the differences between the operation of British and foreign banks, highlighted by both contemporaries and historians, were something of an illusion. Work done on pre-1914 banking systems suggests that a high degree of convergence was taking place as all banks sought to balance their assets and liabilities so as to avoid a liquidity crisis. As one recent scholar has concluded, 'outright condemnation of the British banks and unqualified celebration of the

German banks are clearly unwarranted'.[4] Similarly, in the interwar years, banks the world over tried to limit their exposure to sectors of the economy facing difficult economic conditions because of the risks involved for their survival. Therefore, they applied the strategy of focusing on short-term loans and requesting collateral, when-ever it was possible to do so. When asked by the Macmillan Committee, 'Do I under-stand that the German banker, like the English banker, does not like to have his money tied up permanently in industry?', the German banker Jacob Golschmidt replied, 'No, the German banker dislikes that as much as any banker anywhere else in the world'.[5] He had cause to be worried, since the bank of which he was chair-man, the Darmstädter und National bank, collapsed in July 1931, brought down by the world economic crisis which further undermined a German financial system weak-ened by the hyperinflation of the early 1920s. In both Germany and the United States the banking systems had to be rescued by state intervention because of the difficul-ties they were in. In contrast, though localized difficulties did occur in the British banking system, as in Lancashire with its exposure to the troubled cotton textile industry, there was no crisis and no state intervention. The national nature of the British banking system, and the prudent way it was conducted, allowed even major crises to be surmounted, though they overwhelmed others.

The result of this extensive research has been to transform our understanding of how British banks operated in practice over the 1900–39 period, rather than accept the impressions of ill-informed contemporaries or the views of disgruntled borrowers. Increasingly, it is now recognized that the banking system was powerless in the face of deeper and more general economic difficulties and that it did well to avoid the collapses common elsewhere, which would have created serious additional problems. Weaknesses did exist, as with housing finance, and mistakes were made, as with overseas expansion, but it is difficult to attribute Britain's economic difficulties to these. The consequence of this research has thus been to shift the criticism away from the financial system as a whole, and the banks in particular, to the City of London. In the City of London were to be found not only the head offices of all the major commercial banks, as well as the Bank of England, but also other financial institutions like the London Stock Exchange and a host of financial intermediaries such as the merchant banks and the discount houses. Many of these were involved in financial activities which, taken alone, appeared to have no purpose and could be considered positively harmful to the economy as a whole, such as speculation in the money and securities market. Long before the criticism of historians, contemporaries had targeted the City of London as being out of touch with the needs of the wider British economy and only concerned with its own interests, many of which were to be found abroad. The Labour politician Douglas Jay, writing in 1938, echoed the views of many and not just the left when he stated that:

> Few in the City care whether it is socially desirable that this or that industry should be enabled to develop. Any such motive our financiers would regard as 'political'. Instead they stick to 'business' – which means the attempt to outwit one's neighbour by cunning, luck, inside information, or the deliberate spreading of false rumours. Small wonder that scandals abound, savings are mis-invested, and the small investor continually robbed.[6]

Reflecting these perceived inadequacies of the financial system, by 1928 Labour party policy already favoured the nationalization of the Bank of England and this was extended to include the major commercial banks in the 1930s. They also planned to replace many of the functions of the merchant banks and the Stock Exchange by a National Investment Board, for this would control the activities of the capital market.

Underlying this dissatisfaction with the City of London, which manifested itself with increasing intensity after the First World War, was the fact that the activities undertaken in the City were becoming increasingly remote from the British public. By 1900 the City of London had made the transition from being a national commercial and financial centre to one of global importance. The City of London had flourished for the services it provided were in increasing demand both to coordinate and to integrate activity in the global economy, especially the world's money and capital markets.

However, the result was to remove from the City of London business with which the public could identify and which they could understand, namely the buying, selling and movement of physical goods, or the handling of domestic finance. In their place came activities that were much less visible to the public, much less well understood, and thus much easier to ignore or dismiss as unimportant. The City of London was one of the few centres, if not the only one, with the range and depth of expertise and markets required in the conduct of international trade, but the value of all this essential activity was little understood. Even more difficult to understand was the nature of the financial activities being conducted in the City of London in this period. The composition of this was continually changing before 1914, as some declined or disappeared, while others grew steadily in importance, especially those related to international finance. However, what was growing was extreme functional specialization, with entire firms or even markets devoted to obscure activities, but ones that were vital for international trade and finance. Inevitably, many of the firms in the City were of foreign origin and with foreign connections, attracted by the unrivalled facilities and opportunities it offered. No other financial centre in the world came close to matching the City's international banking connections before 1914, for example with over 1,000 of the world's banks having representation there, while a number had gone so far as to open their own branches. The French bank Société Générale employed 131 people in its London branch in 1912, and it was from there that it conducted much of its operations in international finance.

The result was that the City of London lay at the very centre of the world economy's payments system through which flowed all the transfers between borrowers and lenders, creditors and debtors, and buyers and sellers that were not internal to any single country. Most of the international financial transactions of the United States, stemming from trade and investment, passed through London before 1914. This made the London money market the most important in the world. Around half of all international trade was financed in London. Thus, to those around the world who did understand what the City did, it was valued very highly. The Canadian banker L. D. Wilgress noted shortly before the First World War:

> The London money market is the most important and influential in the world. London is the world's financial centre, and is the clearing house for international payments. The London money market is distinguished from all other money markets by the unparalleled freedom and elasticity which mark the English credit system, and for the fact that London is the only perfectly free market for gold. Money is more easily to be had in London than anywhere else. It has thus become the international loan market.[7]

After the First World War had broken out another Canadian banker reflected that 'although New York, Berlin and Paris have become great money centres they have never been able, despite the adoption of every expedient they could think of, to seriously threaten the paramount position of London as a world market'.[8]

Through occupying such a position, it was only to be expected that the City of London money market would grow rapidly at this time. It also became ever more international, employing short-term money from around the world to finance short-term borrowing from around the world. As the use made of the London money market for domestic purposes declined rapidly from the mid-nineteenth century onwards, with that function being taken over by the big joint-stock banks, it was more than compensated for by the development of an ever-larger international business. At the same time, the Bank of England became much better at recognizing the danger signals when problems arose in this money market, and responding to them in a positive manner, so avoiding major crises and the damage they caused, as has been the case earlier in the century. Crises did continue to occur throughout this period, as was inevitable with a dynamic market-based monetary and financial system, but the collective actions of the Bank of England and other banks and bankers ensured that they were less and less disruptive, both for Britain itself and internationally. All this was done without government intervention or coordination among central banks.

However, this success of the City as a global financial centre has generated sustained criticism that it ignored the financial needs of the British economy. Clearly, any investigation of the London capital market for the period before 1914 reveals it to be heavily oriented towards the issue of securities for foreign governments and railways rather than British business. Much of that was left to provincial centres. This has been seen, not as some natural division within the capital market, but as systematic bias against domestic finance within the City, leaving British industry short of the finance required to fund new enterprises, especially in such technologically important areas as electricity and communications. However, detailed investigations of City–industry relations over this period have revealed strong and flexible links and an absence of any financing difficulties either from bank lending or new issues of securities. Many firms in the City, such as the stockbrokers and the smaller and newer merchant banks, were keen to offer their financial services to British business but were not often given the opportunity. Domestic industry had little need for additional finance owing to its ability to tap family and local sources along with reinvested profits. Consequently, there appears little evidence that the City of London's development as a financial centre before the war was, itself, directly detrimental to the growth of the British economy, through a lack of domestic investment in those sectors of the economy with the greatest potential.

Instead, what emerges is how wide-ranging and sophisticated was the capital market in London in those years. Arranging large loans for foreign governments and corporations was a complex business, requiring a great deal of expertise and effort, and the acceptance of considerable risk. It also took place in a competitive environment both within the City, with new firms always ready to challenge the old, and internationally, as rival centres such as Paris and New York could exploit any reluctance or excessive profit-taking by London. Equally complex and risky was the tailoring of finance for smaller industrial concerns, but that was also not neglected in the City at this time. A growing demand from Canadian industrial companies for finance met a ready response in London, for example, with Canadian financiers migrating there to handle the business. This was typical of the increasingly cosmopolitan nature of international finance before the First World War, in which the City was a magnet for both established and aspiring financiers owing to the unrivalled access it gave to global markets. Though there was a gentlemanly elite in the City that was long established and well connected, this was but a thin veneer masking a vast array of individuals from different countries and backgrounds, who were struggling to create a permanent place for themselves. What had come to exist in the City of London before 1914 was a more complex, varied and sophisticated financial system than in any other financial centre.

Though there can be no doubt that the City of London flourished during the pre-1914 period, offering a range and depth of financial services and markets unrivalled anywhere else in the world, by taking examples from a few specific areas there have been suggestions that it was becoming a less dynamic financial centre, and one increasingly out of touch with industrial Britain. The impression is conveyed that a closed elite dominated the City, and that this financial elite, through education and marriage, was being absorbed into the long-established landed elite of southern England. In turn, this was to the disadvantage of the industrial north of Britain both directly, in terms of access to finance, and indirectly, because this elite was able to exert sufficient social and political influence to ensure that government policy was in its exclusive interest. Evidence of the fusion of wealthy banking families in the City with those from the landed aristocracy can be found to corroborate this trend, giving support to a view that the very success of the City of London was destroying the economy that had created it. However, as the City of London was a much larger and more varied place than one populated by a few merchant banking families, it is difficult to accept that a handful of families could so influence its structure or so direct its affairs for it to ignore any domestic or other opportunities open to it. The success achieved internationally was hardly the product of a complacent and inward-looking culture, but the result of an ability to respond to challenges and seize opportunities. Similarly, though the Bank of England was intimately involved with the government, as it undertook all its banking and monetary functions, this was not true for the rest of the City. Those elsewhere in the City had little direct contact with the government, or any desire to influence its policies other than to be left to get on with their own business. Such a desire was in keeping with the liberal economic ideology of the time rather than a special requirement of the City of London.

On the eve of the First World War the City of London was the leading financial centre in the world. By the end of that war its dominance had been much undermined, especially by New York, though it remained the single most important financial centre across a wide range of activities. The City was always vulnerable to financial crises anywhere in the globe, given its position as the international financial centre, but ways and means to avoid, diffuse and minimize these had been developed over the years. What could not be devised was any simple means of preventing a major crisis created by the outbreak of hostilities between the major imperial powers of the world, as took place in late 1914. The government was aware that a war with Germany, in particular, meant real difficulties for the City of London, as this had been explained to them in evidence given to the Committee for Imperial Defence.

A substantial portion of Germany's foreign trade was financed in the London money market, much of Germany's international investment went through the London capital market, German banks employed their spare funds by lending to London bankers and brokers, the German mercantile fleet was largely insured at Lloyds and employed via the Baltic Exchange, and Germans were probably the most numerous foreign nationality to be found in the City of London. Faced with such overwhelming evidence of the seriousness of such a war for the City, the government's only response was to pass a law on trading with the enemy, while ignoring the problems that would be caused.

Thus, the outbreak of the First World War caught the City of London completely unprepared. The particular problem that arose was the inability of those in the money and securities markets to obtain the money they were owed, or receive the bills and securities they had paid for, from German and other foreign clients. In turn, that had repercussions for others in the money and securities markets through the chain of subsequent deals, so threatening the whole financial structure. Only prompt action by the Bank of England, the commercial banks and the Stock Exchange, supported by the Treasury, averted a crisis that threatened the entire financial system with collapse. By guaranteeing that payments would be made, and by expanding the money supply, sufficient confidence and liquidity was provided to persuade those owed money or securities from pressing for payment. Although that crisis was overcome, the war not only shattered the international payments mechanism, as countries were now at war, but also destroyed the trust upon which so much lending and borrowing, buying and selling, took place. With the collapse of both that mechanism and trust generally, the outbreak of the First World War represented a major blow to the City of London. This was not going to be easily or quickly repaired after four years of intense and costly conflict.

In addition, as the First World War dragged on and on, its effect on the City of London increased. Not only was the connection with Germany destroyed, but growing anti-German hysteria made it almost impossible for those of German birth or recent German origin to operate successfully, so depriving the City of one of its most important and dynamic groups, and one with very strong international connections. At the same time, the war had serious consequences for the City as a commercial centre since it became both dangerous to bring cargoes to Britain for trans-shipment and difficult to organize worldwide distribution from a London base. Thus merchants in countries like the United States and Australia increasingly took control of their own imports and exports rather than using the services of markets and middlemen in the City. Similarly, as the costs of the war rose, the British government absorbed more and more of the money that had once been used in the City to finance international trade. Short-term borrowing by the government came to dominate the business of the London money market. Inevitably, countries outside Britain looked elsewhere for the credit that was necessary if they were to continue to trade, and this was found either within their own financial system or from the United States. However, the war could not be financed from short-term borrowing alone, along with increased taxation. The government also sought to tap the long-term savings of the British population through longer-term borrowing. The national debt, which stood at £706.2 million in 1914, had risen to £7,481.1 million in 1919, or a tenfold increase. Even with this vast increase in borrowing by the government there still remained a need to obtain the foreign exchange necessary to pay for essential food and war materials from abroad. In particular, with so much reliance being placed on supplies from the United States, there was a desperate search for dollars. This was met partly by borrowing from United States investors, and the amount had reached £1.4 billion by the end of the war. The other method used was to sell the foreign assets held by British investors. These had been slowly built up in the fifty years before 1914, with the stocks and bonds of foreign railways being especially popular with British investors, whether they were individuals or institutions like the insurance companies or investment trusts. Even before the government took steps to compel investors to hand over such assets in return for its own securities, sales had been taking place as investors in such countries as the United States, Australia, South Africa and Canada took the opportunity to buy their own securities from their British holders. Altogether, British investors on their own, or through the government, had disposed of securities worth around £850 million by 1921, of which some two-thirds had been issued by US railroads.

Consequently, it is clear that the First World War was very damaging for the City of London. Important sectors of the City experienced a considerable collapse of business, as with those handling and financing international trade or issuing and trading foreign securities. There were compensations for some through the vast increase in government borrowing, but the overall result was both a major disruption to the City and a greatly diminished role in the world economy as foreign countries either looked to their own resources or turned to the United States. In addition, such a radical change in the City could not have been accomplished without a huge increase in government intervention in order to mobilize and channel savings for the war effort. Either directly, through the Treasury, or indirectly, via the Bank of England, the government made its views known and applied pressure so that they would prevail. As the government continued to play an important role in guaranteeing stability, it had the power to ensure that its policies would be implemented. The result was that the operations of the City of London were increasingly directed by the government during the war rather than being responsive to the interaction of national and international forces of supply and demand. Government support had a price and that was to be found in the degree of control exerted, which grew as the costs of the war mounted.

Nevertheless, the City of London was not destroyed by the First World War, having suffered little physical damage, while Britain both escaped invasion and emerged victorious. Thus, the City emerged battered rather than destroyed from the war, ready to rebuild its position as the foremost financial centre, despite the increased importance of New York. The rapid growth of a foreign exchange market in the early 1920s, for example, indicated the City of London's continuing ability to exploit new opportunities and profit from adversity, as with currency instability. However, many in the City were slow to recognize that there was a need to change in the post-war years because the assumption was made that the pre-war business would return. Such a belief was reinforced in the first half of the 1920s when London was regarded as a safe haven for funds fleeing from monetary and financial turmoil in continental Europe, for such funds helped to support an active money market at that time. After 1925, when more stable monetary conditions prevailed with the return of Britain to the gold standard, this advantage of being a safe haven was lost, as was much of the activity in the foreign exchange market. Although the return to the gold standard has been seen as a prime example of City influence, there were many in the City who had little to gain, and much to lose, from a return to fixed exchange rates, especially at the pre-war parity to the dollar which rendered much commercial and financial activity uncompetitive. The return to gold was a policy decision by government, not the City, and so its damaging consequences were the responsibility of the government. Thus, although foreign borrowers did return to the London capital market in the 1920s, for example, they were now largely from the empire, like Australia or the colonies. Many countries like Canada and Japan were able to finance their own investments, while the United States took over Britain's position as the world's largest lender, especially to Latin America and continental Europe, being able to offer larger loans at lower rates. Similarly, though the London money market did revive, its role in the finance of world trade remained much less than pre-war. Not only were other countries no longer reliant upon the credit and expertise available in London, especially the United States, but the continuing need of the British government to borrow heavily, in order to refinance its huge short-term debt, greatly reduced the funds that were available. Activity in the London discount market in the 1920s remained dominated by Treasury bills, as during the war, rather than commercial bills, which had been the case before 1914.

In the face of the reduced international demand for the services in which it specialized, the City of London turned more and more to domestic business finance during the 1920s. The patriotic zeal unleashed by the war had enormously expanded the size of the investing public as all those who could afford to do so bought the securities issued by the government. By the close of hostilities, there were an estimated 17 million investors in Britain and, once introduced to the practice of buying, selling and holding securities, many maintained an interest after the war. At the same time, the war left a legacy of underinvestment in much of British industry, because of the shortage of finance during the conflict. This could not be easily obtained from the traditional sources of retained profits or informal networks because the profits generated during the war were generally low, despite the obvious exceptions of producers of war material, while the greatly increased levels of taxation reduced personal savings among the wealthy. Consequently, many businesses looked to raise funds from outside investors in order to finance both re-equipment and expansion in the immediate post-war years. Though some of the established City firms, whose focus had long been international finance, failed to respond to these opportunities, many others did. Consequently, those in the City who catered for the needs of these new investors, and handled the issues of securities being made by British industrial and commercial businesses in the 1920s, experienced considerable prosperity. There can be no doubt that in the 1920s the City of London was far more involved in domestic finance than before 1914, not only through the need to service the war debt but in response to the needs of British companies and a mass investing public.

Unfortunately for the City this growing involvement was masked by the serious problems experienced by major sectors of British manufacturing. This led many to blame the City for ignoring the plight of British industry rather than recognize the harsh reality that when a business could no longer generate profits it was not attractive to investors, and so could not raise additional finance. Furthermore, the fact that the investing public was now much larger than pre-war meant that, when the speculative boom finally burst in 1929, the City was blamed for the losses incurred by large numbers of inexperienced investors. Inevitably, in any period of speculation, there were those who sought to profit from the investors' belief that all securities, irrespective of their underlying prospects, would rise in price and so could be resold at a profit. This was especially so for those securities issued by newly formed companies with exclusive access to a new technology, as with the rapidly developing record and photography industries. Consequently, many securities were issued that turned out to be worthless, when profits failed to materialize, or could not sustain the valuation that investors put on them. Again, rather than directing blame at those investors that had been willing to buy any rubbish at high prices, in the belief that they could resell for a quick profit, the City as a whole was seen to be at fault because it had failed to stop the issue of worthless securities and the high-pressure sales techniques employed by some. Though more could have been done to police both new issues and subsequent trading, such abuses had always occurred in the past and were impossible to eradicate, unless the market was restricted to issues by long-established companies and to large and experienced investors. If that were the case, the City would then have failed to support new enterprises and ignored the interests of the growing number of small investors.

As it was, the speculative bubble in London burst before the Wall Street crash of October 1929, as it reached a crisis in the September, when the fraudulent schemes of the financier Clarence Hatry collapsed. Hatry had been using money, raised from the issue of local government stocks beyond the amounts authorized, to finance more speculative schemes. When he could no longer meet the interest payments on the additional stocks, he was forced to reveal what he had been doing. This led to a panic in the market, as the fall in the value of those stocks with which he was associated provoked a general collapse. In turn, that was then overtaken by the collapse in New York, bringing down stocks worldwide. If that had been all that had happened it would have been nothing more than a severe but inevitable correction in the market as a speculative boom came to an end. As it was, given the United States' position as the most important creditor nation and the unstable conditions that were a legacy of the war, the collapse on Wall Street caused a general financial panic which had severe international repercussions. Throughout the world national financial systems experienced major problems as banks failed and credit contracted, bringing down businesses and creating depression in its wake. In the past these financial panics would have been stabilized through adjustments in the City of London markets as money and assets flowed between countries, interest rates rose and the prices of securities fell. However, the City of London did not have the financial strength to stabilize the international financial system or even resist damaging speculation against the pound. In September 1931, Britain was forced off the gold standard as the world economy slipped into depression and an era of economic nationalism in which each country erected barriers to restrict the free flow of goods and money. This was exceedingly damaging for the City of London, which had thrived as the financial and commercial centre of an open world economy. Even more than in the 1920s, those firms and markets in the City that relied for their existence on international business suffered very badly. Government intervention, in the shape of exchange controls or a freeze on payments abroad, left many in the City with large losses as they could not recover the money they had lent to clients abroad. Those without adequate reserves either collapsed or barely survived. None of this was the fault of the firms themselves but was due to the completely changed circumstances within which they now operated.

The result of the 1931 financial crisis on the City was to create an international environment that was positively hostile to its operations though trade barriers and exchange controls. This did not affect all in the City equally as those whose business was with the empire, excluding Canada, or more properly the Sterling Area, still performed their traditional role of organizing and financing trade, employing short-term funds, issuing securities and providing markets – though all to a smaller extent than before 1914 or even the 1920s. Conversely, those whose business had been with areas such as continental Europe and the United States, or in sectors like shipping or international credit, suffered badly with the collapse of global commercial and financial transactions. They had no choice but to look elsewhere for business, either in the empire or domestically, if they wanted to survive. Consequently, the City's involvement with the British economy grew even stronger in the 1930s, both through new firms being set up catering for domestic borrowers and established ones undertaking whatever business was available. In the 1920s, for example, most of the new issues for domestic industrial and commercial companies had been left to stockbrokers or smaller and less well-established merchant banks, whereas in the 1930s all in the City were competing for the business. The merchant banking firm Schroders opened an office in Birmingham in 1936, whereas before it had confined its operations to the international sphere. Thus, the new issue market in the 1930s catered increasingly for the issues of industrial companies as the international business died away in the face of government-imposed barriers and world economic instability. Investor preference was for security, and this was to be found in the shape of the shares and debentures issued by British companies either serving the domestic market or producing commodities abroad like gold, oil and rubber, as these were in world demand. By 1939, there were 1,712 publicly quoted British companies with a market value of £2.5 billion. It is thus somewhat curious that the City of London is perceived to be little involved with the British economy in the 1930s when the evidence from recent research indicates that even those merchant banks that had largely confined themselves to international finance were now making issues for domestic industrial firms.

Throughout the interwar years, and especially after the events of 1931, the government had an increasing influence over the City. What had been established during the war was a close relationship between the government, the Treasury and the Bank of England that was much more intimate than in the past. Now the government, through the Treasury, was using the Bank of England to influence or direct the City in line with changing policy requirements. In the 1930s for instance, the discount houses were being used by the Bank of England as a means of controlling lending in the City. For the first time, the British government was seeking to obtain direct benefits for itself from the fact that the world's most important financial centre was located in Britain. This was most obviously seen in the influence the government used to discourage the use of the City of London by international borrowers as this would put pressure on sterling. Both before the return to the gold standard in 1925, and in the aftermath of the financial crisis of 1931, the government was successful in preventing foreign issues in London. Subsequently, with the introduction of exchange controls, after Britain left the gold standard, and the creation of the

Exchange Equalization Account, the government gained control over much of the City's external transactions. Domestically, the government's position as the dominant borrower in both the money and capital markets had already given it an enormous influence over the availability and use of funds by domestic borrowers. The main activity in the London money market in the 1930s became short-term lending to the British government, rather than the finance of international trade and investment. Essentially, the compartmentalization that took place in the world economy in the 1930s, especially through exchange controls and other barriers, gave governments far greater control over their national economies than in the pre-1914 era. Thus it was the British government, acting through the Bank of England, that was in a position to set British interest rates rather than the market, which had been the case before the war.

Generally, the interwar years were difficult ones for many of the small firms that had thrived in the City before 1914 and had made it such a dynamic financial centre. The war itself had left a legacy of hostility towards foreigners, especially Germans, while the far greater level of government control, legislation and taxation affecting domestic and international operations favoured the large banks with permanent clerical and specialist staffs. Nevertheless, many of these smaller firms did find profitable niches for themselves within the City, such as small company finance, while others were able to exploit their established international connections to enter the foreign exchange market. At the end of the 1930s, there were around 140 banks and thirty brokers engaged in foreign exchange dealing in the City of London. Those firms that showed themselves to be flexible and responsive were able to survive while others did not. However, the problems being faced by many in the City were hidden from public view because it was these small, private firms that were suffering the most while the large banks and insurance companies appeared to be prospering, in contrast to much of British manufacturing industry. There was also little public understanding of the causes of exchange rate fluctuations, stock exchange speculation or the cautious lending policies adopted by bankers. Instead, the City was perceived as having failed, both in domestic and international terms, with the only solution being greatly increased state control. This had already grown in importance with the First World War, and then again with the 1931 financial crisis, but it was felt that even more was required if the various institutions, firms and markets of the City were to be made to serve national ends. What this reflected was a general disenchantment with markets. They were blamed for the economic problems experienced by Britain between the war, rather than the unstable conditions that existed at the end of the First World War, and which then plagued the entire interwar period.

Despite all the difficulties it experienced, the City of London remained the most important financial centre in the world even by the end of the 1930s. No other centre could match the network of connections that the City continued to maintain, with around two-thirds of the world's banks having some kind of representation there. This provided the basis for a vast amount and variety of international business, as did the fact that Britain remained a major creditor nation with around £3.5 billion in overseas assets in 1938. Nevertheless, symptomatic of the City's decline as an international financial centre was the fact that the staff employed at Société Générale's London office had fallen to ninety-three in 1935, or by one-third of the pre-war level. However, much of this decline was due to the collapse of international business of all kinds in the world in the 1930s, rather than competition from other financial centres such as New York, Paris or Amsterdam. Rival centres had undermined London's position in the 1920s but the financial and monetary crises in the years after 1929 had done much to reduce this threat, especially that coming from New York. By default, the City of London remained the most important financial centre in the world in the 1930s. Nevertheless, as the City's international business shrank between the wars, both through competition from abroad and from the collapse of such business generally, it became more and more identified with the services that it provided for the British economy. In turn, that exposed it to growing criticism and demands for reform by those who held the City of London responsible for Britain's economic problems, through the failures of its banks and markets to provide sufficient finance and stable conditions. What the research conducted by financial historians over the last few years has now established is that much of that criticism is misplaced. Both the City of London and British banking were as much victims of the economic problems that beset Britain between the wars as were other sectors of the economy, but they proved more resilient and capable of change.

No longer is it acceptable in British history to make sweeping statements condemning either or both British banking and the City of London for the economic misfortunes that overtook the British economy between the wars. Certainly there were weaknesses in both banking and the City. However, such was the magnitude of the economic problems and their global nature that it is unrealistic to blame either banks or the City for them. All economies suffered crises and collapses at this time and, taken over the entire interwar period, Britain's do not seem any worse than those of Germany, France or the United States. Instead, it is possible to see British banking changing and adapting successfully throughout the 1900–39 period, proving itself one of the most robust and successful in the world in the face of severe monetary and financial turmoil. This was true not only domestically, where British banks did not need to be rescued by the state, but also internationally, for British overseas banks surmounted the problems that beset the economies within which they operated.

Even more impressive was the City of London. This had reached a peak of global importance in 1914 that left it without peer. Though seriously affected by the First World War, the City recovered much international business in the 1920s, only to see it decline again in the depression of the 1930s. Nevertheless, the City survived those difficulties better than most other financial centres, especially New York, while increasingly refocusing on domestic business. Therefore, if both banking and the City are examined on their own merits, rather than as an adjunct to an industrial economy, what becomes clear is how successful they were both in profiting from the expansionary times before 1914 and surviving the deflationary years between the wars. Even when studied in terms of their contribution to manufacturing, what emerges is the growth and intensification of contact between the City and industry after the war, but the inability to assist in the face of intractable problems.

NOTES

1   J. M. Keynes, 'The prospects of money, November 1914', *Economic Journal*, 24 (1914), p. 633.

2   A. W. Kirkaldy, ed., *British Finance during and after the War, 1914–21* (London, 1921), p. 115, cf. p. 120.

3   Committee on Finance and Industry, *Report* (London, 1931), p. 161.

4   C. Fohlin, 'Bank securities holdings and industrial finance before World War I: Britain and Germany compared', *Business and Economic History*, 26 (1997), p. 465.

5   Committee on Finance and Industry Q 7285.

6   D. Jay, *The Nation's Wealth at the Nation's Service* (Labour party pamphlet, 1938), p. 6; quoted in R. Coopey and D. Clarke, *3i: Fifty Years Investing in Industry* (Oxford, 1995), p. 14.

7   L. D. Wilgress, 'The London money market', *Journal of the Canadian Bankers Association*, 20 (1912/13), p. 210.

8   W. W. Swanson, 'London and New York as financial centres', *Journal of the Canadian Bankers Association*, 22 (1914/15), p. 198.

FURTHER READING

Best, M. and Humphries, J., 'The City and industrial decline', in B. Elbaum and W. Lazonick, eds, *The Decline of the British Economy* (Oxford, 1986).

Bowden, S. and Collins, M., 'The Bank of England, industrial regeneration and hire purchase between the wars', *Economic History Review*, 45 (1992).

Capie, F. and Collins, M., *Have the Banks Failed British Industry?* (London, 1992).

Collins, M., *Money and Banking in the UK: A History* (London, 1988).

Collins, M., *Banks and Industrial Finance in Britain, 1800–1939* (London, 1991).

Collins, M., 'English bank development within a European context, 1870–1939', *Economic History Review*, 51 (1998).

Daunton, M. J., ' "Gentlemanly capitalism" and British industry 1820–1914', *Past and Present*, 122 (1989).

Garside, W. R. and Greaves, J. I., 'The Bank of England and industrial intervention in inter-war Britain', *Financial History Review*, 3 (1996).

Ingham, G., *Capitalism Divided? The City and Industry in British Development* (London, 1984).

Jones, G., *British Multinational Banking, 1830–1990* (Oxford, 1993).

Kennedy, W. P., *Industrial Structure, Capital Markets and the Origins of British Economic Decline* (Cambridge, 1987).

Marchildon, G. P., 'British investment banking and industrial decline before the Great War', *Business History*, 33 (1991).

Michie, R. C., *The City of London: Continuity and Change since 1850* (London, 1992).

Michie, R. C., *The London Stock Exchange: A History* (Oxford, 1999).

Newton, S. and Porter, G., *Modernization Frustrated: The Politics of Industrial Decline in Britain since 1900* (London, 1988).

Peters, J., 'The British government and the City–industry divide: the case of the 1914 financial crisis', *Twentieth-Century British History*, 4 (1993).

Roberts, R., 'The City of London as a financial centre in the era of the Depression, the Second World War and post-war official controls', in A. Gorst, L. Johnman and W. Scott Lucas, eds, *Contemporary British History 1931–61* (London, 1991).

Roberts, R. and Kynaston, D., eds, *The Bank of England: Money, Power and Influence, 1694–1994* (Oxford, 1995).

Ross, D. M., 'The clearing banks and the finance of British industry, 1930–1959', *Business and Economic History*, 20 (1991).

Ross, D. M., 'Commercial banking in a market-orientated financial system: Britain between the wars', *Economic History Review*, 49 (1996).

Sayers, R. S., *The Bank of England, 1891–1944* (Cambridge, 1976).

Thomas, W. A., *The Finance of British Industry 1918–76* (London, 1978).

Watson, K., 'Banks and industrial finance: the experience of brewers, 1880–1913', *Economic History Review*, 49 (1996).

Williams, D., 'London and the 1931 financial crisis', *Economic History Review*, 15 (1962/3).

Williamson, P., 'Financiers, the gold standard and British politics, 1925–1931', in J. Turner, *Businessmen and Politics* (London, 1984).

CHAPTER SEVENTEEN

Agriculture, Agrarian Society and the Countryside

PETER DEWEY

Introduction and Overview: Agriculture 1900–1939

To place the development of British agriculture in the early twentieth century in a proper historic perspective, one has to go back to the middle of the nineteenth century, and the aftermath of the repeal of the Corn Laws in 1846. In the next few decades, the fears of protectionists that repeal would bring a flood of imported corn failed to materialize. It was not until the 1870s that substantial imports of wheat flowed across the Atlantic from the newly developed plains of the US Midwest. These were accompanied by chilled and frozen beef, lamb and mutton from South America, Australia and New Zealand, and dairy produce from Holland and Denmark. By 1909–13, imports accounted for about 60 per cent of the total supply of calories in the UK, the figure being highest (about 80 per cent) for wheat.[1]

From the national point of view, this situation would pose a serious threat in the event of war. The threat became a reality after 1914. The most serious situation occurred in 1917, when the policy of the German government changed to one of sinking all ships in British home waters. The British government responded with measures to economize on food, and instituted a programme of food production, encouraging farmers to plough up grassland formerly devoted to livestock and grow potatoes and cereals instead. This requirement was backed up by the inducement of guaranteed prices to be paid to growers for wheat and oats. In this way, more people could be fed per acre of farmland. These policies were successful, and 2.13 million acres of grassland in Britain were converted to crops in 1916–18, raising the total area under the plough from 10.23 million acres in 1916 to 12.36 million acres in 1918.[2]

In 1918, the cereal price guarantees were extended for a further six years, since world wheat supplies were still uncertain, having been disrupted during the war. As world prices were rising rapidly, farmers enjoyed a brief boom. This boom turned to bust at the end of 1920, when world food prices collapsed. The price fall was largest in cereals. The government, alarmed at the prospect of having to pay out large sums of compensation to farmers through the operation of the guarantees, responded by dropping the commitment to guarantee cereal prices. Although prices stabilized by the end of 1923, the damage had been done. Farmers' incomes had been lowered substantially, and they were now faced with the problem of converting redundant cereal land back to grass, since the prices of grassland products (meat and milk) had fallen least. To make things worse, many tenant farmers took advantage of their high incomes in 1919–20 to purchase their farms from their landlords. So high mortgage payments were now added to their woes. For the rest of the 1920s, farm incomes were very low, and farmers were scratching around for new ways of making a living.[3]

The next crisis to occur was that of the Great Depression of 1929–32. Once again world prices fell, and in particular the price of cereals. Farm incomes also fell. But this time, the severity of the depression produced a change in national policy. The British government went back to general protection in 1932, when the Import Duties Act imposed a minimum tariff of 10 per cent on imported goods. The agricultural counterpart of this began in the same year, with the Wheat Act, which offered a bounty for farmers growing wheat. It was followed by a variety of marketing schemes and marketing boards for meat, other crops, bacon, potatoes, and most notably milk in the form of the Milk Marketing Board. Agricultural product prices began to recover after 1932, and the worst of the depression was over. But, as in the 1920s, salvation came most immediately to grassland producers. The lot of cereal producers in the 1930s was not easy. In the regions which for climatic or topographic reasons could not easily be converted to grassland, especially those eastern regions of England such as East Anglia, a certain amount of land 'went back', or was in effect abandoned. The final act of the 1930s was the start of renewed preparations for war. Once more farmers would be asked to plough up grassland, and in 1939 the government offered a grant of £2 per acre for farmers to do so.[4]

The continuing dependence on food imports which had developed in the nineteenth century meant that by 1914 about 60 per cent of the British calorie supply was imported. This ratio fell slightly in 1917–19, but thereafter rose again. By 1939, it was about 70 per cent. Thus in spite of the protectionist measures of the 1930s, the British people were less self-sufficient than on the eve of the First World War.[5]

Agriculture

The place of agriculture in the national economy had been shrinking since the beginning of the industrial revolution. By the end of the nineteenth century, in 1891, the income of agriculture had fallen to 8.6 per cent of the total British national income; by 1924 it was down to 4.1 per cent.[6]

The hugely expanding British population of the nineteenth century (from 9 million in 1801 to 40 million in 1911), coupled with rapid urbanization and rising living standards, had changed the demand for British foodstuffs. Farmers had moved away from supplying the 'inferior' foods such as cereals and potatoes to the 'superior' foods of meat, milk and dairy products. By 1914, the structure of agricultural output was dominated by meat and milk. In 1909–13, the value of total British farm output averaged £166 million a year, of which £64 million's worth was meat, and £24 million's worth was milk. Wheat was worth only £8 million, and the three major cereals combined (wheat, oats and barley) only £16 million. In the next couple of decades, the emphasis on meat and milk grew, milk being an especially buoyant market.[7]

Table 17.1 Agricultural land use in Britain, 1900–38 (million acres)

	1900	1918	1925	1932	1938
Permanent grass	16.7	15.9	16.5	17.4	17.4
Arable land	15.7	15.8	13.9	12.4	11.9
(of which, tillage =	10.9	12.4	9.8	8.5	8.5)
All crops and grass	32.4	29.2	30.5	29.8	29.3

Arable land = crops and temporary grassland.
Tillage = land under crops other than grass.
Source: Ministry of Agriculture, *A Century of Agricultural Statistics 1866–1966* (London, 1968), tables 41–44.

The changes in farm output led to changes in land use. Overall, the amount of land available for farming was shrinking, as town and road development expanded into rural areas. The area of farmland in Britain fell, the total area of agricultural land [= all crops and grass] reducing from 32.4 million acres in 1900 to 29.3 million in 1938. But within the 'national farm', there were substantial changes. These can be seen in the changing proportions of grassland, arable land and tillage (table 17.1).

The greatest changes in crops occurred during the First World War and in the post-war readjustment. In 1917 and 1918, the drive to expand cereal production meant that a large area of permanent grass was ploughed up. In those two years, 2.1 million acres of grass were converted to tillage. The acreage of wheat rose from 1.97 million acres to 2.64 million acres, and that of oats from 3.07 to 4.02 million acres. The agricultural crisis of 1920–3 meant the reversal of this process, and the area of grass steadily rose again until the mid-1930s.

There were two new crops of significance in the 1920s. The first was timber; the Forestry Commission was established in 1919, in order to increase home-grown timber supplies. The second was sugar beet; in 1925, to reduce dependence on imports, the government offered a subsidy to sugar beet growers. The new crop took most readily in Norfolk and Suffolk, where it formed a useful offset to the loss of income consequent on the reduction in cereals. By 1935, 375,000 acres of sugar beet were being cultivated, and the temporary subsidy had been made permanent.

Changes in land use were accompanied by changes in livestock. The most notable change was the rise in the numbers of dairy cattle. The dairy herd rose steadily during the 1920s. In 1901–15, there had been an average of 2.19 million cows or heifers in milk or calf; by 1931–5, the average was 2.93 million, and new supplying areas had been developed in the Cotswolds and on the downlands of south-west England. There was also an upsurge of milk production in the midland and eastern counties, especially in the Nene and Welland valleys of Northamptonshire. By 1930, at least 75 per cent of all milk sold off farms was sold into the urban liquid milk market, rather than being made into butter or cheese. The sheep flock diminished, as the old corn-and-sheep systems of the southern downlands proved uneconomic. The national pig herd rose, as demand for pork and bacon grew, although imports proved very competitive. Much attention was given, especially by small producers, to raising poultry and eggs, but this was also subject to stiff import competition. In spite of this, the national poultry flock rose, from 32 million fowls in 1900 to 60 million in 1939.[8]

Technical Advance and Mechanization

For the most part this period was one of hiatus. The broader lines of technical and mechanical advance had been laid down in the late nineteenth century, and the revolutionary advances of post-1940 were yet to come. Although pioneering work was being done on grassland productivity at the Welsh Plant Breeding Institute and at the Jealotts Hill research station in Berkshire, too often grass was the poor relative of cereals when it came to using fertilizers. As ever, the main farm fertilizer was animal manure. 'Artificial' (manufactured) fertilizers had been produced as far back as 1843, and they continued to make progress in this period. Yet the decline in cereals, and the disinterest in grassland fertilization, weakened the market for artificials. In the early 1930s, when ICI's new factory at Billingham for the production of ammonium sulphate came on stream, the world market collapsed, and ICI was left with an unmarketable surplus.

For animal feeding stuffs, the main source was cereals grown on the farm, supplemented with waste grains from breweries and distilleries. The shortage of feeds during the war led to more research on animal nutrition, especially at Cambridge, with the work of Professor T. B. Wood, director of the Research Institute for Animal Nutrition. This publicized the idea that animal feed could be calculated scientifically, in order to maintain the animal's metabolism, and the feed ration varied as required in relation to production targets. These ideas were quickly taken up by the feedstuffs industry, and by the mid-1920s it was producing compounded feeds with guaranteed proportions of starch and protein and of minerals, for dairy cows, pigs and poultry.[9]

Progress in mechanization revolved around the question of the tractor. The bulk of tractive power on farms, whether used directly on the land or in haulage operations, was supplied by the farm horse. Although the numbers of horses on farms declined steadily (especially rapidly after the mid-1920s), from 1,078,000 in 1900 to 649,000 in 1939, they had not been replaced by the tractor. However, these were the official figures, which have been questioned by E. J. T. Collins, who suggests that they may overstate the number of agricultural horses by as much as c.170,000 in 1910. During the First World War, a start had been made with the use of the internal combustion-engined tractor. By the end of the war, farmers had the use of about 9,000 tractors (mainly Fordsons and International Titans) purchased by the government for the ploughing-up campaign, and about 12,000 imported ones, which they had purchased privately in 1917–18. Many observers thought that the tractor would carry all before it. But technically the tractor was not yet suitable. It was prone to break down, its moving parts were too exposed to grit and dust, little thought had been given to designing implements specifically for use with the tractor, and the wheels it used were not suitable for road work. But in the 1930s the market grew, partly due to the reduction in the price of tractors, partly due to the opening of the Fordson tractor factory at Dagenham in 1932, and partly because tractors were improved; low-pressure tyres made them suitable for road and field work, and they became more reliable. By the end of the 1930s, the national stock in Britain had risen to about 52,000.[10]

Two minor mechanical developments are worth mentioning; the progress of milking machines was slowed by technical inadequacies. It was not until the late 1920s that the materials used in their construction were long-lasting enough to withstand steam sterilization, which was essential for hygiene. The other development, which remained something of a curiosity, was the combine harvester, the first of these being employed in 1928. Most machines were imported. But their high cost and limited working season meant that they were not economic propositions in the cereal world of the 1930s. Even in 1942, when the first reliable machinery census was taken, there were only 940 in use.[11]

Farms and Farmers

There was, and is, no adequate definition of what constitutes a farm or a farmer. About a quarter of a million people described themselves as farmers at the population census every ten years, but the annual Ministry of Agriculture returns recorded many more 'agricultural holdings'. In 1925, there were recorded in England and Wales some 406,000 agricultural holdings, of which about 75,000 were between one and five acres. It is probably safe to conclude that these latter were not really farms but accommodation land for butchers and others, parkland, private gardens and so on. Of the remaining holdings, almost all of which must have been farms or parts of farms, 189,000 were between 5 and 50 acres, 128,000 were between 50 and 300 acres and 13,000 were over 300 acres. The contemporary view was that, depending on the type of land, anything under 50 acres (or sometimes 100 acres) would be worked by the labour of a farmer and his family alone, without outside assistance.[12]

Farms and farmers varied across the nation. Generally, there was a correlation between farm size and topography. The smaller farms were found in the upland regions of the west and north-west of Britain. There was also a correlation with type of crop. Farms were largest in the corn belt, which stretched up eastern England from Suffolk, finishing in east Lothian. The larger farms thus tended to be more cereal-specialist and use more machinery; they were the most likely to use tractors.

One of the factors making for differentiation in farmers was the British system of capital provision; tenant farmers were expected to provide their own working capital. On the eve of the First World War this was reckoned at about £10 an acre, and it was much the same after the fall in prices after 1920. Henry Williamson, who bought a run-down 240-acre farm in Norfolk in 1937, paid £2,250 for the farm, and put £1,601 of working capital into it in his first year of farming (including a tractor for £360). There was little to be had in common financially (and socially) between a largish owner like Williamson or a large tenant farmer like A. G. Street, who farmed two farms with a total of 600 acres in south Wiltshire downland after 1918 (he bought them from his landowner later that year), and a smallholder like Joseph Ashby, who worked his way up from being a farm labourer to become a respected small farmer in Oxfordshire. While the larger farmer could take his place as a member of the rural middle class, the small farmer was often little better off financially than agricultural labourers, taking into account the need for a reasonable return on his capital.[13]

Farm Labourers

Although the hired farm labour force had been declining since the 1850s, when there had been over 1 million full-time hired labourers in England and Wales, there were still 685,000 in 1921. Since the smaller farms tried to avoid hiring labour, these labourers were mainly to be found on the larger holdings. The rough rule of thumb before the First World War was that a large mixed farm (part arable, part grass) would require about two labourers to every 50 acres. Since it was the larger farms that bought tractors after 1918, this labour requirement presumably fell, but by how much is unclear. The majority of labourers (about two-thirds) were what is referred to as 'unskilled', although they actually had an impressive range of farm skills. The 'skilled' men were those in charge of animals – horses, cattle and sheep. The aristocrats of the farm, after 1918 as before, were the horsemen. If engaged in ploughing (and most of them were), this meant a long working day: getting up at about 4 a.m., feeding and watering the horses, harnessing them, and leading them to the field, to begin ploughing at about 6 a.m. in the summer. Field work would finish at about 3 or 4 p.m., when the horses would be returned to their stables. After supper there was more evening work, as the horses were given their final feed of the day and prepared for the night. Cattlemen had similar hours and a similar routine. Shepherds had to work long hours also, and spent much time in the open air supervising their flocks. All three were involved in the birth and care of young livestock. The unskilled labourers had the shortest working week, but the lowest wage and the least opportunity to earn more money by working overtime, although there was the possibility of piecework in the growing season and in the hay and corn harvest on the larger arable farms.[14]

The variation in working hours and responsibilities meant that wages were structured accordingly. Those in charge of animals were paid more than the general, 'unskilled' labourers. During the First World War, the government had instituted a central Agricultural Wages Board (AWB), with county sub-boards, which specified minimum wages for all labourers, with standard hours of work and overtime payments accordingly. Many farmers resented the rulings of the AWB. The central AWB was abolished in 1921, to be replaced by county committees, which were largely ineffective. The central AWB was reinstated in 1924, although it was not able to counter the sharp fall in wages that had occurred in the general deflation of 1920–3. During most of the 1920s, the average minimum wage settled at about £1.50–£1.60 a week.[15]

Landowners

By 1900, the well-known tripartite division of effort in British agriculture was established: landless labourers, tenant farmers who provided working capital, and landowners who provided the land, the farmstead and the fixed capital of the farm. Most farmers were tenants; in 1909, it is estimated that only about 13 per cent of all farm holdings in England were owner-occupied. This changed substantially after 1918; rents had been held down during the war, although land values had risen sharply, and many landowners took the opportunity to sell off the farms to their tenants. In their turn, the tenants, who had high incomes to spend, saw this as the opportunity to own their own property. Most of the land sales took place in 1918–21, but there was a continuing trickle during the rest of the interwar period. By 1927, about 37 per cent of all farms were owner-occupied.[16]

The abandonment of farmland by the former owners was a sound move financially; they thus escaped the problems of low agricultural incomes (and thus rents) after 1920. If they invested the resulting capital wisely (e.g. in urban property or newer industries), they improved their financial position. On the other hand, the property-owning classes had lost investments in Europe and further afield during the war, and faced the prospect of higher income taxes, death duties and cost of living after 1918. Some of the more aristocratic took refuge abroad, or took up directorships on company boards. Some of the greatest aristocrats had long since moved out of farming in any case, and were more concerned with realizing the capital value of their urban property. Dorchester House, in London's Park Lane, was replaced by the Dorchester hotel. But for those owners who decided to stay in farmland after 1920, the prospect was bleak. The capital value of land fell even after the deflation had more or less stopped in 1923. Land values fell even more with the depression of the early 1930s, and it was especially the case in the eastern counties. By then, land agents were prepared to let large farms at a little or no rent, merely to have them tenanted and worked. In the early 1930s in Suffolk, a land agent offered the seventeen-year-old Hugh Barrett, a middle-class farm pupil with less than a year's experience, a 200-acre farm tenancy rent free for the first two years.[17]

Incomes and Profits

There are considerable difficulties in working out the value of farm output, and thus of agricultural incomes. The most recent estimate of gross output (i.e., the value of output sold off farms) has the virtue of presenting output at current prices and also in constant prices, thus allowing us to delete the effects of price changes in calculating the volume of output, as well as to get an idea of what the income of the industry was at the time (table 17.2).

Table 17.2 Gross output of British agriculture, 1904–39 (£ million)

	At current prices £ million	At constant (1986) prices £ million	%
1904–10	170	3,400	100
1911–13	188	3,352	99
1914–19	334	3,347	98
1920–2	409	3,265	96
1923–9	284	3,335	98
1930–4	245	3,681	108
1935–9	293	4,134	122

Source: P. Brassley, 'Output and technical change in twentieth-century British agriculture', *Agricultural History Review*, 48, part 1 (2000), table A4.

Table 17.3   Shares of UK farm output, 1920–39

	Wages %	Rent %	Farmers' income %	Total output £ million
1920–2	36	16	48	211
1924–9	43	24	33	180
1930–4	40	23	37	187
1935–9	37	19	44	186

Source: R. Perren, *Agriculture in Depression, 1870–1940* (Cambridge, 1995), table 6.

Table 17.2 shows that the farming industry's current income was rising modestly before the First World War and then rose sharply, especially in the post-war inflation of 1920–2. Thereafter, current income declined considerably, until reviving somewhat in the later 1930s. But even then, the money value of output was less than it had been during the First World War.

Expressing the gross output of the industry in constant price terms (i.e., assuming that the prices of farm products did not change, so that we are measuring the volume of output rather than its value) tells a different story. For most of this period, the volume of output is static and does not begin to rise until the 1930s, the rise being especially rapid in the late 1930s.

Out of this total output/income, farming had to pay for its fixed and variable costs, and provide a living for the three groups of people involved – landowners, farmers and labourers. An estimate for 1909–13 suggests that, after paying for rent and wages, and other current costs such as seed, fertilizer, feed and machinery, farmers could retain about one-third of the gross output of the industry (i.e., that which was sold off farms) as their income. What happened to this share of total farm income after the First World War may be estimated from table 17.3.[18]

The fortunes of the different groups in agriculture fluctuated over this period. In 1920–2, wartime rents had not made good their losses, wage rates had risen, and the residual income available to farmers was high. By the middle of the 1920s, rents had caught up to some extent, wages were even higher as a proportion of the total, and the farmers' residual income was severely squeezed. The proportions had not changed much by the early 1930s, but by the end of this decade the rent proportion had once more fallen; the farm labourers proved unable to raise wages; farmers' residual income rose accordingly.

Agricultural Politics and Policies

The repeal of the Corn Laws in 1846 had dealt a resounding political blow to the agricultural interest. By 1900, the urban electorate was firmly opposed to import duties on food. This was seen clearly in the controversy surrounding the Tariff Reform League, and the associated idea of imperial preference promulgated by Joseph Chamberlain. This advocated tariffs on imported foodstuffs, while allowing the free entry into Britain of food from the British Empire. This proposal was defeated at the general election of 1906. After 1906, a Liberal government was in power, with a large majority in the House of Commons. The Liberal party was clearly opposed to tariffs, was concerned about low wages in agriculture and the poor quality of rural housing, and some sections of it wanted to promote smallholdings for agricultural labourers as a sort of 'farming ladder' by which landless labourers could eventually become farmers. But most of the parliamentary effort of the party was directed to the consequences of Lloyd George's 'people's budget' of 1910. This envisaged a substantial development tax on land values, which was opposed by the Conservative party. The government also raised the level of death duties, and this caused opposition, especially in the House of Lords, with its Conservative majority. Generally, the Conservative party supported landowners and farmers, and was against greater control of farm matters by government. The nascent Labour party did not have a clear policy on agriculture, and different groups in the party supported a nationalized agriculture, the expropriation of landlords, or the promotion of smallholdings.

After 1914, party disagreements on agricultural policy were held in abeyance for a while. By the end of the war, farming had become a controlled industry; cropping policy, food prices, rents and labourers' wages were all controlled by government. Farmers were subject to planning directives and other matters affecting good cultivation from the wartime County War Agricultural Executive Committees, and could even be dispossessed or at least fined for non-compliance. The question of post-war policy now had to be considered. For the time being the County War Agricultural Executive Committees continued in being, although shorn of their compulsory powers. The minimum wage was also maintained. Encouraged by the (somewhat contradictory) reports of a Royal Commission on Agriculture (1919), the government decided to keep the incentives to grow cereals. This was partly because the future of imported corn supplies was uncertain, and partly because it was held unfair suddenly to withdraw support from the farming industry. This decision was enshrined in the Agriculture Act of December 1920, which continued minimum prices to farmers for wheat and oats (although not barley, in deference to the temperance lobby), and committed the government to giving four years' notice to farmers of a decision to withdraw the guarantees. However, almost as soon as the Act was passed, its economic justification disappeared. Large imports of grain were resumed, and cereal prices plummeted. In June 1921, wheat fetched 89s. 3d. (£4.46) a quarter, and this fell to 45s. 8d. (£2.28) in December. The government took fright at the prospect of paying large amounts in guaranteed payments to farmers, especially since it had decided not to assist other industries also affected by the sudden depression, and in June 1921 announced the repeal of the Act, to take effect in August. Compensation amounting to nearly £20 million was paid to farmers in Britain.[19]

The abandonment of the guarantees was not unwelcome to the farming interest. The political cry of a 'Great Betrayal' was raised, but farmers had on the whole not welcomed government control. The prices they had received for their produce in the war had in any case been higher than the official level of guarantees. They also resented the control of wages by the Agricultural Wages Boards, and undoubtedly welcomed the abolition of the central AWB in October 1921.

The brief Labour government of 1924 did little to change agricultural policy. The major innovation was the restoration of the central AWB. Although less effective than its predecessor, it is likely that this mechanism prevented wages falling further in the 1920s than they did; it at least provided some publicity in the more notorious cases of low-paying farmers. For the rest of the 1920s, tariff protection was still ruled out politically; the Conservative party lost the general election of 1923 by adopting it. But there was some assistance given to farming; there was a subsidy for sugar beet farming, initially for ten years, in 1925. There was also some relief from local taxation (= rates), which had risen sharply in the inflationary years since 1914. By 1929, three Agricultural Rates Acts had removed all local taxation on farms in England and Wales. Similar relief from rating was given in Scotland.[20]

The second minority Labour government of 1929–31 was too much preoccupied with the depression that began almost as soon as it took office to evolve a distinctly agricultural policy, although the minister, Christopher Addison, did propose a bill to extend smallholdings. But by the end of 1931, under the impact of the enormous world depression, the political landscape had changed. There was a coalition government, the 'National' government, and it decided upon general protectionist measures. These were enshrined in the Import Duties Act of 1932. This imposed a general tariff of 10 per cent on imports. It was followed by the decisions taken at the Imperial Economic Conference held at Ottawa in the summer of 1932. This gave free entry to products from the empire, while imposing quotas and tariffs on a range of agricultural goods from European and empire countries. After the Ottawa agreements were concluded, practically the only agricultural products with unrestricted entry into the United Kingdom were cotton, wool, hides, skins and rubber. Finally, there were commercial treaties with certain foreign countries – Denmark (1933), Argentina (1933, 1936) and the United States (1938).[21]

In addition to controls over imports, the government took steps to regulate the home market. The Agricultural Marketing Acts of 1931 and 1933 allowed two-thirds of the producers in any branch of farming to adopt a marketing scheme; this then became binding on all producers. It could involve maximum and minimum prices, and restrictions on levels of output. Under these Acts there were eventually subsidies or deficiency payments for beef, pork, butter, cheese, wheat, barley and oats. Milk and bacon had statutory marketing schemes, and milk was subsidized. Hops also had a marketing scheme, and the sugar beet subsidy due to cease in 1934 was made permanent. Two notable innovations were the Wheat Act of 1932 and the Milk Marketing Board of 1933. The former guaranteed farmers a minimum price, up to a certain level of national output; this subsidy was financed by a levy on flour millers. Under this protection the wheat acreage rose by 52 per cent between 1931 and 1935. The acreages of oats and barley, being unsubsidized, fell each by a quarter of a million acres during that period. The Milk Marketing Board was a notable innovation. It was designed to bring order to a disorderly market; the large urban dairy companies had managed to force down the prices paid to farmers. The Board prevented this, and administered a common price for milk to all producers, regardless of efficiency.

The financial value of all these measures of relief taken together – tariffs, deficiency payments, rates relief and market regulation – has been estimated at £45 million in 1933, and the stimulus revived production. As can be seen from table 17.2, farm output rose above its level of the 1920s, although the level of self-sufficiency in foodstuffs was less than in 1913.[22]

One of the notable features of this period was the rise of organized agricultural interest groups. The first of these was the National Farmers' Union (NFU), formed in 1909 out of the earlier Lincolnshire Farmers' Union (1904). It grew rapidly, reaching a membership of 22,000 by 1916, when it was already a national organization, and was accepted as a representative body by the government. However, it is difficult to discern its influence on government policy in this period. It had little influence on policy in the First World War, and the policies of the National and Conservative governments in the 1930s seemed to owe little to its pressure. However, it has been argued by Penning-Rowsell that the union had a strong influence in secret in negotiations over the repeal of the 1920 Agriculture Act, persuading the government to compensate the farmers with generous payments for the 1921 crop and giving them greater freedom in wage negotiations. Thereafter, its influence waned. But in the late 1930s, as the likelihood of war grew, the NFU became much more closely involved with war preparations, and the appointment as minister of agriculture in 1938 of Reginald Dorman-Smith, a recent president of the NFU, was another mark of its increasingly influential position.[23]

The other organization of note was the National Union of Agricultural Workers (NUAW). Agricultural trade unionism had been revived in Norfolk in 1906, and by 1914 the local union had become the NUAW, with a membership of about 9,000. Bolstered by the minimum wage legislation of 1918, it grew enormously. By 1919 it covered most of England and claimed 127,000 members. In Wales, there may have been about 10,000 members in 1920. There was also the Workers' Union, active in the midlands and north of England, which in 1919 claimed 100,000 members in its agricultural branch. But farmworkers had always been difficult to organize, and low wages made it difficult to pay union subscriptions in bad times. The collapse of agricultural prosperity and agricultural wages after 1920 reduced the NUAW to no more than 35,000 between 1924 and 1936. There followed a revival, which took membership to 50,000 by 1939.

In the interwar period, little progress was made with two out of the three questions most agitating the union – low wages and the tied cottage. But there was progress with the third; in 1936, agricultural workers were included in the national insurance scheme, although with lower benefits than other manual groups. On the other hand, like the NFU, the NUAW was now part of the consultative mechanism of government and could not be ignored in the framing of policy.[24]

The Countryside and Countryside Living

By the First World War British society was firmly urban, about 75 per cent of the whole population living in towns. While most of the increase in population in this period occurred in the towns, and thus the rural proportion of the population declined, there was still sufficient growth in the countryside to raise the numbers of rural dwellers, from 8,349,000 in 1911 to 8,963,000 in 1931. Agriculture was no longer the main occupation followed by most people who lived in the countryside. However, it was still much the largest. In 1911 about 36 per cent of those working in rural districts in England and Wales were employed in agriculture, and in 1931 about 30 per cent. Taken with its ancillary industries of malting, brewing, fertilizer, feed and machinery supply, and the services of banks and estate agents, agriculture was clearly still a major force in rural life.[25]

In the country towns and villages, many of the old craftsmen and tradesmen, who were still very numerous in 1900, disappeared rapidly in the twentieth century.

The village wheelwright and miller had more or less disappeared by 1920; the black-smith was in decline. Certain professions and trades remained well entrenched in country towns: doctors, solicitors, estate agents, auctioneers, livestock dealers, corn and feed merchants and seedsmen. But shops were disappearing in smaller country towns and villages, leaving merely a general store/newsagent in place of the former ironmonger's, draper's, grocer's, butcher's, baker's and confectioner's of former times.[26]

The quality of rural housing left a lot to be desired. It had deteriorated in the nineteenth century, when farm labourers had formed a large part of the total rural labour force, and their real wages had been too low to provide a good return for landowners contemplating building cottages for their workers. In many of the older and more picturesque villages and towns, the quality of housing was poor and getting worse. Many commentators bemoaned the lack of piped water supply and mains drainage. This situation persisted into the second quarter of the twentieth century. Whereas in towns local authority house-building became a major feature of urban life, this was less so in the country. Although a large number of new houses were built in rural areas – 871,000 between 1919 and 1943 – most of these were adjacent to towns, and beyond the pocket of the farmworker. Most farmworkers inhabited tied cottages, whose quality was very variable. Local authority house-building in towns had begun in 1919, but there was little specific rural legislation until 1926 when the Rural Workers' Housing Act offered grants for the reconditioning of cottages. The Housing Act of 1930 gave subsidies to Rural District Councils for approved new houses. Overcrowding was tackled by the Housing Act of 1935; under this Act 41,928 rural houses were scheduled as overcrowded. Some grants were also made to improve water supplies. However, conditions still left a lot to be desired. Even in 1939, 25 per cent of English parishes lacked mains water supply, and more lacked mains sanitation; wells, cesspits and earth closets were prevalent.[27]

The developments in transport in this period brought the countryside closer to the towns. By the beginning of the century, the railway network was at its peak, the network British route mileage being some 20,000 miles. Before the First World War the motor car was still a rich man's toy, and there were few lorries or buses outside the towns. In the 1920s, the price of cars and motoring came down and car ownership came within the reach of the middle classes. In the countryside, small farm machinery manufacturing firms and blacksmiths and cycle shops moved into the business of selling and servicing motor vehicles. In addition, motorcycle ownership reached a peak in 1930, when there were more motorcycles on the roads than cars. Finally, the cost of cycling came down; a new bicycle could be purchased for as little as £5 in 1932, or for a few shillings a week on the instalment plan. Public transport also developed; bus services reached into the countryside, and day outings by 'charabanc', a (usually open-topped) single-decked coach, were now feasible. By the 1930s the enclosed coach was more usual, and the range greater; in 1938–9, Southdown Motor Services of Brighton ran day excursions to Oxford and as far as the Bristol area.[28]

Relations between town and country were dominated by several factors. The major one was the physical invasion of the country by towns and roads. By the 1930s, some 60,000 acres a year were being taken from the countryside for these purposes. The greatest expansion was in the London region, where bricks and mortar covered large areas of the home counties. Between 1911 and 1931, Greater London grew by 13 per cent, and by 1931 its population had reached 8.2 million, being the largest capital city in the world. This expansion was facilitated by the expansion of transport systems, chiefly the motor bus and underground railway.

Much of this development took place in ways that were inappropriate to the townsman's vision of the rural idyll. The relatively new phenomenon of 'ribbon development' emerged. There were many examples of this, lining the roads leading from the centre of towns. One notable one was Kidlington, on the northern road leading out of Oxford. The Ribbon Development Act of 1935 attempted without much success to control the process. An outstanding example of inappropriate development in the middle of the countryside was the Peacehaven estate on the downs east of Brighton: advertised as a marvellous place to retire to, it failed to expand as rapidly as anticipated, and gave the impression of a soulless imposition on the countryside.

Little was done to control development in the countryside. A series of Housing and Town Planning Acts, in 1909, 1919 and 1932, gave the local authorities the right to prevent undesirable development, but few could afford the compensation required for owners whose schemes were turned down. Even by 1942, only 3 per cent of Britain was covered by planning schemes. An alternative way of proceeding was to try to get some national and rational form of land use and control unrestricted urban development. By 1938, the idea of a 'green girdle' around London had been accepted, and confirmed in the Green Belt Act of that year.

The pressure to control development in the countryside was encouraged by an increasing awareness of the need for the urban population to have access to the countryside, for health and mental refreshment. New pressure groups emerged, such as the Ramblers' Association and the Youth Hostels' Association. The pressure for access was a development of a longstanding conflict between the rights of the public to use the countryside and the rights of landlords to control access. Anti-landlordism was particularly strong in some areas of Scotland and Wales, and in the northern industrial districts of England. It, and the pressure for public access, was championed by the Labour party and differing groups between the wars. In the 1930s, a campaign developed for the creation of 'national parks'. No government action was taken, but the issue was kept alive by such actions as the (stage-managed) 'mass trespass' on the Kinder Scout moor in the Peak District in 1932, and the Access to the Mountains Act of 1939 foreshadowed a major shift in policy after the Second World War.[29]

There were comparatively few changes in rural recreational pursuits between the wars. Those that did change did so as a result of general social changes rather than particularly rural ones. Those who lived in villages had greater access to the towns, by bicycle, motorcycle and bus or car. Access to public houses was more limited after 1916, as opening hours were restricted by the government, in the town and country alike. Fox-hunting was as popular as ever, especially amongst farmers and landowners, with a proportion of urban hunt followers. A particularly rural innovation was the Women's Institutes. The first was established in Anglesey in 1915, and between the wars new branches opened at the rate of between five and eight a week. They provided a social venue, organized charitable functions and broadened members' intellectual and social outlook through visiting speakers and outings.[30]

Images of the Countryside

By the 1930s, the countryside and country living had various images in the minds of town-dwellers. One image was that of freedom – to hike, cycle or motor, whether just for a day's outing or for an annual holiday. Another was of rustic sentimentality – ancient retired farm labourers quaffing their ale on the bench outside a weatherbeaten and romantic public house. This merged into a kind of 'Olde England', rather Hollywood view of the countryside, perhaps best exemplified in such tourist attractions as the well-preserved village of Broadway in Worcestershire, or in Stratford-upon-Avon, with timber-framed houses and rapidly developing Shakespearean attractions. On a more mundane level, the period saw the development of rustic petrol filling stations and mock-Tudor teashops, provoking the wrath of a self-appointed minority, who made it their mission to defend the rural experience. Such aesthetes, whose enjoyment of the countryside was based on books rather than on personal experience, had a multitude of printed sources to draw on, all describing the precious and cherished heritage of the 'real' England. As *The Morris Owners' Road Book* put it: 'the pretty villages, the farmsteads, and numberless quaint features to be found in our old towns all reach out from those bygone centuries and captivate us with their reminiscences of ancient peace'.[31] A rather romantic view of social relations in the countryside was provided by Mary Webb's novel *Precious Bane*, which drew praise from the prime minister Stanley Baldwin, whose liking for the countryside (and especially keeping pigs) was well known. This literary genre of rural sentimentality was devastatingly satirized by Stella Gibbons's book *Cold Comfort Farm* in 1932. For those unmoved by imaginative literature, the countryside offered a chance to assume a political attitude. Politically, attitudes to the countryside ranged from an emotional nationalism, such as that of Henry Williamson at one end of the political spectrum, to, at the other end, a radical, levelling dislike of private property and landownership in the countryside. Finally, there was a growing feeling in the 1930s that farming had been neglected for too long, and that the heritage of the countryside was at risk. Thus political action to temper the effects of the depression antedated the rise of the Nazi government, although the latter event spurred further action.

NOTES

1 P. E. Dewey, *British Agriculture in the First World War* (London, 1989), table 2.7.

2 Ibid., ch. 8; Ministry of Agriculture, *A Century of Agricultural Statistics 1866–1966* (London, 1968), tables 41–44.

3 E. H. Whetham, *The Cambridge Agrarian History of England and Wales*, vol. 8, *1914–1939* (Cambridge, 1978), ch. 9.

4 Whetham, *Cambridge Agrarian History*, chs 10, 13; R. Perren, *Agriculture in Depression, 1870–1940* (Cambridge, 1995), ch. 5.

5 Dewey, *British Agriculture*, table 2.7; K. A. H. Murray, *Agriculture* (History of the Second World War: Civil Series, London, 1955), p. 242.

6 B. R. Mitchell and P. Deane, *Abstract of British Historical Statistics* (Cambridge, 1962), pp. 60–1, 366; figures are for agriculture, forestry and horticulture.

7 Dewey, *British Agriculture*, appendix D.

8 Ministry of Agriculture, *Century of Agricultural Statistics*, tables 41–44, 64, 65, 69; D. Taylor, 'Growth and structural change in the English dairy industry, *c.*1860–1930', *Agricultural History Review*, 35, part 1 (1987), pp. 62–3.

9 P. E. Dewey, *War and Progress: Britain 1914–1945* (London, 1997), p. 97; Whetham, *Cambridge Agrarian History*, pp. 194–9.

10 E. J. T. Collins, *Power Availability and Agricultural Productivity in England and Wales 1840–1939* (Rural History Centre, University of Reading, Discussion Paper No. 1, 1996), pp. 3, 7; E. J. T. Collins, 'The agricultural tractor in Britain', in K. Winkel and K. Herrmann, eds, *The Development of Agricultural Technology in the 19th and 20th Centuries* (London, 1984).

11 Ministry of Agriculture, *Century of Agricultural Statistics*, table 30; E. H. Whetham, 'The mechanization of British agriculture 1910–45', *Journal of Agricultural Economics*, 21 (1970).

12 Whetham, *Cambridge Agrarian History*, table 8.

13 Ibid., p. 57; H. Williamson, *The Story of a Norfolk Farm* (1941; London, 1986), pp. 38–9, 76, 91; M. K. Ashby, *Joseph Ashby of Tysoe, 1859–1919: A Study of English Village Life* (Cambridge, 1961); J. R. Bellerby, 'The distribution of farm income in the United Kingdom, 1867–1938', in W. E. Minchinton, ed., *Essays in Agrarian History*, vol. 2 (Newton Abbot, 1968), pp. 259–78.

14 P. E. Dewey, 'Farm labour', in E. J. T. Collins, ed., *The Cambridge Agrarian History of England and Wales*, vol. 7, *1850–1914* (Cambridge, 2000), ch. 12.

15 Whetham, *Cambridge Agrarian History*, pp. 157–8.

16 S. G. Sturmey, 'Owner-farming in England and Wales, 1900–1950', in W. E. Minchinton, ed., *Essays in Agrarian History*, vol. 2 (Newton Abbot, 1968), pp. 287–96.

17 H. Barrett, *Early to Rise: A Suffolk Morning* (London, 1967), p. 107.

18 Dewey, *British Agriculture*, table 16.2.

19 E. H. Whetham, 'The Agriculture Act 1920 and its repeal – the "Great Betrayal"', *Agricultural History Review*, 22 (1974); E. C. Penning-Rowsell, 'Who "betrayed" whom? Power and politics in the 1920/21 agricultural crisis', *Agricultural History Review*, 45, part 2 (1997).

20 Whetham, *Cambridge Agrarian History*, pp. 161–2.

21 Perren, *Agriculture in Depression*, pp. 55–7; C. Griffiths, '"Red Tape Farm"? Visions of a socialist agriculture in 1920s and 1930s Britain', in J. R. Wordie, ed., *Agriculture and Politics in England, 1815–1939* (Basingstoke, 2000), pp. 208–14.

22 Perren, *Agriculture in Depression*, pp. 58–60.

23 J. Brown, 'Agricultural policy and the National Farmers' Union, 1908–1939', in Wordie, ed., *Agriculture and Politics*, pp. 178–85; Penning-Rowsell, 'Who "betrayed" whom?', pp. 176–8.

24 R. Groves, *Sharpen the Sickle! The History of the Farm Workers' Union* (London, 1949), p. 245; G. E. Mingay, *Land and Society in England 1750–1980* (London, 1994), pp. 241–3; D. Pretty, *The Rural Revolt that Failed: Farm Workers' Trade Unions in Wales, 1889–1950* (Cardiff, 1989), p. 145.

25 Dewey, *War and Progress*, pp. 159–60.

26 Mingay, *Land and Society*, p. 240.

27 Dewey, *War and Progress*, p. 160; Viscount Astor and B. S. Rowntree, *British Agriculture: The Principles of Future Policy* (Harmondsworth, 1939), p. 215.

28 Dewey, *War and Progress*, p. 197; J. Stevenson, *British Society 1914–45* (Harmondsworth, 1984), p. 392.

29 Stevenson, *British Society*, pp. 232–7.

30 Ibid., pp. 170–1.

31 H. Newby, *Country Life: A Social History of Rural England* (London, 1987), p. 175.

FURTHER READING

Dewey, P. E., *British Agriculture in the First World War* (London, 1989).

Newby, H., *Country Life: A Social History of Rural England* (London, 1987).

Perren, R., *Agriculture in Depression, 1870–1940* (Cambridge, 1995).

Sheail, J., *Rural Conservation in Inter-war Britain* (Oxford, 1981).

Whethan, E. H., *The Cambridge Agrarian History of England and Wales*, vol. 8, *1914–1939* (Cambridge, 1978).

CHAPTER EIGHTEEN

Transport, 1900–1939

COLIN DIVALL

Britain was certainly more mobile in 1939 than at the turn of the century. Entirely new modes of transport which had come into use around 1900 or shortly before – motor road vehicles, electric trains and trams, aeroplanes – largely delivered on their promise to shrink distance. Choices widened as prices fell, speeds got higher, transit times less. People and the goods they manufactured and consumed travelled farther, with wide-ranging consequences for everyday life.

But did this enhanced mobility make Britain a better place in which to live? A straightforward answer is impossible, partly because we have a far from perfect under-standing of the ways in which transport and everyday life shaped each other, and partly because any judgement is essentially a political one, the answer depending on the relative weight given to a whole range of factors. Moving goods and people meant making choices, and the social, cultural, economic, environmental and even ideo-logical consequences of these choices were not neutral. Greater mobility was sim-ultaneously liberating and oppressive, and its considerable benefits and costs were unequally shared across society. Transport exacerbated some social differences and divisions at the same time as it helped to smooth out others.

Transport should thus be at the core of discussions about the nature of British society before 1939. But many historians ignore the subject, or they assume patterns of devel-opment that are inadequately theorized or for which there is little evidence. Take for instance debates about the growing sophistication of Britain as a mass consumer society. Even when transport is acknowledged as an essential aspect of the production and distribution or delivery of consumer goods and services, it is commonly regarded as no more than a utilitarian process governed by narrow economic imperatives. Hardly any historians think about transport as something that was itself consumed, that was increasingly regarded in similar ways to, say, shopping, sport or other leisure activities such as going to the cinema. The streamlined styling of trams, buses and trains in the 1930s, for example, shows how even public transport was caught up in an aesthetic

I am grateful to Dr Gordon Pirie for kindly sharing his continuing research on imperial aviation, and to Dr Karen Hunt for her comments on drafts.

that was itself part and parcel of interwar consumerism. But transport's cultural meanings were nothing new; its symbolic and utilitarian dimensions had always coexisted, although their context, content and relative importance constantly shifted.

This essay looks at the politics of transport in early twentieth-century Britain from both an international and a domestic perspective. Because Britain's sense of national identity was so wrapped up with the nineteenth-century legacy of being a world maritime power, considerable emphasis has been given to how this state of affairs altered with the coming of aviation. In the domestic sphere the politics of transport was worked out at the level of day-to-day choices by ordinary people as well as in more formal political settings such as governments, ministries, local authorities and organized interest groups. Here this chapter can do little more than sketch this politics, not least because most transport historiography deals with the production or provision of transport vehicles, services and facilities, and not with the how and the why of their uptake, or of the effects of this. Space prevents a discussion of important matters such as labour relations, business strategies or technological developments; some indication of the more significant work will, however, be found in the further reading section.

International Transport

The transport of passengers and freight to and from the British Isles was intimately connected with Britain's changing role as an imperial and world power. Prior to 1914 the technologically advanced British merchant marine dominated world trade – in 1900 it carried fully half by volume and value – and symbolized Britain's authority and industrial progressiveness abroad. Such apparent prerogatives were the final flowering of the commercial enterprise and foreign policies of the Victorian era, and in the very different circumstances after 1918 they were severely challenged by the rise of foreign fleets and of state-sponsored aviation.[1]

Throughout the early twentieth century there was a choice of several types of long-distance marine (deep-sea) transport. Steam liners offered fast, regular and generally reliable timetabled services reaching important trading partners and colonial possessions such as the Americas, India, the Far East (including China and Japan) and Australasia. Liners carried passengers – differentiated socially by the class of their accommodation – mail and high-value or perishable goods. Steam tramps provided a cheaper alternative when speed was not of the essence, usually in the case of bulky, low-value freight such as coal or metallic ores, although passengers were carried too; these vessels plied for trade on an ad hoc basis, sailing neither to a timetable nor on regular routes. Sailing ships survived in a handful of deep-sea trades where special circumstances, such as limited port facilities or high seasonality, applied.[2]

Maritime transport to and from Britain was part of an internationally competitive industry, and during the period under review the British state never systematically intervened to any great extent in support of the national merchant marine. The choices open to passengers and shippers were thus shaped by market forces. The market was not an entirely free one, however. Semi-secret cartels – 'conferences' or 'rings' – existed between liner companies on many routes. These were intended to limit competition, to deter new fleets from plying for trade, and to prevent tramp steamers from securing cargoes on an opportunistic basis. Such collusive arrangements tended to strengthen during the depression that overtook world shipping in 1901–11, and they continued during the interwar years. Rings were not necessarily prejudicial to consumers' interests, but we do not know enough about the balance of power between the various parties. Ship ownership was becoming concentrated in fewer hands before 1914, which suggests that the balance might have swung in favour of the shipping companies.[3]

The First World War was an important turning point. Flight became a reality for civilian purposes, although it was not much of a threat to the practical business of moving passengers, mail and freight. Its symbolic importance was, however, considerable, and, as British ships lost their easy technological superiority over those of other nations, aircraft took on much of the mantle of technological nationalism. More research needs to be done on the evolving cultural symbolism of deep-sea shipping, and on how this shaped and was shaped by the British merchant marine's slow decline in the world pecking order. How deeply, for instance, did images of fast and luxurious liners resonate with older associations between maritime travel, modernity and nationalism, and how successfully did shipping companies exploit such perceptions in their competition with one another and with aviation?

Shipping continued to dominate traffic to and from Britain after 1918. Generally, however, changing patterns of travel and trade acted against British interests. Foreign ships, most notably those of the United States, the Scandinavian countries and Japan, became a more common sight in British ports. Worldwide, passenger traffic declined generally in importance, not least because of the curtailment in the 1920s of mass immigration to the United States. It is unclear how much this affected travel from Britain, not least since emigration to the empire remained significant. On the freight side, the worldwide trend away from the use of coal in ships and industry accelerated, as did the development of indigenous fuel resources overseas. Together these trends sharply reduced the volume of coal exports, the single most important factor underpinning the favourable economics of maritime trade to and from Britain before 1914. The effect on British tramp shipping was particularly severe, leading to a reduction in tonnage of over a half between 1913 and 1933.[4]

Empire stood at the heart of British civil aviation overseas for much of the interwar period, although in the 1930s considerations of national prestige led to increasing importance being attached to the development of European routes. High fares meant that flying was only for the wealthy, business people and government officials. Poor regularity and a doubtful safety record, although both gradually improved, also helped to make it the preserve of the intrepid and the adventurous – although airlines did what they could to calm passengers' fears through advertising and the provision of cabin crew. But flying was hopelessly uneconomic and its future secured only thanks to long-term support from the state.

Flight seemed to have huge advantages for linking Britain's colonies and dominions to the imperial centre and, more specifically, London, by virtue of superior speed and reach, promising enhanced administrative supervision and exploitation of the empire and its resources. In practice these advantages were largely negated by low capacity, infrequent flights, routing problems due to geopolitical realities on the ground, and the need for frequent stops for servicing machines and refreshing passengers and crew. But imperial aviation carried a heavy ideological burden. The ways in which civilian aircraft were used and understood were bound up with older notions of empire and maritime sensibilities, and their constructions of class, gender and ethnicity. Through Imperial Airways – established by the government in 1924 as a subsidized monopoly – aviation became an integral part of Britain's efforts to resuscitate and prolong empire, partly by exciting enthusiasm for it through association with the adventure and technology of flight. In all of this it is hard to ignore civil aviation's military origins, or the continuing significance of sporting events such as speed and endurance trials.[5]

Ideologically and politically, imperial aviation flew into turbulence. On the one hand flying could improve awareness of empire among the political, diplomatic, commercial and military elites based in London, and perhaps helped to enhance a sense of belonging to officials and others stationed at the imperial periphery. Yet improved communication also threatened the autonomy of these local elites. The Empire Air Mail Scheme of 1934–8 suggests some of the ways in which such tensions evolved. For Britain the scheme represented an opportunity to encourage or coerce subservient imperial administrations into helping maintain British dominance of the air and empire. By contrast, in Australia the link was both a focus for loyalist sentiment and an opportunity to develop a more equal partnership with the imperial centre, in the process giving white Australia a higher profile in world affairs. These various visions did not always fit happily together.[6]

The symbolism of flight also strongly influenced policy towards overseas aviation outside the empire, which meant flights to continental Europe. Here the excellence of arrangements by short sea crossings and rail meant that the practical advantages of flying were, at best, marginal, particularly once comfort, reliability and safety were added to the equation. Efforts from 1919 to establish commercial operations failed ignominiously within a few years. None the less, considerations of national prestige meant that the state vigorously promoted civil aviation to Europe, settling or heavily influencing decisions over routes, levels of service and aircraft, at first solely through Imperial Airways and then, from the mid-1930s, additionally through British Airways Ltd, a private company rescued from financial ruin by subsidy. Together the two airlines sought to provide Britain with a full network of air services between London and European capitals. State regulation in the pursuit of national prestige had to be balanced against the subsidies paid out, and Britain joined with other European governments in minimizing competition in order to save money. This was achieved through a series of bilateral agreements on destinations, route capacities and fares.[7]

It was not only in the air that flying was seen as a mixed blessing. The construction and operation of airports – such as that at Ringway, on the outskirts of Manchester, or Croydon, London's main facility – lauded by some as symbols of modernity and progress, were vigorously opposed by local residents and landowners fearing environmental degradation and loss of amenity. Much remains, however, to be discovered about how the sophisticated airports of the 1930s evolved from the grass airfields of the 1920s.[8]

Personal Domestic Transport

When it came to moving themselves around the British Isles, people increasingly aspired to personal forms of transport, although it seems probable that public transport contributed more than cars and motorcycles to enhanced levels of mobility. The picture is, however, complicated by the sustained popularity of cycling, and for that matter walking.

Although historians are only just beginning to explore issues relating to the personal ownership, usage and symbolism of motor vehicles, it is clear that all three dimensions were intimately connected. Motoring's surging popularity, particularly after 1918, was driven partly by an aspirational and largely middle-class consumer culture which understood cars and motorcycles as novel (and expensive) consumer durables. Before 1914 high prices and running costs largely restricted vehicle ownership and usage to the upper classes and those segments of the professional and commercial middle classes that could justify a car for work. By 1939 cars were no longer bought just by the elite, although costs were still high enough to restrict ownership of the roughly 2 million cars in Britain – roughly one for every fifth family – to the middle and upper classes. Cars were increasingly sold as symbols of conspicuous consumption; in the 1920s competition in the middle-class market was almost entirely on price, but in the following decade manufacturers offered a range of models that permitted purchasers to make more nuanced statements of their social standing. Working-class desires for mechanized personal transport generally had to be satisfied with cheaper solo motorcycles or 'combinations' of motorcycle and sidecar. From the mid-1930s, however, a growing second-hand market and a willingness to engage in shared ownership enabled a small but significant number of working-class families to acquire cars, often at some sacrifice in other realms of life.[9]

This class dimension was paralleled by one of gender. From the very beginning motor vehicles were identified primarily as masculine technologies, used outside the traditionally feminine and private sphere of the home. Precisely because they were symbols of social or public status, cars and motorcycles allowed men to consume in ways that did not threaten their masculinity. However, in the 1920s cars became a symbol of growing female emancipation, threatening this easy masculine identity with motors and leading to some interesting consequences in the 1930s. Male motoring interests ascribed consumers' increasing concern for comfort and aesthetics to the growing female involvement, and used it to justify the shift to marketing based on repeated model changes. Men's image of themselves as interested primarily in 'masculine' matters such as cost, economy, ruggedness and reliability was thus preserved. At the same time the 'feminization' of the car enabled men to deny the existence of 'feminine' traits in their own behaviour, such as a desire to possess the latest model even though changes were often only cosmetic. Men became as deeply embroiled in consumerism as women, if not more so. The more deeply entrenched masculine image of motorcycles, however, proved to be a great impediment when attempts were made between the wars to market new models to women.[10]

The rising level and increasingly middle-class character of vehicle ownership after 1918 meant that many of the objections raised in the pioneering two decades of motoring either disappeared or were sharply attenuated. When driving was still restricted to a small minority, the clear danger to the lives and limbs of the great majority who did not drive, not to mention the inconvenience and annoyance, particularly in rural areas, occasioned by the use of vehicles at speed on unsuitable road surfaces, made motorists an easy target for popular anxieties.

Opposition to motoring before 1914 was evident in support for restrictions such as the strict enforcement of the universal 20 m.p.h. speed limit (which was widely flouted and eventually abolished in 1930). Such anxieties continued to grow as vehicle usage and road casualties climbed rapidly in the 1920s and early 1930s. But motoring interests effectively countered such opposition through the skilful use of books, films and the specialist and general press, and through organized political lobbying and propaganda. The distressing consequences of being hit by fast motor vehicles were sanitized by the widespread use of the term 'road accident', and these 'accidents' were blamed on a series of scapegoats – often the casualties themselves, including pedestrians, the largest single group of those killed and injured. All of this helped to sustain the idea that motor vehicles were not inherently dangerous and that deaths and injuries could be controlled by educating pedestrians, drivers and other road users in 'road safety'. While speed restrictions were reimposed in urban areas from 1934 and driving tests introduced the next year, the battle for the most influential elements of public opinion was largely won by motoring groups. The physical layout of roads and their surroundings, particularly in urban areas, was increasingly modelled to suit motor vehicles, with detrimental consequences for other road users and communities more generally.[11]

There is some agreement that by the late 1930s personal motor vehicles were used mostly for leisure, with journeys to work still usually made on foot, by pedal cycle or public transport.[12] Leisure use involved contradictions and changes that were resented or opposed by some people. As a means of escaping from one form of collective, commercialized experience, that inherent in the use of public transport, motor vehicles intensified another, the exploitation of places and landscapes to be 'consumed' by tourists; the individualistic ideology of motoring contrasted sharply with the reality of increasing traffic congestion in popular areas. Moreover, the cost of running cars and motorcycles meant that economies were often made by satisfying privately needs that before had involved purchasing services, such as accommodation and catering. Such measures did little to endear motoring to those who made a living from these things, although other people found employment in satisfying the demands of motorists for new or expanded services such as fuel, maintenance and repairs, motoring magazines, car rallies and sports, cheap accommodation, sites for camping and caravanning, driving lessons, road houses and golf courses.[13]

A bicycle was many people's introduction to personal transport, although historians have, like politicians at the time, rather neglected this socially equitable way of travelling. Some of the traits associated with motors – a middle-class pattern of ownership, sporting and recreational usage, growth of the market through advertising and a changing range of models – were already evident in 1900. But with falling prices up to 1914 cycling took on more of a utilitarian character as it became a means of working-class transport for local journeys, a function it retained until 1939, and beyond. Cycling for recreation also mushroomed in popularity between the wars as prices fell and road surfaces, particularly in rural areas, improved. Women were successfully targeted by marketing that suggested that cycling was not only healthy and enjoyable but fashionable. Cycle ownership in the interwar period far outstripped that of cars – indeed, between 1929 and 1935 the number of bikes increased from around 6 to 10 million, proportionally a far larger rise than that for cars.[14]

Public Transport

Since it did not involve ownership of an expensive consumer durable public transport did not offer the same opportunities for social display as motors. But public transport – whether by tram, bus or coach, hackney- or taxi-cab, or train – was of huge practical significance for most people, and it certainly carried wider cultural meanings as well.

The symbolism of internal flight was much more important than its utility as far as society at large was concerned. Planes carried tiny numbers of passengers at large commercial losses, even when they could exploit the advantage of short sea-crossings. After a false start which petered out by the mid-1920s, scheduled internal flights did not recommence until the early 1930s. Although passenger journeys then grew sharply among the social, business and administrative elites, the industry survived only thanks to subsidies provided by the railway companies through their Railway Air Services, established in early 1934, and its policy of ruthless consolidation and tight control of routes.[15] Yet the long-term prospects for domestic aviation were clear enough, and it would be useful to know more about the ways in which it shared in, and perhaps differed from, the cultural symbolism of international flying.

Road was the fastest growing of the more mundane forms of public transport. Indeed, one group of historians judges that passenger travel by commercial operators in the mid-1930s might have exceeded that by private motor vehicles.[16] Yet surprisingly little is known about who used taxis, trams, buses and coaches and for what purposes, and the wider effects these forms of transport had on the people and the places they served.

Between 1900 and 1914 timetabled public transport was almost entirely restricted to urban settlements and the immediately surrounding rural areas. People found it quicker and, on the whole, cheaper to get around as horse, buses, trams and hackneys were rapidly displaced by electric trams and, more slowly, by motorized buses and taxis. The electric tramway was found in all cities and towns of any size, and, since it epitomized modernity and civic pride, in not a few small places where the case on other grounds was at best marginal. Competition with electric tramways led the railways – in those few large cities where they were important for travel within the urban area – to electrify also, with encouraging results; in London, extensions to the electric 'tube' deep underground gave improved access to central districts from the expanding suburbs.

This revolution in transport technology played a part in overcoming the social and physical constraints found in towns and cities where walking, the horse and steam railways had been almost the only travel options. Better housing for the working and lower middle classes was provided by extending urban boundaries and creating suburbs separated from workplaces – a downmarket version of the solidly middle-class migration that had taken place during the previous century. But the true significance of public transport for these important developments is still rather unclear. Cheap travel, stemming particularly from the electrification and widespread municipalization of tramways, was undoubtedly needed, but public transport rarely, if at all, catalysed new suburban development; rather, as in the previous century, provision was made only when demand for journeys into the urban core had been established. Nor do we fully understand the social consequences of enhanced urban mobility. The professional and commercial middle classes probably benefited, if not to such a degree as the working class. Changes to the location of workplaces as well as of residences altered patterns of daily travel, and not all these journeys were of the periphery-to-core model often assumed. The effects on retailing and leisure, particularly as these related to women, are still quite obscure. The department stores that sprang up in city centres clearly relied on public transport for much of their custom, but what, for instance, was the effect on smaller shops elsewhere in urban areas?[17]

Between the wars cheap public transport continued to underpin the flight to the suburbs, although buses tended to displace trams. Municipal policies continued to influence the evolving relationship between the provision of transport, housing, retail and leisure facilities and workplaces. There is some evidence that by the late 1930s cheap fares were under threat from the increased operating costs associated with sub-urban sprawl. And not everyone was pleased with what they found in the suburbs, or with the new patterns of travel forced upon them. For instance, in the 1920s inhabitants of Wythenshawe, a new, largely working-class suburb on the outskirts of Manchester, thought that work, retail and leisure facilities would be available locally, but in fact these were not provided for many years, if at all. Men had to travel in and out of the city for work, although at least they could do this by municipal bus or tram. Their womenfolk had to make lengthy journeys, often on foot across muddy fields, simply to gain access to shops.[18]

There were other problems associated with the actual and envisaged evolution of public transport in towns and cities. Municipal systems played an important part in symbolizing the sense of collective identity and pride held by the urban com-munities they served, but there were always tensions to be found over the ideals of civic community. Historians have long been aware of resistance to the running of electric trams – seen as working-class vehicles – through middle-class residential dis-tricts, but we still know too little about how people divided by class and gender in their perceptions of public transport. There were certainly disagreements among political and professional elites over the desirability of what became the dominant British model of urban core and dependent suburbs. In London, for instance, the railways' part in opening up suburbs was opposed right up to 1939 by the garden city movement and its descendants, which envisaged dispersing the population to smaller, more self-contained settlements. Although this vision enthusiastically embraced environmental considerations, it proved easier to criticize the drawbacks of the existing railways than to anticipate those resulting from the new and widened roads that were planned.[19]

Public transport outside the urban areas must be treated even more briefly since there are surprisingly few detailed studies of consumers' perceptions, and of the social and other consequences of enhanced mobility. Growing levels of business activity as well as higher disposable incomes meant that the market for interurban travel expanded fairly steadily from 1900. Before 1914 this traffic was almost entirely handled by the railways, but after the war there was increasing competition from buses and express coach services. Combined with the increasing use of cars and motorcycles, the effect was to check the absolute rise in passenger usage of the rail-ways (although long-distance traffic grew), which henceforth took a slowly declin-ing share of the overall market. Recognizing this threat to their financial stability, the railway companies invested heavily in bus companies from the late 1920s. There was, however, little attempt to integrate railway and road services, and despite a sharp fall in patronage of many local trains very few were withdrawn and even fewer branch lines closed. From 1930 the fares, frequencies and routes of all timetabled bus ser-vices became subject to regulation by regional traffic commissioners, and some historians argue that this stifled entrepreneurship within the industry, to the detriment of passengers.[20]

Much of the new travel in the interwar period was for leisure. The railways continued to offer numerous excursions to the seaside and other places, and widened the range of cheap tickets for use on ordinary trains. Coach operators started to offer excursions and tours soon after 1918. Road and rail operators saw the need to develop the market by persuading people to make trips that were in a sense unnecessary. They rapidly emulated the practice of oil companies like Shell, which promoted leisure motoring through sophisticated advertising. Railway advertising also looked to the business market, trading on images of modernity, particularly with the introduction in the mid-1930s of prestigious new high-speed services using streamlined locomotives and passenger carriages.[21]

Competition between road and rail was mostly on price, although despite its generally lower cost the quality of road services after 1918 was not always inferior to that on the railways, particularly at times of peak travel when trains were crowded, or for those people without ready access to a mainline railway station. Road services greatly enhanced the mobility of anyone unable to afford a motor vehicle or the railways' fares, but further generalization is dangerous until we know a lot more about who used interurban buses and coaches and what the wider effects were on patterns of work and consumption. The same comment applies to the penetration of motorbus services deep into rural areas between the wars, displacing the horse-drawn carriers' carts of an earlier period that were all that had been available to those without private carriages.[22]

Freight

Few historians have studied the transport of freight around Britain in the early twentieth century, despite its importance for manufacturing and retailing. This reluctance is partly practical, for carrying and haulage were always highly complex and fragmented businesses, even before 1914 when the railways were dominant, and so it is hard to study how freight services were marketed and used, and what their effects were. If anything these problems increase for the period after 1918, for a multitude of often small road hauliers entered the market. There might also be intellectual reasons for the lack of attention given to freight transport, for it seems to be a ruggedly utilitarian activity which lacks the many-layered symbolism of passenger travel and thus is unlikely to attract cultural historians. But few, if any, social activities are entirely free of symbolic meaning, and the history of the movement of freight may yet prove to be more engaging than it appears. A study of the industrial marketing of freight services, for example, might well produce some interesting contrasts with the kind of consumer advertising with which historians are much more familiar.

The bare bones of supply and demand are clear enough. Before 1914 most traders had little option but to send freight by train unless it was fairly light, not too bulky and only travelling a few miles; then carriage all the way by road was a possibility. The only other options for heavy freight or long-distance haulage were coastal shipping or inland waterways.

Coasters offered as sophisticated a range of services as deep-sea shipping, and were formidable competition for the railways in certain markets. By 1910 at the latest, most major ports were served by a network of regular, frequent and fast liner services carrying high-value and perishable goods in small lots (they also carried passengers, albeit in very limited numbers). Regular trades in bulky, low-value products such as coal to London had dedicated services that were also reliable and fairly speedy. Tramp steamers and sailing vessels covered the lower end of the market. Coasters competed with the railways by keeping charges lower, through a combination of restricting competition amongst themselves, technological innovation and economies of scale achieved through mergers. Shipping companies also used sophisticated marketing and sometimes colluded with the railways in order to avoid direct competition. In consequence the volume of traffic handled by coasters increased up to 1913; indeed, it is possible that they handled as large a ton-mileage as the railways. But we do not know very much about how and why traders chose between rail and sea for particular routes or commodities.[23]

Inland waterways were still a viable alternative for some traders. The railways had never succeeded wholly in eclipsing canals and rivers as freight carriers, particularly of low-value, bulky goods, and indeed railway ownership of certain canals was sometimes exploited as the means whereby one company could penetrate the territory of another. Moreover, some inland waterways continued to complement marine activities by offering all-water routes into the industrial heartlands, although the economic advantages already lay with ship canals, such as that serving Manchester, and the larger navigations and canals of north-east England since these all reduced the need for trans-shipment. None the less, trade on inland waterways more or less held up in absolute terms until 1914, although this represented a falling proportion of a growing market and was increasingly restricted to local traffics.[24]

Road haulage offered an even less credible alternative before 1914, except for the strictly local distribution upon which all other forms of transport relied in some degree. The dense network of cartage provided by the railways and other long-distance operators, independent carriers, and by manufacturers, distributors and retailers acting on their own account remained for sound economic reasons the preserve of the horse (although the use of hand-carts, the goods equivalent of walking, was also quite common). From the mid-1900s light petrol-driven vans offered the possibility of speedier deliveries operating over a larger radius, and by 1914 these probably made up most of the 85,000 motorized goods vehicles on the roads. The increasing number of heavy goods vehicles – there were around 1,000 steam wagons by 1904 and from 1905 petrol lorries became available – suggests that longer-distance road haulage was slowly becoming established, but most traffic still went by rail.[25]

Much of the railways' freight traffic had taken on a retail character – comparatively small loads, often of high value, requiring frequent, speedy and reliable transit, often door-to-door – as early as the 1870s. Rates and charges for all freight were, and remained, strictly regulated by the state, and from the 1880s traders had benefited from the consequential high levels of non-price competition between the railway companies – free use of wagons for storage, subsidized warehousing, generous settlements for claims. In 1900–14 the railways' desire to restore profitability led them to withdraw many of these hidden subsidies. Traders were however appeased by real reductions in transport prices, and the railways continued to provide a dense and frequent service particularly suited to retail distribution. In 1911 they were carrying over a fifth more ton-miles than in 1900.[26]

The First World War radically altered the competitive balance, catalysing a huge rise in motorized road haulage that continued more or less unabated through to 1939. Encouraged by the release of some 60,000 war-surplus lorries, a government subvention for lorries which met War Office specifications, and, just as importantly, a flood of ex-servicemen trained as drivers and mechanics, road haulage rapidly took an increasing share of an expanding market, successfully challenging the older transport providers over longer and longer distances as improvements to lorries and road surfaces brought down costs by around a third. Road hauliers were free to undercut the railways' rates, which remained tightly regulated and, perhaps as importantly in the fiercely competitive market, widely publicized. Not all haulage firms were profitable over the long term however, and no historian has yet systematically investigated a claim commonly made by the railways, that hauliers failed to cover the costs of the roads they used or those they imposed on the rest of society through 'accidents' and other causes.[27]

A recent study gives a much clearer picture of just how radically road haulage transformed the structure of freight transport from about 1920. The sector grew very fast until the introduction in 1933 of a national system of licensing which restricted the number of lorries carrying on behalf of other traders; growth thereafter was particularly vigorous among businesses hauling only on their own account. Leaving to one side coal traffic (which still overwhelming went by railway and coaster) and strictly local distribution, motorized road haulage in 1939 accounted for over one-third of all land-borne freight traffic.[28]

This still left the railways as the principal hauliers over medium and long distances, and they did not suffer a very great decline in the absolute volume of freight they handled. Their problem, as historians have long suggested and recent work goes some way to confirm, was that road haulage was taking a greater share of increasing industrial output, particularly that from the newer industries supplying growing markets in consumer goods; these included many high-value cargoes, which commanded premium rates. Retailers increasingly ordered smaller quantities of merchandise at greater frequencies, again making the use of road haulage more likely. By contrast the staple industries (coal, iron, steel and shipbuilding, and the export trade in manufactures), which traditionally provided the railways with profitable traffics, performed poorly.[29]

The other long-established freight hauliers suffered more severely; by the mid-1930s coastal shipping and canals together handled no more than about 10 per cent of domestic freight tonnage, excluding coal. The turn away from coastal shipping after 1918 was dramatic, although it was the railways that did the damage, not road haulage, which was not a serious competitor for most of the coasters' traditional cargoes or routes. The trend started with the diversion of traffic to the railways in 1914–18, partly to avoid losses from enemy action and partly because railway rates were kept artificially low. Since these did not recover between the wars, there was little incentive for the lost trade to return to the sea, although a chronic overcapacity in the coastal trade drove some rates so low that certain long-haul traffics did come back. Coasters were also seriously affected by the decline in staple industries. Many traders also abandoned the canals from the 1920s, partly because road transport offered a more convenient service for non-bulky goods and partly because of cheap railway rates.[30]

It is far less clear how these changing patterns of freight transport shaped, and were shaped by, other aspects of the evolving consumer society of interwar Britain. Motorization after 1918 probably facilitated, rather than initiated, many of the developments in retailing and wholesaling that were already making themselves apparent before 1914. Between the wars the food retailer Sainsbury's, for example, developed its own network of road distribution using motor vehicles rather than relying on the railways as it had done earlier. But apart from such isolated instances, very little is known about what was carried by road hauliers, where, at what cost and with what effect, and this holds good for the other modes of inland transport as well.[31]

The State and Domestic Transport

This chapter has already argued that after 1918, for reasons of national prestige, the state promoted and subsidized the new form of overseas transport, aviation, while leaving shipping largely to the workings of the market. In the domestic sphere matters were more complex. Here the railways, as the dominant mode of transport, were subjected to an increasingly stringent regime of state regulation at the same time as their near monopoly was successfully challenged by motorization on the roads. This challenge was itself furthered by the state which, despite high levels of taxation on the ownership and running of motor vehicles, for many years subsidized road construction.

Until at least the mid-1920s political debate about the railways was framed by attitudes formed in the last two decades of the previous century. Traders' fears that the railway companies would abuse their firm grip on domestic freight had led to their being increasingly tightly regulated. Indeed, by 1900 there were so few areas of managerial responsibility not covered by legislation that one historian argues that it is misleading to describe the railways as private sector companies.[32] Throughout the Edwardian period nationalization was seen by some traders, as well as many in the labour movement, as the logical next step. The experience of government control during the First World War seemed to reinforce the argument that a unified system, perhaps under state ownership, would lead to greater efficiencies. In the event legislation grouped all of the principal companies and most of the minor ones into just four, in 1923. A belief that the railways would continue as near monopolies led to even tighter and more rigid regulation of freight prices, although control of passenger fares was not so strict.

Some of the railways' problems were of their own making or were attributable to changing economic circumstances. Nevertheless, there is a growing consensus among historians that the state's policies considerably hampered the railway companies in their struggle with road transport. Since the railways were modestly, if decreasingly, profitable, the state provided only a little financial assistance, mostly by way of cheap loans for capital improvements in the late 1920s and mid-1930s; in any case these measures were directed more at the relief of unemployment than at improvement of the nation's transport infrastructure. Licensing and regulation of bus and coach operators (1930) and road hauliers (1933) brought a little relief from road competition. Yet railway managers in the late 1930s were probably correct in their feeling that they were faced with obligations on charges and public service not imposed on their road-bound competitors. Redressing the balance would not have stopped the rise of commercial road transport, but it would surely have slackened its pace.[33]

Perhaps the greatest government encouragement to both commercial and personal road transport came from subsidies for road construction and maintenance, although it is important to stress that this was more the consequence of a series of largely unco-ordinated decisions than a coherent and sustained policy. Even after the establishment of the Ministry of Transport in 1919, there was no very clear vision of how the road network ought to be developed. Nevertheless, for many years spending by central government and local authorities on roads exceeded the direct contribution made by road users by way of taxes on ownership and use. By 1910–11 the increased wear and tear from motor vehicles had so forced up costs that the subsidy attribut-able solely to their use had reached some £9.4 million; by the late 1920s perhaps one-third of the annual expenditure on roads of £60 million was not covered by motoring taxes. Only in the early 1930s did these begin to exceed spending on roads.[34]

Even then motorists, bus operators and road hauliers almost certainly did not con-tribute in direct taxation anything like the costs they imposed on the rest of society. As has already been argued, the rising cost of deaths and injuries was politically the most sensitive issue, but there was also concern over pollution. The state treated all motorized road users fairly leniently; government-imposed safety measures in the 1930s were not as stringent as in certain other countries where the road lobby was not as well organized. Governments also discriminated between different kinds of road users, in particular favouring motorists over public transport and, as has already been indicated, own-account over general freight hauliers.[35] On balance, then, the effect of the state's transport policies was almost certainly to encourage the growth of road transport at the expense of rail, and probably to encourage the expansion of individualistic over collective forms of passenger and freight road transport.

Mobility, Accessibility and Transport as Consumption

Did enhanced mobility, then, make the Britain of 1939 a better place to live than in 1900? Yes, for those who could afford to travel and to make use of the goods and services that better transport made possible and accessible. But there were clearly serious drawbacks as well, both for society as a whole and for particular social groups.

One of the most important lessons of recent studies is that transport was rarely, if at all, purely utilitarian. It was not just about moving people or things from A to B – politically, transport's symbolic power was very important. The British sense of nationhood was defined partly through overseas maritime and aeronautical activities; the British people defined themselves through their own mobility, particularly through possession and usage of cars, motorbikes and even pedal cycles. It is not sur-prising therefore that a significant proportion of the higher levels of domestic travel generated between 1900 and 1939, and particularly that by road between the wars, was undertaken voluntarily, often for leisure purposes. People chose to consume more and more transport.

The fact that all forms of personal transport were first taken up by the upper eche-lons of society before being adopted by the middle and working classes may suggest that the process was simply one of emulation. But such a conclusion would be premature. As historians have learnt more about consumption in Britain they have come to realize that the take-up of goods and services by new social groups often involves novel forms of understanding. Consumption is not merely a matter of adoption but also of adaptation. We have already seen, for example, that men and women tended to understand cars in different ways, and more research will almost certainly reveal even more diversity in the cultures of consumption associated with transport.

Transport was not, of course, just about symbolic meanings, important though these are for comprehending the mutual shaping of transport and society in early twentieth-century Britain. It seems likely that the more we study this interaction, the more we shall uncover alternative visions of how the two spheres might have interacted, as well as gaining a better sense of how the benefits and disadvantages of mobility were distributed by gender and social class. To what degree, for instance, did enhanced mobility lead to a reduction in local facilities, such as shops, and thus force people to travel when they would rather have not or, in the extreme, denied them access entirely if they were too poor or too infirm to travel?

To form a rounded judgement on such issues we need both to get inside the minds of contemporaries and to exploit the benefit of hindsight. Understanding more about how people saw transport at the time will help us to avoid making casual judgements about the desirability of this or that development. It might, for instance, be tempting to regard the horse-drawn society of 1900 as environmentally more acceptable than the motorized one of forty years later, but to those who lived with the cruelties, stench, disease and mess of the earlier period the advantages were not always so obvious. On the other hand, transport, like any other sphere of human endeavour, is subject to the vicissitudes of unintended consequences, and we can now see how in the first four decades of the last century the preferences of consumers combined with official policies to produce a society in which individual mobility was fast becoming a cultural and political norm. Understanding the gridlock of modern Britain, and the viability of proposals to alleviate it, demands a fuller appreciation of this fact.

NOTES

1   D. M. Williams, ed., 'Introduction', in *The World of Shipping* (Aldershot, 1997), pp. ix–xii; S. Ville, *Transport and the Development of the European Economy 1750–1914* (Houndmills, 1990), pp. 48–9.
2   Williams, *World of Shipping*, pp. x–xi; Ville, *European Economy*, pp. 54–61.
3   Williams, *World of Shipping*, pp. xii, xv–xvi, xviii–xix; Ville, *European Economy*, pp. 91, 95–6, 109.
4   Williams, *World of Shipping*, pp. xix–xxi; Ville, *European Economy*, pp. 59–61.
5   H.-L. Dienel and P. Lyth, eds, *Flying the Flag: European Commercial Air Transport since 1945* (Houndmills, 1998), pp. 60–1, 63; L. Edmonds, 'Australia, Britain and the Empire Air Mail Scheme, 1934–38', *Journal of Transport History*, 3rd series, 20 (1999), pp. 91–106; B. Burman, 'Racing bodies: dress and pioneer women aviators and racing drivers', *Women's History Review*, 9 (2000), pp. 299–326.
6   Edmonds, 'Empire Air Mail', pp. 103–4.
7   L. Andersson-Skog and O. Krantz, eds, *Institutions in the Transport and Communications Industries: State and Private Actors in the Making of Institutional Patterns, 1850–1990* (Canton, Mass., 1999), pp. 94–5; R. Millward and J. Singleton, eds, *The Polit-*

ical Economy of Nationalisation in Britain 1920–1950 (Cambridge, 1995), pp. 67–9, 74–7; Dienel and Lyth, *Flying the Flag*, pp. 2–3, 50–1.

8   W. M. Leary, ed., *From Airships to Airbus: The History of Civil and Commercial Aviation*, vol. 1 (Washington, DC, 1995), pp. 19–44; C. Simmons and V. Caruana, 'Neighbourhood issues in the development of Manchester airport, 1934–82', *Journal of Transport History*, 3rd series, 15 (1994), pp. 117–24, 140–1.

9   S. O'Connell, *The Car and British Society: Class, Gender and Motoring 1896–1939* (Manchester, 1998), pp. 11–12, 17–38; R. Church, *The Rise and Decline of the British Motor Industry* (2nd edition, Cambridge, 1995), pp. 3–44; J. Foreman-Peck, S. Bowden and A. McKinlay, *The British Motor Vehicle Industry, 1880–1990* (Manchester, 1995), pp. 6–88; Ville, *European Economy*, pp. 172–80, 183–99.

10 O'Connell, *Car and British Society*, pp. 43–76; D. Thoms, L. Holden and T. Claydon, eds, *The Motor Car and Popular Culture in the Twentieth Century* (Aldershot, 1998), pp. 73, 151–64; S. Koerner, 'The British motor-cycle industry during the 1930s', *Journal of Transport History*, 3rd series, 16 (1995), pp. 55–75.

11 Thoms et al., *Car and Popular Culture*, pp. 69–81; O'Connell, *Car and British Society*, pp. 112–49, 185–217; T. C. Barker, ed., *The Economic and Social Effects of the Spread of Motor Vehicles: An International Centenary Tribute* (Houndmills, 1987), pp. 264–80.

12 O'Connell, *Car and British Society*, p. 77; T. C. Barker and D. Gerhold, *The Rise and Rise of Road Transport, 1700–1990* (2nd edition, Cambridge, 1995), p. 91; C. J. Pooley and J. Turnbull, 'Commuting, transport and urban form: Manchester and Glasgow in the mid-twentieth century', *Urban History*, 27 (2000), pp. 360–83.

13 O'Connell, *Car and British Society*, pp. 77–111.

14 R. Lloyd-Jones and M. J. Lewis, *Raleigh and the British Bicycle Industry: An Economic and Business History 1870–1960* (Aldershot, 2000), pp. 9, 31–7, 48–9, 104, 109–14, 130.

15 Millward and Singleton, *Nationalisation in Britain*, pp. 71, 74; Leary, *Airships to Airbus*, pp. 116–17, 124.

16 Foreman-Peck et al., *British Motor Vehicle Industry*, pp. 80–1.

17 See, for example, the introduction and case studies in F. M. L. Thompson, ed., *The Rise of Suburbia* (Leicester, 1982); R. Haywood, 'Railways, urban form and town planning in London: 1900–1947', *Planning Perspective*, 12 (1997), pp. 37–50; M. Barke, 'The middle-class journey to work in Newcastle upon Tyne, 1850–1913', *Journal of Transport History*, 3rd series, 12 (1991), pp. 128–33.

18 W. Bond and C. Divall, eds, *Suburbanizing the Masses: Public Transport and Urban Development in Historical Perspective* (Aldershot, forthcoming 2003); Haywood, 'London', pp. 51–62; A. Hughes and K. Hunt, 'A culture transformed? Women's lives in Wythenshawe in the 1930s', in A. Davies and S. Fielding, eds, *Workers' Worlds: Cultures and Communities in Manchester and Salford, 1880–1939* (Manchester, 1992), pp. 84–6; R. J. Buckley, 'Capital cost as a reason for the abandonment of first-generation tramways in Britain', *Journal of Transport History*, 3rd series, 10 (1989), pp. 99–112; G. C. Dickenson and G. J. Longley, 'Twopence to the terminus? A study of tram and bus fares in Leeds during the inter-war period', *Journal of Transport History*, 3rd series, 7 (1986), pp. 46–7, 53–8.

19 Bond and Divall, *Suburbanizing the Masses*; Haywood, 'London', pp. 50, 58–60, 65–6; Turnbull and Pooley, 'Commuting', pp. 360–83.

20 J. Simmons, *The Railway in Town and Country, 1830–1914* (Newton Abbot, 1986), pp. 235–335; J. Hibbs, *The Bus and Coach Industry: Its Economics and Organization* (London, 1975), pp. 32–57; P. Butterfield, 'Grouping, pooling and competition: the passenger policy of the London and North Eastern Railway, 1923–39', *Journal of Transport History*, 3rd series, 7 (1986), pp. 21–47; Millward and Singleton, *Nationalisation in Britain*, pp. 222, 229.

21   D. N. Smith, *The Railway and its Passengers: A Social History* (Newton Abbot, 1988), pp. 128–35, 155–70; Hibbs, *Bus and Coach Industry*, pp. 71–82.

22   Hibbs, *Bus and Coach Industry*, pp. 32–57, 71–82.

23   Andersson-Skog and Krantz, *Transport and Communications Industries*, pp. 154–60; J. Armstrong, ed., 'Introduction', in *Coastal and Short Sea Shipping* (Aldershot, 1996), pp. xvii–xix, xxi; J. Armstrong, 'Freight pricing policy in coastal liner companies before the First World War', *Journal of Transport History*, 3rd series, 10 (1989), p. 195.

24   G. Crompton, ed., *Canals and Inland Navigation* (Aldershot, 1996), pp. xvi–xvii; C. Hadfield, *Hadfield's British Canals: The Inland Waterways of Britain and Ireland*, rev. J. Boughey (8th edition, Stroud, 1994), pp. 240–54; Ville, *European Economy*, pp. 41–2, 46.

25   Barker and Gerhold, *Rise and Rise*, pp. 81–4; Barker, *Spread of Motor Vehicles*, pp. 39–42.

26   V. N. L. van Vleck, 'Delivering coal by road and rail in Britain: the efficiency of the "silly little bobtailed" coal wagons', *Journal of Economic History*, 57 (1997), pp. 139–60; P. J. Cain, 'Private enterprise or public utility? Output, pricing and investment on English and Welsh railways, 1870–1914', *Journal of Transport History*, 3rd series, 1 (1980), pp. 16, 18–23.

27   Barker and Gerhold, *Rise and Rise*, pp. 85–8; Foreman-Peck et al., *British Motor Vehicle Industry*, p. 82.

28   P. Scott, 'The growth of road haulage, 1921–58: an estimate', *Journal of Transport History*, 3rd series, 19 (1998), pp. 138, 142–4, 149, 152–3.

29   Millward and Singleton, *Nationalisation in Britain*, pp. 118, 125; Scott, 'Road haulage', pp. 152–3.

30   Scott, 'Road haulage', p. 152; Armstrong, *Coastal Shipping*, pp. xix–xx; Hadfield, *British Canals*, pp. 243–5.

31   Ville, *European Economy*, pp. 199–202, 205; Barker and Gerhold, *Rise and Rise*, p. 86.

32   Andersson-Skog and Krantz, *Transport and Communications Industries*, p. 122.

33   G. Crompton, ' "Good business for the nation": the railway nationalisation issue, 1921–47', *Journal of Transport History*, 3rd series, 20 (1999), pp. 141–59; G. Crompton, ' "Efficient and economical working"? The performance of the railway companies 1923–33', *Business History*, 27 (1985), pp. 221–37; G. Crompton, ' "Squeezing the pulpless orange": labour and capital on the railways in the inter-war years', *Business History*, 31 (1989), pp. 66–83; Millward and Singleton, *Nationalisation in Britain*, pp. 116–43, 133–42.

34   Foreman-Peck et al., *British Motor Vehicle Industry*, pp. 31–3, 69, 82–4.

35   Ibid.; Barker, *Spread of Motor Vehicles*, pp. 264–80; O'Connell, *Car and British Society*, pp. 136–43.

FURTHER READING

Bagwell, P. and Lyth, P., *Transport in Britain: From Canal Lock to Gridlock* (London, 2001).

Howell, D., *Respectable Radicals: Studies in Railway Trades Unionism* (Aldershot, 1999).

Chapter Nineteen

Industry and Services: Employment and Unemployment

K. D. Brown

In 1900 Britain was one of the world's most advanced industrial economies, by itself responsible for producing just under a fifth of total manufacturing output. It is true that some 70 per cent of the land area of England and Wales was still under cultivation, while the landscapes of both Scotland and Ireland remained predominantly agrarian. Nevertheless, agriculture was not a major source of either income or employment in Britain. At the turn of the century, less than a tenth of the labour force worked on the land, producing a mere 6 or 7 per cent of total national income. Farming's economic significance had long since been overtaken by both service and manufacturing activity.

Industrial production embraced everything from light consumer goods to heavy capital equipment, but the staple industries of the industrial revolution were still dominant. In 1913, the generally labour-intensive industries of coal, heavy metals, engineering, shipbuilding and cotton textiles between them employed some 40 per cent of the occupied population and generated about a third of national output. While manufacturing was ubiquitous, the staples were regionally concentrated mainly in the north-east, the north-west, south Wales and the Clydeside area of Scotland. The best estimates, for instance, suggest that more than three-quarters of mining employment was in the north, Wales, Scotland, the north-west and the east midlands. The north-west and the Yorkshire Humberside region accounted for slightly more than 70 per cent of workers in textiles. The failure of the manufacturing base to diversify significantly beyond its well-established existing parameters into new sectors such as automobiles or electrical engineering has frequently been cited as evidence of a certain lack of entrepreneurial vigour in the economy. The older staples, too, have been similarly accused of complacency, with firms criticized for slapdash and inflexible marketing, technological conservatism and outmoded structures of internal organization. The proponents of this failure hypothesis have attributed these shortcomings variously to defects in the nature of the education system, the reluctance of financial institutions to support innovative enterprise, the persistence of family ownership and small-scale firms, social snobbery or the restrictive practices of trade unions. Whatever the validity of these hypotheses – and the issue has been

Table 19.1 Distribution of employment in the service sector (%)

	1911	1931
Transport	21.4	16.5
Distribution	22	29.6
Insurance and banking	3.2	4.2
Professions	9.6	9.6
Miscellaneous	38	28.9
Public administration	5.8	11.1

Source: calculated from C. Lee, 'The service industries', in R. Floud and D. McCloskey, eds, *The Economic History of Britain since 1700*, vol. 2, *1860–1939* (Cambridge, 1994), p. 124.

clouded by an underlying confusion between management and entrepreneurship – it was certainly true that the scale of all manufacturing in Britain, whether new or old, was small. In 1907 the country's largest hundred firms employed about 1,400,000 workers, or about 8 per cent of the total labour force between them. The largest single concentration of workers in one plant was probably the 17,300 employed on Tyneside by the engineers Armstrong Whitworths, and the largest single manufacturing firm, Fine Cotton Spinners and Doublers, had a total workforce of about 30,000, but neither was typical of manufacturing as a whole.

Less than half of the top twenty employers of labour were to be found in industry. That eleven were railway companies was testimony to the importance that the service sector had acquired in the economy by the beginning of the century. This reflected not only developments in distribution and transport, but also the growing role of the expert in advanced societies, the expansion of bureaucracy at both local and national level, and the importance of international trade to the British economy. Britain's merchant fleet provided the bulk of the world's carrying service and thus benefited from the massive expansion of international trade from the 1870s. London was the centre of the international money market, earning a substantial income, not least through expanding overseas investments, while growing domestic prosperity also prompted major changes in retailing. Table 19.1 shows the distribution of workers between the various service industries, which altogether provided work for just under a half of the employed population and generated more than half the total national income by 1913. It has also been calculated that by 1900 between a fifth and a quarter of all consumer expenditure in Britain was on services, although this figure varied widely between the differing social classes.[1] Just as with industry, the significance of the service sector was regionally variable. Above-average concentrations of unemployment were to be found in the south-east and south-west, which together accounted for almost a half of all the jobs in the professions. Service employment in East Anglia and the north-west was just under the national average and lowest of all in Scotland, Wales, the midlands and the north.

The manufacturing labour force consisted mainly of adult males. Half-time working whereby children, mainly in the textile districts of Lancashire, the West Riding and Cheshire, alternated their days between school and a local mill, had contracted considerably over the last years of the nineteenth century. By 1910 only about 76,000 were still involved, a fall of more than half since the 1870s. On the other hand, child labour was by no means confined to textiles and an official inquiry of 1901 calculated that some 300,000 children were currently in paid employment. As for women, more than three-quarters of spinsters over the age of fifteen worked for a living. Only about a tenth of married women were in the labour force in 1911, although the pattern of their employment was regionally varied. Charles Booth's surveys revealed that about a third of families in London's East End depended on the wife's income to survive. In Lancashire, the Potteries and the jute city of Dundee, some 30 per cent of married women worked, as against less than 2 per cent in the mining areas.

Textiles provided the most important source of industrial employment for women, although increasingly opportunities were opening up in the burgeoning service sector. The number of women and girls in both transport and factory-based occupations rose at twice the rate of their increase in the population at large between 1891 and 1911. Retailing also offered growing scope as the distributive revolution of the late nineteenth century increased both the number and size of retail shops while at the same time the development of branded goods considerably diluted the traditional skills associated with the grocery trade. Shop work was particularly appealing to women from rural backgrounds and by 1901, London's shops employed twice as many women as its commercial sector. Even so, as H. G. Wells's contemporary novels *Kipps* (1905) and *The History of Mr Polly* (1910) illustrate all too clearly, shop work remained along with professional and clerical occupations as a largely male preserve.

Only in domestic service did women actually outnumber men – by five to one – but here, as in industry, their earning power remained well below that of their male counterparts. Wages for female domestic servants were on a par with those earned by rural male workers, who were near the very bottom of the wages ladder, although the comparison is perhaps misleading in that both groups often received allowances in kind and accommodation. Similarly, women's wages in retailing were about half the level of those earned by men. Lower pay throughout the labour market reflected women's inferior social and economic status. Female weavers in the cotton industry may have been regarded as skilled workers in their own right, but they were the exception. Far more typical were those women who worked in cotton spinning where they were no more than mere appendages to skilled males. On average, women in industrial occupations were being paid at about fifty-eight pence a week, a third of the average male industrial wage.

Although wages in the service industries were unevenly distributed according to both gender and occupation, in the sector as a whole they were generally higher than the average, with the police and utilities workers very near the top of the national wage ladder. Nor were the perceived advantages of service sector work limited to income alone, for it was universally regarded as having a higher social status and, more tangibly, tended to be less volatile. For this reason jobs on the railways or as clerks were much sought after. This was in stark contrast with industry, where labour requirements fluctuated cyclically in accord with changes in the state of the economy. About a third of the world's total manufactured exports were British, with all the staple industries exporting a significant proportion of their output. Consequently, they were vulnerable to shifts in the pattern of international demand and downturns in their fortunes had knock-on effects on their own supplying industries. Given the regional concentration of these industries, it was inevitable that in turn, local labour demand would be heavily influenced by swings in international trade, and in particular the equilibrium of casual labour markets upset. In so far as this affected the general level of activity in the economy, building workers, heavy engineers and other providers of capital and infrastructural goods also suffered. Thus unemployment was consistently higher in the industrial regions of the north and, from the 1880s, Scotland. With the exception of London, the lowest levels were to be found in southern and eastern England. Even at this period, therefore, unemployment was already beginning to assume some of the regional and structural features more usually associated with the interwar period.

It is difficult, however, to be precise about the extent of unemployment in the years before the First World War. The main source of statistical evidence came from the returns made to the Board of Trade by certain trade unions paying unemployment benefit to members. In 1890 these unions were supporting 2.1 per cent of their members. Ten years later the figure had risen slightly to 2.5 per cent. Thereafter it rose to a peak of 6 per cent in 1904 and fell for a year or two before climbing again in 1908 to 7.8 per cent. It then declined annually and by 1913 was back at 2.1 per cent. It might be that these figures exaggerated the incidence of unemployment, as the unions providing them included many of those most vulnerable to cyclical employment, such as engineers, woodworkers, shipbuilders and boilermakers. On the other hand, the contemporary Liberal parliamentarian and economist Leo Chiozza Money argued that these workers were least likely to suffer from unemployment. This was partly because they represented the most skilled sections of the workforce and partly because their high degree of organization meant that they were best placed to resist employers' efforts to cut jobs. In his opinion, the trade union returns underestimated the true level of unemployment.[2]

But in any case, the unions paying unemployment benefit did not even cover all of the unionized workforce, still less the majority, for 90 per cent of workers did not belong to a union at all in 1900. Women and the unskilled were both largely absent from the figures, and thus the available evidence could in no sense be held to provide an accurate representation of either the distribution or the composition of unemployment. At best, therefore, these data give little more than an approximation of the extent of fluctuations in the level of unemployment and its underlying trend. It affords almost no help in calculating its volume, incidence, duration, or in evaluating the extent of underemployment and hidden unemployment. Yet underemployment in particular was a significant feature of the labour market. It may have been most apparent among dock workers and in London's East End, but in most major cities there existed a permanent glut of unskilled labour spread over a wide spectrum of occupations, usually in labour-intensive consumer goods industries. Such industries tended to be characterized by low capital requirements, small profit margins, easy entry and exit, and unstable demand. In order to meet demand peaks, they needed to retain a supply of labour larger than that sustainable in times of more level demand. While there was insufficient work to provide a regular livelihood, there was enough to prevent workers from straying permanently into other occupations. Their mobility was further reduced by high dependence on wives' earnings and on local suppliers of credit in order to make ends meet.

More reliable and more comprehensive information on the industrial and occupational distribution of unemployment did begin to appear after the establishment
of labour exchanges in 1909 and the introduction in 1911 of unemployment insurance. But there were still no trustworthy estimates of unused labour in the economy.
Nor was there much on which to measure the duration of unemployment, or its
relationship with variables such as skill and gender, age and turnover rates. Equally,
attempts to map the regional pattern of unemployment still depended less on statistics and rather more on the subjective and verbal assessments made by employers and
Board of Trade correspondents. The returns made by poor law officials and the
distress committees set up under the terms of the 1905 Unemployed Workmen's Act
were of equally dubious value because while pauperism was certainly related to unemployment, it was by no means synonymous with it. As a result, the relative significance of technological, frictional and structural causes remained largely unclear to
contemporaries.

In the same way there was little systematic or statistically valid analysis of the relationship between unemployment and its victims' personal attributes or backgrounds,
evidence that might have countered some of the deep-seated but ill-founded and
subjective thinking underpinning much of the contemporary approach to unemployment. Typical enough was the opinion of Helen Bosanquet, a major figure in
the Charity Organization Society, the main agent of private philanthropic effort. 'In
charitable work', she wrote, 'we devote ourselves to those who are weak, who have
in some way failed'.[3] Even a radical such as John Burns conceded that 'it is not always
the pig-stye [*sic*]; it is sometimes – yea, too often – the pig'.[4] There was certainly no
real basis for measuring the effects of unemployment, though clearly it had potentially disastrous implications for individuals and families. As Robert Roberts observed
in his recollection of Edwardian Salford, 'Men harboured a dread of sickness, debt,
loss of status; above all, of losing a job, which could bring all other evils fast in train'.[5]
For society at large, unemployment meant lower levels of consumer demand, and
increased the potential for ill health, crime, civil disorder and pauperism, all central
themes in Edwardian public discourse about social policy.

Yet even if the parameters and nature of unemployment were so imperfectly understood, not least in official circles, it was fairly clear that the burden of unemployment
fell most heavily and consistently on the young, the old and the unskilled. These were
the least able to defend themselves against the vicissitudes of the labour market,
a fact which in part may explain their apparent and general resignation. In Robert
Tressell's fictional satire on the contemporary building trades, *The Ragged Trousered
Philanthropists*, for instance, the unskilled were criticized because they 'not only
submitted quietly like so many cattle to their miserable slavery for the benefit of
others, but defended it, and opposed and ridiculed any suggestion of reform'.[6] Before
the advent of old-age pensions in 1908, few unskilled workers were able to make any
provision for old age. If their own families could not support them, they faced the
unattractive choice between charity and the workhouse, or alternatively, if they were
able, of continuing to work. Yet because unskilled labour was invariably manual and
dependent on physical strength, older workers were the most dispensable if employers wished to retrench, as Tressell's novel once again illustrates. Seeking an excuse to
reduce his workforce, the foreman at Rushton and Co., Builders and Decorators,
picks on Jack Linden, 'now really too old to be of much use . . . not worth the money

he was getting'. When Linden protests that he is working appropriately the foreman replies, 'I'm not talking about what you're doing, but the time it takes you to do it!'.[7]

There was a strong perception that the unskilled problem had its roots in adolescence, particularly in the tendency for boys to enter so-called blind-alley occupations. The argument ran thus. Working-class adolescent male school-leavers faced two options in entering the labour market. Either they could seek an apprenticeship in a skilled or semi-skilled trade, or they could opt for blind-alley employment as errand boys, general labourers or in one of the numerous occupations created by the multiplication of low-grade jobs in the expanding retail, commercial and distributive trades. As technological progress had largely deprived apprenticeship of its historic function of inculcating skills to the next generation, it survived in major cities and especially London as little more than a device for controlling the supply of labour in the interests of time-served skilled and highly paid men. Thus even most of those who took up apprenticeships, it was argued, would inevitably remain unskilled, even as adults, thereby helping to sustain the reserve army of casual labour always prone to unemployment. Often, this concern with youth unemployment was presented in terms of character, morals and public order. As one senior Glasgow police officer put it:

> At an early age boys get street employment and become independent to a great extent. They do not obtain the discipline of school and industrial training and their street education unfits them for study work. It is from the youths who have not received industrial training that the majority of hooligans come.[8]

Similar reasons lay behind the strong public response generated by the publication of E. J. Urwick's famous *Studies of Boy Life in Our Cities* (1904), which prompted fears about the implied wastage of manpower and the dilution of the racial stock.

Whatever the moral consequences, the economic arguments about the nature of adolescent unemployment simply did not hold water. For one thing, the relationship between juvenile labour supply and demand varied from region to region, and it was mainly in localities lacking a range of suitable skilled occupations that boys tended to go into blind-alley work. Second, it was not universally the case that apprenticeship had lost its connotation of skill acquisition, for this remained significant, for example in many branches of metal and engineering. Third, because most apprenticeships in the skilled trades were not available until the age of sixteen anyway, many school-leavers went into blind-alley occupations only until they were old enough to take up a formal apprenticeship. Finally, if the argument were true, one would have expected to find some correlation between adolescent work in blind-alley occupations and subsequent adult unemployment. Yet no evidence of any such link emerged from the detailed personal information gathered by local distress committees established under the terms of the 1905 Unemployed Workmen's Act to dispense relief to the unemployed. Nothing suggests that the majority of those applying for help had started their working lives in blind-alley jobs or even that they were still engaged in casual work. The explanation for the prevalence of young men among the unemployed in the 1900s was much simpler: it reflected simply their preponderance in the population as a whole. The 1901 Census of England and Wales indicated that over a half of the population was aged below twenty-five. The figures for the County of London, where the boy labour problem was believed to be most severe, showed that almost 17 per cent of the male workforce of 1,500,000 were adolescents aged between fourteen and twenty. Males in this group generally had no dependants while the frictional and seasonal nature of their work generally ensured that they could soon find a new job. This may help to explain the apparent quiescence of the unemployed noted by contemporaries such as Charles Masterman.

> There was a time when . . . we stood in knots at street corners . . . when work was solicited and solicited in vain. . . . But that time seems long ago. . . . We have no faith in its recurrence . . . we are convinced that tomorrow will see the dawn of a golden age.[9]

Yet if the nature of the boy labour problem was thus largely misunderstood, contemporary interest in it was a further manifestation of the developing concern with social conditions. From the 1880s onwards unemployment as a social phenomenon began to figure more prominently in the public consciousness and social analysis. The word itself (as opposed to 'the unemployed') made its first appearance in the *Oxford English Dictionary* in 1888, the same year as *The Times* (2 February 1888) referred to it as 'the fundamental problem of modern society'. The timing was significant in that it followed hard on the heels of major public disorder in London where unemployed demonstrations had been largely orchestrated by the left-wing Social Democratic Federation (SDF). The same group took up the baton again a few years later when the termination of the Boer War led to a minor economic recession in which reserve and discharged soldiers found it particularly difficult to get work. In 1903 the SDF's protest campaigns led the Conservative government to amend the 1867 Metropolitan Streets Act in order to prevent marchers from collecting money. This had little effect, however, and as unemployment continued to rise, the street campaign intensified. At the same time working-class MPs, some independent, others drawn from the recently formed Labour Representation Committee (LRC), pressed the Conservative government for action by introducing their own legislative remedy. Although this parliamentary effort failed, the outbreak of rioting in a number of cities in 1905 did produce a government response in the shape of the Unemployed Workmen's Act. This legislation was a landmark, representing the first acceptance by government of an obligation to provide for the unemployed. Almost at the same time, and as a direct result of riots in Manchester, the home secretary announced the establishment of a royal commission charged with examining, among other matters, the effectiveness of the poor law in dealing with industrial unemployment. Between 1907 and 1909 a further recession developed, sparked off initially by a banking crisis in the United States. Once again the unemployed appeared on the streets, organized this time mainly by a combination of working-class and left-wing political activists operating under the aegis of the national Right to Work movement. The movement sought to coordinate street marches and public protests with the parliamentary Labour party's efforts to secure the passage of the Right to Work Bill giving the unemployed the right to work or maintenance. The bill was introduced annually between 1907 and 1909 but on each occasion failed to get beyond a second reading.

In part at least this was because by 1909 the Liberal government had produced the first of its own legislative measures. The locally administered poor law rested on the philosophical principle that individuals were basically responsible for their own welfare. This view had become increasingly untenable in the light of the poverty levels uncovered by social investigators such as Seebohm Rowntree and Charles Booth. Furthermore, evidence had long been emerging that a system designed essentially for a rural society could not cope logistically with the unemployment endemic in a free-market industrial economy. The most influential thinker about unemployment was W. H. Beveridge, who argued strongly that casual work was independent of character and training, representing rather a flaw in the organization of the labour market. He also pointed out that unemployment had relatively little to do with character and everything to do with fluctuations in the demand for labour. Accordingly, the mechanism he recommended was the labour exchange, introduced from 1909 to link labour demand and supply more efficiently. Two years later the government introduced a contributory insurance scheme to protect the most vulnerable workers against the income loss incurred during spells of unemployment. Slightly earlier, the introduction of old-age pensions provided a small, guaranteed non-contributory income for those who qualified, effectively releasing many elderly people from the choice of the workhouse or continued employment.

The immediate effects of this legislation remain unknowable. For one thing, it was all introduced against a background of economic boom and relatively low unemployment. For another, the outbreak of war in August 1914 fundamentally distorted the normal workings of the labour market. Initial dislocation caused short-term job losses but employment expanded quickly as strategic industries sought to increase output at a time when significant numbers of workers were being absorbed into the fighting services. Conversely, less important industries such as railway engineering and cotton languished. Otherwise, the most obvious short-term effect was on the gender composition of the workforce. The replacement of men by women was initially slow but gathered momentum after the introduction of military conscription in 1916. The figures are not totally straightforward but in agriculture, for instance, there were 113,000 women workers in July 1918 as against 80,000 four years earlier. Far more entered the tertiary sector – 430,000 in finance and commerce, an extra 200,000 in national and local government, 100,000 in transport, with other services recruiting a further 110,000. As for industry, female numbers in the metal trades rose by 624,000, while another quarter of a million went to work in government docks, factories and arsenals – all this during a period over which the total industrial workforce declined slightly from 8,400,000 to 8,000,000. However, altogether women filled only about a third of total industrial vacancies during the war, while only about a third of those entering the labour market were actually new adult entrants. The majority simply transferred from other occupations or were school-leavers coming onto the market for the first time. It must also be stressed that in manufacturing and services alike, women's pay, status and conditions of service still remained inferior to those of their male colleagues.

Nor did this female colonization of men's occupations long survive the cessation of hostilities. By the time the post-war boom came to an end in the spring of 1920, the gender balance of the British workforce had largely resumed its pre-war shape. As the occupational census of 1921 revealed, only in commerce was there evidence of a permanent change in favour of women, albeit on predictably less favourable terms than those previously enjoyed by the now displaced men. Developments in the civil service were more typical, however. Whereas 56 per cent of its staff in 1918 were female, this had fallen by more than half to about 25 per cent by 1926. More generally it is worth noting that while the aggregate number of women in the workforce rose from 5,700,000 in 1921 to 6,300,000 by 1931, the proportion of the workforce that was female remained only marginally higher than it had been thirty years before.

If the effects of the war on the gender composition of the British labour force were largely temporary, the same could not be said for its impact on the structure of the economy and employment patterns. The ending of the conflict in November 1918 ushered in an economic boom fuelled by restocking and pent-up consumer demand. Initially, heavy industries such as coal and steel prospered because their major European competitors had sustained significant physical damage which took time to restore. Shipbuilding had wartime losses to replace and heavy investment also occurred in cotton in anticipation of continued rising demand. But after the boom broke in the spring of 1920, it gradually became apparent that the favourable international environment in which Britain's staple industries had operated before 1914 had been fundamentally disrupted. Throughout the 1920s, therefore, and despite some productivity improvements, major industries were characterized by low growth, failing exports and high unemployment.

Both the domestic and international demand for coal grew only sluggishly while new sources, first exploited during the war, added to the aggregate supply. With older, generally smaller and more labour-intensive pits, and fractious labour relations, British coal companies found it difficult to compete. Selling coal on the international market was difficult for all producers but the British industry was hardest hit simply because it had always exported a higher proportion of its output. By 1925 unemployment among the country's 1,200,000 miners was running at 11.5 per cent: four years later almost a fifth of them were out of work. By this time they had been joined by almost 13 per cent of employees in the cotton industry, where attempts to regain lost international markets were hampered by technological and organizational conservatism. Relative newcomers such as Japan were making inroads into Britain's major markets in India and China. Shipbuilding at least remained internationally competitive in the 1920s, but war-induced expansion left it with massive overcapacity, given that aggregate demand was squeezed throughout the 1920s by the very slow recovery of world trade, a general improvement in the efficiency of shipping operations, and reductions in domestic naval orders. By 1929 over a quarter of shipbuilders were out of work, although this actually represented something of an improvement, since 43.6 per cent of them had been out of work in 1923. But the difficulties in shipbuilding had adverse implications for the domestic iron and steel industry, which had also expanded massively between 1914 and 1918. Internationally, the growing preference for steel created further difficulties for a British industry specializing in wrought and pig iron and suffering from high production costs arising, in the main, from inefficient organization and obsolete plant. Here, too, unemployment rose, reaching about 20 per cent by 1929.

However, relief of a sort was provided by an increase in demand from domestic producers of automobiles and aircraft. The expansion of these and other related activities such as electrical engineering reflected a shift that was becoming manifest in the country's industrial structure. The older, labour-intensive, small-scale and export-led staples remained dominant, but the most rapid growth was in newer, science-based, capital-intensive and larger-scale industries aimed primarily at domestic consumers. As well as cars and aircraft, there were significant developments in artificial fibres, chemicals and rubber. In each of these industries, a few large enterprises such as Courtaulds, British Celanese, ICI, Ford, Austin and Nuffield accounted for a growing share of output. They also led the way in the move towards increased industrial concentration so that by 1935 more than 75 per cent of workers in factories with more than 100 employees were to be found in just a tenth of the total plants. Because these so-called new industries were capital-intensive, used more female workers and were located away from the traditional areas of heavy industry, they could not compensate adequately for the massive shakeout of labour occurring in the economically depressed staples. It has been calculated that the new industries' share of the total labour force stood at about 10.9 per cent in 1920. While it rose significantly in the course of the decade, it was still only 14.9 per cent in 1929, by which time some 1,200,000 people were officially registered as unemployed in Britain, most of them in the older traditional staples. Worse was to follow, however, as a major cyclical depression, sparked off by the Wall Street crash, swept across the globe, leaving mass unemployment in its wake. In Britain, as in every other industrial country, unemployment reached new heights. The official figure peaked at 2,745,000 in 1932 and did not fall below 2,000,000 until 1936. For the rest of the decade it averaged about 1,600,000.

These figures, however, need careful interpretation. Direct comparisons with the period before 1914 are misleading. For one thing, the workforce was significantly bigger. Between 1921 and 1938 it rose from 15,900,000 to 19,200,000, an increase of about a fifth. Second, the figures were no longer derived from trade union returns but were based on the official returns published by the new Ministry of Labour. These, however, recorded only those covered by the national insurance scheme and who bothered to register at the labour exchanges. In other words, the official statistics ignored the 40 or so per cent of the workforce not included in the scheme, even after it was extended in 1920 and 1921. Furthermore, constant tinkering with the rules over the interwar period meant that individuals became either more or less likely to register. On average, unemployment among the insured workforce between the wars worked out at 14.2 per cent, but it has been estimated that had the uninsured been included then the actual proportion of those out of work would have risen by about 20 per cent.[10] In turn, the partial nature of the interwar data makes comparison with the period after 1945 somewhat misleading, since by that time the returns were far more comprehensive. Making allowance for this by using an appropriate deflator, one calculation has concluded that the real average level of unemployment among insured workers between the wars was only 8.7 per cent.[11] But if this suggests that in historic terms interwar unemployment was not particularly remarkable, it was still two to three times higher than before 1914, and attracted constant attention from contemporaries and historians alike. Furthermore, millions were affected by it. Throughout the 1930s the official returns recorded unemployment rates that never fell below 10 per cent. This translates into 1,200,000 workers. Beveridge reckoned that some 40 per cent of these, rising by 1937 to nearer 50 per cent, were out of work for less than three months.[12] Allowing for this high turnover rate and an average of two dependants each, the official figures alone thus suggest that as many as 12 million individuals may have been affected by unemployment at one time or another.

The official figures also concealed major differences determined by location, age, gender, social class and occupation. Because the majority of insured workers were in manufacturing, it was no surprise that the incidence of unemployment should mirror the regional distribution of industry. Even within the main manufacturing areas, particular districts could suffer disproportionately. In January 1933, for instance, 91 per cent of insured workers in the northeastern village of Saltburn were out of work, while in nearby Jarrow, immortalized in Ellen Wilkinson's book *The Town that was Murdered* (1939), the figure was 77 per cent. In Wales 72 per cent were out at Pontycymmer, 66 per cent in Abertillery. It was clear, too, that older men were more likely to be affected than younger ones. By November 1932, 32 per cent of insured men aged between sixty and sixty-four were registered as unemployed and older men formed a high proportion of those out of work on a long-term basis. Few would now accept uncritically Beveridge's 1944 estimate that the proportion of those out of work for more than a year climbed to 25 per cent in August 1936 as against only 4.7 per cent five years earlier. However, all are agreed that long-term unemployment was an increasingly prominent characteristic of the 1930s. Juveniles were generally less vulnerable, perhaps because they received lower wages and benefits, or because they had higher rates of non-registration.

Male unemployment was also markedly higher than that of women. One reason for this may have been the so-called 'discouraged worker effect'. By this is meant the fact that some female unemployment was effectively masked because, had work been available, it is likely that a greater number of women would have entered the labour market at prevailing wage levels. It is also likely that in some circumstances the absence of equal pay protected them, as did their tendency to work in the service industries, where wages were lower and which were less affected by unemployment anyway. Over three-quarters of the 3 million new jobs created between 1924 and 1938 were in the service sector. In insurance and banking employment rose by a third, slightly more in distribution, and by 400,000 in domestic service. Women were the main beneficiaries of this expansion because by 1931 almost 62 per cent of female workers were in service industries as against about 35 per cent of men. Significantly for unemployment rates, however, wages had not kept pace. In insurance and banking the average annual salary actually fell from £419 to £328. In domestic service the wage bill dropped by 10 per cent, and while it rose in the distributive services, it did so at a lower rate than the labour force expanded.

Finally, the incidence of unemployment fell disproportionately upon manual workers. Social classes I–IV constituted a quarter of the total workforce in 1931 but only 8.3 per cent of the registered unemployed. On the other hand, classes V–VII, comprising skilled, semi-skilled and manual workers, made up almost three-quarters of the workforce but accounted for nearly 92 per cent of the unemployed. Even workers in the newer industries were affected by the cyclical depression of 1929–32, although average unemployment soon reverted to single-figure levels once recovery began. The staples, however, remained characterized by heavy rates of unemployment. At the depth of the depression more than a third of miners were out of work and even by 1939 the proportion was still over 12 per cent. By that date steelworkers were still experiencing rates of 15 per cent, again well down on the 1932 peak of 48 per cent but still high. The trajectory among cotton workers was similar, dropping from 43.2 per cent in 1931 to 16.9 per cent. Shipbuilders suffered worst of all, with almost two-thirds of their number unemployed in 1932 and slightly over a fifth still looking for work by 1939.

Interwar governments were clearly faced with an unemployment problem of unprecedented magnitude and persistence. The predominantly Conservative administrations of the 1920s initially provided some central support for local authority public works schemes through the Unemployment Grants Committee. Yet such programmes were designed essentially to counter cyclical fluctuations, and they were increasingly seen as both costly and irrelevant as the structural nature of unemployment became clearer. Similarly, while the Industrial Transference Act of 1928 aided the movement of some 100,000 individuals in order to find work, it hardly represented a comprehensive or realistic remedy for workers in the staple industries. In any case, few workers were willing to leave the security of familiar communities to face higher housing costs, new forms of work and the likely resentment of residents in areas to which they moved.

In the main, therefore, governments opted to maintain the unemployed rather than create work for them, progressively extending, amending and refining the 1911 National Insurance Act. It was extended in 1920 to cover many more workers, while subsequent amendments lengthened the period over which benefits could be drawn and altered the level of benefits and contributions. As the rate of unemployment settled around 10 per cent, so further steps were introduced to deal with the growing number of claimants who had exhausted their statutory right to benefit. From 1927 they became eligible for transitional benefit, in effect a dole or straightforward destitution relief, paid not from the insurance fund but from the Treasury. Both sources of relief were already hard-pressed even before unemployment was driven to higher levels still in the economic fallout from the Wall Street crash and the ensuing European banking crisis.

Despite its radical pretensions, Ramsay MacDonald's second Labour government, which took office in 1929, had little to offer. Orthodox economics, to which most Labourites subscribed and none more fervently than chancellor of the exchequer Philip Snowden, dictated that budgets should be balanced. Accordingly, calls for higher levels of public spending emanating from the left, the Trades Union Congress (TUC) and the Liberal manifesto, *We Can Conquer Unemployment* (1929), were ignored. Yet with no policy other than awaiting a recovery of world trade and with unemployment rising rapidly, the responsible ministers were forced to seek increased resources for the insurance fund just as the Treasury fund for transitional payments was falling into deficit. In July 1931 the May Committee, set up earlier in the year to examine the state of Britain's public finances, issued its report, forecasting a budget deficit of £120,000,000 and an insurance fund debt of £105,000,000. It could not have appeared at a less auspicious moment, for the collapse of Austria's largest and most prestigious bank precipitated a European banking crisis and led to the substantial withdrawal of funds from London. The May Report merely heightened the loss of international confidence in sterling. Gold poured out of Britain, as much as £60,000,000 in August alone. To stem the flow, the government prepared a broad package of economy measures, including significant reductions in expenditure on unemployment relief. Disagreements about the principle and the means by which these were to be achieved split the cabinet. In August 1931 the government resigned. MacDonald survived as premier in the ensuing National government, which did push the recommendations through. Benefits for men and their wives were reduced, while new regulations requiring the payment of a minimum number of contributions since marriage effectively reduced the number of married women eligible for support. In October transitional benefit was modified to ensure that payments did not exceed the level of insurance benefit, and all applicants were required to submit details of their family's financial circumstances for means testing by Public Assistance Committees (PACs). Young unmarried men living at home had their benefits stopped altogether. Walter Greenwood recollected how his friend Mickmac emerged from an interview with the PAC, 'mesmerised with bewilderment and quite unable to grasp the fact that he had been denied the weekly pittance'.[13] As economic recovery set in from 1932, so more considered measures were introduced. The Unemployment Act of 1934 finally put the insurance scheme on a firm basis by devolving responsibility for its administration and solvency to the Unemployment Insurance Statutory Committee. This ultimately permitted the restoration of some of the 1931 cuts. Those who had lost their entitlement to insurance benefit became the responsibility of the Unemployment Assistance Board, which retained the household means test. On a different tack altogether, a Special Areas Act was passed in 1934 offering tax and other incentives to firms willing to relocate in selected areas of high unemployment. Even so, parsimony still reigned, for by 1938 the Treasury had sanctioned only very modest expenditure of less than £10,000,000.

The National government's economy cuts and the introduction of means testing provoked widespread protest, often violent, in many major towns and there was an upsurge in membership of the Communist-led National Unemployed Workers' Movement (NUWM), which organized a series of hunger marches, especially during the depths of the 1931 crisis. Total membership reached 37,000 by the end of 1931, but still this represented only 1.5 per cent of the registered unemployed and the increase proved to be very short-lived. On the whole the NUWM did its most beneficial work on behalf of the many individuals whose cases it represented to the various authorities administering relief and benefit. Although it certainly helped to keep unemployment firmly in the public mind, it never succeeded in harnessing mass support. Some historians attribute this to a popular suspicion of its Communist connections, for only in a few isolated places did the Communist party secure much tangible political benefit. For similar reasons both the Labour party and the TUC kept their distance from the NUWM, although their endorsement might have gained it much wider popular support. After all, the one march that still lingers in working-class folklore and which attracted the most publicity at the time was the Jarrow March, the only one organized with anything resembling official support from Labour.

Why mass unemployment should have provoked relatively little violence or support for political extremism in Britain has often been seen as something of a puzzle. George Orwell implied that the explanation lay in national character, ascribing to the average Briton a respect for the law and an introversion centring on local community, private life and the family.[14] This at least has the virtue of consistency in that the same sort of traits had been observed among the unemployed before 1914. This cannot be said of W. G. Runciman's theory of relative deprivation. It argues that resentment is not a function of inequality *per se*, but rather of individuals' assessment of their standing relative to that of others with whom they habitually compare themselves. As people tend to measure themselves against those in the same neighbourhood or work environment, the geographical isolation and physical concentration of the interwar unemployed may thus explain their apparent resignation.[15] Wal Hannington, the leading figure in the NUWM, believed that there was a genuine potential for protest but that it was repressed by government action and diverted by private philanthropy.[16] In this context it is perhaps worth noting that the Home Office kept a close eye on the NUWM, penetrating it at a high level with a police agent. It is also significant that having reached Hyde Park at the end of their epic journey, the Jarrow hunger marchers were forcibly dispersed by the police. Among the philanthropic ventures of which Hannington took such a dim view were cash appeals and unemployed clubs, often sponsored by the National Council of Social Service. Some later historians have shared his analysis, arguing that the passivity of the unemployed was more apparent than real and that mass unemployment is better understood as a matter of conflict mediated by social control. More prosaically, perhaps, the explanation lay in the nature of unemployment. Older men were the most likely to be out of work for extended periods and thus the most resentful, but by virtue of their age they were perhaps also the least likely to become actively involved in protest.

Whatever its explanation, the scarcity of violent protest certainly made the task of government easier, although it is a moot point as to whether or not anything more could have been done. It has been argued, for example, that unemployment could effectively have been reduced by raising the level of public expenditure along lines advocated by the economist John Maynard Keynes. However, at best this would have countered cyclical rather than structural unemployment and it would have cut right across orthodox economic opinion in favour of balanced budgets. It is also important to note that the level of government expenditure still represented far too small a proportion of British GNP – about 8 per cent in 1938 – to facilitate outlays of sufficient magnitude to stimulate demand on the scale required. One estimate suggests that to reduce unemployment significantly government expenditure would have required an increase of some 70 per cent, a figure in the realm of political and historical fantasy.[17] Another school of thought has suggested that benefits were set too high relative to wages, effectively allowing individuals to stay out of the labour market for lengthy periods and to be choosy about what work they took.[18] Few accept this analysis, however, for it rests on a fundamental overestimation of the ratio of benefits to wages, while it can also be observed that a higher benefit–wage ratio in the 1960s and early 1970s did not lead to high unemployment. Others have suggested that high unemployment owed something to the high level of real wages.[19] Again, however, it is difficult to see how lower real wages would have increased the labour demand in the export-led staples while lower aggregate demand would undoubtedly have had an adverse effect on domestic demand, particularly on the new industries. None of this is to imply that mass unemployment between the wars was monocausal, although it is evident that structural imbalances were a major contributor.

There have been similar disputes about unemployment's effects. Statistics on real wages, consumption and diet all point to improvement between the wars and the once popular view that long-term unemployment eventually rendered its victims unemployable is not supported by the fact that when the Second World War began they were rapidly reabsorbed into the workforce. Nor can it be assumed that unemployment inevitably involved a reduction of income. For those who were normally low or intermittent wage earners, unemployment benefit could actually represent a more regular and even a higher level of income. A further relevant consideration in this context is that the unemployed benefited in exactly the same way as everyone else from the falling cost of foodstuffs after 1928. Doubt has also been cast on the contemporary opinion that the unemployed suffered unduly from poor health. Yet by their very nature statistical averages obscure the range of experiences they seek to measure, and in so far as the quality of life improved during the interwar years the bulk of the gains went to those living outside the depressed areas. The majority of the unemployed did suffer lower incomes, often falling below what contemporaries regarded as necessary for basic physical maintenance. In York, 86.4 per cent of unemployed families were found to be below the poverty line. Women frequently paid the highest price in terms of stress, diet and ill health, for it was they who had to feed and clothe their families on reduced incomes. The fact that child mortality in Jarrow was 114 per thousand as against 42 in the home counties was widely taken at the time as evidence that the children of the unemployed were similarly vulnerable. Yet some modern writers have denied that the 1930s witnessed any deterioration in the health of women and children, although the main proponent of this view subsequently conceded that there may have been some adverse effect on birth weights in the immediate and longer term.[20] In any case, it might be argued that the greatest effect of unemployment was as a social experience, leaving a great scar on the collective memory and exerting considerable influence on the thinking that produced the welfare state after 1945. This intangible but very real psychological impact was well captured by Orwell's eloquent comment on life in the depressed areas. Leaving Wigan he noticed from the train window a woman trying to clear a drain. On her face was

[t]he most desolate, hopeless expression I have ever seen. . . . She knew well enough . . . how dreadful a destiny it was to be kneeling there in the bitter cold, on the slimy stones of a slum backyard, poking a stick up a foul drainpipe.[21]

NOTES

1 C. Feinstein, 'A new look at the cost of living, 1870–1914', in J. Foreman-Peck, ed., *New Perspectives on the Late Victorian Economy: Essays in Quantitative Economic History, 1860–1914* (Cambridge, 1991), p. 158.
2 L. C. Money, *Riches and Poverty* (London, 1908), pp. 108–9.
3 H. Bosanquet, *The Administration of Charitable Relief* (London, 1898), p. 3.
4 J. Burns, 'Brains better than bets or beer', *Clarion Pamphlet*, 36 (1902), p. 5.
5 R. Roberts, *The Classic Slum: Salford Life in the First Quarter of the Century* (Harmondsworth, 1973), p. 88.
6 R. Tressell, *The Ragged Trousered Philanthropists* (London, 1940), p. 33.
7 Ibid., pp. 28–9.
8 J. Springhall, *Coming of Age: Adolescence in Britain, 1869–1960* (Dublin, 1986), pp. 104–5.
9 C. Masterman, *From the Abyss. Of its Inhabitants. By One of Them* (London, 1901), p. 14.

10   C. Feinstein, *National Income, Expenditure and Output of the United Kingdom, 1855–1965* (Cambridge, 1972).
11   D. Metcalf, S. Nickell and N. Floros, 'Still searching for a solution to unemployment in interwar Britain', *Journal of Political Economy*, 90 (1982), pp. 368–99.
12   W. Beveridge, *Full Employment in a Free Society: A Report* (London, 1944), p. 336.
13   W. Greenwood, *There Was a Time* (London, 1969), p. 181.
14   G. Orwell, *The Road to Wigan Pier* (London, 1937), p. 155.
15   W. Runciman, *Relative Deprivation and Social Justice: A Study of Attitudes to Social Inequality* (London, 1966).
16   W. Hannington, *The Problem of the Distressed Areas* (London, 1937), pp. 194ff.
17   S. Howson, 'Slump and unemployment', in R. Floud and D. McCloskey, eds, *The Economic History of Britain since 1700*, vol. 2, *1860 to the 1970s* (Cambridge, 1972), pp. 265–85.
18   D. Benjamin and L. Kochin, 'Searching for an explanation of unemployment in interwar Britain', *Journal of Political Economy*, 87 (1979), pp. 441–78.
19   S. N. Broadberry, 'The emergence of mass unemployment: explaining macroeconomic trends in Britain during the trans-World War 1 period', *Economic History Review*, 2nd series, 43 (1990), pp. 71–82.
20   J. Winter, 'Unemployment, nutrition and infant mortality in Britain, 1920–1950', in J. Winter, ed., *The Working Classes in Modern British History: Essays in Honour of Henry Pelling* (Cambridge, 1983), pp. 232–56.
21   Orwell, *Road to Wigan Pier*, pp. 16–17.

FURTHER READING

Beales, H. and Lambert, R., eds, *Memoirs of the Unemployed* (London, 1934).

Beveridge, W., *Unemployment: A Problem of Industry* (London, 1909).

Braybon, G., 'The impact of the war on women', in S. Constantine, M. W. Kirby and M. B. Rose, eds, *The First World War in British History* (London, 1995), pp. 141–67.

Brown, K. D., *Labour and Unemployment, 1900–1914* (Newton Abbot, 1971).

Buxton, N., *British Employment Statistics: Guide to Sources and Methods* (Oxford, 1977).

Constantine, S., *Unemployment in Britain Between the Wars* (London, 1980).

Crowther, M. A., *British Social Policy, 1914–1939* (London, 1988).

Deacon, A., *In Search of the Scrounger: The Administration of Unemployment Insurance* (London, 1976).

Garside, W. R., *The Measurement of Unemployment: Methods and Sources in Great Britain, 1850–1970* (Oxford, 1981).

Garside, W. R., *British Unemployment 1919–1939: A Study in Public Policy* (Cambridge, 1990).

Garside, W. R. and Hatton, T., 'Keynesian policy and British unemployment in the 1930s', *Economic History Review*, 38 (1985), pp. 83–8.

Harris, J., *Unemployment and Politics, 1886–1914* (Oxford, 1972).

Howson, S., 'Slump and unemployment', in R. Floud and D. McCloskey, eds, *The Economic History of Britain since 1700*, vol. 2, *1860 to the 1970s* (Cambridge, 1972), pp. 265–85.

Kingsford, P., *The Hunger Marchers in Britain, 1920–1939* (London, 1982).

Macintyre, S., *Little Moscows: Communism and Working-class Militancy in Inter-war Britain* (London, 1980).

McKibbin, R., 'The social psychology of unemployment in interwar Britain', in R. McKibbin, 'The social psychology of unemployment in interwar Britain', in R. McKibbin, *The Ideologies of Class: Social Relations in Britain 1880–1950* (Oxford, 1990), pp. 228–58.

Perry, M., *Bread and Work: The Experience of Unemployment, 1918–1939* (London, 2000).

Pilgrim Trust, *Men Without Work* (Cambridge, 1938).

Southall, H., 'The origins of the depressed areas: unemployment, growth and regional economic structure in Britain before 1914', *Economic History Review*, 41 (1988), pp. 236–53.

Thorpe, A. T., *The Failure of Political Extremism in Inter-war Britain* (Exeter, 1989).

Treble, J., 'Unemployment and unemployment policies in Glasgow, 1890–1905', in P. Thane, ed., *The Origins of British Social Policy* (London, 1982), pp. 147–72.

Winter, J., 'Infant mortality, maternal mortality and public health in Britain in the 1930s', *Journal of European Economic History*, 8 (1979), pp. 439–62.

CHAPTER TWENTY

Industrial Relations in Britain, 1900–1939

Arthur J. McIvor

Industrial relations might be defined as everything that impinges upon the employment relationship, involving a multitude of issues, including wages, working hours, recruitment, supervision, workplace representation and collective bargaining rights. The relationships are between people and the organizations that represent them at the workplace, local and national levels. At the very basic level these are relationships between those providing employment (employers) and those providing labour (workers). This embraces how that relationship was regulated over time and how it was mediated and influenced by subcontractors, management (including foremen), collective organizations on both sides (employers' organizations and trade unions), the state, the law, the economy, politics and society. Moreover, job regulation occurred both at the workplace – where for the majority of this period most workers remained unorganized – and at more formal levels, through, for example, joint rules agreed on wages, working hours and other conditions between the growing trade union movement and employers. Such issues have been the subject of an immense volume of research, especially since the growth of labour history as an academic sub-discipline from the 1960s. This essay provides a brief overview of the major work in this field, investigating continuities and change in industrial relations over 1900–39. Particular emphasis is placed on the role of trade unions, employers' organizations and the state in this process, and on how the First World War and the interwar economic depression affected industrial relations in Britain. For background, readers might like to consult chapters 3, 13, 15, 19 and 21 in this collection, dealing with labour politics, the economy, industry and employment patterns, and social change.

Collective Organization: Extent and Limits

The employment relationship over 1900–39 was the subject of compromise as well as conflict between labour and capital. This was an ongoing power struggle over the distribution of resources in which both sides developed organizations, applied pressure on government and utilized an array of strategies and weapons in an attempt to protect and pursue their respective interests. Undeniably, this was an unequal contest,

Table 20.1 Trade union membership (in millions) and density (as %), by gender in the UK, 1900–39

	Union membership (millions)	Union density (%)		
		total	male	female
1900	2.0	12.7	16.7	3.2
1914	4.1	23.0	29.5	8.0
1920	8.3	45.2	54.5	23.9
1930	4.8	25.4	30.8	13.4
1939	6.3	31.6	38.9	16.0

Source: G. Bain and R. Price, *Profiles of Union Growth* (Oxford, 1980), pp. 37–8.

with employers and their organizations invariably dominating industrial relations before the Second World War. With few exceptions, workers' rights and authority in the workplace were severely prescribed, their say in production matters was limited, whilst employers clung tenaciously to the notion that providing capital conferred upon them the prerogative to manage their firms (and their labour) as they thought fit. However, employers' labour management strategies assumed many forms and recent research has shown that it would be quite wrong to view British employers as monolithic, authoritarian and inflexible.[1] Employer supremacy was incomplete, nor did employer domination go unchallenged. Just as power in the political sphere was shifting, so too was power in the workplace over 1900–39 ebbing and flowing, with labour as the primary beneficiary. The key change was the germination of a powerful trade union movement.

The changing nature of work over the period 1900–39 was a pivotal factor in the incubation of a strong trade union movement in Britain (see table 20.1) and, in turn, workers and their trade unions became increasingly influential agents in the organization and regulation of wages and working conditions. However, the emergence of mass unionization and the rising propensity to strike prompted a counter-response by capital. Employers increasingly became organized in the face of accumulating pressures, not just from the unions, but also from a more hostile product market and more interventionist state. The employers' organizations witnessed mushroom growth, increasing from 336 in 1895 to almost 1,500 on the eve of the First World War, spread widely across the face of the British economy (table 20.2). Numbers of employers' organizations grew further to 2,403 by 1925 and by 1938 around half of all British workers were located in firms that were members of these organizations.[2]

Recent work on the patterns of trade union development has defined more clearly the limits as well as the extent of growth. In an important revisionist piece, Benson has reminded us that prior to 1939 the labour movement meant very little to vast swaths of ordinary working folk outside the union heartlands of coal mining, cotton and the metals and engineering industries.[3] A marked gender differential continued to characterize union membership (see table 20.1), though clearly, over time, the gap was narrowing. The same was true for non-manual workers and for agriculture, where anti-union attitudes amongst employers persisted longer and smaller-scale employ-

Table 20.2   Employers' associations in Britain, 1914

Sectors/industries	Number of associations (local, regional and national)
Building	468
Food, drink and tobacco	166
Paper and printing	116
Cotton textiles	35
Wool and worsted	24
Textile finishing	18
Tailoring	54
Boot and shoe	23
Railways	1
Road transport	40
Water transport	28
Metalworking	144
Engineering	56
Shipbuilding	25
Woodworking and furnishing	52
Mining and quarrying	38
Laundering and dyeing	29
Hairdressing	1
Undertaking	1
Bricks, pottery and glass	25
Agriculture and fishing	10
Chemicals	2
Total employers' associations	1,487

Source: Ministry of Labour, *Eighteenth Abstract of Labour Statistics* (1926), p. 191.

Table 20.3   Manual and non-manual trade union membership, UK, 1900–31

	Manual/density	Non-manual/density
1900	1,830,000 (13%)	78,300 (*c*.3%)
1911	2,730,900 (20%)	398,000 (12%)
1921	5,519,300 (40%)	992,700 (24%)
1931	3,544,000 (24%)	1,025,400 (21%)

Source: G. Bain and R. Price, *Profiles of Union Growth* (Oxford, 1980), pp. 41–2.

ment was less conducive to collective organization before the 1940s (see tables 20.3 and 20.4). Around four out of every five clerical workers, domestic servants, shop workers and agricultural workers were not members of trade unions at the outbreak of the Second World War. There also continued to exist very wide differences in workers' capacity to create and sustain trade unions across different industries (see table 20.4). This, combined with such factors as company size, levels of collective

Table 20.4   Trade union density by industry, 1892 and 1939
(expressed as % of potential membership)

	1892	1939
Agriculture, forestry	3.6	6.8
Fishing	9.8	19.5
Distribution	1.0	11.8
Insurance, banking, finance	1.8	19.5
Food and drink	6.4	23.7
Chemicals	11.2	20.4
Pottery	9.2	33.5
Clothing	6.2	23.6
Construction	7.7	21.3
Woodworking	16.3	21.6
Local government and education	5.1	62.5
Post and telecommunications	19.8	77.8
Cotton, flax and synthetic fibres	23.8	54.4
Other textiles	10.0	26.8
Metals and engineering	31.9	35.5
Footwear	25.4	63.4
Printing	27.7	51.4
Sea transport	26.9	55.9
Coal mining	59.5	81.1
Other mining and quarrying	18.4	27.2
Water transport	61.3	84.2

Source: G. Bain and R. Price, *Profiles of Union Growth* (Oxford, 1980),
pp. 43–76.

organization, labour markets, gender and skill composition of the labour force and
the wide range of different attitudes on the part of employers towards trade unions,
contributed to a broad range of experience in industrial relations in the workplace.

Whilst recognizing the limits of trade union penetration, especially within the non-
manual occupations and female segment of the labour force, none the less the contrast between 1900 and 1939 is quite striking. Moreover, the influence of the trade
unions extended somewhat beyond their numerical membership. This is evident, for
example, in the passage of ameliorative employment legislation which the unions promoted – such as the Workmen's Compensation Acts and Factory Acts – that regulated the work situations of many more workers than just those who were union
members. British trade unionism expanded from a narrow base amongst the skilled
craft artisan elite to embrace a substantial slice of semi-skilled, unskilled, non-manual
and female workers over 1900–39. This changed the nature of industrial relations in
Britain. The skilled unions that dominated the movement before 1914 were joined
and eventually displaced by the omnibus general unions (such as the Transport and
General Workers' Union and the General and Municipal Workers' Union), who
recruited semi-skilled and unskilled workers. Benson's view is a necessary corrective,
but this should not lead us to underestimate the importance of trade unions in British
society and the difference unionization made to workers' lives.

How can this marked growth in the key institution that affected industrial relations be explained? Some studies of the rise of unions and escalating strike action emphasize underlying socio-economic changes creating a more homogeneous working class with a growing awareness of itself as a group with mutual interests diametrically opposed to those who employed their labour power. The engine of growth was firmly located at the point of production.[4] The years from *c*.1880 to the 1930s witnessed an escalating speed-up in production, more draconian workplace discipline and work intensification as employers responded aggressively to declining profitability as competition in markets cranked up. Technological and organizational innovations, task reallocation, the spread of piecework wage payment systems and more systematized direct modes of supervision were elements of a more general process whereby employers were applying pressure upon labour to squeeze more from the wage for effort exchange. These developments helped to fracture deep traditions of deference and loyalty to the company and enervated workers to organize collectively to protect themselves against exploitation. The increasing size of companies depersonalized industrial relations, eroding paternalist relationships and diluting workers' loyalty to the company. Marxist historiography also stressed the key role of individual socialists in helping to form and sustain trade unions, particularly of the lesser skilled. These developments worked to energize trade unionism, alienate workers and ignite industrial militancy, especially when labour markets were tight, notably over the 'radical decade' from *c*.1910–20, as studies of the UK and Scotland have shown.[5]

Other commentators emphasize the relationship between the economic cycle and union implantation and expansion and play down the catalytic influence of socialists and labour process changes in union formation and growth.[6] In such interpretations, growing unionization largely represented an economistic response by relatively conservative workers reacting to eroding real wage levels when the opportunity of tight labour markets raised workers' bargaining power. The preconditions for growth were also laid by a more liberal state, through legislative initiatives (notably the Trades Disputes Act, 1906) providing basic rights to organize, strike and picket.[7] Relative ease of communication, rising levels of literacy, the socialist press, the rising scale of production units, growing awareness of poverty and inequalities and the knock-on effects of successful unionization and strike action are all significant supplementary variables contributing to collective organization. The First World War also had a further catalytic effect, not least because of the accumulating pressures the war economy imposed upon workers. These included rising price inflation, long work hours and exhausting work regimes geared to the war effort, blatant profiteering and growing alienation engendered by state controls such as the Munitions Act, which effectively prevented the free movement of labour and muzzled industrial militancy. The wartime government, moreover, directly encouraged collective bargaining to resolve disputes, thus facilitating the growth in trade union membership.

Industrial Conflict, Compromise and the State

Within the capitalist enterprise at the turn of the nineteenth century most individual workers (with the exception of many skilled craft artisans) lacked effective power, especially in the overstocked urban labour markets. They came to learn, however, especially when demand for labour was high, that through acting in unison they could

Table 20.5 Working days lost through industrial disputes in
Britain, 1893–1942

	Annual average (millions)
1893–1902	8.75
1903–12	8.56
1913–22	20.58
1923–32	20.83
1933–42	2.48

Source: H. Clegg, *A History of British Trade Unions since 1889*, vol. 3,
1934–1951 (Oxford, 1994), p. 421.

exert influence which might mediate grim working conditions and dilute employers'
unilateral control over production. Informal, workplace collaboration, through peer
pressure and the 'customs of the trade', had a long history amongst the artisans,
miners and cotton factory workers, and even extended, as Price has shown, to some
groups of unskilled workers, such as the dockers. Other modes of collective organization and action developed rapidly from the 1880s, though strike propensity was
uneven, with major differences in experience based on occupation and gender, and
fluctuated with external circumstances and economic conditions.[8] Growing resort by
the unions to the strike weapon and by employers to the lockout and more covert
methods of victimization opened the way to a more openly conflictual phase of industrial relations – especially over the period 1910–26 (see table 20.5). This, together
with the outbreak of the First World War, drew the British government into unprecedented degrees of intervention in industrial relations.

However, statistics and accumulated averages do have a tendency to obscure as
much as they illuminate. The recent proliferation of local and regional histories has
pointed to a much broader range of experience, of varying trajectories and of uneven
development across Britain. Apart from the major divide between the urban and rural
experience, there were marked differences in social relations between different parts
of the UK and between different regions, as Reid has shown.[9] Wales and Scotland
were characterized by more conflictual industrial relations, with persistently high
strike proneness in both countries. Whilst the notions of more autocratic employer
behaviour and more radical labour politics (the syndicalism of the Welsh valleys and
'Red Clydeside') have undoubtedly been exaggerated by some writers, none the less
there is something in the concept of a more radical 'Celtic fringe'.[10] In Scotland,
higher levels of popular protest and industrial militancy coexisted with lower levels
of trade union membership, illustrating the point that formal organization was not
necessarily a precondition for active opposition to capitalist exploitation.

The recent work of a clutch of historians has helped to reinstate employers as
significant players on this particular scene.[11] Research here has been multifaceted,
but on a number of counts has contributed to our understanding of the dynamics
of industrial relations. Britain had a long tradition of associational activity amongst
employers as well as workers. None the less, one argument has been that British
employers in general have been weak and disunited, lacking the power of their US
counterparts to smash trade unions.[12] Thus British employers contributed to trade
union growth and the fossilization of 'restrictive practices' through their own

organizational impotence. Recent work on Clydeside and on north-west England, however, suggests a rather different scenario: much more powerful and effective employers' organizations championing class interests as a defensive response to trade unionism.[13] This view is also supported in recent work on the coalowners and road haulage employers between the wars.[14] The relationship was more of a symbiotic one, with an incremental cranking-up of employers' organization at the local, industry and national levels prompting counter-initiatives within the ranks of labour (and vice versa) in an attempt to maintain the balance of power.

Employers' strategies also changed significantly over time. Many of the early British employers' associations tried to root trade unions out, following the American model. However, from the late nineteenth century violent strikebreaking and blackleg importation declined and employers gradually came to recognize and work with unions, developing progressively more sophisticated collective bargaining procedures. Where it occurred, this legitimized the presence of the unions and removed much of the fear of victimization for union activities. This process of accommodation to trade unionism took place slowly and unevenly, however, across the economy, and could be subject to reversals when economic circumstances allowed a more recalcitrant employer stance (e.g. the 1920s). None the less, British employers from the late nineteenth century tended to nurture rather than extirpate the unions. Given the increasing ability of organized labour to disrupt production, particularly in tight labour markets (see table 20.5), this conciliatory strategy was very much in the interests of profit maximization. This concession of union recognition through collective bargaining significantly stimulated union growth, but an increasing number of British employers accepted this in exchange for the other benefits inherent in this policy – including the constraining of industrial militancy, standardizing costs and stabilizing industrial relations. This outcome was most evident after 1926.

Some recent work on comparative industrial relations history corroborates this interpretation. British employers, on the whole, were far less antagonistic towards trade unions than their North American and continental European counterparts.[15] Similarly, recent research suggests that the British state was also less hostile to unionization. The state proved more willing, by the First World War, to treat labour and capital in an even-handed way, at least in principle, if not always in practice. Social stability in a more democratic state, after all, depended upon such a strategy. Having said that, the effective withdrawal of the state from industrial relations in the inter-war period inevitably strengthened the status quo, bolstering the shifting balance of power in the direction of management and employers as the economic recession deepened and persisted through the 1920s and 1930s.[16]

There remained, moreover, significant regional variations in experience. Clydeside stands out as something of an exception. The nature of social relations on the Clyde has been the subject of a long-running debate amongst labour historians for which there is insufficient space here to explore in any depth. Suffice to say perhaps that the revisionism of McLean, who dismissed the phenomenon as a 'legend', has generated a persuasive counter-blast from those who still regard Clydeside as a distinctively militant region in the early decades of the twentieth century.[17]

The expansion of women's history and gender history has also made a vital contribution to our understanding of the development of industrial relations in Britain. Such research has demonstrated the sexist, patriarchal strategies of the British labour movement which worked to limit the implantation (and sustenance) of unionization amongst women workers.[18] By refusing membership, denying access to skills and failing to prioritize issues particularly pertinent to women, British trade unions limited their own effectiveness in industrial relations before the Second World War. None the less, the evidence indicates that despite odds being against them, women increasingly organized and resisted capitalist exploitation in the workplace. A plethora of studies of the role of women at work, in unions and in strike activity has demonstrated the active involvement of women in the employment relationship. This serves to remind us that women workers were not passive in industrial relations and that the employment relationship was subject to challenge and adjustment even where workers were non-unionized. Rising levels of unionization amongst female workers (see table 20.1), moreover, were the product of improving capacities to organize as a result of a series of economic, social and political changes. These included more security in labour markets, the war economy and rising self-confidence as a result of improved status as citizens. Rather than viewing women as subordinate and inactive victims in the workplace, recent research suggests a much more dynamic scenario, where working women were involved in protest and the capacities of women to engage in collective action were advancing significantly over the long term.[19] This was despite the chauvinist policies of the male-dominated trade union movement.

Recent research on trade unions and industrial relations has tended to corroborate the role of the First World War as a primary catalyst for trade union growth. The wartime state encouraged trade unionism and collective bargaining (for example through creating the Joint Industrial Councils and extending the Wages Boards) in response to labour's enhanced bargaining power during wartime. Other commentators have explored the situation within the workplace, arguing that wartime work intensification and the pressures of dilution politicized many craft artisans and incubated a radical shop stewards' movement, fuelling campaigns for work control.[20] The catalytic role of war, however, must be kept in perspective. Union membership was rising, collective bargaining accelerating and state intervention in industrial relations was intensifying in the period 1910–14 before the war broke out, and was sustained thereafter, albeit only until the sharp economic recession in 1921.

Labour historians are now less inclined to see developments in industrial relations characterized by dramatic watersheds, or to perceive the rise of trade unions as either inevitable or all-pervasive. The earlier claims for the 'new unionism' of 1888–90 are now widely accepted as exaggerated, including the view that these organizations were markedly more radical and strike prone before the First World War. Labour historians now tend to stress longer-term changes in union structure, orientation and industrial relations and to emphasize the fact that existing 'old' unions gained considerable numbers of members, moved to the left over these years and continued to dominate the movement until well into the interwar years. There have also been reinterpretations of the role of ideology in the rise of trade unionism. Romanticized notions of an extensive socialist and syndicalist presence within the unions has been placed firmly in perspective in recent work which has shown that syndicalism did not play a major role in union growth, or, indeed, in the massive surge in strike activity that characterized the so-called 'labour unrest' of the years 1910–14. Similarly, there has been an undermining of the idea that the General Strike of 1926 was a pivotal watershed in British industrial relations history.[21]

Table 20.6 Strike settlement by labour replacement, 1891–1919

	% of strikes	% of workers involved
1891–9	14.8	3.1
1900–9	12.9	2.4
1910–19	4.8	0.3

Source: Board of Trade, *Annual Reports on Strikes and Lock-outs, 1891–1913; Abstract of Labour Statistics, 1898–1937.*

Increasingly from the 1890s, industrial relations were regulated jointly through collective agreements struck between the unions and employers' organizations and disputes between management and men orchestrated through stage-by-stage disputes procedures. Employers took the initiative in developing many of these institutional arrangements, which were designed, in part, to strangle strike activity – particularly 'wildcat' unofficial industrial action. By 1920 most of the major industries had embraced national collective bargaining, including cotton, wool, coal, engineering, building, shipbuilding, iron and steel, printing, chemicals, railways and road transport. At this point almost half of all those employed had their basic working conditions regulated by joint agreement. At one level, this thrust towards more conciliatory strategies was reflected in the declining propensity on the part of the bosses to break strikes by importing non-unionized ('blackleg') labour (see table 20.6). What is evident is that the openly conflictual industrial relations of the early twentieth century gave way after a painful period of adjustment in the 1920s to the corporatism and cooperation that characterized industrial relations in the UK in the 1930s.

The state played a key role in all this. From the early 1890s the government directly encouraged workers and employers to regulate work conditions through collective bargaining, seeing this as the best way to stabilize industrial relations in the public interest. With the 'labour unrest' of 1910–14 and the war, the state was drawn into more direct intervention as a mediator in the major industrial disputes. Moreover, collective bargaining was directly extended by the state to many of the poorly organized occupations through the creation of the Whitley Committees (Joint Industrial Councils) from 1917. By 1920, this added around 2 million more workers to the list of those covered by nationally negotiated agreements on wages and work conditions.[22]

What needs to be emphasized, however, is the importance of workers themselves, as an agency capable of regulating employment relations, working conditions and the labour process. Workers responded positively and proactively to changes in production and reacted and adapted to managerial authority and changing employers' strategies.[23] As labour management became more direct and sophisticated over 1900–39, with the decline of subcontracting, foremen drawing nearer to management and the increasing bureaucratization of supervision associated with the (albeit slow and uneven) spread of scientific management ideas (particularly through the Bedaux system), so workers increasingly turned to trade unions – at both the industry and workplace levels – to protect and advance their interests. Over the period 1900–39 it is undeniably the case that trade union influence and control in employment matters extended significantly, though this was uneven and certainly no unilinear process, subject to attack and reversal depending upon prevailing economic, social and political circumstances.

Marxist-inspired notions of capital and labour in perpetual conflict have been eroded in recent research, and replaced by more nuanced theories of the coexistence of cooperation and conflict in employment relations.[24] This is reflected in much of the 'new' labour history, for example of coal mining.[25] Clearly, capital–labour relations did involve violence, conflict and confrontation, and in the early part of this period strikes could be forcibly broken and workers ruthlessly starved into submission. Conflict, however, was episodic and capital–labour relationships were also characterized over long periods by cooperation and peaceful coexistence. In part, this represented a successful strategy on the part of employers to manufacture consent and loyalty to the company. Many employers developed an explicitly welfarist labour relations strategy designed to enhance managerial control over labour. This incorporated the provision of company housing, pension schemes and other company 'perks' (such as medical facilities), as well as the provision of sports and other cultural activities centred around the firm. ICI and Singer provide concrete examples. Fitzgerald has demonstrated the prevalence of such policies across the economy and how they could succeed in drawing workers' attachment away from the union and towards the company.[26]

Moreover, with the growing power of the unions and the prestige of the Trades Union Congress (much enhanced by their cooperative stance during wartime), the political muscle of the trade unions was consolidated. This was reflected in tangible improvements in labour conditions through legislation. It was no coincidence that it was in coal mining – where trade union densities were amongst the highest in Britain in the 1900s and 1910s – that an eight-hour day and a minimum wage (by region) were achieved by legislation before the First World War. The proliferation of workplace legislation also owed much to trade union pressure, and these reforms, though far from perfect, did play a significant part in reducing the death rate through industrial accidents. Between 1900 and 1939 the chance of a worker sustaining a fatal injury whilst at work fell by more than a half.[27] The trade unions were also involved in seesawing guerilla warfare to curb pro-employer judge-made legal decisions and to attain the passage of new employment laws which consolidated and extended the legal rights of the unions. The notable legislation here was the Trades Disputes Act of 1906. This reversed the infamous Taff Vale decision of 1901, reviving the possibility of effective picketing and facilitating unfettered strike action in defence of work conditions and wages.[28] A further expression of the political muscle of the unions was their success in attaining state assurances that pre-war employment conditions would be protected in the Restoration of Pre-War Practices Act (1919). The virtually unopposed implementation of this legislation over 1919–20 speaks volumes for the power of the trade unions in the tight labour markets of the immediate post-war boom years.

In parallel with the increasing role of the unions at the political and industry-wide levels was a marked enhancement of the power of the trade unions at the workplace level. By 1920, shop stewards and workplace committees were well established across a wide range of industries – although most extensively in engineering and metalworking – and were responsible for the day-to-day regulation of many areas of work-shop life. Even before the war, the number of workplace representatives was increasing and their role was widening. In cotton manufacture, for example, the shop representatives were reacting with unofficial action to the myriad grievances over poor-quality raw material ('bad spinning') and were operating as conduits through which millworkers' grievances over the work environment, health and safety (such as lighting, temperature, dust and humidity) were channelled through to management. Again, however, the First World War had a critical impact. In engineering, the shop stewards' negotiating role was formally enshrined and codified in the Shop Stewards' Agreement of 1919.[29]

As unions grew and formalized industry-wide collective bargaining developed, there emerged a wider gulf between the trade union leaders and officials on the one hand, and the mass of workers on the other. Historians disagree on the extent and the implications of this gap between leaders and 'rank and file'. The schematic postulation of a 'reformist' and 'incorporated' leadership contrasted with a revolutionary and dissenting 'rank and file' embedded in much Marxist writing has been much criticized in recent research. Tension invariably existed between national leaders and local activists, examples of which can be found in the syndicalist traditions of the south Wales miners, the rank-and-file railwaymen's committees, and the Minority Movement between the wars. However, to equate the views of the mass of inactive and frequently non-organized workers with the local activists and shop stewards (often themselves active socialists, syndicalists and Communists) is in itself problematic.[30] Be that as it may, what is evident is that the workplace dimension in industrial relations was becoming more important. By 1920 there is clear evidence of the coexistence of two systems of industrial relations; one informal and located in the workplace, the other formal, involving relationships and agreements negotiated between national trade unions and employers' organizations.

Workers, then, could resist and mediate the conditions of labour imposed upon them by capital. However, there were limits beyond which most employers would not go. Direct encroachment by unions and/or stewards into production matters and labour process issues (such as technological innovation and machine staffing) remained rare outside of engineering. An important distinction to be made here, noted by the American observer Carter Goodrich in his seminal study in 1920, is that union controls and influence were much more extensive on issues relating to the labour contract – wages, hours, overtime, holidays etc. – than they were over the organization of work. Even at this time, few bosses were willing to condone direct encroachment into the very kernel of managerial prerogatives. The concessions to the unions on production matters that were made pre-1920, moreover, were largely tactical rather than strategic. Much ground was regained when economic circumstances shifted the balance of power back towards the employers.

Industrial Relations and the Economic Recession, 1920–1939

The interwar years were a period of retrenchment for the trade union movement, traditionally viewed as an era of erosion of union power and authority at the point of production.[31] Certainly, mass unemployment severely circumscribed the capacity of the unions to protect members at all three levels: in the workplace, industry-wide and in relation to the political power of the unions. Despite the centralization of power in the hands of the Trades Union Congress (TUC) and the drift towards more moderate, cooperative and corporatist approaches by the union leaders, the TUC was denied access to the corridors of political power throughout the interwar years. Pro-labour legislation capable of reforming exploitative working conditions was difficult to attain in this period. A new Factory Act, first mooted in 1922, was not made law until 1937. Again, anti-labour legislation – notably the 1927 Trade Union and Trade Disputes Act – circumscribed the capacity of the unions to strike and picket. As union densities dropped as the recession deepened, there was a discernible tendency to drift back to labour contracts struck between the individual worker and employer. Only twenty of the seventy-three Joint Industrial Councils survived the interwar depression.[32] This process was aided by some employers breaking away from their employers' organizations to go it alone in the depression. In two large industries, coal mining and wool manufacture, the system of national collective bargaining broke down and there was a reversion to district bargaining. In the cotton industry, the collective bargaining system collapsed in 1932 and was formally suspended by the employers' associations, leaving millowners the discretion to exploit market circumstances to set wages and conditions at whatever level they thought fit. Elsewhere, across the basic sectors of the economy, an employers' offensive designed to cut labour costs and reassert managerial prerogatives gathered momentum, with power revitalized by the depression. The defeat of the unions in the 1926 General Strike aided this process of disciplining labour and drawing the teeth of the unions, resulting in an under-mining of radical, syndicalist strategies and strengthening the hands of the moderates within the trade union movement.

Furthermore, workplace bargaining and the power of the shop stewards was seriously diminished by a wave of sackings and victimization geared towards the elimination of the wartime activists from positions of influence on the shopfloor. This process was aided by the emergence of the Economic League, a powerful anti-socialist organization operating as a centralized political vetting and blacklisting agency from the mid-1920s. Mass unemployment made it difficult to protest and harder to recruit replacement shop stewards in a climate of fear and chronic job insecurity. Not surprisingly, in the circumstances, workplace representation atrophied and with it the protective matrix provided by the shop stewards.

These developments, however, need to be kept in perspective. Recent research has indicated that it is wrong to view even the 1920s and 1930s as entirely barren years for the unions. Whilst their power was undermined (and severely so across the basic sectors of the economy), the unions remained capable of protecting members' interests and continued to regulate employment relationships, through largely defensive actions in the 1920s, and, increasingly from 1933 on, by again moving on to the offensive. It took fully six years of mass unemployment over 1920–6 to discipline workers and their unions into acceptance of the realities of a changed marketplace. The employers' counter-attack during the years of mass unemployment in the 1920s and early 1930s was neutered by the strength of the unions and the solidarity and residual militancy of labour. This was manifest in lower wage cuts over 1929–32 (compared to 1920–2) and the retention, apart from a couple of notable exceptions (including coal), of employers' commitment to union recognition and collective bargaining. Indeed, what is perhaps surprising is the extent to which collective bargaining survived the 1920s and 1930s. Employers did not, in the main, exploit the opportunity of the deep interwar economic recession to extirpate the unions. Moreover, in the 1930s state intervention aimed at reinforcing collective bargaining systems revived.

In 1933, at the nadir of the depression, it has been estimated that some 7 million workers were covered by voluntary collective agreements and a further 2 million or so by the Trade Boards.[33] This amounted to almost three times the number of workers subject to collectively bargained agreements on wages and working conditions in 1900. Rowe's detailed study of wage determination in 1928 stressed the capacity of the trade unions to regulate wages even in the depression. This he linked to changes in employers' attitudes, with most employers accepting shorter hours and the concept of a minimum wage:

> The general body of employers has swung round from a militant condemnation of trade unionism, to a general recognition of its function in the modern industrial relations system, even though its policies and practices may be the subject of violent denunciation.

He added:

> The modern developments in trade union organisation are the root cause of the numerous changes which have occurred in the whole structure of wages in this country. Trade unionism has been the yeast which has altered the whole shape and nature of the loaf. In 1886 collective bargaining over wages was unusual . . . For the past seven to ten years . . . conditions of ordinary competition have ceased to exist in the market for labour, and have been replaced by conditions of almost bi-lateral monopoly.[34]

A few years later, in the mid-1930s, John Hilton's wide-ranging survey of workplace industrial relations illustrated that the ability of work groups to maintain the power to regulate their work survived, in many cases, the worst ravages of the interwar slump. A whole range of 'restrictive' practices were still effective, including overtime restrictions and bans, opposition to piecework, 'going slow' and apprentice restrictions in engineering, shipbuilding, printing, building and woodworking. Significantly, moreover, Hilton found this to be the case amongst some unskilled groups, for example the dockers, as well as amongst the more skilled in industries such as building, printing and engineering.[35]

Evidence of widespread strikes against the Bedaux system between the wars and recent case studies in engineering and shipbuilding confirm the capacity of local work groups and union branches to maintain their power to regulate industrial relations and mediate transformations of work in the 1920s and 1930s.[36] Moreover, the improvements in pay in coal mining in the later 1930s, the passage of a new Factory Act in 1937 and the Holidays with Pay Act in 1938, the revival of strike activity and unofficial organization and action, are all signs of an energizing of union activities from c.1933 that resulted in tangible gains in the labour contract in the immediate pre-Second World War years. The trade unions may well have had a subordinate role, but evidently were still operating as a protective buffer against overwork and exploitation even during the interwar depression.

Conclusion: Continuity and Change in Industrial Relations

In the first four decades of the twentieth century relations between capital and labour in the UK varied widely in what was a diverse economy supporting many different types of work. A sharp contrast existed in industrial relations between unorganized workers and their employers, and between employers and workforces that were unionized. The extent of the former has tended to be overlooked by labour historians – partly because documentation on industrial relations is less abundant where institutions such as trade unions and employers' organizations did not exist. In the 1930s, two-thirds of all workers were not union members. In most British workplaces, therefore, unilateral regulation of the labour contract by the bosses persisted and management retained firm control over the production process. This was especially so outside the heartlands of strong trade unionism – in offices, shops, small workshops, on the land and in domestic service (the largest single employer of female labour). Right up to the Second World War, unskilled and female workers (outside of the cotton factories) were very unlikely to have had their employment relationships and labour contracts negotiated by trade unions.

The interwar depression facilitated the process whereby employers and their associations reasserted their authority in industrial relations. One steelworker reflected back in 1938: 'Throughout all of this period the feeling of insecurity and uselessness continued. To have a job at all was a privilege'.[37] There still existed a range of industrial relations strategies, from company paternalism through to crude, authoritarian management policies where employers refused any interference in their discretionary power in the workplace. In the main, however, oral and autobiographical testimony suggests that we should not underestimate the persistence of draconian, unilateral, hire-and-fire management, especially in the unorganized sector, right through to the end of the 1930s. It should be emphasized, however, that there is still relatively little systematic study of industrial relations in the unorganized sectors of the economy. This void has undoubtedly contributed to a persistent tendency amongst industrial relations historians to overextrapolate from the organized sector.

State intervention in labour markets and industrial relations did have some ameliorative impact, though historians argue over the degree to which government supported capital, labour, or were neutral in employment relations. The thrust of labour law over 1900–39, despite the more draconian Trade Disputes Act of 1927, improved workers' rights to organize, picket and protest. Moreover, with heightened intervention in the employment relationship, through the factory code, Workmen's Compensation laws, social welfare legislation (such as National Insurance) and the Trade Boards, the state effectively modified and liberalized the nature of industrial capitalism, eliminating many of the worst excesses of the repressive capitalist work regimes of the Victorian era. After the Conciliation Act of 1896, moreover, the state directly encouraged voluntary collective bargaining and stimulated the growth both of 'responsible' trade unions and employers' organizations. However, whilst the state bolstered workers' rights in employment, the capitalist system of production relations remained virtually unscathed. There was no systematic interference in the labour process, nor did the state promote real democracy at work or address effectively the problems of occupational health and safety in the workplace.[38] Inequalities based on class, occupation and gender persisted in industrial relations and whilst workers were cushioned somewhat by a more active state, they remained subject to the vicious vagaries of a fragile economy and the inexorable force of deindustrialization as the interwar depression deepened.

One of the main changes over 1900–39 in industrial relations was the emergence of a mass trade union movement, though historians now are as apt to note the limits of collective organization as well as the extent of union penetration. Employers reacted by strengthening their own collective organizations and both unions and employers' associations became part of the fabric of British society over this period, though the 'forward march' of the unions was neither uniform nor inevitable, as the experience of the interwar depression indicates. The labour movement demonstrated its new-found power, especially over the period 1910–26, challenging capital at a number of levels. What emerged was the institutionalization of industrial relations, with the growth of a system of voluntary collective bargaining that was sanctioned by the state and designed to regulate employment relations and minimize disruption of production through industrial disputes. The bureaucratization of labour relations was strengthened during the 1920s and 1930s and the combined impact of the system and the disciplining effect of mass unemployment operated drastically to reduce time lost through industrial disputes after the General Strike of 1926.

On the eve of the Second World War, the trade union movement in Britain was effectively operating both as a protective buffer against the worst excesses of exploitative capitalism and as policemen against their own rank-and-file activists who were constrained by an institutional framework that strangled discontent and marginalized radical industrial politics. The employment relationship continued to involve tensions and dissatisfaction – even alienation – which episodically boiled over into overt class conflict (as in the General Strike and in cotton textiles over 1929–32). However, mass unemployment helped to shift the balance of power in industrial relations back to the employers, whose successful reassertion of authority in the workplace, whilst incomplete and subject to mediation, characterized the 1920s and 1930s. That said, an outside observer comparing 1939 with 1900 would still be struck by something of a transformation in industrial relations. Coercive managerial policies and confrontational employment relationships were far less in evidence, replaced by a willingness by employers to negotiate and a spirit of consensus and collaboration pervading the major industrial sectors of the economy.

NOTES

1   See A. J. McIvor, *Organised Capital* (Cambridge, 1996); H. Gospel, *Markets, Firms and the Management of Labour in Modern Britain* (Cambridge, 1992); S. Tolliday and J. Zeitlin, eds, *The Power to Manage?* (London, 1991); R. Johnston, *Clydeside Capital* (East Linton, 2000).

2   H. Gospel, 'Employers and managers: organisation and strategy', in C. J. Wrigley, ed., *A History of British Industrial Relations*, vol. 2, *1914–1939* (Brighton, 1987), p. 161.

3   J. Benson, *The Working Class in Britain, 1850–1939* (London, 1989).

4   See E. J. Hobsbawm, *Labouring Men: Studies in the History of Labour* (London, 1964); R. Price, *Labour in British Society* (London, 1986); A. J. McIvor, *A History of Work in Britain, 1880–1950* (London, 2001); W. W. Knox, *Industrial Nation: Work, Culture and Society in Scotland, 1800 to the Present* (Edinburgh, 1999).

5   See, for example, W. Kenefick and A. McIvor, eds, *Roots of Red Clydeside 1910–1914?* (Edinburgh, 1996).

6   See J. Lovell, *British Trade Unions, 1875–1933* (London, 1977); H. Clegg, A. Fox and A. F. Thompson, *A History of British Trade Unions since 1889*, vol. 1, *1889–1910* (Oxford, 1964); D. Matthews, '1889 and all that: new views on the new unionism', *International Review of Social History*, 36, no. 1 (1991).

7   K. D. Brown, 'Trade unions and the law', and C. Wrigley, 'The government and industrial relations', in C. J. Wrigley, ed., *A History of British Industrial Relations*, vol. 1, *1875–1914* (Brighton, 1982), pp. 116–58; W. Hamish Fraser, *A History of British Trade Unionism, 1700–1998* (London, 1999), pp. 97–127.

8   See Price, *Labour in British Society*; J. Cronin, *Industrial Conflict in Modern Britain* (London, 1979); C. J. Wrigley, 'The trade unions between the wars', in Wrigley, ed., *History of British Industrial Relations*, vol. 2.

9   A. Reid, *Social Classes and Social Relations in Britain, 1850–1914* (London, 1992).

10 Knox, *Industrial Nation*; Johnston, *Clydeside Capital*; C. Williams, *Capitalism, Community and Conflict: The South Wales Coalfield, 1898–1947* (Cardiff, 1998).

11 See Gospel, *Markets*; H. Gospel and C. Littler, eds, *Managerial Strategies and Industrial Relations* (London, 1983); J. Melling, 'Scottish industrialists and the changing character of class relations in the Clyde region, *c.*1880–1918', in A. Dickson, ed., *Capital and Class in Scotland* (Edinburgh, 1982).

12 H. Phelps Brown, *The Origins of Trade Union Power* (Oxford, 1983); Tolliday and Zeitlin, *Power to Manage?*

13 McIvor, *Organised Capital*; Johnston, *Clydeside Capital*.

14 P. Smith, 'The road haulage industry 1919–40', *Historical Studies in Industrial Relations*, 3 (March 1997); P. Smith, 'The stupidest men in England?', *Historical Studies in Industrial Relations*, 4 (September 1997).

15 See D. Geary, *European Labour Politics from 1900 to the Depression* (London, 1991); W. Mommsen and H.-G. Husung, eds, *The Development of Trade Unionism in Great Britain and Germany, 1880–1914* (London, 1985).

16 Wrigley, 'Government and industrial relations'; R. Lowe, 'The government and industrial relations, 1919–39', in Wrigley, ed., *History of British Industrial Relations*, vol. 2.

17 See I. McLean, *The Legend of Red Clydeside* (Edinburgh, 1983); J. Foster, 'Strike action and working-class politics on Clydeside, 1914–1919', *International Review of Social History*, 35 (1990); Knox, *Industrial Nation*; Kenefick and McIvor, *Roots of Red Clydeside*; Johnston, *Clydeside Capital*.

18 See, for example, S. Walby, *Patriarchy at Work* (Cambridge, 1986); G. Braybon and P. Summerfield, *Out of the Cage* (London, 1987); E. Gordon, *Women and the Labour Movement in Scotland, 1850–1914* (Oxford, 1991).

19 See Gordon, *Women and the Labour Movement*; M. Glucksmann, *Women Assemble* (London, 1990); McIvor, *History of Work*, pp. 174–99.

20 J. Hinton, *The First Shop Stewards' Movement* (London, 1973).

21 See K. Laybourn, *A History of British Trade Unionism, c.1770–1990* (Stroud, 1992); K. Laybourn, *The General Strike of 1926* (Manchester, 1993).

22 See K. D. Ewing, 'The state and industrial relations: collective laissez-faire revisited', *Historical Studies in Industrial Relations*, 5 (Spring 1998); Wrigley, 'Government and industrial relations'.

23 See Price, *Labour in British Society*; M. Burawoy, *The Politics of Production* (London, 1985).

24 See P. Joyce, 'Work', in F. M. L. Thompson, ed., *The Cambridge Social History of Britain, 1750–1950*, vol. 2 (Cambridge, 1990).

25 See R. Church and Q. Outram, *Strikes and Solidarity: Coalfield Conflict in Britain, 1889–1966* (Cambridge, 1998).

26   R. Fitzgerald, *British Labour Management and Industrial Welfare, 1846–1939* (London, 1988).

27   McIvor, *History of Work*, pp. 116–17, 132–3.

28   J. Saville, 'The Trades Disputes Act of 1906', *Historical Studies in Industrial Relations*, 1 (March 1996).

29   G. D. H. Cole, *Workshop Organisation* (London, 1923), pp. 130–1. See also Hinton, *First Shop Stewards' Movement*.

30   J. Zeitlin, 'From labour history to the history of industrial relations', *Economic History Review*, 40 (1987).

31   N. Branson, *Britain in the 1920s* (London, 1975); J. Hinton, *Labour and Socialism* (Brighton, 1983).

32   Ewing, 'State and industrial relations', p. 18.

33   Clegg, *History of British Trade Unions*, vol. 2; S. Milner, 'The coverage of collective pay-settling institutions in Britain, 1895–1990', *British Journal of Industrial Relations*, 33 (1995), p. 82.

34   J. W. F. Rowe, *Wages in Practice and in Theory* (London, 1928), pp. 176–7, 194–5.

35   J. Hilton et al., *Are Trade Unions Obstructive?* (London, 1935).

36   A. McKinlay and J. Zeitlin, 'The meaning of managerial prerogative', in C. Harvey and J. Turner, eds, *Labour and Business in Modern Britain* (London, 1989); C. R. Littler, *The Development of the Labour Process in Capitalist Societies* (London, 1982); K. Whitson, 'Worker resistance and Taylorism in Britain', *International Review of Social History*, 42 (1997).

37   J. Common, ed., *Seven Shifts* (London, 1938), p. 78.

38   See, for example, G. Tweedale, *Magic Mineral to Killer Dust* (Oxford, 2000); R. Johnston and A. McIvor, *Lethal Work: A History of the Asbestos Tragedy in Scotland* (East Linton, 2000).

FURTHER READING

Benson, J., *The Working Class in Britain, 1850–1939* (London, 1989).

Braybon, G. and Summerfield, P., *Out of the Cage* (London, 1987).

Clegg, H., *A History of British Trade Unions since 1889*, vol. 2, *1911–1933* (Oxford, 1985).

Gospel, H., *Markets, Firms and the Management of Labour in Modern Britain* (Cambridge, 1992).

Gospel, H. and Littler, C., eds, *Managerial Strategies and Industrial Relations* (London, 1983).

Hamish Fraser, W., *A History of British Trade Unionism, 1700–1998* (London, 1999).

Harvey, C. and Turner, J., eds, *Labour and Business in Modern Britain* (London, 1989).

Johnston, R., *Clydeside Capital* (East Linton, 2000).

Knox, W. W., *Industrial Nation: Work, Culture and Society in Scotland, 1800 to the Present* (Edinburgh, 1999).

McIvor, A. J., *Organised Capital* (Cambridge, 1996).

McIvor, A. J., *A History of Work in Britain, 1880–1950* (London, 2001).

Phelps Brown, H., *The Origins of Trade Union Power* (Oxford, 1983).

Price, R., *Labour in British Society* (London, 1986).

Tolliday, S. and Zeitlin, J., eds, *The Power to Manage?* (London, 1991).

Walby, S., *Patriarchy at Work* (Cambridge, 1986).

Williams, C., *Capitalism, Community and Conflict: The South Wales Coalfield, 1898–1947* (Cardiff, 1998).

Wrigley, C. J., ed., *A History of British Industrial Relations*, vol. 1, *1875–1914* (Brighton, 1982).

Wrigley, C. J., ed., *A History of British Industrial Relations*, vol. 2, *1914–1939* (Brighton, 1987).

Readers might also peruse the appropriate journals, especially *Labour History Review, Historical Studies in Industrial Relations, Social History, International Review of Social History, Scottish Labour History* and *Llafur: The Journal of the Welsh Labour History Society.*

CHAPTER TWENTY-ONE

Social Structure, 1900–1939

ANDREW MILES

Introduction

Twenty-five years ago, writing about this subject would have been somewhat easier than it is today. Most social historians at that time could agree that 'social structure' was essentially about 'class' and that early twentieth-century Britain was definitely a 'class society'. Things were perhaps a little more complicated than the influential social theorist Karl Marx had suggested, but while the Marxist overcoat might have become a little loose about the waist and worn at the elbow, it was still serviceable. By the mid-1980s all this had changed. 'Postmodernism' had arrived, and many writers began to question whether the emperor was, in fact, naked.[1] New attention to popular political discourse in the past suggested that the 'language of class' was at best a marginal component. Class analysis, several prominent commentators concluded, was simply part of a 'narrative' – an expression of a particular intellectual and political agenda rather than a useful way of apprehending social reality.

The 'linguistic turn', as it became known, not only called into question the utility of class interpretations of social structure, but also the relevance of social structure itself. For Marx, 'the history of all hitherto existing societies [was] the history of class struggle'.[2] In other words, social structure *explained* social and political change. People's shared economic circumstances underpinned their social identity, which, in turn, strongly influenced what they thought about the world and how they acted. By contrast, postmodern accounts emphasize both the contingent nature of historical change and the importance of the political sphere in this process.

The following account of social structure in Britain between 1900 and 1939 reflects the impact of postmodernist challenges to 'orthodox' accounts of British social history. But it rejects both the idea that social structure played little part in explaining change and the contention that class analysis has little to offer an understanding of social structure in this period. The importance of sources of social identity besides class – age, religion, gender and nationality, for example – must be recognized, but so too the fact that these often interacted with class. Classes themselves are understood here in the broad sense of collectivities defined by their (unequal) access to market resources and life chances. Following E. P. Thompson's famous dictum, classes are not fixed or static categories – 'things' – but dynamic, mutable entities which form and reform in a recursive fashion over time.[3] As such, both social and spatial mobility are considered to be crucial dimensions in the process of class formation, because they underpin the cohesiveness and permeability of class groups. Shared experience of work, education, wealth, living conditions and opportunities for improvement creates the potential for a shared understanding of the world and may lead to the development of class cultures and collective political activities. But, equally, it may not. Nor, if it does, can we predict the outcome.

This chapter is divided into three sections, by chronology. The first part concentrates on the years 1900 to 1914, the second on 1914 to 1921, and the third, 1921 to 1939. In many respects this is an artificial compartmentalization because there were continuities and trends in social structure that lasted across the period as a whole. On the other hand, the relationship between social structure and change was clearly contingent on context and circumstance. In this sense, there was nothing more influential in this period than the coming of war in 1914.

1900–1914

Officially, Britain had no social structure until 1913. This was the year in which the General Register Office (GRO) attempted the first public classification of the nation along social – as opposed to purely occupational or industrial – lines. The registrar general's scheme described a graded system of five 'social classes', based on collections of occupations that were differentiated by their 'general standing in the community'. At the top of this scheme were high-status 'professional' occupations. At the bottom were unskilled manual occupations. This model of the class structure, which was created by the GRO's superintendent of statistics T. H. C. Stevenson to study fertility data from the 1911 Census, was to remain in use for the rest of the twentieth century. But, as Simon Szreter's work has shown, it was as much a product of the changing dynamics of Edwardian society as an accurate depiction of that society's structure.[4]

Stevenson's scheme was developed in a wider context of perceived social crisis. Among many influential Edwardians there was a sense that the fabric of their society was disintegrating in the face of inequality and social division. The rediscovery of poverty, further illuminated by military embarrassment in South Africa and the rise of economic competition overseas, fed anxieties about the state of the British 'race' and its capacity to respond to the challenges of the future. At the same time, the foundation of the Labour party, underpinned by steady expansion of the trade union movement and continuing industrial unrest, seemed only to confirm the polarization of society along class lines.

Against this background, the specific purpose of the 1911 fertility census was to address the claims of an influential group of Darwinian eugenicists that the masses were outbreeding their masters, and that social policy should therefore be used to curtail the reproduction of the hereditarily 'unfit' poor. They were opposed by an alliance of 'environmentalists', made up of social investigators – including the demographers at the GRO – local government officials and Fabian socialists who saw poverty as the product of economic and cultural conditions. While few contemporaries would have placed professionals at the pinnacle of their society, the self-image of this emergent collection of social scientists, academics, administrators and policy makers, Harold Perkin has argued, cast them in the role of society's redeemers. These groups felt that they stood outside of the conflict between capital and labour, and as such were able to articulate an independent identity through their criticism of the negative features of capitalist society.[5]

Perkin's wider argument is that over the course of the twentieth century professional values, emphasizing merit and trained expertise over more traditional forms of property, were to undermine the segregated, class-based character of British society. Meanwhile, he claims, the period 1900–14 represented the 'zenith of class society' in Britain. But to what extent can social structure in the period 1900–14 be understood in this way? Recent accounts have suggested that class rhetoric may have been more significant than class divisions themselves. According to this view, the notion of class conflict in the Edwardian period was as much a product of the discourse of self-interested groups – such as the GRO demographers – and of political parties seeking to mould their constituencies, as a social reality. David Cannadine, for example, has pointed out that there were, and have been throughout the past two centuries in Britain, various competing and sometimes overlapping images of society. Among these, he argues, the dichotomous, adversarial, 'capital versus labour' model derived from the work of Marx was probably the least resonant. Mostly, and most often, he suggests, people also thought of themselves as belonging to a continuous, integrated, status hierarchy, hence the popularity of the monarchy and the aristocratically led Conservative party among many working people.[6]

One reason for the marginality of the two-class model of society in people's subjective understandings of their position in society, it is suggested, is that there was little objective substance to such a model. 'Capital' was comprised of a heterogeneous assortment of interest groups, ranging from the archetypal cotton kings of the north-west, to City of London bankers, and right the way down to the shopkeepers and tradesmen who inhabited virtually every street in the kingdom. Likewise, 'labour' was divided by income, skill, age, gender, ethnicity, location and conditions of work. Equally, the original Marxist model of the class structure in capitalist society took no account of the rapid expansion in white-collar – and indeed professional – employment that occurred from the 1880s onwards. Nor did it accommodate the underclass, or 'residuum', of very poor people revealed by the investigations of Charles Booth and Seebohm Rowntree in the 1890s.

In terms of the number and integrity of classes in Edwardian Britain, it is clear that a simple capital versus labour model is in most respects unhelpful. At the same time, the existence of 'vertical' divisions within class groups does not necessarily mean that they were more important than 'horizontal' divisions between them. Robert Roberts, a commentator often referred to by those who stress the heterogeneity of working-class communities before the First World War, began his autobiographical account of life in early twentieth-century Salford by stressing that, 'No view of the English working class . . . would be accurate if that class were shown merely as an amalgam of artisan and labouring groups united by a common aim and culture'. However, he also writes about the huge gulf ('the real social divide') that existed between the occupants of his slum and the world outside ('between those who, in earning their daily bread, dirtied hand and face, and those who did not').[7]

As to the question of class identity, it is not necessary to have a Marxist view of the world in order to think in class terms, or to be affected by class-based inequalities. Neither the continuing purchase of populist discourse among working people before 1914, nor the phenomenon of working-class conservatism, disproves the 'reality' or influence of class. To suggest this is to apply the same kind of essentialism for which traditional class-based accounts of social structure in this period have been arraigned by their postmodernist critics. Putting aside the theoretical niceties of sociological models for a moment, the priority for working-class people in a capitalist society is to offset the insecurity caused by their lack of resources. In this sense, it could make perfect sense for manual workers to vote for the Conservative party when it lent support to a threatened local industry, or when it represented their anxieties about the impact of Irish immigrants in the local job market.

But if a two-class model is too crude, how and where should the lines be drawn? Historians who view the social structure of this period in class terms have generally preferred to work with a tripolar model of upper, middle and lower or working classes, although disagreements remain about the consistency of the different class groups and the precise location of boundaries between them. A popular starting point in this sense is the contemporary analysis of economic inequality, based on income distributions, which was carried out by the Liberal MP and financier Leo Chiozza Money and published in 1908.[8] Money identified three main groups, categorizing the rich as those earning more than £700 a year and the poor as all of those falling out of the income tax bracket with incomes of £160 or less, with the 'comfortable' falling in between. Altogether the rich and the comfortable amounted to 12 per cent of the population, yet they received virtually the same overall share of the national income as the remaining 88 per cent of the population. In fact, later estimates suggest that Money significantly underestimated the degree of income inequality in Edwardian Britain, and that, in terms of wealth rather than income, the richest 10 per cent of the population owned a staggering nine-tenths of the nation's property.

Economic resources were given social significance, it is argued, by the way in which they were acquired and what was done with them. Considerations of culture and status, in other words, were important in establishing lines of demarcation both within and between classes. In this sense, the 'rich' have been the subject of much recent attention. There is general agreement that the Edwardian period marks the point at which the old division between landed wealth and those making increasingly sizeable fortunes from business came to an end, resulting in a new 'upper-middle-class' elite. This is partly explained by involvement of the landed interest in capitalist enterprise, but also by the diminishing power and status of the aristocracy, as symbolized by the 1911 Parliament Act, which removed the House of Lords' right of absolute veto over legislation passed by the House of Commons. However, while some argue that the elite was now simply a plutocracy – that it was simply the quantity of riches that mattered, rather than the way in which wealth had been acquired – others maintain that the fusion of landed and business wealth excluded manufacturers and industrialists. According to this view, it was the 'gentlemanly capitalists' with interests in the banking and overseas investment activities of the City of London who became the most wealthy and influential group in society.[9]

Another longstanding focus of attention has been the boundary between the 'comfortable' and the 'poor', or between the rest of the middle class and the working class. The gap between those earning £700 and £160 a year was occupied by a very diverse collection of individuals. At the top of this spectrum were lawyers, civil servants, managers, larger-scale merchants and farmers, some of whom had enough wealth to place them on the margins of the elite. At the bottom were shopkeepers, clerks, publicans, elementary schoolteachers and the like who might well earn less than the best-paid manual workers. They were distinguishable from the latter, however, partly by their possession of resources other than income, such as a secondary education, by better career prospects, or by superior conditions and relations of employment, but more obviously by perceived differences, such as the superior prestige of non-manual work, and also by lifestyle and consumption patterns that emphasized their 'respectability', such as the keeping, or at least hiring, of servants.

Another way of thinking about the way in which meaningful social boundaries can be established is to consider the extent to which groups sharing similar market resources form over time through the twin processes of social mobility and social closure. This is an idea that derives from Max Weber and has been developed more recently by the British sociologist John Goldthorpe.[10] Goldthorpe's argument is that formation of stable economic collectivities between generations creates the potential for a shared culture and thereby the possibility of a common institutional response to the problems of class-based inequalities. Conversely, in most cases where the rate of social mobility is high, class membership becomes ephemeral and the salience of class therefore tends to decline.

The pattern of social mobility at the beginning of the twentieth century reinforces the notion of a separate but divided working-class universe.[11] Fewer than 10 per cent of the sons of men in manual work entered non-manual employment, and fewer than one in a hundred transcended the ranks of the lower middle class. Meanwhile, there was a strong tendency for the sons of workers to follow in their fathers' occupational footsteps. This created significant sectional divisions between the skilled and the unskilled, where, in either case, self-recruitment rates were in excess of 50 per cent. Yet when this process is viewed over the longer term, a rather different impression is created, one which suggests that, while the barrier between the classes remained largely intact, internal divisions were steadily declining. Between the 1850s and the 1900s the percentage of workers' sons obtaining non-manual employment rose marginally from 6 per cent to 9 per cent, but the proportion crossing skill sector boundaries doubled from 20 per cent to 40 per cent. A number of developments worked to encourage and reinforce this homogenizing trend. Changes in the division of labour saw male workers increasingly concentrated in manufacturing, mining and transport occupations, where units of production were larger than in the more traditional economic sectors of agriculture and services, and relations between workers and employers more distant. The advent of universal, followed by compulsory, elementary education after 1870 gave fresh impetus to the declining differentials in educational achievement between children from different working-class backgrounds. The continuing shift towards urban living offered a wider range of job opportunities, easier access to information about them, and a more impersonal context for job recruitment than could be found in rural communities.

There was, in addition, an important spatial dimension to this process. Social meanings, identities and forms of organization are constructed on territorial foundations, and where people in a similar economic position are concentrated physically the development of social ties is more likely than if people are widely dispersed. In this sense, the decades leading up to the First World War witnessed important trends in the redefinition of space along class lines in many of Britain's major towns and cities. Starting in the 1880s, the urban middle class began to move out of town centres into specially built suburbs. As they did so, the territory they left behind became increasingly working class by default. By 1900 many of these towns and cities had started to mature as urban expansion slowed. As this happened, population turnover rates fell, providing a basis for the development of settled and more cohesive working-class neighbourhoods.

As this suggests, spatial mobility was also an important factor in the delineation of the Edwardian middle class, with the more prosperous groups moving on to the edge of towns and lower-middle-class groups such as clerks and teachers occupying the inner rings of suburban housing. This combination of separation from but proximity to the working-class community was a more general feature of lower-middle-class life, and was reflected too in the pattern of social mobility. Although a substantial core of this stratum was at least second-generation middle class, 40 per cent of those in the small business sector – or petty bourgeoisie – were upwardly mobile adventurers from the ranks of manual labour, while in the case of clerks, managers and teachers, the proportions were upwards of 50 per cent. Equally, a majority of those growing up in lower-middle-class suburbs faced the prospect of downward mobility into manual employment, if not permanently, then for a considerable part of their careers.[12] Such patterns fit rather neatly with the images of lower-middle-class insecurity and individualism reported by contemporaries like Charles Masterman.[13]

Issues of social and physical exclusion can also be brought to bear on the matter of the Edwardian elite. One part of the argument of those who claim a division between gentlemanly capitalists and the rest, for example, concerns the geographical concentration of landed and financial wealth in London and the south and their separation from the manufacturing heartlands of the north and the midlands. Another highlights the common socialization of gentlemanly groups through a public school system that, in terms of the leading institutions, was far less accessible to the sons of manufacturers.[14] A third vital aspect in this process of social closure, it is argued, involved their integration through the process of intermarriage. Here Cassis's work shows that while it was common for the offspring of bankers and aristocrats to wed, liaisons with the children of industrialists were much rarer.[15]

The question of marriage draws particular attention to the position of women and the impact of gender divisions in Edwardian Britain. Marriage and family life were the defining features of most women's social lives. Between 1901 and 1951 women comprised a more or less constant 30 per cent of the labour force. But the overwhelming majority of women workers were single and working class. Women's work was characterized by low pay, inferior conditions of employment and segregation, while the prevailing domestic ideology dictated that if women worked at all they should cease to do so on marriage. This, officially at least, is what the vast majority did. In contrast to most of their servant-assisted middle-class peers, however, many working-class wives had no choice but to combine an arduous round of domestic duties with part-time work, such as taking in other people's washing or caring for their children.

In terms of their everyday experiences, then, women from different classes shared little. But how did patterns of gender inequality affect the integrity of the classes they belonged to? Here, the weight of argument seems to suggest that, while there were clearly ambiguities in women's relationship to the class structure, inequalities between the men and women of different classes worked as much to underpin as to undermine class divisions. The separation of 'public' (male) and 'private' (female) roles and realms, for example, was a defining feature of middle-class identity. The position of working-class women is perhaps a little less clear. At work, their concentration in traditional areas such as domestic service, combined with expanding opportunities in white-collar work as clerks, shop assistants and schoolteachers, suggests that they had more and closer contact with the middle class than their fathers and brothers. In marriage, too, the daughters of working-class men had better chances of finding a middle-class husband than sons had of obtaining middle-class employment. As for the great majority of women who were left behind, it has also been suggested that the power of working-class wives in the home meant that working-class communities were subject to matriarchal control, and therefore divided along gender lines.[16] Yet it seems equally clear that it was women and the neighbourhood networks they created that provided a vital part of the social and cultural cement which bound such communities together.[17] This was underpinned by the dynamics of the marriage market, which indicate that not only was it a great deal easier for women to cross sectional boundaries within the class than it was to leave it, but that they were also more likely to do so than men. In this sense, then, women seem to have been in the vanguard of working-class formation.

1914–1921

In the first few months after the outbreak of the war against Germany in 1914 a tide of patriotism submerged pre-war divisions as men from all social backgrounds rushed to enlist, and women enthusiastically replaced them in the labour market. Within industry, the bulk of the labour movement supported the official leadership's call for national unity and accepted the compromises enshrined in the Treasury Agreement of March 1915 and the Munitions Act which followed two months later. Nationalism was nothing new in a country whose imperial power, monarchical heritage and racial superiority were impressed upon every schoolchild. Nor was it simply a construction foisted upon an unwitting proletariat by a manipulative ruling class. Indeed, as the conflict in France wore on, patriotism, far from expressing a cohesive national unity, was to play an important part in defining and emphasizing social divisions. The nature and unprecedented scale of the First World War meant that the state was obliged to intervene as never before in order to manage the scarcities resulting from the suspension of the market economy and to coordinate the war effort at home as much as abroad. The resulting 'war economy' led to a significant redistribution of resources which, according to the most thorough and influential study of social structure in wartime Britain, led to a heightened awareness and assertion of class differences.[18]

At the root of this was the impact that the war economy had on the pay and conditions of manual workers. In the first place, labour shortages meant that a large part of the pre-war 'residuum' was absorbed into the workforce, thereby much reducing the problem of poverty. The tight labour market also led to wage rises which, when supplemented by bonuses, overtime and the effects of rationing and rent controls, just about outpaced the roaring inflation of wartime. Workers as a whole made relative economic gains on middle-class groups, and as they did so, mechanization, dilution and substitution substantially reduced the economic differentials between them. Such changes in the economic relations of the working class reinforced the pre-war trend towards greater intra-class social mobility. The resulting homogenization was noted by many, including Robert Roberts: 'Socially, the barriers of caste that had previously existed between the skilled worker and his family and the lower grades were permanently lowered', he writes; 'the artisan felt less superiority, the labourer and skilled man more self-assurance'.[19]

A similar process seems to have taken place among both middle-class and elite groups, although mostly as a result of the deleterious effects of war on their economic position. For example, the fivefold increase in taxation during the war hastened the dispersal of large estates and transfer of landed property that had been started by the Liberals' land campaign in 1909, thereby flattening the top of the wealth pyramid. Meanwhile, the inflation which halved the value of savings and rent controls further depleted urban middle-class incomes. On the other hand, some businessmen – shipowners, munitions contractors, clothiers and farmers, for example – did well out of the war, as did routine white-collar and lower professional groups, so that the overall result was, as in the case of the working class, a tendency towards economic homogenization.

In the case of the middle class, in particular, these developments helped to foster a new and powerful sense of common identity born out of a shared feeling of loss, even among the winners. After the war, Masterman wrote that the middle class was being 'harassed out of existence'. But as De Groot has suggested, the opposite is closer to the mark. The alarming decline in lifestyle, symbolized by the lack of servants, the sense of isolation caused by the loss of only children at the front, and, above all, resentment at gains made by organized labour actually brought it *into* existence as a self-conscious and assertive social group.[20]

Contemporaries detected a similar growth of class consciousness among workers, although this was clearly complicated by both new and continuing sources of division. The undermining of skill differentials could cause resentment rather than fellow feeling, while workers and soldiers inhabited very different worlds. On the face of it, the most significant development of the war in this sense was the increased presence of women in the labour market. This subject has received a great deal of attention since Arthur Marwick concluded that the war liberated British women.[21] Nowadays historians tend to stress the continuities in women's role and status in this period. More women worked during the war, especially married women, but few working-class women had no prior experience or future expectation of employment. There was a redistribution of effort in terms of the sectors women worked in, but most went into jobs that were traditionally female and, by extension, low status and lower paid. In 1918 there were still more female textile workers than munitions workers, and where women did enter previously male preserves they were often treated with hostility.

It is difficult to assess how far gender antagonism at work affected the developing cohesion of the working class. But many working-class women seem not only to have accepted but to have welcomed the prospect of a return to domestic roles after the war. Nor is there much evidence to suggest that the wartime experiences encouraged a common identity between women from different classes. Fewer than 10 per cent of munitions workers came from the middle class or the elite and most of these occupied positions of relative power and privilege in the division of labour, as welfare supervisors, for example. Essentially the distribution of roles between women from different backgrounds seems to have both reproduced the existing social hierarchy and reinforced class prejudice.

Some have suggested that the growing sense of working-class identity was fragmentary and that it had more to do with the state's recognition of working-class institutions and their official leaders than anything else. In other words, that it had only political rather than real social substance.[22] Others, however, argue that it was firmly rooted in labour's positive experiences of the war economy, combining a marked expansion in labour movement organization with growing confidence – and expectation – that state control could be turned to the advantage of working people.[23] Class awareness was heightened by a new sense of relative deprivation, as the mobility of workers sharpened perceptions of inequality. Class assertiveness was reflected in the combination of industrial unrest, which grew out of the new politicized structure of authority in the workplace, with consumption-based conflicts – rent strikes and food protests – rooted in the wider community and often led by women. Both, it is suggested, were increasingly articulated in the form of an 'egalitarian patriotism', an expression of indignation against capitalist 'profiteers' at a time of national sacrifice, which demanded the 'conscription of riches' in return for the conscription of soldiers and workers.

The combination of escalating industrial conflict, civil disorder and serious unrest in the armed forces at the end of the war persuaded many at the time, as it has done since, that Britain was on the brink of revolution. However, a successful appeal to worker patriotism during the 'Hang the Kaiser' election, backed up by plans to create 'a fit land for heroes to live in', helped return a Lloyd George-led but Conservative-dominated coalition in 1918. Gradually, thereafter, the social reform consensus withered and, with the failure of the Triple Alliance to defend the miners' demands for nationalization in the spring of 1921, organized labour's wartime advances came to a shuddering stop.

Critical to the shifting balance of social power in this period was the determination of the newly assertive middle class to reverse its losses. With its grievances represented by organizations such as the anti-waste movement and the middle-class union, and voiced by the *Daily Mail*, it was this group that provided crucial popular endorsement for the City-led, Treasury-supported offensive against the inflationary, interventionist economics of wartime. As Ross McKibbin has shown, a key component of post-war middle-class consciousness was hostility towards the 'unreasonable', 'greedy' trade unionist, a stereotype that was extended to the working class as a whole. By contrast the middle classes identified themselves as the 'public' – defenders of the constitution and of society – an image which the Conservative party, newly released from the obligations of coalition, was ideally placed to articulate.[24]

1921–1939

In terms of economic and social protest, there was nothing in the following two decades to rival either the pre- or post-war periods of unrest. British society was almost alone in resisting the contrasting appeals of fascism and communism, and the 1926 General Strike failed after just nine days, broken in large part by the middle-class 'public' volunteers who helped maintain essential services. Much of the explanation for the relative stability of interwar social relations lies in the political and cultural realms, but these, in turn, were clearly influenced by the structural dynamics of class formation.

McKibbin has written that 'the social peace of the 1930s [and later 1920s] was . . . procured largely . . . at the expense of the working class'.[25] Here the key issue, and one that has dominated discussion about the economy and society of interwar Britain, is unemployment. From the ending of the post-war boom in the summer of 1920 down to the outbreak of the Second World War, there were never less than a million people out of work. Only once in this period did the average annual unemployment rate among insured workers drop below 10 per cent. In the early 1930s, in the wake of the slump, around one-sixth of the total workforce, amounting to almost 3 million people, were out of work.

Concentrated in the highly unionized staple industries of the north and the Celtic 'fringe', in areas that formed the bedrock of the labour movement, unemployment undoubtedly dealt a crushing blow to the organized working class. There is rather less agreement about its effects on the structural and cultural integrity of working-class communities, however. Some accounts, which specify the interwar period as the apogee of the 'traditional' working class, suggest that the shared experience, or risk, of unemployment lowered still further status barriers between different types of worker, reinforced cultural cohesiveness, and nurtured a strong, if defensive, sense of class belonging.[26] Others argue that the unskilled were more adversely affected than the skilled, older men more than younger men, that the tensions it created could undermine family relations, and that those out of work were effectively excluded from the wider cultural life of the community.[27]

The regional, and industry-specific, nature of interwar unemployment meant that, in fact, most working-class people were in work throughout the period. As a result, the majority tended to experience improving living standards as real wages rose and working hours declined. Pointing to the growing opportunities for participation in 'mass' leisure activities, such as cinema-going, which this brought about, some have argued that consumption, either by distraction or via emulation, began to eclipse class-based identities. Others, however, maintain that most of the extra cash that flowed into working-class homes was spent on necessities, participation in the newer commercialized forms of leisure was strongly associated with the lifecycle, and traditional associational pastimes and institutions remained vibrant.[28]

Consumption issues were, it seems, as likely to reinforce as to undermine class divisions in this period. It has been argued, for example, that the changing balance of work and consumption played an important role in the shaping of working-class politics after the war. The Labour party's rapid electoral growth in the 1920s, it is suggested, reflected a shift from a preoccupation with sectional, trade union interests towards more inclusive ward-based activity in which women's concerns about local authority services gained greater prominence.[29] By the same token, the party's close association with municipal government helps to explain the reversal in its fortunes during the 1930s. An essential part of the background to these developments was the wider phenomenon of economic restructuring with which the problem of unemployment was bound up, and the resulting processes of class formation – underpinned by the pattern of social and spatial mobility – which the Labour party drew on to bolster its unstable electoral support.

The interwar years witnessed the intensification of three developments that, together, had a marked effect on the organization of work and, in particular, tended to reduce the autonomy and status of skilled adult men in the labour market. The first was the decline of the staple industries. Those sectors that bore the brunt of depression and unemployment in the 1920s and 1930s – coal, textiles, iron and steel, and shipbuilding – were also notable for their concentration of skilled men who exercised a considerable degree of independence in the workplace. The second was the rise of the large firm, which, although rarely organized on the 'scientific' lines of its American counterpart, increasingly used female and boy labour in an effort to reduce labour costs. Women assembly-line workers were especially prominent in the 'new industries' of the interwar period, such as electrical goods and food production. The third was the increasing bureaucratization of the labour market, evident in the large numbers of people employed by bureaucratic organizations, by the attempts made by firms to detach their supervisory grades from ordinary workers, and by increased state intervention in the labour market. The net effect of this last development was substantially to diminish the power of workers to influence recruitment and training.

The Labour party's origins and early development were the products of a trade union movement, led by skilled male workers, which sought to resist these pressures. By the early 1920s, however, this resistance was effectively at an end, and Labour moved to articulate the broader concerns of a more unified working class. The steady decline in the power of skilled workers to exercise social closure had, by the end of the decade, resulted in a substantial erosion of the barriers to interchange between status groups within the class. Baines and Johnson's recent work on data from the New Survey of London Life and Labour clearly shows that the pre-war trend in intraclass mobility continued into the interwar period.[30] At the same time, there appears to have been little change in the rate of movement between the working and middle classes, again confirming the pre-war pattern. The 1949 London School of Economics mobility survey could find no evidence of a trend in interclass mobility between the wars, and in a smaller study published in 1929, Ginsberg concluded that 'the social ladder so far lifts only relatively small numbers . . . whilst downward movement is slight and nearly constant'.[31]

The metaphor of a 'ladder' was widely used in the interwar period, particularly in relation to educational opportunity. The post-war expansion of the 1907 free places scheme ensured that the numbers of working-class children gaining a place at state-sponsored grammar schools rose faster than the entry rates of middle-class children. This, on the face of it, should have helped to break down barriers to mobility between the classes. However, even at the end of the period, 90 per cent of working-class children were excluded from a grammar school education, while financial constraints or cultural alienation meant that many of those who did win a place left early. It has also been suggested that while education may have increased the chances of mobility into white-collar work at the beginning of a career, the restructuring of the economy meant that traditional routes into the middle class – such as setting up in small business in later life – were becoming harder to follow.[32]

The effect of the interwar restructuring of work on the pattern of social mobility, then, was to consolidate and advance the process of working-class formation. The Labour party responded to this by advancing a wider, welfare-oriented politics based on neighbourhood organization. However, the impact of economic change on social geography in this period appears to have been more disruptive, and what had previously been a robust base for electoral mobilization became, by the early 1930s, something of a liability.

While the first two decades of the century witnessed the maturing of the working-class neighbourhood, developments in the 1920s and 1930s began to destabilize it. In particular, the contraction of traditional industries sponsored a new wave of migration, as people from the depressed regions left to seek out opportunities in the expanding towns of the midlands and the south. Although there is evidence that communities were eventually rebuilt in these areas, the fact that many migrants were young and unmarried suggests considerable social flux in the short term. The flip side of this exodus was that it sapped many of the old established northern conurbations of their vitality, forcing them into decline. The dispersal of the older working-class communities was assisted by post-war housing developments, in particular the huge expansion of council house-building after 1919, which was concentrated in the north and the midlands. New municipal housing was built in suburban locations and designed to accommodate those on higher wages. It was therefore the better-paid workers who were able to move from the centre of the big towns and cities onto the public estates.

While workers gained least from the social settlement of the interwar period, there is little doubt that the main beneficiaries were members of the middle class. By 1923 the pre-war differential between both salaries and wages and salaries and 'riches' had been restored. In the former case, the key issue was the virtual isolation of all but a few middle-class occupations from unemployment. In the latter, it was the return to the pre-war tax regime, which exacted by far the greatest toll on the very wealthy. Against the background of what many came to think of as a 'golden age' of security and progress for the middle class, issues of social and spatial mobility, rooted once more in the wider processes of economic change, were again crucial in shaping its identity in this period.

Externally, the increased 'visibility' of a more homogeneous and physically concentrated working class provided further substance to the negative cultural stereotyping that remained an important ideological cement binding together otherwise disparate middle-class groups. But middle-class cultural cohesion in the interwar period was also founded on new social bases, the most important of which was owner-occupation. The counterpart to the boom in post-war council housing was the even more dramatic rise of speculative private building. In fact, local authorities were responsible for only 1.3 million out of the 4 million new houses built between the wars. The remainder, located mostly in the south, were occupied largely by middle-class owners. Increasingly in this period, then, housing tenure became a symbol of class difference and physical basis for social closure.[33]

The 'brick-box egotism' of the private housing estates perfectly complemented the aspirations for personal mobility that had always been a component of the middle-class mindset. Such aspirations began to be met in new ways during this period, as the foundations were laid for a transformation of the structure of the British middle class. In terms of size, there was a gradual expansion, which quickened in the 1930s. Routh's figures show that in 1921 non-manual employment accounted for just over 20 per cent of the working population, which was slightly more than in 1911, but that by 1951 the figure had grown to 28 per cent.[34] More important than the absolute scale of this expansion, however, was the shifting composition of middle-class employment, and the forces behind it. The main growth point was the rise of salaried, professional occupations at the expense of employers and proprietors. The principal force behind this development was upward mobility, not of working-class children but of those born into the lower reaches of the middle class, those who ultimately gained most from the expansion of the grammar school system.

The consequences of what Perkin has called an 'incipient professional society' were, in the short term at least, probably detrimental to middle-class solidarity. On the one hand, professionalization began to 'nationalize' the middle class. This, it is argued, caused tensions between rootless, anonymous 'spiralists' – managerial and administrative careerists who moved up the promotion ladder by moving around the country between offices, branches or firms – and 'burgesses', the local self-employed businessmen, solicitors and doctors of the traditional middle class. On the other hand, this was a process that was founded on gender divisions. The second key component in the expansion of middle-class employment in the interwar period was the dramatic rise in female clerical employment. Here, recent research has shown how such women were often brought into organizations to carry out routine administrative tasks, for reasons of economy, but also to release middle-class males from career blockages.[35]

Although the growth of the state and the rise of corporate capitalism increased the power and influence of professional groups in this period, human capital did not, on the whole, tend to translate into great wealth. Meanwhile, the rich themselves tended to become a little poorer after the war. It is estimated that between 1911–13 and 1936–8 the share of total personal wealth held by the top 1 per cent of the population fell from 69 per cent to 56 per cent.[36] However, much of the downward redistribution that resulted was accounted for by the transfer of wealth to the heirs of the rich. Equally important was the redistribution that occurred between economic elites, from landowners and financiers on the one hand to those involved in commerce and manufacturing on the other. Although some maintain that the process of assimilation ensured that the values and priorities of gentlemanly capitalism remained prominent within it, most agree that the rising scale and complexity of business in the interwar period helped to create a more inclusive, plutocratic elite. Culturally, this was reflected in the transformation of 'Society', from the largely closed, aristocratic affair it had been before the war to the more glamorous, eclectic, salon-based operation it had become by the 1930s. Politically, the clearest symbol of the restructuring of the elite between the wars was to be found in the post-war amalgamation of propertied interests within and behind the Conservative party.

Conclusion

Social structure has a number of bases. Personal identities are sourced from and articulated in various dimensions of the social realm. Recently, it has become fashionable to downplay the importance of class, as one type of social division, and to insist on the independence of political activity and cultural production from social change.

But caution is required when doubts about the relevance of class to the present are visited on the past. It is all too easy to forget the extent to which the everyday lives and opportunities of earlier generations were shaped by unequal access to market resources.

In this chapter, I have argued that class formation – understood as a dynamic process rooted in patterns of social and spatial mobility – remained at the core of British social structure in the first half of the twentieth century. I have also suggested that while there is no necessary or predictable relationship between this process and change in the cultural and political spheres, the fortunes of political parties in this period, together with the popular belief systems that underpinned electoral allegiance, were crucially influenced by the remaking of class structures and relations.

The main changes in British social structure in the first half of the twentieth century occurred within rather than between classes. The boundaries marking off the territory of the three main class groups – upper, middle and working – remained largely intact. Internally, it can be argued that each became, for at least part of the period under consideration, more cohesive, although there were always complicating factors and countervailing tendencies. In this sense, while certain trends were already in train, the experience of the First World War seems to have been pivotal in generating class awareness and shaping social relations.

Perhaps the most cohesive group by the end of the interwar period was the social elite, still rich and powerful, but now, with the decline of the aristocracy and the travails of the financiers, a more unified plutocracy. Structurally, the most internally differentiated was the middle class, spanning a broad range of occupations, economic interests and status groups, and, at the end of the period, still in transition as the harbinger of Perkin's 'professional society'. Nevertheless, middle-class stratification was largely overcome by its post-war, ideological unity in the face of the perceived threat from organized labour – through which it found common cause with the elite in its support for the Conservative party – and the utilization of the private housing market as a new basis of social identity and exclusion. The process of working-class formation began in the second half of the nineteenth century and was accelerated by the war economy. The defeat of the trade union movement, which had mobilized politically for the first time in order to resist the downward mobility of skilled men, gave rise to a still more homogeneous class and encouraged the development of a broader-based, working-class politics. As this process proceeded, however, it began to be undermined by the dispersive effects of post-war economic restructuring on urban working-class communities.

NOTES

1 See R. E. Pahl, 'Is the emperor naked? Some questions on the adequacy of sociological theory on urban and regional research', *International Journal of Urban and Regional Research*, 12 (1988).
2 K. Marx and F. Engels, *The Communist Manifesto* (Harmondsworth, 1967), p. 79.
3 E. P. Thompson, *The Making of the English Working Class* (Harmondsworth, 1968), pp. 8–10.
4 S. Szreter, *Fertility, Class and Gender in Britain, 1860–1914* (Cambridge, 1996), pp. 182–280.

5 H. Perkin, *The Rise of Professional Society: England since 1880* (London, 1990), pp. 117–18, 161.

6 D. Cannadine, *Class in Britain* (London, 1998), pp. 19–20, 106–26.

7 R. Roberts, *The Classic Slum: Salford Life in the First Quarter of the Century* (Harmondsworth, 1973), pp. 13, 19.

8 L. C. Money, *Riches and Poverty* (London, 1908), pp. 41–3.

9 The definitive statement of this position is by P. J. Cain and A. G. Hopkins, *British Imperialism*, vol. 1, *Innovation and Expansion 1688–1914* (London, 1993).

10 J. H. Goldthorpe (in collaboration with C. Payne and C. Llewellyn), *Social Mobility and Class Structure in Modern Britain* (Oxford, 1987), p. 330.

11 See A. Miles, *Social Mobility in Nineteenth- and Early Twentieth-century England* (Basingstoke, 1999), pp. 22–34.

12 Ibid., pp. 23–6, 70–3.

13 C. F. G. Masterman, *The Condition of England* (London, 1909), pp. 66–7.

14 On the former, see W. D. Rubinstein, 'Wealth, elites and the class structure of modern Britain', *Past and Present*, 76 (1977); on the latter, H. Berghoff, 'Public schools and the decline of the British economy', *Past and Present*, 129 (1990).

15 Y. Cassis, 'Bankers in English society in the late nineteenth century', *Economic History Review*, 38 (1985).

16 C. Chinn, *They Worked all their Lives: Women of the Urban Poor in England, 1880–1939* (Manchester, 1988), chs 1 and 2.

17 E. Ross, 'Survival networks: women's neighbourhood sharing in London before World War I', *History Workshop*, 15 (1983).

18 B. Waites, *A Class Society at War: England 1914–18* (Leamington Spa, 1987), pp. 88, 279–80.

19 Roberts, *Classic Slum*, p. 200.

20 G. J. De Groot, *Blighty: British Society in the Era of the Great War* (London, 1996), p. 294.

21 A. Marwick, *The Deluge: British Society and the First World War* (London, 1965), part 3.

22 For example, A. Reid, 'World War I and the working class in Britain', in A. Marwick, ed., *Total War and Social Change* (Basingstoke, 1988).

23 J. E. Cronin, *Labour and Society in Britain 1918–1979* (London, 1984), ch. 2.

24 R. McKibbin, *The Ideologies of Class: Social Relations in Britain, 1880–1950* (Oxford, 1990), pp. 270–4, 298–300.

25 R. McKibbin, *Classes and Cultures: England 1918–1951* (Oxford, 1998), p. 68.

26 For example, Cronin, *Labour and Society*, pp. 79–82.

27 For example, A. Davies, *Leisure, Gender and Poverty: Working-class Culture in Salford and Manchester, 1900–1939* (Buckingham, 1992), pp. 43–8.

28 For a review of this debate, see J. Benson, *The Rise of Consumer Society in Britain 1880–1980* (London, 1994), ch. 9.

29 M. Savage and A. Miles, *The Remaking of the British Working Class, London, 1840–1940* (London, 1994), ch. 5.

30 D. Baines and P. Johnson, 'In search of the "traditional" working class: social mobility and occupational continuity in interwar London', *Economic History Review*, 52 (1999), pp. 702–4.

31 D. V. Glass and J. R. Hall, 'Social mobility in Britain: a study of intergenerational change in status', in D. V. Glass, ed., *Social Mobility in Britain* (London, 1954); M. Ginsberg, 'Interchange between social classes', *Economic Journal*, 39 (1929), p. 565.

32 A. Little and J. Westergaard, 'The trend of class differentials in educational opportunity in England and Wales', *British Journal of Sociology*, 15 (1964).

33 McKibbin, *Classes and Cultures*, p. 101.

34   G. Routh, *Occupations and Pay in Great Britain 1906–79* (London, 1980), p. 5.
35   K. Stovel, M. Savage and P. Bearman, 'Ascription into achievement: models of career systems at Lloyds bank, 1890–1970', *American Journal of Sociology*, 102 (1976).
36   *Royal Commission on the Distribution of Income and Wealth* (1975), cited in P. Dewey, *War and Progress: Britain 1914–1945* (London, 1997), p. 65.

FURTHER READING

Bourke, J., *Working-class Cultures in Britain 1890–1960: Gender, Class and Ethnicity* (London, 1994).
Braybon, G., *Women Workers in the First World War: The British Experience* (London, 1981).
Cannadine, D., *The Decline and Fall of the British Aristocracy* (London, 1990).
Crossick, G., 'The emergence of the lower middle class in Britain', in G. Crossick, ed., *The Lower Middle Class in Britain 1870–1914* (London, 1977).
Gittins, D., *Fair Sex: Family Size and Structure 1900–1939* (London, 1982).
Halsey, A. H., *Change in British Society* (Oxford, 1986).
Hobsbawm, E. J., 'The making of the working class 1870–1914', in E. J. Hobsbawm, *Worlds of Labour: Further Studies in the History of Labour* (London, 1984).
Johnson, P., *Saving and Spending: The Working-class Economy in Britain, 1870–1939* (Oxford, 1985).
Joyce, P., 'The end of social history?', *Social History*, 20 (1995).
Lawrence, J., 'The First World War and its aftermath', in P. Johnson, ed., *Twentieth-century Britain: Economic, Social and Cultural Change* (London, 1994).
Lewis, J., *Women in England 1870–1950: Sexual Divisions and Social Change* (London, 1984).
Masterman, C. F. G., *England After the War* (London, 1922).
Mowat, C. L., *Britain Between the Wars 1918–1940* (London, 1968).
Pollard, S., *The Development of the British Economy, 1914–1950* (London, 1962).
Priestley, J. B., *English Journey: Being a Rambling but Truthful Account of What One Man Saw* (London, 1934).
Roberts, E., *A Woman's Place: An Oral History of Working-class Women 1890–1940* (Oxford, 1984).
Rubinstein, W. D., *Elites and the Wealthy in Modern British History: Essays in Social and Economic History* (Brighton, 1987).
Sanderson, M., *Educational Opportunity and Social Change in England* (London, 1987).
Stevenson, J., *British Society 1914–45* (Harmondsworth, 1984).
Thompson, P., *The Edwardians: The Remaking of British Society* (London, 1992).

CHAPTER TWENTY-TWO

Consumption and Consumer Behaviour

SUE BOWDEN

Introduction

What is consumption, how do we explain the phenomenon, what are its main features and what are the implications of consumption for the individual, the household and the economy? Consumption affects each and every one of us. It has been a basic fact of life throughout history; throughout the centuries our ancestors sought to satisfy their basic needs to survive and their less basic wants to seek gratification through the ownership and enjoyment of goods.

This chapter explores how and why consumption patterns defined the lives of people in the first half of the twentieth century, assessing how and why 'wants' and 'needs' changed and how these changes affected the lives of the people. We consider the main features of consumption patterns during these years, standard explanations of those patterns, their impact on the quality of life for the majority of the populace and the implications for the economy, the household and the individual.

I

Consumption refers to the expenditure of a nation or an individual on consumer goods and services. Private consumption is defined as the expenditure of consumers on goods and services, such as food, drink and entertainment. It does not usually include capital assets. We normally view consumer expenditure as relating to the acquisition by private individuals, and households, of a range of durable and non-durable goods, and class the distinction between the two as relating to the frequency of purchase and the life of the good in question. Non-durable goods are bought on a frequent basis and for immediate use. Food is one such example. Clothing is semi-durable because it is not bought that regularly and can be made to last (notwithstanding, of course, fashion victims); durable goods meanwhile are purchased for use over a relatively long period of time. Motor cars are one such example.

Between 1900 and 1938, the bulk of consumers' expenditure was directed towards perishable goods. The perishable goods were dominated by a variety of foods and, to a lesser extent, drink and tobacco, food and light. Four trends were important: considerably more was spent on food, less was spent on alcohol, more was spent on tobacco and increasing amounts were spent on fuel and light (table 22.1). Before the First World War, perishables accounted for over half of total consumers' expenditure. In the following decades, the total amount spent on these goods increased. In percentage terms, however, perishables accounted for a smaller (albeit still the largest) share of total expenditure.

In the early years of the twentieth century we became a nation of smokers; between 1900 and 1913, the number of cigarettes bought quadrupled; during the war (and despite the price increases of these years), consumption of cigarettes nearly doubled. Smoking was to continue its dubious appeal after the war. Meanwhile, from 1902, the amount spent on and the amount of alcohol consumed began to fall, reflecting a decline in expenditure on spirits and on wine; beer meanwhile enjoyed rising popularity. This trend continued after the war. During the first three decades of the century, the populace, in other words, was consuming more (and a greater variety of) food, smoking more and drinking less: a mixed message of course in terms of well-being!

By contrast, expenditure on semi-durables and other services remained relatively constant in their shares of total expenditure. The amount spent on clothing grew, but its share of total expenditure remained the same. The other popular items of a semi-durable nature were furniture, drapery, fittings and a variety of household equipment, reflecting growing purchases of crockery, cutlery, a variety of ironmongery goods and small items of furniture.

The declining *share* of perishable and semi-durable goods in total consumers' expenditure was the result of increased amounts of expenditure on durable goods. After the First World War, the rate of growth of expenditure on durable goods far exceeded that for any class of good. Two sectors accounted for the bulk of this increased expenditure: transport and communications and durable household goods.

This was the age that witnessed the beginnings of the communication revolution, marked in its initial stages by the advent of telephones in the home. Prior to the First World War, communication between private individuals was largely by letter and telegram. Such was the usage of this method of communication that post was delivered several times a day. Instant and direct communication, however, became the norm after the war as telephones became commonplace. Communication was also enhanced by the growth of transport. In the early years of the century, private transport was dominated by the growing popularity of the bicycle. Expenditure on this mode of travel dwarfed that on private motor cars (table 22.2). Bicycles were cheap to buy and to maintain. They were, moreover, gender neutral. The bicycle thus became an ever-popular mode of transport, both for men and women and for all classes. Wider ownership of the motor car postdates the war.

A third category of durable goods promised to make substantive changes to both work and leisure within the home. The first was the growing use of gas and then electricity for a range of applications in the home. At the beginning of the period, coal was the standard fuel for heating. Gas was increasingly used for lighting and for a variety of cooking and water-/space-heating appliances. Gas became, and was to remain, a popular source of power for cooking and heating for all classes. The

Table 22.1 Consumers' expenditure at constant (1938) prices in the UK between 1910 and 1938

	1910–14		1920–4		1925–9		1930–4		1935–8	
	£m	% total	£m	% total	£m	% total	£m	% total	£m	% total
Food	981.9	28.64	1,002.3	29.84	1,116.7	30.24	1,231.1	30.98	1,285.9	29.38
Alcoholic drink	502.5	14.66	351.8	10.47	320.5	8.68	264.6	6.66	286.4	6.54
Tobacco	84.0	2.45	113.0	3.36	123.6	3.35	137.8	3.47	163.3	3.73
Rent, rates and water	333.7	9.73	368.3	10.96	393.4	10.65	428.9	10.79	471.7	10.78
Fuel and light	137.3	4.01	138.7	4.13	155	4.20	163.7	4.12	182.7	4.17
Clothing	367.2	10.71	356.7	10.62	388.8	10.53	403.1	10.14	434.8	9.93
Durable household goods	134.7	3.93	176.9	5.27	218.0	5.90	258.5	6.51	289.4	6.61
Transport and communications	131.5	3.84	188.5	5.61	241.9	6.55	258.2	6.50	326.1	7.45
Other goods	164.1	4.79	204.3	6.08	219.9	5.95	243.6	6.13	293.4	6.70
Other services	591.0	17.24	458.5	13.65	515.4	13.96	584	14.70	643.4	14.70
Total	3,427.9	100.00	3,359.0	100.00	3,693.2	100.00	3,973.5	100.00	4,377.1	100.00

Source: R. Stone and D. Rowe, *The Measurement of Consumers' Expenditure* (Cambridge, 1966), vol. 2, table 56, p. 125.

Table 22.2 Consumers' expenditure on private transport, 1900–19

Year	Number of new bicycles purchased	New cars purchased for personal use	Price (£) per cycle	Expenditure (£m) on bicycles	New cars purchased	New cars purchased for personal use	Average price (£) per car
1900	350,000	700	10.00	3.50	800	700	385
1901	375,000	1,300	10.00	3.80	1,500	1,300	390
1902	400,000	2,400	10.00	4.00	2,800	2,400	395
1903	425,000	3,400	10.00	4.30	4,000	3,400	400
1904	450,000	7,200	10.00	4.50	8,500	7,200	405
1905	475,000	7,100	10.00	4.70	8,400	7,100	410
1906	500,000	9,900	8.60	4.30	11,600	9,900	415
1907	522,000	9,400	7.88	4.10	11,000	9,400	420
1908	420,000	8,100	7.34	3.10	9,500	8,100	420
1909	350,000	6,600	6.93	2.40	7,800	6,600	420
1910	350,000	16,300	6.58	2.30	19,200	16,300	420
1911	350,000	15,100	6.40	2.20	17,800	15,100	420
1912	385,000	20,000	6.61	2.60	23,500	20,000	420
1913	400,000	28,700	6.42	2.60	33,800	28,700	340
1914	400,000	20,800	6.34	2.60	24,500	20,800	340
1915	250,000	6,000	6.85	1.70	15,000	6,000	370
1916	50,000	1,600	7.54	0.40	4,000	1,600	500
1917	50,000	1,200	9.02	0.50	3,000	1,200	600
1918	100,000	2,000	11.20	1.10	5,000	2,000	700
1919	400,000	34,000	15.05	6.00	45,000	34,000	800

Source: A. R. Prest, *Consumers' Expenditure in the United Kingdom, 1900–1919* (Cambridge, 1954); bicycles, table 89, p. 139; motor cars, table 91, p. 142.

interwar years were characterized by a move to electric lighting and an increased use of electricity in the home. In 1932, fewer than 32 per cent of homes were wired for electricity; by 1938 just under two-thirds had electric lighting. Specific electrical appliances for cleaning (the vacuum cleaner), laundry (the wash boiler, washing machine and electric iron), heating (the electric space heater) and cooking (the electric oven and kettle) never promised to replace housework, but they did offer the potential of reducing some of the manual labour involved in housework at the time. The '1900s house' was extremely hard work for the people who had to do the housework; the '1930s house' was still hard work – but less so.

One durable good stands out as offering the potential for leisure within the home: the radio. The radio offered music, news, information and entertainment, all within the privacy of the home and at a fraction of the cost of entertainment outside it. Not surprisingly, its popularity grew at a significant rate. In 1922, there were 5.8 radio licences per 1,000 families; by 1930 this had grown to 37.1. At the end of the 1930s, there were 68.3 radio licences per 1,000 families.[1]

It is for this reason that many historians have viewed this period as marking the beginning of the mass market for a range of consumer durables. For these scholars, the interesting features are the reasons for and the implications of the increased expenditure on durable goods for the household and, in particular, for the individuals who used them.

II

The increased ownership of consumer durables is of interest for three distinct, not necessarily mutually exclusive, areas of enquiry: what explains their diffusion through society, what are the implications for the economy and society as a whole, and how did this impact on the everyday lives of the household and the individual? The answers to these questions are to be found in a wide range of historical work, including that of social historians seeking to assess the impact of changing patterns of leisure, of feminist historians working on the use of time in the home and women's labour force participation, of economic historians seeking to explain the reasons for and effects on the economy of the rising expenditure on consumer goods, as well as of business historians working on technological change in industry. The following pages of this chapter will refer to this important body of work.

Three main theories have been used to explain the diffusion of consumer goods through society: macroeconomic analyses of consumer demand, epidemiological diffusion models and new home economics.[2] The 'macro' approach concentrates on explaining expenditure on durable goods over time through the effects on demand of a variety of economic factors. These studies have identified price, income, depreciation, existing stocks and household formation as the important influences.

The increased acquisition of consumer durables in this period has been explained in terms of the lowering of both the purchase prices and running costs of the goods and increased real incomes (for the majority of the population), a growing need for new and replacement goods and the increase in the number of household units. Although the prices of the 'new' goods fell (the price of electric washing machines, for example, fell by 50 per cent in the 1930s), purchase prices remained too high for most people's budgets. The cost of running the goods acted as a further deterrent;

Table 22.3 Average weekly expenditure of the working class,
1937–8

Region	Total average expenditure on all non-food items (£)	Total average expenditure on food (£)
South-east	2.88	1.78
South-west	2.74	1.99
North	2.95	1.46
North-west	2.23	1.64
London	2.85	2.03
North-east	2.57	2.29
Midlands	1.97	1.60

Source: Ministry of Labour, 'Weekly expenditure of working-class
households in the United Kingdom, 1937–1938', *Ministry of Labour
Gazette* (London, December, 1940, January 1941 and February
1941).

people only switched from solid fuel and/or gas to electricity once the cost of running
electric appliances compared favourably with that of gas or solid fuel goods.[3]

What of the effect of incomes on the demand for consumer durables? Two effects
are important in this respect: the growth of incomes over time and the distribution
of income. The early part of the century was marked by a highly skewed distribution
of income; £250 per annum was regarded as the dividing line marking out, in income
terms, the working classes from the rest of society. Households in receipt of less than
£250 a year constituted about three-quarters of all households in the UK in the
1930s. The skewed distribution of income became ever more apparent in the interwar years as economic problems led to widescale unemployment. Those who were
in work (and enjoyed regular, well-paid incomes) enjoyed an improved standard of
living. For those who endured unemployment, short-time working and low-paid
employment, the situation was bleak. The result was that the majority of the population survived on low (and until 1934) falling wages that gave them a weekly income
of less than £5 a week. The budgets of such families were dominated by the costs of
the basic necessities of life (e.g. food).[4] Consumerism for such people remained a
dream rather than a reality (table 22.3).

It was the more affluent members of society who enjoyed the 'new' consumer
goods: the professional, salaried middle classes whose high and rising incomes allowed
the luxury of a range of transport and communication, household appliances and
privatized leisure goods. The average annual income of a general practitioner, for
example, grew from £756 between 1924 and 1929 to £1,094 between 1930 and
1940.[5] Most middle-class families were not operating under the budget constraints
experienced by the working classes: their incomes gave them access to the full range
of new durable goods. Food remained an important part of the budget of the middle
classes, but increasingly 'other items' constituted a large part of their expenditure
(table 22.4). Entertainment, holidays, clothing, motoring, eating out, a variety of
household appliances all became part of the normal expenditure of the middling-
income groups.

Table 22.4 The average weekly expenditure patterns of middle-class households in 1938–9

Selected items	Annual income £250–350	Annual income £350–500	Annual income £500–700	Annual income £700+
Food	1.78	2.10	2.63	3.23
Housing	0.95	1.00	1.29	1.74
Clothing	0.62	0.77	1.02	1.33
Fuel and light	0.42	0.51	0.64	0.81
Entertainment	0.10	0.13	0.20	0.26
Total weekly expenditure	6.80	8.67	11.39	16.09

Source: P. Massey, 'The expenditure of 1360 British middle-class households in 1938–1939', *Journal of the Royal Statistical Society*, 95, part 3 (1942), pp. 159–85, table XXII, p. 185.

At first sight, the emphasis on replacement goods in the 'macroeconomic' approach seems strange given the fact that many of the goods were new. It was the *source* of the *power* rather than the good itself that was new. Ovens, water- and space-heating appliances had existed for centuries. What was new about the twentieth century was the extended use of electricity in the home – first for lighting purposes, and later for a range of consumer goods. Not only were more people being connected to electricity supply, but also each consumer was using increasing amounts of electricity.

The second approach is that of the diffusion model. Diffusion models were initially based on the work of epidemiologists in their study of the spread of disease through society. The spread of consumer durables was likened to the spread of an infectious illness, was plotted as an S-shaped curve and drew attention to specific stages in the development of markets for such goods (figure 22.1). Seen in these terms, the spread of ownership through society is not a smooth, continuous process but is marked by specific turning points, each inaugurating distinct periods of ownership growth.

A three-stage process was identified: initially the goods are expensive, are perceived as luxuries and are bought only by the most affluent. This stage relates to the Edwardian period when consumer durables were the privilege of the wealthy minority. In figure 22.1 this relates to the early years of stable growth and low levels of ownership given high purchase prices. The second stage is associated with diffusion through the 'middling' ranks of society and would aptly describe the growth in durable ownership amongst the middle classes during the interwar years. Ownership, however, did not become a mass-market phenomenon. The second turning point marks the end of this middling stage. It inaugurates the third stage of mass production for mass markets which, for consumer durables, refers to the period after, not before, the Second World War. Finally, saturation is reached once all the potential consumers have been 'infected' and become owners.

Diffusion models add technological change as the instrumental variable, which causes inflection points in the curve leading to different stages in the process. It is technology which leads to the price reductions which make the goods affordable first to the middling classes and then ultimately to the majority of the population. This would suggest that there were changes during the interwar years, which enabled

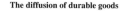

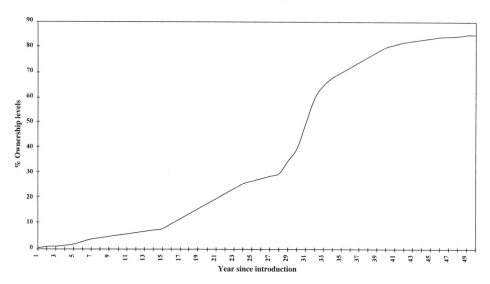

Figure 22.1   A stylized illustration of the diffusion of durable goods.
Year since introduction refers to the number of years from the launch of the product onto the
market.
% ownership refers to the percentage of households owning one appliance.

In recent decades, the trend has been towards ownership of more than one of the relevant good
per household (e.g. a household owning more than one television) and towards individual ownership of some goods (e.g. several members of a household each owning and running a motor car).
Key inflection points can be dated from about year 15, marking the beginning of the second stage
of the diffusion curve, and from about year 28, marking that of the third stage. As the text indicates, the dating of the inflection points differs between durable goods, with leisure goods showing
a more rapid growth curve and higher ownership levels than time-saving goods.

purchase prices and running costs to be reduced. One such key change was the extension of electricity supply through the country. The provisions of the Electricity
(Supply) Act of 1926 gave the Central Electricity Board the powers to operate a
newly constructed national grid of high-tension transmission lines. Work on the
project began the following year and by the end of 1934, the grid was operating in
most of the country, delivering electric power to most households. This, in turn,
created a market for electric appliances, which encouraged manufacturers to increase
output and reap the economies of scale, which led to purchase price reductions.[6]
Likewise, once manufacturers such as Herbert Austin and William Morris decided to
increase motor vehicle production and explicitly adopted a strategy to produce large
numbers of cars for the middle-class markets, economies of scale were realized and
purchase prices were reduced – thereby realizing their plans to create demand from
the middle classes.[7]
  An important additional insight from the diffusion approach is its identification of
'contagion'. This stresses the importance of understanding how and why consumers

learn of new goods and acquire the desire to own them. Diffusion theories see the spread of ownership of durable goods as depending on 'infection', that is, they see the desire to own such goods as largely a matter of learning, imitation and information. Contemporary manufacturers certainly believed they faced consumer resistance, which would have to be overcome by 'educating' the market. Not surprisingly, advertising, the role of the media and cultural norms thus become key components of our understanding of how and why consumers in this period, and indeed later, acquired the information and the taste for consumer durable acquisition. Both the electrical and the motor industry engaged in heavy marketing campaigns; newspapers, journals and magazines were all used to advertise the benefits of the new goods, as advertisers took advantage of the potential audience (and hence consumers) that followed as a result of the introduction of new magazines for women in these years. The cinema also offered a new and important site for advertisements, as weekly audiences grew for this new and exciting form of popular entertainment.[8]

Advertising for motor cars was directed at men; that for electrical appliances at women. The electricity industry embarked on advertising campaigns designed to persuade women to acquire their goods. A recurrent theme was that electrical appliances would help women to become 'better' housewives. Three features were featured prominently in the advertising: the potential of the appliances to reduce hard physical work, to reallocate time to the 'caring' aspects of housework (which included being a 'model mother') and to raise standards of cleanliness. The industry linked its products to contemporary concerns about health and hygiene; electrical goods promised to realize high levels of cleanliness.

The third approach used to explain the growth of expenditure on durable goods is grounded in household supply decision where consumer durables are treated as an input into household production. Instead of income and price effects, this approach stresses household formation, the allocation of work in the home and the labour supply decision of household members. It is this approach that has prompted some of the most exciting work on this period, not least given the obvious questions it raises about the use of and value placed on women's time and the role of women in the economy and society (see below).

III

What were the implications of these changes in consumption patterns for the economy and society? Several themes are important in this respect: the role of the 'new' industries in stimulating economic recovery in the 1930s, the link between the durable goods industries and innovations in the financial sector, and the implications of the durable goods for female labour market participation.

In the 1960s it was fashionable to claim that the 'new' industries played a pivotal role in Britain's recovery during the 1930s and laid the basis for the post-Second World War boom as electrical goods, chemicals and motor vehicles came to dominate the economy in terms of output, exports and employment. The thesis that the 'new' industries were an important development block, which regenerated the economy, was first postulated in a series of articles by Richardson and Aldcroft. They adopted a quasi-Keynesian approach, arguing that the building boom of the period (see below) created a demand for a range of household goods. Both created employ-

ment opportunities, which in turn created additional income with which to acquire
the new goods.[9]

Revisionist work since this time has questioned how 'new' these 'new' industries
were, has queried their contribution to the economic recovery of the 1930s, and has
emphasized constraints on their growth. Electrical engineering, chemicals and motor
vehicle production all dated back to the late nineteenth century and comprised 'old'
as well as development sectors.[10] The growth of ownership of a range of consumer
durables did not constitute the emergence of any mass market and, given the collapse of the international economy at this time, added little to import earnings. In
1935, the gross value of output of the 'new' chemical industry was £206.2 million,
that of the 'new' motor vehicle engineering industry £129.5 million and that of the
'new' electrical engineering industry £55.8 million; meanwhile, the 'old' industries
of textiles produced a gross output valued at £442.9 million. In 1924, the UK produced 116,600 motor cars of which it exported 15,700. In 1936, 367,200 cars were
produced, and 65,000 (17.7 per cent) exported.[11] The large majority of motor cars
were produced for and consumed by the home market.

Some historians, given the constraints on the growth of mass markets in the first
three decades of the century, have used the 'new' industries to argue for continuity
in obstacles to productivity growth in the UK. The key argument in this respect is
that manufacturers in the UK 'failed' to introduce mass production methods on
American Fordist lines, by which is meant the manufacture of standardized products
in huge volumes using special-purpose machinery and unskilled labour.[12] Other
historians, however, have argued that the decision not to apply Fordist production
methods was entirely rational. They argue that it did not make sense to invest in the
machinery needed for the production of large output volumes when the mass market
did not exist.[13]

A longstanding debate in British economic industry surrounds whether, and to
what extent, the 'City' is to blame for the misfortunes of industry.[14] Research on
consumer durables, however, has identified the innovative and crucial role played by
financial institutions in introducing new finance schemes, which enabled consumers
to acquire the new goods. What was new about this period was the extent of the use
of hire purchase amongst the middle classes and the increasingly social respectability
of this form of credit. Hire purchase was introduced into the UK in the early nineteenth century, having developed first in Paris in the early 1800s and then in New
York in 1807. In the 1860s, the Singer Sewing Machine Company began to sell its
machines on credit terms. In the Victorian period hire purchase was largely used for
furniture, pianos and sewing machines. By 1891, it is estimated that there were about
1 million hire purchase agreements in existence.[15] In the interwar years, new forms
of finance for a wider group of society were introduced and, increasingly, gained
respectability. As the middle classes began to take up mortgages to acquire their own
homes, so credit assumed a respectability amongst this group that had been absent
before. This provided the framework from which new financial institutions developed
to promote hire purchase of consumer durables.

Mortgages to finance house acquisition, funded by building societies, were increasingly used by the middle classes to buy homes. Whereas in the Edwardian years the
majority of people leased or rented homes, by the end of the interwar years it was
common practice amongst the middle and upper classes to buy homes via mortgage

facilities. In 1914, private rented housing accounted for 80 per cent of the housing stock; council and owner-occupied housing accounted for 1 and 10 per cent respectively. By 1939, private rented accommodation accounted for only 46 per cent of the total stock, whereas council and owner-occupied housing accounted for 14 per cent and 21 per cent respectively.[16] Increasingly, owner-occupation became an accepted form of life for the middling classes and mortgages a respectable way of financing owner-occupation. The increasing social acceptability of mortgages was used by 'new' financial institutions known as the finance houses to promote the acquisition of a range of consumer goods by hire purchase. Hire purchase was marketed as a form of saving, akin to a mortgage, and as such quite distinct from the 'unrespectable' working-class credit known as 'check clubs' and 'tick'.[17] Schemes were designed to appeal to, and taken up by, the business and professional classes. The first recorded sale of a motor car on hire purchase terms in the UK was in 1912, but it was not until the 1920s that the schemes were widely used to acquire cars. Hire purchase became viable only when purchase prices fell. By the early 1930s, the combination of the fall in purchase prices and the wider availability of hire purchase schemes meant that many middle-class families could afford to buy a car.

Innovation from private financial institutions was accompanied by innovation in financing methods from public authorities, namely, local councils. Prior to nationalization, electricity supply was owned and run by a mixture of private and public authorities. From 1926, the legal restrictions that had prevented public undertakings from offering hire and hire purchase schemes were raised. Thereafter, it became commonplace for undertakings to offer these schemes – and for consumers to acquire electric wiring and goods by such means. By the mid-1930s, electric cookers could be hired for as little as 4.62d. a week. Technological change was not the only factor that caused inflection points in the diffusion curve: innovation from the financial institutions also played a key role. Culturally, this was an era when the use of credit became socially acceptable – because it was marketed and accepted as a form of saving. Investment in consumer durables, whether by hire purchase of cars or consumer durables, became an accepted and respectable part of life.[18]

The household supply decision explanation of changing patterns of consumer durable expenditure might suggest that the increased acquisition of household appliances would be related to changes in the labour supply decision of members of the household in general and, in particular, to the potential for women to enter the labour market if and when their housework duties were alleviated. The impact of durable goods on the use of women's labour market participation may be broken down into three distinct but interrelated questions: their effect on the supply of female labour, the implications for the demand for female labour, and finally, changes in a specific traditional form of female work: that of domestic service.

In theory, the introduction of domestic electric appliances into the home might be expected to reduce the drudgery and physical labour of housework, thereby reducing the amount of time a woman had to spend in cleaning, washing and laundry. It might also be predicted that the time saved might be used to enter the paid labour market. The evidence suggests, however, that the potential was not realized in this period, not least because the majority of women did not own the appliances. In addition, the low income women could earn in the labour market did not persuade them to enter it – unless of course household income was so constrained that they had little choice. Historically, women have been treated as a secondary labour force, used to meet short-term emergency needs in the economy and/or to provide a low-paid, temporary, unskilled labour force. The early twentieth century was no exception; this was not a period of labour shortage and hence did not create any stimulus to reallocate married women's work outside the home.[19] There was little demand for female labour and what work was available was, relative to men, poorly paid.[20] Whilst women were excluded from many occupations and industries, and whilst their earnings were significantly lower than men's, there was little incentive to undertake paid work outside the home. Nor did the 'new' industries constitute a major source of employment for women. At the turn of the century, female employment was concentrated in the textile and clothing trades. By the end of the interwar years, textile and clothing still employed far more women than did the 'new' industries of motor vehicle and electrical engineering and radio and telecommunications manufacture.

Electric household appliances did, however, impact on the other traditional form of female employment: that of domestic service. From the turn of the century, the number of women seeking domestic work had been falling; in the commuter areas of London 'the number of servants per 1,000 households had been 24.1 in 1911, by 1921 it was already down to 12.4 and continuing to fall'.[21] The middle classes did not eliminate domestic help in these years; they changed the nature of the work by replacing the full-time live-in servant with casual, informal help in the form of a 'daily'. Electric consumer durables, by reducing the need for the live-in servant, may have speeded up the process and, as such, contributed to the continuance of the segregation of women into low-paid, unskilled work.

IV

Human development is about widening people's choices and the level of their well-being. The key components of this are to be able to lead a long and healthy life and enjoy a decent standard of living. Given such assumptions, one might well question the level of human development achieved by a large proportion of the population of the UK by the end of the third decade of the twentieth century. At its most basic level, well-being is affected by having sufficient to eat and having a range of food intake, which satisfies basic nutritional requirements.

In quantitative terms, the evidence would certainly suggest an improvement in the amount and variety of foods consumed during these years. For the country as a whole, the figures suggest a better-fed population, enjoying a greater amount and wider range of foods which supplied basic calorific, vitamin, mineral and protein needs (table 22.5). The nation, so it would appear, was enjoying a better diet of fresh fruit and vegetables.

Aggregate figures, however, can conceal a variety of experiences. There was a world of difference between the nutritional intake of those at the top and those at the bottom of the income scale. The top 10 per cent of the population consumed over 3 lbs of meat, nearly 2.5 lbs of fruit and 2.25 lbs of vegetables each a week, the bottom 10 per cent, 1.5 lbs of meat, 1 lb of vegetables and less than 1 lb of fruit each a week (table 22.6). A professional man consumed 3.04 lbs of meat, 1.26 lbs of fish and game, 3.17 lbs of fruit and 4.39 lbs of vegetables a week. An unemployed man consumed 1.25 lbs of meat, 0.44 lbs of fish and game, 0.30 lbs of fruit and 2.68 lbs of

Table 22.5 Estimated annual consumption per head of certain foods in the UK at three periods

	1900–13	1924–8		1934	
	Quantity (lbs)	Quantity (lbs)	As % of 1900–13	Quantity (lbs)	As % of 1900–13
Fruit	61	91	149	115	188
Vegetables (other than potatoes)	60	78	130	98	164
Butter	16	16	100	25	157
Eggs	no. 104	no. 120	115	no. 152	146
Cheese	7	9	128	10	143
Margarine	6	12	200	8	133
Sugar	79	87	110	94	119
Meat	135	134	99	143	106
Potatoes	208	194	93	210	101
Wheat flour	211	198	94	197	93

Source: J. Boyd-Orr, Food, Health and Income (London, 1937), table II, p. 24.

vegetables.[22] Nutrition impacts on the health and well-being of the population, not only in terms of being a basic requirement for a long and healthy life, but also enabling an individual to function. By this definition, large numbers of people were suffering from malnutrition, with serious nutritional deficiencies in a range of minerals and vitamins as well as in basic protein, fats and calories (table 22.7). Human development, measured in terms of the nutritional well-being of a significant proportion of the population, was still a major problem by the end of the 1930s.

We have already noted that similar trends may be discerned in the ownership of the 'new' durable goods. For the majority of the population, motor car ownership was out of the question. The motor car was a gender as well as a class good, bought and used by middle-class men. By 1937, the car had become a necessity as a proper occupational asset amongst the professional male middle classes (e.g. doctors).[23] To own a car was a mark of social and professional status. Ownership of the motor vehicle offered not only a new way of travelling to work (and as such encouraged the growth of the commuter town), but also a new form of leisure. This was the era of 'weekend' drives to the countryside and the seaside, of travel in pursuit of leisure and entertainment. Consumerism was not only about purchase of goods for the home, but included goods that permitted greater, more flexible, more personalized travel away from the home.

The gender implications of the diffusion of household consumer durables have provided one of the most fruitful avenues of research in recent years, reflecting in part the profusion of work by feminist historians seeking to understand continuity and change in women's lives over time. Scholars have demonstrated that household technology did not reallocate work in the home away from women, nor did it necessarily release their time: consumer durables never questioned cultural norms that housework was 'women's work'. Nor did they necessarily reduce the time spent on

Table 22.6 Estimated quantities of food consumed per head per week at different income levels in the UK

	Group I	Group II	Group III	Group IV	Group V	Group VI	Weighted of groups	National average
Proportion of the population	10	20	20	20	20	10		
Average food expenditure per week	4s.	6s.	8s.	10s.	12s.	14s.	9s.	
Beef and veal (ozs)	10.5	14.5	17.2	18.9	19.5	18.9	17.0	20.0
Mutton and lamb (ozs)	3.1	5.6	7.2	9.4	11.6	13.9	8.4	9.0
Bacon and ham (ozs)	4.3	6.3	6.8	7.3	7.8	9.4	7.0	7.8
Other meats (ozs)	5.2	5.2	5.9	5.9	5.9	7.2	5.8	7.2
Total meat (ozs)	23.1	31.6	37.1	41.5	44.8	49.4	38.2	44.3
Bread and flour, including biscuits and cakes (ozs)	66	68	68	67	65	60	66	61
Fresh milk (pints)	1.1	2.1	2.6	3.1	4.2	5.5	3.1	2.8
Condensed milk (pints)	0.7	0.6	0.55	0.5	0.4	0.3	0.5	0.5
Eggs (no.)	1.5	2.1	2.6	3.2	3.6	4.5	2.9	2.9
Butter (ozs)	3.0	6.5	7.5	8.5	9.5	11.0	7.8	7.8
Cheese (ozs)	1.8	2.5	3.1	3.6	3.6	2.6	3.0	3.2
Margarine (ozs)	4.5	3.5	2.5	2.0	1.6	1.3	2.5	2.4
Tea (ozs)	2.2	2.7	2.9	3.0	2.9	2.7	2.8	2.8
Potatoes (ozs)	53.0	56.0	57.0	57.0	57.0	54.0	56.0	64.0
Lard, suet and dripping (ozs)	2.7	3.6	4.2	4.4	4.3	3.5	3.9	2.7
Fish (ozs)	2.7	5.5	8.2	10.4	12.2	13.5	8.9	13.2
Sugar purchased as such (ozs)	13.5	16.0	18.0	19	19.5	19.5	17.8	27.7
Jams, jellies, syrup, etc. (ozs)	4.3	5.3	5.2	5.4	5.8	5.5	5.2	
Sugar consumed in other forms (ozs)	6.5	7.5	8.5	9.5	10.5	11.5	9.0	
Fruit (ozs)	14.0	21.7	25.8	27.9	30.5	39.3	26.5	35.1
Vegetables exc. potatoes (ozs)	16.0	20.0	27.2	30.6	32.3	34.0	27.0	30.2

Source: J. Boyd-Orr, *Food, Health and Income* (London, 1937), table II, appendix VI, p. 73.

housework itself. Personal and domestic cleanliness, together with the strict ordering of the household, had emerged in the nineteenth century 'as an important way of marking off the middle class from those below them' and was 'part and parcel of the behaviour and attitudes bundled together in that imprecise but vital concept, respectability'. Such middle-class values were emulated and had become part of the aspirations of the working-class woman by the Edwardian period and were to increase over the next two decades.[24]

Table 22.7 Composition of the diet (per day) by income group of the population

Composition of diet	Group I (g)	Group II (g)	Group III (g)	Group IV (g)	Group V (g)	Group VI (g)	SRUP[a] (g)
Protein							
Plant	40.9	43.5	44.0	43.8	42.8	40.5	
Animal	22.5	32.5	39.6	45.6	51.6	57.8	
Total	63.4	76.0	83.6	89.4	94.4	98.3	68.0
Fat							
Plant	20.9	17.9	14.5	13.3	12.2	11.1	
Animal	50.7	80.9	95.1	107.3	118.3	130.4	
Total	71.6	98.8	109.6	120.6	130.5	141.5	98.0
Carbohydrate	348	381	395	403	406	396	
Minerals							
Calcium	0.37	0.52	0.61	0.71	0.83	0.95	0.6[b] 0.9[c]
Phosphorus	0.81	1.04	1.17	1.28	1.42	1.54	1.23
Iron	0.008	0.0099	0.011	0.012	0.0127	0.0137	0.0115
Vitamins	IU	IU	IU	IU	IU	IU	IU[d]
Vitamin A	774	1,250	1,624	2,015	2,210	2,875	1,900
Vitamin C	838	1,134	1,314	1,577	1,832	2,323	1,400
Calories	2,317	2,768	2,962	3,119	3,249	3,326	2,810

[a] SRUP = standard requirements per unit of the population
[b] minimum for positive balance
[c] minimum plus 50 per cent for safety margin
[d] IU = international units
Source: J. Boyd-Orr, *Food, Health and Income* (London, 1937), table VII, p. 40.

In the interwar years acceptable standards of homecare rose. Magazines, newspapers and the radio extolled the virtues of the perfect wife. Advertisements and articles played on a woman's responsibility for the health of her family. This was hardly a new responsibility. What was new in these years was the emphasis on responsibility for the physical and mental, future and present health of the offspring – and what this entailed. This was partly the outcome of the popularization of Freudian ideas about childcare, but also, and increasingly, a reaction to public concerns about prevailing levels of infant illness and mortality. Few stressed the relevance of the poor diets of many women; rather, the emphasis was on the germs that abounded in a dust-laden atmosphere. Contemporary opinion, as presented in the media, placed much of the blame upon housewives who 'failed' to clean their houses properly. Women were told in no uncertain terms that dust carried disease germs and that it was their responsibility to rid the house of this disease-inducing substance. Cleaning became almost an obsession as the media popularized the 'germ theory of disease'. Both working- and middle-class women's magazines went to great lengths to elaborate 'germ warfare' timetables for housework – on a daily, weekly and monthly basis. Thursday, for example, was the day for cleaning the bedroom, which involved sweeping the floor surface, washing down the windows and paintwork, as well as dusting and polishing every surface and ornament. The emphasis was on scrupulous cleanliness and efficiency.

Did women believe this mass onslaught of advice from the media? Contemporary accounts suggest that women spent nearly a third of their time cleaning and the same amount of time cooking.[25] It would take a strong mind to resist (and reject) the cultural messages, especially when presented in pseudo-scientific terms. If germs and badly cooked and prepared meals caused disease, and housewives were responsible for the well-being of family members, it would have been difficult if not impossible to ignore such advice. Time saved by using appliances was spent on achieving higher standards of cleanliness in the home and on realizing increased expectations of acceptable norms of childcare. Electrical goods allowed women to reallocate their time and to obtain ever-increased standards of acceptable cleanliness and orderliness. In the wider scheme of economic and social analyses, fertility control, access to education and a reduction of discrimination in the workplace have been more important in women's lives than have consumer durables. Now, as in the past, women perform most housework, whether or not they are in paid work outside the home.

There was, however, one consumer durable that did make a large impact on both genders, all age groups and every income group: the radio. Analyses of patterns of consumption have suggested that households have assigned greater priority to leisure goods rather than to housework goods, a preference for time-using rather than time-saving goods.[26] The radio offered drama, music and current affairs; it gave its listeners contact with the wider outside world. For many, living on limited incomes, it was an escape from the tedium of everyday life. Some historians have therefore seen the radio as playing a key role in the privatization of leisure within the home and, whilst only one such appliance was acquired, to more leisure time being enjoyed in a family setting.[27]

The radio as a low-cost, high-utility good was used and enjoyed by the vast majority of the population: 'radio was magic to child and adult alike, keeping families indoors almost every evening'.[28] Such was the popularity of the radio that 'cinema and theatre managers found their Wednesday evening receipts fell, in some cases, by as much as a third' because of that evening's radio programmes.[29] It was working-class women who benefited most from the radio. For such women, leisure was a relative term. Leisure for these women meant listening to the radio at the end of the day whilst they did the sewing, knitting and mending. For such women, the radio was seen as their one luxury; it did not eliminate or even reduce their housework, but it did relieve the monotony of their daily lives and gave them entertainment and communication with the outside world.[30]

Conclusion

In the past decade, economists have been excited by the notion of measuring the success of an economy less in terms of economic growth *per se* and more in terms of human development. This has produced a new global forum for measuring current changes in human development and growing interest in the measurement, implications of and explanations for differences in human development between countries, genders and regions.[31] It is a subject to which economic and social history has much to offer.

Human development is about the process of widening people's choices and the level of their achieved well-being, most importantly their ability to lead a long and healthy life, to be educated and to enjoy a decent standard of living.[32] Changes in consumption patterns, for example, may lead to improved (or diminished) calorific and nutritional intake, which will have direct effects on the health of the individual. For historians, the key questions arising from the trends in expenditure on perishable goods relate to the implications of changing patterns of consumption on perishable goods for the health and well-being of the population.

Consumption in the first three decades of the twentieth century is dominated by two themes: that of the skewed distribution of income and its consequent implications for the expenditure patterns of the population, and second, the promise of the growth of a mass market for consumer durables. As this chapter has shown, the distribution of income was such that the majority of people did not benefit from the introduction of a large number of the new consumer durables. Goods were also gendered: the motor car promised a new and convenient way to travel for the middle-class male; electrical appliances allowed middle-class women to rely on part-time 'daily' help in the home, but also to realize increased expectations of housewifery.

For the large majority of the population life in the first three decades of the twentieth century was harsh. Consumption was then, as it had been in the nineteenth century, a matter of providing for the basic necessities of life. Food, fuel and shelter accounted for, and continued to account for, the large majority of their expenditure. Low wages, irregular employment and unemployment characterized the lives of many people. Life was concerned with ensuring that the family got enough to eat. Evidence on nutrition would suggest that many did not even realize this.

There were none the less some important exceptions. Many working-class women were able to participate in a world where 'fashionable' dress (albeit cheap copies) became part of their lives. It is, however, the radio that had the most significant impact on everyday life. The radio opened up a new world for many people, a world of music, drama and current affairs within their own homes. Entertainment and information were now available, at a low cost, to all. This more than anything else marks out the importance of this period in the history of consumption, not least because that entertainment and information were made available to the working-class housewife, even if they were enjoyed whilst she was doing housework. Leisure and communication have characterized the history of consumption in the twentieth century: these years were pivotal to that development.

A long-run perspective would also suggest that the early twentieth century marked the important second stage in the development of the mass market for consumer durables. The mass market for consumer durables is located after the Second World War, but we can see in the first three decades of the twentieth century the transition from the 'luxury' to the 'middle' stage in the evolution of mass demand. The transition was important, not least since people acquired a taste for the goods. Advertising and marketing became part of everyday life and the potential of electrical appliances to reduce the drudgery of housework the dream of many women. These years saw the beginning of the emergence of a culture of mass consumption: the realization of ownership, however, had to wait until after the Second World War.

NOTES

1 British Broadcasting Corporation, *Annual Report* (London, 1938), p. 73.
2 See A. Deaton and J. Muellbauer, *Economics and Consumer Behaviour* (Cambridge, 1980) and F. G. Pyatt, *Priority Patterns and the Demand for Household Goods* (Cambridge, 1964).
3 S. Bowden, 'The new consumerism', in P. Johnson, ed., *Economic, Social and Cultural Change in Twentieth-century Britain* (London, 1994), pp. 242–62.
4 See B. Eichengreen, 'Unemployment in interwar Britain', *ReFRESH*, 9 (1989).
5 A. A. Jackson, *The Middle Classes, 1900–1950* (Nairn, 1991), appendix A, pp. 336–7.
6 Economies of scale is the term used to describe a situation when increasing the scale of production leads to a lower cost per unit of output.
7 See J. Foreman-Peck, S. Bowden and A. McKinlay, *The British Motor Vehicle Industry, 1880–1990* (Manchester, 1995).
8 *Ideal Home* was launched in 1920, *Woman and Home* in 1926, and *Homes and Gardens* in 1916. The circulation and readership of these magazines extended to most middle-class women. See N. Beauman, *A Very Great Profession: The Woman's Novel, 1914–1939* (London, 1983), p. 109 and Jackson, *Middle Classes*, pp. 116–17. The annual expenditure on cinema admissions rose from £186.7 million in 1924 to £262.5 million by 1938. Cinema admissions accounted for 66 per cent of the number of admissions for all entertainments. See R. Stone and D. Rowe, *The Measurement of Consumers' Expenditure* (Cambridge, 1966), vol. 2, table 36, p. 91; table 38, p. 92; table 45, p. 110. See also A. Davies, 'Cinema and broadcasting', in Johnson, ed., *Economic, Social and Cultural Change*, pp. 263–80.
9 The articles were subsequently collected and published in book form: D. H. Aldcroft and H. Richardson, *The British Economy, 1870–1939* (London, 1969).
10 See for example the collected works in N. K. Buxton and D. H. Aldcroft, *British Industry between the Wars: Instability and Industrial Development, 1919–1939* (London, 1979).
11 Board of Trade, *Census of Production for 1951* (London, 1956), summary tables, part 1, table 1, pp. 4, 6, 8, 16, 18. See also S. Bowden, 'Demand and supply constraints in the interwar UK car industry: did the manufacturers get it right?', *Business History*, 33 (April 1991), pp. 242–67.
12 See W. Lewchuk, *American Technology and the British Motor Vehicle Industry* (Cambridge, 1987).
13 Bowden, 'Demand and supply'.
14 See, for example, W. Hutton, *The State We're In* (London, 1995).
15 *Consumer Credit* (The Crowther Report), Report of the Committee, vol. 1: *Report* (London, March 1971), Cmd. 4596.
16 S. Glynn and J. Oxborrow, *Interwar Britain: A Social and Economic History* (London, 1976), pp. 221, 227.
17 Crowther Committee, *Report*, para 2.1.51, pp. 46. See also M. Tebbutt, *Making Ends Meet: Pawnbroking and Working-class Credit* (London, 1983).
18 S. Bowden, 'Credit facilities and the growth of consumer demand for electric appliances in England in the 1930s', *Business History*, 32, no. 1 (1990), pp. 52–75.
19 A. T. Mallier and M. J. Rosser, *Women and the Economy: A Comparative Study of Britain and the USA* (London, 1987), p. 47; G. Joseph, *Women at Work: The British Experience* (Oxford, 1983), pp. 126–7; S. Walby, *Theorising Patriarchy* (Oxford, 1990), pp. 24–40.
20 See E. Roberts, *Women's Work, 1840–1940* (London, 1988); S. Bowden and A. Offer, 'Gender and the culture of consumption: women and the market for domestic electrical

appliances in interwar England', in V. de Grazia and E. Furlogh, eds, *The Sex of Things: Gender and Consumption in Historical Perspective* (California, 1996), pp. 244–74.

21 J. Burnett, *A Social History of Housing 1815–1970* (London, 1980), p. 258.

22 Medical Research Council, *A Dietary Survey in Terms of the Actual Foodstuffs Consumed* (London, 1936), table VII.

23 S. Bowden and P. Turner, 'The UK market and the market for consumer durables', *Journal of Economic History*, 53, no. 2 (1993), pp. 244–58 and 'Some cross-section evidence on the determinants of the diffusion of car ownership in the interwar UK economy', *Business History*, 35, no. 1 (1993), pp. 55–69.

24 L. Davidoff, 'The rationalisation of housework', in D. L. Barker and S. Allen, eds, *Dependence and Exploitation in Work and Marriage* (London, 1976); A. Ravetz, 'Modern technology and an ancient occupation: housework in present-day society', *Technology and Culture*, 6, no. 2 (1965), pp. 256–60; R. S. Cowan, 'A case study of technological and social change: the washing machine and the working wife', in M. S. Hartman and L. Banner, eds, *Clio's Consciousness Raised* (New York, 1989), pp. 245–53; S. J. Kleinberg, 'Escalating standards: women, housework and household technology in the twentieth century', in F. J. Coppa and R. Harmond, eds, *Technology in the Twentieth Century* (Iowa, 1983), pp. 1–29.

25 Political and Economic Planning, *The Market for Domestic Household Appliances* (London, 1945), p. xiii.

26 S. Bowden and A. Offer, 'Household appliances and the use of time: the United States and Britain since the 1920s', *Economic History Review*, 47, no. 4 (1994), pp. 725–48.

27 H. Cunningham, 'Leisure and culture', in F. M. L. Thompson, ed., *The Cambridge Social History of Britain, 1750–1950*, vol. 2, *People and their Environment* (Cambridge, 1990), pp. 278–339; see esp. p. 317.

28 Jackson, *Middle Classes*, p. 277.

29 R. Graves, R. Hodge and A. Hodge, *The Long Weekend: A Social History of Great Britain, 1918–1939* (London, 1940).

30 M. S. Rice, *Working-class Wives* (1939; rpt. London, 1981).

31 Thus from 1990 the United Nations Development Programme has published an annual *Human Development Report*. The work is related to the work of the Nobel prize winner Amartya Sen. See A. Sen, *Development as Freedom* (Oxford, 1999).

32 United Nations Development Programme, *Human Development Report* (1999), 'Analytical tools for human development', p. 1.

FURTHER READING

The key sources of statistical information for consumption patterns from 1900 to 1938 remain the seminal works by A. R. Prest, *Consumers' Expenditure in the United Kingdom, 1900–1919* (Cambridge, 1954) and R. Stone and D. Rowe, *The Measurement of Consumers' Expenditure* (Cambridge, 1966). In-depth articles on middle-class and working-class budgets are P. Massey, 'The expenditure of 1360 British middle-class households in 1938–1939', *Journal of the Royal Statistical Society*, 95, part 3 (1942), pp. 159–85, and Ministry of Labour, 'Weekly expenditure of working-class households in the United Kingdom, 1937–1938', *Ministry of Labour Gazette* (London, December, 1940, January 1941 and February 1941). A. A. Jackson, *The Middle Classes, 1900–1950* (Nairn, 1991) and M. S. Rice, *Working-class Wives* (1939; rpt. London, 1981) give narrative weight to the reality of life on middle-class and working-class incomes respectively.

Economic approaches that centre on the role of the producers of the 'new' goods can be consulted in D. H. Aldcroft and H. Richardson, *The British Economy, 1870–1939* (London,

1969) and N. K. Buxton and D. H. Aldcroft, *British Industry between the Wars: Instability and Industrial Development, 1919–1939* (London, 1979). W. Lewchuk, *American Technology and the British Motor Vehicle Industry* (Cambridge, 1987) provides the key reading for a negative interpretation of the performance of the motor industry. The key text for economic analyses of demand is A. Deaton and J. Muellbauer, *Economics and Consumer Behaviour* (Cambridge, 1980). Specific analyses of the demand for different consumer goods in the inter-war years can be found in S. Bowden, 'The new consumerism', in P. Johnson, ed., *Economic, Social and Cultural Change in Twentieth-century Britain* (London, 1994), pp. 242–62.

The role of entertainment and leisure is analysed to great effect by H. Cunningham, 'Leisure and culture', in F. M. L. Thompson, ed., *The Cambridge Social History of Britain, 1750–1950*, vol. 2, *People and their Environment* (Cambridge, 1990), pp. 278–339, and A. Davies, 'Cinema and broadcasting', in P. Johnson, ed., *Economic, Social and Cultural Change in Twentieth-century Britain* (London, 1994), pp. 263–80, whilst S. Bowden and A. Offer, 'Household appliances and the use of time: the United States and Britain since the 1920s', *Economic History Review*, 47, no. 4 (1994), pp. 725–48, consider the diffusion of time-saving and time-using goods. There are many high-quality feminist works on the lives of women at this time. A key text in this respect, which makes excellent use of the insights revealed by oral history, is E. Roberts, *Women's Work, 1840–1940* (London, 1988). S. Bowden and A. Offer, 'Gender and the culture of consumption: women and the market for domestic electrical appliances in interwar England', in V. de Grazia and E. Furlogh, eds, *The Sex of Things: Gender and Consumption in Historical Perspective* (California, 1996), pp. 244–74, C. Hardyment, *From Mangle to Microwave: The Mechanization of Household Work* (Oxford, 1988), A. T. Mallier and M. J. Rosser, *Women and the Economy: A Comparative Study of Britain and the USA* (London, 1987) and S. Walby, *Theorising Patriarchy* (Oxford, 1990) are all first-class works which consider, from a variety of approaches, the reality of women's experience at home and in the labour force.

What human development means, how it has changed over time, and how (and why) it differs between countries, between regions within countries, and between men and women can be consulted via the United Nations' *Human Development Report* (annual from 1990), a text that offers insights of great importance to historians, and to which historians have much to offer.

Chapter Twenty-Three

Social Welfare: Public and Private, 1900–1939

Keith Laybourn

The early twentieth century saw a remarkable change in the balance of social welfare provision in Britain, from a position whereby the voluntary and philanthropic/private contribution rivalled that of the state to the point where the state provision became dominant. Whilst the balance of public and private provision changed dramatically, it is also clear that this became necessary given the failings of the Poor Law and philanthropy in the Edwardian age, the rising political challenge of the Labour party, the First World War, and the immense problem presented by unemployment during the interwar years. Although Tony Blair's 'New' Labour government has revived the idea of both private and state cooperating in future social welfare provision, it is obvious that, during the first decade of the twentieth century, the combination of philanthropy and limited state action was insufficient to deal with the rising social problems faced by the British working classes. Indeed, the rapid extension of state provision became essential in the attempt to tackle poverty, and its causes, in the early twentieth century, even if it was driven more by expediency and political need than by a coherent strategy for social policy.

1900–1914

The emergence of state intervention, through the medium of the Liberal social reforms of 1905–14, was the most important development in the decade before the First World War, largely because it challenged and undermined both local control and the philanthropic efforts that had been the basis of British social provision until the early twentieth century. Indeed, Derek Fraser has reflected that '[w]hatever historical perspective is used, one cannot escape the conclusion that Liberal social policy before the First World War was at variance with the past and an anticipation of radical changes in the future'.[1] Nevertheless, one should be cautious of suggesting that there was any clean break between the past and the present for relations between the two forces of social provision overlapped for many years. In addition, the voluntary sector varied in its response to the state. The London-based Charity Organization Society (COS) was reluctant to accept that poverty was anything other than a personal failing and was hostile to David Lloyd George's state insurance scheme (the 1911 National Insurance Act), which was forcing voluntary bodies to become an authorized sub-service of the state.[2] In contrast, the Guild of Help, a new philanthropic body that emerged in Bradford in September 1904 and quickly superseded the COS as the largest voluntary body in Britain, recognized the challenge that was coming, and inherent in its 'new philanthropy' was a commitment to working with public bodies. Its aim was to check the pace of state intervention by demonstrating the way in which voluntary help could become more effective in acting as the friend of the poor. In the end neither the approach of the COS nor that of the Guild of Help succeeded, particularly as the First World War swallowed up voluntary help, which became a mere adjunct to, rather than a partner with, state social welfare. The state became ubiquitous and the voluntary sector declined. Yet, for a decade or more there was the possibility of overlap and cooperation between the state and philanthropic help.

The Edwardian years were clearly ones of transition which saw the state assume new and wider responsibilities. But why did state intervention widen? There have been many explanations. Some historians have suggested that it was the product of ideals and idealists,[3] New Liberals such as David Lloyd George who were committed to social reform in order to reduce the social differences within society and bring social harmony. Others have noted the failure of philanthropy which necessitated state involvement.[4] Yet others have suggested that welfare capitalism might have had an impact,[5] that the emergence of the political power of the working class was shaping events, or, on the contrary, that the impact of the rise of labour has been exaggerated.[6] In this whirl of ideas it has become obvious that many forces helped to shape the evolution of the welfare state. However, whilst each has a claim to influence, and it is clear that whilst philanthropy was ineffective and the Labour party and working-class demands were becoming more pressing, the real problem was that the Poor Law was failing under the burden of an increasing level of poverty and unemployment.

Philanthropy was an essential part of social provision in the 1890s and early twentieth century. Indeed, Frank Prochaska has written that

> No country on earth can lay claim down to a greater philanthropic tradition than Great Britain. Until the twentieth century philanthropy was widely believed to be the most wholesome remedy for the nation's ills, a view not without its adherents today.[7]

Indeed, millions of pounds were spent to relieve the poor, if not the destitute, in the late 1890s and early twentieth century. No one knows the precise level of philanthropic help, but one estimate suggests that in London alone in the 1890s the thousand leading charities raised and spent more than £7,000,000.[8] Yet the problem of poverty remained more acute than ever, and was amplified by the severe economic depression that occurred between 1902–4 and 1908–9. In these conditions doubts began to develop about the effectiveness of the philanthropic approach to the poor. The COS had failed to make a significant impact upon poverty in London and its influence outside London and Liverpool was negligible, there being only twenty-six COS organizations with forty-four paid and 235 voluntary organizers in the north of England serving about 3.5 million people in various towns at a cost of £16,000 per year.[9] There were many local charities in the towns and communities of Britain but they often lacked coordination in their relief activities. As a consequence co-ordinated charitable relief, which was increasingly considered to be a feature of a 'scientific' approach to charity, was missing.

Faced with the clear failure of the 'old philanthropy', efforts were made to modernize charity and to stave off the threat of increasing state control and intervention. Although there were several movements in this direction, the most important attempt to make philanthropy more effective was that associated with the Guild of Help. Formed in Bradford in September 1904, the Guild of Help spawned more than eighty semi-autonomous organizations by the time of the First World War. Its aim was to build up an effective community structure to deal with poverty. Indeed, according to *Help*, the organ of the Bradford Guild,

> The Guild of Help is the practical expression of the civic consciousness and the embodiment of the new philanthropy. The old was clearly associated with charity in a narrow sense, and between those who gave and those who received was a great gulf fixed; the 'lady bountiful' attitude has received its death blow, the Guild worker does not go as a visitant from another world but as a fellow creature to be helpful.[10]

Organized on the basis of local volunteer helpers, working through the municipal ward system of the towns, Bradford and other guilds sought to develop a pattern of social casework designed to alleviate the sufferings of the poor by giving advice, arranging necessary health, clothing and holiday provision, organizing employment exchanges and offering a variety of other activities. The Halifax Guild encouraged the local authority to appoint health visitors and in Bolton, Bradford and Halifax, as well as in other areas, the guilds contributed to the provision and distribution of school meals.[11] Unlike the old philanthropy, the new philanthropy espoused by the Guilds of Help emphasized the need to work with public bodies, the need to reflect the local community, and the need to accept that it was often society rather than the individual who was to blame for poverty. These views suggested that a new, more socially oriented type of philanthropy was emerging. Nevertheless, the appeal and influence of the new movement barely lasted a decade. Most guilds lacked the resources to tackle the high level of poverty caused by unemployment, found that their support came from the middle classes rather than from the whole of the community, and failed to develop good relations between all the various charity organizations in their area. The movement also lacked an effective national organization and public bodies were not always willing to work closely with them.

The efforts of such organizations as the Guild of Help were greatly challenged by the emergent political Labour movement, through such bodies as the Independent Labour party (ILP) and the Labour party, which had been formed as the Labour Representation Committee (LRC) in February 1900. Committed to both municipal and parliamentary change, these organizations accepted that progress would be slow, even after the Labour party's position in the 1906 general election rose to thirty MPs. James Ramsay MacDonald, one of its leading figures, mounted the right to work movement throughout 1908, based upon similar earlier movements, and there was clearly increasing pressure upon the Liberal governments of the pre-war years to do something about social reform. However, the working classes and even the Labour party and the trade unions were often suspicious of social reforms, such as the creation of employment exchanges and the introduction of national insurance, in the hands of the Liberals, and some historians have played down the commitment of the working class to social reform.[12] Even at the municipal level Labour activists recognized that the pace of change had to be slow. Indeed, Fred Jowett, one of the leading Bradford socialists, concluded that '[t]he future must grow out of the present; it cannot be created to fit with a plan', adding that the socialist being 'by conviction a democrat, his inclination to chafe soon gives way to a feeling that on the whole it is better so [to accept delay], because progress in advance of the public opinion of the day rests on a very unsafe foundation'.[13]

Philanthropy was failing and the Labour challenge was rising, but the most serious and immediate problem facing the pre-war Liberal governments of Henry Campbell-Bannerman and Herbert Henry Asquith was the deep economic crisis between 1902–4 and 1909–9, which saw a rapid rise in those seeking help from the Poor Law and the decision to form the Royal Commission on the Poor Law and the Relief of Distress (1905–9). It was clear that the 1834 Poor Law Amendment Act, and the New Poor Law it bequeathed, was no longer relevant to the Edwardian age and the twentieth century. The task of deterring the poor by the imposition of a workhouse test was no longer feasible in a climate where the extension of democratic rights was on the political agenda and when philanthropy had clearly failed to deal adequately with the poor, if not the destitute. The 'New' Liberal reformers were forced to accept that they had to intervene to organize a coherent attack upon rising poverty and continuing inequality, and because of the divided final conclusions of the Royal Commission. The Poor Law structure was thus to be left alone, although the burden on the Poor Law was to be reduced by a variety of social measures, the cost of poor relief having increased from £8.1 million in 1881 to £8.6 million in 1906.

In a forlorn attempt to reduce the pressure of unemployment the Conservative government had introduced the Unemployed Workman's Act of 1905, which, amongst other things, allowed for the creation of distress committees in all metropolitan boroughs and urban districts with a population of more than 50,000. Unfortunately, the implementation of the Act did not work well. In addition, the Royal Commission on the Poor Law produced two reports in February 1909. The Majority Report wished to retain the Poor Law but to operate it more closely with charitable and philanthropic bodies and to emphasize the importance of moral rescue and 'restoring people to a higher status of life'. In the final analysis it was prepared to retain a Poor Law more tightly tied in with more efficiently organized local authorities (the Public Assistance Committees of the 1930s). In contrast, the Minority Report wanted to break up the Poor Law into specialist bodies (dealing with sickness, old age and the like) administered by a committee of the elected local authority, although unemployment was to be dealt with by central government.

In the end, it proved impossible to change the Poor Law before the First World War, civil servants were resistant to change and there were difficulties in ensuring that local finance would be changed and equalized between different areas. As a result the Liberal social reforms aimed to dismantle the Poor Law by removing needy groups by a series of measures, such as the introduction of old-age pensions, the creation of employment exchanges (recommended by both the Majority and Minority reports), the introduction of the National Insurance Act of 1911, and child welfare legislation.

The introduction of non-contributory old-age pensions occurred from 1 January 1909. The 1908 Act had offered 5 shillings (25p) per week at the age of seventy, and introduced sliding-scale arrangements for those with incomes from 8 to 12 shillings (40–60p) per week, or between £21 and £31.10s. per annum, provided that those of seventy and over had not been imprisoned for any offence, including drunkenness, during the ten years preceding their claim. These pensions were to be paid through the Post Office rather than the Poor Law. In other words, the pensions were given as a right of citizenship and were not tainted with the moral stigma of the Poor Law. It was, as Pat Thane suggests, 'a pension for the very poor, the very respectable and the very old'.[14] It certainly did help relieve the Poor Law of some of its elderly inmates, and the government found that in the first year the cost was £8 million rather than the estimated £6.5 million.

Child poverty was catered for in a number of ways. Most obviously, the Education (School Feeding) Act of December 1906 paved the way for the introduction of school feeding and free school meals. In addition, the Children's Act of 1908 consolidated and codified existing legislation concerning children and in 1909 the Local Government Board obliged every Poor Law Union to set up a boarding-out committee, which had to appoint salaried female visitors to visit those children who were boarded out and women and children who were on outdoor relief. Indeed, the number of boarded-out children had risen from 2,799 in 1885 to 11,596 in 1914, by which time it represented about 14 per cent of all children in care.[15]

Employment exchanges also came into operation in 1909 in order to provide details of job vacancies for the unemployed. However, potentially the most important measure impacting upon poverty, and the Poor Law, was the National Insurance Act of 1911. On 4 May 1911 Lloyd George, chancellor of the exchequer, offered his national insurance scheme to the House of Commons, stating that 'In this country . . . 30 per cent of pauperism is attributable to sickness', noting that a considerable percentage more was added by unemployment.[16] The message was clear: the National Insurance Act, part I of which dealt with health and part II with unemployment, was designed to deal with two major causes of poverty and destitution, which impacted upon the Poor Law. As a result Lloyd George introduced forms of insurance which, although limited by the vested interests of friendly societies, trade unions and insurance companies, introduced a system of state-encouraged insurance provision that was to be widened during the First World War and the interwar years to act as the basis of the social welfare provision made by the state. On health insurance, the workers had to contribute 4d. per week (3d. for females), the employer 3d. per week and the state 2d., all of which would be paid into an accumulating fund to finance benefits. Those eligible for health insurance had to be aged between sixteen and sixty-five and had to earn less than £150 per year. When it came into operation on 15 January 1913, the scheme provided sickness benefits of 10s. (50p) per week for men and 7s.6d. (37.5p) for women for the first thirteen weeks of sickness, although nothing would be paid for the first three days. After the first thirteen weeks 5s. per week was paid to both men and women. There was a disability pension of 5s. per week, and a maternity benefit of 30s. (£1.50) was paid to the wives of insured men. As for unemployment insurance, each insured worker contributed 2.5d. (1p) per week, as did the employer, and the state contributed 1.67d. (0.6p). Unlike health insurance, which covered most of the nation, the scheme was compulsory only for certain industries (such as building, mechanical engineering and ironfounding) and the benefits were to be 7s. (35p) per week for up to fifteen weeks, with the possibility of subsidies to trade unions who ran their own schemes. In the final analysis, about 2.25 million men were to be protected against unemployment and the whole scheme came on to the statute book without much parliamentary rancour. The first contributions were paid on 1 July 1912, and the first benefits from 1 January 1913.

It is difficult to be exact about the precise impact of such measures in easing the burden of the Poor Law. Nevertheless, Pat Thane suggests that the measures for the aged and the sick reduced the number of paupers from 916,377 in 1910 to 748,019 in 1914.[17] As far as unemployment insurance is concerned, its impact was undoubtedly restricted by the small proportion of workers that it covered, all of whom were in trades that expected only a low level of unemployment in the normal course of events. The provision of employment exchanges in 1909 might have been more effective for there were 423 employment exchanges by February 1914, with appointed management boards containing worker representatives. By 1914 they were registering over 2 million workers per year and finding 3,000 jobs per day. Although the majority of the registered never got their jobs through the exchanges and unemployment insurance was limited, the exchanges and insurance undoubtedly reduced the numbers of able-bodied workers applying for Poor Law relief.

The cost of reducing the burden of the Poor Law was substantial and forced the chancellor of the exchequer Lloyd George to introduce the controversial 'people's budget' of 1909 to make good a £16 million deficit. This was resisted by the House of Lords and not passed until April 1910, amidst a constitutional crisis in which the Liberal government threatened to create new Liberal peers and to reduce the political powers of the House of Lords. Once passed, this budget raised the basic rate of income tax on earned income to 1s. 6d. in the pound (7.5p) and imposed a super-tax on incomes above £3,000 per year. Death duties were also increased on estates of over £5,000 and taxes were levied on land. It was these land taxes which invited the wrath of the Lords for they raised 20 per cent of the unearned increment in land values, levied on the sale of land. In order to help families on lower incomes, Lloyd George also introduced a £10 tax allowance for each child under sixteen for taxpayers earning £500 per year or less. This established firmly the principle of progressive taxation. The 'people's budget' was thus clearly designed to make some small redistribution of the wealth of the country through taxation and was indicative of the Liberal commitment to reducing the poverty of the mass of the people by a relatively modest taxing of the rich. Indeed, at the end of the budget speech, Lloyd George stated that 'This is a War Budget. It is for raising money to wage implacable warfare against poverty and squalidness'.[18]

The years 1900 to 1914 thus saw an immense extension of the role of the state in social welfare and created a new balance between the state and philanthropic bodies. By 1914 it was accepted that the voluntary and philanthropic efforts were insufficient to deal with the immense social problem of poverty and that social reforms had to be introduced to reduce the pressure of the destitute upon the wilting Poor Law. Both the new approach of the state to welfare and the balance between the public and private sectors were further legitimized by the experience of war.

The First World War, 1914–1918

The First World War affected the balance of the new relationship that was being struck between the voluntary sector and the state in the immediate pre-war years. It ensured that the state became dominant and the voluntary sector a subsidiary force in welfare. The wartime situation made this necessary since the state needed to organize and control the lives of millions of people to win the war with the help of voluntary bodies.

The immediate and widespread dislocation of military men and the plight of their dependants led to the call of the Prince of Wales's appeal to voluntary societies on 6 August 1914, as a result of which the National Relief Fund was formed. New volunteers joined existing voluntary societies and helped to form over 300 Local Representative Committees (LRCs) to administer monies and coordinate relief, encouraged by the Government Committee for the Prevention and Relief of Distress. Out of this development voluntary societies were now forced to cooperate more effectively than ever before. In the words of M. J. Moore, 'The pressure of war had forced the co-ordination that had previously eluded voluntaryists, and they recognised a valuable chance to build an effective organisation'.[19] Indeed, the wartime experience did force many of the voluntary societies, including the Guild of Help and the COS, into the National Council of Social Services in 1919, the forerunner of the present National Council of Voluntary Organizations, although many remained separate bodies. New organizations were formed. Most obviously there was the Soldiers' and Sailors' Families Association (SSFA), formed from a variety of voluntary bodies to ensure that the families of soldiers and sailors were not left destitute and to check upon those qualified for war pensions which the government had passed on to it through the War Pensions Act of July 1916. The Queen's Committee, later renamed the Central Committee on Women's Employment, organized voluntary relief and training, with both government and voluntarily raised funds, to those women who lost employment as a result of the war. It set up workshops for those women to produce army blouses and earn an income.[20] Thus the SSFA now became a 'handmaiden of the War Pensions Committee'.[21] Other voluntary bodies played a similar role.

The dominating presence of the state was evident for all to see. In 1914 parliament passed the Defence of the Realm Act (DORA), greatly extending the powers of the government, which could now control industry and make munitions work a priority over private orders. The government increased the national debt from £650 million to £7,500 million to conduct the war between 1914 and 1918 and imposed military conscription in January 1916. The government began to plan for post-war developments through a Ministry of Reconstruction, set up by Dr Christopher Addison in 1917, and proposals for post-war housing, health, education and unemployment were discussed. Thus the Ministry of Reconstruction paved the way for future social policies, cultivating the so-called 'wartime socialism'. David Lloyd George's election pledge of 'Homes Fit for Heroes' had a genuine ring about it in 1918, but the post-war years and economic dislocation that occurred for the staple industries, and thus for governments, ensured that social policy was an area characterized more by expediency than by continuity and clear structure, one factor in which was the 1918 Franchise Act, which increased the electorate from about 7 million to 21 million and forced all governments to become more aware of the working-class electorate and the women's vote.

The Interwar Years, 1918–1939

The years between 1914, rather than 1918, and 1939 saw the end of the destitution policies that had dominated Victorian and early Edwardian thinking and the development of selective policies to deal with the problems of specific social groups. However, faced with a high level of unemployment, the 'intractable million', successive interwar governments created a confused and complex pattern of social security which barely alleviated the condition of a large proportion of the unemployed and the poor. The years between 1914 and 1939 can thus be seen as some type of transition period between the destitution policies of the Victorians and the universalism of Beveridge and the post-war Attlee Labour governments.

At first the good economic conditions of the immediate post-war years encouraged Lloyd George's post-war coalition government to extend the Liberal reforms. In 1919 it was decided that the 1911 Unemployment Insurance Scheme would be extended to all workers, except for agricultural labourers and domestics, with earnings of less than £250 per year. Thus the number of workers covered by unemployment insurance rose from 2 million in 1913 to 12 million in 1919. However, after an Indian summer of post-war prosperity, unemployment rose in most of Britain's basic industries as it became obvious that export markets had been lost. Unemployment amongst the insured sections of the nation rose to more than 1 million, beyond the means of the Unemployment Fund. Unemployment occasionally reached levels of up to 3 million, as in 1930 and 1931, and many unemployed workers had insufficient contributions to be entitled to benefits. It was in this situation that the Lloyd George coalition government decided to offer its form of outdoor relief, without the Poor Law, which went under several titles, although it was popularly known as the 'dole'.

The 'dole' cut across the insurance principle but did have the advantage that it relieved the Poor Law from the problem of having to deal with some of the impact of mass unemployment. The problem was that the sheer cost of saving the Poor Law was enormous. Nevertheless, some means of subsistence had to be provided to deal with the unemployed. The problem was that whilst unemployment insurance could deal with normal cyclical unemployment, it could not deal with the structural unemployment resulting from the collapse of the major industries. This problem was compounded by the fact that the 1921 Unemployed Workers' Dependants (Temporary Provisions) Act provided additional benefits of 5s. (25p) for a wife and 1s. (5p) for each child, thus adding to the financial burden.

It was this system of national insurance and the dole – formally known as uncovenanted benefit (1921), extended (1924) and transitional benefit (1927), and then transitional payments (1931) – which survived until the 1934 Unemployment Act created the Unemployment Assistance Board and attempted to separate the long-term and the short-term unemployed. The structure that evolved was inconsistent and varied according to the political party in power and the economic conditions that prevailed.

David Lloyd George's post-war coalition government accepted the need to provide uncovenanted benefit. The Labour government of 1924 increased unemployment benefit and attempted to introduce limitless access to unemployment insurance and uncovenanted or extended benefit. The Baldwin government of 1924 to 1929 set up the Blanesburgh Committee to examine unemployment insurance and extended benefit. It suggested that unemployment insurance/the new standard benefit should be unlimited but based upon thirty contributions in two years, thus breaking the 1911 arrangement, which related the number of contributions to the amount of benefit. It attempted to offer an actuarially sound scheme based upon 6 per cent unemployment levels, and offered transitional payments for those who could not meet the 'thirty in two' requirement. William Beveridge denounced the scheme and stated that '[i]t was the Conservative government of 1927 which on the bad advice of the rather stupid Blanesburgh Committee made the insurance benefit unlimited in time and formally divorced the claim of benefit from payment and contributions'.[22] Nevertheless, the Conservative government did extend the 'genuinely seeking work test', to prevent abuse and to eliminate the 'scrounger', since the principle of proportionality set up by the National Insurance Act (of one benefit for five contributions in 1911 and one to six in 1920) had been swept away. A form of 'genuinely seeking work' test had been applied since March 1921. By 1924 about 10 per cent of claimants were being rejected, 17 per cent by early 1927, and about 33 per cent between 1927 and 1930, under the more stringent 'genuinely seeking work test' advocated by the Blanesburgh Committee. The test was suspended by the Labour government in 1930 and transitional benefits/transitional payments became a charge on the Treasury, not the Unemployment Fund.

Despite the insurance and dole provisions many unemployed still fell on the Poor Law and throughout the 1920s about 350,000 to 400,000 workers received outdoor relief, although the General Strike of 1926 pushed this up to 1,500,000 because of the denial of unemployment and dole benefits to the strikers. The action of some guardians, such as West Ham, Poplar, Chester-le-Street and Bedwellty, in providing generous outdoor relief to the unemployed or benefits to those involved in the General Strike pushed Neville Chamberlain, minister of health, to speed up the end of the Poor Law. Chamberlain's Local Government Act of 1929, plus a similar act in Scotland, and the Labour government's Poor Law Act of 1930 ended the existing Poor Law arrangements. As a result the Poor Law was replaced by local authority bodies known as Public Assistance Committees (PACs) for the relief of the destitute and poor. Poor Law hospitals were also handed over to the local authorities. Although local control seemed embedded in the new structure, the government continued to control the direction of policy since it provided 50 per cent of the expenditure.

By 1930, then, there were three types of benefit: unemployment insurance based upon thirty contributions in two years, transitional benefit paid by the Treasury, and public assistance paid through PACs funded by both local authorities and the state in a 50–50 per cent arrangement. Unemployment provision was thus confused and increasingly expensive, and the Labour government took John Maynard Keynes's advice of October 1930 to restrict unemployment insurance. It set up a Royal Commission on Unemployment Insurance under Judge Holman Gregory in December 1930, which first reported in June 1931 that unemployment benefits should be cut by 30 per cent and that 'anomalies' should be eliminated, that unemployment benefit should only be paid for twenty-six weeks in the year, and that those on transitional benefit should be means tested. All the Labour government did was introduce an Anomalies Bill, which reduced the rights of casual workers and married women to benefits. Nevertheless, the issue of benefits arose with the financial crisis of 1931, which saw the collapse of Ramsay MacDonald's Labour government, because the Sir George May Committee, an all-party committee set up to look into government finances, suggested cuts of 20 per cent on the standard benefit and means testing of transitional benefit. The collapse of the Labour government over the issue of cutting benefits by 10 per cent paved the way for a National government which introduced a Household Means Test on transitional payments (formerly transitional benefits) in September 1931. In addition, standard benefits were reduced from 17s. (85p) to 15s. 3d. (76p), about 10 per cent, and restricted to twenty-six weeks. The National government effectively introduced, in scaled-down form, the preliminary Gregory recommendations. The deserving poor faced with long-term unemployment would now become the undeserving poor, and by November 1931 400,000 applicants for relief were subject to the Household Means Test.

During the early 1930s unemployment levels rose to more than 3 million of the insured workers, and towns such as Jarrow, which lost its shipyards, faced horrendous unemployment levels of 70 per cent.[23] At first the National government did little to tackle this problem beyond offering some public works and introducing the Special Areas Act of 1934, which established special areas status for southern Scotland, the north-east, Cumberland and south Wales. Even this measure was limited, since two commissioners were appointed to spend £2 million a year to help local authorities carry out amenity schemes and attract firms into their areas. In the end, however, the financial cost of unemployment benefits forced the National government to reorganize benefit arrangements for the unemployed, even if it could do little about the level of unemployment.

Driven by the desire of the chancellor of the exchequer Neville Chamberlain to distinguish between long-term and short-term unemployment, a position endorsed by the final Gregory Commission report in December 1932, it was decided that the Unemployment Act of 1934 would be introduced. Part I of the Act put the Unemployment Insurance Scheme on a sounder footing and set up the Unemployment Insurance Statutory Committee to administer it. Employer, employee and the state made equal contributions to the fund, which paid out benefits to claimants for twenty-six weeks. The 13 million people covered by the scheme in 1936 were those less likely to be affected by unemployment and unlikely to be a drain on the resources of the Unemployment Fund. In contrast, the long-term unemployed were to be dealt with by the Unemployment Assistance Board (UAB), whilst the PACs would deal with the elderly and sick. The UAB was to produce its own regulations, scales of benefit and means test arrangements. However, because of the strong opposition that emerged throughout the country to the lower benefits of the UAB, a 'standstill' Act was introduced in 1935 to allow the long-term unemployed to choose between the PAC and UAB scales, and the Act was not fully introduced until April 1937.[24]

Financial needs and political demands had shaped government policy towards the overriding issue of dealing with the unemployed during the interwar years. Yet though the state played a dominant role in the provision of unemployment relief, it is clear that the voluntary/private sector also played its part. The Central Committee on Women's Training and Employment (as it became in 1920) offered courses

in domestic skills to unemployed women and, through Violet Markham, a committee member and later vice-chairwoman of the UAB, transferred these ideas to the
Unemployment Assistance Board. In addition, the National Council of Social Services encouraged the formation of clubs for the unemployed, of which there were
900 for men and 500 for women by 1938, offering social recreation and craft
classes.[25] Although space does not permit a detailed examination of other areas, and
some, such as old-age pensions, will be omitted altogether, it is clear that the private
sector still contributed significantly in other areas of social provision.

In recent years there has been a major debate about the standard of health of the
British people during the interwar years. One body of historians suggests that the
health of the nation improved enormously,[26] whilst another suggests that the health
of a significant minority of the nation, and particularly women, did not improve.[27]
In a sense, neither alternative in the debate is incompatible with the other: general
health conditions undoubtedly did improve, but a significant proportion of the
working classes, perhaps half (about 37 or 38 per cent of the population as a whole)
did experience continued high death rates because of unemployment, consequent
poverty and a deterioration in their standard of living. Both sides can accept the findings of B. S. Rowntree's social investigation of York, *Poverty and Progress* (conducted
in 1936 and published in 1941), which indicate that living standards had risen about
30 per cent between the 1890s and 1930, and the other poverty surveys that suggested improvements.[28] There is little doubt about the improving nature of many of
the vital statistics. The question is one of degree – how pervasive were such improvements? Whatever the outcome of that debate, and there is evidence that the improvements in the conditions were exaggerated and that the unemployed faced a 50 per
cent higher death rate than those who were employed, it is clear that there were some
structural improvements in health provision during these years.[29]

As Noel Whiteside has suggested, there was a steadily rising incidence of sickness
and disability among working people which ran parallel to growing unemployment
during the interwar years in Britain, and economic factors helped to influence contemporary perceptions of sickness and health in such a way as to ensure that both
those who were genuinely sick as a result of unemployment, and those who regarded
themselves as being so, were able to obtain health insurance. Indeed, Whiteside adds
to the debate by noting that claims and payments in health benefits increased steadily
throughout this period – though she qualified this by stressing that such statistics
might be, as contemporaries commented, only claims rather than illness and noted
that less than half the population was covered by health schemes in the late 1930s.[30]
The thrust of her argument is that it is very difficult to distinguish between those
genuinely suffering ill health and those who were 'malingerers'; clearly unemployment caused ill health just as ill health caused unemployment. However, there was a
clear reluctance by the authorities to prevent unemployed people from applying for
health relief and a marked tendency for those who were unemployed to remain in
health insurance, since the rights of the unemployed under the health insurance
scheme were safeguarded whilst the rights of the long-term sick to statutory unemployment were not. In addition, with the Anomalies Act and other actions working
against women who it felt 'abused' the system of unemployment relief, many women
felt safer on health as opposed to unemployment insurance. In other words, it is quite
likely that some, possibly many, unemployed families used health insurance as an alter-

native to drawing the standard benefit offered by unemployment insurance, the various types of 'dole', or the Poor Law.

Unlike unemployment insurance, health insurance was very largely worked jointly by the state and the private sector. The health provision that existed between the wars was based upon part I of the National Insurance Act of 1911. By 1920 the scheme was paying 15s. (75p) per week for men and 12s. (60p) per week for women, with basic medical treatment for twenty-six weeks a year for all members of the scheme earning less than £250 per year, in return for contributions from the employer, the employee and the state. After six months those who were still ill could claim disability benefit at half the previous rate. The system operated through approved societies, such as friendly societies, trade unions and insurance companies, whose schemes had to be non-profit-making, and there was great duplication of effort since the workforce of the factory might be insured by many different approved societies. All the societies had to pay statutory benefits and paid a panel of doctors to care for their members. Yet they often provided discretionary extras, some societies offering hospital and consultant services. Dental and ophthalmic services were generally provided as extras, whilst convalescent and nursing allowances were less common. The health schemes were variable but provided a permanent form of income for many, and during the interwar years the numbers on the scheme doubled from 11.5 million in 1912 to 20.36 million in 1938 (from 3.68 million women in 1912 to 7.1 million in 1938).

The state did consider removing the approved societies from health provision, but the Minority Report of the Royal Commission on National Health Insurance (1924–6) was ignored, Neville Chamberlain reflecting that 'the political power and the influences of the Approved Societies make it desirable in present circumstances to meet their views'.[31] The influence of private provision in health was also evident in the areas of hospital provision, where of the 210,000 beds available 83,000 were provided by the voluntary hospitals and 123,000 by local authority and the old Poor Law hospitals, which were transferred to the local authorities in 1929.

In housing, the political demands of both Conservative and Labour governments ensured that differing legislation favoured both the private builder and the construction of houses by local authorities in the 1920s and the 1930s. It is impossible in this short essay to go into the details of housing provision, but it is sufficient to suggest that the Chamberlain Act of 1923 favoured the construction of houses by private builders (362,700 private and 75,300 local authority built), whilst the Labour government's Wheatley Housing Act of 1924 favoured local authority building (504,500 houses were built by local authorities and 15,800 by private builders). During the interwar years as a whole, 4 million houses were built in Britain, 1,100,000 by local authorities, 400,000 by private builders, both with subsidies from the state, and another 2,500,000 were built by private builders alone. In terms of housing provision, both the state and the private sector made a significant contribution to Britain's house-building programme.[32]

Conclusion

Between 1900 and 1939 there had been a fundamental change in the balance of social provision between the private/voluntary sector and the state. In 1900 the Poor

Law was the chief weapon of the state in tackling destitution. Voluntary and philanthropic bodies were concerned to prevent poverty becoming destitution. The state also assumed some responsibility for a few more areas of social concern, particularly the education of the working classes. However, in the first decade of the twentieth century attitudes towards the treatment of the poor and destitute in British society were changing, particularly as the Labour party emerged, and high unemployment demanded that governments do something about the Poor Law, which was under enormous strain. The Liberal reforms were a response to this situation and ensured that state powers and responsibilities would increase. The First World War emphasized the changing balance of social responsibilities, emphasizing further the power of the state, and shaped the future responsibilities of interwar governments.

All the governments of the interwar years faced problems of how to continue to move from the destitution policies of the Victorian state towards developing selective policies to deal with specific groups of people. Different problems, governments, strategies and the need for expedient measures from time to time ensured that the pattern of social security that emerged was both complex and confused. There was still a streak of hostility towards the idea that the unemployed and the poor should be treated in a generous manner in case this reduced the incentive to work. The Poor Law as an institution disappeared in 1930, but the mentality behind its operation – the view that it must be a final deterrent – lingered on in the Household Means Test, the Anomalies Bill and other legislation. The interwar years reveal that the nation was still not yet ready for the redistribution of income and wealth that was necessary if those in poverty were to be relieved. It was not until the Second World War that such a change of attitude came about. In the meantime, millions of working-class families failed to benefit fully from the social provision that had been introduced. Their benefits were means tested and their incomes did not necessarily allow them to enjoy the improvement in housing provision, which was central to the evolution of social welfare policies affecting working-class living standards. In other words, 'Policy had . . . evolved pragmatically, was uncoordinated and still far from universal'.[33] Nevertheless, it was increasingly dominated by the state rather than by private and voluntary bodies. This situation developed over the next forty years before Margaret Thatcher and Tony Blair sought to reduce the dominance of state control and encourage, in their own ways, more balance between both private and public provision. Yet up to, and during, the interwar years voluntary bodies continued to fill the gaps in state provision.

NOTES

1   D. Fraser, *The Evolution of the British Welfare State* (London, 1983), p. 163.
2   M. J. Moore, 'Social work and social welfare: the organisation and philanthropic resources in Britain, 1900–1914', *Journal of British Studies* (Spring 1977), p. 96.
3   J. Harris, 'Political thought and the welfare state 1870–1914: an intellectual framework for British social policy', *Past and Present*, 135 (May 1992).
4   K. Laybourn, *The Guild of Help and the Changing Face of Edwardian Philanthropy: The Guild of Help, Voluntary Work and the State, 1904–1919* (Lampeter, 1994).
5   J. Melling, 'Welfare capitalism and the origins of the welfare states: British industry, workplace welfare and social reform c.1870–1914', *Social History*, 17 (1992), pp. 453–78.

6   H. Pelling, 'The working class and the welfare state', in H. Pelling, *Popular Politics and Society in Late Victorian Britain* (London, 1968); P. Thane, 'The working class and state "welfare" in Britain 1880–1914', *Historical Journal*, 27 (1984), pp. 877–900.

7   F. K. Prochaska, 'Philanthropy', in F. M. L. Thompson, ed., *The Cambridge Social History of Britain 1750–1950*, vol. 3, *Social Agencies and Institutions* (Cambridge, 1990).

8   F. Prochaska, *Philanthropy and the Hospitals of London: The King's Fund, 1897–1990* (London, 1992), p. 2.

9   E. W. Wakefield, 'The growth of charity organisation in the north of England', *Charity Organisation Review*, 34 (1908), p. 40.

10 *Help*, 4, no. 2 (November 1908).

11 Laybourn, *Guild of Help*.

12 Note 6.

13 F. W. Jowett, *The Socialist and the City* (London, 1907), pp. 2–3.

14 P. Thane, *The Foundations of the Welfare State* (London, 1982), p. 83.

15 Ibid., p. 79.

16 *Hansard*, 4th series, 4 May 1911.

17 Thane, *Foundations*, p. 91.

18 *Hansard*, 29 April 1909.

19 Moore, 'Social work and social welfare', p. 102.

20 The Violet Markham Papers section in the British Library of Political and Economic Science provide the detailed papers and minutes of the Central Committee on Women's Employment.

21 County Borough of Bolton Guild of Help, *Thirteenth Annual Report, 1918*, p. 8.

22 Beveridge to Churchill, 5 February 1930, Beveridge Papers, LII, 218, British Library of Political and Economic Science.

23 E. Wilkinson, *The Town that was Murdered: The Life Story of Jarrow* (London, 1939).

24 Markham Papers, 7/10, 'The Progress of Legislation of the Standstill'.

25 National Council of Social Services, *Out of Adversity* (1939), copy in Markham Papers, 14/3, British Library of Political and Economic Science.

26 D. H. Aldcroft, *Inter-war Economy: Britain 1919–1939* (London, 1970); J. Stevenson and C. Cook, *The Slump* (London, 1977).

27 C. Webster, 'Healthy or hungry thirties?', *History Workshop*, 13 (1982); M. Mitchell, 'The effects of unemployment on the social conditions of women and children in the 1930s', *History Workshop*, 19 (1985), pp. 105–27.

28 A. L. Bowley and M. Hogg, *Has Poverty Diminished?* (London, 1925).

29 G. C. M. M'Gonigle and J. Kirby, *Poverty and Public Health* (London, 1936).

30 N. Whiteside, 'Counting the cost: sickness and disability among working people in an era of industrial recession, 1920–1939', *Economic History Review*, 40 (1987), pp. 228–46, particularly pp. 230 and 237, respectively, for the later quotes.

31 B. B. Gilbert, *British Social Policy, 1914–1939* (London, 1970), p. 283.

32 K. Laybourn, *The Evolution of British Social Policy and the Welfare State* (Keele, 1995), pp. 201–5.

33 Fraser, *Evolution*, p. 206.

FURTHER READING

Deacon, A., *In Search of the Scrounger: The Administration of Unemployment Insurance* (London, 1976).

Fraser, D., *The Evolution of the British Welfare State* (London, 1983).

Gilbert, B. B., *British Social Policy, 1914–1939* (London, 1970).

Gladstone, D., *The Twentieth-century Welfare State* (London, 1999).

Laybourn, K., *Britain on the Breadline* (Gloucester, 1990).

Laybourn, K., 'The Guild of Help and the changing face of Edwardian philanthropy', *Urban History* 20 (April 1993), pp. 43–60.

Laybourn, K., *The Guild of Help and the Changing Face of Edwardian Philanthropy: The Guild of Help, Voluntary Work and the State, 1904–1919* (Lampeter, 1994).

Laybourn, K., *The Evolution of British Social Policy and the Welfare State* (Keele, 1995).

Mitchell, M., 'The effects of unemployment on the social conditions of women and children in the 1930s', *History Workshop*, 19 (1985), pp. 105–27.

Moore, M. J., 'Social work and social welfare: the organisation and philanthropic resources in Britain, 1900–1914', *Journal of British Studies* (Spring 1977).

Page, R. M. and Silburn, R., eds, *British Social Welfare in the Twentieth Century* (London, 1999).

Pelling, H., 'The working class and the welfare state', in H. Pelling, *Popular Politics and Society in Late Victorian Britain* (London, 1968).

Thane, P., *The Foundations of the Welfare State* (London, 1982).

Thane, P., 'The working class and state "welfare" in Britain 1880–1914', *Historical Journal*, 27 (1984), pp. 877–900.

Webster, C., 'Healthy or hungry thirties?', *History Workshop*, 13 (1982).

Whiteside, N., 'Counting the cost: sickness and disability among working people in an era of industrial recession, 1920–1939', *Economic History Review*, 40 (1987), pp. 228–46.

CHAPTER TWENTY-FOUR

Housing and Town Planning, 1900–1939

HELEN MELLER

In the dark days of the First World War, prime minister David Lloyd George called on his trusty colleague Dr Addison to be minister of reconstruction, a move that gave a much greater political profile to the Reconstruction Committee set up by Asquith. Addison's brief was to draw up plans for the peaceful future evolution of British society. What that meant was clear. It was to provide a non-revolutionary model of the future in which the masses would benefit from measures of social reform. The central focus of reconstruction had already been established by the previous committee. It was to be housing for the working classes. Addison's task was to give that intention some form. He transformed what had been a housing panel of advisers into a committee, under the chairmanship of the MP Sir John Tudor Walters. The committee was asked to draw up guidelines on how, working with the Local Government Board, local authorities should set about building public housing.

A key figure on the committee was Raymond Unwin, Arts and Crafts architect, designer of Ebenezer Howard's Garden City at Letchworth, advocate of town planning and, since 1914, chief town planning adviser to the Local Government Board. Another was civil servant George Pepler, who had been appointed to the Local Government Board to assist the previous town planning adviser, Thomas Adams, and was a committed supporter of modern housing and town planning.[1] Pepler and Unwin were a formidable duo who were to have the greatest impact on housing design and town planning in the whole period from 1900 to 1930. One of the sources of that influence was the Tudor Walters report, 'On Questions of Building Construction in connection with the Provision of Dwellings for the Working Classes', which was submitted in 1918.[2] It was to be a landmark in the history of housing and town planning in Britain in the first half of the twentieth century. In the context of reconstruction, it was fired with a vision of the future and set standards beyond the dreams of many working-class families. It was the product of a peculiarly British response to questions of housing and town planning.

All the European belligerents in the First World War were concerned with the problem of low-cost housing. All had been involved in the nascent town planning movement which, from its inception, had been international. Yet each responded differently to these issues, according to their culture, history and political institu-tions.[3] In Britain, Lloyd George, secure in the knowledge of the work of the Tudor Walters Committee, used the slogan 'Homes for Heroes' as propaganda in his elec-tioneering for the 'khaki' election held immediately after the war. He won the elec-tion, but the National government that he headed was not able to deliver on social reform. Economic turbulence in the post-war era, especially the slump of 1921, put paid to any government financing of schemes to promote the happiness and comfort of the masses. The collapse of social reform measures after the war has been well charted.[4] Nothing was more dramatic than the failure to provide homes for heroes.[5]

Britain's role as the greatest imperial nation in the world and hub of the interna-tional economy was given precedence over all other considerations. Policies of high interest rates and deflation in the 1920s kept house-building in both the public and private sector at low levels. Hopes for the implementation of a more rational plan-ning system across the country failed to materialize. Housing reformers and town planners found themselves still in their nineteenth-century roles of lobbyists, trying to get a hearing from politicians with other things on their minds. Unlike their nineteenth-century counterparts, however, the need for public involvement in these matters was much clearer. At stake was the very future of both cities and the British countryside, fast disappearing with unbridled and unplanned development.[6]

This chapter is devoted to an exploration of those elements that influenced the British response to the modernization of the urban environment. It is divided into the following sections. First, there is an exploration of the housing problem before the First World War, and then an outline of the evolution of modern town planning in Britain. Then there is a section devoted to the crucial interrelationship between housing and town planning over the whole period. The final section discusses housing and town planning in the interwar years. Between 1900 and 1939, housing and town planning were much more closely linked together than either before or after this time. The early years of professional town planning were clearly defined by the demands of town extension schemes to accommodate new housing. Only in the last few years before the Second World War did physical planning come to inhabit a broader brief, related to economic and social planning as a whole.[7]

The Housing Problem before the First World War

The only nineteenth-century Royal Commission on the Housing of the Working Classes, appointed in 1884, presented its final report in 1889, and in 1890 a new Housing Act was passed. This was to set the official framework of legislation on working-class housing until the First World War, collecting and codifying all the pre-vious nineteenth-century legislation.[8] All this legislation had had one aim: to regu-late the market for housing in such a way that what was built to house the increasing population would not contribute to the problem of insanitary housing, which was a social problem to be found in varying degrees in all towns and cities.[9] The 1890 Act made one concession to the findings of the previous Royal Commission. The com-missioners had reluctantly recognized that poverty was a prime cause forcing people to endure insanitary and unhealthy living accommodation.

The Act included a provision empowering local authorities to purchase land and to erect or convert suitable buildings as dwellings for the working classes. The Public

Works Loan Commissioners were given powers to make advances for this purpose. Virtually no local authorities asked for a loan. Municipal debt was already considerable with Public Works loans for water supplies, sewers, roads and so on, and above all there was no public consensus that municipal housing was the answer to the housing problem. Britain had had the longest experience of mass urbanization in the world with more than 50 per cent of the population living in cities since 1851. By 1901, this proportion had risen to 77 per cent in England and Wales and was still rising. Not only did most people live in towns, most lived in large towns. London, still the largest city in the world in 1901 with more than 4 million inhabitants, was not the only city of more than a million inhabitants in Britain. Manchester, Birmingham and Glasgow had already passed this landmark.[10]

This massive transformation had taken place without any interference in the housing market. In many respects, the play of market forces had served people well. Most people of all classes rented their accommodation in 1900. Houses for people with adequate income were available and landlords were ready to invest in new housing for the future. The problem lay with the poor, who either had to live in central areas to be close to often irregular work (such as dock labour) or who earned insufficient to be able to pay more than the lowest rent, or both. The intensity of the problem varied in different cities according to the local economic structure and the housing stock available at any particular time. The considerable local variations in the relationship between wages, rents and the retail price of food were revealed in a Board of Trade national investigation in 1908.[11]

For those in steady employment, however, matters had improved over the previous quarter of a century. With increasing internationalization of trade and the application of new technology such as refrigeration, the cost of food had actually fallen in many instances in the last three decades.[12] The opposite happened to rents. The problem with a free market in property in city centres was that it was not really geared to providing residential accommodation. There were competing uses for land, such as commercial offices and retail outlets, which could command greater financial resources and could afford higher rates, a crucial factor for cash-strapped local authorities. The return on housing developments was fixed by the level of rent. The amount of rent that people could pay was determined by their wages, and yet wage levels were unrelated to the cost of housing.

All cities had had boundary extensions in the two decades leading up to the First World War. There were improvements in roads and public transport. The great exodus to the suburbs accelerated. But for those with low or inadequate income, there was the poverty trap. Proximity to work was vital and the cost of travel was beyond the means of the poorly paid. Accommodation in city-centre areas was reduced by redevelopment. The poor crammed themselves into what was left, with two results: desperate levels of overcrowding in the poorest-quality housing; and the possibility for landlords to make substantial profits. It was to produce a potentially inflammable political response. In the two decades before the war, struggles between tenants and landlords became more highly organized.

The work of Melling and Englander has revealed the importance of rent strikes against profiteering from rents, especially in the early days of the First World War.[13] The fear of industrial unrest and the need to protect the interests of essential munition workers prompted the government into action. It took two forms. First, the

Table 24.1(a) House-building in Great Britain, 1880–1940: houses built in Great Britain 1880–1920 (all tenures)

Year	Houses built (all tenures)
1880	83,100
1885	76,700
1890	75,800
1895	89,800
1900	139,700
1905	127,400
1910	86,000
1915	30,800
1920	29,700

Table 24.1(b) House-building in Great Britain, 1880–1940: houses built in Great Britain 1919–40[a] (divided by tenure)

Year	Houses built for local authorities		Houses built for private owners	
1 April–31 March	England and Wales	Scotland	England and Wales	Scotland
1919/20	576	–	_[b]	_[b]
1920/21	15,585	1,201	_[b]	_[b]
1921/22	80,783	5,796	_[b]	_[b]
1922/23	57,535	9,527	_[b]	_[b]
1923/24	14,353	5,233	71,857	_[b]
1924/25	20,624	3,238	116,265	3,638
1925/26	44,218	5,290	129,208	5,639
1926/27	74,093	9,621	143,536	7,496
1927/28	104,034	16,460	134,880	6,137
1928/29	55,723	13,954	113,809	5,024
1929/30	60,245	13,023	141,815	5,011
1930/31	55,874	8,122	127,933	4,571
1931/32	70,061	8,952	130,751	4,766
1932/33	55,991	12,185	144,505	6,596
1933/34	55,840	16,503	210,782	10,760
1934/35	41,593	15,733	287,513	6,096
1935/36	52,357	18,814	272,503	7,086
1936/37	71,740	16,044	274,313	7,757
1937/38	77,970	13,341	259,632	8,187
1938/39	101,744	19,162	230,616	7,311
1939/40	50,452	19,118	145,510	6,411

[a] Various categories of housing are excluded from the figures. See source for details.
[b] S. Merrett, *Owner-occupation in Britain* (London, 1982), p. 346, estimates an annual average of 25,727 private completions in Britain 1919–23.
Source: B. R. Mitchell, *British Historical Statistics* (Cambridge, 1988), pp. 390–2.

government financed new housing estates for munition workers, the largest direct input of government resources into housing to date. Then, in 1915, a Rent Restriction Act was passed, freezing rents at their pre-war level. By accident, in the midst of the stresses of war, the government had taken a step which meant that a new solution to the housing problem had to be found.[14] After the war, rent control became a political 'hot potato' which no government in the early post-war years was prepared to deregulate. At the same time, building costs rose, making the provision of cheap housing for rent a financial impossibility. The government was left looking at the problem identified by the Royal Commission on the Housing of the Working Classes in 1889: the problem of poverty.

This was a question far wider than the matter of working-class housing. The surveys of Charles Booth in London in 1889 and B. S. Rowntree in York, published in 1902, both gave statistical evidence that inadequate wages left 10 per cent of the population without sufficient means for barest survival and a further 17–20 per cent lived on or close to a 'poverty line'. Rowntree's further elaboration of a poverty cycle made greater sense of these bald statistics. He found that poverty was an everyday experience of the majority of the working classes at different points in their lives. In their childhood, in large families, they experienced poverty. In early adulthood, when they could earn and contribute to family income, times were better. Poverty re-emerged in old age, when earning capacity had decreased and sickness was prevalent. As if to confirm what these experiences meant in terms of a nation's health, more than three-quarters of the volunteers in Manchester for the Boer War were declared unfit on medical grounds. When the war was over, the government set up an Interdepartmental Committee (not a Royal Commission, as it was fearful of the cost implications of recommendations) to investigate the Physical Deterioration of the Working Classes.

Regardless of government machinations, its report, published in 1904, still confirmed what everyone was beginning to believe: that the quality of the urban environment in Britain's cities was not conducive to health and at the heart of the matter was inadequate and insanitary working-class housing. The government shied away from the problem and focused instead on exploring the efficacy of the provision of poor relief with a massive Royal Commission enquiry into the working of the Poor Laws which took place between 1905 and 1909. To allay public fears, the Liberal government meanwhile passed a number of social welfare measures: the medical inspection of schoolchildren and the feeding of necessitous children in Acts of 1906 and 1907 and old-age pensions in 1908. National insurance schemes on a revised adaptation of what had already been achieved in Germany several decades previously were on the statute book by 1911.[15] Bad-quality housing, or 'slums', had to wait.

This was due partly to the huge capital cost of housing, partly to a legacy of nineteenth-century thinking on the problem of poverty. The Majority Report of the Poor Law Royal Commission of 1909 went along with the views of the most influential philanthropic lobby, the Charity Organization Society (COS) of London. The COS secretary C. S. Loch was still of the opinion that poverty was the 'responsibility' of the individual, caused by moral failings, that the poor were inferior people and that poverty had to be dealt with as such, not as a matter of low wages or, in the case of housing, insufficient decent accommodation to rent. The concept of the 'slum' was still deeply ingrained with the idea of moral depravity. Alan Mayne's work,

The Imagined Slum, has highlighted the cultural assumptions made about slums and the ways in which such assumptions were transported through the media, especially the newspapers, around the European-dominated world.[16] A professor of moral economy at the University of Glasgow could address a meeting in that city in 1902 (which had one of the highest proportions of the worst-quality housing), on the subject of housing, suggesting that 'in the absence of special circumstances, it is no part of the work of a municipality to build houses at all. But the undoubted duty of every municipality is to provide police and sanitary control'.[17]

His views were not exceptional amongst many of the middle classes. There were, however, those who were prepared to view the matter differently. Councillors and local government officials in the London area and major provincial cities found themselves responsible for working-class housing. A prime example is councillor J. Nettlefold, chairman of Birmingham's Housing Committee before the First World War. Following the Report of the Interdepartmental Committee on the Physical Deterioration of the Working Classes in 1904, Birmingham's Housing Committee had commissioned its own report on the city's housing problems, which reported in 1906. Nettlefold, as a steel magnate, had learnt in his own business that 'free' markets do not always work, and he was prepared to find a role for his committee that would enable the market to work better to meet demand.

He wrote a number of books on housing and town planning because he thought he had found an answer.[18] It was that city councils should buy land on the city's periphery and adopt the town planning principles already used in German cities for the layout of the land and the provision of essential services. Within this context, private initiatives and cooperative ventures of better-off working men could then provide the capital to develop the land and provide excellent quality housing at reasonable rents. When they moved into this new property, their old homes, closer to the city centre, would become available to those currently forced into overcrowded properties and thus, in stages (and related to the market economy and rewarding the better workers first), the housing problem would be solved. Another example, William Thompson, an alderman of Richmond in Surrey, had also made the connection between problems of the housing market and the need for town planning. He gave evidence to a parliamentary committee set up in 1906 to explore the need for legislation on town planning since he had come to believe that only through a synthesis of a number of different activities could an efficient public response be made to the problem of working-class housing.[19]

John Burns, the Labour MP who worked with the Liberal government, had been appointed to the Local Government Board in 1905. Thomas Coglan Horsfall had written his popular work, *The Improvement of Dwellings and Surroundings of the People: The Example of Germany*, in 1904 in which he detailed the superior regulations in force in Germany controlling house-building and town planning.[20] Lobbying parliament for town planning legislation was to reach a crescendo in the next three years, culminating in the passing of the Housing and Town Planning Act of 1909, the first piece of modern town planning legislation in Britain. The Act offered the framework for the kind of actions that Nettlefold had envisaged in Birmingham. Local authorities would be responsible for controlling the acquisition and layout of town extensions, private capital could be used for the building of houses. In the absence of private capital, the option still existed for local authorities to borrow funds

for building purposes. For all its modesty in defining the possible role of town planning, in solving social problems, the Act was a landmark in the evolution of a new
professional activity: that of modern town planning.

But thinking about the future of working-class housing was not only in the hands
of the lobbyists for town planning. An important contribution had been made on
the subject of working-class housing, was being made, and would continue to be
made after the war by a group of people largely unconnected with the town planning lobbyists. If Nettlefold and his counterparts can be referred to as 'city fathers',
this other group might be called 'city mothers' as it was constituted of philanthropists
and social workers, amongst whom women had made an outstanding contribution.
With pioneers like Octavia Hill (working in London from the mid-1860s), who
trained her lady volunteers to be professional rent collectors, in which role they
gained access to working-class homes and could offer help and advice in times of
trouble, these women had worked to improve homes of the poor and their inhabitants together.[21]

Groups of women were to be found following similar activities in towns and cities
all over Britain.[22] They were undertaking their role as 'citizens', the only role left to
them since the 1867 Reform Act had deliberately ruled out the enfranchisement of
women. 'Social citizenship' became recognized as a crucial element in philanthropic
activity, one where women's 'altruistic' natures were particularly valued. The gendering of responses to the problems of cities, working-class housing and the poor
was to lead to fruitful interactions between professionals (mostly male), volunteers
(mostly female) and lobbyists throughout the first three decades of the twentieth
century. It worked well as long as the women did not overstep gender-determined
boundaries.[23]

The philosopher T. H. Green had inspired a whole generation of men at Oxford
and Cambridge from the 1880s to devote themselves to 'social citizenship' and build
a united nation. The University Settlement Movement, pioneered by the Rev. Samuel
Barnett in Whitechapel, was an outstanding male-dominated example of a practical
result of this doctrine.[24] But by the first decade of the twentieth century, many of
the university and denominational settlements in the provincial cities, for instance in
Bristol, Manchester and Liverpool, were to be run by women. They had the time,
energy, patience and, most recently, skills (as a tiny few benefited from the provision
of university education for women). They were prepared to continue initiatives that
were no longer making headline news, though still valuable to local communities.

The next generation of female philanthropists, while sustaining all the old initiatives in poor areas of cities, did develop new concerns, especially about the health of
mothers and babies. Their work was part of the drive, in the decade before the war,
against the constant high rates of infant mortality.[25] Part of their self-imposed brief
was how to define a 'healthy home' in a healthy environment. Alongside these efforts,
there was a movement to greater coordination of voluntary activities and volunteers
signed up for the League of Social Service, which was organized on a city basis, and
other such organizations. In 1918 women over thirty were given the vote and, at
last, the franchise was given equally to all men and women in 1928. The National
Union of Women's Suffrage Societies became the National Union of Societies for
Equal Citizenship. Women as volunteers, and increasingly as professionals, were to
continue in their supporting role, making crucial contributions to understanding the

problems of poverty, poor health, working-class housing and, most importantly, community development. Since the interwar years were to witness such a massive building boom, their work was to remain hugely in demand until the Second World War.[26]

The Evolution of Modern Town Planning in Britain

The task of deciding what constituted a healthy home for the working classes in the first half of the twentieth century, however, remained a male prerogative. It was a matter of design and a matter of management, and male architects and industrialists were totally dominant in these matters. The design of the housing in London's 'cottage estates' of the 1920s and the public housing built in Birmingham and Manchester, and many other cities in the 1930s, offered a considerable contrast to much housing for the working classes built in the rest of Europe.[27] There was a distinctly British style, articulated by Unwin, but widely copied and repeated in both the public and private sector. Its wholesale acceptance rested on an historical legacy unique to Britain. It was shaped by a number of factors,[28] overlaid by the coming together of two quite different traditions, each shaped by Britain's distinctive experience of industrialization. On the one hand, since the earliest days of water power in the late eighteenth century, factory masters had faced problems with labour management.[29] From this time, factory masters used the idea of a factory 'village' built by the factory master, equipped with well-appointed cottages, a school, almshouses, a community centre and recreation grounds, as a means of attracting, controlling and keeping a steady workforce.

Paternalistic employers, acting as individuals outside any legislative framework, continued to use and modify this method throughout the late nineteenth and early twentieth centuries. Sir Titus Salt built Saltaire, just outside Bradford, in the late 1850s; William Lever, the soap manufacturer, built Port Sunlight a couple of decades later. His ideal village was featured in the Manchester Civic Exhibition of 1888 as the epitome of modernity, despite its mock-Tudor style of architecture. The Quaker Cadbury and Rowntree brothers were making fortunes out of the luxury trade of chocolate manufacturing. George Cadbury built Bournville from the mid-1890s onwards, a model industrial village in the countryside outside Birmingham; the Rowntrees began building their model village in New Earswick, outside York, soon afterwards. What these mainly nonconformist, paternalistic industrialists had achieved was an image of the ideal home for the working classes of the future as one rooted firmly in a past ideal: that of the idyllic rural village, human in scale, rustic in nature.[30]

On the other hand, the totally different tradition feeding into ideas on the image of the healthy home for the working classes came from the rebellious Arts and Crafts movement, led by John Ruskin and William Morris. Their hatred for industrialization and its most obvious manifestation, the industrial city, stimulated them to study the urban form of pre-industrial periods. The Middle Ages became a passion, but so too did the early modern period, especially the little towns of the Cotswolds in England, built in honey-coloured stone, organic in form, beautiful to behold. Raymond Unwin was to use the model of the Cotswold town as the epitome of good design in his book *Town Planning in Practice* (1909), which was the first British textbook on the subject.[31] Unwin was to become the figure through whom the two traditions of what constituted healthy homes for the working classes were to be brought together. He was commissioned to build New Earswick with his partner and brother-in-law Barry Parker, and he was invited to design an important extension in Bournville. Above all, however, he and his partner were appointed architects to the Garden City Co., established in 1903, and produced the plans for the entire development.[32]

The form they gave to their model town and the architecture of the houses was to have a worldwide influence. Why Unwin was so influential was due to many factors, not least that he was a pioneer among a new group of professionals.[33] Problems of controlling the urban environment and the construction of homes for the working classes that were healthy and would remain so were matters on which there was little professional expertise. Elsewhere in Europe, different paths to gaining this expertise were followed. In Germany after 1870, the mayors of the great cities had the power to appoint experts of all kinds to deal with urban problems. Architects, engineers and surveyors worked together to develop expertise on town extensions and urban improvements. Germany in this respect led the field.[34] In France, civil servants and municipal officials banded together in associations of local government, of hygiene, of sanitary engineering, and in so doing developed the expertise for urban development and control.[35]

In Britain, while there was an important growth in municipal services with their attendant professionals, the impetus for developing ideas for the future had for decades been in the hands of public health officials. Imagining a wholly new form for the future was left to voluntary effort and philanthropy, stimulated by a small number of individuals who spotted a chance to develop new careers for themselves in this developing area. Men such as Thomas Adams (Garden City propagandist and town planner),[36] T. H. Mawson (landscape architect) and Patrick Geddes (professor of botany, sociologist and influential figure in the international town planning movement)[37] were to find fame and sometimes fortune in town planning activities. These were not only in Britain but more especially in the empire: in India, Canada, Australia and New Zealand; and also elsewhere, in America, in Greece and Palestine, and wherever opportunities beckoned.

In 1902 Thomas Adams, as the new and energetic secretary of the Garden City Association set up to promote Ebenezer Howard's concept of the Garden City, organized a national conference in Bournville. It was attended by municipal officials, by architects and surveyors, by interested parties, even by George Bernard Shaw! They tramped around the model village in the mud, as much of it was still under construction.[38] What they wanted was a view of the future and how to achieve it. An immediate practical concern was town extensions, since every large city was pushing back its boundaries to extend the land area available for building. New extensions needed planning to prevent future decline. Ebenezer Howard, however, had looked to a future beyond that. As an inhabitant of London and passionate about the welfare of this great city, Howard believed that the nineteenth-century pressures that had created great cities had to be reversed.

New technologies of transport and communication meant that people could be moved right away from the original city, to live in a new ordered environment, a Garden City, which would be better for them in terms of health and well-being. It would also mean that the new suburbs would not continue for ever, strangling the original city as it became further and further divorced from its rural hinterland. This latter insight became a matter of urgency for Howard's disciples in the interwar period. Viewing the fate of London, which expanded dramatically in the 1920s and 1930s, they lobbied vigorously for a 'green-belt' policy to preserve open space around even the largest cities.[39] Their reward was the Green Belt (London and Home Counties) Act of 1938, which was to become a crucial element in British town planning after the Second World War. In effect, Howard was demanding the building of new towns in which the problems of Victorian cities were to be eliminated from the start by careful planning.

His vision was exciting, modern and easily grasped (he was a brilliant propagandist), though the history of the first Garden City, begun at Letchworth in 1903, is a saga of disappointments for Howard as his social aspirations for the new town were sacrificed on the altar of expediency.[40] Howard's searching questions about what makes a healthy environment and the answers he produced were very much drawn from the context of his time. He saw salvation for the working classes in terms of a petty bourgeois ideal of domesticity: a happy family life, in a healthy home, located in the midst of a small-scale, well-integrated community. The best defence against creating a future slum was to build decent cottages with gardens. The best defence against crime was to create leisure activities all could share, stable local communities where everyone was known, and the close proximity of nature whose soothing presence would enhance the quality of daily life.

The Interrelationship between Housing and Town Planning

Howard's hopes for social reform, and the form that Parker and Unwin gave to his ideal, touched a nerve in the English body politic. They had articulated what everyone wanted: a combination of town and country, family homes with gardens and some privacy, pleasant, salubrious surroundings. For a honeymoon period, for a decade before the First World War, this is what social reformers, housing reformers, architects and planners believed was possible, not just for the rich but for everyone. After many false dawns, the state gave its approval to this dream by passing the first Housing and Town Planning Act of 1909, which gave local authorities permissive powers to plan town extensions. The Royal Institute of British Architects set up what they called the first International Exhibition of Town Planning in London in 1910, though the Germans also had a town planning exhibition in the same year.[41] Raymond Unwin was asked to chair a committee to organize an international exhibition to go alongside the conference papers. He wanted to keep alive the social objectives of modern planning, to insist that plans should be judged not on whether they looked beautiful but whether they also worked in economic and social terms. He invited Patrick Geddes, the sociologist and environmentalist who had made the study of cities and their development his speciality, to represent Britain.

In his Cities and Town Planning exhibit, Geddes produced an historical and geographical illustration of the evolution of cities over long periods of time. But his interest was not only in achieving a perspective on present problems. He also wanted to harness the new knowledge being produced by the nascent social sciences to the service of 'city development'. By this term, he believed he had encompassed the prospect of the enhancement of city and people together. But such an approach was alien to the British political environment. No politician, nor indeed any pioneering women pushing back barriers controlling women's public roles, wished to be constrained by Geddes's vision.

But Geddes, in partnership with Unwin, did find one group receptive to his ideas, an unusual group at the top of the British governing classes. These were the governors of troublesome colonies.[42] The viceroy of Ireland, for example, or the governors of the great states in India, were finding it increasingly hard to quell unrest and agitation, especially in the cities. Lord Aberdeen was viceroy of Ireland and his wife was a deeply philanthropic lady concerned with the welfare of women and children. Together they invited Unwin and Geddes to come and study the problems of Dublin. The lack of housing for the poor was top of the agenda. The colonial context highlighted what was to be a major constraint of town planning in Britain for the entire first half of the twentieth century. Only in a colonial context could planners be given the freedom to 'plan' a city, unencumbered by the democratic process and the problems of private property.

The two men were in their element, comprehensively tackling the problems of a large city. Geddes wanted to build a new Catholic cathedral to compensate for the confiscation of the old one by the Anglicans as a means of healing the rifts of the Anglo-Irish Union. Unwin was planning working-class housing estates at low densities of not more than twelve houses per acre, the ideal that he was to expound in his most influential town planning pamphlet, *Nothing Gained by Overcrowding*, in 1912.[43] It was to become one of the dominant ideas in British town planning until well after the Second World War. All the funding promised by government and philanthropists to help Dublin came to an abrupt end in 1914 when very little had been accomplished. Geddes actually believed that the Easter Rising might have been averted if the housing programmes had been given top priority and the people had been massively rehoused. There is no way of assessing such a counterfactual conditional. Yet by this time it was recognized in Britain, as well as in the colonies, that some form of town planning was a matter of vital necessity to the future peaceful evolution of cities.

Geddes persuaded Abercrombie, Pepler and others that planning was a practical activity rooted in place. Each plan must be preceded by a survey of the specific economic, social and cultural features of that particular place. Then the planner needed to develop a regional perspective to put each plan into context.[44] Geddes's influence was limited but others were recognizing the need for planners to have some professional expertise. The Town Planning Institute, a lesser mirror of the Royal Institute of British Architects, was founded in London in 1913. It was made up of architects, surveyors and civil engineers, and Geddes was the only founder member who called himself a social scientist. The idea that town planning would take its place among the tools to improve the economic and social context of society as well as its health and well-being, however, never fully materialized. In fact, the First World War marked the end of this honeymoon period of British planning before its legislative and political limitations were exposed.

However, through Unwin, who was appointed adviser to the Local Government Board in Housing and Town Planning during the war, its legacy was stamped indelibly on the interwar period. It was Unwin who had actually drafted the recommendations of the Tudor Walters Report. Addison's Housing Act of 1919 required all local authorities to draw up plans and made the permissive legislation of 1890 manda-tory. These Acts also made the Tudor Walters building regulations mandatory. They provided the yardstick for both private and public housing, though both sectors of the market found them hard to implement because of cost. Most local authorities failed to fulfil housing objectives, not only because of the cost but also because of a lack of trained personnel to carry out schemes and, in some cases, a lack of political will. The housing revolution of the interwar period, when it came, was to have little to do with government action or the new planning profession.

Housing in the Public and Private Sector in the Interwar Period

The sheer statistics of house-building in the interwar period are quite astonishing. Between 1919 and 1939, 4 million new houses were built. Of these, about one-quarter were built by the public sector, and it was this sector which adopted more planning controls. By 1940, one-third of all houses had been built since 1918. The face of urban Britain had been irrevocably changed. What happened in Britain was also quite different from what happened elsewhere in Europe. Building in the 1920s was limited because of high costs and low investment. Britain was severely hit by the Great Depression, triggered by the American Wall Street crash of 1929. But Britain was the first of the European countries to recover, not because of government policy but because of an investment boom, made possible by low interest rates. Housing, as an industry dependent on heavy capital investment, was a leading sector.

In many ways, Britain built itself out of depression, feeding the pent-up demand that had not been met in the 1920s. The market, however, was a particular one. The largest group of people who were better off than before were those with modest but permanent incomes. Over the course of the depression with falling prices, there was a net gain for those who remained in work of around 8 per cent in real wages. These people wanted homes and could now afford them. The class dimension to this demand was that it was much boosted by those from the modest middle classes to the skilled working classes. The great change in this range of the market was a marked shift away from renting to homeownership. This was made possible by a dramatic fall in the cost of building houses and by a revolution in the means of financing their construction.

There was a transformation in the century-old system of building societies. Instead of small, locally based societies dependent on the loyalty of their tiny bands of members, the numbers of building societies decreased dramatically as amalgamations took place that greatly strengthened financial assets. At the same time, land was more readily available. In the course of the First World War, a quarter of the entire agri-cultural land in Britain changed hands because of the imposition of death duties on the landed classes. The final boost to the building boom was the evolution of modern transport, the suburban railway, the electric tramway and the car. The suburban railway system, especially around London and the home counties, had been decant-ing commuters to rural homes for the previous half-century. But what had once been a privilege for the rich became a commonplace experience for the modestly well-off.

Railways and electric tramways made daily commuting commonplace. Both, however, were to be surpassed by the motor car. The crucial turning point was the period of the Great Depression. In the 1920s, cars of 10 horsepower or more had

Table 24.2   Building societies in Great Britain, 1900–50

Year	Number of societies	Total assets (£m)
1900	2,286	60
1910	1,723	76
1920	1,271	87
1930	1,026	371
1940	952	756
1950	819	1,256

Source: Building Societies Fact Book (1986), p. 5.

dominated the market. From the early 1930s, the invention of the small car was to be a runaway success. Locations ten, twenty or even thirty miles from city centres became instantly accessible whether or not there was a rail link. Much development took place along the country main roads to such an extent that in 1935 legislation was passed, the Restriction of Ribbon Development Act, which required developers to build more compact estates leading off main roads. But state efforts to control the private sector were modest and usually too late. The interwar period was a golden age for the small entrepreneur, the modest builder (and Britain's building trade was still dominated by thousands of small firms employing fewer than ten workmen). The anti-urban stance of the Arts and Crafts movement became like an epidemic that was caught by the entire nation. Couples on the fringe of even the lowest levels of the housing market were to be found, way out of town, or by the seaside, building their own bungalows themselves and achieving their own ideal of heaven.[45]

But there were still those who fell below that threshold. For those who could only dream of homeownership and could afford a rent of between five and eight shillings a week, the interwar period was no halcyon era. Indeed, E. D. Simon, an ex-lord mayor of Manchester and former chairman of the Housing Committee, wrote a book in 1929 on *How to Abolish the Slums*. His argument was that there was no evidence that the 'filtering-up' process (where slum-dwellers were able to occupy homes vacated by those who moved further out) had taken place. On the contrary, the amount of housing available to the poor had actually been reduced by redevelopment of city centres and that overcrowding was worse than it had ever been. After the post-war failure of Addison's Act of 1919, a more conservative measure, Chamberlain's Act of 1923, had been passed which cut the subsidy available for public housing, in the hope that 'filtering up' would take place. Yet in every major city in Britain, appalling housing conditions existed for the poor. In London, Birmingham, Manchester and Newcastle, there was poverty and bad housing, and also in towns and cities of every size in the 'depressed areas', where the collapse of coal, iron and steel and the shipbuilding industries had plunged whole areas into poverty.

The first minority Labour government of 1923, with its commitment to labour, tried to do something about this. Wheatley's Act of 1924 set up more generous subsidies. Those that benefited from this were the larger cities where the rateable values had not collapsed and the London County Council (LCC). The latter, following on from its pre-war building efforts, continued to try to disperse the poor in 'cottage estates' built in the countryside and connected to the city by rail. By 1939 the LCC had built twenty 'cottage estates', mostly on a small scale, with one exception, the mighty estate at Becontree. This consisted of 2,770 acres and over 25,800 houses and flats of between one and six rooms. It was the size of a substantial provincial town. Yet the thinking behind the development was very limited. There were no jobs there and the development was fortuitously saved when the Ford plant was located there in 1931.

The problem of the slums was seen as divorced from economic and social realities. Healthy homes were a matter of abundant light and air and contact with natural surroundings. Low-density cottages were built with indoor plumbing and gardens. The new tenants were simply decanted into them from some inner-city area, usually the East End. Apart from one or two schools and some shops, very little was done to help them acclimatize to such a dramatic change of environment. Many returned to the older houses in the city where rents were cheaper and there were no transport costs, regardless of the insanitary conditions of the houses themselves. However, oral testimony from those who went as children in families to the new 'cottage estates' paints a more optimistic picture of what life was like.[46]

The 1 million new houses built by the public sector in the interwar period were largely accounted for by the massive building efforts of major cities, especially Birmingham, Manchester, Liverpool and Sheffield. Birmingham, having followed the Nettlefold line, had a complete change of heart in 1924 and began building public estates on a massive scale, outstripping all other local authorities. When the next minority Labour government came to power in 1929, there was hope that at last a nationwide system of housing and town planning would reach the statute book. Arthur Greenwood, as minister of health with a responsibility for housing, introduced a Housing Act of 1930 designed to make public funds available for rehousing people in overcrowded accommodation. A Town and Country Planning Act was to follow, but the vagaries of politics in the Great Depression led to the fall of Labour. The 1932 Act that followed under the auspices of the National government was a watered-down affair. It still brought more land under state control for future planning purposes, but it fell far short of developing an integrated system for town and country planning.[47]

In 1930, when Arthur Greenwood was still minister of health, he visited Birmingham to open the 30,000th house built by the Corporation. It was in Kingstanding, one of the largest public housing estates outside London, which, when completed, had 4,802 houses. It exhibited many of the characteristics of public housing of the interwar period. The estate was built on a greenfield site and displayed new design features such as roundabouts, cul-de-sacs, wide grass verges, low-density and low-rise development with gardens and much public space for sports and recreation. For the new tenants, the transition from their former homes to the new conditions was not an easy one to make. They asked for help from socio-religious workers who had helped them in the inner city. Both the Congregationalists and Methodists sold inner-city chapels and devoted the proceeds to building new settlements on the estate, largely staffed by women volunteers. Women volunteers were similarly involved in making Wythenshawe work, Manchester's largest interwar housing estate and E. D. Simon's dream of a municipal Garden City.

This ensured that the input by women in the housing world continued, albeit still as the weaker partners in the gender divide. Municipal officers, surveyors, architects and a very few planners had brought the new physical environment into being; it was up to the women to make it work. Women rose to the challenge, some even gaining some sort of professional status as they wrestled with the problems. They worked in the new estates and in the cities. In London, the Kensington Council for Social Service set up the Kensington Housing Association in 1925 to work for action against the problem of severe overcrowding. It was fortunate to recruit Elizabeth Denby, who had taken a professional course in social work at the London School of Economics, to act as its professional secretary. Denby was particularly interested in dealing with the problem of housing by renovating and renewing old properties. Between 1931 and 1938, she was the prime mover in the organization of five major New Homes for Old Exhibitions held in London.[48] Denby also worked with the modern architect group MARS on the design of modern housing incorporating new technology, especially the use of electricity.

In fact, probably one of the greatest transformations in housing over the whole interwar period was the increased use of gas and electricity for household tasks. Whereas, for example, the rich would formerly pay servants or washing women to do the weekly laundry and the poor would use the municipal baths and washhouses, now washing was done individually in each house with the aid of gas hot-water systems and small boilers. Electrical appliances were expensive and electricity not widely available until the development of the national grid in 1926,[49] but by the end of the interwar period almost every home had an electric iron. All this amounted to vast changes in the lives of all women, even the rich, as the number of domestic servants declined dramatically.

There had been a further stage in the demographic revolution and average family size had massively shrunk amongst all social classes. Social ambitions became centred on the desire for homeownership, privacy and happy family life.[50] It was a dream bolstered by media propaganda, from the Ideal Homes Exhibitions held throughout the period to the development of women's magazines. For example, *Good Housekeeping* was founded in 1922, *Woman and Home* in 1926, *Woman's Own* in 1932, and *Woman* in 1937. They mark a cultural revolution in terms of expectations of home and family life. The Tudor Walters Report of 1918 had raised aspirations. Raymond Unwin and his Arts and Crafts colleagues had given these a particular form and many women, as wives and mothers, as professional housing managers and philanthropists, had made the new developments work. The slums in the big cities, however, were still there, if reduced in size, and dealing with that problem after the Second World War was, finally, to break the cultural mould that had produced the outcomes of the first three decades of the twentieth century.

NOTES

1   G. Cherry, 'George Pepler 1882–1959', in G. Cherry, ed., *Pioneers in British Planning* (London, 1981), pp. 72–102, 131–49.
2   J. Burnett, *A Social History of Housing 1815–1985* (London, 1986), pp. 222–6.
3   C. Pooley, ed., *Housing Strategies in Europe, 1880–1930* (Leicester, 1992), pp. 1–8, 325–48.
4   P. Abrams, 'The failure of social reform', *Past and Present*, 24 (1963).

5   M. Swenarton, *Homes Fit for Heroes: The Politics and Architecture of Early State Housing in Britain* (London, 1981).

6   C. Williams-Ellis, ed., *Britain and the Beast: A Survey by Twenty-six Authors* (Letchworth, 1937).

7   H. Meller, *Towns, Plans and Society in Modern Britain* (Cambridge, 1997), pp. 66–70.

8   S. M. Gaskell, *Building Control, National Legislation and the Introduction of Local Bye-laws in Victorian England* (London, 1983).

9   J. Morton, 'The 1890 Act and its aftermath: the era of "model dwellings"', in S. Lowe and D. Hughes, eds, *A New Century of Social Housing* (Leicester, 1991), pp. 13–32.

10 C. M. Law, 'The growth of urban population in England and Wales 1800–1911', *Transactions of the Institute of British Geographers* (1967).

11 M. J. Daunton, ed., *Housing the Workers: A Comparative History 1850–1914* (Leicester, 1990), pp. 1–8.

12 P. Johnson, *Saving and Spending: The Working-class Economy in Britain, 1870–1939* (Oxford, 1985).

13 J. Melling, *Rent Strikes: People's Struggle for Housing in West Scotland 1890–1916* (Edinburgh, 1983), pp. 59–73; D. Englander, *Landlord and Tenant in Urban Britain 1838–1918* (Oxford, 1983), pp. 140–61.

14 M. Bowley, *Housing and the State 1919–1945* (London, 1945).

15 See chapter 23.

16 A. Mayne, *The Imagined Slum: Newspaper Representation in Three Cities 1870–1914* (Leicester, 1993), pp. 1–17.

17 Quoted in S. Damer, 'State, class and housing: Glasgow 1885–1919', in J. Melling, ed., *Housing, Social Policy and the State* (London, 1980), p. 84.

18 For example, *Practical Housing* (Letchworth, 1908).

19 W. Ashworth, *The Genesis of Modern British Town Planning* (London, 1954), pp. 176–7.

20 M. Harrison, 'Thomas Coglan Horsfall and the example of Germany', *Planning Perspectives*, 6 (1985), pp. 297–314.

21 O. Hill, *Homes of the London Poor* (London, 1875; rpt. 1970), pp. 38–53.

22 M. Simey, *Charitable Effort in Liverpool in the Nineteenth Century* (Liverpool, 1951), pp. 62–81.

23 J. Lewis, 'Women, social work and social welfare in twentieth-century Britain: from (unpaid) influence to (paid) oblivion', in M. Daunton, ed., *Charity, Self-interest and Welfare in the English Past* (London, 1996), pp. 203–23.

24 J. Walkowitz, *City of Dreadful Delight: Narratives of Sexual Danger in Late Victorian London* (London, 1992), pp. 59–61.

25 J. Lewis, *The Politics of Motherhood: Child and Maternal Welfare in England, 1900–1939* (London, 1980), pp. 61–117.

26 E. Macadam, *The New Philanthropy* (London, 1934).

27 Pooley, *Housing Strategies*, pp. 325–48.

28 S. M. Gaskell, '"The salubrious suburb": town planning in practice', in A. Sutcliffe, ed., *British Town Planning: The Formative Years* (Leicester, 1981), pp. 16–22.

29 S. Pollard, *The Genesis of Modern Management* (Cambridge, Mass., 1965).

30 Ashworth, *Genesis of Modern British Town Planning*, pp. 118–46.

31 R. Unwin, *Town Planning in Practice: An Introduction to the Art of Designing Cities and Suburbs* (London, 1909), ch. 3.

32 M. Miller, 'Raymond Unwin 1863–1940', in Cherry, ed., *Pioneers in British Planning*.

33 M. G. Day, 'The contribution of Sir Raymond Unwin (1863–1940) and R. Barry Parker (1867–1947) to the development of site-planning theory and practice, c.1890–1918', in Sutcliffe, ed., *British Town Planning*, pp. 156–200.

34   B. Ladd, *Urban Planning and Civic Order in Germany 1860–1914* (Cambridge, Mass., 1990).

35   S. Magri and C. Topalov, 'L'habitat du salarié en France, Grande-Bretagne, Italie et aux Etats-Unis, 1910–25', in Y. Cohen and R. Baudouï, eds, *Les Chantiers de la Paix Sociale (1900–1940)* (Fontenay/St Cloud, 1995), pp. 223–54.

36   M. Simpson, *Thomas Adams and the Modern Town Planning Movement, Britain, Canada and the United States, 1900–1940* (London, 1985).

37   H. Meller, *Patrick Geddes: Social Evolutionist and City Planner* (London, 1990).

38   D. Hardy, *From Garden Cities to New Towns: Campaigning for Town and Country Planning 1899–1946* (2 vols, London, 1991), vol. 1, pp. 46–7.

39   F. J. Osborn, *Green-belt Cities: The British Contribution* (London, 1946).

40   R. Beevers, *The Garden City Utopia: A Critical Biography of Ebenezer Howard* (London, 1988).

41   C. C. Collins, 'City planning exhibitions and civic museums: Walter Hegemann and others', in V. Welter and J. Lawson, eds, *The City after Patrick Geddes* (Bern, 2000), pp. 113–32.

42   Meller, *Patrick Geddes*, pp. 182–235.

43   R. Unwin, *Nothing Gained by Overcrowding: How the Garden City Type of Development May Benefit Both Owner and Occupier* (London, 1912).

44   D. Massey, 'Regional planning 1909–1939: "The experimental era"', in P. Garside and M. Hebbert, eds, *British Regionalism 1900–2000* (London, 1989).

45   D. Hardy and C. Ward, *Arcadia for All: The Legacy of a Makeshift Landscape* (London, 1984).

46   A. Rubinstein et al., *Just Like the Country: Memories of London Families who Settled the New Cottage Estates 1919–1939* (London, 1991).

47   S. V. Ward, *Planning and Urban Change* (London, 1994), p. 47.

48   E. Darling, '"Enriching and enlarging the whole sphere of human activities": the work of the voluntary sector in housing reform in inter-war Britain', in C. Lawrence and A.-K. Mayer, eds, *Regenerating England: Science, Medicine and Culture in Inter-war Britain* (Amsterdam, 2000), pp. 149–78.

49   B. Luckin, *Questions of Power: Electricity and Environment in Inter-war Britain* (Manchester, 1990).

50   A. Ravetz, *The Place of Home: English Domestic Environments 1914–2000* (London, 1995).

FURTHER READING

Lloyd George, D., *War Memoirs of Lloyd George* (2 vols, London, 1938).

Melling, J., ed., *Housing, Social Policy and the State* (London, 1980).

Miller, M., *Raymond Unwin: Garden Cities and Town Planning* (Leicester, 1992).

Simon, E. D., *How to Abolish the Slums* (London, 1929).

Sutcliffe, A., ed., *The Rise of Modern Urban Planning 1800–1914* (London, 1980).

Sutcliffe, A., ed., *British Town Planning: The Formative Years* (Leicester, 1981).

Sutcliffe, A., *Towards the Planned City: Germany, Britain, the United States and France 1780–1914* (Oxford, 1981).

CHAPTER TWENTY-FIVE

Medicine and Public Health, 1900–1939

STEVEN CHERRY

Introduction

The record of this country in its health and medical services is a good one. . . . Achievements before the war – in lower mortality rates, in the gradual decline of many of the more serious diseases, in safer motherhood and healthier childhood . . . all substantiate it.

1944 White Paper, *A National Health Service* (Cmd 6502)

[Concerning] existing health services . . . it is inherent in their more or less haphazard and sectional growth that they do not constitute a national health policy. The first essential is to integrate the separate services.

1935–6 Committee on Scottish Health Services, Report (Cmd 5204, vol. 11)

Few people would deny that medical knowledge and public sanitation, formal health-care systems and the management of illness and disease all improved in Britain between 1900 and 1939. Most would also recognize that the associated benefits were inequitably distributed and linked with features such as social class background, gender, age and geographic area. For much of the population the trauma of accident or disease was still accompanied by the additional stresses of income loss, worries concerning doctors' or hospital fees and the residual stigma attached to Poor Law or charitable treatments. Their responses to such crises are an essential part of history, rather under-represented in historical writing. In part, this is because the relevant evidence is diverse and fragmentary. It nevertheless suggests that people were not merely victims of illness, or recipients of orthodox medical care or users of alternative medicines, but were also procurers and even organizers of medical services. There is ample evidence of declining death rates over the period, with rather less on recorded patterns of disease. However, the avoidance of death and information on causes of mortality are a poor guide to the experiences of more routine illnesses and still less of health levels. In 1946 the World Health Organization defined health as 'a state of complete physical, mental and social well-being, not merely the absence of disease or infirmity'. Historians have tended to surmise about health from mortality data or medical constructions of disease rather than from popular experiences. At least until 1946, people probably considered themselves fortunate to avoid serious illness or incapacity and there are no statistics and little personalized recording of positive or 'good' physical or mental health. Moreover, any broader sense of 'feeling well' was likely to encompass lifestyles, social roles and expectations often difficult to express, let alone quantify.

Given all this, investigations of social policy formulation and the respective contributions of income, social intervention and nutrition relative to medical effort in improving health remain important. Questions such as the impact of the Great War upon civilian health, or the consequences of economic change for general levels of health in the 1930s, attract controversy. So does the role of the medical profession and its exercise of power, in hospital and asylum or in public life. Features such as health risks, coping with illness, accessing medical facilities and reforming health care in the four decades before the National Health Service (NHS) also need to be considered, not least from grassroots perspectives.

Mortality and Morbidity

British mortality rates continued their decline, but at decelerating rates and with some lag in Scotland. Rural rates were lower than urban, though preventive measures and services exerted a containing effect in towns and cities. With reductions in birth rates and infant mortality rates, more children survived to become adults and, typically, half of these lived beyond the age of sixty. So the population structure aged: over 7 per cent of the population were aged seventy-five years or more in the middle 1930s, compared with under 5 per cent in 1900. Overall, female mortality was less than male, between 15 and 25 per cent lower among infants, slightly less among children, roughly the same among young adults, and then appreciably lower after the age of thirty-five. Social class variations continued too. Death rates among men and women in the professional and business classes were roughly one-quarter below those among unskilled men and women workers in the 1930s. Infant mortality among unskilled working-class families was roughly double that among the upper and middle classes in 1900, and still 75 per cent higher in the 1930s.[1]

Mortality data suggest an epidemiological transition, with fewer deaths from infectious diseases and more from the chronic or degenerative illnesses affecting an older population.[2] Most water-borne and airborne infections were reduced, but TB affected at least 250,000 people in 1900 and roughly 50,000 annually in the 1930s, with nearly 60 per cent fatality. Heart disease and circulatory conditions accounted for one in four of adult deaths by then, with breast cancer prominent among women and lung cancer among men. Neonatal mortality, reflecting congenital malformations and prematurity, persisted among the newborn, and babies remained vulnerable to gastrointestinal infections. But the combination of health visiting, better baby milk substitutes and improved hygiene meant fewer deaths, particularly from diarrhoea. Table 25.1 shows the reduction in infant mortality: between 1913 and 1935 death rates among two- and three-year-olds fell by two-thirds, and among those aged four and five by half. In 1939 mortality among infants and young children was respectively one-third and one-tenth of levels a hundred years earlier. Childhood diseases remained a threat, with 50,000 cases of diphtheria annually in the 1930s, for example, and TB still killed older children and young adults.

Table 25.1 Population and trends in crude death rates (CDR per 1,000 living) and mortality (IMR per 1,000 live births) in census years, 1901–39

	England and Wales			Scotland		
	Population (000)	CDR	IMR	Population (000)	CDR	IMR
1901	32,612	16.9	151	4,479	17.9	129
1911	36,136	14.6	130	4,751	15.1	112
1921	37,932	12.1	83	4,882	13.6	90
1931	39,988	12.3	66	4,843	13.3	82
1939	41,460 (est.)	12.1	51	5,007	12.9	69

Source: B. R. Mitchell, *British Historical Statistics* (Cambridge, 1988), pp. 12, 58–9.

National morbidity data were not compiled before 1945 but limited evidence shows major differences between illnesses and causes of death. The earlier sources have their problems; for example, the diseases that required public notification were usually infectious and hospital records focused in detail only upon the seriously ill. Friendly society, health insurance and general practitioners' records are skewed towards male family breadwinners who had greatest access to such facilities. Until the state national health insurance (NHI) scheme commenced in 1913 there were fewer medical consultations, but probably no less sickness. Unknown but considerable numbers of sick people did not seek medical attention or become patients as such. Those who did reported mainly with bronchitis, tonsilitis, colds and influenza, which accounted for 35 per cent of all illnesses between the wars. Rheumatism and lumbago, digestive disorders, sepsis, skin conditions and nervous disorders were also prominent, with men additionally vulnerable to physical injuries. Women were particularly affected by debility and neuralgia but, with less access to formal health care, much of their poverty- and stress-related illnesses went unreported. The potential of fertility control measures in reducing illegitimate births and their attendant risks or the threat of extra children to women's health, family incomes or overcrowding also went understated in medicine and social policy. Children were particularly vulnerable and contemporary investigations, by the National Birthday Trust in south Wales or by medical officers of health in north-east England, showed large families, low income, poor accommodation and inadequate nutrition to be closely linked. Official and medical explanations focused upon maternal or parental neglect, but these were no substitute for positive measures. Nor did they resolve grim considerations of cost and likely outcomes of medical treatment made when children were sick and incomes were insufficient.[3]

The onset of the decline in mortality is conventionally explained in terms of improved social intervention and public health measures, or rising nutritional levels, or some combination of these.[4] A resultant twentieth-century rise in longevity might not lead to more healthy lives, however, if the incidence of sickness increased with age. Yet if falling death rates do not always signify reduced levels of illness, they suggest more recoveries from it. Improved sanitation was vital in combating water- and food-borne infection, but it did not prevent continuing exposure to disease.

As will be seen, more than the gestation of nineteenth-century social investment was required to reduce infant mortality. Before 1900 factory reforms or measures to reduce atmospheric pollution had little effect, although there were patchy improvements in occupational health measures by 1939. Arguments for better housing and reduced overcrowding are also stronger by then. More recoveries from diseases suggest more resilient populations, aided by better nutrition, but such optimism must be tempered by evidence of considerable poverty and malnutrition and associated disease, notably TB, rickets, bronchitis and anaemia.[5]

Medicine and Medical Effort before 1914

What scope did this leave for medical effort? In medicine as in so much else, the period reviewed is one of contrasts. Advances in medical knowledge and, in the late 1930s, major breakthroughs in treatments needed general application in order to be effective. This required more personnel and services, but provision varied and access to it was still more uneven. Although services expanded, they were frequently uncoordinated, not least because professional, commercial and ideological interests often produced sectional approaches and rivalries, for example between voluntary and public hospitals or between salaried 'public health' doctors and contract-based general practitioners (GPs). These operated at the expense of comprehensive approaches to health services or broader considerations of health. Thus the planning, potential and best practice examples of services ran parallel with conservatism, lags in service delivery and even neglect in many areas.

By 1900 hospitals had become associated with more advanced forms of medicine as a more sophisticated understanding of body cell structures, bacteriology and aseptic procedures developed. New aids to diagnosis, such as the X-ray, blood and urine testing, were used to gather information about the patient's body, to ascertain his or her condition, suitable remedial procedures and a likely prognosis. Although people might dread serious illness and treatment in what must have seemed an increasingly alien hospital environment, such facilities were strongly supported, if the financial evidence and resort to outpatient departments are any guide. Teaching and larger urban voluntary hospitals offered complex treatments and became centres for new technologies and specialisms, seen as superior to the GP's surgery, nursing home or domiciliary attendance. New hospital departments used X-rays, light and electrotherapy with forms of manipulation and massage by 1914. Salvarsan, employed in the treatment of syphilis after 1910, was the first drug that directly combated the process of infection. After the 1911 National Insurance Act improved access to primary health care, the possibility of systematic referral to hospitals arose. Ironically, the need for such procedures was demonstrated in the extreme conditions of the Great War, when attempts were made to assess sick or wounded troops and move them to appropriate levels of care.[6] With the standing of hospital treatments further enhanced, the paying middle classes also sought access, broadening the patient clientele and recasting the hospital as a genuine community institution.

Medical developments during the 1920s involved the use of insulin in controlling diabetes and liver extract in cases of pernicious anaemia. Kidney dialysis was followed by radium therapy, skin-grafting techniques and blood transfusions in the 1930s. Less spectacularly, growing awareness of the significance of vitamins led to new therapies using vitamins C and D in cases of scurvy and rickets, respectively. However, the major medical breakthrough was the discovery of sulphonamide drugs that could combat the spread of infection in the body. Early successes included the control of puerperal fever from 1936, pneumonia from 1938 and the use of streptomycin against TB. The range of bacteristatics, chemical compounds which enfeebled target micro-organisms, and antibiotics, which used one bacterial form (e.g. penicillin) to control others that were more dangerous to their human host, expanded. These were initially seen as magic bullets, enabling medical practitioners to win the war against disease, but few of the new weapons could be directed at heart disease or cancers and the adaptability of 'hostile' micro-organisms was understated.

Disease and poverty were allies and this war had many fronts. Around 1900 medical practitioners were usually involved in family doctoring for commercial fees and sometimes lower-grade 'sixpenny doctoring', or they were employed in forms of friendly society, workplace and club medicine. General practice still included surgical work and some dentistry, and referral of poor patients to hospital was very limited. The family GP was a source of advice, often based on a holistic approach, although most club patients experienced primary care in the form of 'bottle doctoring', linctuses, expectorants, tonics and so on. Most of this was later regarded as ineffective, dealing with symptoms rather than underlying causes, though such relief, placebo effects, faith in qualified practitioners or knowledge that some remedial action had been taken may have been beneficial. Opium derivatives and chloral were increasingly replaced by aspirin for general use in pain relief. Specifics included quinine for malaria, iron preparations for anaemia, the use of antitoxins against diphtheria and tetanus, and digitalis for some heart conditions.[7] In best-case examples the diffusion of these new treatments made an appreciable difference, but a characteristic of inter-war general practice was its diversity, with poor, ill-equipped surgeries another persistent feature.

By 1900 Poor Law medical services were largely under medical control. They were available without disfranchisement in London and were municipalized in Sheffield in 1906, with Glasgow setting new standards for Scotland. Provincial Poor Law dispensaries were restricted by financial stringency and the promotion of self-help ideologies, however. English and Welsh rural provision often depended upon solitary part-time medical officers and almost 10 per cent of Scottish parishes still relied upon payments to GPs for visits or services deemed necessary. In such areas the urban transition from workhouse sick ward to infirmary and public hospital was rarely emulated: some 300 rural Poor Law infirmaries characteristically lacked basic medical supplies, surgical equipment and qualified nursing staffs.[8]

Public health efforts to contain infectious diseases in the decades around 1900 were increasingly shaped by some 1,800 medical officers of health and extended from sanitation to the establishment of isolation hospitals. Local authorities already provided one-sixth of hospital beds in England and Wales and one-third of those in Scotland by 1911. These represented a community service and a non-stigmatized individual facility, a better indication of proto-public sector potential than the Poor Law. Similar combinations were offered in local authority provision for maternity, infant and child welfare. Attempts to test and trace TB victims and provide pure milk supplies were followed by legislation covering the training and conduct of midwives in 1902. Early infant welfare centres opened in north London, Sheffield and

Leicester, the emphasis often upon advice rather than material aid. Health-visiting services, targeting new mothers, reflected high infant mortality and fears of a degeneration of the population, as did municipal efforts to promote health awareness and personal hygiene. The 1907 Education (Administrative Provisions) Act required the medical inspection but not necessarily treatment of schoolchildren and reflected similar concerns, but, more positively, three-quarters of local authorities were developing services by 1914.

Another legislative landmark was the 1911 National Insurance Act (Part I). Its compulsory health insurance, for 12.7 million manual workers aged between sixteen and seventy years and earning less than £160 annually, covered their registration with a doctor chosen from a listed panel, medical attendance, drugs and treatment. Sickness and disability benefits and, in theory, TB treatment were also provided. Although the scheme was oriented upon male family breadwinners, their dependants were excluded, with the significant exception of maternity payments for wives. Consequently, Poor Law provision remained part of twentieth-century health care. Hospital facilities were neither provided nor funded, although they were occasionally offered at the discretion of some 'approved societies', the commercial insurance companies, friendly societies and trade unions which administered the state scheme. In extending personal health care, the NHI scheme aimed primarily to offset the pauperizing effects of sickness. It was neither comprehensive nor capable of addressing issues in preventive medicine, but 'Lloyd George's Ambulance Wagon' shaped general practice and was the largest of a series of uncoordinated health services through the interwar years.[9]

Health policy formulation or legislation did not guarantee improvements or services, however. Public sector models, based upon a unified county or borough health service, were promoted by London County Council by 1900, endorsed by the Minority Report of the 1905–9 Poor Law Commission and adopted by the Labour party after 1911. They were not necessarily socialistic, for they attracted support on national efficiency criteria or as an opportunity to develop preventive medicine. However, central government was unenthusiastic. There was no Ministry of Health to offer the possibility of service coordination, let alone an integrated health-care system. Suggestions that 'maintenance of personal health had become a specific responsibility of society', or that a national health service for the poor was already emerging before 1914, impart social justice commitments to what were variable motives and they telescope and oversimplify reform processes.[10]

They also understate the scale and consequences of social risks. On the whole, popular responses to sickness throughout the period examined remained private rather than public, local not national, but collective or solidaristic rather than individualistic. Not all sufferers became patients, nor were all healers doctors. People relied upon self- or family diagnosis and their assessments might be followed by self-medication, using herbal or patent medicines or visits to alternative healers, such as homoeopaths or bone-setters. The number of retail outlets for patent medicines quadrupled over forty years, to 40,000 in 1905. Vigorous advertising by 'toadstool millionaires' preyed upon the desperate, offering abortifacients and spurious cures for venereal diseases (VD), TB or cancer. Defending professional as well as public interests, the British Medical Association (BMA) exposed these 'secret remedies' in 1909 and 1912, but effective regulation only commenced with the 1917 Venereal

Diseases Act.[11] Annual turnover of patent medicines approached £30 million, or one-fifth of all health-care spending, in the 1930s.

Yet there was significant resort to qualified medical practitioners. Relatively few could afford family doctors, but over 4 million friendly society members and some of their dependants were eligible for medical care and 9 million for sickness benefit in 1900. Provident dispensaries, offering medical attention and medicines for twopence or so weekly, were also popular. The *Lancet* estimated that two-thirds or more of urban populations obtained medical attention through sick clubs and other arrangements, with one-half of all doctors involved in club practice. Scottish friendly society membership neared half a million and cheap or sixpenny doctoring was extensive. Many mining and industrial centres had works clubs or participated in Hospital Saturday networks, which often covered access to hospital facilities for workers and their dependants. The scale of such institutions has been recognized more than their utility. New research on friendly society records confirms that occupational illnesses contributed less to sickness than background socio-economic features. To focus upon adult male breadwinners was inappropriate, but the general conclusion is that increased access to qualified medical services was a benefit when management of disease and illness was improving. This not only helped individual sufferers but, more controversially, may have been 'the crucial factor in mortality decline'.[12]

Professionals

For most of the nineteenth century a university medical training and hospital experience preceded qualified medical practice. The formal registration of qualified doctors under the 1858 Medical Act and amending legislation in 1886 also gave the profession's senior members control of the processes defining competence and regulating conduct. Restriction of public medical office to the qualified and the requirement of minimum standards served wider public interests, but the expense, duration and nature of medical education produced an entrant range restricted in social class, discriminatory in attitudes towards women and likely to perpetuate establishment values. Nor was university- and hospital-based education, removed from wider economic and social conditions and familiarity with minor or common illnesses, the best preparation for popular general practice.

Table 25.2 Registered medical practitioners in Britain, 1890–1945[a]

	Britain and Ireland[a]	*England and Wales*	*Scotland*	*Women doctors*
1890	23,027	18,092	2,658	101
1900	29,044	23,023	3,462	212
1910	31,868	25,398	3,228	477
1920	34,519	26,619	4,544	1,200?
1930	41,904	31,936	5,905	3,331
1940	48,504	39,210	6,336	
1945	54,844	42,041	8,133	7,000?

[a] Includes retired practitioners but excludes those in the armed services and overseas.
Sources: *Medical Directory* (1946), tables I, II; J. Brotherston, 'Evolution of medical practice', in Nuffield Provincial Hospitals Trust, *Medical History and Medical Care* (Oxford, 1971), p. 99.

Conventionally, the provision of medical care is demarcated between GPs, responsible for primary care, and the increasing numbers of hospital consultants or specialists providing advanced care for the seriously ill. In theory GPs screened patients for hospital consultants, referring only those who required higher levels of facilities or attention. Yet this model describes a professional division by no means complete by 1939 and unfamiliar to most patients, who were insufficiently wealthy or interesting as medical cases to attract consultant services.[13] Developing from family doctoring and club medicine, general practice was boosted by the 1911 NHI scheme, which required certification by qualified panel doctors prior to claims for sickness benefit. But without guarantee of secondary care in hospital facilities or even payments to the hospitals under the NHI scheme, panel patients and their dependants had no right to hospital treatment. GPs were not obliged to refer and hospitals, without alternative funding, were not compelled to accept those referred.

Many GPs carried out surgical procedures themselves or retained their more wealthy patients by attending them in cottage hospitals. These were established in smaller towns, suburbs and dormitory towns as well as in rural areas and they provided over 10,000 beds by 1935. There were strong therapeutic arguments for basic localized hospital care, convenient for patients and visitors, but cottage and smaller district hospitals also represented a professional benefit to the GP. They offered a certain status, the opportunity to enhance skills and access better equipment. GPs might also perform surgery on schoolchildren under the Schools Medical Service or in maternity complications cases on behalf of local authorities. Even in 1938–9, they controlled one in five hospital beds and conducted 2.5 million operations, to the consternation of hospital specialists who sought to monopolize such work. Away from teaching hospitals and urban centres, depictions of the GP as subordinate to the hospital consultant in the medical division of labour are probably inaccurate.

Some doctors were also directly employed by local authorities or retained by Poor Law, later Public Assistance, Committees. These areas of medical practice, usually focused upon the poorest, allegedly encroached upon the professional ideal of family doctoring. Salaried medical officers of health, whose management of public health medicine had widened to include the supervision of personal medical services, were seen as another threat. However, if the medical profession was not all-powerful or monolithic, the economic benefits which most GPs derived from combining NHI panel work with private practice were considerable.[14]

Nursing as an occupation expanded more rapidly than did the proportion of qualified nurses between 1900 and 1939 and nursing shortages remained endemic. A formally identifiable profession emerged from the 1919 Nurses Registration Act, but qualified nurses were underrewarded and the part-qualified went poorly paid and largely unrecognized.

Contrary to popular perceptions, under one-third of nurses were hospital-based in 1901 and most of the remainder attended the wealthy. Legislation in 1902 and 1925 required midwives and health visitors respectively to undergo training and further unqualified practice was prohibited. The 1907 Notification of Births Act and the 1918 Maternity and Child Welfare Act stimulated municipal provision, though local authority midwifery services were not formally required until the 1936 Midwives Act. Some 8,000 district nurses covered nearly all the English counties and most of those in Wales. There were also 5,800 health visitors, with over 1,000 more

Table 25.3 Nursing as an occupation, 1901–39

	Women nurses	All nurses	Trained/Registered nurses
1901	64,030	69,200	12,500
1911	77,060		18,000 (1916)
1921	110,040	122,050	25,000
1931		153,670	50,000
1939		160,000	60,000

Sources: C. Maggs, ed., *Nursing History: The State of the Art* (London, 1987), pp. 8, 9, 24; B. Abel Smith, *The Hospitals* (London, 1964), pp. 57, 117; B. Abel Smith, *A History of the Nursing Profession* (London, 1960), pp. 85, 162.

in Scotland, the latter often doubling as district or school nurse. Although the 1919 Act instituted a three-year nurse training programme, only one-third of those employed as nurses at the 1931 Census were registered as fully qualified. Hospitals used the training of probationary nurses as a means of staffing their wards and between one-third and one-half of probationers failed to complete their training. Work in a voluntary hospital probably carried most status for nurses, although numbers and standards of nursing improved more rapidly in Poor Law and local authority hospitals over the interwar period. Whereas the average hospital nurse worked a seventy-hour week in 1900, the ninety-six-hour fortnight had been attained by just one-fifth of local authority nurses and only one-eighth of voluntary hospital nurses by 1938.[15] What was seen as a vocation by some, including the Royal College of Nursing itself, was interpreted as cheap labour by others.

Developments, Contrasts and Lost Opportunities to 1939

Although the range of health facilities improved between the wars, the economic context was often discouraging and governments were reluctant to initiate or fund reform. Failure to implement planning opportunities, to achieve more comprehensive services or to generalize best practice and improved health levels characterized the period. In turn, this provided arguments rather than an 'enlightened consensus' concerning the need for a national health service.

The impact of the Great War upon civilian health and social policy remains controversial and its short-run consequences for medical facilities were mixed.[16] Amidst the horrific loss of life, a significant reorganization of medical care for service personnel occurred. The sick or injured received emergency treatments and were assessed at casualty stations, with serious cases referred to field hospitals set behind the front lines. Those able to withstand long-distance transportation were evacuated to war and auxiliary hospitals in Britain. Many war hospitals were former mental hospitals and Poor Law institutions, temporarily appropriated by the War Ministry, and some derived longer-term benefits from improved facilities and equipment. They provided 29,000 and 35,000 beds respectively, with 100,000 more auxiliary beds.[17] With some failings, this system coped with large numbers of the sick and injured and was soon regarded as a model for civilians. Over 13,000 doctors volunteered or were enrolled for war service, leaving an equivalent number to attend the civilian population. Their absence was not critical, though the depletion of hospital resources was felt during the first influenza outbreak in 1918.

An increasing threat from VD and TB to military and civilian personnel eventually led to legislation which provided new, free public services. Following the 1913–16 Royal Commission, government grants under the 1917 Venereal Diseases Act encouraged local authorities to establish clinics and the advertising of spurious remedies was prohibited. Following the 1921 Tuberculosis Act, 17,000 sanatorium beds were available in England and Wales and 5,000 in Scotland by 1935. Central government grants under the 1918 Maternity and Child Welfare Act and the establishment of the Schools Medical Service in 1919 were among the few tangible benefits of the post-war social reform package. War work meant full employment and, on balance, better female and child health, but the opportunity to extend the NHI scheme to significant numbers of women workers was not taken.

Among reform advocates Robert Morant and George Newman at the Board of Education, Sir Arthur Newsholme, the chief medical officer, and Lord Rhondda, president of the Local Government Board, all favoured the creation of a Ministry of Health and a public hospital service. Sympathetic proposals to the Ministry of Reconstruction were opposed by the insurance societies, which feared competition and sought to retain their hold on the NHI scheme, and the Local Government Board, which was determined to safeguard its own powers. Thus the Ministry of Health, established in 1919, symbolized state involvement in health care and the prospect of qualitative improvements, but it embraced an unreconstructed Poor Law, it lacked control over NHI arrangements and, with restricted funding, could neither coordinate nor expand services.[18]

These shortcomings were quickly revealed. In 1919 the first minister of health, Christopher Addison, established a consultative council on medical and allied services. Chaired by Bernard Dawson, its interim report of 1920 drew upon wartime experiences, proposing GP-staffed health centres with health promotional functions but also with inpatient and surgical facilities. These would provide primary health care, referring patients to larger hospitals for specialist staff and facilities.[19] How this potentially attractive plan was to be implemented and funded was unclear. The voluntary hospitals, which had most of the special facilities, were in financial difficulties, the medical profession was suspicious and the approved societies were uncooperative. The doctors' alternative, endorsed by the Scottish Medical Consultative Council, was to extend the NHI scheme. This was considered by the 1924–6 Royal Commission, which advocated more uniform services, including hospital and maternity care, funded from the pooled resources of the approved societies. But the latter were unwilling to spend their accumulated surpluses, which deteriorated as unemployment levels increased, and central government provided neither funding nor reform impetus, so these were forlorn hopes.[20]

Covering 13.3 million people in 1922, the NHI scheme grew incrementally and was extended to young workers in 1938, then reaching 20.3 million or 54 per cent of the adult population. Their access to qualified GPs aided the earlier diagnosis and management of illness, with potential therapeutic advantages, but serious defects remained. The interwar average of 900 to 1,000 panel patients per doctor was misleading. At least 5,000 doctors remained outside the NHI scheme, and some within it derived most of their income from private patients, supplementing this with NHI capitation payments. In poorer areas, doctors loaded up with panel patients; a GP employing an assistant could have up to 4,000 such patients, and 2,500 for a single doctor was commonplace.[21] In such circumstances doctors had little time for each individual panel patient. Total patient attendances at doctors' surgeries doubled between the wars, but only one-half of panel patients saw their doctor in any one year. Allegations concerning cursory consultations and preferential treatment for private patients were routine, as was the common reckoning that 'a minute of the doctor's time was more valuable than an hour of the patient's'. Access to care and its standard varied, though recent research shows that bad practice was much the same in poor areas in Glasgow or Swansea as in Leeds or London: wherever poor patients had low expectations, these were likely to be fulfilled.[22]

The NHI scheme failed to guarantee hospital care or other 'additional benefits'. By 1939 twelve commercial concerns dominated the approved societies; their restrictions on medication and intrusive promotion of private business were greatly resented. More generally, as health insurance did not integrate services or help 'bad risks', the chronic sick, elderly or economically inactive, it remained a heavily qualified success. Medical provision for the 15 million dependants of NHI contributors and others excluded from state insurance was conditioned by income. Some GPs participated in Public Medical Services, covering over 600,000 people in 1935, or ran sick clubs, and friendly societies and works clubs often reoriented upon the provision of family benefits. Despite the prompting of the Industrial Welfare Society, health promotion and other efforts in industrial life were patchy. Corporate support for medical research into heart disease, rheumatism or alcoholism was often motivated by loyalty and labour productivity concerns, and employer contributions to works clubs, hospitals and convalescent schemes were very limited.

A few local authorities organized direct medical services using salaried doctors. Glasgow employed thirty-six doctors in this way by 1935; Oxford and Mansfield were good English examples. Most met only their statutory obligations, notably regarding infant and maternity care. Again provision varied: one-seventh of babies were hospital-delivered in 1927 and one-quarter by 1939; four-fifths in London in the 1930s, but only one-tenth in Norfolk. After the Midwives and Maternity Services (Scotland) Acts of 1936 and 1937 health care improved, although arrangements for the two to five age group barely existed and Schools Medical Services remained rudimentary.

Most women were excluded from state and local authority services. The Ministry of Health insisted that worrying evidence concerning their health, nutrition and maternal mortality rates did not reflect poverty and depression.[23] For all the state's focus upon motherhood and infant welfare, the maternal mortality rate actually reattained the 1900 level of 4.1 per 1,000 births in 1935. In south Wales and Scotland it exceeded 6 per 1,000, reaching 10 in some districts. New drugs against sepsis, implicated in one-third of maternal mortality and in abortion attempts, blood and plasma transfusions and enhanced midwifery services from 1936 were more effective. Generally, insurance companies considered women's 'natural' or biological needs a bad risk, making commercial provision expensive and NHI coverage unlikely. Chief medical officer Sir George Newman privately acknowledged the mass of 'dull diseases' affecting women but publicly prioritized spending controls, fearing that 'the demonstration of a great mass of sickness and impairment attributable to child-

Table 25.4 Hospital bed provision, 1891–1938

	England and Wales				Scotland		
	Voluntary	Poor Law	(Separate infirmary)	Local authority	Voluntary	Poor Law	Public health
1891	29,500	60,800	12,100	10,400	6,000	4,500	1,500
1911	43,200	80,300	40,000	31,800	10,500	6,900	7,900
1921	56,600	83,800	36,500	51,700			
1938	87,200	56,000	44,600	84,300	14,100	5,600	15,400

Sources: R. Pinker, *English Hospital Statistics*, table 1, p. 49; table 12, p. 75; table 14, p. 81; I. Levitt, *Poverty and Welfare in Scotland, 1890–1948* (Edinburgh, 1988), appendix 2, p. 208.

birth . . . would create a demand for organised treatment by the state'.[24] Others were even less concerned: a Rotherham midwife with rheumatism was advised by her doctor: 'all women get backache round about 40, so why worry?'[25]

NHI primary care was inadequate and GP provision remained inequitable: research conclusions that few doctors had over 3,500 patients by 1939 are hardly reassuring.[26] Provision beyond the state scheme reflected charitable or commercial interests or specific, statutory requirements upon local authorities. The latter provided most services but inevitably, with 1,400 responsible authorities in England and Wales and 1,900 in Scotland in 1929, unevenness, political and territorial rivalries all featured. Given these limitations, services were cost-effective, with some coordination in urban areas. Positive health concepts were for the future: meanwhile, most medical officers of health shrank from public acknowledgement of deficiencies in health, criticisms of services or demands for reform.

By 1910 roughly one-sixth of all deaths, in London one-third, occurred in medical institutions of some sort. Although hospitals were an essential in twentieth-century life, they were not fully integrated into a system of health care or even a national hospital service by 1939. Voluntary hospitals began as philanthropic institutions but, faced with rising treatment costs and inflation during the Great War, had introduced almoner-assessed charges for most patients. Increasingly, they were funded through patient payments and quasi-insurance arrangements and focused upon the acute sick. The duration of their inpatient treatments fell by one-quarter, to an average of eighteen days, from 1921 to 1938 and their bed provision per 1,000 population doubled between 1911 and 1938. Consequently, they treated roughly 12 inpatients per 1,000 population in 1911 and 35 by 1938, sufficient to affect national mortality rates. There were then thirty teaching hospitals averaging over 500 beds each, with forty-five larger hospitals exceeding 200 beds and 600 smaller hospitals, many of them cottage hospitals with fewer than twenty beds, in the voluntary sector.[27]

From 1921 the Voluntary Hospitals Commission promoted the regional organization of services around base hospitals, providing specialist facilities, medical education and nurse training, supported by district hospitals and satellite cottage hospitals. Regionalization and efficiency became watchwords, but service integration varied. The smaller hospitals boosted access to treatments but did not serve as the health centres, though some referred serious cases to larger hospitals.[28] Specialist facilities were inequitably distributed and expensive equipment was often used ineffec-tively, while intensive treatments contrasted with inadequate after-care services. Vol-untary hospital authorities and medical staffs too readily asserted their independence or assumed superior status and were frequently accused of 'dumping' chronic sick patients on the public sector. This soured their relations with public authorities and undermined opportunities to assess or meet area health needs, although limited co-operation with former Poor Law hospitals in major cities occurred.

Financially, voluntary hospitals were not sustainable in the long term. Some of the larger London hospitals had been wrestling with debts before 1914, and their prob-lems were compounded by wartime inflation and the withdrawal of central govern-ment grants. Most provincial and Scottish hospitals were not in debt, however; some had invested funds and most attracted considerable new income from hospital con-tributory schemes and direct patient payments. More private patients were admitted during the 1920s and private wards, blocks and insurance schemes rapidly followed. The hospitals received little help from the approved societies or insurance compa-nies, but benefited from local authority service contracts for VD, schools and mater-nity services. Although traditional 'windfall' legacies still funded new hospital building and extensions, their capacity to sustain improvements or meet additional demands was limited by 1939. Moreover, new funds rarely came without strings: the Voluntary Hospitals Commission's conciliatory attitude towards the London County Council reflected efforts to gain contracts and reduce public sector competition. In Manchester, new professional opportunities in public as well as voluntary hospitals led hospital consultants to promote their coordination.[29] Hospital contributory schemes also influenced services and the demarcation of treatments, for example, facilitating patient transfers or relieving waiting lists. Yet overall, voluntary hospitals skimped on their contribution to integrated health care.

As services of last resort for the chronic or infectious sick or disturbed, the ex-Poor Law and local authority hospitals and asylums should not be undervalued. Qualitative improvement, new functions and lost opportunities feature in the history of public hospitals in this period. More medically specific beds were provided in separate hospitals, often because of positive civic or ideological commitment to public sector medicine. Again, such developments were uneven: three-quarters of London's public hospital patients but fewer than one-third of provincial patients were accom-modated in this way by 1925.

Poor Law medical services and former sanitary authority functions were transferred to county and county borough councils under the 1929 Local Government Act. This provided another opportunity for health service integration, but suitable facilities, financial resources and political resolve were scarce and only one-fifth of Poor Law infirmaries – 109 – were appropriated as general hospitals.[30] Hospital beds under local authority control were often in outmoded infectious diseases institutions. Some conversion for sanatorium or mental hospital accommodation was possible, although this hardly amounted to the development of community medicine. Corresponding Scottish legislation produced little change outside Glasgow, so, as in rural England and Wales, Poor Law facilities and attitudes often continued in the guise of public assistance provision. An improving public hospital sector provided two-thirds of hospital beds, but had just one-third of medical staffs and one-half of nursing staffs. Surveys for 1938/9 indicated that public sector hospital facilities were more equitably distributed than voluntary, but 50 per cent shortfalls in beds and nursing provision featured in some areas, with intra-regional variations equally pronounced. Meanwhile, as a future chief medical officer noted, the concept of hospitals as a supporting service for community care remained underdeveloped.[31]

Similar conclusions applied with mental health. Medical and judicial authorities largely determined the numbers of those considered to be mentally ill or with special needs, while cost and social order considerations affected provision for them. The 1890 Lunacy Act revised procedures for asylum certification and stimulated office-based entrepreneurial psychiatry for the better off, but the number of people 'of unsound mind' rose from 116,000 in 1900 to over 146,000 by 1914.[32] The vast majority of patients remained in asylums, with others in workhouse infirmaries and, in Scotland particularly, lodged 'with friends'. Measures to reduce the stigma surrounding mental illness, using outpatient clinics or voluntary procedures, were probably nullified by expanding concepts of 'moral insanity', which included insufficiencies in self-help or self-control. The 1913 Mental Deficiency Act similarly applied local authority protection for those 'subject to be dealt with', aged seven years upwards, pregnant girls and young unmarried mothers on poor relief, but not all were removed from asylums.

Fewer than one-tenth of asylum buildings in use in 1930 had been constructed since 1914, with a similar proportion temporarily converted to military hospitals during the Great War. Asylum overcrowding increased dramatically, making out-patient provision desirable on economic as well as therapeutic grounds. The 1930 Mental Treatment Act encouraged voluntary treatments and outpatient attendance at local authority clinics but, six years later, 95 per cent of 155,500 mental patients in England and Wales were still certified and 80 per cent of Scotland's 21,000 patients were still designated as paupers.[33] Even under reforming regimes, elderly homeless people or those requiring various forms of care became institutionalized in mental hospitals. Others were kept inappropriately in public assistance accommodation and one-quarter of the 40,000 people classified as mentally retarded were similarly confined. These were truly the last places in the hierarchy of medical resort and hospital provision.

Costs and Payments

The proliferation of health-care services was associated with changed patterns of funding and public perceptions of accountability and entitlement, a relatively neglected issue.[34] Poor Law medicine was always subject to financial restraints, but the doubling of new infirmary bed costs and medicines expenditure in the two decades to 1905 indicates improving standards here, as with the sanitary infrastructure. Public sector health spending in England and Wales rose from £5.7 million in 1911 to £22.9 million in 1921 and £48.3 million in 1939; corresponding figures in Scotland were £0.55, £2.2 and £3.5 million.[35] These increases reflect new maternity and child-care services but also, after the 1929 Local Government Act, the inclusion of former Poor Law spending areas and central government block grants. The real cost of private care is unknown, but that for patent medicines approached £30 million in 1939. Predominant in the voluntary sector, the combined incomes of voluntary hospitals rose from £4.3 million in 1910 to £9.44 million in 1920 and £18.55 million in 1938. Health service spending represented 1.1 per cent of gross national product in 1921 and averaged 1.8 per cent over the 1930s. Most of the £150 million total in 1939 was rate-financed by local authorities, though voluntary effort remained important. The money was split roughly between doctors' fees (37 per cent) and hospital services (public, 18 per cent; voluntary, 12 per cent; mental, 8 per cent). Spending on self-medication (17 per cent) far exceeded that on NHI scheme medicines (3 per cent).[36]

Three per cent of working-class household expenditure went on medicines and services additional to NHI contributions in the 1930s. Hospital contributory schemes were the popular response to patient charges and the continuing absence of NHI hospital cover. Their membership exceeded 6.25 million in 1932 and 10.3 million plus dependants in 1938, when it provided over £8 million, mainly to voluntary hospitals. Taken with the earlier extensive support for friendly societies and sick clubs, this suggests positive interest in the consumption and organization of health care. Independent contributory schemes participated in hospital policy making, raising fears that 'one class of the community' – presumably the 'wrong' class – might assume control in some areas.[37] The 1941 Hospital Almoners' Association survey noted that contributory scheme patients, like ratepayers in public hospitals, frequently expected treatment as of right.[38] This point is often overlooked by accounts that focus upon traditional charitable provision by the enlightened wealthy for deferential or grateful patients. Depictions of the rise of public sector alternatives, driven by national efficiency considerations or by socialist ideas, may also understate such grassroots initiatives. Such lay effort also has consequences for explanations that emphasize professional power and control because the shaping of health services thereby affected health professionals. However, the scope for lay influence was gradually reduced within professionally dominated state services and was, ironically, minimized in the genuinely popular NHS.

Conclusions

What conclusions should be drawn about health care by 1939? Optimistic surveys of provision, such as the 1944 White Paper, highlighted causal links between health service improvements and reduced mortality or the better management of illness. Vitality in the voluntary sector and the potential of the developing public sector could also be stressed: coordinating their efforts to generalize health-care improvements was difficult but not impossible. Pessimistic views noted gaps, persistent variation and poor coordination of provision. Several remedial opportunities had been missed and the promotion of positive health, rather than sickness services, had hardly begun.

But where to begin? Discourse on a national health service began with the territorial, ideological and professional interests of participants rather than any consideration of health or well-being. The 1937 PEP Report noted the 'bewildering variety' of agencies responsible for services and the precondition of adequate nutrition and accommodation for improvements, centred upon GP-oriented services, regionally coordinated with the hospitals. This dovetailed with BMA proposals, dating from 1930 and restated in 1938, for an insurance-based service, available to all barring those paying for private medical care. The British Hospitals Association, concerned with the independence of its voluntary members, finally accepted the need for a national hospital service.[39] Their common ground was their opposition to socialized medicine, based on health centres and controlled by local authorities. This was promoted by the Socialist Medical Association and adopted by the Labour party in 1935, though the Trades Union Congress looked to more equitable service provision rather than organizational principles. The 1936 Committee on Scottish Health Services also favoured public services but, because the record of Scottish local authorities was poor and the threat of wartime emergencies was both urgent and real, state management of services and direct provision of hospitals soon featured here. An impending contribution from the Luftwaffe also committed the British government to regionally based emergency hospital schemes, as part of the state-funded wartime Emergency Medical Service. In this decisive step towards the NHS, 'the Luftwaffe achieved in months what had defeated politicians and planners for at least two decades'.[40]

There is another perspective. Popular suspicion of intrusive or bureaucratic health care, including Poor Law services, compulsory state health insurance and health visiting in the early 1900s, was strengthened by the experience of means testing in public and voluntary sectors between the wars. People expected to encounter illness and, considering their resources, sought forms of medical expertise and remedy. They endorsed improved medical services and better treatments, whatever other professional or ideological objectives these served. PEP and the 1940 Nuffield Reconstruction Survey noted the popularity of hospital contributory schemes precisely because they were neither intrusive nor commercial.[41] But did people resent less bureaucratic local authority or state facilities? Municipal appropriation of Poor Law infirmaries was endorsed where it signalled better facilities and non-stigmatized usage. The prospect of optimum standards of freely available treatment, provided by the state mainly from general taxation, was novel but met these traditional objectives. And heavy usage of the new NHS simply confirmed the extent of previous deprivations in health and medicine, experienced by those who did not shape policy and who had so few choices in medical markets.

NOTES

1 H. Hendrick, *Children, Childhood and English Society 1880–1990* (Cambridge, 1997), p. 21; H. Jones, *Health and Society in Twentieth-century Britain* (London, 1994), p. 75.
2 P. Weindling, 'From infectious to chronic diseases', in A. Wear, ed., *Medicine and Society* (Cambridge, 1992), pp. 303–16.
3 M. Pollard and S. B. Hyatt, *Sex, Gender and Health* (Cambridge, 1999), p. 104.
4 S. Szreter, 'The importance of social intervention in Britain's mortality decline *c*.1850–1914', *Social History of Medicine*, 1 (1988), p. 25; S. Guha, 'The importance of social intervention in England's mortality decline: the evidence reviewed', *Social History of Medicine*, 7 (1994), p. 101.
5 E.g. G. C. M. M'Gonigle and J. Kirby, *Poverty and Public Health* (London, 1936), p. 98. Evidence produced on heights as an indicator of improved nutrition in this period remains less eye-catching than reported social class differences in height and weight, but see R. Floud, K. Wachter and A. Gregory, *Height, Health and History* (Cambridge, 1990), pp. 306–24.
6 R. Cooter, *Surgery and Society in Peace and War* (London, 1990), pp. 105–36; A. Hardy, *Health and Medicine in Britain since 1860* (London, 2000), pp. 47–76.

7   A. Digby, *The Evolution of British General Practice 1850–1950* (Oxford, 1999), pp. 17, 222; I. Loudon and M. Drury, 'Some aspects of clinical care in general practice', in I. Loudon, C. Webster and J. Horder, *General Practice under the National Health Service 1948–1997* (Oxford, 1997), p. 100.

8   M. A. Crowther, *The Workhouse System 1834–1929* (London, 1981), p. 178.

9   N. Eder, *National Health Insurance and the Medical Profession in Britain* (New York, 1982), p. 360.

10 J. Brand, *Doctors and the State* (Baltimore, 1965), p. 231; R. Porter, *Disease, Medicine and Society* (Cambridge, 1993), p. 57.

11 P. Vaughan, 'Secret remedies in the late nineteenth and early twentieth centuries', in M. Saks, ed., *Alternative Medicine in Britain* (Oxford, 1992), p. 109; Saks, *Alternative Medicine*, p. 15.

12 J. C. Riley, *Sick, Not Dead* (Baltimore, 1997), p. 272.

13 Cf. R. Stevens, *Medical Practice in Modern England* (New Haven, Conn., 1966), p. 33.

14 A. Digby and B. Bosanquet, 'Doctors and patients, 1913–38', *Economic History Review*, 41 (1988), pp. 76–7.

15 B. Abel Smith, *A History of the Nursing Profession* (London, 1960), pp. 137, 139.

16 L. Bryder, 'The First World War: healthy or hungry', *History Workshop*, 24 (1987), pp. 141–55; J. M. Winter, *The Great War and the British People* (London, 1986).

17 Crowther, *Workhouse System*, p. 182; B. Abel Smith, *The Hospitals* (London, 1964), p. 267.

18 F. Honigsbaum, *The Struggle for the Ministry of Health 1914–19* (London, 1970).

19 J. Lewis, *What Price Community Medicine?* (Brighton, 1986), pp. 18–21.

20 N. Whiteside, 'Private agencies for public purposes', *Journal of Social Policy*, 12 (1983), pp. 165–94; F. Honigsbaum, 'The interwar health insurance scheme', *Journal of Social Policy*, 12 (1983), pp. 515–24.

21 Digby and Bosanquet, 'Doctors and patients', pp. 82–3.

22 Digby, *General Practice*, p. 214.

23 C. Kenner, *No Time for Women: Exploring Women's Health in the 1930s and Today* (London, 1985), p. 35; C. Webster, 'Healthy or hungry thirties?', *History Workshop*, 13 (1982), p. 122.

24 Cited in Webster, 'Thirties', p. 122.

25 M. S. Rice, *Working-class Wives* (1939; rpt. London, 1981), p. 92.

26 M. Powell, 'A tale of two cities: a critical evaluation of the geographical provision of healthcare before the NHS', *Public Administration*, 70, no. 1 (1992), pp. 67–80, 71.

27 S. Cherry, *Medical Services and the Hospitals in Britain, 1860–1939* (Cambridge, 1996), pp. 44–8, pp. 60–3.

28 M. Emrys-Roberts, *The Cottage Hospitals 1859–1990* (Motcombe, 1991).

29 G. Rivett, *The Development of the London Hospital System, 1823–1982* (London, 1986), p. 222; J. V. Pickstone, *Medicine and Industrial Society* (Manchester, 1985), p. 260.

30 Ministry of Health, *Report*, 19 (1937–8), pp. 76–7. Just eleven of these were by county councils, excluding Middlesex and Surrey.

31 M. Powell, 'Hospital provision before the NHS: a geographical study of the 1945 hospital surveys', *Social History of Medicine*, 5 (1992), pp. 483–504, 498–9; Sir George Godber participated in the wartime hospital surveys in Sheffield and was chief medical officer from 1960 to 1974.

32 K. Jones, *Asylums and After* (London, 1993), pp. 116, 124; A. T. Scull, *The Most Solitary of Afflictions* (New Haven, Conn., 1993), p. 362.

33 Political and Economic Planning, *Report on British Health Services* (London, 1937), pp. 275–6.

34 S. Cherry, 'Accountability, entitlement and control issues *c*.1860–1939', *Social History of Medicine*, 9 (1996), pp. 215–33.

35 Annual spending on hospitals and asylums (£ million, maintenance accounts)

1900	1.0	2.3	0.96	0.21	0.11	0.13
1911	1.8	3.9	1.25	0.38	0.17	0.14
1921	13.6	9.3	6.55	1.25	0.90	0.72
1931	16.1	10.8	9.75	1.29	1.31	0.98
1939	33.3	15.0	11.66	1.96	1.60	1.13

Sources: B. R. Mitchell, *British Historical Statistics* (Cambridge, 1988), XI Public finance, table 12, pp. 614, 616; table 15, pp. 626, 628; S. Cherry, 'Before the NHS: financing the voluntary hospitals 1900–1939', *Economic History Review*, 50 (1997), table 2, p. 311.

36 C. Webster, *The National Health Service: A Political History* (Oxford, 1988), table 1, p. 13.

37 *The Hospital*, 24 February 1900.

38 (H. Rees), *Hospital Almoners' Association Survey* (1941), p. 103.

39 British Hospitals Association, *Report* (1939–41), p. 11.

40 Webster, *National Health Service*, p. 6.

41 PEP, *Report*, p. 213; J. Harris, 'Did British workers want the welfare state?', in J. M. Winter, ed., *The Working Class in Modern British History* (London, 1983), pp. 200–14.

FURTHER READING

Bryder, L., 'The First World War: healthy or hungry', *History Workshop*, 24 (1987), pp. 141–55.

Cherry, S., *Medical Services and the Hospitals in Britain, 1860–1939* (Cambridge, 1996).

Cherry, S., 'Before the NHS: financing the voluntary hospitals 1900–1939', *Economic History Review*, 50 (1997), pp. 305–26.

Cooter, R., *Surgery and Society in Peace and War* (London, 1990).

Crowther, M. A., *The Workhouse System 1834–1929* (London, 1981).

Digby, A., *The Evolution of British General Practice 1850–1950* (Oxford, 1999).

Gordon, P. and Humphries, S., *A Labour of Love: The Experience of Parenthood in Britain 1900–50* (London, 1993).

Guha, S., 'The importance of social intervention in England's mortality decline: the evidence reviewed', *Social History of Medicine*, 7 (1994), pp. 89–113.

Hardy, A., *Health and Medicine in Britain since 1860* (London, 2000).

Hendrick, H., *Children, Childhood and English Society 1880–1990* (Cambridge, 1997).

Honigsbaum, F., *The Struggle for the Ministry of Health 1914–19* (London, 1970).

Jones, H., *Health and Society in Twentieth-century Britain* (London, 1994).

Jones, K., *Asylums and After* (London, 1993).

Kenner, C., *No Time for Women: Exploring Women's Health in the 1930s and Today* (London, 1985).

Levitt, I., *Poverty and Welfare in Scotland 1890–1948* (London, 1988).

Lewis, J., *What Price Community Medicine?* (Brighton, 1986).

Loudon, I. and Drury, M., 'Some aspects of clinical care in general practice', in I. Loudon, C. Webster and J. Horder, eds, *General Practice under the National Health Service 1948–1997* (Oxford, 1997), pp. 92–127.

Political and Economic Planning, *Report on British Health Services* (London, 1937).

Pollard, M. and Hyatt, S. B., *Sex, Gender and Health* (Cambridge, 1999).

Powell, M., 'Hospital provision before the NHS', *Social History of Medicine*, 5 (1992), pp. 483–504.

Rice, M. S., *Working-class Wives* (1939; rpt. London, 1981).

Riley, J. C., *Sick, Not Dead* (Baltimore, 1997).

Scull, A. T., *The Most Solitary of Afflictions* (New Haven, Conn., 1993).

Szreter, S., 'The importance of social intervention in Britain's mortality decline *c*.1850–1914', *Social History of Medicine*, 1 (1988), pp. 1–37.

Vaughan, P., 'Secret remedies in the late nineteenth and early twentieth centuries', in M. Saks, ed., *Alternative Medicine in Britain* (Oxford, 1992), pp. 101–11.

Webster, C., 'Healthy or hungry thirties?', *History Workshop*, 13 (1982), pp. 110–29.

Webster, C., 'Labour and the NHS', in N. Rupke, ed., *Science, Politics and the Public Good* (London, 1988), pp. 184–202.

Winter, J. M., *The Great War and the British People* (London, 1986).

Chapter Twenty-Six

Education, 1900–1939

ROY LOWE

The period 1900 to 1939 may seem, on the face of it, to have been one of consolidation for the education system in Britain. The previous thirty years had seen the coming of universal elementary schooling in all parts of the British Isles, a restructuring of secondary education, the appearance of new civic universities and the origins of a system of further education as well as a complete overhaul of the administration of education. Similarly, the period following the Second World War was to experience further dramatic change. After 1944 secondary schooling became universal, the university sector as well as further education expanded dramatically and changed almost beyond recognition in character, whilst the administration of education was revamped by the 1944 Education Act. Beyond this, as its economic and social significance became increasingly apparent, education itself became nothing short of a political football before the end of the century.

What, then, of the years 1900 to 1939? As will be argued in this chapter, they witnessed equally significant transformations of the education system and the politics of education was no less fiercely contested than had been the case in the late nineteenth century and was to be the case after the Second World War. But what is perhaps most significant is the ways in which educational developments reflected and echoed the social and economic changes of the period as well as the increasingly significant regional and local variations that were such a deep-seated feature of twentieth-century life in Britain. It is impossible to comprehend fully the nature and significance of educational change without first considering the nature of the society in which it occurred, and this is nowhere more true than of the United Kingdom during the early twentieth century.

The transformation of Britain that took place in the early twentieth century had several interlinked characteristics, all of significance for education. First, the economy continued to diversify and become more complex, posing ever-more difficult challenges for the education system. The old industries of the first industrial revolution had already defined the character of many northern towns and cities, and these were sustained by the demands of world war from 1914 to 1918. Alongside them the new industries of the late nineteenth century (petrochemicals, car manufacture and electronics particularly) became increasingly important. They had their own new localities for growth and made new demands of schooling, requiring a more highly trained labour force than had the industries of the first industrial revolution.

At the same time, the accelerating growth of the tertiary sector of the economy, of the service industries, led to a proliferation of new jobs in minor professional positions, in banking, accountancy, insurance, as well as the increasing bureaucratization of existing industries. Institutions such as banks became larger in scale, their working practices more bureaucratized and their labour force gendered. There were parallels right across these growing service industries. All of this preconditioned the demands made locally of schools and institutions of further and higher education by potential employers and by parents.[1]

These economic changes meant the continuing transformation of the social structure itself. Suburbanization continued apace, with many urban areas assuming nothing short of a new character between 1900 and 1939. The addition of new housing stock at the periphery of existing towns meant not just the rise of commuting for the first time in modern Britain on any significant scale (transport systems underwent their own transformations during these years), but also the adoption of new lifestyles as the closely interdependent extended families of the nineteenth century gave way to smaller nuclear groupings with new social and cultural loyalties. For the first time council estates began to appear around the larger cities.[2] The redefinition of social class that this involved had clear implications for schooling. It meant, in particular, that the demand for different forms of schooling was unevenly distributed.

This all linked to the ongoing secularization of society. If the nineteenth century had been that in which almost every educational initiative was underpinned by the theme of interdenominational rivalry, the twentieth was that in which the religious issue became an anachronism, as the churches steadily lost their hold over the popular psyche and ultimately their influence on the political process. But 'the religious issue' continued to be reflected in the structure and administration of the education system, particularly since the turn-of-the-century educational settlement ensured the survival of the dual system by allowing support for church schools from local rates. Each of these phenomena was important for schooling as educators found themselves confronted by changing expectations of and attitudes towards schooling.

It is important to make two further preliminary points about the social transformations of these years. First, as has been hinted above, they were not geographically uniform. If anything Britain became more socially diverse as the regional impact of all these changes began to be felt. Some localities became those with high expectations of schooling, with higher staying-on rates after the end of compulsory schooling, with a more natural assumption of access to university and with a higher uptake on school places in the private rather than the state sector. This also correlated with the geographical distribution of public and preparatory schools, which were predominantly in the home counties of England.

Second, these transformations were not uniform over time. It is possible to identify several 'sub-periods' even within this relatively brief span of years. The Edwardian 'building boom' gave way to a relative economic decline in the years immediately preceding the First World War. Whilst the war itself involved an overstimulation of the old industries, it led almost inexorably to a period of heightened expectations but of economic instability and turmoil. In some cities, because of their commitment to new industries (Coventry and Bristol are striking examples), the high unemployment rates that afflicted south Wales and the industrial north seemed light years away. It was only during the late 1930s that the economic upturn that was reflected among other things in large new Art Deco school buildings was fairly widely felt. This patchwork over time and by region makes any simplistic account of educational change an impossibility.

In this diverse and quickly changing situation what happened within education was, quite simply, that the state, with new agencies and greater powers than ever before, sought to control the working of schools and colleges and to impose a template of national homogeneity which was increasingly obsolescent and increasingly dysfunctional. Thus, it is possible to argue, many of the key issues that have been central to educational debate in the period since the Second World War and that reverberate today stem from, or are in large part explicable in the light of, what happened in the early years of the twentieth century. This argument, which is central to this chapter, will be worked out by showing, first, the growing forces of centralization within British education, second, some of the developments that took place at local level appearing to defy increasingly national planning, and finally, ways in which different sectors of the educational provision took on their own characteristics during these years. In conclusion, this chapter will try to examine and explain the overall educational and social outcomes of these changes.

The Making of Educational Policy

At the beginning of the twentieth century, the setting up of the Board of Education and of the new local education authorities (LEAs), together with new political groupings, led to a redefinition and a restatement of educational policy in the United Kingdom, ushering in a fairly lengthy period during which, by and large, people had faith in the efficacy of popular schooling. It is appropriate, therefore, to examine first the growth of government, the state and 'statist' thinking in respect of education during these years.

The establishment of the Board of Education in 1899 proved to be a hinge-point in this respect. Its Consultative Committee became an important agency for devising educational policies in the shadow of civil servants and of the government of the day. The appointment of Robert Morant as first permanent secretary of the Board meant that a firm hand was at the tiller of policy making from the start. Under his influence, the Consultative Committee set about confirming the need to differentiate boys' and girls' curricula in state schools. It also worked to confirm the strict divide between elementary and secondary education, preserving the nineteenth-century practice of having two sets of regulations, one for each type of school.[3] The survival of this element of policy into the twentieth century was to have vital repercussions when secondary education became universal after 1944. Once the significance of the Consultative Committee had been established, it continued to play a major part in policy making throughout the period under review. In 1924 it reported on the use of intelligence tests, which were fast becoming the tool used by local authorities to select pupils for secondary schooling. In 1926 its report on *The Education of the Adolescent* set a seal of official approval on the steady drift towards universal secondary schooling. A few years later it gave support to a more 'child-centred' approach to elementary education. Finally, in 1938, its report on *Secondary Education* provided the template for a tripartite system of secondary schooling to be set up in the years following the 1944 Act. This indirect influence on policy was given a cutting edge through a series of circulars and directives from the Board. Morant used these ruthlessly to impose his personal vision of what popular education might mean in practice. In particular his 1904 *Regulations on Secondary Education*, although in force for only three years, imposed a curriculum on secondary schools that survived throughout the century and was, as numerous commentators have pointed out, echoed in the 1988 National Curriculum. Further, the 1907 Free Place Regulations, which insisted that any secondary school in receipt of public finance must offer at least a quarter of its places to non-fee-paying pupils, placed the eleven-plus scholarship at the heart of educational debate for the following century. Changes to the school building regulations in 1907 meant that the appearance of schools was to change irrevocably, with cross-ventilated classrooms and quadrangular plans becoming the new orthodoxy.[4]

From 1902 the new LEAs, established by the Education Act of that year, were able to carry more political clout than the smaller and far more numerous school boards they replaced. Fourteen of these new local authorities, aware of their responsibility under the terms of the 1902 Act for the provision of secondary schooling, commissioned Michael Sadler to write research reports which reflected his rather patrician vision of a three-tier system of secondary schools. These reports proved widely influential and undoubtedly helped keep the torch of selectivity burning brightly into the new century. On some issues pioneering local authorities ran ahead of national policy and forced its modification. This was the case in respect of school building design, of the provision of central and intermediate schools, of health care and of school meals provision.

There were other important agencies at work at this time establishing the view that it was the right and responsibility of the state to oversee and guarantee the provision of the people's education. At the start of the century the drive for 'national efficiency' was largely the brainchild of the Fabians, who saw education as one of the keys to its realization. Sidney Webb's vision of an educational 'capacity catching machine' also popularized the idea of identifying a meritocracy through the use of examinations.[5] Webb was one of the many intellectuals of this period who fell under the influence of leading eugenicists such as Francis Galton. His Eugenic Education Society, with its focus on hereditarianism and on those inborn characteristics that distinguished individuals and ethnic groups, led to the downplaying of 'environmentalist' approaches to child-rearing and to an emphasis on the need to select and to separate at every level of education.[6] Another leading eugenicist was Cyril Burt. He and a group of associates were among the country's first educational psychologists. As one of the high priests of intelligence testing Burt had a massive impact on educational policy making, at both national and local level, whilst at the same time distorting the development of educational psychology in Britain, so that it quickly took on a very different aspect from that discipline as studied elsewhere in Europe.[7]

But perhaps the most significant agency impacting upon educational policy in Britain during our period was the Labour party. Slow to develop coherent identified policies right across the political spectrum (for the very good reason that it was an amalgam of pre-existing organizations with no clearly identified shared policy), the

Labour party set about the process of policy definition in earnest after the First World War.[8] R. H. Tawney authored *Secondary Education for All* to articulate the party's aims. Whilst the slogan he gave the party seemed in itself to be radical enough, Tawney's own background, as a lifelong Christian socialist steeped in the gradualism of the Oxbridge-dominated adult education movement, ensured that the details of policy adopted left scope for a system of secondary schooling which, one way or another, would contain within it significant divisions and hierarchies. Although Tawney's goal was equality, the pervasive impact of the psychometrists and the eugenicists meant that it was all too easy to construe equality in practice as equality of opportunity to pursue an appropriate track within the education system. This blurring resulted in long-term fissures and tensions in respect of educational policy making within the Labour party that were to be of massive significance given the steadily growing perception of the importance of educational policy at the heart of the party's agenda. It also helps explain why, in the post-war years, the party's implementation of universal secondary schooling was through a tripartite system that earned immediate censure from groups to the left of the party.

The overall impact of all of these agencies was to confirm the widespread belief in society at large that it was the job of the state, whether through local or national agencies, to take responsibility for the provision of education and that, by and large, solutions could be applied nationally. Underpinning the debate, and the whole process of policy making in education, was the general acceptance that education was a public good, that its effects were, on the whole, beneficial, and that it was one of the keys to the establishment of a better society and a successful economy. It is hardly surprising, therefore, that the first half of the twentieth century saw virtually no deschooling movement, but that dissent was centred on the need to provide forms of schooling that were more progressive and more child-centred. The strength of the deschooling movement since the Second World War, and in recent years in particular, may derive in part from its almost complete absence between 1900 and 1939. This is why the word 'statist' was used earlier in this section. In brief, policy making in education during these years can be summarized as the high point for 'statist' solutions, policies which saw the state as paramount in educational policy making and which had few qualms about the uniform application of policy across the country as a whole.[9]

The Structure and Development of Education

Elementary education had become universal by the end of the nineteenth century. The key issue in the early twentieth century was precisely what form it should take, although it is probably true to say that, for the vast majority of children passing through the elementary schools during these years, very little appeared to change. The Revised Code, although greatly extended, had placed a premium on the three Rs, on the core curriculum, and had marked out the Inspectorate as figures of authority rather than mentors to most teachers. Often working with little guidance on how to proceed beyond their own memories of schooling and some words of advice from their head teacher (who was usually male), elementary schoolteachers remained repetitious, heavily dependent on drill, often focused on arithmetical tables, basic literacy and numeracy, and the development of a good writing hand. By the time of the Second World War almost all schools had access to pen and ink for their pupils, visual aids were few, and the overall atmosphere of the elementary classroom was one of formality. Corporal punishment and caning remained the norm. Probably the most significant change was a steady drift away from the nineteenth-century practice of separating boys and girls towards mixed classrooms, although, as will be argued below, this did not necessarily mean uniformity of curriculum.

The tone of the Board of Education was permissive: its first handbook for elementary schoolteachers appeared in 1905 and it stressed that 'the only uniformity of practice the Board . . . desire to see . . . is that each teacher shall think for himself, and work out for himself such methods of teaching as may use his powers to best advantage'. This was in tune with much educational thinking at this time. Numerous 'progressives', perhaps most notably Maria Montessori (whose work was available in translation in English from 1912), sought to place the need of the child at the heart of classroom practice. As Richard Selleck has shown, there were numerous educational experiments along these lines, mostly (but not all) in the private sector.

But for the vast majority the realities were very different. The growing prevalence of eleven-plus testing to select pupils for secondary schools led to greater resort to streaming in elementary schools. Although the half-time system was ended by the 1918 Education Act, so that no pupils had exemption from school below the statutory leaving age, the realities of the slump, and in particular the 1921 Geddes cuts and the 1931 May Committee retrenchment, meant that there was little scope for experimentation of any kind in the elementary sector. True, the period saw some consolidation of the school meals service and of the medical inspection and treatment of schoolchildren, but the overall picture of elementary schools during this period is a bleak one. This was relieved only by a growing number of experiments in higher elementary education during the mid- and late 1930s as local authorities struggled to implement the 1926 Hadow recommendation that there should be a break in schooling at eleven years of age. In so doing they provided the template for a cheap version of universal secondary education after 1944, when most of these became secondary modern schools, with all that that implied for selectivity and differentiation.

Economic stringency also meant that there was to be no major shift in the pattern of teacher training during the first half of the twentieth century. Although the pupil–teacher system effectively collapsed during the first few years of the twentieth century, and several of the new LEAs made efforts to set up teacher training colleges, it was Morant's introduction of the 'student–teacher' scheme in 1907 which in reality ensured that most elementary teachers were trained through a system analogous to the recently discarded pupil–teacher scheme. In place until 1937, and used by some LEAs beyond that date, the student–teacher scheme ensured that the provision of teachers was inexpensive and their training largely 'on the job'.[10] It can be of little surprise, given this parsimonious approach to teacher education, that there was relatively little pedagogic innovation in elementary schools between 1900 and 1939.

It can hardly be surprising, too, that in this situation elementary school teaching became increasingly the domain of lower-middle-class women. At the turn of the century over 100,000 female teachers were recognized by the Board of Education. Although pay levels were ahead of those available to women in factories, and teaching was seen as a 'respectable' profession, the establishment of the Equal Pay League in 1904 placed the issue of the remuneration of female teachers at the heart of the politics of education for the first half of the twentieth century. This initiative led to the establishment of the National Union of Women Teachers (NUWT) in 1919 and to a semi-permanent fracturing, along gender lines, of teacher unionism.[11]

If anything, given the fears of racial deterioration which were widespread after the Boer War, there was also a reinforcement of the gendering of the elementary school curriculum itself. This gendering had already been evident during the nineteenth century but was sustained into the twentieth both by government policy and practice on the ground. The Board of Education's 1905 *Suggestions for Teachers* stressed that 'the course of instruction in household management must include cookery, laundry work and practical housewifery . . . to fit girls, by repeated practice, to undertake when they leave school the various household duties which fall more or less to all women'. This was reinforced by a succession of school textbooks which were becoming increasingly available in the elementary sector. The *Royal Princess Reader*, published in 1901 and widely used in elementary schools, included a chapter on 'obligingness', a female attribute which schoolgirls were to aspire to: they were to become 'the good fairy' who made herself indispensable to the rest of the family. Thus, in summary, those changes that did take place in the elementary schools can only be seen as sustaining problems and issues that had developed during the nineteenth century into the twentieth.

In contrast, the secondary sector underwent significant change between 1900 and 1939, as the impact of 'second-phase' industrialization was felt by the education system. The need for generally higher levels of education resulted in a steady drift towards universal secondary schooling, so that, when it came, the 1944 Act was only legitimating what was already happening in practice on the ground.

The first phase of this early twentieth-century growth pattern involved the establishment of municipal secondary schools in most of the industrial towns and cities between 1902 and 1914. In 1904 there were a total of 575 secondary schools recognized for grant by the Board of Education. By 1914 this figure had risen to 1,027. This facilitated, inadvertently, the stratification of secondary education that commentators like Sadler were calling for, since few if any of the municipal schools were seen as rivalling the pre-existing grammar schools in either prestige, intake or academic standards.

This was also to have a massive impact for girls, because many of these municipal secondary schools were intended for female pupils. In 1904, 292 of these recognized schools were for boys and only ninety-nine for girls. Of the rest, which were returned as coeducational, almost all ran as two separate schools (one for boys and one for girls) under one roof. By the outbreak of the First World War, these figures had been transformed. Now there were 349 recognized girls' schools alongside the 397 for boys, with 281 coeducational. Thus, the municipal secondary school was the main vehicle for the expansion of girls' secondary schooling. So, almost by accident, girls' secondary education (with the exception of a few major public and GPDST schools) came to be seen as of lower status than that of boys. It was an inheritance that took the best part of a century to eradicate.

The development of separate secondary schooling for boys and girls made it possible for there to be an even more marked distinction of girls' curricula in the secondary sector than was the case in the elementary schools. During the Edwardian period the Board of Education took an increasingly close interest in the curriculum of the girls' secondary school. Its 1904 Regulations spelt out that 'a common curriculum for both boys and girls will not as a rule be approved'. For girls 'a practical training for home duties' was to be the norm. A few years later the Board was advocating that housework might be allowed to substitute for mathematics in girls' schools and that matriculation examinations in domestic science could be introduced. Whilst there might, during the previous century, have been numerous pioneering Victorian headmistresses who would have opposed any such trend, there were a growing number of heads during the Edwardian era who both supported this tendency and promoted it in their own schools. In 1911 L. M. Faithfull, headmistress of Cheltenham, wrote that there had been, in recent years, 'a widespread movement' to bring the secondary education of girls into relation with their future work as homemakers. 'We want our girls to grow up into sensible, practical, methodical women, able to direct, intelligently and practically, the manifold duties of the home.' Similarly, at Manchester High School for Girls, Sara Burstall introduced both technical and domestic education, arguing that mathematics should be kept to a minimum for girls 'since it does not underlie their activities as it does so many of the activities of men'. Burstall was clearly influenced by the ideas of the eugenicists, going on to add that, for her, 'evolutionary ideas' made it vital to use the girls' schools to protect the progress of the race. Thus the expansion of secondary education in the years before the First World War was only achieved at the cost of its becoming more clearly gendered than ever before.[12]

The reality of the development of secondary education during the interwar years contained its own inherent contradictions and these were to set the agenda for the politics of secondary schooling for the rest of the century. On the one hand, there were clear signs of investment in secondary education, reflecting the growing demand from the new middle classes for some sort of secondary schooling for their children. Manchester Grammar School, King Edward's, Birmingham, Bolton School, King George VI School, Southport, Queen Mary's, Lytham and Merchant Taylor's School, Northwood, were among the better known of a large number of secondary schools that relocated to new suburban sites in magnificent, expensively designed premises.[13] But, at the same time, many of the local education authorities of the growing industrial and commercial towns were pre-empting the growth of secondary education by establishing either central schools or senior elementary schools to meet the growing demand for staying on within the elementary school regulations, a ploy which was, of course, cheaper than investing in fully fledged secondary schools. The result was a patchwork of provision for pupils of eleven years and above that anticipated the ways in which universal secondary education was to be realized after the war. The precedent of differing class size, different levels of investment and contrasting prestige made it relatively easy for the post-war LEAs to defend a tripartite system of universal secondary education (involving grammar, technical and secondary modern schools) as being an improvement on what had gone before.

Similarly, in respect of post-school education, the first part of the twentieth century witnessed a confirmation of class and status divisions which have clouded the debate on higher education ever since. On the one hand, the growing demand for some form or other of higher education (which stemmed naturally from this growing system of secondary education and the changing demands of the workplace) was met by the recognition of the nineteenth-century university colleges as fully fledged universities in their own right. The redbrick universities became one of the key tokens of the respectability of the major industrial cities. Birmingham was the first to be given a charter in 1900; by 1914 the others had followed suit.

However, on the other hand, the urgent necessity to provide more intensive technical education, particularly in those parts of the country feeling the full impact of 'second-phase' industrialization, was met more in the new technical colleges funded from the rates than by the civic universities. Much of that provision was through part-time evening work and did not receive the recognition of full university awards. Ironically, the redbrick universities, all of which had been founded on a tide of rhetoric that emphasized their contribution to their local economies, at the moment of full recognition, without exception, fought to model the curricula of Oxford and Cambridge. Their quickest expansion was in Faculties of Arts, and, although several of them developed significant reputations for their work in the applied sciences, the view that the first duty of a university was to pursue 'pure' knowledge for its own sake became widely accepted during this period and coloured the major reports on higher education that appeared immediately after the Second World War.[14] The binary system that developed subsequently, and which so bedevilled the face of British higher education in the later twentieth century, owed its origins to the policy initiatives of the early twentieth century.

It is worth adding, too, that the period 1900 to 1939 was the golden age of the civic universities as regional institutions. Oxford and Cambridge, London and Durham were already established nationally, drawing their students from across the United Kingdom and from abroad. This was not so with the redbricks. They provided, until the coming of mandatory student grants after the Second World War, the apex of these emergent regional education systems. Many of their students remained non-residential. Most of their graduates found their way into the local professions.[15] The conversion of their day training departments into fully fledged Education departments during the early twentieth century confirmed the rift between elementary and secondary schooling in modern Britain as well as the gender imbalance between the two sectors, with the more prestigious secondary sector attracting a far higher proportion of male entrants to teaching. The student teachers who went on to teach in the elementary schools were predominantly female; the majority of entrants to the one-year postgraduate teacher training year were, until the Second World War at least, mostly male, although this did prove an increasingly attractive route for female graduates from the growing Arts departments of these new universities.

The beginning of the twentieth century also saw the adult education movement take on its modern form, and this, too, involved a series of social and political tensions. The sponsorship of extension lecturing by both Oxford and Cambridge in the closing years of the nineteenth century resulted in numerous industrial townships developing a clientele from among the growing lower middle class for this sort of teaching. Oxbridge summer schools gave students a taste for what the universities had to offer. Equally, the prospect of developing this work held out the prospect of Oxford and Cambridge being seen to widen their catchment without having to undergo radical internal change. Extension lecturers such as R. H. Tawney developed the tutorial class to give greater continuity to extension work, and Rochdale in Lancashire and Longton in north Staffordshire became the two centres where this mode of delivery was first tried. Meanwhile an extension student, W. H. Mansbridge, set about the establishment of an organization (the Workers' Educational Association) which became the vehicle for much of this work. By 1910 the Board of Education had offered funding support, so that, within a few years, an educational movement had appeared that seemed to offer some prospect for at least a few of its cohort drawing close to Oxbridge.[16]

Significantly, political content was disallowed within this movement, an omission which left the growing trade union movement, increasingly drawn to syndicalist ideas, with no viable educational outlet of its own. The establishment of Ruskin College at Oxford in 1899, with its encouragement of the social sciences and of trade union representatives, appeared to be set fair to meet this want. Ruskin quickly became the focus of a national system of Labour Colleges. But Oxford University's determined take-over and incorporation of Ruskin College in 1908 served both to damp down the sharp contrast between these two strands of the nascent adult education movement and also to make it far more difficult for oppositional political ideas to be disseminated through educational agencies. The muted theme of education for its own sake became that which predominated in adult education for most of the twentieth century: self-improvement rather than political effectiveness was the watchword.

An Emerging Politics of Education

It will be seen from this account of the developing education system that its politics was hardly likely to be uncontroversial during these years. In reality the period witnessed a steadily increasing definition of the main lines of educational policy at governmental level, and much of this definition was in response to the lobbying of the increasingly articulate labour movement. At the start of the century, the debate was largely monopolized by the Fabians, dedicated to national efficiency and the establishment of meritocratic routes through the education system. Webb's publication in 1899 of a Fabian tract, *The Education Muddle and the Way Out*, argued for 'local administrative unity' in education and placed him for the next few years at the heart of the debate on what form the new local authorities should take and what their duties should be. He was also closely involved in the negotiations leading to the establishment of the London County Council Education Committee as part of the 1902 Education Act. Set alongside these attempts to develop a more rational structure of educational administration, there was a growing sense that the schools should be responsible for more than simply instruction. Initiatives taken in several towns and cities (Bradford and London were leading exemplars) resulted in a patchwork introduction of school meals and medical inspection, leading in some cases to treatment. Margaret Macmillan was a pioneer in this movement and doctors such as Alfred Eichholz and Ralph Crowley were also leading figures. Individuals such as these became well known for their work in the provinces but later in their careers moved to London and became influential behind the scenes. Their life histories reflected the increasing significance of London politics and the centrality of educational policy making at this time.

Similarly, the drive for more hygienic school buildings, which resulted in major changes to the building regulations before the First World War, stemmed from an alliance of members of the medical and architectural professions and began largely in the provinces. The move away from central hall schools towards quadrangular building plans with all classrooms being cross-ventilated was largely the outcome of a one-man crusade by George Reid, the chief medical officer for Staffordshire, which he communicated to fellow enthusiasts working in other parts of Britain.

Much of this was meat and drink to the nascent Labour party, and its first significant electoral gains in 1906 resulted in legislation on both issues. Local authorities were given the power to provide school meals as a result of a private members motion in 1906, and a year later the Board of Education's medical department was established with the brief to monitor the health of the nation's children. Thus the key policy shift of the Edwardian period was undoubtedly the widespread recognition that the physical welfare of children as well as their instruction was the proper preserve of educators.

The 1902 Education Act, by putting the church schools on the rates, also regenerated the sectarian conflicts that had raged throughout the nineteenth century. Before the end of the year the National Passive Resistance League had been set up and the government found itself confronted by the prospect of having to jail defaulting local councillors in strongly nonconformist rural areas when they refused to implement the 1902 legislation. The outcome was the 1904 Local Authorities Default Act giving the government power to insist on the full implementation of the legislation. Thus, for a few years at least, the power struggle between educational modernizers and traditionalists appeared to have a sectarian undertow and gave renewed life to tensions between Anglicans and nonconformists in respect of the provision of education.

But it was not until after the First World War that the Labour party set about the process of policy definition in earnest. Arthur Henderson's attempt to bring coherence to the party's policy making resulted in the establishment at the end of 1918 of the Advisory Committee on Education, and it was this committee which commissioned R. H. Tawney to develop a coherent set of proposals. His *Secondary Education for All*, which appeared in 1922, not only gave the party a clear and identifiable policy target, but also had the effect of shifting the issues of the extent and structure of secondary schooling to the heart of the educational debate. If elementary education had been the key issue of the nineteenth century, Tawney's publication confirmed that the debate had now moved on, irreversibly, towards the secondary arena.

It was not many years before some party members began to look beyond Tawney's laudable and widely accepted general aim, and to worry that his gradualism might result in various forms of secondary schooling being developed alongside each other. Tawney served on the Consultative Committee under Hadow and was one of the authors of the 1926 report on *The Education of the Adolescent*. This stressed that 'there are diversities of gifts, and for that reason there must be diversity of educational provision. Equality, in short, is not identity . . . education should not attempt to press different types of character and intelligence into a single mould'. Although the Hadow Report won plaudits from the press, the National Union of Teachers' response was more muted, and involved a plea for the establishment of multilateral schools to pre-empt the need to select pupils for different kinds of secondary education.

Thus emerged the great educational issue of the mid-twentieth century, the question of selection for secondary education. In 1930 the National Association of Labour Teachers, which had emerged from the 1927 take-over by Communists of the Teachers' Labour League, published *Education: A Policy*, calling for 'common schools' and a broadening of the curriculum of the existing grammar schools even if it was at the cost of academic success. Throughout the 1930s there was a growing feeling, particularly among the more politically active members of the teaching profession, that the multilateral school was the key to delivering universal secondary schooling. The National Association of Labour Teachers, which had a strong London power base, Barbara Drake being one of its key activists, was ideally placed to promote these ideas in Labour circles. Changes in the membership of the party's Education Advisory Committee in 1937 saw Drake, Brian Simon and Lionel Elvin drafted in, and by the beginning of 1939 they had reworked Labour party policy to involve a commitment to 'the general development of multilateral schools as the goal of a long-term policy'. Thus, by the end of the period under review, the main lines of post-war development were already anticipated.

Complicating this issue, even within the labour movement, was the response of the National government to the economic crisis of the early 1930s. As part of the programme of cuts in educational expenditure, in 1932 it was announced that the 1907 Free Place Regulations, which for a generation had ensured the availability of grammar school places for at least some children whose parents had been only to elementary school, were to be discontinued. Instead, a less expensive sliding scale of grant support was to be introduced which offered no guarantees of working-class entry to the grammar schools and seemed likely to result in places at these schools becoming far too expensive for many parents. For many in Labour circles, the issue immediately became that of defending working-class access to the grammar schools, and thereby implicitly, defending the grammar schools themselves.

Thus, during the interwar period, there was a common consensus that education in general, and secondary schooling in particular, were for the general good, but no clarity or common agreement, even among radicals, of what form they should take. In this confusion lay the seeds of the educational politics of the post-Second World War era. It has been argued that struggles over access to secondary education, over its content and over who should control it, which reached their zenith at this time, resulted in a more or less complete neglect of alternatives, a loss of any sense of popular possession of schooling and, ultimately, in widespread disappointment at the failure of state education to transform society in the ways that many of its supporters had hoped.[17]

In this sense the period 1900 to 1939 may be seen as the high point for this 'statism' in respect of educational politics. It was easy to construe Tawney and the radical alliance of Labour workers and schoolteachers that he gathered around him as heroic figures in a social class war, fighting a series of rearguard actions against educational cuts imposed by a succession of Conservative-minded governments. But it should not be overlooked that their ultimately successful fight for universal secondary schooling may have been won at the cost of a sense of vision as to just what popular education might mean in practice.

The first half of the twentieth century was the period when educational solutions were increasingly imposed on the populace rather than derived from them, when templates of what constituted a sound education were drawn up with growing confidence by administrators and politicians, but when social and economic development was such as to make uniform provision more and more inappropriate and questionable. In different parts of the United Kingdom, there were growing contrasts in the educational provision as local education authorities responded each in its own way to its particular situation. Wide disparities in the provision of secondary school places, in the uses to which selective and intelligence tests were put and in the development of ancillary services became more apparent as the period progressed. The essentially regional nature of the economic slump of the interwar years served only to heighten these differences.

Those involved in the debate on education between 1900 and 1939 may well have come up with solutions to some, if not all, of the problems of the late nineteenth century, but in so doing, they generated the educational crisis of the modern era. That is why it is so important for us to have some understanding of both the development and the politics of education between 1900 and 1939.

NOTES

1   H. Perkin, *The Rise of Professional Society: England since 1880* (London, 1989).
2   F. M. L. Thompson, ed., *The Rise of Suburbia* (Leicester, 1982).
3   N. Daglish, *Education Policy Making in England and Wales: The Crucible Years, 1895–1911* (London, 1996), pp. 405–11.
4   M. Seaborne and R. Lowe, *The English School: Its Architecture and Organisation, 1870–1970* (London, 1977), chs 4 and 5.
5   E. J. T. Brennan, 'Educational engineering with the Webbs', *History of Education*, 1, no. 2 (1972).
6   D. J. Kevles, *In the Name of Eugenics* (Harmondsworth, 1985); R. A. Soloway, *Demography and Degeneration: Eugenics and the Declining Birth Rate in Twentieth-century Britain* (Chapel Hill, NC, 1995).
7   L. S. Hearnshaw, *Cyril Burt, Psychologist* (London, 1979), esp. chs 3, 4, 5 and 7.
8   R. Barker, *Education and Politics, 1900–1951: A Study of the Labour Party* (Oxford, 1972), pp. 26–64.
9   See on this Centre for Contemporary Cultural Studies, *Unpopular Education: Schooling and Social Democracy in England since 1944* (London, 1981), pp. 33–57.
10 The significance of this scheme has recently been identified by Peter Cunningham and Phil Gardner: their book on the subject is forthcoming.
11 See F. Widdowson, *Going Up into the Next Class: Women and Elementary Teacher Training, 1840–1914* and D. M. Copelman, *London's Women Teachers: Gender, Class and Feminism, 1870–1930*.
12 C. Dyhouse, *Girls Growing Up in Late-Victorian and Edwardian England* (London, 1981).
13 Seaborne and Lowe, *The English School*, ch. 9.
14 R. D. Anderson, *Universities and Elites in Britain since 1800* (Basingstoke, 1992), ch. 3.
15 Ibid., ch. 4.
16 R. Fieldhouse et al., *A History of Modern British Adult Education* (Leicester, 1996), esp. ch. 7.
17 See Centre for Contemporary Cultural Studies, *Unpopular Education*, esp. pp. 41–6.

FURTHER READING

Anderson, R. D., *Universities and Elites in Britain since 1800* (Basingstoke, 1992).

Andrews, L., *The Education Act, 1918* (London, 1976).

Barker, R., *Education and Politics, 1900–1951: A Study of the Labour Party* (Oxford, 1972).

Bernbaum, G., *Social Change and the Schools, 1918–1944* (London, 1967).

Centre for Contemporary Cultural Studies, *Unpopular Education: Schooling and Social Democracy in England since 1944* (London, 1981).

Daglish, N., *Education Policy Making in England and Wales: The Crucible Years, 1895–1911* (London, 1996).

Dent, H. C., *1870–1970: Century of Growth in English Education* (London, 1970).

Dyhouse, C., *No Distinction of Sex? Women in British Universities, 1870–1939* (London, 1995).

Fieldhouse, R. et al., *A History of Modern British Adult Education* (Leicester, 1996).

Gordon, P., Aldrich, R. and Dean, D., *Education and Policy in England in the Twentieth Century* (London, 1991).

Gordon, P. and Lawton, D., *Curriculum Change in the Nineteenth and Twentieth Centuries* (London, 1978).

Green, A., *Education and State Formation* (London, 1990).

Hearnshaw, L. S., *Cyril Burt, Psychologist* (London, 1979).

Hurt, J. S., *Elementary Schooling and the Working Classes, 1860–1918* (London, 1979).

Parkinson, M., *The Labour Party and the Organisation of Secondary Education, 1918–1965* (London, 1970).

Rubinstein, D. and Simon, B., *The Evolution of the Comprehensive School, 1926–1966* (London, 1969).

Sanderson, M., *The Universities and British Industry, 1850–1970* (London, 1972).

Seaborne, M. and Lowe, R., *The English School: Its Architecture and Organisation, 1870–1970* (London, 1977).

Selleck, R. J. W., *The New Education: The English Background, 1870–1914* (London, 1968).

Selleck, R. J. W., *English Primary Education and the Progressives* (London, 1972).

Sherington, G., *English Education, Social Change and War, 1911–1920* (Manchester, 1981).

Simon, B., *Education and the Labour Movement, 1870–1920* (London, 1965).

Simon, B., *The Politics of Educational Reform, 1920–1940* (London, 1974).

Stephens, W. B., *Education in Britain, 1750–1914* (Basingstoke, 1998).

Sutherland, G., *Ability, Merit and Measurement: Mental Testing and English Education, 1880–1940* (Oxford, 1984).

Wooldridge, A., *Measuring the Mind: Education and Psychology in England, 1860–1990* (Cambridge, 1994).

Wright, A., *R. H. Tawney* (Manchester, 1987).

CHAPTER TWENTY-SEVEN

Crime, Police and Penal Policy

CLIVE EMSLEY

In 1931 the Buckinghamshire village of Brill had a population of 869, and the Census suggests that this was declining. Nevertheless, Brill remained the centre of a county petty sessions division covering fifteen other parishes with a total population of 4,803, and it had its own police station. The Occurrence Book of that police station[1] lists only eight offences for the year 1931: one instance of wilful damage and seven others listed initially as theft. Two of the latter remained undetected, but no other occurrence resulted in a prosecution. The victim of the wilful damage, a local gentleman, declined to prosecute the two boys, aged nine and seven, and two girls, aged six and four, who had broken his windows. In the detected instances of theft, one woman refused to prosecute the domestic servant who had taken clothing and bedlinen, a father would not prosecute his eleven-year-old daughter for taking a £1 note, and an uncle would not prosecute his fourteen-year-old nephew for taking three £1 notes. A spare wheel, reported stolen from a car, appeared rather to have fallen off in the road. Nineteen sheep reported stolen by their owner had, in fact, been properly delivered to his slaughterhouse by two of his labourers.

Brill cannot be taken as typical of England and Wales in the first third of the twentieth century, though its rural setting is reminiscent of that portrayed by many of the authors of popular detective fiction during the period. Nor is 1931 a typical year in the Occurrence Book of Brill police station. Usually there were rather more offences listed, including the occasional case of violent sexual assault. But if the setting resembles Agatha Christie's St Mary Mead, the murder rate was quite different. The Occurrence Book lists no murders and only one instance when murder was attempted; this was in 1904, when a seventy-year-old man tried to kill his equally aged wife. Christie's Miss Marple would have been bored to death in Brill, for here the predominant offence was petty theft and the usual offenders were juveniles and young people; to this extent the pattern of crime in Brill does appear similar to that of the rest of the country.

The Pattern of Crime

Crime is a slippery subject. There are crime statistics which politicians, police officers, the media and others use, and have used, to underline the success or failure of particular policies, to argue the case for more resources, to demonstrate, particularly amongst the young, a moral decline. But crime statistics are also one of the best ways of exposing the subject's slipperiness.

Since the early nineteenth century judicial statistics listing crimes and prosecutions have been published annually for England and Wales. The statistics for the period 1900 to 1925 show a relatively steady pattern of around 100,000 indictable crimes recorded as 'known to the police'. These then move steadily upwards to 150,000 in 1930, 250,000 in 1935 and 300,000 in 1939. If these statistics are computed as the number of offences per 100,000 of the population, the pattern appears as moving from around 250 at the beginning of the century to just under 600 before the Second World War. Violent offences, such as the murders by Dr Crippen (1910) or Alfred Arthur Rouse (1930) and the shootings and outrages involving foreign 'anarchists' between 1909 and 1911, are the kinds of crime that frighten people and provide the best copy for the media, but these were always few in number. The annual average of murders and attempted murders 'known to the police' hovered around 100 for each of these offences and, in both instances also, the figures showed signs of a slight decline towards the end of the 1930s. 'Malicious wounding' appeared to be on the increase from the mid-1920s, rising from around 500 cases each year to three times that number ten years later. This increase was assumed at the time to be largely the result of the introduction of summary jurisdiction; the assumption was that the move to the smaller magistrates' courts, where the proceedings were generally much quicker and less formal, had encouraged more prosecutions. Some of the sexual offences listed as known to the police increased during the interwar years, notably homosexual offences and indecent assaults on women and girls. Rape, however, was rather different; here the instance was roughly the same as that of murder, and relatively static. The overwhelming majority of those crimes known to the police for which an offender could be proceeded against on an indictment were not violent attacks on individuals but were crimes against property, particularly theft, and here the statistics show a steady rise, particularly after the First World War. There was also a significant rise in non-indictable offences. The biggest increase here was in traffic violations reflecting the growth of motor car ownership; but while there were periodic outcries against 'carbarians', few people viewed the 'road hog' as a dangerous, professional criminal.

The initial problem with the judicial statistics is that of the 'dark figure' of those crimes that were never reported. The logical assumption might be made that individuals reported crime in much the same way year after year, and that, therefore, the pattern remains relatively accurate in shape if not in absolute numbers. But this remains an assumption, and it may be that there were changes and events which encouraged the reporting of crime in much the same way that it might be supposed that there were changes and events which encouraged crime itself. The growth of insurance and the depression provide good but very different examples. It was suggested, in 1931, that the increasing popularity of insurance, together with the insurance companies' requirements that all thefts for which claims were made be reported to the police, had led to an increase of reported crimes; and, four years later, the commissioner of the Metropolitan Police argued that people became careless of their property once they were insured.[2] Economic hardship may have encouraged some among the desperate to steal. Those responsible for compiling the judicial statistics

in the Home Office thought that 'bad trade and hard times' in some degree contributed to larceny and fraud.[3] The stoppage in the colliery districts in 1926 was seen
similarly, and coal theft did indeed constitute half of the reported indictable crime in
Merthyr Tydfil in the mid-1920s.[4] At the same time, economic hardship among the
victims of petty theft, or the fear of potentially dangerous predators lurking amongst
the unemployed, might have acted as a spur to individuals to report incidents which,
at other times, they may have been inclined to ignore.

Methods of recording the statistics could also affect the numbers. In his annual
report as one of His Majesty's Inspectors of Constabulary in 1921, Sir Leonard
Dunning made the point that chief constables might be reluctant to record a crime
as 'known' if there was little chance of putting an offender alongside it.[5] Changes in
the collection of the statistics probably improved this situation. In a move considered at the time to be establishing increasing sophistication, the police were allowed
to record 'crimes known' that had been cleared up without a prosecution – because
the perpetrator had been convicted of another crime but had confessed to other
offences that were taken into consideration at the time of sentence; because
the victims declined to prosecute or assist in a prosecution; because the victims or
the offenders were dead. A Metropolitan Police order of 1 June 1932 directed that
the Suspected Stolen Book kept in London police stations be abolished. Much
missing property, probably stolen, was recorded in these books and omitted from the
offences known to the police forwarded to the Home Office for inclusion in the
judicial statistics. The order probably contributed to the statistical rise in indictable
offences from 159,278 in 1931 to 208,175 in the following year; but to what extent
it contributed is impossible to know. The commissioner of the Metropolitan Police
himself estimated 'that if the figures for 1932 had been compiled on the same basis
as for 1931, the increase would only have been about 5 per cent for all indictable
offences and about 12 per cent for cases of "breaking and entering"'.[6]

In addition to the problems of the dark figure of crime there is also the suspicion
that, on occasions, the police may have manipulated the crime figures to their own
ends, and even that the amount of money available to the criminal justice system may
have distorted the way in which offences were categorized and processed. At the
beginning of the century there was a relatively optimistic attitude in the Home Office
about the state of crime. The police forces, which numbered just under 200, were
essentially local organizations, but they received one half of their pay and clothing
costs from central government; and they were not considered a priority when it came
to the distribution of Treasury money. Following the police strikes of 1918 and 1919,
central government assumed responsibility for half of the total funding of the police,
and police officers themselves received a significant pay rise, but this led to pressures
to cut police numbers. It has been forcefully argued that provincial police forces
fought back against these pressures by raising crime statistics and thus raising the
profile of their tasks on the political agenda. A key figure in this process was Sir
Leonard Dunning, who wanted uniformity in the way that the police forces recorded
crime and who was convinced that crime, in particular theft, was rising. One of the
issues which he stressed in his evidence to the Desborough Committee on the Police
in 1919 was how the parsimony of local government police authorities sometimes
compelled their police forces to take no action against offenders simply because of
the costs of prosecution.[7]

Particular events and the direction of the economy are commonly assumed to affect the pattern of crime, yet even if the judicial statistics are accepted as giving an approximation of the pattern of crime, statistical relationships are not causal relationships, and the most common assumptions remain difficult to prove with statistics alone. In the immediate aftermath of the First World War, there were anxieties that, in the words of *The Times*, 'familiarity with bloodshed' had brought about a 'decreased regard for the sacredness of human life'.[8] 'In the terrible ordeal where a man is placed upon a pedestal the greater the number of lives taken by him,' declared the *Sheffield Mail*, 'it is not easy, indeed it is not sensible, to expect to bring him back to the adequate appreciation of the standards compatible with order and civilisation'.[9] Some commentators and sections of the press linked what they saw as a growing number of sexual assaults and brutality towards children with men returning from the war mentally unbalanced by their experiences.[10] More generally, newspapers wrote of a 'crime wave' and MPs asked questions about how the home secretary intended to deal with 'the alarming increase in the number of brutal crimes'. The home secretary responded that he knew of no such increase,[11] and the statistics do not bear out the notion of a generation of young men returning from the trenches so brutalized that they assaulted and murdered in greater numbers than before the war. In the introduction to the judicial statistics for both 1923 and 1924, it was suggested that the war had, in some way, contributed to an increase in fraud and crimes against property, especially those involving violence. The war, it was stated, 'had long continued debasing effects', while the wartime opportunities 'for getting rich quick' may have brought about 'a decay in commercial probity'.[12] The eminent criminologist Hermann Mannheim developed this theme at the beginning of the Second World War, suggesting that the previous conflict had brought about a 'gradual diminution of the individual's respect for the State' since military service gave men the idea 'that the State was under a moral obligation to supply them with everything they needed. If the State failed to fulfil this duty, they had the right to help themselves'.[13] But all of this was presented without any empirical evidence other than the slight but steady increase in the statistics.

Mannheim also suggested that a rise in sexual offences during the interwar period was possibly linked with mental instability caused by the war, though he did not suggest how this might be proven.[14] Moreover he ignored, or simply missed, the fact, noted by those at the Home Office responsible for compiling the judicial statistics, that during the 1930s about one-third of the sexual offences were committed by persons, generally males, under twenty-one years old, few of whom can have been directly affected by the war.[15] Mannheim also insisted that economic factors, especially unemployment, had an impact on crime. He was not alone in such beliefs since many, including statisticians in the Home Office as noted above, anxiously eyed the depression and the General Strike as heralds of increasing crime. Yet, when it came to assessing the statistical data of the interwar years, the only conclusion that Mannheim felt could be drawn safely was 'that unemployment as a causative factor of crime seems to play a widely varying role in different districts'. In some areas there appeared 'an almost complete harmony between the fluctuations of unemployment and crime', but elsewhere 'not even the slightest analogy exists'.[16] Mannheim suggested that psychological explanations might provide answers here; but it could equally be argued that such psychological explanations as to why individuals, or groups of individuals, commit offences should be put before any assessment of the trade cycle and unemployment in the first place.

In the end, whatever their inherent problems, the statistics are the only historical trace remaining to assess the pattern of crime for a given period. The judicial statistics for the years 1900 to 1939 reveal, first, property offences to have been the most predominant form of crime, and second, a steady increase in crime from the end of the First World War. Even though the problems inherent in these statistics were recognized by many contemporaries, it was generally assumed that this pattern generally reflected some sort of reality. Similarly, while it was difficult to demonstrate how world war and economic depression affected crime, such events served as useful explanatory scapegoats.

Offenders

In March 1916 the *Justice of the Peace* noted a significant drop in convictions since the beginning of the war and extrapolated from this a corresponding drop in crime. The war, explained the journal, had led to a large number of criminals, 'or the class from which our criminals come', joining the army. 'This class . . . often makes excellent soldiers.' Moreover, the number of foreigners had been reduced; 'a large number of crimes in this country are committed by foreigners'. There was full employment with good wages, and while the latter often fostered drunkenness, the new licensing regulations seemed, successfully, to have controlled this. As well as causing crime, poverty and drink were 'among the principal causes of lunacy'; and the journal noted that 'the number of lunatics in asylums has also decreased since the outbreak of war'. The journal hoped that, with the restoration of peace, this progress achieved in war could be maintained.[17] The article reflects some of the perceptions of the 'criminal' developed during the Victorian period, together with a more liberal perception which was already being manifested in new, liberal penal legislation and which survived both the war and the economic troubles of the 1920s and 1930s.

Victorian perceptions of the criminal had shifted from broad concerns about a 'class' of such offenders who committed crime because it suited their preference for a hedonistic life avoiding respectable labour, to equally broad beliefs that 'criminals', and particularly recidivists, were inadequate individuals shaped by forces extrinsic to their personal will.[18] Such perceptions were informed by social Darwinism and new sciences such as psychiatry. In 1913 Charles Goring, a doctor working in the prison service, published a study based on the examination of nearly 4,000 convicts in English prisons which showed up as crude the positivism of early criminologists like Cesare Lombroso but which, nevertheless, portrayed offenders as individuals whose physical, mental and moral world made them susceptible to what he termed 'the criminal diathesis'.[19] Goring's work was received with ambivalence by the British politicians and civil servants who had encouraged it. While they often applauded its scientific excellence, they were unconvinced by his focus on heredity and by his eugenicist solutions. The experience of the First World War helped continue the shift in perceptions of criminality away from the notion of an hereditary, degenerate residuum of unemployables. 'Criminals', as the *Justice of the Peace* and others concluded, appeared to make good soldiers; and people worked when there was work. Moreover, the statistics of shell-shock demonstrated that fit young men, educated in public schools, could break down in proportionately greater numbers than, though in slightly different ways from, the rank and file. Thus, while there were occasional scares about 'bag-snatchers', 'cat-burglars', 'motor-bandits' and razor gangs, and while certain districts continued to be regarded as problem areas where the population had little regard for the police and the state's ideas of law and order,[20] the overall image of the offender in the interwar period was relatively restrained. He – and overwhelmingly criminal offenders were male – was principally seen as inadequate rather than dangerous.

There were what might be called 'professional' criminals in the first part of the twentieth century who sought to make a significant part of their livelihood from various forms of law-breaking. A quick glance through the records of any law court trying the more serious offences – a county assize court, quarter sessions or London's Old Bailey – reveals a string of recidivists charged, again and again, with offences against property. There were also criminal entrepreneurs who provided generally law-abiding citizens with illicit pleasures. London's Soho district, for example, became the centre of vice in the metropolis where drugs (principally cocaine), pornography and prostitutes could be found. Criminal syndicates, notably the Messina brothers, systematized the organization of vice in Soho from the early 1930s. There was also an underworld involved in drinking clubs, boxing and, above all, gambling. Syndicates operated as off-track bookmakers taking bets illegally in the streets, in shops, in certain houses; they also ran protection rackets seeking to control the legal betting conducted at race tracks. The Darby Sabini gang, operating out of London's Clerkenwell, appears to have achieved a degree of dominance by the early 1920s, and not without considerable violence.[21] Nor were such activities confined to the capital. The principal rival to the Darby Sabini gang, until it was overwhelmed, was based in Birmingham. In Sheffield, the best-known provincial example, there was also serious gang violence, even murder, between groups struggling for control of gambling, particularly the pitch and toss rings, in the city.[22]

In addition to the professional criminals there were also some professional men who were criminal. The Victorian desire to classify offenders in terms of class led to difficulties when assessing the white-collar offender. The latter tended to be seen as a rotten apple, the exception that proved the rule of the respectable middle-class world where the businessman's word was his bond. There were commentators who took a rather more critical view, and the recurrent scandals caused by business and financial fraud, together with the increasing acceptance of psychological explanations for crime, fostered a more realistic recognition of the problem. Charles Goring noted that, among his convicts, there was a disproportionate number of professional men imprisoned for forgery and fraud. In the same year that Goring's book appeared, the Rev. J. W. Horsley published *How Criminals are Made and Prevented*, in which he suggested that commercial morality could encourage criminal behaviour. The Victorian faith in the effectiveness of the free market and good business in driving out corrupt behaviour had kept regulation to a minimum. Yet there had been periodic scandals during the Victorian and Edwardian periods involving business and financial fraud, and similar frauds created similar scandals in the interwar years. In 1923 Gerard Lee Bevan was exposed as having used the funds of City and Equitable Insurance to support his stockbroking firm. The collapse of the share market in 1929 exposed the massive frauds of Lord Kylsant at the Royal Mail Steam Packet Company and of Clarence Harty at the Austin Friars Trust.[23] In 1937 the *Report of the Depart-mental Committee* on 'sharepushing' focused on continuing fraudulent behaviour in the City where, according to the City of London Police, between 1910 and 1936 some 177 firms were either known to be or suspected of selling worthless shares or deliberately mismanaging an investor's money for their own profit. There had been, however, only thirty-seven successful prosecutions, primarily because in such cases the victim was required to initiate and underwrite legal action. The Board of Trade's committee condemned 'English-speaking aliens' as the principal sharepushers, but an analysis of the eleven prosecutions between 1927 and 1938 gives a rather different picture. The thirty-eight persons convicted seem to have been generally outwardly respectable, middle-aged English gentlemen, including a baronet, a lieutenant colonel and graduates of some of the best universities.[24]

If there was one group of offenders which stood out as a main and growing concern during the first forty years of the twentieth century, it was juvenile delin-quents. Statistically, the First World War period witnessed a significant increase in juvenile offending. This upsurge had begun before the war and was possibly the result, partially at least, of more interventionist behaviour on the part of private and state agencies, coupled with a less retributionist attitude towards the young offender in the law. The statistical increase during the war, which peaked in 1916, was attrib-uted by contemporaries to the disruption attendant on the conflict. It was concluded that parental discipline had broken down with fathers away in the armed forces and mothers out at work. At the same time, the demands of war were blamed for a short-age of adult supervisors for clubs and parks where the young might normally be expected to expend their energies. Moreover, the wartime reduction of street light-ing was seen as providing opportunities for vandalism and theft. It is, however, far from clear to what extent these causes did function as assumed. Married men from the poorest households, where delinquency seemed most apparent, were not promi-nent among the volunteers of 1914 and 1915 when the rise in the juvenile offend-ing rate was at its sharpest. A case might be made that the increase was as much a result of a moral panic and a reflection of what contemporaries feared would happen, leading in turn to a greater sensitivity and greater concerns about young people's, and particularly young men's, behaviour.[25]

This concern about rising rates of juvenile delinquency during the war did not lead to harsher laws and penalties. Nor did the concerns, expressed with increasing fre-quency during the interwar period, about the suspect 'excitement' that the new cinema was thought to generate among the young, especially the gangster films imported from America. Rather, these concerns served to stimulate the calls for the introduction of the progressive ideas prevalent before the war for more specialist juvenile courts, more probation and less institutionalization. There were some who called for harsher penal-ties, but the prevailing opinion was that 'boys would be boys'. Lord Baden-Powell argued in such a way both before and after the war, and he advocated the Boy Scouts as the ideal place for civilizing and moulding hooligans into 'useful' men. In 1925, in his pathbreaking study *The Young Delinquent*, the influential psychologist Cyril Burt declared delinquency to be 'nothing but an outstanding example of common childish naughtiness'.[26] It became a commonplace to hear similar arguments put by youth workers and magistrates who, like Basil Henriques in 1937, could condone petty theft, fiddling slot machines and joyriding by juveniles as 'perfectly innocent'.[27]

A final point is worth noting in this section – the image of the offender in the popular literature of the day was, generally speaking, very different from that of the offender who appeared daily before the courts. The 1920s and 1930s were a golden age for detective literature in England. The stories of these years usually involved murder and the offender was only revealed in the very last act by the brilliant deduction of the detective, who was quite often an aristocrat – Dorothy Sayer's Lord Peter Wimsey, Margery Allingham's Albert Campion – genteel or donnish – Agatha Christie's Miss Marple, Nicholas Blake's (C. Day Lewis's) Nigel Strangeways – or a foreigner – Agatha Christie's Hercule Poirot. Even when the detective was a serving policeman he was aristocratic – Ngaio Marsh's Roderick Alleyn – or donnish – Michael Innes's John Appleby. What these stories did get right was the fact that the murders were often committed 'in the family', or at least by people well acquainted with their victims. But the essential raison d'être of these stories was to provide a puzzle with a satisfying resolution of the status quo in an England of traditional values and class structure. Only occasionally did a novelist seek to break out of the genre, most notably Graham Greene with his exploration of the motivation of the young thug Pinkie in *Brighton Rock* (1938).

Police

Politicians, political and social commentators and senior police officers lionized the bobby as a member of 'the best police in the world' throughout the period; and foreign tourists were regularly reported as commenting on how 'wonderful' English policemen were.[28] Yet the police service faced a series of problems in the first four decades of the twentieth century, not all of which were confronted and overcome.

The largest of the police forces, the Metropolitan Police of London, was, through its commissioner, directly responsible to the home secretary. County police forces were responsible to Standing Joint Committees comprised of elected county councillors and unelected magistrates; and well over half of the chief constables appointed in the counties during the interwar years continued to be drawn from the military or from imperial, often paramilitary, police forces. Borough police forces were responsible to watch committees appointed by and from the elected representatives on the town councils. The 'head' or chief constables of most towns were generally career policemen who had worked their way up through the ranks. They began the century with less autonomy than their counterparts in the counties but, increasingly, the professionals in the Home Office were looking to bypass the amateur councillors on the watch committees and to liaise directly with the professional policemen. This policy was boosted during the First World War, and especially in its aftermath, when concerns for the maintenance of public order strengthened the ties between the Home Office and police chiefs. Significantly also, when chief constables clashed with their local civilian committees during the interwar years, they were able to fall back on Home Office support. The controversial ruling of Judge Macardie in the case of Fisher versus Oldham Corporation in 1930 gave a powerful legal underpinning to the idea of police independence from local government in operational matters.[29]

Policing began the century as a working-class trade. It was unskilled, though, through their trade journals, notably the *Police Review*, policemen saw themselves as on a level with respectable, semi-skilled or even skilled workmen. There were some perks to the job, most importantly the pension to which a man was entitled at the end of his service, but the hours were long and hard, and the pay, while varying a little from force to force, was not particularly good. Immediately before the First World War there was unrest and talk of unionizing. The pressures of policing in wartime – extra duties, the reduction in manpower as reservists and young, fit police constables left for the front – increased dissatisfaction and contributed to the police strikes of 1918 and 1919. The first of these strikes brought about the creation of a committee under Lord Desborough to investigate the service as a whole. The second strike, manipulated by Lloyd George, brought about the total destruction of the National Union of Police and Prison Officers.

The recommendations of the Desborough Committee led to standardized conditions of service and standardized pay rates across the police forces of England and Wales. It also led to the creation of the Police Federation, an integrated organization involving all ranks in all forces, to defend policemen's interests but without the right to strike. The new rates of pay meant an increase for most police officers, but upset local councillors wary of what the rate increases necessitated by new pay rates might do to their local popularity and hence to their chances of re-election. Some Labour councillors in London also objected to paying the Metropolitan Police precept out of their rates, when they had no control over how the money was spent or on how their districts were policed. The central government itself, mindful of the country's financial state following the war, decided to save money by cutting police pay temporarily by 2.5 per cent in 1922, and making the cut permanent four years later. Throughout the 1920s central government was also prepared to see many police vacancies left unfilled as another means of saving money.

The shortage of jobs during the depression appears to have led to an influx of recruits into the police service who were rather better educated than their predecessors. Opportunities were also taken to weed out old sweats and/or officers whose behaviour did not measure up to the levels desired. Even though the police were 'the best in the world', there was a series of scandals both before and after the war which prompted official enquiries. In 1908 a Royal Commission was established to investigate how the Metropolitan Police dealt with street offences. Evidence was provided of police corruption and of some rough and brutal police behaviour but, overall, the commission gave the force a clean bill of health.[30] Twenty years later similar complaints about police behaviour led first to a parliamentary enquiry, chaired by Hugh Macmillan MP, and second to another Royal Commission on Police Powers and Procedure. The Royal Commission found 'isolated incidents' of police wrongdoing but, once again, and relying heavily on the testimony of local and judicial authorities, the institution was found to be satisfactory in its overall conduct and efficiency.[31]

The Royal Commission of 1928–9 recommended the use of more policewomen. First introduced during the First World War to supervise, in particular, young women factory workers and girls and young women in the vicinity of military camps, women police were resented by some policemen of all ranks who considered that policing was no job for a woman. The financial restrictions and the embargoes on filling vacancies were used by some chief constables as a way of removing women from the service, or at least keeping their numbers very small. Such women police as continued to exist during the interwar years had their duties confined to dealing with women, offenders and victims, and children.

The ordinary English bobby of the nineteenth century had rarely found himself confronting members of the middle class. The growth of motor vehicle ownership, however, made such confrontations increasingly common. In desperation, because the law was so often broken, the Road Traffic Act of 1930 abolished the speed limit which had prompted so many clashes between police and public. Four years later, in part at least because of the increase in accidents and injuries, speed limits were reintroduced. At the end of the 1930s the Treasury agreed to an initial investment in a scheme to establish 'courtesy cops', whose key task was to educate motorists in the new Highway Code rather than bringing them, in ever greater numbers, before the courts.[32] But, new road traffic problems apart, the job of the English policeman in the first four decades of the twentieth century was much the same as that of his Victorian predecessor. He was expected to patrol his beat at a steady pace; he was to prevent crime by his presence, getting to know the householders and shopkeepers on the beat who might pass him information. But the suburbs increased enormously after the First World War and, as a consequence, beats were longer and the police presence was much thinner on the ground. Moreover, much working-class entertainment shifted from the street to cinemas, dance halls, sports stadia and even the home. It was, however, not until well after the Second World War that new systems of patrolling were developed to try to take account of these changes. Nor was the beat the only area in which change was slow. In 1933 the home secretary established a committee to investigate detective policing. It spent five years on its task and concluded that English police detectives were some way behind those of other countries in their use of scientific aids. The report, and a slightly earlier assessment of the Metropolitan CID, urged greater cooperation and communication between the detective departments of different police forces as well as within the Metropolitan Police divisions, and between detective departments and uniformed police. It also required better, more systematic, standardized record keeping, and led eventually to a more uniform basis of detective training.[33]

Penal Policy

Changes in the police and policing strategies throughout the period were generally reactive or were prompted by concerns that 'the best police in the world' might not be 'the best' in a particular respect. In contrast, changes in penal policy were more often proactive, driven by a liberal optimism, by a desire to keep people out of prison and to develop systems of reformation relevant to different kinds of offender.

The 1895 Departmental Committee chaired by Herbert Gladstone, then parliamentary under-secretary at the Home Office, has commonly been taken as the starting point of a new, more humanitarian penal policy. Yet the committee, established to investigate how the English and Welsh prison system was functioning, built on ideas of improvement and philanthropy inherent in the teachings of the liberal Oxford philosopher T. H. Green and which were already fostering increasing social regulation in the workplace, and with regard to children, and unfortunates such as inebriates and mental defectives.[34] A succession of young men were profoundly influenced by Green's ideas and several of these, notably Evelyn Ruggles-Brise, who served as chairman of the Prison Commission and Convict Directorate from 1895 to 1921, were to play significant roles in promoting liberal reform at the heart of government.

But also important in pressing ahead with, and promoting the tone for, penal reform were the first two home secretaries of the pre-First World War Liberal government, Herbert Gladstone himself and then Winston Churchill. In 1907 Gladstone saw through parliament the Probation of Offenders Act, which formalized a system of probation that had been developing over the preceding quarter of a century. In the following year juvenile courts were established under the Children Act in a continuing attempt to dissociate young offenders from adult criminals, while the Criminal Justice Act set up both the Borstal system for sixteen- to twenty-one-year-olds and a system of preventive detention for persistent adult offenders. Churchill's significance lay in the way that, during his twenty months as home secretary, he provided plans and a momentum for legislation passed shortly before the war which diverted those with mental illness away from prison and required magistrates to give petty offenders some time in which to pay a fine rather than promptly incarcerating them for immediate failure. Moreover, his analysis of the results of the new but illiberal system of preventive detention led to an amelioration of the way that it was employed and, consequently, to a considerable reduction in the numbers imprisoned under it. Overall, the reforms and tone set by Gladstone, Churchill and their administrators brought a reduction in the daily average prison population from around 20,000 at the turn of the century to around 10,000 in the middle of the war, and the numbers hovered between 9,000 and 13,000 throughout the interwar years. At the same time, the number of local prisons was reduced from fifty in 1914 to twenty-six in 1930.[35]

While there was a pronounced liberal optimism underpinning penal policy in the first two decades of the century, there was no let-up in criticism of the prison system for severity. The imprisonment of suffragettes before the war and of conscientious objectors during the war produced a clutch of articulate critics with first-hand knowledge of prisons from the inside. Several of the most powerful critics contributed to *English Prisons Today*, begun under the auspices of the Labour party research department, denied assistance by the Prison Commission, and edited by two ex-prisoner 'conchies', Stephen Hobhouse and Fenner Brockway. While recognizing that some reforms had taken place for the better, the essays in the book challenged Ruggles-Brise's assertions that the intellectual, moral and physical care of prisoners was developing well. A steady rather than striking and rapid process of reform continued under Ruggles-Brise's successors: prison floggings declined until there were none; conversation was permitted in prison workshops; compulsory chapel attendance was suspended; and entertainments were introduced in the shape of the wireless, film shows and concerts. An experiment in open prisons was begun with men working and sleeping out of doors at New Hall Camp near Wakefield in May 1936. At the same time, Alexander Paterson, another Oxford convert to T. H. Green's brand of progressive liberalism and whose career and missionary zeal has eclipsed the chairmen of the Prison Commission under whom he served, developed further the Borstal system for young persons.

It is, of course, one thing to pass legislation and to create systems, and another to have them implemented as the legislators would have wished. The probation system established in 1907 was still not functioning fully in the early 1920s; over a fifth of courts still had not appointed probation officers by 1922. Different courts used the system differently. Thus in 1933 the percentage of those found guilty of indictable offences who were put on probation ranged from 5 per cent to 40 per cent depending on the court. The Borstal system established for girls lagged behind that for boys, with little thought being put into their training other than preparing them for domestic tasks. Moreover, while a liberal, progressive ethos pervaded penal policy and survived shocks such as the Dartmoor prison mutiny of January 1932, conservative opponents could still win important victories. The 1927 Departmental Committee on the Treatment of Young Offenders, for example, did not recommend the abolition of prison for young persons under the age of twenty-one in spite of Paterson's confidence. Six years later the House of Lords successfully removed a clause that would have abolished the whipping of young offenders from what became the Children and Young Persons Act of 1933.[36]

The general liberal atmosphere towards penal policy, together with the coming to power of the first Labour government, helped revive the campaign against capital punishment largely dormant for half a century. On this emotive issue there was some division on party lines, and a general nervousness about quite how far to press the issues by different governments. A Select Committee met in 1930 and recommended an experimental abolition for five years. All of its Conservative members dissented; and the Labour home secretary, J. R. Clynes, who had established the committee, made no move to follow its recommendation. A Criminal Justice Bill introduced in 1938 also ignored the recommendation. Sir Samuel Hoare, then home secretary, subsequently insisted that a clause providing for even an experimental abolition could have endangered the whole bill. Abolitionists put down a motion to implement the recommendation at some future unspecified date, and this was carried on a free vote. But the government took no action and the Criminal Justice Bill itself, with a series of other liberal reforms relating to, for example, flogging, was shelved on the outbreak of war.[37]

Halcyon Days?

In the first forty years of the twentieth century, crime, police and penal policy were never the political footballs that they were to become at the end of the century. In the Conservative party election manifesto of 1924, under the heading 'Women and Children', Stanley Baldwin promised to reform and develop the probation system, and he added that 'the number of women police should be increased, and the penalties for criminal assaults against women and children made adequate to the offence'.[38] But such a reference in an electoral statement was unique. Moreover, developing the probationary service and introducing more women police – whose job, after all, remained the care and supervision of children and of female offenders and victims – can both be said to fit within the broadly liberal and optimistic attitudes towards crime and penal policy that characterized the period. While there were concerns about the effects of war and economic depression on criminality, neither politicians, policemen nor more general commentators expressed great and continuing concerns about crime during these years. Geoffrey Pearson has warned about the ways in which successive generations look back to a more tranquil past when assessing current concerns about crime.[39] Yet it is difficult to come to any conclusions other than that crime was not an issue that unduly worried the people of Edwardian and interwar England, and the progressive penal policy, which resulted in the closure of virtually half of the local prisons, continued with little hindrance into the aftermath of the Second World War where eventually, and for a variety of reasons, it did founder.

NOTES

1 Bucks CRO BC/5/1.

2 A. Locke, 'Criminal statistics', *Police Journal*, 4 (1931), pp. 188–96; *Report of the Commissioner of the Metropolitan Police* (London, 1935), p. 16.

3 *Judicial Statistics for England and Wales for 1921* (London), p. 5; *Judicial Statistics for 1922*, p. 7.

4 *Judicial Statistics for 1926*, p. 5; D. J. V. Jones, *Crime and Policing in the Twentieth Century: The South Wales Experience* (Cardiff, 1996), pp. 65–6.

5 *Report of His Majesty's Inspectors of Constabulary* (London, 1921), p. 12.

6 *Judicial Statistics for 1932*, p. 8.

7 H. Taylor, 'The politics of the rising crime statistics of England and Wales, 1914–1960', *Crime, Histoire et Sociétés/Crime, History and Societies*, 2, no. 1 (1998), pp. 5–28; H. Mannheim, *Social Aspects of Crime in England Between the Wars* (London, 1940), pp. 59–60.

8 *The Times*, 21 January 1920, p. 12.

9 *Sheffield Mail*, 2 December 1920, p. 2.

10 S. K. Kent, *Making Peace: The Reconstruction of Gender in Interwar Britain* (Princeton, NJ, 1993), pp. 97–101.

11 *The Times*, 21 January 1920, p. 12, 22 January 1920, p. 12, 18 February 1920, p. 9; *Parliamentary Debates*, 21 March 1921, vol. 152, col. 279, and 30 March 1921, vol. 152, col. 1532.

12 *Judicial Statistics for 1923*, p. 10; *Judicial Statistics for 1924*, p. 6.

13 Mannheim, *Social Aspects of Crime*, pp. 112–13.

14 Ibid., p. 122.

15 *Judicial Statistics for 1933*, p. xiv; and see also *Judicial Statistics for 1935*, p. x, where it is noted that 20 per cent of such offenders were under seventeen years.

16 Mannheim, *Social Aspects of Crime*, p. 147.

17 *Justice of the Peace*, 18 March 1916, p. 134.

18 M. J. Wiener, *Reconstructing the Criminal: Culture, Law, and Policy in England, 1830–1914* (Cambridge, 1990).

19 C. Goring, *The English Convict: A Statistical Study* (London, 1913).

20 J. White, *The Worst Street in North London: Campbell Bunk, Islington, between the Wars* (London, 1986); H. Daley, *This Small Cloud: A Personal Memoir* (London, 1986), p. 93.

21 P. Jenkins and G. W. Potter, 'Before the Krays: organized crime in London, 1920–1960', *Criminal Justice History*, 9 (1988), pp. 209–30; R. Samuel, *East End Underworld: Chapters in the Life of Arthur Harding* (London, 1981), pp. 182–5 and 328–9.

22 J. P. Bean, *The Sheffield Gang Wars* (Sheffield, 1981).

23 G. Robb, *White-collar Crime in Modern England: Financial Fraud and Business Morality 1845–1929* (Cambridge, 1992), pp. 122–4 and 142–6.

24 E. Smithies, *The Black Economy in England since 1914* (Dublin, 1984), pp. 56–9; *Share-pushing: Report of the Departmental Committee Appointed by the Board of Trade* (Cmd 5539, London, 1937).

25 D. Smith, 'Juvenile delinquency in Britain in the First World War', *Criminal Justice History*, 11 (1990), pp. 119–45; B. Weinberger, 'Policing juveniles: delinquency in late nineteenth- and early twentieth-century Manchester', *Criminal Justice History*, 14 (1993), pp. 43–55.

26 C. L. Burt, *The Young Delinquent* (London, 1925), p. viii.

27 G. Pearson, *Hooligan: A History of Respectable Fears* (London, 1983), pp. 34–5, 40–7 and 108–14.

28 C. Emsley, 'The English bobby: an indulgent tradition', in R. Porter, ed., *Myths of the English* (Oxford, 1992).

29 C. Emsley, *The English Police: A Political and Social History* (2nd edition, London, 1996), pp. 160–5.

30 *Report of the Royal Commission upon the Duties of the Metropolitan Police* (Cmd 4156, London, 1908).

31 *Report of the Royal Commission on Police Powers and Procedure* (Cmd 3297, London, 1929).

32 C. Emsley, ' "Mother, what *did* policemen do when there weren't any motors?" The law, the police and the regulation of motor traffic in England, 1900–1939', *Historical Journal*, 36 (1993), pp. 357–81.

33 *Report of the Departmental Committee on Detective Work* (London, 1938); PRO Mepo 12/5, Correspondence on the reorganization of the CID, 1929–34.

34 C. Harding, 'The inevitable end of a discredited system? The origins of the Gladstone Committee Report on Prisons 1895', *Historical Journal*, 31 (1988), pp. 591–608.

35 W. J. Forsythe, *Penal Discipline, Reformatory Projects and the English Prison Commission 1895–1939* (Exeter, 1990); L. Radzinowicz and R. Hood, *The Emergence of Penal Policy in Victorian and Edwardian England* (Oxford, 1990).

36 Forsythe, *Prison Discipline*; V. Bailey, *Delinquency and Citizenship: Reclaiming the Young Offender 1914–1948* (Oxford, 1987), esp. pp. 104–9.

37 J. B. Christoph, *Capital Punishment and British Politics: The British Movement to Abolish the Death Penalty 1945–57* (London, 1962), pp. 19–21; E. O. Tuttle, *The Crusade against Capital Punishment in Great Britain* (London, 1961), pp. 34–44; V. Bailey, 'The shadow of the gallows: the death penalty and the British Labour government, 1945–51', *Law and History Review*, 18 (2000), pp. 305–49.

38 I. Dale, ed., *Conservative Party: General Election Manifestos, 1900–1997* (London, 2000), p. 35.

39 Pearson, *Hooligan*.

FURTHER READING

There has been relatively little academic research into the history of crime in twentieth-century England, but the following should enable most of the issues covered in this essay to be followed up, at least in part.

Bailey, V., *Delinquency and Citizenship: Reclaiming the Young Offender 1914–1948* (Oxford, 1987).

Emsley, C., ' "Mother, what *did* policemen do when there weren't any motors?" The law, the police and the regulation of motor traffic in England, 1900–1939', *Historical Journal*, 36 (1993), pp. 357–81.

Emsley, C., *The English Police: A Political and Social History* (2nd edition, London, 1996).

Forsythe, W. J., *Penal Discipline, Reformatory Projects and the English Prison Commission 1895–1939* (Exeter, 1990).

Jenkins, P. and Potter, G. W., 'Before the Krays: organized crime in London, 1920–1960', *Criminal Justice History*, 9 (1988), pp. 209–30.

Jones, D. J. V., *Crime and Policing in the Twentieth Century: The South Wales Experience* (Cardiff, 1996).

Mannheim, H., *Social Aspects of Crime in England Between the Wars* (London, 1940).

Pearson, G., *Hooligan: A History of Respectable Fears* (London, 1983).

Robb, G., *White-collar Crime in Modern England: Financial Fraud and Business Morality 1845–1929* (Cambridge, 1992).

Smith, D., 'Juvenile delinquency in Britain in the First World War', *Criminal Justice History*, 11 (1990), pp. 119–45.

Smithies, E., *The Black Economy in England since 1914* (Dublin, 1984).

Taylor, H., 'The politics of the rising crime statistics of England and Wales, 1914–1960', *Crime, Histoire et Sociétés/Crime, History and Societies*, 2, no. 1 (1998), pp. 5–28.

Weinberger, B., 'Policing juveniles: delinquency in late nineteenth- and early twentieth-century Manchester', *Criminal Justice History*, 14 (1993), pp. 43–55.

CHAPTER TWENTY-EIGHT

Leisure and Sport in Britain, 1900–1939

PETER J. BECK

During the 1930s escalating international rivalries placed a premium upon projecting the right sort of national image to reaffirm Britain's great power status, and particularly to counter impressions of decadence fostered by hostile German and Italian propaganda. Kingsley Martin, who edited the *New Statesman*, described one example.

> In September 1937 I visited a great Paris Exhibition which symbolised national aspirations. It was dominated by the German and Soviet pavilions . . . Britain was modestly housed in something that looked like a white packing-case. When you went in, the first thing you saw was a cardboard Chamberlain fishing in rubber waders and, beyond, an elegant pattern of golf balls, a frieze of tennis rackets, polo sets, riding equipment, natty dinner jackets and, by a pleasant transition, agreeable pottery and textiles, books finely printed and photographs of the English countryside. I stared in bewilderment. Could this be England?[1]

Martin's reaction, quite apart from illuminating more overt foreign propaganda, reflected regret that Britain's low-key exhibit – the prime minister shown as an angler, not an appeaser, at leisure in a 'nice' and 'entirely upper-class' country – ignored contemporary realities like factory chimneys and football. Despite having attended Rugby School, Neville Chamberlain was no great lover of sport. Nor did he show any interest in association football, the sport of the working man, who played, watched, talked and read about the game, and also did the football pools. For the 'flat caps', depicted vividly in J. B. Priestley's novel *The Good Companions* (1929), ninety minutes of football aroused greater interest and commitment than fifty hours of work.

Nevertheless, most histories of Britain overlook the central role of leisure and sport in industrial urban culture. Frequently, these activities are written out of the national past regardless of their intrinsic historical interest, prominent role in the everyday life of all sections of twentieth-century British society, and relevance to a wide range of political, social, economic, cultural and other historical themes. Their history is often treated as a world apart, meriting neither integration nor parity with historical studies of, say, high politics, foreign policy or the economy. And yet we live in a society attaching high priority to both activities; indeed, politicians prove willing advocates of their prominent place in both the national heritage and present-day life. In 1995, John Major (prime minister, 1990–97) challenged historians.

> Some people say that sport is a peripheral and minor concern. I profoundly disagree ... Sport is a central part of Britain's National Heritage. We invented the majority of the world's great sports ... Nineteenth-century Britain was the cradle of a leisure revolution every bit as significant as the agricultural and industrial revolutions we launched in the century before.[2]

Tony Blair, his successor, agreed that 'sport matters'; indeed, sport was given a lead role in his government's rebranding Britannia exercise, since – to quote the British Council – 'Britain is particularly strongly placed to use sport as a means of communicating messages about itself' to help 'improve its international standing and build relationships'.[3]

In this manner, sport has become a powerful instrument of cultural propaganda, that is, a form of 'soft power', as opposed to 'hard' military and economic power, capable of crossing state and other boundaries in support of the national interest. Moreover, looking back over the past century and notwithstanding the impression given by most histories of Britain, sport was never mere play. Rather, it proved an integral part of images of Britishness projected to both domestic and external audiences. Britain's undoubted role as an originator, leader and teacher of football, cricket and many other modern games meant that sport proved both a cause and an effect of the extension of British ideas, influence and prestige. James Douglas, writing in 1929 as editor of the *Sunday Express*, was not alone in expressing great pride in 'our position as the greatest exporters of sport in the world. We teach other nations to play our national games, and they prove such apt pupils'.[4] Sport's domestic role in helping to define class, county, gender, local and national identities appropriate to a rapidly changing urban industrial society was complemented by its use externally to propagate British values (e.g. fair play) and images of national greatness. Also, as highlighted by Tony Mangan, sport helped to build and hold together a far-flung empire.[5] From this perspective, the cricket bat or football seemed as powerful as the gun in propagating the imperial message and extending British influence and rule.

During the late 1920s Rudolf Kircher, a German observer, was fulsome in his praise of Britain as a sporting nation: 'Sport is immediately and inseparably bound up with the whole life of the people ... All peoples have their play, but none of the great modern nations has built it up in quite the same way into a rule of life and a national code'.[6] Even so, he was baffled by cricket's appeal: 'anyone who is neither an Englishman nor a cricketer finds this slow motion film tedious after half an hour'. By contrast, for Siegfried Sassoon, cricket captured the essence of *his* past. Of course, his semi-autobiographical *Memoirs of a Fox-hunting Man* (1928) articulated the views of a poet whose privileged social background and private income allowed him to hunt and to play cricket or golf, not work. Cocooned in a first-class rail carriage, Sassoon gave little thought to the leisure of the lower classes living in London's squalid slums spreading out alongside the railway line into his beloved Kentish countryside. Sir John Simon, foreign secretary from 1931 to 1935, echoed Sassoon's claims about cricket's quintessentially national character. Like Kingsley Martin and Kircher, he conflated Englishness and Britishness in the typical manner noted by Linda Colley.

The observant and judicious foreigner, if asked to select the two institutions of our country which are most characteristic of the English spirit, would unhesitatingly reply – 'Cricket' and 'the House of Commons' . . . Cricket furnishes a storehouse of the most delightful memories which will remain with us as long as life lasts . . . The Frenchman thinks of his early love affairs; the American gloats over his most successful speculation; the Hindu contemplates his previous existence; and the happy Englishman dreams of cricket.[7]

Simon, who also captained the St Andrew's Royal and Ancient Golf Club (1936–7), typified the sporting elitism criticized by Kingsley Martin. Unsurprisingly, association football, the undoubted game of the masses, failed to figure in his thinking and lifestyle, although the four British football associations were equally capable of stating how their game epitomized national values and rivalled Shakespeare as one of Britain's most successful cultural exports.

Perceptions do not necessarily reflect realities, but they provide an invaluable framework for this chapter, most notably by establishing Britain's status as a sporting nation in the eyes of both Britons and foreigners, sport's prominence in British leisure, and inequalities of access to leisure and sport within Britain. In addition, these examples suggest the perceived contemporary significance of what represents still a peripheral, even missing, element in most national histories. Of course, there are exceptions, most notably Barbara Tuchman, who claimed that '*homo ludens*, man at play, is surely as significant a figure as man at war or at work. In human activity the invention of the ball may be said to rank with the invention of the wheel'.[8] In this vein, pioneering histories by Richard Holt, Stephen Jones, Tony Mason, Tony Mangan, Wray Vamplew, John Walton and James Walvin, among others, opened up leisure and sport in Britain as valid topics for historical investigation, particularly as viewed within their defining social historical context. By contrast, political, economic and international historians have proved far less forthcoming in following Peter Clarke's acknowledgement of sport's historical significance:

For some people, the joke goes, sport is not a matter of life and death: it is more serious than that. When it is referred to as a religion, the comment may be suggestive as well as ironic. The ability of sport to capture the popular imagination, to infuse a sense of common commitment in the outcome of an epic contest, to provide a strong narrative line – even when busy people can only eavesdrop on the story on the back page of a newspaper or snatch at the latest Test score – this is not just a trivial matter. In twentieth-century Britain organised mass sport may have filled some of the psychic space which was being evacuated by organised mass Christianity.[9]

A British Leisure and Sporting Revolution

The period 1900–39 saw a further phase in Britain's evolution from a traditional rural country to a modern industrial urban society characterized by an expanding economy. Within this context, the late Victorian and Edwardian periods witnessed a major transformation in the pace, nature and scale of Britain's leisure and sporting cultures; indeed, Tranter and Walvin, among others, have referred to a leisure and sporting 'revolution' following on from those affecting agriculture and industry.

Alternatively, Lowerson, inspired by the 'Scramble for Africa', refers to a pre-1914 'Scramble for Sport'. But is the term 'revolution' an appropriate descriptor for changes occurring over a fifty-year time span? Neither 1900 nor 1939 represent significant turning points for leisure and sport. Rather, late nineteenth-century trends continued seamlessly into the 1900s, just as the late 1940s exhibited strong elements of continuity from the 1930s.

In reality, the late Victorian, Edwardian and interwar years exhibited the usual historical blend of continuity and change. New forms of leisure and sport emerged, but more often represented modern variants of pre-industrial activities; thus, association football and boxing developed from the frequently violent, disorganized and discredited traditional sports of folk football and prize fighting respectively. Nor did everything change, as evidenced by the prevalence even upon the eve of the Second World War of Victorian public house and street-based leisure. Unsurprisingly, specific activities experienced varying rates of advance and regression; indeed, perhaps any 'revolution' should be viewed more accurately as a series of separate overlapping, occasionally cyclical, rises and falls.

Leisure in Britain

Late Victorian and Edwardian leisure must be viewed against a backdrop of urban, industrial and demographic change, most notably Britain's prevailing conditions of life. Reductions in working hours and the increased consumer power consequent upon rising real incomes proved key enabling factors, but changes in housing and health, communications, technology and materials, legislation (e.g. Factory Acts; 1871 Bank Holiday Act) and trade union pressure contributed to the dramatic emergence of a recognizably modern leisure allowing people the freedom to do, or not to do, what they wanted in non-working hours. Leisure extended well beyond the confines of the traditional 'leisured class', whose conspicuous consumption of leisure was described in Thorstein Veblen's *The Theory of the Leisure Class* (1899). Expectations, even of the less prosperous, broadened to embrace the ideal of having a worthwhile life distinct from the world of work. Walvin, pointing to surveys conducted during the 1890s by Charles Booth (*Life and Labour of the People in London*) and B. Seebohm Rowntree (*Poverty: A Study of Town Life*), identified a 'national urge for leisure': 'By the turn of the century . . . it was now widely accepted that everyone had a right to the enjoyment of leisure'.[10]

In part, the shape of the 'leisure revolution' was influenced by the 'rational recreation' visions of the growing middle class, even if Huggins, pointing also to historians' concentration hitherto upon the working classes, stresses the need to move on from treating the middle classes as a single undifferentiated group.[11] Having discovered leisure and sport, the middle classes assimilated these activities into their lifestyle to display status and wealth in a manner emulating Veblen's leisured class. Leisure was endowed with a purposive rationale adjudged beneficial not only for their class but also for the nation in general; thus, it became an instrument for promoting social control and Gramscian notions of 'cultural hegemony'. Moreover, the resulting improvements in physical, mental and moral well-being were deemed to help national efficiency by boosting economic productivity and military preparedness. As a result, the industrial proletariat was pushed by employers and the church, among others, towards acceptable, educational and 'improving' forms of leisure – these included brass bands, choral societies, municipal parks, public libraries, organized, codified modern sports and various activities provided by voluntary associations with church and chapel affiliations – offering preferable alternatives to drink, crime and gambling. In practice, 'rational recreation' schemes often foundered or lost their hegemonial impact because of the reluctance or refusal of the working classes to be conditioned in their leisure time. Indeed, their growing power as consumers led the proletariat to create their own leisure forms or to adapt middle-class schemes to their own circumstances, as evidenced by the professionalism and tribalism characteristic of football.

In this vein, Stedman Jones and Hobsbawm identified a distinctive uniform pattern of British working-class culture characterized by men who wore flat caps, ate fish and chips, watched association football and the music hall, gambled on horses and holi-dayed in Blackpool.[12] In turn, this leisure-centred lifestyle, diverting people's ener-gies away from revolutionary agitation, much to the annoyance of political activists, has been interpreted as helping to explain the reformist character of British politics. As G. K. Chesterton commented in his novel *The Return of Don Quixote* (1927) about their penchant for betting, working men cared 'a damn sight more about the inequality of horses than about the equality of men'! However, Davies painted a more diverse picture in his in-depth case study of Salford and Manchester, whose experi-ence between 1900 and 1939 possesses a broader relevance for other areas of urban deprivation, since the most vivid historical, literary and visual portrayals of 'tradi-tional' working-class life in Britain – these range from Friedrich Engels's *The Con-dition of the Working Class in England in 1844* (1845), Walter Greenwood's *Love on the Dole* (1933) and Robert Roberts's *The Classic Slum: Salford Life in the First Quarter of the Century* (1973) to the art of L. S. Lowry – have given these places a symbolic importance for working-class studies.

Notwithstanding the enduring appeal of many traditional pleasures, by 1900 the British leisure pattern reflected the availability of an ever-wider range of opportu-nities. Hoopdriver's cycling adventures, as related in H. G. Wells's *The Wheels of Chance* (1896), highlighted the enhanced mobility enabled by bicycles as well as by trams, trains and ships. Trips through the countryside were complemented by seaside holidays and excursions. Cycling's popularity, though dependent upon the usual enabling factors affecting hours and income, was largely a function of the economic and technological change responsible for the growth of an industry producing pneumatic-tyred safety bicycles as consumer durables for a mass market. Rubinstein, inspired by *The Times*'s claim about a resulting 'social revolution' (15 August 1898), argued that 'the bicycle brought a new dimension to British social life in the 1890s . . . few corners of British society remained untouched by cycling'.[13]

Paradoxically, as provision became more diverse and extensive, leisure became more homogenized across the nation through increased commercialization alongside a concentration by time defined principally by Saturday half-days and bank holidays. In turn, this emergent mass leisure, reinforced by the rise of newspapers with a growing national readership crossing geographical and social boundaries, provided the foundation for new leisure industries at a time when British industry in general seemed to be losing its lead or failing to change with the times. Even so, their impact was limited in both scale, at an estimated *c.*3 per cent of gross national product, and geographical coverage, as suggested by, say, the concentration of cycle production in Birmingham, Coventry, London and Nottingham. Likewise, deerstalking emerged in the Scottish Highlands but failed to remedy the region's fundamental lack of development aggravated by the decline in sheep farming.[14] Nevertheless, the pace of change was accelerating, not slackening, as evidenced by the speed with which the cinema expanded to become by 1914 the most popular form of commercialized public entertainment providing a temporary escape from everyday realities for a broad cross-section of the population. As one London magistrate commented, 'for the few hours at the picture palace at the corner they [the masses] can find breathing space, warmth, music (the more the better), and the picture where they can have a real laugh, cheer and sometimes a shout. Who can measure the effects on their spirits and bodies?'[15] Also, the cinema, establishing itself as an integral part of national culture, proved instrumental in shattering the blinkered horizons of Edwardian Britain. Nor, despite the focus of historians upon the more easily researched commercialized public leisure, did all activities take place outside the home; thus, the vogue for musical instruments, most notably the accordion and piano, as well as hobbies, like gardening or pigeon fancying, reflected a growing trend towards individual, informal home-based leisure.

Between 1914 and 1918 Britain's mobilization for the needs of total war disrupted, even temporarily terminated, certain activities. Even so, leisure, though often regarded as unpatriotic unless undertaken in a restrained manner, remained important in entertaining troops on leave and upholding civilian morale. For many, particularly women, like Vera Brittain, wartime yielded additional resources and opportunities for leisure. As a result, the First World War, far from reversing the leisure revolution, provided a springboard for further advances, most notably by the cinema.

The interwar years have attracted less research than those prior to 1914, but the history of leisure was marked by continued expansion in a manner frequently reinforcing and extending pre-war trends; for example, Blackpool, claiming over 7 million visitors per annum during the 1930s, improved its infrastructure and amenities to remain the leading seaside resort. Whether or not British leisure consolidated, 'matured' or was 'recast, if not transformed' remains debatable, but in July 1937 the *Listener* felt justified in claiming that 'the major social gain of our day is the increase which has taken place in the individual's leisure time'.[16] The leisure–work balance was transformed as employment became a less dominating experience of people's lives. Indeed, in 1935 *The New Survey of London Life and Labour*, updating Booth's pioneering study, acknowledged the contemporary significance of leisure in people's lives by devoting a whole volume to 'Life and Leisure'.[17] Readers wishing to go beyond this chapter's inevitable generalizations will find such contemporary surveys, alongside oral testimony and *Mass Observation* reports, an interesting read in spite of the retrospective character of oral testimony and the fact that *Mass Observation* reports often reveal more about the observers than the observed![18]

Although the new leisure industries were not fully insulated from depression, Jones argues that they offered alternative economic opportunities at a time when older industries were in decline.[19] Naturally, sections of the population failed to share in such advances, but greater access to leisure resulted from rising real wages, reduced working hours – the post-war average of forty-eight hours per week compared favourably with the pre-war figure of fifty-four hours – declining family size, improved welfare benefits, the Trades Union Congress's campaign for holidays with pay, and legislative changes regulating hours and holidays with pay (e.g. the 1937 Factory Act, 1938 Holidays with Pay Act). Transport improvements further enhanced mobility and recreational opportunities; indeed, by the mid-1920s, when Sir Arthur Balfour claimed that the bicycle had become a necessity for the working classes, the motor-cycle was becoming more popular, and car ownership was filtering down through the upper and middle classes with the production of smaller 'family' models. By 1937, c.1.8 million cars and nearly half a million motorcycles were in use.

Spectacular growth in commercialized forms of leisure was centred upon the cinema, wireless broadcasting, dance halls, gramophone records and sport. The cinema, which 'slaughtered all competitors' to become 'the essential social habit of the age' (A. J. P. Taylor), led the advance in a manner showing the impact of improved technology and investment.[20] Thus, the industry moved on rapidly from silent films to talkies – Al Jolson's *Jazz Singer* (1927) was the first such film – and then colour films. 'Flea pits' remained, but purpose-built cinemas, linked to the development of national chains, like Odeon, led to the Art Deco architecture still surviving (albeit often as bingo halls) on some British high streets. By the late 1930s over 23 million people visited cinemas each week, with many going more than once. Annual admissions totalled 987 million by 1938. Wireless broadcasting was another growth area following the commencement of broadcasting in 1922 by the BBC (British Broadcasting Company, later Corporation). Within a decade or so over 70 per cent of British households had a licence, although any semblance of mass provision must be qualified by the BBC's lack of a populist approach and the fact that posses-sion of a wireless remained a symbol of relative affluence. As one of Davies's interviewees observed, depression meant that either people could never afford to buy a wireless or were forced to sell or pawn their set: 'you *were somebody* if you had a wireless'.[21]

Commercialization, and especially the powerful cultural impact of film and broad-casting, fostered, it is argued, a more homogeneous British experience and outlook, even if, notwithstanding the protective quota introduced in 1927, the vogue for American films qualified elements of Britishness. Certainly, the wireless, albeit viewed paradoxically as a cause of fragmentation through its central place in home-based leisure, generated a vast national audience for cricket and football commentaries, the Christmas carol service from King's College, Cambridge, or the monarch's Christ-mas message. Overriding distance and social differences, broadcasting proved a major force for temporal regimentation through shared national rituals as millions of Britons undertook the same leisure activity at exactly the same time through the mediation of a wireless set.

Despite laissez-faire images, central and local government had always impacted upon British leisure, such as through the provision of municipal parks and swimming baths or the regulation of working hours. The state's role increased dramatically during and after the First World War, when leisure came to be viewed, like educa-tion, as politically sensitive and hence as a political fact of life. Indeed, the cinema's perceived power meant that state regulation went beyond safety and licensing ques-tions, as indicated by Pronay's study of the British Board of Film Censors, a non-governmental body under Home Office patronage.

Instead of powerful, emotionally backed calls for taking matters into their own hands, for viewing the government as their enemy 'class' or otherwise, and their plight as the result of the system of government, they [the people] were encouraged to regard their economic and social condition as a personal and not a political problem . . . Censorship ensured that . . . there were no alluring visions of new orders.[22]

As always, it is difficult to evaluate film's actual impact upon attitudes and values – Pronay's view, though supported by Tony Aldgate and Jeffrey Richards, was challenged by Jones – but arguably censorship, combined with restrictions on showing Soviet films and the rejection of certain scripts (e.g. *Love on the Dole*), accentuated the cinema's role in moulding an acceptable apolitical social consensus during a difficult decade, providing a cheap and agreeable outing transporting people to a dream world, and offering an environment favoured by courting couples.

Like other depressed regions, Salford and Manchester shared only partially in the wholesale transformation of British leisure between 1900 and 1939. Unemployment, alongside age, family circumstances and gender, meant that even during the relatively more prosperous late 1930s leisure remained rooted in cheap or cost-free Victorian survivals, centred upon the public house, working men's clubs and street-based activities like gambling, 'sitting out' on doorsteps, 'monkey parades' (i.e., promenading), gangs, street entertainers and markets. Nor did the ban imposed by the 1906 Street Betting Act – this represented another example of social control – stop gambling on greyhound and horse racing becoming major working-class pursuits, as verified by both the 1934–5 London *New Survey* and Rowntree's 1938 York report (*Poverty and Progress*, 1941). Also, the football pools emerged as a national pastime during the interwar years.

According to Davies, 'gender was central to the division of leisure in working-class districts', where the principal activities were male-dominated; thus, photographs of football crowds show numerous 'flat caps' but few women.[23] Generally speaking, the virtual exclusion of women from leisure conducted outside the home proved a function of power relations within the family, their relative lack of resources, and the heavy demands made by housework and washing clothes. In turn, male expenditure on drink, gambling and other leisure activities was instrumental in aggravating the impact of poverty and causing household strife. Despite Davies's claim that commercialized leisure barely affected many women, even in 1939, the post-1918 period witnessed a general improvement for working-class women, who discovered the cinema as an affordable and accessible form of leisure. Leisure reflected, reinforced and created masculine identities and networks for other sections of British society, even if structuring by gender proved less rigid for the upper and middle classes. For example, Vera Brittain, though resenting the separate spheres of men and women and the preferential treatment given to her brother, enjoyed much greater access to leisure than her lower-class counterparts.

For the rest of 1912 and the first half of 1913, I went to more dances, paid calls, skated and tobogganed, played a good deal of Bridge and a great deal of tennis and golf, had music lessons and acted in amateur theatricals; in fact, I passed my days in all those conventional pursuits with which the leisured young woman of every generation has endeavoured to fill the time that she is not qualified to use.[24]

Nevertheless, despite the political, economic and social changes ushered in during and after the First World War and the greater opportunities furnished by commercialized leisure, women remained second-class citizens as far as leisure and sport were concerned.

Therefore, the general advance in people's expectations and access to leisure failed to override significant variants and inequalities occasioned principally by class, wealth and gender. Social differences, albeit blurred, endured; indeed, just as one type of leisure rated more highly in social terms than another, so significant gradations existed within any one activity. Britons rushed increasingly to the seaside, but travelled in different ways for different periods to different resorts and enjoyments; for example, Lytham St Anne's, not Blackpool, was often the preferred choice of the middle classes. Likewise, for golf, by 1900 membership of a club, or rather a *particular* club, recorded an individual's social standing.

British Sport

When studying British leisure between 1900 and 1939, it is difficult to avoid sport's prominence as a recreational activity appealing to an ever-larger number of Britons as both participants and watchers and giving greater pleasure than either politics or most rival leisure activities. Indeed, sport, defining community, gender and social class, has been presented as one of the 'most significant' and 'most powerful' cultures in British society.[25]

Britain, the first industrial country, became also the first modern sporting nation in which codification and institutionalization transformed fragmented and localized 'games' into national 'sports'. According to Tranter, 'as a general rule, the more industrialised and commercial the economy the greater the extent of organised sport and the earlier its inception. It was no accident that Britain, the first country to industrialise, was also the first country to introduce a codified, institutionalised and highly commercialised sporting culture'.[26] Significantly, Lancashire, Britain's first industrial region, led the way in commercialized sport as well as in the new holiday industry centred on Blackpool. Generally speaking, sport's advance proved a function of the leisure revolution, and hence of the various enabling factors mentioned earlier. But why did an ever-larger number of Britons devote a substantial proportion of their additional income and free time to sport rather than to some other leisure activity? Of relevance here is the manner in which late Victorian and Edwardian Britain, glossing over the sheer pleasure of being a player or spectator, endowed sport with a range of purposes and values of national utility – these included 'muscular Christianity' – which served also to assuage any feelings of guilt occasioned by the pursuit of leisure rather than work.

British sport's organizational revolution was based essentially upon a series of developments, which were not necessarily sequential:

- the formation of national administrations for individual sports;
- regulation and ordering through the adoption of standard written national rules;
- the formation of clubs, and the proliferation of local, regional and national league and cup competitions;
- the extension of the administrative structures' spatial parameters locally, regionally, nationally and internationally.

	England	**Northern Ireland**	**Scotland**	**Wales**
National association established	Football Association (FA) 1863	Irish Football Association (IFA)[a] 1880	Scottish Football Association (SFA) 1873	Football Association of Wales (FAW) 1876
Cup competition introduced	1871	1880	1873	1877
League introduced	1888	1890	1890	1902/1992
Membership of Fédération Internationale de Football Association (FIFA), founded 1904	1905–20 1924–8 1946–	1911–20 1924–8 1946–	1910–20 1924–8 1946–	1910–20 1924–8 1946–
First international match	1872	1882	1872	1876

[a] Initially, the IFA claimed jurisdiction over the whole of Ireland.

Figure 28.1   British football: a brief chronology.

Association football displayed perhaps the fullest development of these points (figure 28.1), but as ever, there were exceptions; for instance, cricket's governing body, the Marylebone Cricket Club (MCC), like the game's laws, dated back to the eighteenth century. Equally important in justifying the revolutionary descriptor was a series of general characteristics. First, there occurred a dramatic increase in the number of sports, even if many were modern variants of traditional sports and there were isolated cases of decline (e.g. shinty). Second, the pace and scale of growth, though varying by sport and difficult to quantify accurately, were unprecedented. Nor was it merely a matter of playing a sport, given the rapid advance of spectating and the large-scale interest taken in sport through everyday conversation, the press, wireless broadcasting and cinema newsreels. Third, common leisure hour patterns, most notably the Saturday half-day, enabled mass participation and attendance as well as enhanced commercialization, including professionalism.

Although cricket was often presented as the national sport central to literary constructions of Britishness – A. G. Macdonnell's *England, their England* (1933) remains an excellent example of this genre – and county, pastoral and imperial identities, association football soon emerged as both the most popular sport, whether measured by number of players or spectators, and the principal unifying force in working-class culture: 'the industrial working class was neither politically nor culturally homogenous, but love of football united them almost more than anything else'.[27] By 1914, the British people's game *par excellence* was also en route to becoming the undoubted world sport. The Irish Football Association's *Annual Report 1903–4* reminded readers that 'the game has increased in popularity, going steadily onwards, gathering new adherents every day, and conquering new districts, until it would appear there is nothing that can stem the onrushing force of Association Football as the popular game in town and country'. An even faster period of growth occurred during the next decade, when annual reports of the Scottish Football Association (SFA) reaffirmed repeatedly 'the enormous increase' in the sport's popularity. Between 1910–37 the number of clubs affiliated to the Football Association (FA) in England rose from 12,000 to 37,000. Although cricket and horse racing occasionally attracted large crowds, association football saw the most spectacular growth in spectating. By 1909 around 1 million people watched the game on a Saturday afternoon, with average first division (now the Premier League) attendances rising from 23,115 in 1913–14 to 30,659 in 1938–9. Cup finals and Scotland–England home internationals attracted even larger crowds, with the 1914 Scotland–England match, played in Glasgow, recording a 127,000 attendance. Nor should the novelty of such 100,000-plus gatherings be taken for granted, since traditionally the assembly of large numbers of the lower classes in one place would have been interpreted as having the potential for serious disorder. Despite occasional rowdy outbursts, football, having been civilized by public schools and formally regulated by associations controlled by the upper and middle classes, was now treated by political elites as a respectable sport – in 1919 the Home Office listed sport as a major stabilizing force – even if their preferred sports remained cricket, golf or rugby union.[28]

Football established a nation-wide culture giving Britons a sense of community and civic pride at a time when urbanization and industrialization were undermining the sense of belonging characteristic of the earlier period. For many Britons, as Priestley observed in *The Good Companions*, football was the prime conversational resource: 'a man who had missed the last home match of "t' United" had to enter social life on tiptoe'. Frequently, the local team would be the nearest Football League side – unlike today, most players also resided locally – but Davies found that, despite reduced admission prices for the unemployed, economic circumstances prevented many people in Manchester and Salford from watching either Manchester City or Manchester United. More likely, they watched, even played for, local pub teams. International football developed after 1900, even faster during the interwar years, thereby allowing national teams to represent Britain versus the world, even if the home international tournament, inaugurated in 1883, allowed football to become one of the more visible markers of Irish, Scottish and Welsh national consciousness struggling against English hegemony. However, a recently coined phrase, 'ninety-minute patriots', suggests the need for caution when assessing football's devolutionist credentials.[29]

Unsurprisingly, football, catering to a mass public, proved the most commercialized sport, but clubs frequently prioritized sporting success over profit maximization. For players, the prospect of making money through sport was attractive, even during a period when professional footballers were subjected to a maximum weekly wage (£8 in the 1930s) and a restrictive contract, enjoyed only a brief and insecure career, and were rarely able to use the game as a platform for subsequent material and social advancement. Of course, professional footballers remained a minority; for example, in 1910 the FA claimed 300 professional clubs with 6,000 registered professionals as compared to over 12,000 affiliated amateur clubs and over half a million amateur players. At this time, the SFA recorded ninety-eight professional clubs with 1,637 professional players. Nevertheless, this failed to prevent either heated debates about professionalism in sport or public schools opting for amateur games like rugby union at a time when the Olympic movement operated a strict definition of amateurism and British elites upheld the amateur ethic. Their strong antipathy to professionalism was epitomized in 1903 by Abell, who lamented that association football, far from serving as an instrument of rational recreation, had been devalued by 'the infection of the working classes . . . and the part played in it by money'.[30] Professionalism also represented a major divide in cricket, whose elitist ethos explained the relative lack of commercialization and the pronounced gulf between 'gentlemen' and 'players' compelled to use separate ground entrances, changing rooms and hotels. Moreover, as suggested by Lord Hawke's famous plea – 'Pray God, no professional may ever captain England' – professionals rarely captained a county or national team.

As sport expanded, it was taken up by a broader social range of participants; indeed, growth is viewed frequently in terms of downward diffusion by class. Nevertheless, golf, polo, rowing, rugby union football and tennis, among others, remained sectarian sports whose elitist image was reinforced through convention and high participation costs as well as by social exclusion, as practised by the Amateur Rowing Association's Henley Regatta until 1936. Nor does the social diffusion model take account of the fact that the impetus for the spread of organized sport came from below or that sport remained differentiated, often sharply, along class lines. In particular, sport, having helped to make the English middle classes, represented a major element used to differentiate their 'more superior' suburban lifestyle from 'inferior' working-class variants.

Women's experience of sport is gradually being recovered by historians, who have concentrated hitherto upon the vote and other aspects of the emancipation movement, in spite of the fact that women proved a peripheral sporting presence. Indeed, the very masculine character of the late Victorian and Edwardian sporting revolution is emphasized by Lowerson through chapter headings entitled 'manly games' and 'lesser breeds', defined principally as women! Admittedly, participation levels of upper- and middle-class women increased dramatically during the pre-1914 period; indeed, writing in 1912, one observer asserted that, following a 'great spurt' in recent years, 'woman is coming on in sport'.[31] Yet, numbers for the more popular women's sports, like golf, hockey or lawn tennis, remained modest as compared with those for men. Moreover, relatively few middle-class women engaged in sport after college, and even fewer after marriage. Nor did they participate in any one sport on the same terms as men. Sport reinforced rather than challenged gender stereotypes, and it remained difficult for women either to infiltrate key sports defining masculinity or to undermine existing perceptions of womanliness. Women were firmly excluded by most sports associations, which, like the FA or MCC, remained all-male preserves or, like the Men's Hockey Association, made abortive attempts to prevent the estab-lishment of a women's counterpart. Likewise, women golfers were excluded from leading clubs as well as from parts of the clubhouse, particularly the bar, or might be expected to give way to men when playing out on the course. The vogue for cycling prompted vigorous debate about both its alleged gynaecological dangers and implications for female dress. To some extent, the acceptance of women as cyclists depended upon the adoption of new ideas of womanliness reconciling sport and femininity in a manner preserving existing gender distinctions, such as in terms of ensuring the healthy bodies required for their domestic and child-rearing roles. Unsurprisingly, working-class women participated far less in sport, even during the interwar years, since the usual domestic and financial constraints were accentuated by the reluctance of upper- and middle-class women as well as working-class men to share their sport with them.

Britain was distinguished, even as late as the 1980s, by traditional images of the separation of politics and sport. Despite a strong voluntarist tradition and the lack of a minister of sport until the 1960s, laissez-faire was always a myth, as shown by the longstanding impact of central and municipal government upon working hours and employment patterns, sport in schools, and the provision of playing fields and swim-ming baths. During the pre-1914 period increased anxiety about Britain's power and place in the world in the face of foreign challenges prompted debate about both the merits of sport and the government's role therein. Did sport improve national fit-ness, efficiency and prestige or exert more negative impacts, as argued by Arthur Shadwell, who saw the 'distinctive' and growing British obsession with sport as a problem distracting political and business leaders, encouraging workers' absenteeism, and undermining national preparedness.

> We are a nation at play. Work is a nuisance, an evil necessity to be shirked and hurried over as quickly and easily as possible in order that we may get away to the real business of life – the golf course, the bridge table, the cricket and football field or some other of the thousand amusements which occupy our minds.[32]

Likewise, Robert Graves, looking back in *Goodbye To All That* (1929) to his pre-1914 years at Charterhouse school, attacked the fact that greater prestige was attached to selection for the cricket or football eleven than for being a scholar.

The 1937 National Physical Training and Recreation Act – the resulting 'National Fitness Campaign' was designed to meet Chamberlain's aim 'to raise the quality of those who are in future to carry on the race' – typified the increasingly interven-tionist role of British governments towards sport, including the way in which domes-tic considerations (e.g. evidence of poor national standards of physical fitness) were reinforced by the need to respond to the enhanced politicization of sport by Germany and Italy. Nor did British governments forgo the opportunity of using sport for foreign policy reasons, most notably to prevent the exploitation of sport for hostile propaganda – in 1930 the British government refused visas for a Soviet football team – or to foster relations with another country and raise national prestige through sport-ing success, as happened with the 1938 Germany–England football international played at Berlin.[33]

Conclusion

In 1899, when Veblen discussed leisure's exclusivity, Britain was already moving towards a more generalized leisure society combining work, leisure, education and family life in an ever-changing manner.[34] References to dramatic, even revolutionary, change suggest that by 1939 the pattern of leisure and sport in British society was very different from that prevalent in 1900. Essentially, this involved more of one activity, even more of another and less of something else, even if, in reality, the process occurred in a somewhat erratic and complex manner over time and space. Despite being combined frequently in the same phrase, leisure did not necessarily mean sport, especially as over time Britons were bombarded with an ever-increasing range of attractive alternatives to occupy their free time. Even so, sport, whether being played, watched, read about in the press, discussed in everyday conversation or listened to in a wireless commentary, remained 'the tip of the leisure iceberg'.[35]

Respecting leisure in Britain, the period 1900–39 saw major advances in access, opportunities, commercialization and uniformity of experience, but a sense of perspective is required when viewing its history, given evidence also of restricted access, limited opportunities, Victorian survivals and diversity of experience. As Royle observed, class, gender and wealth remained influential:

> The working class whom Rowntree studied in 1938 still lived, despite a World War, in an intellectual and social climate which was recognisably 'Victorian'. A labourer aged 50 worked five days a week and Saturday morning. His main leisure pursuit was looking after his hens and his allotment; he spent one night at the pub, one at the club, and Saturday afternoon watching football; he took his wife out on Saturday night, and visited relations with her on Sunday night. She washed, dried and ironed the clothes, cleaned the house and did the shopping.[36]

Leisure and sport displayed the familiar mixture of old and new, with Victorian survivals coexisting alongside more recent developments. Television, a 1930s invention, had yet to make an impact. Moreover, despite their dramatic growth since 1900, leisure and sport grew even faster after the Second World War, when – to quote Addison – 'the post-war boom in leisure witnessed the zenith of old or established pastimes rather than the introduction of new ones'.[37]

Meanwhile, the history of leisure and sport in Britain between 1900 and 1939 remains in urgent need of both more research – this point has been argued forcefully by Holt, Huggins and Tranter – and further integration into the historical mainstream, as exemplified already by the work of Jeffrey Hill or Martin Polley. Neither leisure nor sport, representing cultural products of a stratified and hierarchical society, can be studied meaningfully in isolation from broader political, economic, social and cultural trends. Also, far from being marginal activities ignored by most national histories, they proved major preoccupations for many Britons and exerted a pervasive influence shaping the development of British society, most notably by giving meaning to gender, national and social identities. Indeed, one leading social historian asserted that 'the history of societies is more widely reflected in the way they spend their leisure than in their work or politics'.[38] Certainly, leisure and sport offer invaluable windows through which to study Britain between 1900 and 1939, given their role in illuminating continuities and changes in living standards and social structures, offering evidence of people's status and wealth, and serving as powerful reminders and reinforcers of integrative and contested class, gender, local, national and other identities in British society.

NOTES

1   K. Martin, *Editor: Kingsley Martin: A Second Volume of Autobiography, 1931–45* (London, 1968), p. 209.
2   Department of National Heritage, *Sport: Raising the Game* (London, 1995), p. ii.
3   Department of Culture, Media and Sport, *A Sporting Future For All* (London, 2000), p. 2; British Council, *Sprint: A Report on the Relationship between Sport and Society, Education, the Arts and Gender* (London, 1999), pp. 3, 24–8.
4   *Daily Express*, 3 January 1929.
5   J. Mangan, *The Games Ethic and Imperialism: Aspects of the Diffusion of an Ideal* (London, 1998).
6   R. Kircher, *Fair Play: The Games of Merrie England* (London, 1928), pp. 3–6, 63.
7   Quoted in P. J. Beck, *Scoring for Britain: International Football and International Politics, 1900–1939* (London, 1999), p. 28; L. Colley, *Britons: Forging the Nation, 1707–1837* (London, 1994), p. 162.
8   B. Tuchman, *Practising History: Selected Essays* (New York, 1982), p. 234.
9   P. Clarke, *Hope and Glory: Britain 1900–1990* (London, 1996), p. 53; Beck, *Scoring*, pp. 10–13. One exception is Martin Polley. Note his forthcoming book entitled *Sport and British Diplomacy: The Foreign Office and International Sport, 1896–2000* (London, 2003).
10 J. Walvin, *Leisure and Society, 1830–1950* (London, 1978), pp. 63–9, 125.
11 M. Huggins, 'Second-class citizens? English middle-class culture and sport, 1850–1910: a reconsideration', *International Journal of the History of Sport*, 17, no. 1 (2000), pp. 28–30.
12 E. J. Hobsbawm, *Worlds of Labour: Further Studies in the History of Labour* (London, 1984); G. Stedman Jones, *Languages of Class: Studies in English Working-class History 1832–1982* (London, 1983).
13 D. Rubinstein, 'Cycling in the 1890s', *Victorian Studies*, 21, no. 1 (1977), pp. 47–9, 71.
14 W. Orr, *Deer Forests, Landlords and Crofters: The Western Highlands in Victorian and Edwardian Times* (Edinburgh, 1982), pp. 147–8.
15 Quoted in Walvin, *Leisure*, p. 133.
16 S. G. Jones, *Workers at Play: A Social and Economic History of Leisure, 1918–1939* (London, 1986), pp. 17, 198.
17 *The New Survey of London Life and Labour*, vol. 9 (London, 1935), pp. 1–7.
18 *The New Survey of London Life and Labour*, vol. 1 (London, 1934), vol. 9; S. B. Rowntree, *Poverty and Progress* (London, 1941); A. Davies, *Leisure, Gender and Poverty: Working-class Culture in Salford and Manchester, 1900–1939* (Buckingham, 1992); G. Cross, *Worktowners at Blackpool: Mass-Observation and Popular Leisure in the 1930s* (London, 1990); P. Schweitzer, ed., *The Time of Our Lives: Memories of Leisure in the 1920s and 1930s* (London, 1986).
19 S. G. Jones, *Sport, Politics and the Working Class: Organised Labour and Sport in Interwar Britain* (Manchester, 1988).
20 A. J. P. Taylor, *English History 1914–1945* (Oxford, 1965), p. 313.
21 Davies, *Leisure*, p. 40.

22 N. Pronay, 'The first reality: film censorship in liberal England', in K. Short, ed., *Feature Films as History* (London, 1981), p. 125.

23 Davies, *Leisure*, p. 55; C. M. Parratt, 'Little means or time: working-class women and leisure in late Victorian and Edwardian England', *International Journal of the History of Sport*, 15, no. 2 (1998), pp. 47–8.

24 V. Brittain, *Testament of Youth* (London, 1978), p. 51.

25 E. J. Hobsbawm, 'Mass producing traditions: Europe 1870–1914', in E. J. Hobsbawm and T. Ranger, eds, *The Invention of Tradition* (Cambridge, 1983), p. 298; R. McKibbin, *Classes and Cultures: England 1918–1951* (Oxford, 1998), p. 332.

26 N. Tranter, *Sport, Economy and Society in Britain, 1750–1914* (Cambridge, 1998), p. 29.

27 McKibbin, *Classes*, p. 340; D. Russell, 'Sport and identity: the case of Yorkshire county cricket club, 1890–1939', *Twentieth-century British History*, 7, no. 2 (1996), p. 206; J. Williams, ' "One could literally have walked on the heads of the people congregated there": sport, the town and identity', in K. Laybourn, ed., *Social Conditions, Status and Community, 1860–c.1920* (Stroud, 1997), pp. 123–6.

28 Jones, *Workers*, p. 180.

29 G. Jarvie and G. Walker, eds, *Scottish Sport in the Making of the Nation: Ninety-minute Patriots?* (Leicester, 1994); M. Cronin, *Sport and Nationalism in Ireland: Gaelic Games, Soccer and Irish Identity since 1884* (Dublin, 1999); J. Sugden and A. Bairner, 'Northern Ireland: sport in a divided society', in L. Allison, ed., *The Politics of Sport* (Manchester, 1986); G. Williams, 'How amateur was my valley: professional sport and national identity in Wales, 1890–1914', *British Journal of Sports History*, 2, no. 3 (1985), pp. 248–69; M. Johnes, *Soccer and Society in South Wales, 1900–1939* (Cardiff, 2002).

30 H. F. Abell, 'The football fever', *Macmillan's Magazine*, 89 (1904), p. 276.

31 'An Oxford Blue', 'Are women approaching men in sport?', *C. B. Fry's Magazine*, 16 (1912), p. 209.

32 A. Shadwell, *Industrial Efficiency: A Comparative Study of Industrial Life in England, Germany and America*, vol. 2 (London, 1906), pp. 264–6, 454.

33 Beck, *Scoring*, pp. 4–7, 137–42.

34 R. Dahrendorf, 'Towards the twenty-first century', in M. Howard and W. Roger Louis, eds, *The Oxford History of the Twentieth Century* (Oxford, 1998), p. 340.

35 Jones, *Workers*, p. 56.

36 E. Royle, *Modern Britain: A Social History 1750–1997* (London, 1997), p. 286.

37 P. Addison, *Now the War is Over: A Social History of Britain, 1945–51* (London, 1995), p. 114; Jones, *Workers*, p. 199.

38 H. Perkin, 'Teaching the nations how to play: sport and society in the British Empire and Commonwealth', *International Journal of the History of Sport*, 6, no. 2 (1989), p. 145.

FURTHER READING

Bailey, P., *Leisure and Class in Victorian England: Rational Recreation and the Contest for Control, 1830–1885* (London, 1978).

Beck, P. J., 'Projecting an image of a great nation on the world screen through football: British cultural propaganda between the wars', in B. Taithe and T. Thornton, eds, *Propaganda: Political Rhetoric and Identity, 1300–1990* (Stroud, 1999), pp. 265–84.

Beck, P. J., *Scoring for Britain: International Football and International Politics, 1900–1939* (London, 1999).

Davies, A., *Leisure, Gender and Poverty: Working-class Culture in Salford and Manchester, 1900–1939* (Buckingham, 1992).

Dewey, P., *War and Progress: Britain 1914–1945* (Harlow, 1997).

Hill, J., *Sport, Leisure and Culture in Twentieth-century Britain* (Basingstoke, 2002).

Holt, R., *Sport and the British: A Modern History* (Oxford, 1989).

Holt, R., 'Sport and history: the state of the subject in Britain', *Twentieth-century British History*, 7 (1996), pp. 231–52.

Horne, J., Tomlinson, A. and Whannel, G., *Understanding Sport: An Introduction to the Sociological and Cultural Analysis of Sport* (London, 1999).

Jones, S. G., *Workers at Play: A Social and Economic History of Leisure, 1918–1939* (London, 1986).

Lowerson, J., *Sport and the English Middle Classes, 1870–1914* (Manchester, 1993).

Mangan, J. A., *Athleticism in the Victorian and Edwardian Public School* (London, 2000).

Marwick, A., *A History of the Modern British Isles, 1914–1999* (Oxford, 2000).

Mason, T., ed., *Sport in Britain: A Social History* (Cambridge, 1989).

Mason, T., 'Sport and recreation', in P. Johnson, ed., *Twentieth-century Britain: Economic, Social and Cultural Change* (London, 1994), pp. 111–26.

Russell, D., *Football and the English: A Social History of Association Football in England, 1863–1995* (Preston, 1997).

Tranter, N., *Sport, Economy and Society in Britain, 1750–1914* (Cambridge, 1998).

Walton, J. K., *The British Seaside: Holidays and Resorts in the Twentieth Century* (Manchester, 2000).

Walvin, J., *Leisure and Society, 1830–1950* (London, 1978).

Walvin, J., *The People's Game: The History of Football Revisited* (Edinburgh, 1994).

Williams, J., *Cricket and England: A Cultural and Social History of the Inter-war Years* (London, 1999).

CHAPTER TWENTY-NINE

Religion, 1900–1939

STUART MEWS

One of the criticisms made of A. J. P. Taylor's *English History 1914–45* when it appeared in 1965 was its almost total neglect of religion. There should have been no surprise in this because Taylor, like most of his contemporaries (he lived from 1906 to 1990), was not a churchgoer, though he would go out of his way to visit churches and cathedrals, which in itself raises questions about what is meant by 'being religious'. With religious institutions manifestly in numerical decline in the twentieth century, a historian with limited space cannot be blamed for downplaying an area of human life that must have seemed of only marginal relevance. Yet Taylor's memories of his own childhood suggest that in the opening years of the twentieth century religion still had significance, if only for tracing inherited attitudes, personal identity and social control.[1] However, it is important to note that church membership was growing until 1927, when the churches together had 6 million names on their rolls.

In providing historical interpretations of the first half of the twentieth century most historians have followed Taylor in giving little or no place to religion. A notable exception is Ross McKibbin, especially in *Classes and Cultures: England 1918–1951*, where in addition to a chapter on religion and belief, there is an awareness of the religious dimension of other areas of social existence. For the earlier pre-First World War period Jose Harris's *Private Lives, Public Spheres: A Social History of Britain 1870–1914* also takes religion seriously as a vital force in the lives of people and in the working of institutions. Both, however, hive religion off to a separate chapter rather than integrate it into the social flow of the periods they are covering.[2] In this they are in step with those sociologists who believe that religion in the twentieth century went through a process of differentiation, in which having formerly been integrated with other aspects of life, the religious sphere became increasingly separated out, and consequently lost relevance to national social and political life.

Since around 1980 the interpretations of the social functions of religion by historians have been radically revised, which has made it an exciting area in which to work. The academic pioneer in this field is Hugh McLeod, who since 1974 has published a steady stream of books and articles on urban religion in the late nineteenth and early twentieth centuries, beginning with London but moving on to comparisons with Berlin and New York. McLeod wanted to find out who went to church, why they went, and what led to lapses in attendance. Starting with church attendance surveys, the impressions of clergy, journalists and city missioners, he moved on to oral history archives. Having mainly focused on class in his first book, McLeod moved on to extend his researches by also considering age and gender.[3] Further area studies by Stephen Yeo on Reading, Jeffrey Cox on Lambeth, Jeremy Morris on Croydon and Simon Green on Halifax have deepened understanding of the processes by which religion peaked and then declined.[4] Two important approaches should be mentioned. Callum Brown has broken away from the pack of social historians by arguing that urbanization, far from being a secularizing force, in fact assisted religious bodies to maintain and increase their congregations. He argues that in moving from country to town, people were moving out of areas of traditional domination by squire and parson and were now able to use their free time as they wished. First generations of town-dwellers might, like first-generation Americans, seek a church or chapel that had links with the old world they had left. For families from Lincolnshire, where late nineteenth-century villagers often had dual loyalties to both the parish church and the Methodist chapel, migration might result in attachment just to the chapel, which in a strange town could offer a warmer welcome in a more egalitarian worshipping community.

In his study of churchgoing in Reading, Stephen Yeo has shown that the religious organizations were sharing in the common problems of all the town's voluntary organizations. In Lambeth Jeffrey Cox has pointed to what the Edwardian bishop Edward S. Talbot called *diffuse* religion, but also draws attention to the strength of religious organizations. In Edwardian England, religious organizations were close to working people because they were major providers for people's physical as well as spiritual needs. This could lead to an unhealthy dependence on church charities, which could produce servility and resentment. The parish church of St Mary in the London suburb of Barnes had a high church vicar, who by 1913 had set up thirty funds to plug the gaps in social provision. These included a parish nurse, a coal club, a clothing club, a children's shoe club, a women's boot club, a blanket club, a soup kitchen, children's dinners, a maternity society, as well as more specifically church-related causes such as foreign missions. Not surprisingly, the vicar was constantly appealing for money in the magazine. In its outreach into the community, St Mary's was fairly typical of most churches and chapels of the time. As well as being a provider of welfare, Edwardian religious bodies also tried to respond to the demand for recreational and youth facilities: choirs, mothers' meetings, men's institutes with snooker tables, football and cricket clubs, Boys' Brigade, Boy Scouts, Girl Guides.

Bishop Talbot's distinction between *diffused* and *embodied* religion has been found helpful by some recent historians. It was his high church way of justifying the Church of England's retention of its status as the established national church. He believed that Christians were leaven in the lump. In his charge in 1903 to the diocese of Rochester, which then included the whole of south London, he spoke about the church's failures, the low level of church attendance, and the gulf between the church (*embodied*) religion and the working class with its basic beliefs. He drew comfort, however, from the many signs that the English people did have elemental conceptions of right and wrong, a willingness to offer help to a needy neighbour, and appreciation of a warm community spirit. This he saw as *diffused* Christianity. The English people were, in his eyes, Christians of the *diffused* kind, which he saw as a base on which to build an informed Christian faith. The aim of high churchmen like Talbot was to deepen the understanding of the faith that people already had through encouraging more regular participation in the sacramental services of the church. As his friend Charles Gore said, 'What we want most is not more Christians, but better Christians, not more Churchmen, but better Churchmen'. Better churchmen in Gore's view were episcopally confirmed weekly communicants. This high church view was to become the dominant ideology of the ministry of the Church of England in the period from around 1920 to around 1975.

A crucial requirement in Gore's and Talbot's eyes in creating better church-people were church schools where children were grounded in the catechism and creed. To maintain church schools, many in declining villages, Talbot arranged a lunch at which Robert Morant persuaded Unionist leader A. J. Balfour to take up the ideas which appeared in the 1902 Education Act. The most controversial clauses, the scrapping of elected School Boards and introduction of rate support for denominational schools (mainly Anglican and Roman Catholic), provoked Free church outrage and direct action in the form of a refusal to pay that part of the rate deemed to pay for church teaching. Free churchmen had given up their own schools in 1870 and resented having to pay for 'Rome on the rates', especially as the Unionist government had obtained its majority mainly on the issue of the Boer War and had no mandate to change education. Passive resistance involved bailiffs seizing goods and auctioning them. Almost 200 Free churchmen were absolutists and served prison sentences between 1902 and 1914. Their methods influenced M. K. Gandhi in the struggle from 1920 for an independent India.

Some historians have followed the French functionalist sociologist Emile Durkheim in holding an inclusive view of religion, that is, that every society has over-arching values which can be described as its religion. In this view, the faith or world-view of an Englishman might be Christian in one of that faith's many varieties but is never confined to some illusory pure version. Some people's personal ideologies might be an amalgam of some Christian virtues with nationalism, possibly royalism, possibly socialism, possibly folk culture. 'This is indeed, *par excellence* the age of faith or rather of faiths', claimed J. N. Figgis in 1909. A new wave of historians now claim that accounts of the religiosity of the nation must include the entire range of its religious beliefs and practices, even though many might take a popular form which falls outside orthodox Christian theology. This has led Sarah Williams to interview old people in Southwark and enabled her to reconstruct the cosmologies of south Londoners.[5] Folk beliefs, superstitions, lucky charms, bad omens and effective rituals are mixed up with church ceremonies, Bibles, crucifixes and communion. For many, possession of an unread family Bible was an important way of hallowing and protecting a home. Williams insists that her study is not primarily about religion but about people and the way in which their needs find religious expression, often 'by depute' – women representing the family.

Sarah Williams like McLeod begins as did the German sociologist Max Weber with people trying to make sense of their situation. Why has my husband/wife/child died? Why was I the unlucky one who didn't get a job today? Experiences like these lie behind the religious concerns of many people and were significant factors in working-class theodicies. But religion does not just console the deprived, it also legitimizes the achievements of the successful. Both start from the individual's need to explain in intellectually and emotionally satisfying terms his or her own peculiar circumstances.

But religion in this period did more than simply respond to individual needs. An alternative starting point has come from John Wolffe, who draws on Durkheim with his stress on the social character of religion and on the importance of ritual and ceremony for reinforcing beliefs and community. Wolffe has impressively argued his case in a book focusing on the social impact of the deaths and emotional arousal caused by the funerals and services of commemoration of famous people, such as Queen Victoria and King Edward VII.[6]

Wolffe's work can usefully be considered alongside that of David Cannadine, whose recent work on imperialism, and earlier work on the invention of tradition, are important keys for unlocking the role of religion.[7] The ideology of empire from around 1880 to 1920 was welcomed by most religious leaders as confirming that the British were a people chosen by God to take the true religion to pupil races. All the denominations accepted the 'white man's burden' with pride. Christian imperialism, fuelled by the evangelical Keswick convention revivalism, provided the stimulus for a new generation to seek 'the evangelization of the world in this generation'.

At the apex of empire was the monarch, whose significance was enhanced by the popular pageantry of the 1890s and Edwardian years. The Anglo-Boer War brought out the patriotism of the Church of England – so much so that it was the prime minister, the marquis of Salisbury, himself an Anglican high churchman, who wrote in June 1900 to the archbishop of Canterbury to ask for the toning down of a public pronouncement which spoke in glowing tones of the expansion of the empire.[8] For Anglicans having to face both the aggressive threats from self-confident Free churchmen, who wanted nothing less than the disestablishment of the Church of England, and the internal battles between high and low Anglican churchmen, the former led by Viscount Halifax and the latter by Sir William Harcourt and Lady Wimborne, it seemed providential to rally to the call of the empire. Even Dr B. F. Westcott, bishop of Durham, the leading Christian socialist and long-term advocate of European disarmament and peace, embraced the British cause against the Boers with ardour. All this contrasted with the divisions about the South African War to be found in the chapels. The Wesleyan Methodists, the largest of the Free church denominations, largely took the Conservative and Liberal imperialist line, whilst the Baptists and Primitive Methodists followed Dr John Clifford and the young radical MP David Lloyd George in criticizing the British methods of warfare and internment.

The Church of England was quick to grasp the value of popular monarchy and the special ties between throne and altar. The death of Queen Victoria and the coronation of the new King Edward VII provided new possibilities for cementing the traditional relationship between the church and the crown. No one had a keener awareness of this than Randall Davidson, bishop of Winchester, who as archbishop of Canterbury from 1903 to 1928 was the religious leader who towers over the period. Personally selected for high office by Queen Victoria, who had a weakness for young Scotsmen, he became the first modern archbishop, visiting the United States shortly after his appointment, and creating a centralized bureaucracy.[9] But Davidson also wanted to mobilize tradition, preserve the monarchy by humanizing it, maintain its ecclesiastical links and strengthen its hold on popular loyalties. To bring the king closer to the people he approved a proposal to allow press photographs of the coronation ceremony in 1910; it was his suggestion that the title 'queen mother' be invented for Queen Alexandra; he proposed (to no avail) the lying-in-state of the dead king in Westminster hall so that Londoners could pay their last respects. He has been described in a recent study as one of the most important contributors to the establishment of the modern monarchy.[10] His fellow archbishop, Cosmo Lang at York, did his bit by suggesting (successfully) that the new king, George V, should tour politically crucial Lancashire. A twentieth-century Anglican slogan might be, 'No king, no bishop'.

The royal link was one way in which the Church of England with considerable success carved a new role for itself as royal confidante, bestowing and receiving blessings and so ensuring a place in the national civil religion. National and local religious rituals (coronations, mayoral services, memorials) were ways of maintaining a place for religion in a nation that was slowly abandoning the habit of Sunday worship. McLeod would not, in my view, reject Wolffe's interpretation, and vice versa. Both approaches clearly contribute to the bigger picture. So also do narrative history and biographical studies. Just as the political history of this period cannot ignore the people who brought about change – a Lloyd George or Churchill – so religious history needs to take account of the views and actions of leaders of the Anglican episcopate such as Davidson and Gore, or the Congregationalist R. J. Campbell. Events such as wars, industrial disputes and natural disasters can shake people's confidence in the stability of their world and require religious responses. What follows is an outline of some of the highlights, trends and significant personalities of the period from 1900 to 1939.

There were many reasons for the decline in churchgoing, relative to the increase of population. The leisure revolution, elementary education for all, the challenge of labour and the assertiveness of women had implications for the churches. The invention of the bicycle provided opportunities that were blamed for taking people away from churches, while the motor car not only disturbed the peace of the Edwardian Sunday, but also encouraged the weekend habit amongst the middle class. Even more threatening were the mass spectator sports like football, which by claiming Saturday afternoon encouraged a Sunday morning lie-in.

Evangelicalism, which had set the tone for early and mid-Victorian society, was being rejected for its lack of joy and humanity, as well as its intellectual crudeness. Christianity was by the 1890s being domesticated through the rejection of the concept of a God who seemed to be more concerned with punishing sinners than in sharing his love. Even in Scotland and Wales Calvinism was in retreat. Liberal theology, powerfully influenced by German scholars like Albrecht Ritschl and Adolf von Harnack, presented a God who was the father of all people, not just the predestined few. Gradually the idea spread that Jesus had come not just to save individual souls but to inaugurate a kingdom of love characterized by the fatherhood of God and the brotherhood of man. Nonconformity was particularly receptive to these ideas and they were powerfully developed in the sermons of ministers who combined Liberal theology with Christian socialism. The Rev. Frank Ballard was a Wesleyan minister, Christian apologist and Christian-socialist controversialist in the Sheffield area. He believed that the best defence of Christianity was by holding public question-and-answer sessions and through the publication of cheap tracts. He was particularly

aroused by the anti-Christian campaigns built around the socialist Robert Blatchford's *God and My Neighbour*, published in 1903.

The best-known preacher in Edwardian England was R. J. Campbell, minister of
the City Temple, the leading Congregational chapel in London, who regularly
preached to congregations of 3,000. His sermons were picked up by the *Daily Mail*
and collected together in a book, *The New Theology*, published in 1907. His gospel
was a blend of liberal Protestantism, mysticism, pantheism and the socialism of the
Independent Labour party: 'Jesus was Divine, but so are we', 'the wagon of
Socialism must be hitched to the star of religious faith', 'Go with Keir Hardie to the
House of Commons, and listen to him pleading for justice to his order, and you see
the Atonement'.

In the pits and mills, what can loosely be called socialist ideas were getting a more
receptive hearing. 'There is a strong new wine working in the hearts and brains of
thousands today', declared the bishop of London, A. F. Winnington-Ingram. 'They
are tired of hearing of a heaven in another world; they believe they were promised a
heaven on earth.' Anglican clergy founded the Christian Social Union to press for
collective action by government for better wages and conditions, but it rarely reached
down into the parishes. Other denominations had parallel Christian socialist ginger
groups. In a study of pit villages in Co. Durham, Robert Moore has shown the
tension between the generations in the Primitive Methodist chapels, leading to the
young Methodists who had now become socialists being driven out of membership.[11]
Yet if promotion of socialism in Pleasant Sunday Afternoon meetings in chapels was
discouraged and sometimes banned, this did not keep Methodists out of trade unions
in which many of them, like Peterlee in Co. Durham, rose to positions of trust. A
Methodist like Arthur Henderson could move out of Liberalism and find greater
opportunities in the Labour party, but after 1918 was unable to persuade it to adopt
his lifelong commitment to temperance. The Labour party after 1918 was wary of
giving hostages to fortune by adopting the faddist notions of the Victorian Liberals'
Newcastle Programme.

Figgis's observation about living at a time of faiths should be a reminder that
beyond the main historic denominations were minority groups and fringe cults.[12] The
immigration of poor east European Jews to London, and in smaller numbers to Manchester, Leeds and Glasgow, trebled the number of Jews in Britain between 1881
and 1905. The estimated Jewish population of London rose from 47,000 in 1883
to 180,000 in 1914. Most of the newcomers were concentrated in poor Yiddish-
speaking clusters in Spitalfields and Whitechapel, where their presence was resented
by longstanding residents who feared competition for jobs and homes. Their worries,
fanned by xenophobic politicians, led to the Aliens Act of 1905. Older historians
have told an optimistic story of the acceptance of Jews and their achievements in
politics, business and law, but recent work has focused on anti-Semitism, the processes
of acculturation, women, prostitutes and trade unions. Comfortably off, assimilated
middle-class Jews who had moved to suburban Finchley or St John's Wood had
doubts about the open-door policy, but the pogroms in Russia in 1903 and 1904
made them more sympathetic. Most Jews in England were Ashkenazim with east
European roots and the rabbi of London's Great Synagogue was regarded as their
spokesman. But there was also a Jewish intelligentsia, often of Sephardic or Spanish
origin. Under the leadership of Claude Montefiore, who had taken a first-class degree

at Balliol College, Oxford, and Lily Montagu, the Liberal Jewish Synagogue was founded in 1911. Liberal Judaism was rejected by both orthodoxy and by visionary Zionists who dreamt of a return to Palestine. This was the life-goal from 1895 of Theodore Herzl, a Budapest-born Viennese journalist and playwright, and was taken up by Chaim Weizmann, a Manchester University biochemist, but treated with scorn by the *Jewish Chronicle*. Liberal Jews saw it as aiming for 'a restoration of primitiveness'. Montefiore warned that the Zionist movement was harmful to 'the development of Judaism as a religion'. An indication of the failure of the Zionist vision to catch fire can be found in the paltry £500 raised for Zionist funds from British Jews in 1916. The following year Lloyd George's cabinet, in a bid to sway American opinion, agreed to the letter the foreign secretary A. J. Balfour had written to Lord Rothschild supporting the idea of a Jewish 'national home' in Palestine subject to the preservation of the civil and religious rights of existing Arab communities.[13]

Knowledge of eastern religions was slight in England before the Great War. A mosque had been built in Woking in 1889 for Indian Muslims, where the teaching of Islam was available. More acceptable to the western mind was the teaching of the Bahais, who began in Tehran as a sect within Shi'ite Islam but soon developed into a semi-pacifist universal religion that was condemned by every branch of Islam. They caught the attention of a Cambridge orientalist, E. G. Brown, who publicized their teaching and sufferings. In 1911 and 1912 the leader of the faith, 'Abdu'l-Baha, spoke in London at the City Temple and an Anglican church, and small groups were formed. However, interest in eastern mysticism was confined to small numbers, though there seems to have been some interest in the Hindu idea of reincarnation.

Many people in Wales felt disoriented at the start of the twentieth century. A majority of them, brought up in a chapel-centred nonconformist culture, felt threatened. The arrival of non-Welsh speakers in the industrial areas in the south, together with rural depopulation in the north, weakened national self-confidence. Sermons deplored increasing worldliness and longed for religious revival. It came in 1904 in the form of a mass movement triggered by the prophetic visions of Evan Roberts, a twenty-six-year-old ex-miner who had been training for the ministry. Though the catalyst for revival, Roberts was not its leader. Spiritual fervour spread spontaneously; meetings were held without structure; anyone could start a chorus, give a testimony or interpret a vision. Some 100,000 converts were claimed in Wales and the spiritual repercussions spread to India and California. This was the climate in which Pentecostalism – speaking in tongues and spiritual healing – flourished. The movement was not in any obvious way political, but Dr Rhodri Hayward, following Michel Foucault and Michel de Certeau, argues that what was believed to be prophecy was always subversive. In Wales the revival swept aside the normally accepted authority figures in the community, ministers, chapel deacons and parents; young men like Roberts and young women like Anne Davies who followed him were empowered by their inspired utterances, and given a status in the revival which defied their worldly social standing. Even the admonitions of children were taken seriously. Roberts had a nervous breakdown and the revival petered out, but it left hundreds with the belief that they had sampled first-century Christianity with its absence of hierarchy and its egalitarian lifestyles. This was the dynamic that inspired A. J. Cook, the Welsh ex-Baptist lay preacher – twenty-one in 1904 – who was to become the fiery leader of the Welsh miners in the General Strike of 1926.[14] It is difficult not to conclude that the revival contributed to the atmosphere which in Wales produced the 1906 electoral landslide.

The new parliament was regarded as a triumph by the nonconformists, who looked to the new Liberal government to introduce changes to the 1902 Education Act and to the licensing laws, and to disestablish the Anglican church in Wales. They had hoped that the way forward would follow the French pattern, where religious institutions had been secularized in 1904. Obstruction in the House of Lords blocked all Liberal measures close to Free church hearts and some nonconformists began to lose heart. Their national secretary Thomas Law, depressed and overworked, drowned himself in 1910.

F. B. Meyer, a Baptist minister, took Law's place and sought to rally his troops by leading them into battle in a moral crusade against a heavyweight boxing match planned for London in 1911. The two antagonists were a former British soldier, Matt Wells, and a black American, Jack Johnson, likened by the BBC's Harry Carpenter to Mike Tyson. Long the target for moral reform groups in America, where his victories had left a trail of injury and death in the subsequent street brawls, Johnson now became the target of a campaign instigated by the Free churches, but which drew support from other groups, Anglican bishops, headmasters and MPs. Bishop Edward Talbot wrote to deplore the racial aspect of the conflict. After a public meeting, press and letter campaign, Winston Churchill, then home secretary, intervened and the fight was called off.[15]

In Edwardian England, it was important for the Free churches to stand up and be counted. Not only did some of them feel frustrated by the Liberal government's inability to right their grievances, but there was concern at the growth of Roman Catholicism. It was estimated that in 1900 there were 2,061,000 Roman Catholics in Britain, as against 5,056,000 Protestants. In the twentieth century Catholics were becoming more visible in English life. The Wesleyans felt they were staking their claim to become the alternative to the Church of England when they built Westminster Central Hall opposite Westminster Abbey in 1900, but the Catholics provided Westminster Cathedral in 1903. Winston Churchill blamed the opposition of Catholic priests for the loss of his seat in Manchester in 1908, and later in the same year British Catholics caught the attention of the world when the outdoor procession to round off the International Eucharistic Congress was banned by the government, following protests to the king by Ulster Unionist MPs. The newly appointed archbishop of Westminster, Francis Bourne, won his spurs by wrongfooting the government and forcing the resignation of a Catholic cabinet minister, the marquis of Ripon, and the transfer of the home secretary Herbert Gladstone. To try to make amends, Asquith agreed to the removal of the offensive anti-Catholic oath in the coronation service for 1910, but Bourne smarted from the outburst of anti-Catholicism and bided his time, which was to come in 1926.

The years between 1910 and 1914 saw the welfare reforms of the Liberal government, the consolidation of the Labour party and the crucial consciousness-raising of the women's suffrage movement. These three developments were to be critical for religious organizations. All the denominations had societies in support of votes for women by constitutional means. The Anglican high church Community of the Resurrection in Yorkshire, founded by Charles Gore to train boys from poor homes for the priesthood, provided a platform for the militant suffragette Christabel

Pankhurst. The leading Anglican woman of the time was a bishop's widow, Louise Creighton, who before 1914 opposed votes for women, putting her efforts instead into promoting higher education for women. Among younger Anglican women, Maude Royden campaigned not just for the vote but also for opening the Anglican priesthood to women. Recent research has revealed that in Liverpool, normally a cockpit for sectarianism, the campaign for votes for women crossed the usual divisions between constitutionalists and militants, as well as that between Catholics and Protestants.[16]

What has been called 'the threat of Europe' created a pervasive sense of anxiety. Nonconformists had been enthusiastic supporters of the Anglo-German Society for promoting friendship through the churches. The perennial belief of middle- and upper-class pessimists that the country was going to the dogs was fed by the wave of strikes, the militant women's campaign of window-breaking, and the fears of insurrection in Ulster. Many Anglican clergy looked to compulsory national service to instil discipline at home and deter invasion from abroad. The Anglican Church Congress had debated the subject in 1910 when, according to a press report, 'the militarists ran away with the meeting'. Despairing of the restoration of Victorian values, Dean Inge came to the conclusion that the only solution was war. 'War', he declared in 1911, 'would purge the middle class and discipline the working class.' 'We are certainly moving to great calamities in this country', thought Hensley Henson, dean of Durham in 1912.[17]

When war was declared with Germany in 1914, the churches rallied to the national cause and used their positions and pulpits to justify the war and aid recruitment. Before 1914 the sympathies of most British churchgoers lay more with Germany, which was seen as Protestant and progressive, than with France, often viewed as either Catholic or infidel. Belgium before 1914 was regularly condemned, especially by nonconformists, for atrocities committed by King Albert's agents in the Congo. Now the German invasion of Belgium with its cynical disregard for treaty obligations outraged the nation, and especially those placed in positions of religious leadership. A Cambridge Free church minister noted 'the frequency in which in private gatherings the religious official is the most belligerent person present'.[18] According to a French observer, 'in the history of the war no fact has more "shocked" the English conscience' than 'that the enemy does not consider himself bound by a treaty'.[19]

Bishop Winnington-Ingram of London was an ardent patriot who excelled in persuading men to enlist. In June 1915 he announced that the nation was engaged 'in a Holy War'. 'Christ died on Good Friday for Freedom, Honour and Chivalry, and our boys are dying for the same thing . . . They have all died a martyr's death and passed to glorious reward.' The bishop's language was disowned by some younger clergy who had experience of trench warfare and who suspected that this kind of rhetoric came better from Muslims. The veteran Christian socialist Scott Holland, now an Oxford professor, urged that the clergy should not be asked 'to become Mad Mullahs preaching a Jehad (sic)', but the following week's paper said that correspondence was overwhelmingly with the bishop of London.[20] The clergy of all denominations urged their young men to join up. Free church ministers preferred voluntary enlistment, but many Anglicans were advocates of compulsion. Michael Furse was high church bishop of Pretoria, who came back to England to rally the nation. In May 1915 he told the boys of Eton that every man, woman and child should be at the service of the state, demanding in a letter to *The Times* conscription for both the army and munitions factories.[21] He was one of many clergy who convinced themselves that the army in the field was being let down by slacking at home. Soldiers' wives were denounced for drinking away their allowances. Shipyard workers on the Clyde were criticized for persistent absenteeism – thought to be caused by drink. In an astute move both to placate nonconformist critics and to react to the reported shortfalls in production, Lloyd George introduced restrictions in licensing hours that were to remain in place for most of the rest of the century, and persuaded King George V to abstain from alcohol in public for the duration of the war.[22]

'The clergy have never worked harder or with greater self-denial or with more whole-hearted devotion', protested a puzzled church journal in 1916, 'and yet the Trades Union Congress at its recent sitting gave them a rude slap in the face.' The issue debated by the TUC was the exemption of the clergy from military service. Medieval canon law had been clear that a priest should not shed blood, but the anomalies in government policy after the introduction of conscription inevitably caused resentment. Ben Tillett, the London dockers' leader, proposed a motion regretting 'the unfair privilege' granted by exempting the clergy from military service. Opposition to him came from another dockers' leader, James Sexton, a cradle Roman Catholic from Liverpool, who questioned the crude anti-clericalism behind Tillett's assault. Despite a reasoned explanation of clerical exemption, Tillett's resolution was carried by 1,379,000 to 1,200,000, itself an interesting indication of the attitudes of working-men's organizations, which seem to have voted on gut feelings rather than the strength of argument. 'What is the secret of the animosity of Labour towards the Church?' wailed *The Churchman*.[23]

Conscription posed serious problems of conscience for some young men who were Quakers or who had taken pre-war liberal theology seriously. They now found support in the Fellowship of Reconciliation and the No Conscription Fellowship. Free church ministers were particularly disturbed by reports of the ill treatment of conscientious objectors (COs), who were liable to be sent to France where they were told that persistent refusal to obey orders in the field was punishable by death. The Free church secretary F. B. Meyer was horrified and, though pro-war, devoted time and trouble to intercede for fair treatment for prisoners of conscience, even tracing a group of COs to Boulogne where he addressed them and then rushed back to warn Asquith of the public consequences if they were shot.

Evidence of a small demand for religion in the services was a great disappointment to the chaplains. After the war a report based on questionnaires was compiled by a committee chaired by E. S. Talbot, now bishop of Winchester. In an echo of his pre-war comment distinguishing between diffused and embodied religion, the report highlighted the view, widely shared by the chaplains and already mentioned, that 'the soldier has got religion. I am not sure that he has got Christianity'. Chaplains discovered that soldiers were 'amazingly *ignorant* of the Christian religion' and unable to name the four gospels. Yet at the back of their minds was a vague, imprecise belief: 'they are conscious of being in the hands of a Power which controls the world; they are conscious of their impotence and littleness'. When an Edinburgh minister, John Kelman, set out the soldier's creed he put fatalism at the top. How was it that one man was shot and another spared? 'Oh fate', the men would answer, '– *Kismet*. In this we are Muslims.' The close comradeship of army life was another recurrent theme in replies. 'They feel they have got something worth keeping, and Church-people at home will do well to remember it.'[24] In these totally unforeseen circumstances, many chaplains floundered. One of them remarked in 1918 that the war was breaking down no class barriers; officers and men lived in different worlds, 'and the chaplain lives in the officer's world'.[25] Unlike Anglicans, Roman Catholic chaplains usually came from the same social class as the men to whom they had to minister, and were free to concentrate on their pastoral role instead of organizing concerts or canteens. The usually accepted view is that the reputation of the Roman Catholic church was enhanced by the war, whereas that of the Church of England was diminished.

There is little evidence to suggest that the Christian beliefs of the nation, such as they were, were consciously repudiated as a result of war, but social and spatial movement did disrupt settled habits. Soldiers got out of the habit of going regularly to church, but the nation remembered its holy days and holy places. The eleventh hour of the eleventh day of the eleventh month was to become in the 1920s and 1930s a solemn day of national remembrance. Every town and village had its memorial, though the style of commemoration sometimes changed during that time. In London the dean of Westminster conceived the idea of burying an unknown warrior in the abbey to lie in what was becoming a national Valhalla.

War memorials offered lessons for social harmony: 'Remember the men of Cheltenham, who gave their lives for you in the Great War. If they were strangers to one another here in their common home they served and fought and died in many lands near and far as a band of brothers. Learn from them to live and die'. The language of brotherhood resonated with old soldiers but also held out the goal of an organic society which might have implied a contrast with both the past conflict of strangers and the danger of future class conflict. Jay Winter has insisted that while recent semiological analysis has identified war memorials as sites of symbolic exchange 'where the living admit a degree of indebtedness to the fallen which can never be discharged', their primary historical significance should not be overlooked. This was to enable the dead to be suitably commemorated and to provide space for grief and mourning. However, moving beyond the immediate need for sites of memory and mourning, Adrian Gregory has shown that the meaning of Remembrance Day was continually being contested. He quotes a Birmingham paper as saying that the silence was 'emphatically a moment for the Quaker ideal of worship to predominate'. The archbishop of Canterbury had a battle with Lloyd George and Curzon, who had wanted a wholly secular service at the unveiling of the Cenotaph, which he eventually won. In most places an interdenominational service was used and Remembrance Sunday and the local memorial became an accepted liminal space. But there were significant exceptions. When a village war memorial was erected in the public cemetery in Streatham, near Ely, the vicar refused to dedicate it, even though it included the name of his own son. In the 1920s village memorial crosses sometimes became rallying points for striking workers.[26]

The involvement of royalty in remembrance brought an added ingredient. Receipt of the king's telegram of sympathy in thousands of homes was both a message from beyond most people's domestic world and at the same time brought the king down to their level. Under George V Britain became a family monarchy with the king as respected *paterfamilias*. The king and an Anglican bishop led the nation's annual tribute to the fallen and their appearance together reinforced their roles as national leaders of state and church. But George V was not only supreme governor of the Church of England but was beginning to reach out to those outside the established church. In July 1917 the king was represented at a memorial service at Westminster Cathedral for fallen French soldiers. In November 1918 the king and queen attended a Free church service of thanksgiving at the Albert Hall. By 1918 the monarch was already on the way towards becoming Defender of Faiths. The link between monarchy, the nation and the fallen in a religious context was reinforced when the future King George VI was married in Westminster Abbey and his bride, Elizabeth Bowes-Lyon, with a sureness of touch that never deserted her, after the service left her bouquet on the tomb of the unknown warrior.[27]

The invention of the wireless was both a help and a hindrance to the churches. It enabled the nation to gather together as families and listen to the king's Christmas Day broadcast, which alongside Remembrance Sunday became fixed points in the religion of the period. Under its first managing director John Reith, a Scottish Presbyterian minister's son appointed in 1922, the infant BBC aimed at uplifting and enlightening the public. The appointment of the Religious Advisory Committee with Anglican, Free church and Roman Catholic members demonstrated that it was possible in 1923 to achieve for broadcasting the working across denominational boundaries that had not been possible in education. The first church service was broadcast in 1924 and provided comfort for sick and elderly people, but also gave an excuse for others to stay at home. 'BBC Religion' became the sacred canopy covering the nation's armchair religion.

Messages from beyond came not just by wireless and telegram but in the 1920s through highly publicized spiritualist mediums. The huge loss of life in the war and from the worldwide influenza epidemic in 1918 left millions grieving and anxious to be reassured about their loved ones. Spiritualism has been described by David Cannadine as 'the private denial of death', though Jay Winter more correctly asserts that the movement 'was anything but private'.[28] The Methodist peripatetic controversialist Frank Ballard recalled that he was asked to deal with spiritualism most frequently in 1920. Body, mind and spirit were topics that aroused much interest in a generation with so many broken bodies, disturbed minds and restless spirits. In 1924 spiritual healing burst into the headlines through a series of missions held by an Anglican layman James Moore Hickson. Tales of discarded crutches and abandoned wheelchairs raised high hopes, but a committee set up by the archbishop concluded that there had been no physical healing, though some functional disorders had been cured. On a different social level Christian Science, the faith of the American Mary Baker Eddy, which denied matter and rejected doctors, made surprising converts including the Astors, Lord Lothian and Viscount Lee. Meanwhile, Lee's former coalition cabinet colleague H. A. L. Fisher was busy exposing the cult in *Our New Religion*, published in 1929.[29]

The Empire Exhibition held at Wembley in 1924 included a symposium on 'Living Religions within the Empire' at which speakers from all the great faiths explained their teaching. One of the organizers was Sir Francis Younghusband, explorer, soldier, diplomat and mystic. Born in India, he negotiated a treaty with Tibet in 1904, explored the Afghan border and revised the gazetteer of Kashmir. A devout Christian and mystic, he inquired into the religions and philosophies of the East, especially Hinduism and Buddhism. His religious philosophy, which accepted the underlying unity of experience beneath the surface differences between religions, appeared in *Life in the Stars* (1927). In 1936 he founded the World Congress of Faiths, which now has a permanent headquarters in London.

The political significance of religion after 1920 was less visible than before the war for several reasons. There was the electoral eclipse of the Liberal party and the departure of the Irish Nationalists. The extension of the franchise gave votes to working men who were unlikely to be churchgoers or to have their vote decided by religious issues. The new importance given to bread-and-butter politics over the former great issues of principle gave little room for a distinctively religious view. Moreover, on the main issues of the interwar years, unemployment, peace and war, the differences divided the denominations. However, Bishop Talbot's distinction between defused and embodied Christianity has its political equivalents in the interwar years. This has been well brought out in Philip Williamson's study of Stanley Baldwin, a man who, like archbishop Davidson, had imbibed the notion of service at Harrow school. Frequent themes in Baldwin's speeches were character, service and Christianity. Descended from generations of Methodists (his parents transferred and became churchgoers), Baldwin saw himself as heir to both the Anglican and Wesleyan traditions. Though not identified with official Anglicanism, he made an effective appeal to the millions of respectable and responsible people who might or might not be churchgoers but had almost certainly tuned in to BBC religion.

The long-feared clash between capital and labour in the General Strike of 1926 did bring Christian responses from Archbishop Davidson, backed by the Free churches but countered by Cardinal Bourne. The archbishop called for compromise, was banned from saying so on the BBC, but was cheered in the streets. Bourne backed the government and condemned the strike as a sin, and having been eulogized in the West End clubs went on to persuade Baldwin to grant parliamentary time for a new bill that would prevent the 1908 ban ever falling on Catholic processions again.[30]

In the interwar years the Church of England became effectively a denomination, though retaining the trappings of a national church. The growth of the Catholic movement amongst Anglicans reached a high point in 1933 when 70,000 attended the Catholic Congress. The Parish Communion movement aimed at replacing the non-sacramental service of matins with a central service of holy communion. This was a service that appealed to the committed but left many casual attenders feeling excluded. There was, however, an awareness of the power of sacred space as manifested in the cathedrals. It was F. S. M. Bennett, a high churchman who was appointed dean of Chester in 1920, who began the cathedral renaissance by abolishing all charges and positively encouraging people to come in. Cathedrals were in the van of what David Lowenthall has called 'the heritage crusade', which spread in the 1930s to country houses and in the 1990s became, in his words, 'a newly popular faith'.[31] Perhaps the best visual image to sum up the concerns of this chapter is the photograph of the dome of St Paul's Cathedral, standing proudly and majestically, surmounted by the cross, amidst the devastation caused by German bombs in 1941. St Paul's, even for non-churchgoing Cockneys, stood for Christian England. Perhaps in his visits to cathedrals A. J. P. Taylor was not quite as irreligious as might be supposed, but he should have given religion more of a mention in his *English History*.

NOTES

1   A. J. P. Taylor, *A Personal History* (London, 1984), *English History, 1914–45* (Oxford, 1965), *A. J. P. Taylor, Letters to Eva: 1969–83*, ed. E. H. Taylor (London), pp. 120, 364, 420.

2   R. McKibbin, *The Ideologies of Class: Social Relations in Britain 1880–1950* (Oxford, 1990), *Classes and Cultures: England 1918–1951* (Oxford, 1998); J. Harris, *Private Lives, Public Spheres: A Social History of Britain 1870–1914* (London, 1993).

3   H. McLeod, *Class and Religion in the Late Victorian City* (London, 1974), *Religion and the People of Western Europe 1789–1970* (Oxford, 1981), *Religion and Society in England 1850–1914* (London, 1996), *Piety and Poverty: Working-class Religion in Berlin, London and New York 1870–1914* (New York, 1996).

4   S. Yeo, *Religion and Voluntary Organisations in Crisis* (London, 1976); J. Cox, *The Churches in a Secular Society: Lambeth 1870–1930* (Oxford, 1982); J. Morris, *Religion and Urban Change: Croydon 1840–1914* (London, 1992); S. J. D. Green, *Religion in the Age of Decline* (Cambridge, 1996); J. Whale, *One Church, One Lord* (London, 1975), p. 156.

5   S. C. Williams, *Religious Belief and Popular Culture in Southwark c.1880–1939* (Oxford, 1999).

6   J. Wolffe, *Great Deaths: Grieving, Religion and Nationhood in Victorian and Edwardian Britain* (Oxford, 2000).

7   D. Cannadine, *Orientalism: How the British Saw their Empire* (London, 2001), 'The context, performance and meaning of ritual: the British monarchy and the "invention of tradition"', in E. Hobsbawm and T. Ranger, eds, *The Invention of Tradition* (Cambridge, 1983), pp. 101–65.

8   A. Roberts, *Salisbury: Victorian Titan* (London, 1999), p. 667.

9   S. Mews, 'Randall Thomas Davidson', in *New DNB* (Oxford, forthcoming); K. A. Thompson, *Bureaucracy and Church Reform* (Oxford, 1970).

10 W. M. Kuhn, *Democratic Royalism: The Transformation of the British Monarchy, 1861–1914* (London, 1996).

11 *Expository Times*, 23, 2 November 1911; R. Moore, *Pitmen, Preachers and Politics: The Effects of Methodism in a Durham Mining Community* (Cambridge, 1974).

12 J. N. Figgis, *The Gospel and Human Needs* (London, 1913), p. 3.

13 D. Cesarani, *The Jewish Chronicle and Anglo-Jewry 1841–1991* (Cambridge, 1994), p. 86; S. A. Cohen, *English Zionists and British Jews: The Communal Politics of Anglo-Jewry 1895–1920* (Princeton, NJ, 1982); G. Alderman, *Modern British Jewry* (Oxford, 1992); E. J. Bristow, *Prostitution and Prejudice: The Jewish Fight against White Slavery 1870–1939* (London, 1983).

14 R. Hayward, 'From the millennial future to the unconscious past: the transformation of prophecy in early twentieth-century Britain', in B. Taithe and T. Thornton, eds, *Prophecy: The Power of Inspired Language in History 1300–2000* (Stroud, 1997), pp. 161–80; C. R. Williams, 'The Welsh religious revival, 1904–5', *British Journal of Sociology*, 3 (1952), pp. 242–9.

15 S. Mews, 'Puritanicalism, sport and race: a symbolic crusade of 1911', in G. J. Cuming and D. Baker, eds, *Popular Belief and Practice* (Cambridge, 1972), pp. 303–31; D. Batchelor, *Jack Johnson His Times* (London, 1990), foreword by H. Carpenter, p. 7.

16 S. Fletcher, *Maude Royden: A Life* (Oxford, 1989); K. Cowman, 'Crossing the great divide: inter-organisational suffrage relationships on Merseyside, 1895–1914', in C. Eustace, J. Ryan and L. Ugolini, eds, *A Suffrage Reader: Charting Directions in British Suffrage History* (London, 1999), pp. 37–52.

17 *Church Family Newspaper*, 22 May 1911; H. H. Henson–W. Sanday, 3 June 1912 (Bodleian MS Res.d.19/159).
18 J. Oman, *The War and its Issues* (Cambridge, 1915), p. 7.
19 A. Chevrillon, *Britain and the War* (London, 1917), p. 55.
20 S. Mews, 'Spiritual mobilization in the First World War', *Theology* (June 1971), pp. 258–64.
21 M. Furse, *Stand Therefore!* (London, 1953), p. 78.
22 S. Mews, 'Drink and disestablishment in the First World War', in D. Baker, ed., *The Church in Town and Country* (Oxford, 1979), pp. 444–79.
23 *The Churchman*, 30 (1916), pp. 610–13; *The Times*, 8 September 1916.
24 D. S. Cairns, ed., *The Army and Religion* (London, 1919), pp. 9, 109, 23, 132; J. Kelman, *The War and Preaching* (London, n.d.), p. 103.
25 L. Creighton, ed., *Letters of Oswin Creighton* (London, 1920), p. 219.
26 J. Winter, *Sites of Memory, Sites of Mourning* (Cambridge, 1998), p. 94; A. Gregory, *The Silence of Memory: Armistice Day 1919–1946* (Oxford, 1994), p. 187; N. Mansfield, 'Class conflict and village war memorials, 1914–24', *Rural History*, 6 (1995), p. 79.
27 *The Universe*, 18 January 1918; J. Marchant, *Dr. John Clifford* (London, 1924), p. 235.
28 D. Cannadine, 'War and death, grief and mourning in modern Britain', in J. Whaley, ed., *Mirrors of Mortality* (London, 1981); Winter, *Sites of Memory*, p. 57.
29 S. Mews, 'The revival of spiritual healing in the Church of England, 1920–26', in W. J. Sheils, ed., *The Church and Healing* (Oxford, 1982), pp. 299–331.
30 P. Williamson, 'The doctrinal politics of Stanley Baldwin', in M. Bentley, ed., *Public and Private Doctrine: Essays in British History presented to Maurice Cowling* (Cambridge, 1995), pp. 181–208; S. Mews, 'The churches', in M. Morris, ed., *The General Strike of 1926* (Harmondsworth, 1976), pp. 318–37.
31 D. Lowenthall, *The Heritage Crusade and the Spoils of History* (London, 1996), p. 1.

FURTHER READING

Alderman, G., *Modern British Jewry* (Oxford, 1992).
Ceadal, M., *Pacifism in Britain 1914–45* (Oxford, 1980).
Chadwick, O., *Hensley Henson: A Study in the Friction between Church and State* (Oxford, 1983).
Fletcher, S., *Maude Royden: A Life* (Oxford, 1989).
Green, S. J. D., *Religion in the Age of Decline* (Cambridge, 1996).
Hastings, A., *A History of English Christianity 1920–90* (London, 1991).
Kent, J., *William Temple* (Cambridge, 1993).
McLeod, H., *Religion and Society in England 1850–1914* (London, 1996).
Maloney, T., *Westminster, Whitehall and the Vatican: The Role of Cardinal Hinsley 1935–43* (London, 1985).
Mews, S., ed., *Modern Religious Rebels* (London, 1993).
Moore, R., *Pitmen, Preachers and Politics: The Effects of Methodism in a Durham Mining Community* (Cambridge, 1974).
Williams, S. C., *Religious Belief and Popular Culture in Southwark c.1880–1939* (Oxford, 1999).
Winter, J., *Sites of Memory, Sites of Mourning* (Cambridge, 1998).
Wolfe, K. M., *The Churches and the British Broadcasting Corporation 1922–1956* (London, 1984).
Wolffe, J., *Great Deaths: Grieving, Religion and Nationhood in Victorian and Edwardian Britain* (Oxford, 2000).

CHAPTER THIRTY

Culture in the Sceptr'd Isle

ANTHONY SUTCLIFFE

Recent British Culture as a Historical Problem

Definitions of 'culture' are now so numerous that this chapter requires a working definition. Following Arthur Marwick's approach in 1991, it will concentrate on 'the arts, intellectual activities, entertainments and leisure pursuits'.[1] It will deal with the entire population and will not favour the working class, ethnic minorities, women, gays or lesbians, or any other group within society. Nor will it essay distinct treatments of Ulster, Wales or Scotland.

Culture springs from leisure, and leisure rests on wealth. Britain entered the twentieth century as one of the richest countries in the world. Relatively impoverished by the First World War and the rise of industrial rivals such as the United States and Germany, Britain remained a very rich country in 1939. Of course, its wealth was very unevenly distributed. It reflected Britain's social structure, which fell, for the purposes of this chapter, into the following categories:[2]

1   *The upper classes*
    Royal family and titled people
        (royalty, aristocracy, bishops, senior judges)

    The gentry
        (minor landowners, senior military officers)

    The upper middle class
        (major professionals, major employers, people living on private incomes)

2   *The lower middle class*
    (white-collar workers, minor professionals, farmers, minor traders)

3   *The working class*
    (skilled workers, semi-skilled workers, unskilled workers)

The author wishes to thank C. J. Wrigley for his careful and generous attention, and for providing a number of very helpful references.

Britain's rejection of continental absolutism in the seventeenth century left it without strong central guidance in cultural matters. A leisured aristocracy of builders and collectors was challenged during the nineteenth century by the cultural preferences of an achieving middle class of talent and education. Britain's wealth and liberal traditions drew talented immigrants from all over the world. Meanwhile, the working class struggled to find the time and energy to develop any culture separate from simple leisure. On the other hand, the working class retained more of a local and regional culture than did the rich.

Change and Tradition

In 1900 much of Britain's most vital culture was a product of its wealthy classes and institutions, its origins going back as far as the Norman Conquest. As Standish Meacham has shown, England's great cathedrals and castles, its Lake District and its cliffs of Dover, were seen as expressions of English aspirations and values which had come to be part of imperial consciousness.[3] Frequent ceremonies, from Westminster Abbey weddings or a lord's annual reception of his tenants to rough street parties for royal visits or national occasions, all justified music, texts, decorations and robes whose origins lay in the past, even if it was – as David Cannadine has revealed – sometimes a very recent past. British industrialization in the eighteenth and nineteenth centuries generated increasing wealth and the people to enjoy it, and by 1900 a great cultural structure had been built up with a large additional contribution from the upper middle class.

The twentieth century, nevertheless, saw a movement away from the culture and attitudes of the Victorian era, which had been largely linked to the empire, to British history and to nature. The term 'modern', once used of Victorian deeds and thought, began to be applied to forms of art and thinking that rejected the norms of the nineteenth century. These innovations often implied uncertainty or criticism. Non-representational or abstract art, and 'modern' architecture, had a more indirect effect. In both cases the origin or the inspiration came largely from the continent, as many British artists chose to study or live in France and Germany. In Britain, the impact of old and new tended to produce compromises. Public opinion and taste remained conservative, with the upper classes, who bought the new works of art, in a position of great influence.

The Culture of the Rich and Educated

As we shall see, the biggest cultural changes after 1900 occurred in the ranks of the working class and the lower middle class. The upper class, the gentry and the upper middle class, much smaller in numbers, retained the culture that they had inherited from the nineteenth century. Some experienced declining resources during parts of this period, but this upper cultural structure survived.[4] On the other hand, innovation was rare, partly perhaps because the rich had more leisure than they knew what to do with, and little stimulus.

The culture of the rich and educated rested on two foundations. The culture of the royal court, the great landed estates and their London homes, and of the gentry was a mighty structure of landed wealth and status. The members of this group were often impressive experts in art and architecture in relation to the decoration or repair of their own homes, but they filled most of their leisure with pursuits that dated back to the Norman aristocracy. 'Huntin', shootin' and fishin'' were the core, but later developments, including horse racing, golf, bridge and other card games, together with gambling, did not greatly alter it. Flying interested some of the younger aristocrats between the wars, including young women,[5] and skiing in the Alps, though cheaper, still excluded the mass of the country's youth. Amy Johnson's rise from office worker to world aviatrix was unique and rested on her hard-earned skills in navigation and mechanics. Newsreels nevertheless chart the progress of her accent from the flat Yorkshire of her Hull birthplace to a 'county' accent after her marriage to a richer but inferior flyer, James Mollison, introduced her to the gentry. Music and the theatre did not greatly interest the royal family, who merely tolerated the many galas and special performances that they had to attend. They preferred family games, such as billiards and cards, and shooting when staying at their country homes. The upper classes were often seen at church, partly to demonstrate status and influence, and partly to set an example. Society weddings also brought them out in large numbers, both in London and the country. The ladies' attempts at fashionable dress on these occasions influenced the whole of the upper stratum via fashionable magazines.

The second foundation was provided by the universities of Oxford and Cambridge, London University and distinguished universities in Scotland. The royal family and many of the great landed heirs did not favour university education, but many younger sons and gentry went on from Eton and other exclusive public schools to the two great English universities where their rank, status or wealth were welcomed, generation on generation. These superior graduates then progressed into the forces, the upper ranks of the civil service, the Church of England, or (for the more able) the law. The university teaching staff (dons) were of a high standard and there was a strong basis for intellectual activity. Between 1900 and 1939 little of this purest milk of scholarly knowledge was allowed to spread outside the two universities and a few outposts which had been founded in the nineteenth century, but Britain had a firm basis of scholarship that sustained a vital culture of knowledge at the upper levels of society.

These foundations were shaken by the First World War. The deaths of so many young men in the officer class deprived Britain of many creative spirits, such as Wilfred Owen and Rupert Brooke. The sense of loss and uncertainty, which had partly replaced the pre-1914 confidence and creativity, affected much cultural creation after 1918. British culture became less self-sufficient, moving much more in international currents and modernity.

Complex Currents in Literature

The main cultural expression of the upper classes was literature. Book production, purchase and consumption increased throughout the period. The number of titles published increased from 8,666 in 1914 to 14,904 in 1939. Nearly all of these were hardback editions and private purchase was rare outside the upper classes. The majority of these titles were novels and women remained the main readers. However, the numerous literary critics were predominantly men. Already before 1914 a number of serious novels had dealt with change and social problems, like those of H. G. Wells, but the shock of the First World War and the threats of unemployment and fascism gave a sombre tone to some fictional and non-fictional writing between the wars. The rich and learned 'Bloomsbury set' both wrote and encouraged young writers. D. H. Lawrence, a miner's son, gave a new realism to human relationships, in the context of working-class life and improvement. Virginia Woolf, a sad, Bloomsbury depressive, wrote introspective novels of boredom and social immobility.

The Victorian world that had helped produce the First World War was often ridiculed or castigated. Lytton Strachey's *Eminent Victorians*, four biographical essays delving slyly into the psyche of previously unimpeachable figures, was a landmark when it appeared in 1918. It ended literary hagiography and marked the beginnings of destructive journalism. A more pessimistic, cynical novel emerged between the wars. The idea of a 'lost generation', uniquely entertained in Britain, applied to literature as much as to politics.[6] War books were numerous, with a peak of twenty-nine published in 1929.[7] The growing danger of a new war emerged in the 1930s, notably in *The Shape of Things to Come* by the internationalist H. G. Wells, which the author helped turn into a film, and in James Hilton's *Lost Horizon*, which dreamed of a Shangri-la of utter peace and satisfaction. Sex also became a more respectable subject for literature in the work of James Joyce and D. H. Lawrence, though subject to occasional interference by the censor. From 1935, the Lane brothers' Penguin books, augmented by Pelicans from 1937, helped create a permanent literary culture based on selected classics and stimulating new writing. *Fact*, a socially committed monthly, was launched in 1937 by Raymond Postgate and other London intellectuals.

Established institutions and beliefs came under attack and the upper classes were often a subject of derision, as in P. G. Wodehouse's Bertie Wooster stories from the early 1920s, or of cynicism, as in the novels of Evelyn Waugh from 1928. Middle-class childhood, previously a myth of happiness and endeavour, was undermined in the crippled Richmal Crompton's 'Just William' stories from 1922. A. J. Cronin, the leading popular author of the 1930s, wrote powerful novels based on struggle and perseverance. Meanwhile, there was much reading of the classics, stimulated by the growth of education. French novels, especially, were read in translation. Much of this reading of the classics was based on library borrowing, paperbacks and through the cheap series of reprints offered by the *Daily Mail* and other newspapers.

Although the electorate generated only two brief Labour governments between 1900 and 1939, there was a leftward change in the politico-cultural climate to which writing made a big contribution. It was linked to perceptions of a changing Britain in which landscapes, people and customs were at last recognized and valued in human terms, much as John Ruskin had once desired. The Left Book Club, founded in 1936 by a group of London intellectuals, sought to create a tradition of concern with monthly book publications, a newsletter and local groups. J. B. Priestley's books about a changing England probably made the greatest impact. The most popular was *The Good Companions* (1929), a picaresque story of roving young actors. His *Angel Pavement* (1930), a rich, London novel, was followed by a piece of regional reportage, *English Journey* (1934). Priestley, a Yorkshireman with a deep, modulated regional accent, liked to introduce his readers to the British regions, their cultures and the strength of the people who lived in them. Later, Priestley would play a big part in the literary and broadcasting side of the British war effort and would refuse both a knighthood and a peerage.

The Victorian style of poverty enquiry continued into the 1920s in York and London, and Mass Observation, an independent sociological research unit founded in 1937, produced a big study of life in 'Worktown' (Bolton) in 1937.[8] Socialist George Orwell's *Road to Wigan Pier* (1937) was an odyssey of poverty based on the author's stays as a lodger with poor people. Also popular was Winifred Holtby's *South Riding* (1937), a tale of ordinary people at odds with local government in the Hull region. Like A. J. Cronin's *The Citadel*, Holtby's novel was quickly made into a film. Novels directly about social problems were rare, but Walter Greenwood's *Love on the Dole* (1933) was widely read. The British Board of Film Censors, active since 1912, refused to allow it to be made into a film for fear of unrest. It was finally filmed in 1941 when mass support was necessary for the war effort, but the delay indicated some of the constraints on social debate in the 1930s.

Poetry was less popular than before 1914 but war poetry, with its sense of lost opportunities, was valued. T. S. Eliot, a young American who chose to settle in England, charmed the Bloomsbury set and wrote much gloomy verse between the wars. His grim reflections on modern existence recalled the novels of Virginia Woolf, while his Anglo-Catholicism set him slightly apart from the main currents of English culture, much as the Catholicism of Graham Greene tinged some of Britain's finest novels of the 1930s. W. H. Auden was affected more directly by politics. Once a brilliant Oxford undergraduate, he turned to the issues of unemployment and fascism in the 1930s and produced some gritty poems about industrial life. Auden underwent a kind of conversion, to Anglo-Catholicism, in 1940, but his Marxism largely survived it.[9]

How far poetry and other elite literature reached the general public must be uncertain, but urbanized Britain had the best system of lending libraries in the world. Most loans were no doubt of popular novels to married women of the Laura Jesson ilk, but the whole system supported school and college study, language learning and skill acquisition. Public libraries lent more books after 1900 and private circulating libraries like Boots did more business. In 1911 public libraries issued 54.3 million books, when six people out of ten were within reach of one, and, in 1939, 247.3 million books.[10]

The newspaper and magazine press greatly expanded. More than any other large European country and the United States, Britain was served by national newspapers and Sunday newspapers. In 1939, 69 per cent of the population over the age of sixteen read a national newspaper, and 82 per cent read one of the national Sunday papers. Regional and local daily and Sunday newspapers greatly declined in numbers after 1900. Sales of national dailies increased from 4.5 million in 1910 to 10.5 million in 1939.The newspapers of the rich and the well educated altered little, carrying society announcements as well as news, but working-class and lower-middle-class publications multiplied. Entertaining newspapers aiming at the lower middle class and the working class did best – the *Daily Express* circulation rose from less than half a million in 1910 to 2.5 million in 1939. Cartoons and competitions were a feature of this and other mass newspapers like the *Daily Mail*, the *Daily Herald* and the *Daily Mirror*. Crosswords were popular in all social classes. Layout and content were simplified on American lines from the 1920s. Broadcasting and cinema publications multiplied, along with leisure and hobby magazines. Children's papers, or 'comics', were the main growth area. This unique British phenomenon was due in part to house delivery, which was available to all except country folk.

The Stage

The theatre was mainly for the upper middle class. There was little of it outside London, except the touring productions of London companies during the summer, though the first repertory theatre, set up in 1908 in Manchester, was followed by a number of provincial repertory theatres between the wars. Attendance was boosted in the winter when the aristocracy and gentry moved to their London homes. Music hall, however, suffered a rapid death after about 1923.[11] Theatregoing peaked around 1900 and the virtual absence of new professional theatres in London after 1914 is enough to indicate the theatre's failure to generate fresh demand. The plays of Shaw, W. S. Gilbert and foreign playwrights such as Ibsen and Gorki could set a serious note, but the theatre columns of Max Beerbohm, a cultured and intelligent observer, in the *Saturday Review* from 1898 to 1910, suggested that most plays were light entertainment for the leisured and the clever.[12]

Little changed after 1918. However, the Shakespeare Memorial Theatre at Stratford-upon-Avon, opened in 1932, set new standards for all of British theatre. Opera enjoyed a similar stimulus. The British National Opera Company was formed in 1922, and the Sadler's Wells theatre, built in 1931, catered for a variety of performances, many associated with Ninette de Valois. Then, in 1934, the opera house was founded at Glyndebourne.

Theatre and opera did not generate change, however. The plays reflected upper-class, conservative tastes, and operas were the same old classics year after year. There were many musical shows, some of them imported from New York. Noel Coward's entertaining tales of the rich and idle showed a complete lack of concern for the issues of the day and for ordinary people. J. B. Priestley's 'time' plays were among the most serious produced between the wars, but their implications of guilt and change were probably lost on most audiences.

The West End theatre and the universities nurtured an extraordinary phenomenon, the assertive upper-class accent, which, though undoubtedly present in Britain before 1900, seems to have become more exaggerated after 1918.[13] Many actors developed extravagant upper-class accents. In its most extreme form, the speaker used the front of the mouth to produce a high-pitched, sometimes sneering tone. Vocabulary and syntax were little affected but charged expressions such as 'ay seeay!' and 'look he-eah!' were rarely heard outside the upper classes. This superior braying was often referred to as an 'Oxford' or 'cut-glass' accent, but Richmal Crompton's 'super-county-snaring accent' caught it very well. The radio and the public schools, and some films based on West End plays, tended to disseminate the accent, which had no equivalent in the United States, France or Germany at this time. British people were accustomed to it and were not especially offended, this being the last era in which the 'toff' was a recognized and respected social type. However, when J. B. Priestley and Wilfred Pickles were allowed to broadcast during the war, the difference was widely noted.

Music

Britain had a strong tradition of classical music. It was linked to choral and religious participation in the industrial towns of the nineteenth century, though Germanic composers, led by Mendelssohn, were the most admired. Choirs and brass bands were still strong after 1900, especially when based in local communities, but with Parry, Elgar, Holst, Delius and many others, a unique British tradition of classical composition emerged at the turn of the century. With Elgar becoming part of the Establishment after 1900, classical music became more fashionable in the upper classes. Sir Henry Wood's Promenade Concerts, held in London from 1895, extended classical music to the whole of the middle class, but the intelligentsia remained the core of its support.

The emergence of Edward Elgar as a composer of world, or at any rate imperial, stature in the early 1900s helped a new generation of British composers to acquire confidence after 1918, and to express a national identity which had emerged from the nineteenth century and which differed from the previous Germanic tradition. Elgar moved sharply from the music of empire, as expressed in his Second Symphony of 1911, to his poignant Cello Concerto of 1919, followed by reflective composing until his death in 1934. Bliss and Walton could compose in an imperial style reminiscent of Elgar as they matured after 1918, especially on royal occasions, but Delius, though resident in France, composed impressionistic poems to nature and life which British listeners hailed as tributes to the English countryside. The younger composers Vaughan Williams, Gerald Finzi and Frank Bridge also developed pastoral music, following the new British interest in the countryside as a recreational resource and an expression of national sentiment after 1918.[14] Folk music was already in decline among countryfolk by 1900, but it was the object of preservation efforts by the new generation of composers. Paradoxically, the sylvan efforts of Cecil Sharp and his followers further reinforced national identity, which was linked to the countryside. Bax also valued traditional culture, but he composed prolifically on the theme of Arthurian and Nordic myth, without greatly moving the British public. Foreign music continued to be as popular as it had been before 1914, however, and foreign companies and directors did much to make ballet more popular after 1918.

The BBC broadcast much classical music from its creation in 1922, and especially after John Reith, a determined Scot, was promoted from general manager to director general in 1927. Reith wanted to encourage a national identity and culture and saw serious music as a means to this end. In 1930 the BBC Orchestra was founded. Improvements in the design of gramophones, including electrical drive, allowed classical music to be much more widely appreciated after 1918.

Painting and Sculpture

Painting and sculpture were liberated after 1900 from the solemn world of the Victorian municipal art gallery, if not from the cluttered walls of the ancestral seat. The rich bought more and more pictures from the Paris shows, or from London galleries dealing with the continent. Study abroad became common, while the Slade School of Art produced regiments of effective draughtsmen.[15] No British school emerged from this maelstrom, though the distinctive British Impressionists pressed doggedly on in a world without bright light.[16] Cubism affected many, while Mark Gertler and others drew on the critical, expressionist German painting of the 1920s. The idiosyncratic Augustus John and Stanley Spencer, and later Wyndham Lewis and Francis Bacon, drew inspiration from abroad but retained a British realism and criticism.[17] Spencer, Paul Nash, C. R. W. Nevinson and many other painters were affected by their work, official or unofficial, in the First World War, and religious images and bleak landscapes survived in some of their work until the 1930s, when the threat of war once again began to influence British painters. Landscape painting moved on from the traditional British school of blue skies, cloud and meadows to scarred subjects recalling war or industrial destruction. The work of the leading British sculptors, led by Jacob Epstein and Henry Moore, took a similar course.

The Changing Culture of the Masses

The culture of the working classes was bound to be relatively impoverished because of their limited wealth, leisure and education. In 1900, for most, it was a culture of poverty and discomfort, but it was just as self-confident as the culture of the upper classes – public houses, Woodbines, football, cheap reading and repetitive seaside holidays. In some regions minority hobbies required investment and skill; brass bands, whippets and pigeon racing were the most demanding. The skilled workers had some interest in self-improvement, which was linked to part-time education that brought them into contact with the lower middle classes. The lower middle classes had similar incomes and hours of work, but they were suspicious of working-class culture. They distinguished themselves by church attendance, suburban residence, participation in sport and commitment to formal education. Self-confidence was not a feature of the lower middle classes. They had a position to protect, a position that was threatened by the taint of the lower classes and the disdain of the upper classes.

By 1939 this cultural structure had changed. Most important of all, the birth rate halved between 1900 and 1939 while average real earnings rose by about one-third. The rise of new industries had increased the numbers of high-paid skilled workers, many of whom became houseowners in the 1930s after the slump had reduced interest rates. The spread of motor vehicles – from 110,000 in 1919 to 2 million in 1939 – encouraged many middle-class and even working-class people to move out into distant suburbs where they became involved in painting, car cleaning, minor repairs, visits to roadhouses and church attendance.[18] The spread of the semi-detached house, a product of post-war town planning convention, brought more than 10 million people into contact with a semi-rural way of life in which tending front and back gardens became a virtual obligation.[19] New household equipment, much of it financed by hire purchase and powered by electricity, helped liberate women from drudgery.[20] By 1939, two-thirds of British homes had electric power.[21]

These changes released massive resources and time for new consumption and leisure activities. High levels of unemployment in the 1930s meant that up to 10 per cent of the population at any time lived at reduced living standards. However, their reduced purchasing power did not seriously undermine the structure of demand and supply, as savings, unemployment pay, poor relief and juvenile employment did much to sustain family incomes.

Nature

The growing interest of the middle and working classes in nature meant that the upper classes ceded part of their traditional role as guardians and exploiters of the countryside. Huntin', shootin' and fishin' stagnated or declined, while hiking, walking, climbing, cycling and birdwatching expanded, mainly as middle-class, youth activities. Working-class contact with nature was mainly encouraged by charabanc excursions and allotments. Cheap seaside residence on 'plotlands' such as Peacehaven also appealed to the working class and the lower middle class. Here, a way of life rather than a culture grew up.[22] As Michael Bracewell, most recently, has stressed, British culture was strongly 'arcadian'.[23] This meant youth, innocence, purity, nature and a distrust of the city.

British interest in and use of the countryside followed trends in Germany. The Youth Hostels Association was founded in 1930, and calls for the defence of the countryside against sprawling building expanded after 1930. The growing middle-class taste for fresh air led on to the innovation of the seaside holiday camp, which became something of a cult in the 1930s, and not just among poor people. Similar was the open-air lido, many of which were built from the 1920s by local authorities in or near the big cities, and which attracted families, young and old, from a range of social classes, despite the cold water.

Religion

Formal religion (see also chapter 29) interested the working classes only in remote regions such as south Wales and parts of industrial Scotland. The lower middle classes were more assiduous, partly for status reasons. They did not attend Anglican churches as much as the upper classes. Their favoured churches often generated serious thought about God and social issues. Religion created even more doubt and struggle than it had before 1914, as secularism and modernism expanded. Meanwhile, the losses in the First World War helped spiritualism to survive its Victorian origins, with more mediums and a better publicity network. Interest could be found in all social classes, but especially in the lower middle class, even though some of the more notorious mediums were charged with fraud by the police.[24] Altogether, the affairs of the spirit seemed to generate uncertainty and insecurity between the wars, in strong contrast to their role as a social foundation before 1914.

Radio

Radio was enjoyed by all social classes, except the very poor who apparently could not afford to buy sets and licences. The number of licences rose from 36,000 in 1922, when the BBC was established, to over 8 million in 1939. The basic radio set, usually known as the crystal set, interested mainly enthusiasts, but the addition of valves and a speaker allowed the radio to become a family entertainment and a rapid source of information. By the 1930s whole families would gather around the radio in the evenings, with the evening news programme an especial focus. Many family discussions were promoted by the radio. Outside broadcasts such as the Crystal Palace fire in 1936, the abdication speech or Chamberlain's announcement of war with Germany were remembered by all, but regular outside broadcasts like the Cup Final and the Boat Race became common events for many people, which they heard with their families or groups of friends or workers. Many working and young people wearied of John Reith's improving fare and turned their dials to a distant Radio

Luxembourg with its diet of dance music. The radio, nevertheless, helped strengthen a national experience based on portentous news bulletins and shared occasions. The BBC television service, launched in 1936, served only a few hundred rich subscribers in the London area by 1939.

Cinema

Cinema shows for the general public spread rapidly from the initial London experiments in 1895. At first this form of entertainment was crude, and although a number of picture houses were built in the early 1900s, the audience was mainly working class. American films, led by the Hollywood work of the producer-director D. W. Griffith from 1908, were generally better than the British products. Cinema attendance had expanded by the end of the First World War, partly because it was cheap relative to a night at the pub and partly because official films brought news from the front.

Cinema entertainment continued to expand after the war. Working people remained the main clients, but middle-class attendance seems to have grown in the 1920s, with many films of an artistic or dramatic character imported from abroad. Film clubs, designed to secure showings for films with limited commercial appeal, spread from London from the 1920s, encouraged by the creation of the British Film Institute in 1933. Distinguished British directors, led by Alfred Hitchcock, began to appear, his *The Lodger* (1926) being a film of distinctive British artistic character. A number of new cinemas were built, especially in the later 1920s. Most of the feature films shown came from Hollywood, however, with British films accounting for fewer than 5 per cent of the films shown in 1926.[25]

This artistic development was encouraged, together with mass attendance, by the arrival of sound in 1929. The increased audience remained mainly working class, but the lower middle class of the new suburbs attended the spate of new sound-equipped cinemas built in the early 1930s. Most of these cinemas were modernistic in style. The work of cinema architects like Harry Weedon for the Odeon circuit, founded in 1933, associated architectural distinction with quality film-making.

Young people were attracted to the Hollywood image and they picked up styles of dress and hair. Certain American interjections and catchphrases were in common use among them by the later 1930s. Women attended the cinema more often than did men, and some of the more sentimental films were aimed directly at them. British films like *Things To Come* (1936) and *The Stars Look Down* (1939) dealt with major themes of the day and attracted interest from a wide social range. However, American films were more popular than British ones. The British Board of Film Censors, tougher than its American equivalents, kept the more controversial subjects and scripts off the screen. The fact that some had been produced on the West End stage under the censorship of the Lord Chamberlain suggested that some social classes were more social than others.

Dancing

Women played a bigger part in social life than before 1900. Dancing, including the luxurious post-war Palais de Danse, became more popular. Dance music began to establish itself in the early 1900s. Gramophone records and sheet music reinforced it.[26] Night clubs, for young and single people, appeared in London from the 1920s and there were a few examples in some of the bigger provincial cities. Dance music provided the main background for encounters between single young people.

Toys

There was a big development of children's toys. German penetration of the British toy market before 1914 has been exaggerated, but the domestic industry was in a much stronger position in 1918 after wartime rationalization and problems in Germany.[27] Dolls, teddy bears and cuddly animals were mass produced by firms such as Britains' and Merrythought. Traditional hobbyhorses and wheeled horses were still made from wood. Tinplate models of cars and trains began to give way to diecast in the 1930s, with Dinky Toys in the lead. Bakelite and plastic were coming in by the end of that decade. Clockwork drive spread in the 1920s with Hornby clockwork trains on sale from just after the war, but electric traction, especially for model trains, was coming in by the end of the 1930s. Bassett-Lowke trains, made in Northampton from the early 1920s, kept up with the best techniques, while the owner encouraged the architecture of the leading Glasgow modernist Charles Rennie Mackintosh. Hornby trains and cars, Dinky diecast vehicles (the first in the world) and Meccano metal construction sets were among the best in the world, at prices attractive to the lower middle and skilled working classes. Pedal cars and children's bicycles, in use among the royal family and the aristocracy, had scarcely penetrated below the upper middle class by 1939. Toy soldiers and guns, still made mainly with lead, survived the horrors of the First World War. Some of these toys were durable enough to be passed from generation to generation among the poor. Rag dolls were the main self-made toy. If K. D. Brown's assertion that children are the main beneficiaries of rising living standards is correct, children's play may well have been the main area of social change in Britain during our period.[28]

Sport

Most people's acquaintance with sport was as spectators.[29] Association football, like the pub, was mainly the preserve of the working class, as was rugby league on its home ground in the north. Professionalism was the key to sporting appreciation, with sports stars gripping the masses much as film stars did. Six million attended first division football matches in 1908–9, but the total had risen to 14 million in 1937–8.[30] Rugby union, an amateur sport, appealed mainly to the middle classes and did not attract large crowds. However, it increasingly displaced football at the public schools and aspiring grammar schools. Cricket attracted all social classes and went through a boom between the wars, encouraged by tours and Test matches. Certain newer activities, such as golf, tennis and athletics, attracted participants from the middle classes but had few spectators.

International matches created growing interest, linked to radio commentaries from 1922. In most sports, all four home countries were separately represented but England, with the world's best football and cricket teams, had the biggest following. Large crowds at these events produced national enthusiasm, as did football internationals in Scotland. Normal attendances at Wembley of 100,000, and of 134,000 at

Hampden Park, reflected a national cultural unity unique in the world. The FA Cup, above all, drew multitudes of supporters from across the country. London became the first national magnet of the industrial era. Life, work and leisure combined there in a great cultural wave.

Public Houses

The public house continued as the main working-class place of leisure after 1900. A larger type emerged in the spreading suburbs after 1918, and motoring led to the creation of roadhouses on the main roads outside the big cities. Some large cities, such as Birmingham, terminated the licences of many small outlets in slum districts, in return for approving large pubs with better facilities in the new suburbs. Drinking thus tended to become a more genteel pastime.

The volume of drinking declined with the general extension of wartime restrictions and higher prices.[31] Convictions for drunkenness declined and pub attendance became more of a subculture. Female attendance increased, and pub decor became more comfortable and even – in the case of the roadhouses – elegant. The lower middle classes made more use of pubs, and in the spreading suburbs the brewers built a more refined form of pub to attract them. Regular pub attendance declined among the working class, becoming more a matter of choice. Shorts, cocktails and fruit juice became more popular, while beer consumption dropped. During the 1930s beer production was about half the pre-war level, while tea and coffee drinking increased.[32] Tea, with its moderate caffeine content, remained the national reviving and soothing drink.

Smoking, encouraged in the forces and armaments industries during the war, continued to increase after 1918. The number of cigarette brands increased, some of them appealing to women and young people.[33] Annual per capita consumption of tobacco rose from 2.19 lbs in 1914 to 4.0 lbs in 1938. Heavy smoking cannot have sharpened the palate or stimulated the appetite, but good food was not a feature of British life, whatever the social class. The rich could afford good materials, but even in the finest restaurants little was served except prime cuts of cooked meat and fish, with steamed vegetables and few prepared sauces. Oysters were a delicacy for the rich but were normally eaten raw. Foreign cooking made little impact, however much the rich enjoyed it in Paris, Nice or Monte Carlo. Yorkshire seems to have boasted just one Indian restaurant by the 1920s, the Yorkshire Curry Restaurant in Leeds.

The middle and working classes ate reduced forms of upper-class fare. Labour-intensive meals such as stews were not popular, except among the poorest. It was normal to cook vegetables in boiling water, destroying taste and goodness. Salads were not widely eaten, even in summer. Fresh food, including milk, butter, meat and fish, was difficult to keep fresh before the mass onset of the refrigerator after 1945. Some relief was granted by tinned food, which became much more varied after 1918. Tinned peas were mostly of the 'mushy' type which, incredibly, became a delicacy. By the 1930s frozen and chilled meat were adding to the range of foods open to working people.[34] Cooked ham was the only 'tasty' meat. Pork pies were also 'tasty'. Lard and margarine were a constant presence in the kitchen, with lard generated by the universal fried breakfast. Heavy, sugary puddings were much appreciated. Fish and chips, one of the first takeaway foods, dating from about 1870, were eaten by young people outside the home, and were bought as a family meal at least once a week. Men out for the evening in pubs ate whelks and other portable seafood, together with another surprising delicacy, pork scratchings. Salt and vinegar were used in frightening quantities as the main seasoning, though bottled sauces were used by the richer households. The consumption of confectionery grew, and the types of these products increased. Social observers questioned the cooking ability of working-class wives, but the latter were little aware of their limitations.

Gambling

Before 1914 gambling had for the most part revolved around horse racing, but after 1918 dogtracks and football pools had made gambling more convenient for the working-class urbanite. It has been estimated that 10 million coupons were returned by the late 1930s.[35] In the 1930s gambling was an opiate for unemployment and general poverty.[36] Carl Chinn's highly informed book on street bookmaking, one of the few academic histories of an illegal activity written by a participant, shows how most betting on horses went through 'bookie's runners', who took bets on the streets and in pubs or in rudimentary 'betting shops'.[37] For a working man to bet legitimately, he had to go to the racecourse itself, which explained the numerous meetings and huge attendances throughout our period. A richer man with an account with an established bookmaker could legally place a bet over the telephone, but few members of the working or lower middle classes qualified for this luxury. By the 1930s, the police were aware that their pursuit of street betting was undermining their generally good relations with working people, and the way was opening up to the general legalizing of betting and gambling in the 1950s and 1960s.[38]

Architecture

British architecture at first followed much the same path as its late Victorian predecessor. Until the 1920s it was a mixture of historicism and eclecticism, reworking traditional British styles, though with more reference after 1900 to contemporary American and continental architecture. The imperial theme persisted, together with developments of the English cottage and the English country house of the Augustan age.

Traditional British architecture was challenged from about 1920 by 'modern architecture', sometimes known as 'the international style', which was imported mainly from the continent. Émigré architects, from Russia and later from Germany, were able to build pure examples of modernism and some of the younger British were influenced. The Russian émigré Berthold Lubetkin was required by the Royal Institute of British Architects to set up a partnership, Tecton, with some young English colleagues. Tecton had built some of the finest modern buildings in Britain by the later 1930s. Walter Gropius, fleeing from Hitler's Germany, worked in a similar partnership before moving on to America. Some new office blocks in London adopted steel and glass construction, or, as at the *Daily Express* in Fleet Street, a combination of Streamline Moderne, modern and the Art Deco that had briefly flourished in the 1920s under French influence. Garden design also began to move away from the picturesque and the classical to create angular, more geometric shapes.

The new cinemas of the 1930s also made a sharp break with the past, though their combination of styles and building techniques did not impress the architects of the Modern movement. Meanwhile, house design in the new suburbs did not diverge significantly from Edwardian and even Victorian models, and church design evolved very little. Only the big roadhouses and some of the new suburban public houses used horizontal lines, white stucco and Crittall windows to create impressions of high speed and ultra-modernity.

Interior design was influenced by French Art Deco in the later 1920s, and increasingly by the American Streamline Moderne in the 1930s. There was a switch here from ornate decoration (though with geometric structures) to an expressionist, 'machine age' aesthetic using chrome application and moulded glass. Opulence changed to efficiency. In design as a whole, foreign influence was greater than before the war, and continental Europe was added to North America as a source.

Holidays

Motor cars, as Sean O'Connell has shown, were bought mainly for leisure and status.[39] Sunday driving was a big feature of car use, and motor holidays opened up many a small village and region like the Cotswolds. Skindles built a car park on the Thames and employed parking attendants at weekends. Country cottages offering cream teas spread through the home counties.

The spread of motor touring diverted British holidaymaking to some degree from the ubiquitous seaside resort. Seaside holiday camps, beginning in modest form in the 1920s as an extension of 'plotland' development, multiplied in the 1930s, with the first Butlin's opening at Skegness in 1937.[40] They became something of a cult in the 1930s, and not just among poor people. Cheap hotels, boarding houses and landladies multiplied at the seaside, with more working people going away for annual seaside holidays. The number of workers enjoying paid holidays increased from 1.5 million in the early 1920s to over 11 million by 1939, though most of this increase occurred from the mid-1930s and was limited to one week only.[41] Over 20 million visitors went to the English seaside resorts by the late 1930s, though most favoured local or regional resorts that permitted day trips or short stays. Scottish resorts, less frequented, generally offered a combination of sea and mountain pleasures, as at Fort William and Rothesay. The big working-class resorts, led by Blackpool, provided a higher standard of facilities.[42] The great southern resorts, led by Torquay, provided an elegant, metropolitan environment. The rich continued their pre-war practice of travelling to the French and Italian Mediterranean, or to the Alps.

Conclusion

How may we sum up the culture of this 'sceptr'd isle'? The most embattled part of it, Ulster, was part of another, 'emerald' isle. Ulster's experience between 1900 and 1939 was a weary extension of Ireland's sad calvary in the nineteenth century. Part Irish, part Scottish, riven by religious obsessions, and poorer than England, Ulster's culture was *sui generis*, linked to the mainland more by Protestant support for Scottish football teams than anything else. Scotland, also, was poorer than England, its urban workers marked by heavy drinking and its country people affected by depopulation, poor soil and a dire climate. Middle-class values were sustained by religious observance in the Protestant church, and this was linked to the value attached to education. But with rewarding careers at a premium in Scotland, medicine attracted many men and not a few women. After 1900 Scottish culture developed very much as before, independently from England. At least Scotland had a proud and independent culture; Wales had very little, with the coal and iron districts of the south being essentially a recent English promotion. There was little sign of a national culture here. This chapter has dealt mainly with English culture, it is true, but how could we have done better?

One thing united this cluster of isles – the climate. As the clouds strode eastward across the North Atlantic, they created a north European climate of damp, mist and gloom. Britain's sceptr'd status did not spare it from the fate of north Germany, the Baltic states, Poland and southern Scandinavia. Dark winters, grey summers, Scotch mist and rain aplenty produced a pale, hunched populace. By the 1930s middle-class men normally carried raincoats over their arms in summer, while working men wore them in winter for lack of an overcoat. Though the home of the seaside resort, Britain's rainy, windy coasts kept holidaymakers in pubs, shelters and funfairs most of the time. Fish and chips was the standard diet on holiday in boarding houses and front cafés, to the delight of most people who normally ate them only once a week. A tradition of cheap coal kept open fires popping, cracking and puffing in nearly every home across the nation, from pauper to prince. Their deficiencies as a source of heat did not undermine a universal belief in them as a British cultural inheritance. Nor did the drudgery which only the servant-employing classes were spared.

A permanent damper was the gloomy Sunday. Local by-laws and practices meant that little was open on Sunday except the churches. The cinemas, that great innovation, were sometimes open on Sunday afternoon and Sunday evening, though the churches campaigned to see that children were driven into Sunday school. Jewish owners like Oscar Deutsch could ignore this policy, together with the half-serious joke that they should close their houses on Saturday, which they never did.

Saturday afternoon was the weekly cultural festival of the nation, thanks to the late Victorian half-day, and to professional football. Shops generally closed at Saturday midday, so women and children had less fun than the men, but a special tea was put on for the returning spectators, often with some 'tasty' ham and bullet-like tomatoes, or . . . fish and chips.

In 1900 much of Britain's culture was still based on its past and its upper classes. By 1939 it was increasingly based on change among the middle and working classes. The People's War would confirm that tendency in ways that none could yet suspect.

NOTES

1   A. Marwick, *Culture in Britain since 1945* (Oxford, 1991), p. 1.
2   This differs from the most commonly used Census definition structures, which relate to occupation rather than culture. See e.g. R. Crompton, *Class and Stratification: An Introduction to Current Debates* (Cambridge, 1998), pp. 58–61.
3   See S. Meacham, *Englishness and the Early Garden City Movement* (London, 1999).
4   W. D. Rubinstein, 'Modern Britain', in W. D. Rubinstein, ed., *Wealth and the Wealthy in the Modern World* (London, 1980), pp. 57–8.

5 D. Cannadine, *Aspects of Aristocracy* (London, 1994), pp. 67–72.

6 R. Wohl, *The Generation of 1914* (Cambridge, Mass., 1979), p. 85.

7 Ibid., p. 106.

8 The Worktown study was never published, but *The Pub and the People*, published in 1943 and republished by the Cresset Press in 1987, drew on it.

9 C. Osborne, *W. H. Auden: The Life of a Poet* (London, 1983), pp. 202–3.

10 T. Mason, 'Sport and recreation', in P. Johnson, ed., *Twentieth-century Britain: Economic, Social and Cultural Change* (Harlow, 1994), p. 112; J. Stevenson, *British Society, 1914–1945* (Harmondsworth, 1984), p. 398.

11 D. F. Cheshire, *Music Hall in Britain* (Newton Abbot, 1974), pp. 52–60.

12 See e.g. M. Beerbohm, *Around Theatres* (1924; London, 1953).

13 Just two days before the delivery of this chapter, a *Times* report on changes in Her Majesty the Queen's rendering of English revived interest in upper-class accents; *The Times*, 21 December 2000.

14 W. Mellers, *Music and Society: England and the European Tradition* (London, 1946), pp. 105–32.

15 W. Gaunt, *A Concise History of English Painting* (London, 1964), p. 207.

16 See D. Messum, *British Impressions: A Collection of British Impressionist Paintings, 1880–1940* (London, 1988).

17 See J. Rothenstein's intimate biographies of the cohort of painters born in the 1880s and 1890s in his *Modern English Painters: Lewis to Moore* (London, 1956).

18 H. Perkin, *The Age of the Automobile* (London, 1976), pp. 129, 136–7, 147–51.

19 P. Newby and M. Turner, 'British suburban taste, 1880–1939', in R. Harris and P. J. Larkham, eds, *Changing Suburbs: Foundation, Form and Function* (London, 1999), pp. 32–55.

20 J. Walvin, *Leisure and Society, 1830–1950* (London, 1978), pp. 139–40.

21 S. Bowden, 'The new consumerism', in Johnson, ed., *Twentieth-century Britain*, p. 245. See chapter 22 in this volume.

22 See D. Hardy and C. Ward, *Arcadia for All: The Legacy of a Makeshift Landscape* (London, 1984).

23 See M. Bracewell, *England is Mine: Pop Life in Albion from Wilde to Goldie* (London, 1997), pp. 8–28.

24 J. Hazelgrove, *Spiritualism and British Society between the Wars* (Manchester, 2000), pp. 13–24.

25 Stevenson, *British Society*, p. 418.

26 Ibid., p. 397.

27 K. D. Brown, *The British Toy Business: A History since 1700* (London, 1996), p. 64.

28 Ibid., p. 58.

29 See chapter 28 in this volume.

30 A. Davies, 'Cinema and broadcasting', in Johnson, ed., *Twentieth-century Britain*, pp. 263, 271–2.

31 Bowden, 'New consumerism', p. 244.

32 Stevenson, *British Society*, p. 383.

33 M. Hilton, *Smoking in British Popular Culture, 1800–2000* (Manchester, 2000), pp. 84–111.

34 N. Branson and M. Heinemann, *Britain in the Nineteen-thirties* (London, 1971), p. 203.

35 Davies, 'Cinema and broadcasting', p. 264.

36 C. Mowat, *Britain between the Wars, 1918–1940* (London, 1955), p. 487.

37 C. Chinn, *Better Betting with a Decent Feller: Bookmaking, Betting and the British Working Class, 1750–1990* (Hemel Hempstead, 1991).

38 Ibid., pp. 270–6.

39 S. O'Connell, *The Car in British Society: Class, Gender and Motoring, 1896–1939* (Manchester, 1998), pp. 77–107.

40 C. Ward and D. Hardy, *Goodnight Campers! The History of the British Holiday Camp* (London, 1986), pp. 23–51.

41 Stevenson, *British Society*, p. 193.

42 J. K. Walton, *Blackpool* (Edinburgh, 1998), pp. 46–134; J. Stevenson and C. Cook, *Britain and the Depression: Society and Politics, 1929–39* (Harlow, 1994), p. 34.

FURTHER READING

Blake, A., *The Land Without Music: Music, Culture and Society in Twentieth-century Britain* (Manchester, 1997).

Gray, A. and McGuigan, J., eds, *Studying Culture: An Introductory Reader* (London, 1993).

Johnson, P., ed., *Twentieth-century Britain: Economic, Social and Cultural Change* (London, 1994).

Stevenson, J., *British Society, 1914–1945* (Harmondsworth, 1984).

Stevenson, J. and Cook, C., *Britain and the Depression: Society and Politics, 1929–39* (Harlow, 1994).

Turner, G., *British Cultural Studies: An Introduction* (2nd edition, London, 1990).

Ward, C. and Hardy, D., *Goodnight Campers! The History of the British Holiday Camp* (London, 1986).

CHAPTER THIRTY-ONE

The Impact of the First World War

CHRIS WRIGLEY

The horrors of the western and eastern fronts, Gallipoli and Mesopotamia were seared into the collective consciousness of the twentieth century. Images of trench warfare and of the soldiers who experienced sectors of high military activity became widely understood symbols of human suffering and endurance. Such images were powerful later in such plays as R. C. Sherriff's *Journey's End* (1928), television series such as 'Sapphire and Steel' (1979), and television documentaries such as John Terraine's twenty-six-part 'The Great War' (1964, repeated in 1974). The twentieth century had many later horrors, but images of the First World War remained among the most powerful at the century's end.

Economic, social and political changes that occurred after 11 November 1918 should not simply be ascribed to the impact of the First World War. That changes came after the war does not necessarily involve a causal connection. In many instances striking changes of the First World War era, such as in art and literature, were under way before the war. Often the First World War appears as an accelerator of change rather than an initiator of change. This is especially so in such areas as science, technology and medicine. Also some adverse and some beneficial changes occurred in the post-war boom, 1919–20, and for some aspects of British history there is a clearer break in 1921 than in 1918.

Short-term Economic Impact

The war transformed government intervention in the economy. Before 1914 this had been limited, even if growing notably in social welfare. With a major European conflict, which spilt over to other parts of the world, the government came to take very extensive controls over much of the economy.

As the war developed into a lengthy conflict, clearly not 'over by Christmas', the government intervened in response to increasing scarcities in the economy. Often intervention in one area led to intervention in other areas. Control of one commodity or economic sector had knock-on effects for others. As the war continued, it was apparent that such a war between industrialized nations stretched Britain's financial and industrial resources nearly to their limits, with the government needing to arbitrate between competing priorities.

Labour was a critical area from early in the war. Without adequate labour of the right skill at the right place the war could be lost. There was an early urgent need for men for the army to assist the French army to contain the German army, and supplying reinforcements remained a priority until the end of the war. The advent of conscription in two stages in January and April 1916 and the coming of the Schedule of Reserved Occupations gave the government tighter control over the allocation of labour between the armed forces, priority war production, maintaining vital services, food production and export industries.

By the end of the war some 5.7 million men had joined the armed forces. This was a large proportion of the pre-war male labour force, which had numbered 12.6 million at the time of the 1911 Census. In 1916 28 per cent and in 1918 36 per cent of the pre-war male labour force had left civilian employment. In the early part of the war voluntary recruitment was indiscriminate (in being blind to wartime civilian employment priorities), with 2 million men enlisting by July 1915. In essential war occupations there were substantial losses from the labour forces: 23.8 per cent in chemicals and explosives, 23.7 per cent in electrical engineering, 21.8 per cent in coal and other mining, 19.5 per cent in engineering, 18.8 per cent in iron and steel, and 16.5 per cent in shipbuilding.[1] These were all sectors in which Britain could ill afford to lose any skilled labour. In the case of the crucial metal trades, the lost labour had to be replaced and much more labour found. Here the numbers employed rose by 34 per cent between July 1914 and July 1918, while the overall numbers in civil employment fell by 12 per cent. Lloyd George commented in a speech at Bangor in February 1915, 'This is an engineers' war, and it will be won or lost according to the efforts of the engineers'.

The substantial transfer of labour, finance, iron and steel and other resources to engineering was greatly facilitated by state action. In the case of iron and steel there were nine stages of controls between October 1915 and January 1917. The sheer scale of demand for munitions quickly revealed that market forces in wartime would inflate prices but not secure sufficient additional output. The government's National Shell Factories thereby not only helped to achieve a greater output but provided cost returns which provided substantial evidence to secure reduced prices from private suppliers. Of 162,708,100 shells manufactured in Britain during the war, the National Shell Factories produced 64,376,900 (40 per cent). With more effective accounting (the Ministry of Munitions accounts department growing from thirty-five to 3,500 between July 1915 and the Armistice), much keener prices were fixed from late 1915 with a reasonable rate of profit on cost of production being 10 per cent or less (not the 20 per cent suggested by Vickers). With £3 million a week being spent on munitions in autumn 1915, it is perhaps not so astounding that a review of past transactions carried out in mid-1917 resulted in a recovery of £39 million.[2]

While engineering, metals and chemicals were industries that expanded in Britain and other belligerent countries during the First World War, there were other sectors that were crucial. Coal was one, another industry where voluntary recruiting in the first year of the war (taking some 22 per cent of the men by July 1915) caused serious labour shortages later. Lloyd George, with characteristic hyperbole, told representatives of the Miners' Federation of Great Britain on 29 July 1915,

In peace and in war King Coal is the paramount Lord of Industry. It enters into every article of consumption and of utility. It is our international coinage. We buy goods abroad, food and raw material. We pay, not in gold, but in coal. In war it is life for us and death for our foes. It not merely fetches and carries for us; it makes the material and machinery which it transports. It bends, it moulds, it fills the weapons of war.[3]

Coal was essential for much power (steam and electricity), including for the non-oil-powered larger part of the British navy, for production of toluol (part of TNT) and for her Allies (most of the French coal mines being in German occupied areas). By 1918 shortages of labour and levels of output were threatening the capacity of Britain to continue her role as a major industrial supplier had the war gone on into 1919 or 1920. Lloyd George informed Georges Clemenceau on 30 August 1918 that Britain could not provide more soldiers, observing, 'The only way in which we can liberate more workers is if you and your Allies can dispense with the shipping, the coal, the steel and other supplies which are sent to you at the present time'.[4]

Severe shortages of materials, especially those imported, led to the government allocating supplies and regulating firms' levels of output. An example of such a shortage was wool, needed for the uniforms of the huge new army. In June 1916 the War Office took on purchasing and distribution of the whole wool clip of the British Isles, and later in the year bought up the entire outputs of Australia and New Zealand.[5] By the later part of the war the government was the sole overseas purchaser of many raw materials.

Shortages also led the government to encourage the expansion of several industries and to promote industrial research and development. Several products needed for the war had previously been imported from Germany; these included several chemical products, optics and ball bearings. The government sponsored research from mid-1915, with its efforts being centred from 1916 in the Department of Scientific and Industrial Research. The extension of government control over industries under the Munitions of War Act 1915 or Defence of the Realm Acts' regulations accelerated the spread of many best practices in British industry, including cost accounting, wider use of electric power and better welfare provision.[6]

Further state intervention to ensure major transfers of resources was brought about by the German submarine campaign which became notably effective from 1916. When the German U-boat campaign became unrestricted in February 1917, the numbers of ships sunk increased markedly. In February–April 1917, 401 British ships and 487 Allied and neutral ships, some 2 million tons of shipping, were sunk primarily by submarines (a few by mines or surface ships). As a result of submarine warfare, shipbuilding became a high priority, allocation of precious shipping space between competing priorities an important task for senior ministers, even greater care had to be taken in selecting shorter journeys for vessels rather than longer (North America, even if the cost of the supplies was higher, rather than South America), and there had to be more import substitution. The seriousness of the situation was alleviated by the introduction of convoys and by the United States' entry into the war in April 1917. Shortly afterwards, when addressing an American audience in London, Lloyd George declared, 'The road to victory, the guarantee of victory, the absolute assurance of victory, is to be found in one word – ships! In a second word – ships! In a third word – ships!'[7]

Shortages of shipping space and foreign exchange forced the government into securing greater food production in Britain. Roughly half of British shipping was requisitioned early on in the war for moving troops and supplies to France and elsewhere. As a result, even before U-boat action caused further loss of capacity, shipping prices soared. Andrew Bonar Law, the Conservative party leader, told parliament of his embarrassment at earning £7,500 return in two years (in 1915–17) on an invested £8,000 in shipping.[8] In 1916 the tonnage of the UK's food imports had fallen by a third. With the Corn Production Act 1917, domestic output was increased, with a switch away from livestock and dairy produce to higher nutritional value grain and potatoes. Fear of shortages was tackled by price controls, beginning with wheat, meat and sugar in July 1917, and local rationing of meat, margarine, butter, tea, bacon and cheese but national rationing of sugar from December 1917. The consumer was also helped by subsidized domestic coal prices under the state control of the mines (south Wales from 1915, other areas from 1916).

The war effort drew massively on Britain's financial strength. Public expenditure took roughly 50 per cent of the national income by the end of the war, up from the pre-war 8 or 9 per cent. Britain funded not only a fourfold increase in expenditure on the fighting services between 1915 and the end of the war, but also increased expenditure on food and shipping and loans of £1,741 million to her Allies. Over the war years (1914–15 to 1918–19) government revenue met 28.5 per cent of expenditure, the rest being covered by internal and external borrowing. The British government raised loans in the United States on the security of British investments there, and eventually 20–25 per cent of her foreign capital assets were sold to pay for the war. Britain also borrowed £1,365 million, over three-quarters of which came from the United States.

The other European belligerent countries had to make similar economic responses to the needs of the war. Britain was unusual in that foreign armies did not invade her homeland (though they did fight on empire soil) and that civilian casualties other than at sea were relatively few. Apart from explosions in munitions works and other accidents, some 1,400 people were killed and 3,400 wounded during air raids in Britain and others killed when German battleships shelled the north-east coast in December 1914. The power of the British navy guarded against invasion.

The most notable economic feature of Britain was that her economy could respond so strongly to the shock of a European war and provide very substantial assistance to her Allies, especially before the entry of the United States into the war in April 1917. In contrast, Russia, with a less advanced industrial economy, was shattered by the war, her transport infrastructure unable to meet the needs of her big cities and armies. Britain had some transport problems, with the railway lines to the south coast ports seriously congested by the end of the war, but experienced no such crisis.

Long-term Economic Impact

Although the British economy was weakened by the First World War, it was not affected in the long term to the extent that it was by the Second World War. In several respects the First World War accelerated problems that were already developing before August 1914.

It has been estimated that European manufacturing output was set back by eight years by the First World War. This conclusion was reached by the economist W. Arthur Lewis by projecting pre-war trends into the 1920s, thereby finding that the actual level of output in 1929 would have been achieved in 1921. In summarizing Lewis's findings, Ingvar Svennilson argued that more significant was European countries' 'failure to keep up to date as regards new products and new methods of production', and cited as examples the United States taking the lead in motor cars and rubber.[9]

Britain was notably slow in moving into dynamic new industrial sectors. The First World War saw a continuation of the decline of Britain's share of world trade. In this Britain was a notable part of a European relative decline, with some shift of world economic activity towards the United States, Canada and Japan. In terms of value Europe's share fell from 58.5 to 48 per cent between 1913 and 1926, while in these years the North American share rose from 14 to 19 per cent and Asia's from 12 to 17 per cent. In terms of volume of exports as a percentage of 1913 volumes, Britain's total fell to 38 per cent in 1918 and reached 81 per cent in 1929, while the United States' total rose to 120 per cent in 1918 and 158 per cent in 1929, and Japan's rose to 212 per cent in 1918 and 258 per cent in 1929.[10]

An outstanding feature of Britain's declining share of trade was a severe fall in textiles. India took some 40 per cent of Lancashire's exports of cotton but during the war production of cotton in Britain was curtailed, in large part because of shortages of shipping space. In India production rose by about 40 per cent during the war and Japanese inroads into the Indian market accelerated. Apart from India and cotton, British exports dropped markedly elsewhere during the war, notably Australia, New Zealand, South Africa and Japan.

Britain, like other parts of Europe, was much affected by industrial developments in other parts of the world; this resulted in a lessening of their demand for imported basic industrial goods while increasing the competition in other markets. The situation was exacerbated for British exports by a much more sluggish rate of growth of world trade after 1920 compared to before 1914 and by more tariff barriers. The expansion of capacity in such industries as engineering, steel and shipbuilding during the war and post-war boom (1914–20), often financed with loans at relatively high rates of interest, added to British industry's problems. There is much truth in the traditional structural explanation that British industry was too committed to the nineteenth-century staple industries – coal, cotton, iron and steel, shipbuilding and heavy engineering – and became too dependent on selling in the favourable empire markets rather than competing in products for which there was considerable growth in demand, often consumer industries. However, more recent writing has emphasized that some sectors of 'old industries' remained buoyant, but often as a result of being more oriented to the domestic market where there was substantial growth in consumer demand.[11]

British exports grew more slowly than her European competitors' from the mid-1920s. This may well have been due to sterling being overvalued after the return to the gold standard in 1925 at the old pre-war parity to the dollar. There has been much debate over J. M. Keynes's estimate that sterling was overvalued by 10 per cent. This has been disputed, especially the degree of overvaluation. Others have argued that shorter working hours and higher real wages damaged British competitiveness and led to high unemployment. While labour costs may have had an adverse impact on competitiveness in 1919–20, it is less likely that they did after 1921. However, there is much to suggest that sterling was one of several currencies (including the French and Belgian francs) that was overvalued, in sterling's case taking five years to decline to roughly the level comparable to competitors' price levels.[12]

Britain's pre-war primacy in overseas investment was much weakened by the war. Some £850 to £1,000 million of foreign capital assets were liquidated to pay for the war (over £500 million in the United States), but after the war there was very substantial renewed overseas investment. By 1920 earnings from overseas investments amounted to some £200 million per year and by 1925 to £250 million per year, a higher figure than pre-war but in real terms worth less. However, after the war the United States overshadowed Britain as an international creditor. Between 1924 and 1929 United States overseas lending was nearly double that of Britain, some $6.4 to $3.3 billion.

The First World War saw New York overtake the City of London as the pre-eminent financial centre. During the war there were delays or defaults by many international borrowers, resulting in major strains on London banks. International seekers of capital increasingly looked more to New York than to London and sterling was weaker as a currency for funding international trade. As a result much international financial business moved permanently to New York.

The war started and centred in Europe, with massive devastation of resources. The relative economic weakening of Britain in international economic relations was not a peculiarly British phenomenon. Europe as a whole was weakened relative to other parts of the world. That said, Europe (including Britain) remained the most powerful economic bloc, even if the United States, Japan and other countries' share of world economic activity grew markedly during the war. British and European relative decline was under way anyway. The First World War accentuated it and made the changes very apparent. British pre-war pre-eminence in various areas of the international economy would have continued longer without the war, but such pre-eminence would have ended in due course.

Short-term Social Impact

The removal of 4,970,000 men into the army, 407,000 into the navy and 293,000 into the air force, with the massive increase in demand for armaments and other war supplies, had an inevitable major impact on British society. The scale of its impact on different groups in society has been much debated ever since.

The enormity of the First World War encouraged reflections, often linked to comparisons with the impact of the French and Napoleonic Wars (1793–1815), of the greater the involvement of the population in war, the greater the social impact. The distinguished sociologist Stanislas Andrzejewski argued in *Military Organisation and Society* (1951) that where societies pushed beyond an optimum ratio of military participation in war (famously dubbed the 'military participation ratio'), wider social groups than existing elites experienced social gains. Subsequent historical writing rejected this formula as far too simplistic. The historian Arthur Marwick published a series of articles and books exploring war and social change, which increasingly backed away from specific generalizations but argued that wars accelerated many social trends in British and other societies.[13] His *The Deluge* (1965) was the influential and attractively written social history of Britain during the First World War against which other historians in the late twentieth century reacted. The work of Gail Braybon, Bernard Waites, J. M. Winter and others offered more complex and nuanced interpretations.

Those who place greater emphasis on primarily economic than sociological explanations tend to see the social impact of the First World War not as unique to the 'total war' phenomenon but as having the characteristics of an accentuated upturn in the trade cycle. The economic historian W. H. B. Court has written of the wartime economic boom compared to pre-war economic expansion,

> Public spending on this scale reversed the pre-war trend of the trade cycle . . . The wartime industrial expansion of 1915–18 had a very different root, but a similar mode of growth. It arose out of public expenditure and the growth of production to satisfy it. The public sector of the economy had been increasing in size before the war. Now it took an immensely sharp upward turn.[14]

The downturn of such war-induced booms was post-war depression, as after the Napoleonic, Crimean and Boer Wars, and a loss of most of labour's gains. Lloyd George, when introducing his war budget on 17 November 1914, predicted a wartime and a post-war reconstruction boom but warned, 'When that period is over, we shall be face to face with one of the most serious industrial situations with which we have ever been confronted'.[15] Hence, historians have needed not just to look at labour market and other social changes during the war but to assess the extent to which these survived the severe 1921–2 recession.

From early on in the war one of the most commented on developments in the labour market was changed employment patterns for women. There was a substantial number of working women who changed employment during the war. Some sectors, such as fish-gutting, shed labour and many women took the opportunity of shortages of labour to leave domestic service. Often they moved from one traditional female job into another. However, commentators then and subsequently suggested that gender barriers in employment were tumbling down like the walls of Jericho. This is an exaggeration. It was brought about during the war by the most being made of women being in jobs usually not carried out by women. Photographs appeared not only in the press and as postcards but also on posters and leaflets issued to promote women's war work. The notion of novelty was also underlined at the time and later by the writings of middle-class women for whom such employment, or in many cases any employment, was noteworthy. Moreover, the range of women's work experienced before the war was frequently overlooked in appraisals of 'new work' for women in wartime. Similarly, there was substantial underrecording of women's pre-war paid employment.[16] Even ignoring the pre-war underestimates, women's employment rose significantly but not as massively during the war as is often thought, by just under a quarter between July 1914 and July 1918.

Whether or not the war marked 'a sudden and irreversible advance in the economic and social power' of working women, as Marwick claimed in *The Deluge*, has been much discussed. All generalizations concerning women's experiences in the First World War need to be made cautiously, given the varying experiences between different parts of Britain, different occupations, different age groups and different classes.[17] The war did offer women more work alternatives, many could migrate to higher-paid work and, like Lancashire cotton textile workers before the war, some relatively well-paid single women enjoyed spending their disposable income on leisure and modest luxuries. Yet, there is much to suggest that the status of the women in male employers', male employees' and probably in many women's views did not change.

During the war, in spite of much talk of equal pay for equal work, employers and trade unions alike kept women out of male areas of employment as long as they could and maintained substantial gender differentials in pay. Before the war women in textiles had been kept out of higher-paid tasks by spurious arguments about their physiques and their attire. During the war similar arguments were mobilized. Often what had been impractical and unacceptable earlier in the war became necessary and successful when labour shortages ensured women were employed on such tasks. This was notably true of sorting the mail in London, where the London Postal Service soon had to operate with women sorters after rejecting the possibility in 1914.[18] There were ample opportunities for women's work to be deemed not equal to that of men. In engineering the subdivision of tasks under dilution of labour plus increased mechanization resulted in modified jobs. There were substantial changes to working practices in other employment. The result was that significant gender differentials in pay continued and that usually, where work was subdivided, women continued to be allocated monotonous and mundane tasks which men believed women were especially suited to carrying out. While women's pay usually improved (relative to what women had earned earlier), their earnings remained lower than men's and their status was not dissimilar to before 1914. That this was so was demonstrated by the vigour of the post-war campaigns to get women out of 'men's jobs' and back to 'women's tasks'.

The experience of women in the post-war labour market indicates the importance of assessing not just the war years but the whole of the boom (1915–20) and the ensuing depression (1921). During the war the government gave fifteen pledges to restore pre-war trade union conditions, which included the removal of female and unskilled male labour from engineering. The Restoration of Pre-War Practices Act 1919 gave employers up to two months in which to return to pre-war practices, and then required that they be maintained 'for one year after such restoration is effected'. This removed remaining women in the autumn of 1919 and the economic downturn of late 1920 reinforced employer and trade union hostility to their return. However, in some areas women maintained wartime gains in work opportunities. This was notably so in clerical and other white-collar employment, including in banking, but generally in such work women were kept in the lower-paid, more mundane work and were far less likely than men to be promoted. Some women also found continuing employment in retailing, pottery, printing, book binding, light metals and the police.

During the war the greatest amount of replacement labour for those withdrawn from the labour market to the armed forces was male. The influx of unskilled and semi-skilled labour into skilled work and the spread of piecework rates and various bonuses linked to output gave rise to some erosion of wage differentials during the war. The Commission of Enquiry into the May 1917 engineering unrest found many 'instances . . . in which unskilled workers, labourers, women and girls were earning more than double that of skilled men'. There were similar complaints in building, the railways and other sectors of the economy.[19] However, several historians have cautioned against taking too rosy a view of improved living standards for the unskilled workers and their families. They have queried the extent to which unskilled workers in such trades as shipbuilding and printing gained relative to skilled workers, and also emphasized that wartime escalating prices hit their real wages.[20]

While those in the wartime labour market may have had their real wages eroded by inflation, the extra hours worked generally ensured that they did not suffer in terms of take-home pay. However, during the war there were losers who were on fixed incomes or low wages. The issue of wartime poverty has sometimes been overlooked when authors have focused on aggregate demographic data. The most distinguished study of broad trends in civilian health in the war is J. M. Winter's *The Great War and the British People* (1986). Winter offered the paradox that while there was horrendous military slaughter, the war 'was the occasion of a completely unanticipated improvement in the life of the civilian population', which he argued was 'primarily on account of the demands of the war economy'. He went on to claim, 'This benefited all classes . . . The general rule was that the worse off a section was before 1914, the greater were its gains in life expectancy'. The improved infant mortality figures (from 110 to 82 per 1,000 live births between 1910 and 1920) were a notable and surprising aspect of British wartime statistics.[21]

Some aspects of Winter's impressive study have been questioned. His aggregate figures cloak any marked regional, industrial or class variations. His analysis depended on the mortality records of the Prudential Assurance Company, which while covering 'about one-half of the male population which manned the war economy' thereby did not cover the multitudes who did not benefit directly from the war boom and were those hardest hit by price inflation. High tuberculosis rates may well be linked to wartime overcrowding in industrial areas and bad working conditions. Moreover, while the infant morality rates were good, there was a deterioration among young (10–29) and elderly (75–79) women.[22]

Overall, the picture of wartime health and poverty is complex. There is a strong case for believing that for many people in urban areas there was an improvement in nutrition, especially with rationing in the later stages of the war. Although not popular, the decline in consumption of sugar, butter and meat and increased consumption of bread and potatoes was a healthy development.[23] Some 900,000 workers in munitions factories benefited from food in canteens, while alcohol was less available and beer weaker. The Education (Provision of Meals) Act 1914 made it compulsory for local authorities to feed necessitous children. In Scotland expenditure on feeding children reached £29 million in 1918–19, up from £7 million in 1912–13. However, the war economy lifted many parents out of poverty. In Bristol, the number of daily meals provided by the city council for needy children fell from 1,445 to 114 between March 1915 and March 1916.[24]

Yet those on fixed incomes or low pay were adversely affected by the war. The elderly faced escalating food and fuel prices, while receiving a rise in pensions from the pre-war five shillings to seven shillings and sixpence (for those most in need in 1916, for all in 1917). While the government frequently raised allowances and pensions for the dependants of men in the armed forces, these rises trailed behind price rises and in practice the authorities seem to have felt charitable and voluntary organizations would meet the shortfall. A soldier's wife with three children complained in December 1916,

> Give us a fair allowance, or it will be found necessary to add an extra wing to the workhouse, for the day of miracles is past, and we come to the final conclusion that we cannot compete with the constant 'going up' of food prices.[25]

The withdrawal of a large sector of the male labour force also had an impact on the young. In Britain, as in Germany, concern was expressed over the adverse effect on the discipline of boys given the removal of fathers and vigorous male teachers into the armed forces. By mid-1916 roughly half the pre-war male elementary teachers had enlisted and the numbers of male students in teacher training colleges had fallen from 4,242 to 700.[26] They were frequently replaced with women, retired male teachers and clergymen.

Schoolchildren were despatched to agricultural and urban work. By 31 May 1916, 15,753 children aged eleven to fourteen, mostly boys, had been issued with exemptions from school and were working as agricultural labourers. There was considerable concern about eleven-year-olds missing their education and in February 1916 a Board of Education circular said that this age group should only be excused in 'entirely exceptional' circumstances. Given widespread fears that schoolchildren were used because they were cheap, the circular

> suggested that the urgency of the need for the labour of school children may, to a certain extent, be tested by the amount of wages offered, and as a rule it may be taken that if the labour of a boy of school age is not worth at least six shillings (30p) a week to the farmer, the benefit derived from the boy's employment is not sufficient to compensate for the loss involved by the interruption of the boy's education.

Far fewer were released for industrial or miscellaneous work; between September 1914 and February 1915, only 178 (of whom thirty-one were for industry).[27] However, in urban areas large numbers of boys were working out of school hours, as much as 40 per cent in one town in 1917.

Another notable feature of the wartime high demand for labour was substantial labour mobility. This was a massive change for men (and some women) across Europe. People who normally might never expect to travel more than twenty or thirty miles from their birthplace travelled vast distances to fight or substantial distances to take up priority war work.

Some Long-term Political and Social Impacts

Although there were many politicians, civil servants, academics and even businessmen who hoped that the more interventionist state policies of the war would continue, there was a powerful impulse to return to the pre-war world. Rationalization of production and industrial efficiency were again to be left to market forces.

Yet the war with its massive demand for industrial goods had strengthened labour, not only in the market, but also politically. UK membership of trade unions rose by 58 per cent between 1914 and 1918, from 4,135,000 to 6,533,000, and more than doubled (102 per cent) between 1914 and 1920, from 4,135,000 to 8,348,000. The trade unions also emerged from the war financially strong, with sizeable political funds. Trade union organization provided an urban framework for the Labour party, and unions such as that of the railwaymen provided a focus in many rural con- stituencies. Although the Labour party did not perform very well in the 1918 general election, there was much in Arthur Henderson's comment afterwards that in the patriotic fervour of that election the Labour party had polled its minimum vote. Even so, it was the largest opposition group to take its seats in the House of Commons, and it went on to be the official opposition in 1922 and to form a government in January 1924.

The Labour party's swift emergence as a party of office after the war was due in large part to the war. Before 1914 it had been an auxiliary group to the Liberals, much dependent on a parliamentary election pact for most of its seats. Although its strength was growing through the unions and in municipal politics, it was not immi- nently likely to increase markedly its parliamentary representation. In contrast, the war brought about divisions in the Liberal party and undercut part of the party's support.

The war also helped the Conservative party recover further from its three succes- sive general election defeats. The Conservatives were strengthened by their ability to be associated with vigorous prosecution of the war. They were the party of conscription, of unstinted support for the generals, of empire and British naval supremacy.

The war also ended the thirty-year aspiration that devolution ('Home Rule') would meet Irish political aspirations. The British making martyrs of the leaders of the Easter Rising in 1916, Lloyd George's attempts to secure further concessions in order to carry out Home Rule (which had already been on the statute book in 1914), and the passage of legislation for conscription in Ireland ended the politics of Home Rule and undercut the Irish Parliamentary party, bringing about its replacement by Sinn Fein. Most of Ireland went its own way after 1921, leaving the issue of Ulster for later in the century.

The war years marked one of many alleged watersheds for women. Although many women gained the vote in 1918, women's status was only temporarily improved, and then attitudes were not substantially altered. Other watersheds would come and go, in the Second World War and in the 1960s, but much inequality remained entrenched at the end of the century.

The war was traumatic for many who fought in it. The post-war world had many men in it who were maimed or damaged by shell shock. In 1921 1,187,450 men were in receipt of pensions for war disabilities, with a fifth of these having suffered serious loss of limbs or eyesight, paralysis or lunacy.

The war was marked by triumphal celebrations mixed with sadness. The sadness was not only for the deaths of so many relatives, friends and neighbours, but also expressed a sense of the loss of the relative stabilities of the pre-war world combined with some anxiety as to what the post-war years would hold. As Jay Winter has observed, 'commemoration was a universal preoccupation after the 1914–18 war. The need to bring the dead home, to put the dead to rest, symbolically or physically, was pervasive'.[28] Following a decision by the War Office in 1915, very few of the dead were physically returned home, but symbolically there remained a strong need to put them to rest. For some there was even a drive to try to communicate with the dead, with a resurgence of interest in spiritualism.

Huge numbers of war memorials were built after the Armistice. Most of these were unveiled in the first half of the 1920s, though some were much later, notably that at Mumbles of 30 July 1939.[29] With the mass graves abroad, the memorials provided places for grieving, both individually and as a community. In many parts of Britain there were particular large groups of men, and some women, to grieve for. For instance, the Chorley Pals Company, which became Y Company of the 11th Battalion, the East Lancashire Regiment, suffered the loss of 758 officers and men. The death toll at Gallipoli was devastating for the Lancashire Fusiliers and a town such as Bury, as well as for ANZAC troops and Australia and New Zealand.[30]

For the communities, the war memorials, whether monuments, hospital wings, gardens or playing fields, provided an opportunity for the living to express their indebtedness to the dead. The local leaders of society often required their communities to respond to patriotic remembrance just as earlier they had exerted much social pressure to maximize voluntary responses to recruiting. At the many inaugurations or memorials, Armistice Days and Remembrance Sundays, the message delivered was one of duty, of serving King, Country and God. The dead were to be revered and respected as role models by the young. Generally, as Mark Connelly has observed, 'the Armistice message was . . . one of teamwork and hierarchy'. Remembrance was pervasive, with sometimes multiple commemorations of the dead: at their former school, college, workplace, church or chapel and at a civil memorial.[31]

As after the Second World War, the First World War was followed by much idealized nostalgia for wartime social bonding. The bishop of Stepney, in a school address in July 1925, declared, 'What was needed to make the country great was to bring the spirit of the trenches into our social and industrial life'. The Toc H movement was one Christian attempt to build on wartime comradeship.[32]

Remembrance was long made very tangible, not only by the monuments, but also by human reminders of the war, the ex-servicemen, the fit as well as the mutilated. School remembrance services frequently involved staff who themselves were veterans, and this was so until the early 1960s. Even the literature ambiguous in its attitude to, or outrightly critical of, the First World War, much in vogue in the late 1920s, reinforced younger generations' awareness of what their predecessors had experienced. In the interwar years and to the end of the century, the First World War generation was one that was pitied yet respected by its successors.

Like the ex-servicemen's organizations themselves in various countries, remembrance of the First World War was not always attached to the political right.[33] In working-class areas the contrast between the high rhetoric at the civic memorials and the penury the heroes' widows suffered was sometimes all too apparent. There was also much bitterness among long-term unemployed ex-servicemen, with Armistice Day in some places and in some years being an occasion to highlight that unemployment, not 'a land fit for heroes to live in', was their post-war experience.

The war had its cultural impact. This has often been viewed as enormous, most memorably in Paul Fussell's *The Great War in Modern Memory* (1975). However, there has been substantial challenge to seeing the war as the major cause of change in the style and direction of writing. Ecksteins argued that war in some way was a response to modernism and that the cult of the irrational was present before July

1914. Hynes, Winter and the contributors to the Roshwald and Stites collection on European culture all point to the complexities of the relationship between the war and culture. Winter, in studying bereavement, argues that 'the war gave a new lease of life to a number of traditional languages expressed both conventionally and in unusual and modern forms'.[34] As with the international economic impact of the war, recent reassessments of the cultural impact confirm that it was significant but suggest less of a sharp discontinuity than some earlier writers assumed.

In the twenty-first century the First World War retains its fascination for writers, film-makers, artists and the general public. After the war, for many participants there was a need to express their feelings. Jay Winter has captured this well, observing, 'The soldier-writers' task was . . . that of trying to find a way to glorify those who had died in war without glorifying war itself'.[35] Subsequent generations have tried to empathize with the experiences of combatants. Works such as J. L. Carr's *A Month in the Country* (1978) and Pat Barker's *Regeneration* (1991) found large appreciative audiences. Similarly, there has been a sizeable market for almost any historical works on that war. Although often depicted in stereotypes by both novelists and the less careful historians, the First World War remains very alive in the western world's imagination.

NOTES

1 P. E. Dewey, 'Military recruiting and the British labour movement during the First World War', *Historical Journal*, 27 (1984), pp. 199–233.

2 HM Government, *History of the Ministry of Munitions* (London, 1922), vol. 2, part 2, pp. 42–8; vol. 3, part 1, pp. 43–8 and part 2, pp. 26–44. (This was printed but not published.)

3 D. Lloyd George, *Through Terror to Triumph* (London, 1915), pp. 178–9.

4 C. Wrigley, *David Lloyd George and the British Labour Movement* (Hassocks, 1976), p. 231.

5 E. M. H. Lloyd, *Experiments in State Control* (Oxford, 1924), pp. 118–19.

6 R. MacLeod and K. MacLeod, 'Government and the optical industry in Britain 1914–18', in J. M. Winter, ed., *War and Economic Development* (Cambridge, 1975); C. Wrigley, 'The Ministry of Munitions: an innovatory department', in K. Burk, ed., *War and the State: The Transformation of British Government 1914–1919* (London, 1982).

7 D. Lloyd George, *The Great Crusade* (London, 1918), pp. 82–3.

8 T. Wilson, *The Myriad Faces of War* (Oxford, 1986), p. 222.

9 I. Svennilson, *Growth and Stagnation in the European Economy* (Geneva, 1954), pp. 19–20.

10 A. Maddison, *Dynamic Forces in Capitalist Development: A Long-run Comparative View* (Oxford, 1991), pp. 316–18; League of Nations, Economic and Financial Section, *Memorandum on Production and Trade, 1913 and 1923–6* (Geneva, 1928), p. 51.

11 B. Eichengreen, 'The inter-war economy in a European mirror', in R. Floud and D. McCloskey, eds, *The Economic History of Britain since 1700* (2nd edition, London, 1994), vol. 2, p. 236.

12 J. Redmond, 'The sterling overvaluation of 1925: a multilateral approach', *Economic History Review* (1984).

13 A. Marwick, 'The impact of the First World War on Britain', *Journal of Contemporary History*, 3, no. 1 (1968). For a later assessment, A. Marwick, *War and Social Change in the Twentieth Century* (London, 1974).

14 W. H. B. Court, 'The years 1914–18 in British economic and social history', in W. H. B. Court, ed., *Scarcity and Choice in History* (London, 1970), pp. 61–126 (at p. 102).

15 Lloyd George, *Through Terror to Triumph*, p. 23.

16 D. Thom, *Nice Girls and Rude Girls: Women Workers in World War I* (London, 1998), pp. 87–9.

17 G. Braybon, *Women Workers in the First World War* (London, 1981); A. Wollacott, *On Her Their Lives Depend* (Berkeley, Calif., 1994).

18 G. Braybon, 'Women, war and work', in H. Strachan, ed., *The Oxford Illustrated History of the First World War* (Oxford, 1998), pp. 149–62; G. Braybon, 'The impact of the war on women', in S. Constantine, M. W. Kirby and M. B. Rose, eds, *The First World War in British History* (London, 1995).

19 B. Waites, *A Class Society at War: England 1914–1918* (Leamington Spa, 1987), pp. 137–40.

20 A. Reid, 'The impact of the First World War on British workers', in R. Wall and J. M. Winter, eds, *The Upheaval of War: Family, Work and Welfare in Europe, 1914–1918* (Cambridge, 1988).

21 J. M. Winter, *The Great War and the British People* (London, 1986), pp. 2 and 279; D. Dwork, *War is Good for Babies and Young Children* (London, 1987).

22 L. Bryder, 'The First World War: healthy or hungry?', *History Workshop Journal*, 24 (1987), pp. 141–57; G. De Groot, *Blighty: British Society in the Era of the Great War* (London, 1996).

23 P. E. Dewey, 'Food production policy in the United Kingdom 1914–1918', *Transactions of the Royal Historical Society*, 5, no. 20 (1980), pp. 73–8.

24 Wilson, *Myriad Faces of War*, pp. 756–7.

25 *Loughborough Echo*, 1 December 1916.

26 G. Sherington, *English Education, Social Change and War, 1911–20* (Manchester, 1981), pp. 48–50.

27 I. O. Andrews and M. A. Hobbs, *The Economic Effects of the War upon Women and Children in Great Britain* (Oxford, 1918), pp. 147–9.

28 J. M. Winter, *Sites of Memory, Sites of Mourning* (Cambridge, 1995), p. 28.

29 A. Bruce, *Monuments, Memorials and the Local Historian* (London, 1997); C. McIntyre, *Monuments of War: How to Read a War Memorial* (London, 1990); C. Moriarty, 'Private grief and public remembrance: British First World War memorials', in M. Evans and K. Lunn, eds, *War and Memory in the Twentieth Century* (Oxford, 1997), pp. 125–39.

30 J. Garwood, *Chorley Pals* (Manchester, 1989); G. Moorhouse, *Hell's Foundations: A Town, its Myths and Gallipoli* (London, 1992).

31 M. Connelly makes these points in his excellent study *The Great War, Memory and Ritual: Commemoration in the City and East London, 1916–1939* (Suffolk, 2002), esp. pp. 66–84 and 172.

32 Ibid., pp. 88 and 201.

33 S. R. Ward, ed., *The War Generation: Veterans of the First World War* (Port Washington, NY, 1975); G. Wootton, *The Politics of Influence: British Ex-Servicemen, Cabinet Decisions and Cultural Change, 1917–1957* (London, 1963).

34 Winter, *Sites of Memory*, pp. 4–8 and 18; R. Prior and T. Wilson, 'Paul Fussell at war', *War and History*, 1 (1994), pp. 63–80; M. Ecksteins, *Rites of Spring: The Great War and the Birth of the Modern Age* (New York, 1989); S. Hynes, *A War Imagined: The First World War and British Culture* (London, 1991); A. Roshwald and R. Stites, eds, *European Culture in the Great War* (Cambridge, 1999).

35 Winter, *Sites of Memory*, p. 304.

FURTHER READING

Andrews, I. O. and Hobbs, M. A., *The Economic Effects of the War upon Women and Children in Great Britain* (Oxford, 1918).

Braybon, G., *Women Workers in the First World War* (London, 1981).

Burk, K., ed., *War and the State: The Transformation of British Government 1914–1919* (London, 1982).

Connelly, M., *The Great War, Memory and Ritual: Commemoration in the City and East London, 1916–1939* (Suffolk, 2002).

De Groot, G., *Blighty: British Society in the Era of the Great War* (London, 1996).

Gillis, J. R., ed., *Commemorations: The Politics of National Identity* (Princeton, NJ, 1994).

Milward, A. S., *The Economic Effects of the Two World Wars on Britain* (London, 1970).

Sherington, G., *English Education, Social Change and War, 1911–20* (Manchester, 1981).

Tanner, D., *Political Change and the Labour Party, 1900–1918* (1987; Cambridge, 1990).

Thom, D., *Nice Girls and Rude Girls: Women Workers in World War I* (London, 1998).

Waites, B., *A Class Society at War: England 1914–1918* (Leamington Spa, 1987).

Wall, R. and Winter, J. M., eds, *The Upheaval of War: Family, Work and Welfare in Europe, 1914–1918* (Cambridge, 1988).

Wilson, T., *The Myriad Faces of War* (Oxford, 1986).

Winter, J. M., *The Great War and the British People* (London, 1986).

Winter, J. M., *Sites of Memory, Sites of Mourning* (Cambridge, 1995).

Winter, J. M. and Robert, J.-L., eds, *Capital Cities at War: Paris, London, Berlin 1914–1919* (Cambridge, 1997).

Wollacott, A., *On Her Their Lives Depend* (Berkeley, Calif., 1994).

Wrigley, C., ed., *A History of British Industrial Relations*, vol. 2, *1914–1939* (Brighton, 1987).

Wrigley, C., ed., *Challenges of Labour: Central and Western Europe 1917–1920* (London, 1993),

Wrigley, C., ed., *The First World War and the International Economy* (Cheltenham, 2000).

CHAPTER THIRTY-TWO

Britishness

JOHN K. WALTON

Questions of Britishness attained a high profile and generated fierce controversy at the beginning of the new millennium. The Runnymede Trust's Commission into the Future of Multi-ethnic Britain, whose report was launched (but not entirely endorsed) by home secretary Jack Straw in October 2000, not only cast doubt on the robustness of Britishness as a focus for loyalty and national identity in an age of devolution, globalization, ethnic diversity and the dissolution of old certainties, but also argued that the concept itself was divisive and exclusive, privileging particular groups (the white Anglo-Saxon Protestant middle and upper classes) and (relatedly) geographical areas, most obviously in southern England, against the rest of the nation and its inhabitants. Englishness, indeed, was often used as an even narrower surrogate for Britishness, and the prevalence of multiple identities within the 'imagined community' of Britain was played down. The national curriculum in history was blamed for perpetuating views of the British past which minimized the importance of imperial conflicts and cross-currents and ignored racial and cultural differences. The Commission urged the rejection of nationalist models of state, culture and society, which imposed assimilation through conformity to established norms, and promoted debate between liberal models (political unity with acceptance of cultural diversity) and pluralist ones (flexible political spheres responding to continuous cultural flux). Responses varied across the political spectrum, with Conservative guardians of older nationalist assumptions displaying aggressive rhetorics of dismissal as they restated what they saw as the older truths of an established majority, and the nationalist campaigns to keep the pound and to deter asylum seekers resonated with the ironclad certainties of a Norman Tebbitt or a *Daily Mail* editorial. Meanwhile, less committed voices were heard to bemoan the challenge to the legitimacy of the only national identity they had, whether hyphenated or not, and to reclaim it against 'political correctness'.

The Commission contained no professional historians, as such, but its findings drew on a growing volume of debate within as well as beyond the discourses of history. Its agenda cannot be ignored as we look back to examine ideas about Britishness in the early decades of the twentieth century, the heyday of the empire whose ramifications lie at the core of the current debates, and whose periphery, as seen from London, was at least as important as the core in establishing and contesting the values that danced around the word, even before the dissolving post-war empire sent its offspring on the *Empire Windrush* and by a host of subsequent routes, from the Mediterranean and directly from India and Africa as well as via the Caribbean, to enrich and complicate metropolitan notions of what it might be to be British. The report and controversy reveal both the vulnerability of Britishness as a concept and its importance in defining individual identities in the absence of other labels at the turn of the millennium; and we need to look carefully at the roots of this paradox. Many of them are to be found in the early decades of the twentieth century.[1]

British identity, as such, was in most respects and for most of the time a surprisingly fragile construct during the years between the death of Queen Victoria and the outbreak of the Second World War, although it derived strength from pride, adversity and external threat, and found a collective expression that transcended internal divisions most convincingly when questions of empire or the demands of war were at issue: in other words, perhaps, when it mattered most. Ireland apart, British unity was least threatened on the political stage, where the monarchy, laws and representative institutions of the United Kingdom claimed almost unchallenged loyalty and recognition of legitimacy even where economic depression and despair bit deepest. The limited extent of popular antagonism towards the House of Lords during the conflict over Lloyd George's 'people's budget' in 1909–10 is a particularly remarkable example, as is the way in which so many trade union leaders in the General Strike of 1926 pulled back from seeming to challenge the constitution itself. By then, of course, the socialist or anarchist 'others' that could be conjured up rhetorically to frighten constitutional dissenters into acquiescence, partly through emphasis on their alien origins and nature, had been potently supplemented (indeed, for most purposes, supplanted) by the spectre of Bolshevism, godless, violent, founded in obscure foreign philosophies and destructively revolutionary. The otherness of fascism, Nazism and related creeds was to come more firmly into focus at the end of the 1930s, but despite attempts to pull such ideologies into line with (especially) traditionally Conservative visions of hierarchical, paternalist Britishness through corporatism, active adhesion to them (even to the extent of casual flirtation on the streets or at the ballot box) remained the preserve of a minute minority.[2]

From 1931, especially, the 'National government' sought to pull the classes together under a banner which identified Britishness with moderation and stability. Even under the most difficult interwar conditions, and in the most depressed local economies, neither Communists nor fascists made significant headway, while republicanism kept its head below the parapet; even socialism could be systematically represented as unBritish, with predominant success; and the members of the first Labour cabinet in 1924 were notoriously eager to don fancy (or court) dress for their inaugural presentation at the palace.[3] Regional divisions had economic and cultural but hardly political dimensions; or at least, the varying colours of the political map did not pose a threat to the integrity of Britain as a political nation.[4] But divisions based on culture, class, language, landscape, settlement, architecture and consumer preferences undermined any attempt at presenting a unified British identity in other respects, and where such claims were made they almost invariably assumed that Englishness (and certain kinds of southern Englishness at that) could stand in for

Britishness, while promoting a view from the privileged classes that defined the British more successfully in terms of who they were not (proposing superiority to the 'otherness' of lesser breeds, inferior races and godless ideologies) than in any convincing unifying portrayal of who they were. But these general introductory statements require amplification; and we begin with the symbols of national identity and the shared values that pulled Britain together, acting as centripetal forces against the cultural, social and economic divisions that challenged notions of national unity.

The twin pillars of war and Protestantism, which Linda Colley identified as underpinning the rise of a sense of Britishness between the Act of Union and the beginnings of Victoria's reign, experienced very different fates during the intervening years.[5] By the early twentieth century Protestantism had long been fading to the margins of the picture, despite residual attachments to aspects of its public trappings, and continuing vigour in sectarian guises in specific geographical locations, especially northern Ireland, Liverpool and the west of Scotland; but war as a unifier against external 'others' remained as powerful here as anywhere, despite the long Victorian interlude of European peace. The new century was ushered in by the riotous popular celebrations of the relief of Mafeking, and the jingoistic patriotism associated with the South African campaign and stoked by the new popular press soon found deeper expression through the First World War and the private and public commemorations of its slaughter which produced new calendars and topographies of remembrance and commemoration. The Germans replaced the French as the external 'other' against which Britishness was tested and defined, along with the indigestible colonial opponents of 'British interests' who had to be repressed from time to time, in campaigns that might be celebrated in the popular media and the public school classroom. Teutonic otherness was constructed in abstract terms as cold, calculating, efficient and ambitious, and more concretely through (for example) representations of German holidaymakers as fat sauerkraut-guzzlers who took the best positions on the beach as of right (and this in 1912).[6] The First World War did pull together English, Welsh and Scots across class boundaries, marginalizing a tiny minority of conscientious objectors and generally equating Britishness with active and appropriate participation in the war effort. It also perpetuated and crystallized notions of British 'freedom' that needed to be defended against alien despotisms, transferring the anti-French rhetoric of the late eighteenth and much of the nineteenth centuries to attack new targets. The subsequent collective recognition of sacrifice through the rituals of Remembrance Day, the Cenotaph, the cult of the war memorial and the tours to battlefields and war graves kept the British virtues of the stoical, self-deprecating, unsung hero of the trenches or the battleship engine-room in view, providing an enduring point of reference for the underlining of patriotic allegiance and commitment.[7]

Ireland, of course, remained outside this frame. When the question of Irish Home Rule was reintroduced into parliament in 1912, it sparked off a chain of events that precipitated the departure of most of Ireland from the United Kingdom, and the exposure of the fault-lines which left Irish identities of every kind outside the pale of Britishness. Already in January 1913, L. S. Amery was regretting in his diary that 'not a soul throughout these debates ever says anything to suggest that he feels that the United Kingdom really is a nation' in which Ireland was incorporated. Unionists in southern Ireland might have much in common with English Conservatives, as J. H. Grainger suggests; but they were a wealthy minority, and it was Protestant industrial Ulster that showed itself prepared to fight to stay within a greater United Kingdom, challenging the legitimacy and indeed the British fairness of the political manoeuvrings that sought to exclude it.[8] This was, however, a last-ditch attachment to Britain (in defiance of its elected government) that was visibly founded in a culture which had few counterparts on the larger island, and in which Protestant religious attachment (across various sects and with diverse reinforcing motivations) was much more powerful and salient in political and cultural terms than current notions of Britishness could accommodate. Despite the vocal support they received, from Conservative circles that considered themselves to be repositories of traditional upper-class British virtues, the Ulster Protestants were all too visibly 'other' when viewed from the metropolis whose allegiance they espoused and whose support they demanded.

This exceptional case underlines the extent to which, across most of the rest of Britain, Protestantism in itself had ceased to be a potent signifier of Britishness. For most people, attachment to the Church of England had become residual where it was still claimed; the established church in Scotland had always been Presbyterian; the Anglican church in Wales was disestablished in 1920 (when an Act of 1914 was brought into force); and a kaleidoscopic variety of belief, attachment and practice left the map of religious allegiance across Britain looking so colourful as to be difficult to read. This was an increasingly secular society, despite the continuing role of the Church of England on occasions of national celebration or mourning and the surviving English episcopal presence in the House of Lords, and despite the remarkable continuing acceptance of restrictions on public and commercial enjoyments on Sundays, which nevertheless had its lacunae, especially at Blackpool.[9] The inclusion of 'Holding up a Minister of Religion to ridicule' among the cinema censors' justifications for intervention arguably owed more to the likelihood of subversive mirth among the audience than to widespread deep acceptance of the sacred nature of the office: a Blackpool entrepreneur was apparently willing to pay £100 per week to exhibit the unfrocked rector of Stiffkey to the holiday crowds under humiliating circumstances.[10] Attachments to the details of the Anglican liturgy, or to the church as expression of traditional rural innocence, were reserved for a nostalgic minority, and their associations were with a particular brand of Englishness rather than a broader British canvas. Keith Robbins's researches uncovered a 'high' Scottish Presbyterian who advocated a United Church for the British Empire in 1902, and urged in 1918 that such a development would 'seal and consecrate the union of the British Empire'; but, as Robbins remarks, 'his voice was a lonely one'. Roman Catholics, of course, could never have been included in this Protestant ecumenical embrace, and nor could (for example) Unitarians or (a fortiori) Jews; but by the early twentieth century there was no threatening religious 'other' in England, Wales or Scotland against which to define and reinforce a British religious identity, despite (generally) residual anti-Catholicism and endemic but usually low-key anti-Semitism. Religion as a positive marker for national identity was of limited significance and in continuing decline, despite occasional rhetoric to the contrary, although it did serve to reinforce the legitimacy of the monarchy in its guise as defender of a Protestant faith which was not necessarily seen as stopping short at the Church of England.[11]

In peace and war alike, indeed, the royal family probably constituted the strongest cement for a British identity that transcended divisions, pulling in Scots, Welsh and working-class allegiances and making them visible at points of carefully orchestrated commemoration and ceremonial such as weddings, coronations and Jubilees. This was a new development in the late nineteenth and early twentieth centuries, as David Cannadine has demonstrated. Victoria's Jubilees and the ceremonial of the new Empire of India inaugurated a novel interest in regal pageantry, responding to the new opportunities offered by improved means of communication to show the royal family to the people and place the monarchy at the core of Britishness, with (under Edward VII and afterwards) the king as father to the nation. Cannadine argues plausibly that this was only possible because the crown had disengaged itself from the realities of power and government, floating above mundane quotidian political conflicts. The 'dignified' aspects of monarchy had become exalted even as its role in the 'efficiency' of government had dissolved, in sharp contrast with the ceremonial regimes associated with empires, monarchs and dictatorships elsewhere in Europe. Dignity was enhanced by an appeal to the archaic, well exemplified in the elaborate horse-drawn carriages used on ceremonial occasions; and traditions of recent invention swiftly became invested with legitimacy and a sense of awe.[12]

By 1935 such an aura had enveloped even George V, not obviously the most charismatic of monarchs, who found himself overtaken by a flood of popular enthusiasm when his Silver Jubilee was celebrated. Philip Gibbs, a well-connected commentator whose opinions were broadly but not entirely predictably Establishment in tone, began his 'panorama of the English scene' in that year with an extended pen-portrait of Jubilee in the streets, the 'half-million people who went surging towards Buckingham Palace on Jubilee nights . . . until suddenly on the balcony the King appeared with the Queen and his family, gazing down upon this vast sea of faces, . . . astonished, perhaps even awestruck, by this tremendous demonstration of popular affection'. This was, apparently, not just a metropolitan enthusiasm, as 'thousands of country cousins came to town' and 'suburban populations surged to the West End after office hours to see the decorations and the lighting effects', while the 'slums' harboured bunting and dancing in the streets. As these remarks hint, the celebrations were an excuse for high jinks and time off work, and over much of northern England just as much fun and disruption to routine had been engendered by the entirely secular Blackpool Carnivals of 1923 and 1924, for example; but Gibbs evoked a wider mystique through the pioneering royal Jubilee broadcast, the king 'speaking to the peoples of the British Empire as the Father of the Family', and through the chain of bonfires which brought the occasion to 'thousands of villages far from the glare and traffic of London . . . not only in England but from Wales to the north of Scotland, as when the beacons were lit in the days of Elizabeth when the Armada was sighted'. This conjuring up of the shared memory of war as national unifier was mixed with a portrayal of quiet, unpretentious pride in perceived English virtues of decency, democracy and security, as England once again did duty for Britain in the phrasing of most of this paean of praise. This kind of writing was a commonplace of these years, and played its own part in constructing a rhetoric of national identity that could inoculate against discontent and danger, in part because it acknowledged deprivation and grievance and praised the restraint of the sufferers while reminding them that things were worse elsewhere.[13] Jubilee symbolism and commemoration appropriated invented traditions and associated them with the most contemporary and glamorous of modernities: the London and North Eastern Railway named its streamlined Anglo-Scottish express the Silver Jubilee, while the London, Midland and Scottish inaugurated a whole new 'Jubilee' class of express locomotives, naming them after colonies, dominions, admirals, sea battles and naval vessels. Royal family names were reserved for the most high-powered of the top link engines, in the 'Princess' and 'Coronation' classes, and the Great Western already had its imposing 'Kings', which first took to the rails in 1927. The politics of locomotive naming, a highly visible public relations exercise when express rail travel still symbolized power, glamour and command over resources, would repay further investigation alongside other constructed associations between modernity and these incarnations of British-ness (which extended, in the case of the railways, to the celebration of regiments, stately homes, public schools and racehorses).[14]

The role of the monarch as symbol and core of British identity survived the abdi-cation crisis of 1936, when the challenge embodied by an incoming king who was prepared to put his attachment to an American divorcee before prevailing concep-tions of personal and constitutional duty was successfully overcome, thereby pre-empting more serious potential problems that might have arisen from Edward VIII's closeness to the Nazi regime in Germany. George VI overcame his stammering shyness, continued the broadcasts to nation and empire, and provided sustenance for the ideal of the monarch as decent, unostentatious, quietly courageous family man who embodied 'respectable' attributes of masculine (and familial) Britishness for a respectful nation.[15]

The sense of Britishness which the monarchy was seen to embody reached out beyond Britain itself, of course: pride in empire also pulled the component parts together, across class, party (generally) and geographical lines, drawing sustenance from a sense of an imperial civilizing, pacifying and law-giving mission to peoples whose 'otherness', through its absences as well as its visible distinguishing charac-teristics, helped to define what was valuable about the export of British values to a necessitous world. That such global definitions of Britain's mission helped to gen-erate conflict with other imperial powers, thereby providing further reinforcements through combative contact with what the British were 'not', reinforces the inter-locking nature of these strands. That they were founded in attitudes which later generations were to characterize as racist, a set of stereotypes which was reinforced through everything from school geography lessons to children's fiction, imperial exhi-bitions and the advertising of colonial produce, would go without saying were it not so necessary to say it; and reactions to the stirrings of nationalist movements, espe-cially in India, were tainted by such assumptions and expectations. And the 'white settler' Dominions, which were represented so readily in terms of manliness, inde-pendence and the taming of distant wilderness, also saw the indigenous peoples, on whom they imposed their new legal and economic order and their self-serving defi-nitions of property, reduced to quaintness and exoticism for metropolitan consump-tion. The dominant representations of empire, through (for example) the advertising campaigns of the Empire Marketing Board of the 1930s, accepted the economic importance of imperial links and preferential tariffs (especially as staple British exports lost ground in world markets) while remaining blind to the exploitation of indige-nous peoples on which the edifice was founded, a set of transactions in which British virtues of decency, fairness and the rule of law were often suspended or redefined.[16] The far-flung reach of the empire at its fullest stretch fed back into glorification of the navy, and of shipping and the sea more generally, with an aura of Britishness surrounding the seaside holiday, the Royal National Lifeboat Institution, the inshore fishermen and the picturesque eccentricities of their much-painted and photographed warrens of harbourside cottages, the hardy trawlermen who hunted through the seas to supply the 'national' dish of fish and chips, as well as the ostensibly unsung heroes of the merchant marine (as anthologized in the poet laureate John Masefield's poem 'Cargoes') and the bluejackets themselves. Empire reinforced the place of the sea at the core of romanticized British identity, although there were two sides to some of the imagery: fishermen could, after all, be lazy, their quarters dirty and subject to slum clearance orders; trawlermen, like the lower deck, were notoriously prone to binges and immorality; and fish and chips, whose production united fire and air with earth and water, was equally ambiguous as symbol of domestic slackness and lack of thrift and patience.[17] But the land, as mediated into Britishness through the evocative idea of 'countryside', was also as problematic as it was potent in the construction of shared identities.

The monarchy might flourish as an effective focal point for national and imperial identity, but the territorial aristocracy was having a hard time. The landed estate and stately home, as symbols of an elite version of Britishness (with a strong English accent), founded in early Victorian times and later to be revived through an idealized version of a hierarchically organized, cap-doffing countryside with a dominant aesthetic of the great house in its park, the nucleated village with medieval church, green and pond, and the endless patchwork of enclosed fields and copses, were in eclipse in the early twentieth century. The roots of the malaise lay in a combination of the agricultural depression of the later nineteenth century and a deepening (mainly urban) radical estrangement from the idle rich and their parasitic consumption, a frame of mind which encouraged increasingly determined and effective taxation regimes, culminating in the demanding taxation policies of successive governments on either side of the First World War. The notion that country houses (and landed families) were a legitimate part of a notional national heritage, and that they and their contents deserved to be preserved as part of the patrimony of the British, gradually gained ground during the interwar years, fostered especially by the National Trust; but to make headway it required some concessions to democratic notions of public access and enjoyment which cut across the notion that the aristocratic Englishman's home was emphatically his castle. In practice, access to parties of visitors tended to be withdrawn from the late nineteenth century onwards, and did not begin to revive, modestly, until the 1930s. The landowning assumption that the absolute property rights of the landed estate were themselves part of British heritage came under continuing attack, and rival, more democratic versions of the relationship between countryside(s) and Britishness gained growing credence.[18]

These were identified above all with the rise of rambling and its more assertive, athletic cousin hiking as popular pursuits from the late nineteenth century, again peaking in the 1930s, and with a belated popularization of the pre-war intelligentsia's Arts and Crafts-based predilection for the 'unspoiled', unmodernized village community, which also made headway in commercial guise in the interwar years. All this owed little to Stanley Baldwin, who, as Peter Mandler comments, 'has inexplicably gained a reputation as the man most responsible for fixing national identity firmly in the rural past'. Rhetoric apart, he was more closely attuned to the spread of suburbia, the notion of combining the advantages of town and country and copying the outward trappings of cosy cottagey timbered architecture which took hold so strongly in the 1920s and 1930s, marching in step with the popularity of 'the countryside' as a destination for motorists and cyclists as well as rail-borne, footslogging ramblers.[19] Walking in the countryside as a popular pursuit was not an interwar invention: it had (in organized form) late Victorian antecedents in (especially) northern England and western Scotland, and its ideologues went beyond associations with fresh air, healthy recreational exercise and good fellowship to urge the importance of popular access to and enjoyment of the pathways and open spaces that were held to be part of every Britisher's birthright. Such values, often associated with romantic socialism and (in the interwar years) with the Communist party at play (which was also work), constituted an alternative identification of countryside with Britishness that found assertive expression in the mass trespasses in the Peak District of the early 1930s, which themselves had antecedents in rights of way disputes and access campaigns that gathered momentum in Lancashire where industrial towns abutted on hills and moorland from the 1870s onwards.[20]

The Kinder mass trespass of 1932 pitted rival versions of the relationship between Britishness and countryside against each other to particularly resonant effect. It expressed the bringing to a head of long-held grievances about lack of access to Peak District uplands between Manchester and Sheffield, an area that had attracted ramblers from the two cities in large numbers since the turn of the century; and prominent among its organizers were members of the British Workers' Sports Federation, an affiliate of the Communist party. Several of them, including Benny Rothman, a conspicuous leader of the demonstration, were also Jewish. So the demonstration, which pitted large numbers of hikers against police and gamekeepers who were trying to prevent them from penetrating Kinder Scout, also set rival conceptions of Britishness and countryside head to head. On the one hand were devotees of 'traditional' (but recently invented, in their current form) rural blood sports and of the sanctity of the private property of the landed estate; on the other hand was an urban and mainly working-class group that sought to reclaim open land from those whom they regarded as illegitimate usurpers of the people's patrimony, drawing on a populist history which highlighted conquest and enclosure as stealing the land from the people. Six demonstrators were tried at Derby Assizes, before a hostile judge and a jury of landowners and retired army officers; and Rothman's attempt to defend himself 'from a historical and legal point of view, not as a barrister would do, on legal and technical grounds' proved unavailing. The judge's summing-up emphasized that 'it was the pride of the country to give a man even-handed justice, whatever his name, race, nationality or religion', and he 'was sure that the jury would not be prejudiced by the foreign-sounding names of two or three of the defendants'. 'There was no country in the world in which expression of opinion, however extreme, was so free or in which demonstrations of every kind were so little interfered with.' Thus was an ideal of British fair play, justice and equity summoned up to justify the imprisonment of five demonstrators (one was discharged), who were presented (in this paradoxical manner) as representatives of an alien ideology and ethnic group, and who represented an urban tradition of democratic enjoyment of the countryside that was no less British than the values the judge chose to deploy on the other side. Not that the trespass was generally supported by the leaders of mainstream ramblers' organizations, most of whom regarded it as dangerously illegal and counterproductive; but it did help to crystallize out the conflicting rhetorics of rival versions of the proper relationship between Britishness and countryside, and to demonstrate the ways in which either side might appeal to their own assumptions on the issue.[21]

This episode brings out fault-lines in the notion of Britishness that were widely reproduced elsewhere: questions of class, ethnicity, geographical divisions, attitudes to sport and leisure, the presentation of self, and access to and use of the institutions that were supposed to epitomize British ideals. In the first place, class divisions remained important throughout these years, and working-class conceptions of Britishness, in particular, might diverge widely from those entertained by their 'betters'. Respect for private property might take on a different dimension for those who had nothing to sell but their labour, for example, and the attitudes of trade unions and the parties of the left towards British identity had to be worked out very gingerly, especially as core values were contested rather than consensual within the working class itself. The emergent Labour party, and especially the Independent Labour party (ILP), espoused their own version of patriotism, drawing on William Morris, Edward Carpenter and an idealized vision of the sunny uplands of a happy pre-capitalist Britain, and promoting the revival of craftsmanship and 'folk-song' as a fulfilling alternative to the industrial town and commercial popular culture. This alternative Britishness (much of which was expressed in a vocabulary in which English and British were interchangeable) negotiated uneasy relationships with war and empire. Opposition on the left to the Boer War was tainted with anti-Semitism, and the early Labour party effectively adopted Ramsay MacDonald's 'Imperial Standard', 'not anti-imperialism but an alternative imperialism, . . . based on assumptions, if not of British superiority then at least of a British genius for government and adminis- tration that was of benefit to the colonised'.[22] The First World War divided the left, just as had questions of arming and naval development in face of 'the German menace'. Only the ILP actually opposed the war, arguing that true patriotism lay in preferring informed democracy to the secret diplomacy on which the war was blamed, and condemning the suppression of British liberties, especially through the intro- duction of conscription. Here the Labour party joined the opposition, defining con- scription as 'against the spirit of British democracy and full of dangers to the liberties of the people', even though most of its leaders were active in recruiting campaigns for the armed forces. Wartime attacks on the right to strike similarly drew out alter- native patriotisms, which equated Britishness with democratic freedoms. On the other hand, there were the 'super-patriots' of the left, the most outspoken of whom, Robert Blatchford, formed his own National Socialist party, which attracted very limited support. Questions of class were never far from these debates. C. H. Norman expressed his position thus: 'I am on the side of the British people, not the side of the British ruling classes'. These, again, were to be enduring divisions.[23]

The anti-Semitism within the Edwardian left, which was directed against working- class immigrants from eastern Europe to London's East End as well as international capitalists, was an indicator of the exclusions that were often entailed in construct- ing even radical and oppositional British identities, which could not be done without staking a claim on patriotism and defining Britishness partly in terms of what it was not. Mosley's Blackshirts were able to draw on anti-Semitic traditions in London's East End in the 1930s. The Catholic Irish, who had been the favourite targets of dis-

crimination and intermittent violence in the mid-Victorian years, faded from the
picture after the spate of Liverpool riots which culminated in 1909, as perceived competition in job markets eased and fear of Catholicism and papal imperialism receded
in a more secular society, although prejudice persisted in a lower key. From time to
time particular environments and circumstances produced flashpoints involving other
ethnic groups, which illuminated endemic tensions. Cases in point included the riots
in Lancashire (and especially Liverpool) directed against German pork butchers (and
other traders with equivocal surnames) in the aftermath of the sinking by torpedo of
the *Lusitania* in 1915, which broadened their targets to include other 'alien' groups,
especially the Chinese; or the riots against Yemeni seamen in South Shields in 1919
and 1930, in which, here as elsewhere, the National Union of Seamen and its pre-
cursors were prominent in raising 'racial' issues under Havelock Wilson; or the attacks
on black seamen in Liverpool and the Bristol Channel ports in 1919. Examples could
be multiplied.[24]

As the empire attained its fullest extension after the First World War, with 450
million people worldwide living under British rule, questions about the relationship
between 'race' (or skin colour) and Britishness thus came to the fore. Riotous conflict tended to be triggered by competition for jobs on vessels, and by sexual tensions over the perceived impropriety of relations between 'black' men (a very broad
generic term) and local women; and such explosions led to the public articulation
(in letters to the press, for example) of stereotypes that denied the true 'Britishness'
of men (almost invariably) who had migrated from the empire and contributed to
the war effort but who could not make themselves acceptable to their entrenched
detractors: they were cowards who had been the first to run for the lifeboats, they
were dirty (and used the darkness of their skin to hide their unwashed state), and
they had migrated into places like Aden to lay claim to membership of an empire in
whose component parts they had not been born. On the other hand, spokesmen and
women for the small 'black' populations (which had put down firm roots in their
localities, and were actually subdivided into a multiplicity of ethnic and religious
groups) asked to be incorporated into a society that promised British fairness and
justice, even as officialdom (especially in the Home Office) sought to deny their
British status by requiring impossible documentary proof. In practice, most of their
claims were accepted, although the conflicts brought forth assertive and articulate
expressions of bitter feeling from the threatened parties: if 'blacks' from the empire
should be sent 'home', then white British colonials should abandon their mission of
exploitation and return to Britain in exchange. But official acceptance that it was at
least politic to allow 'blacks' to be brought within the canons of Britishness combined appeals to principle and self-interest, was articulated (with a sequence of deli-
cious ambiguities) by the bishop of Liverpool in 1919: 'As members of the British
Empire, on which the sun never sets, we are bound for our own welfare and for the
sake of our own kith and kin, to deal fairly and humanely with our fellow subjects
and with those to whose countries (*sic*) our own people are at present living. The
story of deeds of violence wrought in Liverpool circulate (*sic*) like wildfire throughout the world . . . They rouse the worst passions of a hot-blooded race . . . They will
lead to the shedding of the blood of defenceless men and women of their own race.
They bring a slur on our name and a stain on our flag. They lower our prestige'.
This rhetoric set 'our fellow subjects' against 'our own race' and 'our prestige' against

'the worst passions of a hot-blooded race', and brought out the uneasiness of the negotiation between Britishness and the extended empire; but it was, at the time, sufficient for its purpose.[25]

Not that Britishness found uniform expression within England, Wales and Scotland. Britain lacked the well-developed regional identities that were so much in evidence within the shifting map of European nation-states. Scotland and Wales had some of the characteristics of a 'nation without a state', especially the former, with its own legal and educational systems and Presbyterian religious establishment. Scots were prominent in Westminster politics and in the administration (and 'exploration') of empire. Wales, meanwhile, had a stronger politics of language but a less-articulated set of quasi-national institutions otherwise; and it lost its established church without replacing it, although its culture was strongly influenced, cumulatively, by Methodists and Baptists of various hues. Political nationalisms were stunted and of late development in this period, and there was nothing in terms of ideology or political clout to come near to (for example) Basque or Catalan nationalism in Spain.[26] Regional consciousness within England itself showed even less political articulation: people might have a sense of belonging to 'the midlands', or (more so) 'the north', or (even more so) to smaller and more distinctive areas like Cornwall or Geordieland, but the stronger geographical loyalties were normally to town (rather than county) and locality. Britishness, where expressed, often found articulation through these more immediate ties, and pride in local industry was in practice at least as potent as pride in countryside (of which there were anyway many versions, with northern uplands attracting as many devotees as southern downs and patchwork quilts of fields). Thus might Widnes issue postcards celebrating the smoke of the chemical industry that gave it such life, identity and prosperity as it might claim.[27]

Regional identities were cross-cut by those of class, as expressed especially through the varieties of working-class accent and popular culture. The English language was a pillar of British identity (despite Welsh, Scots Gaelic and the Cornish revival), and when elegantly deployed it could disarm prejudice against (for example) Indian barristers or other graduate professionals; but the ruling definitions of elegance, founded as they were in class-inflected preferences for the distinctive accents of the 'King's English', could exclude working-class Glaswegians, Brummies or Geordies much more readily than it embraced 'well-spoken' colonials.[28] Reith's BBC sought to propagate 'received pronunciation' as 'standard English', stigmatizing those who spoke otherwise in the process; and Cockney or Lancashire accents evoked stereotypes about working-class 'characters' that might also promote condescension. Gracie Fields and George Formby did become national stars with Lancashire accents in the 1930s, giving working-class characters a measure of agency and power to subvert, while the music hall continued to celebrate local differences within national frameworks of provision; but manners of speaking continued to divide as well as unite even within the nominally common linguistic community that embraced most of Britain and exported the English language to the empire.[29] Here, of course, it might be even more divisive, a point symbolized by Havelock Wilson's assertion in 1914 (apropos Chinese sailors) that 'we shall soon be having "Rule Britannia" sung in pidgin English'.[30]

The growing interest in spectator sport, perhaps the most important development in popular culture in this period, also divided as well as uniting. On the one hand, interest in football became very widely shared among (especially) working-class men across the whole of urban Britain. Eric Hobsbawm used it as a marker for what he saw as the new, national, homogenized (but essentially masculine) working class that was created in the late nineteenth century, with its cloth-cap uniform, its weekly routines of work and leisure, its mass-produced newspapers and conventionalized holidays and entertainments, and its shared thraldom to spectator sport providing a common culture right across the country.[31] In practice, however, underneath the shared surface and common idioms were wide variations in popular foodstuffs (fish and chips differed noticeably in West Yorkshire, Lancashire, the north-east and London, for example), senses of humour (the comedian Frank Randle was unable to make audiences laugh outside his Lancashire stronghold), living arrangements (two-up-and-two-down terraces, Tyneside flats, London multi-occupancy, Leeds back-to-backs, all with different implications for how neighbours socialized, and only gradually being challenged by the greater homogeneity of the new council estates), and much else besides.[32]

Sport is similarly a complex matter. Scotland had its own League, Cup and Football Association, and England, Scotland and Wales had separate international teams that played each other, drawing attention to divided loyalties within Britain rather than to Britishness as a whole. Primary loyalties were to local clubs rather than to countries, and often to highly parochial rivalries within cities or regions. Playing styles were said to vary regionally and between amateurs (middle class, mainly southern) and professionals (drawn disproportionately from the industrial north and Scotland), although this was difficult to pin down; and within England football was certainly a vehicle for rivalries between north and south, nebulous though those entities were at the margins on the map. Cricket drew on local and county loyalties, failed to gain much purchase in Scotland or Wales, had a much stronger middle-class identity (despite the fiercely contested and well-attended Saturday afternoon matches of the northern leagues), and channelled national identification into England. Rugby was also, for most purposes, divided by class, region and country. On a broader stage, it was cricket that began to colonize the empire, while rugby became important to the 'white settler' Dominions and football was exported successfully to almost everywhere except the empire.[33] All this, of course, tended to leave women on the margins, despite a great upsurge of interest in women's football at the end of and just after the First World War; and the notion of Britishness was disproportionately a matter for the constructed masculinity of the 'public sphere', despite the rhetoric of some of the suffrage campaigners.[34]

The growing, even obsessive popularity of sports played to common rules, the acceptance of the shared authority of rules and referee or umpire, and the perceived Britishness of the ideals of fair play and gentlemanly conduct in sport, all helped to unite the participants behind a common set of values, even as they struggled for supremacy. When the rules were strained in pursuit of victory, as in the 'bodyline' bowling controversy in the Australia–England cricket Tests of 1932–3, arguments about what constituted British fair play might escalate to affect relationships between governments within the empire, with added poignancy when (as in this case) it was the British who were accused of going beyond consensual acceptability.[35] But the importance of the common code of expectations that lay behind such crises, and helped to resolve them, is a reminder of sport's power to reinforce values identified with Britishness even as it expressed and emphasized social and geographical fault-lines within nation and empire.

It is easy to reduce the apparent significance of an overarching concept like 'Britishness' by adopting the posture of a 'splitter', in J. H. Hexter's terminology: one who prefers to divide, to take apart, in a sense to deconstruct, rather than to 'lump' together mounds of material to give shape and direction to argument, especially when theory-driven. It is obviously the case, as Linda Colley acknowledged for her earlier, formative period, that Britishness was experienced differently in different parts of the United Kingdom, and that attachments to Scottish, Welsh, Cornish or northern identities, for example, and to county, locality, neighbourhood and family, counted for much more, most of the time, in most people's lives.[36] So might the solidarities of trade, social circle, religious denomination, sporting allegiance, lifestyle, gender and (not forgetting) class. But the idea of Britishness was pervasive enough to affect outcomes profoundly, even though the characteristics ascribed to it were often expressed in terms of Englishness, the terms frequently being used interchangeably. Britishness was constructed and represented in terms of fairness, decency, moral and economic superiority, freedom, democracy, tradition, stability, chivalry and the rule of law. Some of these myths people lived by can easily be demonstrated to have no basis 'on the ground', such as (up to 1918, most obviously) the belief that Britain was more fully democratic than other western nations. But the languages or key-words of Britishness made a difference: people mobilized around them and went to war for them; arguments about policy and morality were inflected through them. Britishness constructed the rhetorics people used, even though versions of it might be deployed on both sides of contending arguments; and (like the ideology of the rule of law in Hanoverian England, so effectively laid bare by Edward Thompson and Douglas Hay) the currency of the ideals meant that, to some extent, those who conjured them up to justify their actions had to seem to live by them.[37] Perhaps this necessity also helped to nurture the cult of official secrecy which sought (and seeks) to hide governmental falls from grace, and which is part of that darker side of Britishness that sometimes reminds us that we are subjects rather than citizens; and it was certainly easier to let the gap between the rhetoric of Britishness and the activities of government widen at a distance from the metropolis, whether in suppressing unemployment marchers in Salford or repressing colonial independence movements.[38] So the role of Britishness as unifying and justificatory rhetoric itself has ambiguities; but that, in conclusion, emphatically does not make it unimportant.

NOTES

1 *Guardian*, 11 and 21 October 2000.
2 R. Thurlow, *Fascism in Britain: A History, 1918–1985* (Oxford, 1987), pp. 298–9.
3 R. McKibbin, *The Ideologies of Class: Social Relations in Britain 1880–1950* (Oxford, 1990); see also his *Classes and Cultures: England 1918–1951* (Oxford, 1998).
4 N. Kirk, ed., *Northern Identities* (Aldershot, 2000); E. Royle, ed., *Issues of Regional Identity* (Manchester, 1998).
5 L. Colley, *Britons: Forging the Nation, 1707–1837* (London, 1994), pp. 364–9.
6 S. Fisher, ed., *Recreation and the Sea* (Exeter, 1997), pp. 51–2.

 7 J. M. Winter and E. Sivan, eds, *War and Remembrance in the Twentieth Century* (Cambridge, 1999).

 8 J. H. Grainger, *Patriotisms: Britain, 1900–1939* (London, 1986), pp. 244, 251.

 9 K. Robbins, *Nineteenth-century Britain* (Oxford, 1989), ch. 3.

10 N. Hiley, ' "No mixed bathing" ', *Journal of Popular British Cinema*, 3 (2000), p. 14; G. Cross, *Worktowners at Blackpool: Mass-Observation and Popular Leisure in the 1930s* (London, 1990), pp. 199–200.

11 Robbins, *Nineteenth-century Britain*, pp. 83–4.

12 D. Cannadine, 'The context, performance and meaning of ritual: the British monarchy and the "invention of tradition", *c*.1820–1970', in E. J. Hobsbawm and T. Ranger, eds, *The Invention of Tradition* (Cambridge, 1983), pp. 101–64.

13 P. Gibbs, *England Speaks* (London, 1935), part 1.

14 F. Burridge, *Nameplates of the Big Four* (Oxford, 1975).

15 Cannadine, 'Context, performance and meaning'.

16 E. Said, *Orientalism* (Harmondsworth, 1985); J. M. Mackenzie, *Propaganda and Empire* (Manchester, 1984); S. Constantine, *Buy and Build* (London, 1986); A. McClintock, *Imperial Leather* (London, 1995).

17 J. K. Walton, 'Fishing communities', in D. J. Starkey, ed., *A History of the Fisheries of England and Wales* (London, 2000).

18 P. Mandler, *The Fall and Rise of the Stately Home* (New Haven, Conn., 1997), chs 4–7.

19 Ibid., p. 241.

20 H. Taylor, *A Claim on the Countryside* (Edinburgh, 1997).

21 T. Stephenson, *Forbidden Land* (Manchester, 1989), pp. 153–63.

22 P. Ward, *Red Flag and Union Jack: Englishness, Patriotism and the British Left, 1881–1924* (London, 1998), p. 70.

23 Ibid., ch. 7.

24 P. Panayi, ed., *Racial Violence in Britain in the Nineteenth and Twentieth Centuries* (revised edition, Leicester, 1996), chs 2, 4–6; R. J. Lawless, *From Ta'izz to Tyneside* (Exeter, 1995); L. Tabili, *'We Ask for British Justice': Workers and Racial Difference in Late Imperial Britain* (Ithaca, NY, 1994).

25 Quotation from N. Evans, 'Across the universe: racial violence and the post-war crisis in imperial Britain, 1919–25', *Immigrants and Minorities*, 13 (1994), p. 77. See also Tabili, *British Justice*, and Lawless, *Ta'izz to Tyneside*, pp. 88–98, 118–19, 180–7.

26 Grainger, *Patriotisms*, pp. 50–2.

27 Royle, *Regional Identity*; R. Colls and B. Lancaster, eds, *Geordies* (Edinburgh, 1992).

28 L. Mugglestone, *Talking Proper: The Rise of Accent as Social Symbol* (Oxford, 1995).

29 J. Richards, *Stars in Our Eyes* (Preston, 1994), pp. 22–32.

30 Tabili, *British Justice*, p. 91.

31 E. J. Hobsbawm, *Worlds of Labour: Further Studies in the History of Labour* (London, 1984).

32 J. K. Walton, *Fish and Chips and the British Working Class* (Leicester, 1992); J. Nuttall, *King Twist* (London, 1978); M. J. Daunton, *House and Home in the Victorian City: Working-class Housing 1850–1914* (London, 1983); S. Muthesius, *The English Terraced House* (New Haven, Conn., 1982).

33 R. Holt, *Sport and the British* (Oxford, 1989); D. Russell, *Football and the English* (Preston, 1997); J. Williams, *Cricket and England: A Cultural and Social History of the Inter-war Years* (London, 1999).

34 A. Melling, ' "Ladies' football": gender and the socialization of women football players in Lancashire, *c*.1906–1960' (Ph.D. thesis, University of Central Lancashire, 2000).

35 Williams, *Cricket and England*, pp. 81–2.

36 Colley, *Britons*, pp. 372–3.

37 E. P. Thompson and D. Hay, eds, *Albion's Fatal Tree* (Harmondsworth, 1975).
38 D. Vincent, *The Culture of Secrecy: Britain 1832–1998* (Oxford, 1998).

FURTHER READING

Cannadine, D., 'The context, performance and meaning of ritual: the British monarchy and the "invention of tradition", *c.*1820–1970', in E. J. Hobsbawm and T. Ranger, eds, *The Invention of Tradition* (Cambridge, 1983), pp. 101–64.

Colley, L., *Britons: Forging the Nation, 1707–1837* (London, 1994).

Colls, R. and Dodd, P., eds, *Englishness: Politics and Culture 1880–1920* (London, 1986).

Gibbs, P., *England Speaks* (London, 1935).

Grainger, J. H., *Patriotisms: Britain, 1900–1939* (London, 1986).

Hechter, M., *Internal Colonialism* (London, 1975).

Joyce, P., *Visions of the People* (Cambridge, 1991).

Kirk, N., ed., *Northern Identities* (Aldershot, 2000).

Mackenzie, J. M., *Propaganda and Empire* (Manchester, 1984).

Mandler, P., *The Fall and Rise of the Stately Home* (New Haven, Conn., 1997).

Moorhouse, G., *Hell's Foundations: A Town, its Myths and Gallipoli* (London, 1992).

Panayi, P., ed., *Racial Violence in Britain in the Nineteenth and Twentieth Centuries* (revised edition, Leicester, 1996).

Robbins, K., *Nineteenth-century Britain* (Oxford, 1989).

Samuel, R., ed., *Patriotism: The Making and Unmaking of British Identity* (3 vols, London, 1989).

Taylor, H., *A Claim on the Countryside* (Edinburgh, 1997).

Thurlow, R., *Fascism in Britain: A History, 1918–1985* (Oxford, 1987).

Ward, P., *Red Flag and Union Jack: Englishness, Patriotism and the British Left, 1881–1924* (London, 1998).

Bibliography of Secondary Sources

Abrams, P., 'The failure of social reform', *Past and Present*, 24 (1963).

Adams, R. J. Q., *Arms and the Wizard: Lloyd George and the Ministry of Munitions 1915–1916* (London, 1978).

Agriculture, Ministry of, *A Century of Agricultural Statistics 1866–1966* (London, 1968).

Alberti, J., *Beyond Suffrage: Feminists in War and Peace* (London, 1989).

Alberti, J., *Eleanor Rathbone* (London, 1996).

Aldcroft, D. H., *Inter-war Economy: Britain 1919–1939* (London, 1970).

Aldcroft, D. H., *From Versailles to Wall Street 1919–1929* (Harmondsworth, 1987).

Aldcroft, D. H. and Richardson, H., *The British Economy, 1870–1939* (London, 1969).

Aldcroft, D. H., 'The disintegration of Europe 1918–1945', in D. H. Aldcroft and A. Sutcliffe, *Europe in the International Economy 1500 to 2000* (Cheltenham, 1999).

Alderman, G., *Modern British Jewry* (Oxford, 1992).

Alexander, S., 'Men's fears and women's work: responses to unemployment in London between the wars', *Gender and History*, 12, no. 2 (July 2000).

Alford, B. W. E., *Britain in the World Economy since 1880* (Harlow, 1996).

Alford, B. W. E., *Depression and Recovery? British Economic Growth 1918–1939* (London, 1972).

Allen, C., ed., *Tales from the Dark Continent: Images of British Colonial Africa in the Twentieth Century* (London, 1979).

Al-Sayyid-Marsot, A. L., *Egypt and Cromer* (London, 1968).

Alter, P., *The Reluctant Patron: Science and the State in Britain 1850–1920* (Oxford, 1987).

Anderson, R. D., *Universities and Elites in Britain since 1800* (Basingstoke, 1992).

Andersson-Skog, L. and Krantz, O., eds, *Institutions in the Transport and Communications Industries: State and Private Actors in the Making of Institutional Patterns, 1850–1990* (Canton, Mass., 1999).

Andrew, C., *Secret Service: The Making of the British Intelligence Community* (London, 1985).

Andrews, I. O. and Hobbs, M. A., *The Economic Effects of the War upon Women and Children in Great Britain* (Oxford, 1918).

Andrews, L., *The Education Act, 1918* (London, 1976).

Armstrong, J., 'Freight pricing policy in coastal liner companies before the First World War', *Journal of Transport History*, 3rd series, 10 (1989), pp. 180–97.

Armstrong, J., ed., 'Introduction', in *Coastal and Short Sea Shipping* (Aldershot, 1996).

Arnold, A. J., 'Profitability and capital accumulation in British industry during the transwar period, 1913–1924', *Economic History Review*, 52 (1999).

Ashby, M. K., *Joseph Ashby of Tysoe, 1859–1919: A Study of English Village Life* (Cambridge, 1961).

Ashworth, W., *The Genesis of Modern British Town Planning* (London, 1954).

Astor, Viscount and Rowntree, B. S., *British Agriculture: The Principles of Future Policy* (Harmondsworth, 1939).

Aubel, F., 'The Conservatives in Wales, 1880–1935', in M. Francis and M. Zweiniger-Bargielowska, eds, *The Conservatives in British Society* (Cardiff, 1996).

Augustijn, J., *From Public Defiance to Guerilla Warfare: The Experience of Ordinary Volunteers in the Irish War of Independence, 1916–1921* (Dublin, 1996).

Bagwell, P. and Lyth, P., *Transport in Britain: From Canal Lock to Gridlock* (London, 2001).

Bailey, P., *Leisure and Class in Victorian England: Rational Recreation and the Contest for Control, 1830–1885* (London, 1978).

Bailey, V., *Delinquency and Citizenship: Reclaiming the Young Offender 1914–1948* (Oxford, 1987).

Bailey, V., 'The shadow of the gallows: the death penalty and the British Labour government, 1945–51', *Law and History Review*, 18 (2000), pp. 305–49.

Bain, G. and Price, R., *Profiles of Union Growth* (Oxford, 1980).

Baines, D., *Migration in a Mature Economy* (Cambridge, 1985).

Baines, D. and Johnson, P., 'In search of the "traditional" working class: social mobility and occupational continuity in interwar London', *Economic History Review*, 52 (1999).

Ball, S., 'Asquith's decline and the general election of 1918', *Scottish Historical Review*, 61 (1982), pp. 44–61.

Ball, S., *Baldwin and the Conservative Party: The Crisis of 1929–1931* (New Haven, Conn., 1988).

Ball, S., *The Conservative Party and British Politics 1902–1951* (London, 1995).

Barke, M., 'The middle-class journey to work in Newcastle upon Tyne, 1850–1913', *Journal of Transport History*, 3rd series, 12 (1991), pp. 107–34.

Barker, R., *Education and Politics 1900–1951: A Study of the Labour Party* (Oxford, 1972).

Barker, T. C., ed., *The Economic and Social Effects of the Spread of Motor Vehicles: An International Centenary Tribute* (Houndmills, 1987).

Barker, T. C. and Gerhold, D., *The Rise and Rise of Road Transport, 1700–1990* (2nd edition, Cambridge, 1995).

Barrett, H., *Early to Rise: A Suffolk Morning* (London, 1967).

Bartlett, C. J., *British Foreign Policy in the Twentieth Century* (Basingstoke, 1989).

Baston, L., 'Labour local government 1900–1999', in B. Brivati and R. Heffernan, eds, *The Labour Party: A Centenary History* (Basingstoke, 2000).

Beales, H. and Lambert, R., eds, *Memoirs of the Unemployed* (London, 1934).

Bean, C. and Crafts, N., 'British economic growth since 1945: relative economic decline . . . and renaissance?', in N. Crafts and G. Toniolo, eds, *Economic Growth in Europe since 1945* (Cambridge, 1996).

Bean, C. E. W., *Official History of Australia in the War*, vols 1–6 (Sydney, 1933).

Bean, J. P., *The Sheffield Gang Wars* (Sheffield, 1981).

Beauman, N., *A Very Great Profession: The Woman's Novel, 1914–1939* (London, 1983).

Beaumont, C., 'Citizens not feminists: the boundary negotiated between citizenship and feminism in mainstream women's organisations in England, 1928–39', *Women's History Review*, 9, no. 2 (2000).

Beck, P. J., 'Projecting an image of a great nation on the world screen through football: British cultural propaganda between the wars', in B. Taithe and T. Thornton, eds, *Propaganda: Political Rhetoric and Identity, 1300–1990* (Stroud, 1999), pp. 265–84.

Beck, P. J., *Scoring for Britain: International Football and International Politics, 1900–1939* (London, 1999).

Beckett, I. F. W., *The Army and the Curragh Incident, 1914* (London, 1986).

Beer, S. H., *Modern British Politics* (London, 1980).

Beesly, P., *Room 40: British Naval Intelligence 1914–1918* (London, 1982).

Beevers, R., *The Garden City Utopia: A Critical Biography of Ebenezer Howard* (London, 1988).

Bellerby, J. R., 'The distribution of farm income in the United Kingdom, 1867–1938', in W. E. Minchinton, ed., *Essays in Agrarian History*, vol. 2 (Newton Abbot, 1968), pp. 259–78.

Beloff, M., *Imperial Sunset*, vol. 1, *Britain's Liberal Empire, 1847–1921* (London, 1969), vol. 2, *Dream of Commonwealth, 1921–42* (London, 1989).

Benjamin, D. and Kochin, L., 'Searching for an explanation of unemployment in interwar Britain', *Journal of Political Economy*, 87 (1979), pp. 441–78.

Bennett, G. H., *British Foreign Policy during the Curzon Period, 1919–24* (Basingstoke, 1995).

Benson, J., *The Working Class in Britain, 1850–1939* (London, 1989).

Benson, J., *The Rise of Consumer Society in Britain 1880–1980* (London, 1994).

Bentley, M., 'Liberal politics and the Grey conspiracy of 1921', *Historical Journal*, 20 (1977), pp. 461–78.

Bentley, M., *The Liberal Mind 1914–1929* (Cambridge, 1977).

Bentley, M., *The Climax of Liberal Politics 1868–1918* (London, 1987).

Bentley, M., 'Liberal Toryism in the twentieth century', *Transactions of the Royal Historical Society*, 6th series, 4 (1994), pp. 177–201.

Berghoff, H., 'Public schools and the decline of the British economy', *Past and Present*, 129 (1990).

Berman, B. and Lonsdale, J., *Unhappy Valley: Conflict in Kenya and Africa* (London, 1992).

Bernbaum, G., *Social Change and the Schools, 1918–1944* (London, 1967).

Bernstein, G. L., 'Sir Henry Campbell-Bannerman and the Liberal imperialists', *Journal of British Studies*, 23 (1983), pp. 105–24.

Best, A., 'Constructing an image: British intelligence and Whitehall's perception of Japan, 1931–39', *Intelligence and National Security*, 11, no. 3 (1996), pp. 403–23.

Best, M. and Humphries, J., 'The City and industrial decline', in B. Elbaum and W. Lazonick, eds, *The Decline of the British Economy* (Oxford, 1986).

Bettez, D. J., 'Unfulfilled initiative: disarmament negotiations and the Hague Peace Conference of 1899 and 1907', *Journal of the Royal United Services Institute*, 133, no. 3 (1988).

Beveridge, W., *Unemployment: A Problem of Industry* (London, 1909).

Beveridge, W., *Full Employment in a Free Society: A Report* (London, 1944).

Bew, P., *Ideology and the Irish Question: Ulster Unionism and Irish Nationalism, 1912–1916* (Oxford, 1994).

Biagini, E. F., ed., *Citizenship and Community: Liberals, Radicals and Collective Identities in the British Isles, 1865–1931* (Cambridge, 1996).

Bialer, U., *The Shadow of the Bomber: The Fear of Air Attack and British Politics 1932–1939* (London, 1980).

Bidwell, S. and Graham, D., *Firepower: British Army Weapons and Theories of War 1904–1945* (London, 1982).

Blackaby, F. T., ed., *British Economic Policy 1960–1974* (Cambridge, 1978).

Blake, A., *The Land Without Music: Music, Culture and Society in Twentieth-century Britain* (Manchester, 1997).

Blake, R., *The Conservative Party from Peel to Churchill* (London, 1970).

Blewett, N., 'The franchise in the United Kingdom, 1885–1918', *Past and Present*, 32 (1965), pp. 27–56.

Blewett, N., *The Peers, the Parties and the People: The General Elections of 1910* (London, 1972).

Bond, B., *British Military Policy between the Two World Wars* (Oxford, 1980).

Bond, W. and Divall, C., eds, *Suburbanizing the Masses: Public Transport and Urban Development in Historical Perspective* (Aldershot, forthcoming, 2003).

Booth, A., 'Britain in the 1930s: a managed economy?', *Economic History Review*, 40 (1987), pp. 499–522.

Bosanquet, H., *The Administration of Charitable Relief* (London, 1898).

Bourke, J., *Working-class Cultures in Britain 1890–1960: Gender, Class and Ethnicity* (London, 1994).

Bowden, S., 'Credit facilities and the growth of consumer demand for electric appliances in England in the 1930s', *Business History*, 32, no. 1 (1990), pp. 52–75.

Bowden, S., 'Demand and supply constraints in the interwar UK car industry: did the manufacturers get it right?', *Business History*, 33 (April 1991), pp. 242–67.

Bowden, S., 'The new consumerism', in P. Johnson, ed., *Economic, Social and Cultural Change in Twentieth-century Britain* (London, 1994), pp. 242–62.

Bowden, S. and Collins, M., 'The Bank of England, industrial regeneration and hire purchase between the wars', *Economic History Review*, 45 (1992).

Bowden, S. and Offer, A., 'Household appliances and the use of time: the United States and Britain since the 1920s', *Economic History Review*, 47, no. 4 (1994), pp. 725–48.

Bowden, S. and Offer, A., 'Gender and the culture of consumption: women and the market for domestic electrical appliances in interwar England', in V. de Grazia and E. Furlogh, eds, *The Sex of Things: Gender and Consumption in Historical Perspective* (California, 1996), pp. 244–74.

Bowden, S. and Turner, P., 'Some cross-section evidence on the determinants of the diffusion of car ownership in the interwar UK economy', *Business History*, 35, no. 1 (1993), pp. 55–69.

Bowden, S. and Turner, P., 'The UK market and the market for consumer durables', *Journal of Economic History*, 53, no. 2 (1993), pp. 244–58.

Bowley, M., *Housing and the State 1919–1945* (London, 1945).

Bowman, J., *De Valera and the Ulster Question, 1917–73* (Oxford, 1982).

Boyce, D. G., *Englishmen and Irish Troubles: British Public Opinion and the Making of Irish Policy, 1918–1922* (London, 1972).

Boyce, D. G., *The Irish Question and British Politics, 1867–1996* (2nd edition, London, 1996).

Boyce, D. G., *Decolonisation and the British Empire, 1775–1997* (London, 1999).

Boyce, R. W. D., *British Capitalism at the Crossroads 1919–1932: A Study in Politics, Economics and International Relations* (Cambridge, 1987).

Boyce, R. W. D., 'Creating the myth of public consensus: public opinion and Britain's return to the gold standard in 1925', in P. L. Cottrell and D. E. Moggridge, eds, *Money and Power: Essays in Honour of L. S. Pressnell* (London, 1988).

Bracewell, M., *England is Mine: Pop Life in Albion from Wilde to Goldie* (London, 1997).

Branson, N., *Britain in the 1920s* (London, 1975).

Branson, N. and Heinemann, M., *Britain in the Nineteen-thirties* (London, 1971).

Brassley, P., 'Output and technical change in twentieth-century British agriculture', *Agricultural History Review*, 48, part 1 (2000).

Braybon, G., *Women Workers in the First World War: The British Experience* (London, 1981).

Braybon, G., 'The impact of the war on women', in S. Constantine, M. W. Kirby and M. B. Rose, eds, *The First World War in British History* (London, 1995), pp. 141–67.

Braybon, G., 'Women, war and work', in H. Strachan, ed., *The Oxford Illustrated History of the First World War* (Oxford, 1998), pp. 149–62.

Braybon, G. and Summerfield, P., *Out of the Cage* (London, 1987).

Bristow, E. J., *Prostitution and Prejudice: The Jewish Fight against White Slavery 1870–1939* (London, 1983).

Broadberry, S., *The British Economy between the Wars: A Macroeconomic Survey* (Oxford, 1986).

Broadberry, S. N., 'The emergence of mass unemployment: explaining macroeconomic trends in Britain during the trans-World War 1 period', *Economic History Review*, 2nd series, 43 (1990), pp. 71–82.

Brodrick, G. C., 'A nation of amateurs', *Nineteenth Century and After*, 48 (Oct. 1900), pp. 521–35.

Brooke, S., *Labour's War: The Labour Party during the Second World War* (Oxford, 1992).

Brown, G., *Maxton* (Edinburgh, 1986).

Brown, I., ed., *The Economies of Africa and Asia in the Inter-war Depression* (London, 1989).

Brown, J., 'Agricultural policy and the National Farmers' Union, 1908–1939', in J. R. Wordie, ed., *Agriculture and Politics in England, 1815–1939* (Basingstoke, 2000).

Brown, J. M., *Gandhi: Prisoner of Hope* (New Haven, Conn., 1989).

Brown, J. M. and Louis, W. R., eds, *The Oxford History of the British Empire*, vol. 4, *The Twentieth Century* (Oxford, 1999).

Brown, K. D., *Labour and Unemployment, 1900–1914* (Newton Abbot, 1971).

Brown, K. D., ed., *The First Labour Party 1906–14* (London, 1985).

Brown, R. C. and Cook, R., *Canada, 1896–1921: A Nation Transformed* (Toronto, 1974).

Bruce, A., *Monuments, Memorials and the Local Historian* (London, 1997).

Bruley, S., *Women in Britain since 1900* (London, 1999).

Bryant, C., *Stafford Cripps: The First Modern Chancellor* (London, 1997).

Bryder, L., 'The First World War: healthy or hungry', *History Workshop*, 24 (1987), pp. 141–55.

Buchan, W., *John Buchan: A Memoir* (1982; London, 1985).

Buckland, P., *Irish Unionism*, vol. 1, *The Anglo-Irish and the New Ireland, 1885–1922* (Dublin, 1972), vol. 2, *Ulster Unionism and the Origins of Northern Ireland, 1885–1922* (Dublin, 1973).

Buckland, P., *The Factory of Grievances: Devolved Government in Northern Ireland, 1921–1939* (Dublin, 1997).

Buckley, R. J., 'Capital cost as a reason for the abandonment of first-generation tramways in Britain', *Journal of Transport History*, 3rd series, 10 (1989), pp. 99–112.

Burawoy, M., *The Politics of Production* (London, 1985).

Burk, K., ed., *War and the State: The Transformation of British Government 1914–1919* (London, 1982).

Burman, B., 'Racing bodies: dress and pioneer women aviators and racing drivers', *Women's History Review*, 9 (2000), pp. 299–326.

Burnett, J., *A Social History of Housing 1815–1985* (London, 1986).

Burns, J., 'Brains better than bets or beer', *Clarion Pamphlet*, 36 (1902).

Burt, C. L., *The Young Delinquent* (London, 1925).

Butterfield, P., 'Grouping, pooling and competition: the passenger policy of the London and North Eastern Railway, 1923–39', *Journal of Transport History*, 3rd series, 7 (1986), pp. 21–47.

Buxton, N., *British Employment Statistics: Guide to Sources and Methods* (Oxford, 1977).

Buxton, N. K. and Aldcroft, D. H., *British Industry between the Wars: Instability and Industrial Development, 1919–1939* (London, 1979).

Cain, P. J., 'Private enterprise or public utility? Output, pricing and investment on English and Welsh railways, 1870–1914', *Journal of Transport History*, 3rd series, 1 (1980), pp. 9–23.

Cain, P. J. and Hopkins, A. G., *British Imperialism*, vol. 1, *Innovation and Expansion 1688–1914* (London, 1993), vol. 2, *Crisis and Deconstruction 1914–1990* (London, 1993).

Cairncross, A., *The British Economy since 1945: Economic Policy and Performance, 1945–1990* (Oxford, 1992).

Cairncross, A. and Eichengreen, B., *Sterling in Decline: The Devaluations of 1931, 1949 and 1967* (Oxford, 1983).

Campbell, J., *The Goat in the Wilderness, 1922–31* (London, 1977).

Campbell, J., *Nye Bevan and the Mirage of British Socialism* (London, 1987).

Cannadine, D., 'The context, performance and meaning of ritual: the British monarchy and the "invention of tradition", *c.*1820–1970', in E. J. Hobsbawm and T. Ranger, eds, *The Invention of Tradition* (Cambridge, 1983), pp. 101–64.

Cannadine, D., *The Decline and Fall of the British Aristocracy* (London, 1990).

Cannadine, D., *Class in Britain* (London, 1998).

Canning, P., *British Policy towards Ireland, 1921–1947* (Oxford, 1985).

Capie, F. and Collins, M., *Have the Banks Failed British Industry?* (London, 1992).

Cassis, Y., 'Bankers in English society in the late nineteenth century', *Economic History Review*, 38 (1985).

Castles, S. and Kosack, G., eds, *Immigrant Workers and Class Structure in Western Europe* (Oxford, 1985).

Ceadal, M., *Pacifism in Britain 1914–45* (Oxford, 1980).

Centre for Contemporary Cultural Studies, *Unpopular Education: Schooling and Social Democracy in England since 1944* (London, 1981).

Cesarani, D., *The Jewish Chronicle and Anglo-Jewry 1841–1991* (Cambridge, 1994).

Chadwick, O., *Hensley Henson: A Study in the Friction between Church and State* (Oxford, 1983).

Charmley, J., *Chamberlain and the Lost Peace* (London, 1989).

Cherry, G., 'George Pepler 1882–1959', in G. Cherry, ed., *Pioneers in British Planning* (London, 1981).

Cherry, S., *Medical Services and the Hospitals in Britain, 1860–1939* (Cambridge, 1996).

Cherry, S., 'Before the NHS: financing the voluntary hospitals 1900–1939', *Economic History Review*, 50 (1997), pp. 305–26.

Cheshire, D. F., *Music Hall in Britain* (Newton Abbot, 1974).

Childs, D. J., *A Peripheral Weapon? The Production and Employment of British Tanks in the First World War* (Westport, Conn., 1999).

Chinn, C., *They Worked all their Lives: Women of the Urban Poor in England, 1880–1939* (Manchester, 1988).

Christoph, J. B., *Capital Punishment and British Politics: The British Movement to Abolish the Death Penalty 1945–57* (London, 1962).

Church, R., *The Rise and Decline of the British Motor Industry* (2nd edition, Cambridge, 1995).

Church, R. and Outram, Q., *Strikes and Solidarity: Coalfield Conflict in Britain, 1889–1966* (Cambridge, 1998).

Churchill, R. S., *Winston S. Churchill*, vol. 2 (London, 1967).

Clarence-Smith, G., 'The effects of the Great Depression on industrialisation in Equatorial and Central Africa', in I. Brown, ed., *The Economies of Africa and Asia in the Inter-war Depression* (London, 1989), pp. 170–202.

Clarke, P., *Lancashire and the New Liberalism* (Cambridge, 1971).

Clarke, P., 'The electoral position of the Liberal and Labour parties, 1910–1914', *English Historical Review*, 90 (1975), pp. 828–36.

Clarke, P., *Liberals and Social Democrats* (Cambridge, 1978).

Clarke, P., *The Keynesian Revolution in the Making 1924–1936* (Oxford, 1988).

Clarke, P., *Hope and Glory: Britain 1900–1990* (London, 1996).

Clavin, P., 'The World Economic Conference 1933: the failure of British internationalism', *Journal of European Economic History*, 20 (1991).

Clayton, A., *The British Empire as Superpower, 1919–1939* (London, 1986).

Clegg, H., *A History of British Trade Unions since 1889*, vol. 2, *1911–1933* (Oxford, 1985).

Clegg, H., Fox, A. and Thompson, A. F., *A History of British Trade Unions since 1889*, vol. 1, *1889–1910* (Oxford, 1964).

Cline, P., 'Winding down the war economy', in K. Burk, ed., *War and the State: The Transformation of British Government, 1914–1919* (London, 1982).

Cockett, R., 'The party, public and the media', in A. Seldon and S. Ball, eds, *The Conservative Century: The Conservative Party since 1900* (Oxford, 1994), pp. 547–64.

Coen, T. C., *The Indian Political Service: A Study in Indirect Rule* (London, 1971).

Coetzee, F., *For Party and Country* (Oxford, 1990).

Cohen, M. J. and Kolinsky, M., eds, *Britain and the Middle East in the 1930s: Security Problems, 1935–39* (London, 1992).

Cohen, R. and Bains, H. S., *Multi-racist Britain* (Basingstoke, 1988).

Cohen, S. A., *English Zionists and British Jews: The Communal Politics of Anglo-Jewry 1895–1920* (Princeton, NJ, 1982).

Cole, G. D. H., *Workshop Organisation* (London, 1923).

Collette, C., *For Labour and for Women: The Women's Labour League, 1906–1918* (Manchester, 1989).

Collette, C., *The International Faith* (Andover, 1998).

Collette, C., 'Questions of gender', in B. Brivati and R. Heffernan, eds, *The Labour Party: A Centenary History* (London, 2000).

Collette, C. and Bird, S., eds, *Jews, Labour and the Left* (Andover, 2000).

Colley, L., *Britons: Forging the Nation, 1707–1837* (London, 1994).

Collini, S., *Liberalism and Sociology: L. T. Hobhouse and Political Argument in England, 1880–1914* (Cambridge, 1979).

Collins, C. C., 'City planning exhibitions and civic museums: Walter Hegemann and others', in V. Welter and J. Lawson, eds, *The City after Patrick Geddes* (Bern, 2000).

Collins, E. J. T., 'The agricultural tractor in Britain', in K. Winkel and K. Herrmann, eds, *The Development of Agricultural Technology in the 19th and 20th Centuries* (London, 1984).

Collins, E. J. T., *Power Availability and Agricultural Productivity in England and Wales 1840–1939* (Rural History Centre, University of Reading, Discussion Paper No. 1, 1996).

Collins, M., *Money and Banking in the UK: A History* (London, 1988).

Collins, M., *Banks and Industrial Finance in Britain, 1800–1939* (London, 1991).

Collins, M., 'English bank development within a European context, 1870–1939', *Economic History Review*, 51 (1998).

Collins, P., ed., *Nationalism and Unionism: Conflict in Ireland, 1885–1921* (Belfast, 1994).

Colls, R. and Dodd, P., eds, *Englishness: Politics and Culture 1880–1920* (London, 1986).

Common, J., ed., *Seven Shifts* (London, 1938).

Connelly, M., *The Great War, Memory and Ritual: Commemoration in the City and East London, 1916–1939* (Suffolk, 2002).

Constantine, S., *Unemployment in Britain Between the Wars* (London, 1980).

Cooper, A. F., *British Agricultural Policy 1912–36: A Study in Conservative Politics* (Manchester, 1989).

Cooper, F., *Decolonization and African Society: The Labor Question in French and British Africa* (Cambridge, 1996).

Cooper, M., *The Birth of Independent Air Power: British Air Policy in the First World War* (London, 1986).

Cooter, R., *Surgery and Society in Peace and War* (London, 1990).

Cooter, R., Harrison, M. and Sturdy, S., eds, *War, Medicine and Modernity* (Stroud, 1998).

Corner, D. C., 'Exports and the British trade cycle: 1929', *Manchester School*, 26 (1956).

Court, W. H. B., *British Economic History, 1870–1914: Commentary and Documents* (Cambridge, 1965).

Court, W. H. B., 'The years 1914–18 in British economic and social history', in W. H. B. Court, ed., *Scarcity and Choice in History* (London, 1970).

Cowan, R. S., 'A case study of technological and social change: the washing machine and the working wife', in M. S. Hartman and L. Banner, eds, *Clio's Consciousness Raised* (New York, 1989), pp. 245–53.

Cowling, M., *The Impact of Labour 1920–1924: The Beginning of Modern British Politics* (Cambridge, 1971).

Cowling, M., *The Impact of Hitler: British Politics and British Policy 1933–1940* (Cambridge, 1975).

Cowman, K., 'Women's suffrage campaigns in Britain', *Women's History Review*, 9, no. 4 (2000).

Cowman, K., 'Crossing the great divide: inter-organisational suffrage relationships on Merseyside, 1895–1914', in C. Eustace, J. Ryan and L. Ugolini, eds, *A Suffrage Reader: Charting Directions in British Suffrage History* (London, 1999), pp. 37–52.

Crafts, N. and Mills, T. C., 'Europe's golden age: an econometric investigation of changing trend rates of growth', in B. van Ark and N. Crafts, eds, *Quantitative Aspects of Post-war European Economic Growth* (Cambridge, 1996).

Crafts, N. F. R. and Thomas, M., 'Comparative advantage in U.K. manufacturing trade 1910–1935', *Economic Journal*, 96 (1986), pp. 629–45.

Craig, F. W. S., *British Electoral Facts 1832–1980* (Chichester, 1981).

Crompton, G., '"Efficient and economical working"? The performance of the railway companies 1923–33', *Business History*, 27 (1985), pp. 221–37.

Crompton, G., '"Squeezing the pulpless orange": labour and capital on the railways in the inter-war years', *Business History*, 31 (1989), pp. 66–83.

Crompton, G., ed., *Canals and Inland Navigation* (Aldershot, 1996).

Crompton, G., '"Good business for the nation": the railway nationalisation issue, 1921–47', *Journal of Transport History*, 3rd series, 20 (1999), pp. 141–59.

Cronin, J., *Industrial Conflict in Modern Britain* (London, 1979).

Cronin, J. E., *Labour and Society in Britain 1918–1979* (London, 1984).

Cronin, M., *Sport and Nationalism in Ireland: Gaelic Games, Soccer and Irish Identity since 1884* (Dublin, 1999).

Cross, G., *Worktowners at Blackpool: Mass-Observation and Popular Leisure in the 1930s* (London, 1990).

Crossick, G., 'The emergence of the lower middle class in Britain', in G. Crossick, ed., *The Lower Middle Class in Britain 1870–1914* (London, 1977).

Crowe, S. and Corp, E., *Our Ablest Public Servant: Sir Eyre Crowe 1864–1925* (Newton Abbot, 1993).

Crowther, M. A., *British Social Policy, 1914–1939* (London, 1988).

Crowther, M. A., *The Workhouse System 1834–1929* (London, 1981).

Cullerton, C., *Working-class Culture, Women and Britain, 1914–1921* (London, 2000).

Cunningham, H., 'Leisure and culture', in F. M. L. Thompson, ed., *The Cambridge Social History of Britain, 1750–1950*, vol. 2, *People and their Environment* (Cambridge, 1990), pp. 278–339.

D'Ombrain, N., *War Machinery and High Policy: Defence Administration in Peacetime Britain 1902–1914* (Oxford, 1973).

Daglish, N., *Education Policy Making in England and Wales: The Crucible Years, 1895–1911* (London, 1996).

Dale, I., ed., *Conservative Party: General Election Manifestos, 1900–1997* (London, 2000).

Daley, H., *This Small Cloud: A Personal Memoir* (London, 1986).

Damer, S., 'State, class and housing: Glasgow 1885–1919', in J. Melling, ed., *Housing, Social Policy and the State* (London, 1980).

Dangerfield, G., *The Strange Death of Liberal England* (London, 1936).

Darling, E., ' "Enriching and enlarging the whole sphere of human activities": the work of the voluntary sector in housing reform in inter-war Britain', in C. Lawrence and A.-K. Mayer, eds, *Regenerating England: Science, Medicine and Culture in Inter-war Britain* (Amsterdam, 2000).

Daunton, M. J., *House and Home in the Victorian City: Working-class Housing 1850–1914* (London, 1983).

Daunton, M. J., ' "Gentlemanly capitalism" and British industry 1820–1914', *Past and Present*, 122 (1989).

Daunton, M. J., ed., *Housing the Workers: A Comparative History 1850–1914* (Leicester, 1990).

Davenport-Hines, R. P. T., *Dudley Docker: The Life and Times of a Trade Warrior* (Cambridge, 1984).

Davidoff, L., 'The rationalisation of housework', in D. L. Barker and S. Allen, eds, *Dependence and Exploitation in Work and Marriage* (London, 1976).

Davies, A., *Leisure, Gender and Poverty: Working-class Culture in Salford and Manchester, 1900–1939* (Buckingham, 1992).

Davies, A., 'Cinema and broadcasting', in P. Johnson, ed., *Economic, Social and Cultural Change in Twentieth-century Britain* (London, 1994), pp. 263–80.

Davies, D. H., *The Welsh Nationalist Party 1925–45: A Call to Nationhood* (Cardiff, 1983).

Davies, S. and Morley, B., *County Borough Election Results in England and Wales 1919–1938: A Comparative Analysis* (2 vols, Aldershot, 1999, 2000).

Davis, L. E. and Huttenback, R. A., *Mammon and the Pursuit of Empire: The Political Economy of British Imperialism, 1860–1912* (Cambridge, 1987).

Day, M. G., 'The contribution of Sir Raymond Unwin (1863–1940) and R. Barry Parker (1867–1947) to the development of site-planning theory and practice, *c.*1890–1918', in A. Sutcliffe, ed., *British Town Planning: The Formative Years* (Leicester, 1981).

Deacon, A., *In Search of the Scrounger: The Administration of Unemployment Insurance* (London, 1976).

Deaton, A. and Muellbauer, J., *Economics and Consumer Behaviour* (Cambridge, 1980).

De Cecco, M., *Money and Empire* (Oxford, 1974).

De Groot, G., *Blighty: British Society in the Era of the Great War* (London, 1996).

Denman, T., *Ireland's Unknown Soldiers: The 16th (Irish) Division in the Great War* (Dublin, 1992).

Denniston, A. G., 'The Government Code and Cipher School between the wars', *Intelligence and National Security*, 1, no. 1 (1986), pp. 48–70.

Denniston, R., 'Diplomatic eavesdropping, 1922–44', *Intelligence and National Security*, 10, no. 3 (1995), pp. 423–48.

Dent, H. C., *1870–1970: Century of Growth in English Education* (London, 1970).

Dewey, P. E., 'Food production policy in the United Kingdom 1914–1918', *Transactions of the Royal Historical Society*, 5, no. 20 (1980).

Dewey, P. E., 'Military recruiting and the British labour movement during the First World War', *Historical Journal*, 27 (1984), pp. 199–233.

Dewey, P. E., *British Agriculture in the First World War* (London, 1989).

Dewey, P. E., *War and Progress: Britain 1914–1945* (London, 1997).

Dewey, P. E., 'Farm labour', in E. J. T. Collins, ed., *The Cambridge Agrarian History of England and Wales*, vol. 7, *1850–1914* (Cambridge, 2000).

Dickenson, G. C. and Longley, G. J., 'Twopence to the terminus? A study of tram and bus fares in Leeds during the inter-war period', *Journal of Transport History*, 3rd series, 7 (1986), pp. 45–60.

Dienel, H.-L. and Lyth, P., eds, *Flying the Flag: European Commercial Air Transport since 1945* (Houndmills, 1998).

Digby, A., *The Evolution of British General Practice 1850–1950* (Oxford, 1999).

Dilke, C., *The British Empire* (London, 1899).

Dimsdale, N. H., 'British monetary policy and the exchange rate 1920–1938', *Oxford Economic Papers*, 33 (1981), pp. 306–49.

Dockrill, M. L., *Peace without Promise: Britain and the Peace Conferences 1919–23* (London, 1981).

Doerr, P. W., *British Foreign Policy, 1919–1939* (New York, 1998).

Donnachie, I., Harvie, C. and Wood, I., eds, *Forward! Labour Politics in Scotland, 1888–1988* (Edinburgh, 1989).

Douglas, R., *The History of the Liberal Party 1895–1970* (London, 1971).

Dow, C., *Major Recessions: Britain and the World, 1920–1995* (Oxford, 1998).

Dow, J. C. R., *The Management of the British Economy 1945–1960* (Cambridge, 1965).

Dowie, J. A., '1919 is in need of attention', *Economic History Review*, 2nd series, 28 (1975).

Drummond, I. M., *British Economic Policy and the Empire, 1919–1939* (London, 1972).

Drummond, I. M., *Imperial Economic Policy 1917–1939: Studies in Expansion and Protection* (London, 1974).

Drummond, I. M., *The Gold Standard and the International Monetary System 1900–1939* (Basingstoke, 1987).

Drummond, I. M. and Hillmer, N., *Negotiating Freer Trade: The United Kingdom, the United States, Canada and the Trade Agreements of 1938* (Waterloo, Ontario, 1989).

Durbin, E., *New Jerusalems: The Labour Party and the Economics of Democratic Socialism* (London, 1985).

Dutton, D., 'John Simon and the post-war Liberal party: an historical postscript', *Historical Journal*, 32 (1989), pp. 357–67.

Dutton, D., *His Majesty's Loyal Opposition: The Unionist Party in Opposition, 1905–1915* (Liverpool, 1992).

Dutton, D., *Simon: A Political Biography of Sir John Simon* (London, 1992).

Dwork, D., *War is Good for Babies and Young Children* (London, 1987).

Dyhouse, C., *No Distinction of Sex? Women in British Universities, 1870–1939* (London, 1995).

Eddy, J. and Schreuder, D., eds, *The Rise of Colonial Nationalism: Australia, New Zealand, Canada, and South Africa First Assert their Nationalities, 1880–1914* (Sydney, 1988).

Edgerton, D., 'Liberal militarism and the British state', *New Left Review*, 185 (1991), pp. 139–69.

Edmonds, L., 'Australia, Britain and the Empire Air Mail Scheme, 1934–38', *Journal of Transport History*, 3rd series, 20 (1999), pp. 91–106.

Edwards, R., *Victor Gollancz: A Biography* (London, 1987).

Egan, D., 'A cult of their own: syndicalism and *The Miners' Next Step*', in A. Campbell, N. Fishman and D. Howell, eds, *Miners, Unions and Politics, 1910–47* (Aldershot, 1996).

Eichengreen, B., *Sterling and the Tariff, 1929–32* (Princeton Studies in International Finance, No. 48, 1981).

Eichengreen, B., ed., *The Gold Standard in Theory and History* (London, 1985).

Eichengreen, B., *Golden Fetters: The Gold Standard and the Great Depression, 1919–1939* (Oxford, 1992).

Eichengreen, B., 'The gold standard since Alec Ford', in S. N. Broadberry and N. F. R. Crafts, eds, *Britain in the International Economy* (Cambridge, 1992).

Eichengreen, B., 'The inter-war economy in a European mirror', in R. Floud and D. McCloskey, eds, *The Economic History of Britain since 1700* (2nd edition, London, 1994).

Eichengreen, B., 'The origins and nature of the great slump revisited', *Economic History Review*, 45 (1994).

Ellis, M. and Panayi, P., 'German minorities in World War One', *Ethnic and Racial Studies*, 17, no. 2 (1994).

Emrys-Roberts, M., *The Cottage Hospitals 1859–1990* (Motcombe, 1991).

Emsley, C., 'The English bobby: an indulgent tradition', in R. Porter, ed., *Myths of the English* (Oxford, 1992).

Emsley, C., ' "Mother, what *did* policemen do when there weren't any motors?" The law, the police and the regulation of motor traffic in England, 1900–1939', *Historical Journal*, 36 (1993), pp. 357–81.

Emsley, C., *The English Police: A Political and Social History* (2nd edition, London, 1996).

Englander, D., *Landlord and Tenant in Urban Britain 1838–1918* (Oxford, 1983).

Evans, N., 'Across the universe: racial violence and the post-war crisis in imperial Britain, 1919–25', *Immigrants and Minorities*, 13 (1994).

Evans, N., 'Immigrants and minorities in Wales 1840–1990', in C. Holmes, ed., *Migration in European History* (Cheltenham, 1996), pp. 293–314.

Feinstein, C., *National Income, Expenditure and Output of the United Kingdom, 1855–1965* (Cambridge, 1972).

Feinstein, C., 'A new look at the cost of living, 1870–1914', in J. Foreman-Peck, ed., *New Perspectives on the Late Victorian Economy: Essays in Quantitative Economic History, 1860–1914* (Cambridge, 1991), pp. 151–79.

Feldman, D., 'The importance of being English: Jewish immigration and the decay of liberal England', in D. Feldman and G. Stedman Jones, eds, *Metropolis. London: Histories and Representations since 1800* (London, 1989), pp. 56–84.

Fergusson, T. G., *British Military Intelligence, 1870–1914* (London, 1984).

Ferris, J., 'The theory of a "French air menace", Anglo-French relations and the British Home Defence Air Force Programmes of 1921–25', *Journal of Strategic Studies*, 10, no. 1 (1987), pp. 62–83.

Ferris, J., 'Treasury control, the Ten-Year Rule and British service policies 1919–1924', *Historical Journal*, 30, no. 4 (1987), pp. 853–83.

Ferris, J., 'Whitehall's Black Chamber: British cryptology and the Government Code and Cipher School, 1919–1929', *Intelligence and National Security*, 2, no. 1 (1987), pp. 54–91.

Ferris, J., 'Before "Room 40": the British Empire and signals intelligence, 1898–1914', *Journal of Strategic Studies*, 12, no. 4 (1989), pp. 431–57.

Ferris, J., *Men, Money and Diplomacy: The Evolution of British Strategic Policy 1919–26* (Ithaca, NY, 1989).

Ferris, J., ' "The greatest power on earth": Great Britain in the 1920s', *International History Review*, 13, no. 4 (1991), pp. 726–50.

Ferris, J., *The British Army and Signals Intelligence during the First World War* (London, 1992).

Fieldhouse, R. et al., *A History of Modern British Adult Education* (Leicester, 1996).

Finlay, R. J., *A Partnership for Good? Scottish Politics and the Union since 1880* (Edinburgh, 1997).

Fisher, K., ' "Clearing up misconception": the campaign to set up birth control clinics in south Wales between the wars', *Welsh History Review*, 19 (1998).

Fitzgerald, R., *British Labour Management and Industrial Welfare, 1846–1939* (London, 1988).

Fitzpatrick, D., 'Militarism in Ireland, 1900–1922', in T. Bartlett and K. Jeffery, eds, *A Military History of Ireland* (Cambridge, 1996).

Fleisig, H., 'The US and the non-European periphery during the early years of the Great Depression', in H. van der Wee, ed., *The Great Depression Revisited* (The Hague, 1972).

Fletcher, S., *Maude Royden: A Life* (Oxford, 1989).

Flint, J. E., 'Frederick Lugard: the making of an autocrat, 1858–1943', in L. H. Gann and P. Duignan, eds, *African Proconsuls: European Governors in Africa* (New York, 1978).

Floud, R., Wachter, K. and Gregory, A., *Height, Health and History* (Cambridge, 1990).

Fohlin, C., 'Bank securities holdings and industrial finance before World War I: Britain and Germany compared', *Business and Economic History*, 26 (1997).

Foreman-Peck, J., 'The British tariff and industrial protection in the 1930s: an alternative model', *Economic History Review*, 2nd series, 34 (1981).

Foreman-Peck, J., *A History of the World Economy: International Economic Relations since 1850* (2nd edition, Hemel Hempstead, 1995).

Foreman-Peck, J., Bowden, S. and McKinlay, A., *The British Motor Vehicle Industry, 1880–1990* (Manchester, 1995).

Forsythe, W. J., *Penal Discipline, Reformatory Projects and the English Prison Commission 1895–1939* (Exeter, 1990).

Foster, J., 'Strike action and working-class politics on Clydeside, 1914–19', *International Review of Social History*, 35 (1990), pp. 33–70.

Fowler, D., *The First Teenagers: The Lifestyle of Young Wage-earners in Interwar Britain* (London, 1995).

Francis, H., *Miners Against Fascism* (London, 1984).

Francis, H. and Smith, D., *The Fed: A History of the South Wales Miners in the Twentieth Century* (London, 1980).

Francis, M., *Ideas and Policies under Labour 1945–51* (Manchester, 1977).

Francis, M., 'Labour and gender', in D. Tanner, P. Thane and N. Tiratsoo, eds, *Labour's First Century* (Cambridge, 2000).

Francis, M. and Zweiniger-Bargielowska, I., eds, *The Conservatives and British Society 1880–1990* (Cardiff, 1996).

Fraser, D., *The Evolution of the British Welfare State* (London, 1983).

Fraser, T. G., *Partition in Ireland, India and Palestine* (London, 1984).

Freeden, M., *Liberalism Divided: A Study in British Political Thought 1914–1939* (Oxford, 1986).

French, D., 'Spy fever in Britain, 1900–1915', *Historical Journal*, 21 (1978), pp. 355–70.

French, D., 'Sir John French's secret service in France, 1914–1915', *Journal of Strategic Studies*, 7, no. 4 (1984), pp. 423–40.

French, D., *British Strategy and War Aims, 1914–1916* (London, 1986).

French, D., *Raising Churchill's Army: The British Army and the War against Germany, 1919–1945* (Oxford, 2000).

Fry, M., *Patronage and Principle: A Political History of Modern Scotland* (Aberdeen, 1987).

Fuller, J. G., *Troop Morale and Popular Culture in the British and Dominion Armies 1914–1918* (Oxford, 1991).

Gailey, A., 'Failure and the making of the New Ireland', in D. G. Boyce, ed., *The Revolution in Ireland, 1879–1923* (London, 1988).

Garner, R., 'Ideological impact of the trade unions on the Labour party 1918–31' (Department of Politics, University of Manchester, occasional paper, 1989).

Garside, W. R., *The Measurement of Unemployment: Methods and Sources in Great Britain, 1850–1970* (Oxford, 1981).

Garside, W. R., *British Unemployment 1919–1939: A Study in Public Policy* (Cambridge, 1990).

Garside, W. R. and Greaves, J. I., 'The Bank of England and industrial intervention in interwar Britain', *Financial History Review*, 3 (1996).

Garside, W. R. and Hatton, T., 'Keynesian policy and British unemployment in the 1930s', *Economic History Review*, 38 (1985), pp. 83–8.

Garson, N. G., 'South Africa and World War One', *Journal of Imperial and Commonwealth History*, 8, no. 1 (1979).

Gaskell, S. M., '"The salubrious suburb": town planning in practice', in A. Sutcliffe, ed., *British Town Planning: The Formative Years* (Leicester, 1981).

Gaskell, S. M., *Building Control, National Legislation and the Introduction of Local Bye-laws in Victorian England* (London, 1983).

Geary, D., *European Labour Politics from 1900 to the Depression* (London, 1991).

Gibbs, N. H., *Grand Strategy* (London, 1976).

Gibbs, P., *England Speaks* (London, 1935).

Gilbert, B. B., *British Social Policy 1914–1939* (London, 1970).

Gilbert, B. B., *David Lloyd George: A Political Life. The Architect of Change, 1863–1912* (London, 1987).

Gilbert, M., *Winston S. Churchill*, vol. 4 (London, 1975).

Gillis, J. R., ed., *Commemorations: The Politics of National Identity* (Princeton, NJ, 1994).

Ginsberg, M., 'Interchange between social classes', *Economic Journal*, 39 (1929).

Gittins, D., *Fair Sex: Family Size and Structure 1900–1939* (London, 1982).

Gladstone, D., *The Twentieth-century Welfare State* (London, 1999).

Glass, D. V. and Hall, J. R., 'Social mobility in Britain: a study of intergenerational change in status', in D. V. Glass, ed., *Social Mobility in Britain* (London, 1954).

Glucksmann, M., *Women Assemble* (London, 1990).

Glynn, S. and Howells, P., 'Unemployment in the 1930s: the Keynesian solution reconsidered', *Australian Economic History Review*, 20 (1980), pp. 28–45.

Glynn, S. and Oxborrow, J., *Interwar Britain: A Social and Economic History* (London, 1976).

Goldman, C. S., ed., *The Empire and the Century: A Series of Essays on Imperial Problems and Possibilities by Various Writers* (London, 1905).

Goldstein, E., *Winning the Peace: British Diplomatic Strategy, Peace Planning, and the Paris Peace Conference, 1916–1920* (Oxford, 1991).

Goldstein, E., 'The evolution of British diplomatic strategy for the Washington Conference', *Diplomacy and Statecraft*, 4 (1993).

Goldthorpe, J. H. (in collaboration with Payne, C. and Llewellyn, C.), *Social Mobility and Class Structure in Modern Britain* (Oxford, 1987).

Gollin, A. M., *The Observer and J. L. Garvin* (London, 1960).

Gollin, A. M., *Proconsul in Politics: A Study of Lord Milner in Opposition and in Power* (London, 1963).

Gooch, G. P. and Temperley, H., *British Documents on the Origins of the War 1898–1914* (11 vols, London, 1926–8).

Gooch, J., '"Hidden in the Rock": American military perceptions of Great Britain 1919–1940', in L. Freedman, P. Hayes and R. O'Neill, eds, *War, Strategy and International Politics: Essays in Honour of Sir Michael Howard* (Oxford, 1992).

Gopal, S., *British Policy in India, 1885–1905* (Cambridge, 1965).

Gopal, S., *Jawaharlal Nehru: A Biography*, vol. 1 (London, 1975).

Gordon, D. C., *The Dominion Partnership in Imperial Defence 1870–1914* (Baltimore, 1965).

Gordon, E., *Women and the Labour Movement in Scotland, 1850–1914* (Oxford, 1991).

Gordon, P., Aldrich, R. and Dean, D., *Education and Policy in England in the Twentieth Century* (London, 1991).

Gordon, P. and Humphries, S., *A Labour of Love: The Experience of Parenthood in Britain 1900–50* (London, 1993).

Gordon, P. and Lawton, D., *Curriculum Change in the Nineteenth and Twentieth Centuries* (London, 1978).

Goring, C., *The English Convict: A Statistical Study* (London, 1913).

Gospel, H., 'Employers and managers: organisation and strategy', in C. J. Wrigley, ed., *A History of British Industrial Relations*, vol. 2, *1914–1939* (Brighton, 1987).

Gospel, H., *Markets, Firms and the Management of Labour in Modern Britain* (Cambridge, 1992).

Gospel, H. and Littler, C., eds, *Managerial Strategies and Industrial Relations* (London, 1983).

Grainger, J. H., *Patriotisms: Britain, 1900–1939* (London, 1986).

Graves, P., *Labour Women: Women in British Working-class Politics 1918–1939* (Cambridge, 1994).

Graves, R., Hodge, R. and Hodge, A., *The Long Weekend: A Social History of Great Britain, 1918–1939* (London, 1940).

Gray, A. and McGuigan, J., eds, *Studying Culture: An Introductory Reader* (London, 1993).

Grayson, R. S., *Austen Chamberlain and the Commitment to Europe: British Foreign Policy 1924–29* (London, 1997).

Grayzel, S. R., ' "The outward and visible sign of her patriotism": women, uniforms and national service during the First World War', *Twentieth Century British History*, 8, no. 2 (1997).

Greasley, D. and Oxley, L., 'Discontinuities in competitiveness: the impact of the First World War on British industry', *Economic History Review*, 49 (1996).

Green, A., *Education and State Formation* (London, 1990).

Green, E. H. H., *The Crisis of Conservatism: The Politics, Economics and Ideology of the British Conservative Party, 1880–1914* (London, 1995).

Green, S. J. D., *Religion in the Age of Decline* (Cambridge, 1996).

Greenwood, W., *There Was a Time* (London, 1969).

Gregory, A., *The Silence of Memory: Armistice Day 1919–1946* (Oxford, 1994).

Gregory, R., *The Miners and British Politics, 1906–1914* (Oxford, 1968).

Griffith, P., *Battle Tactics of the Western Front: The British Army's Art of Attack, 1916–18* (London, 1994).

Griffiths, B., *Saunders Lewis* (Cardiff, 1989).

Griffiths, C., ' "Red Tape Farm"? Visions of a socialist agriculture in 1920s and 1930s Britain', in J. R. Wordie, ed., *Agriculture and Politics in England, 1815–1939* (Basingstoke, 2000).

Griffiths, J., *Pages from Memory* (London, 1969).

Grigg, J., *Lloyd George* (3 vols, London, 1973).

Groves, R., *Sharpen the Sickle! The History of the Farm Workers' Union* (London, 1949).

Guha, S., 'The importance of social intervention in England's mortality decline: the evidence reviewed', *Social History of Medicine*, 7 (1994), pp. 89–113.

Gwynn, S. and Tuckwell, G. M., *The Life of the Rt. Hon. Sir Charles Dilke* (2 vols, London, 1918).

Hadfield, C., *Hadfield's British Canals: The Inland Waterways of Britain and Ireland*, rev. J. Boughey (8th edition, Stroud, 1994).

Hall, L. A., *Sex, Gender and Social Change in Britain Since 1880* (Basingstoke, 2000).

Hall, S. and Schwarz, B., 'State and society, 1880–1930', in M. Langan and B. Schwarz, eds, *Crises in the British State 1880–1930* (London, 1985).

Halsey, A. H., *Change in British Society* (Oxford, 1986).

Hamish Fraser, W., *A History of British Trade Unionism, 1700–1998* (London, 1999).

Hancock, W. K., *Survey of British Commonwealth Affairs*, vol. 2, *Problems of Economic Policy, 1918–1939, Part 1* (Oxford, 1940).

Hannah, L., *The Rise of the Corporate Economy* (2nd edition, London, 1983).

Hannam, J., 'Women and politics', in J. Purvis, ed., *Women's History: Britain, 1850–1945* (London, 1995).

Hannington, W., *The Problem of the Distressed Areas* (London, 1937).

Harding, C., 'The inevitable end of a discredited system? The origins of the Gladstone Committee Report on Prisons 1895', *Historical Journal*, 31 (1988), pp. 591–608.

Hardy, A., *Health and Medicine in Britain since 1860* (London, 2000).

Hardy, D., *From Garden Cities to New Towns: Campaigning for Town and Country Planning 1899–1946* (2 vols, London, 1991).

Hardy, D. and Ward, C., *Arcadia for All: The Legacy of a Makeshift Landscape* (London, 1984).

Hardyment, C., *From Mangle to Microwave: The Mechanization of Household Work* (Oxford, 1988).

Harkness, D. W., *The Restless Dominion: The Irish Free State and the British Commonwealth of Nations, 1921–31* (London, 1969).

Harris, J., *Unemployment and Politics, 1886–1914* (Oxford, 1972).

Harris, J., 'Political thought and the welfare state 1870–1914: an intellectual framework for British social policy', *Past and Present*, 135 (May 1992).

Harris, J., *Private Lives, Public Spheres: A Social History of Britain 1870–1914* (London, 1993).

Harris, P., *Men, Ideas and Tanks: British Military Thought and Armoured Forces, 1903–1939* (Manchester, 1995).

Harrison, B., *Prudent Revolutionaries: Portraits of British Feminists Between the Wars* (Oxford, 1987).

Harrison, M., 'Thomas Coglan Horsfall and the example of Germany', *Planning Perspectives*, 6 (1985).

Harrison, R., *Before the Socialists: Studies in Labour and Politics 1861–1881* (London, 1965).

Harrison-Place, T., 'British perceptions of the tactics of the German army, 1938–40', *Intelligence and National Security*, 9, no. 3 (1994), pp. 495–519.

Hart, P., *The I.R.A. and its Enemies: Violence and Community in Cork, 1916–1923* (Oxford, 1998).

Harvey, C. and Turner, J., eds, *Labour and Business in Modern Britain* (London, 1989).

Hastings, A., *A History of English Christianity 1920–90* (London, 1991).

Hatton, T., 'The outlines of a Keynesian solution', in S. Glynn and A. Booth, eds, *The Road to Full Employment* (London, 1987), pp. 82–94.

Haym, R., 'The British Empire in the Edwardian era', in J. M. Brown and W. R. Louis, eds, *The Oxford History of the British Empire*, vol. 4, *The Twentieth Century* (Oxford, 1999).

Haywood, R., 'Railways, urban form and town planning in London: 1900–1947', *Planning Perspective*, 12 (1997), pp. 37–69.

Hazelgrove, J., *Spiritualism and British Society between the Wars* (Manchester, 2000).

Hearnshaw, L. S., *Cyril Burt, Psychologist* (London, 1979).

Hechter, M., *Internal Colonialism* (London, 1975).

Henderson, F., *The Labour Unrest: What it Is and What it Portends* (London, 1911).

Hendrick, H., *Children, Childhood and English Society 1880–1990* (Cambridge, 1997).

Hennessey, T., *Dividing Ireland: World War and Partition* (London, 1998).

Henry, D., 'British submarine policy, 1918–1939', in B. McL. Ranft, ed., *Technical Change and British Naval Policy, 1860–1939* (London, 1977).

Herwig, H., 'Admirals versus generals: the war aims of the Imperial German Navy, 1914–18', *Central European History*, 5, no. 3 (1972), pp. 208–33.

Hewins, W. A. S., *Apologia of an Imperialist* (London, 1929).

Hibbs, J., *The Bus and Coach Industry: Its Economics and Organization* (London, 1975).

Hiley, N., 'The failure of British espionage against Germany, 1908–1914', *Historical Journal*, 26, no. 4 (1983), pp. 867–89.

Hill, J., *Sport, Leisure and Culture in Twentieth-century Britain* (Basingstoke, 2002).

Hill, O., *Homes of the London Poor* (London, 1875; rpt. 1970).

Hilton, J. et al., *Are Trade Unions Obstructive?* (London, 1935).

Hilton, M., *Smoking in British Popular Culture, 1800–2000* (Manchester, 2000).

Hinton, J., *The First Shop Stewards' Movement* (London, 1973).

Hinton, J., *Labour and Socialism* (Brighton, 1983).

Hirshfield, C., 'Fractured faith: Liberal party women and the suffrage issue in Britain, 1892–1914', *Gender and History*, 2 (1990), pp. 173–97.

Hobhouse, L. T., *Liberalism* (London, 1911).

Hobhouse, S. and Brockway, A. F., eds, *English Prisons Today* (London, 1922).

Hobsbawm, E., *Labouring Men: Studies in the History of Labour* (London, 1964).

Hobsbawm, E. J., 'Mass producing traditions: Europe 1870–1914', in E. J. Hobsbawm and T. Ranger, eds, *The Invention of Tradition* (Cambridge, 1983).

Hobsbawm, E. J., 'The making of the working class 1870–1914', in E. J. Hobsbawm, *Worlds of Labour: Further Studies in the History of Labour* (London, 1984).

Hobsbawm, E. J., *Worlds of Labour: Further Studies in the History of Labour* (London, 1984).

Holford, J., *Reshaping Labour: Organisation, Work and Politics in Edinburgh during the Great War and After* (London, 1988).

Holland, R. F., *Britain and the Commonwealth Alliance 1918–1939* (London, 1981).

Hollins, T., 'The Conservative party and film propaganda between the wars', *English Historical Review*, 96 (1981), pp. 359–69.

Holmes, C., *Anti-Semitism in British Society 1876–1939* (London, 1979).

Holmes, C., *John Bull's Island* (Basingstoke, 1988).

Holmes, C., ed., *Migration in European History* (2 vols, Cheltenham, 1996).

Holmes, J. and Urqhart, D., eds, *Coming into the Light: The Work, Politics and Religion of Women in Ulster, 1840–1940* (Belfast, 1994).

Holt, R., *Sport and the British: A Modern History* (Oxford, 1989).

Holt, R., 'Sport and history: the state of the subject in Britain', *Twentieth-century British History*, 7 (1996), pp. 231–52.

Holton, S. S., *Feminism and Democracy: Women's Suffrage and Reform Politics in Britain, 1900–1918* (Cambridge, 1986).

Holton, S. S., 'The making of suffrage history', in J. Purvis and S. S. Holton, eds, *Votes for Women* (London, 2000).

Honigsbaum, F., *The Struggle for the Ministry of Health 1914–19* (London, 1970).

Horne, J., Tomlinson, A. and Whannel, G., *Understanding Sport: An Introduction to the Sociological and Cultural Analysis of Sport* (London, 1999).

Horner, A., *Incorrigible Rebel* (London, 1960).

Howard, M., *The Continental Commitment: The Dilemma of British Defence Policy in the Era of the Two World Wars* (London, 1972).

Howard, M., *War and the Liberal Conscience* (London, 1978).

Howe, A., *Free Trade and Liberal England 1846–1946* (Oxford, 1997).

Howe, S., *Anticolonialism in British Politics: The Left and the End of Empire, 1918–1964* (Oxford, 1993).

Howe, S., 'Labour and international affairs', in D. Tanner, P. Thane and N. Tiratsoo, eds, *Labour's First Century* (Cambridge, 2000).

Howell, D., *British Workers and the Independent Labour Party 1888–1906* (Manchester, 1983).

Howell, D., *Respectable Radicals: Studies in Railway Trades Unionism* (Aldershot, 1999).

Howson, S., 'Slump and unemployment', in R. Floud and D. McCloskey, eds, *The Economic History of Britain since 1700*, vol. 2, *1860 to the 1970s* (Cambridge, 1972), pp. 265–85.

Howson, S., *Domestic Monetary Management in Britain 1919–1938* (Cambridge, 1975).

Howson, S., 'The management of sterling 1932–1939', *Journal of Economic History*, 40 (1980), pp. 53–60.

Howson, S., *Sterling's Managed Float: The Operation of the Exchange Equalisation Account 1931–1939* (Princeton Studies in International Finance, No. 46, 1980).

Huggins, M., 'Second-class citizens? English middle-class culture and sport, 1850–1910: a reconsideration', *International Journal of the History of Sport*, 17, no. 1 (2000).

Hughes, A. and Hunt, K., 'A culture transformed? Women's lives in Wythenshawe in the 1930s', in A. Davies and S. Fielding, eds, *Workers' Worlds: Cultures and Communities in Manchester and Salford, 1880–1939* (Manchester, 1992), pp. 74–101.

Hunt, K., 'Negotiating the boundaries of the domestic: British socialist women and the politics of consumption', *Women's History Review*, 9, no. 2 (2000).

Hurt, J. S., *Elementary Schooling and the Working Classes, 1860–1918* (London, 1979).

Hutchison, I. G. C., *A Political History of Scotland, 1832–1924: Parties, Elections, Issues* (Edinburgh, 1986).

Hutchison, I. G. C., 'Scottish Unionism between the two world wars', in C. Macdonald, ed., *Unionist Scotland 1800–1997* (Edinburgh, 1998).

Hutchison, I. G. C., *Scottish Politics in the Twentieth Century* (Basingstoke, 2001).

Hutton, W., *The State We're In* (London, 1995).

Hynes, S., *A War Imagined: The First World War and British Culture* (London, 1991).

Ingham, G., *Capitalism Divided? The City and Industry in British Development* (London, 1984).

Jackson, A., *The Ulster Party: Irish Unionists in the House of Commons, 1884–1911* (Oxford, 1989).

Jackson, A. A., *The Middle Classes, 1900–1950* (Nairn, 1991).

Jalal, A., *The Sole Spokesman: Jinnah, the Muslim League and the Demand for Pakistan* (Cambridge, 1985).

Jalland, P., *The Liberals and Ireland: The Ulster Question in British Politics to 1914* (Brighton, 1970).

Jarvie, G. and Walker, G., eds, *Scottish Sport in the Making of the Nation: Ninety-minute Patriots?* (Leicester, 1994).

Jarvis, D., 'British Conservatism and class politics in the 1920s', *English Historical Review*, 111 (1996), pp. 59–84.

Jarvis, D., 'The shaping of the Conservative electoral hegemony 1918–39', in J. Lawrence and M. Taylor, eds, *Party, State and Society: Electoral Behaviour in Britain since 1820* (Aldershot, 1997).

Jeffery, K., 'The eastern arc of empire: a strategic view 1850–1950', *Journal of Strategic Studies*, 5, no. 2 (1982), pp. 531–45.

Jeffery, K., *The British Army and the Crisis of Empire, 1918–1922* (Manchester, 1984).

Jeffrey, R., ed., *People, Princes and Paramount Power: Society and Politics in the Indian Princely States* (Delhi, 1978).

Jeffreys, S., *The Spinster and her Enemies: Feminism and Sexuality, 1880–1939* (London, 1997).

Jenkins, D., *A Nation on Trial* (Cardiff, 1998).

Jenkins, P. and Potter, G. W., 'Before the Krays: organized crime in London, 1920–1960', *Criminal Justice History*, 9 (1988), pp. 209–30.

Jennings, H., *Brynmawr: A Study of a Distressed Area* (London, 1938).

John, A., *Our Mothers' Land: Chapters in Welsh Women's History, 1830–1939* (Cardiff, 1991).

Johnes, M., *Soccer and Society in South Wales, 1900–1939* (Cardiff, 2002).

Johnson, P., *Saving and Spending: The Working-class Economy in Britain, 1870–1939* (Oxford, 1985).

Johnson, P., ed., *Twentieth-century Britain: Economic, Social and Cultural Change* (London, 1994).

Johnston, R., *Clydeside Capital* (East Linton, 2000).

Johnston, R. and McIvor, A., *Lethal Work: A History of the Asbestos Tragedy in Scotland* (East Linton, 2000).

Joly, D. and Cohen, R., eds, *Reluctant Hosts: Europe and its Refugees* (Aldershot, 1989).

Jones, B., *Welsh Elections, 1885–1997* (Talybont, 1999).

Jones, D. J. V., *Crime and Policing in the Twentieth Century: The South Wales Experience* (Cardiff, 1996).

Jones, G., *British Multinational Banking, 1830–1990* (Oxford, 1993).

Jones, H., *Health and Society in Twentieth-century Britain* (London, 1994).

Jones, H., *Women in British Public Life, 1914–1950: Gender, Power and Social Policy* (Harlow, 2000).

Jones, K., *Asylums and After* (London, 1993).

Jones, R. M. and Jones, I. Rh., 'Labour and the nation', in D. Tanner, C. Williams and D. Hopkin, eds, *The Labour Party in Wales, 1900–2000* (Cardiff, 2000), pp. 241–63.

Jones, S. G., *Workers at Play: A Social and Economic History of Leisure, 1918–1939* (London, 1986).

Jones, S. G., *Sport, Politics and the Working Class: Organised Labour and Sport in Inter-war Britain* (Manchester, 1988).

Joseph, G., *Women at Work: The British Experience* (Oxford, 1983).

Joyce, P., 'Work', in F. M. L. Thompson, ed., *The Cambridge Social History of Britain, 1750–1950*, vol. 2 (Cambridge, 1990).

Joyce, P., *Visions of the People* (Cambridge, 1991).

Joyce, P., 'The end of social history?', *Social History*, 20 (1995).

Kenefick, W. and McIvor, A., eds, *Roots of Red Clydeside 1910–1914?* (Edinburgh, 1996).

Kennedy, P. M., *The Rise of the Anglo-German Antagonism 1860–1914* (London, 1980).

Kennedy, W. P., *Industrial Structure, Capital Markets and the Origins of British Economic Decline* (Cambridge, 1987).

Kenner, C., *No Time for Women: Exploring Women's Health in the 1930s and Today* (London, 1985).

Kent, J., *William Temple* (Cambridge, 1993).

Kent, S. K., *Making Peace: The Reconstruction of Gender in Interwar Britain* (Princeton, NJ, 1993).

Keogh, D., *Twentieth-century Ireland: Nation and State* (Dublin, 1994).

Kershen, A. J., *Uniting the Tailors* (Ilford, 1995).

Kershen, A. J., ed., *London the Promised Land? The Migrant Experience in a Capital City* (Aldershot, 1997).

Kershen, A. J., ed., *Language, Labour and Migration* (Aldershot, 2000).

Keynes, J. M., *The Economic Consequences of the Peace* (New York, 1920).

Keynes, J. M., *The Economic Consequences of Mr Churchill* (London, 1925).

Keynes, J. M., *Essays in Biography* (London, 1961).

Kindleberger, C. P., *The World in Depression, 1929–1939* (London, 1973).

Kingsford, P., *The Hunger Marchers in Britain, 1920–1939* (London, 1982).

Kinnear, M., *The British Voter* (London, 1981).

Kirby, M. W., 'The Lancashire cotton industry in the inter-war years: a study in industrial organisation', *Business History*, 16 (1974), pp. 145–59.

Kirby, M. W., *The British Coalmining Industry, 1870–1946: A Political and Economic History* (London, 1977).

Kirby, M. W., *The Decline of British Economic Power since 1870* (London, 1981).

Kirby, M. W., 'Industrial policy', in S. Glynn and A. Booth, eds, *The Road to Full Employment* (London, 1987), pp. 125–39.

Kirby, M. W., 'Supply side management', in N. F. R. Crafts and N. Woodward, eds, *The British Economy since 1945* (Oxford, 1991), pp. 236–60.

Kirby, M. W., 'Railway development and the role of the state', in R. Ambler, ed., *The History and Practice of Britain's Railways: A New Research Agenda* (Aldershot, 1999), pp. 21–35.

Kirby, M. W. and Rose, M. B., 'Productivity and competitive failure: British government policy and industry, 1914–19', in G. Jones and M. W. Kirby, eds, *Competitiveness and the State: Government and Business in Twentieth-century Britain* (Manchester, 1991), pp. 20–39.

Kirk, N., ed., *Northern Identities* (Aldershot, 2000).

Kirkaldy, A. W., ed., *British Finance during and after the War, 1914–21* (London, 1921).

Kitson, M. and Solomou, S., *Protectionism and Economic Revival: The British Inter-war Economy* (Cambridge, 1990).

Kleinberg, S. J., 'Escalating standards: women, housework and household technology in the twentieth century', in F. J. Coppa and R. Harmond, eds, *Technology in the Twentieth Century* (Iowa, 1983), pp. 1–29.

Knox, W. W., *Scottish Labour Leaders, 1918–39* (Edinburgh, 1984).

Knox, W. W., *James Maxton* (Manchester, 1986).

Knox, W. W., *Industrial Nation: Work, Culture and Society in Scotland, 1800 to the Present* (Edinburgh, 1999).

Knox, W. W. and Mackinlay, A., 'The re-making of Scottish labour in the 1930s', *Twentieth Century British History*, 6 (1995), pp. 134–53.

Koerner, S., 'The British motor-cycle industry during the 1930s', *Journal of Transport History*, 3rd series, 16 (1995), pp. 55–75.

Koss, S., 'Lloyd George and nonconformity: the last rally', *English Historical Review*, 89 (1974), pp. 77–108.

Koss, S., *Asquith* (London, 1976).

Kuhn, W. M., *Democratic Royalism: The Transformation of the British Monarchy, 1861–1914* (London, 1996).

Kushner, T. and Knox, K., *Refugees in an Age of Genocide* (Ilford, 1999).

Ladd, B., *Urban Planning and Civic Order in Germany 1860–1914* (Cambridge, Mass., 1990).

Laffan, M., *The Partition of Ireland, 1911–25* (Dundalk, 1983).

Laffan, M., *The Resurrection of Ireland: The Sinn Fein Party, 1916–1923* (Cambridge, 1999).

Lahiri, S., *Indian Visitors in Britain 1880–1930* (Ilford, 2000).

Larson, R. H., *The British Army and the Theory of Armoured Warfare 1918–40* (Newark, NJ, 1984).

Law, C., *Suffrage and Power: The Women's Movement 1918–1928* (London, 1997).

Law, C. M., 'The growth of urban population in England and Wales 1800–1911', *Transactions of the Institute of British Geographers* (1967).

Lawlor, S., *Britain and Ireland, 1914–1923* (Dublin, 1983).

Lawrence, J., 'Class and gender in the making of urban Toryism, 1880–1914', *English Historical Review*, 108 (1993), pp. 629–52.

Lawrence, J., 'The First World War and its aftermath', in P. Johnson, ed., *Twentieth-century Britain: Economic, Social and Cultural Change* (London, 1994).

Laybourn, K., *Britain on the Breadline* (Gloucester, 1990).

Laybourn, K., *A History of British Trade Unionism, c.1770–1990* (Stroud, 1992).

Laybourn, K., 'The Guild of Help and the changing face of Edwardian philanthropy', *Urban History* 20 (April 1993), pp. 43–60.

Laybourn, K., *The General Strike of 1926* (Manchester, 1993).

Laybourn, K., *The Guild of Help and the Changing Face of Edwardian Philanthropy: The Guild of Help, Voluntary Work and the State, 1904–1919* (Lampeter, 1994).

Laybourn, K., *The Evolution of British Social Policy and the Welfare State* (Keele, 1995).

Laybourn, K., *A Century of Labour: A History of the Labour Party 1900–2000* (Stroud, 2000).

Leary, W. M., ed., *From Airships to Airbus: The History of Civil and Commercial Aviation*, vol. 1 (Washington, DC, 1995).

Lee, J. M., *Colonial Development and Good Government: A Study of the Ideas Expressed by the British Official Classes in Planning Decolonization 1939–1964* (Oxford, 1967).

Lees, H. L., *Exiles of Erin: Irish Migrants in Victorian London* (Manchester, 1979).

Leneman, L., *A Guid Cause: The Women's Suffrage Movement in Scotland* (Aberdeen, 1991).

Levitt, I., *Poverty and Welfare in Scotland 1890–1948* (London, 1988).

Lewchuk, W., *American Technology and the British Motor Vehicle Industry* (Cambridge, 1987).

Lewis, J., *The Politics of Motherhood: Child and Maternal Welfare in England, 1900–1939* (London, 1980).

Lewis, J., *Women in England 1870–1950: Sexual Divisions and Social Change* (London, 1984).

Lewis, J., *What Price Community Medicine?* (Brighton, 1986).

Lewis, J., 'Women, social work and social welfare in twentieth-century Britain: from (unpaid) influence to (paid) oblivion', in M. Daunton, ed., *Charity, Self-interest and Welfare in the English Past* (London, 1996).

Lewis, S., 'The principles of nationalism', in H. Pritchard Jones, ed., *Saunders Lewis: A Presentation of his Work* (Illinois, 1990), pp. 29–40.

Liddington, J. and Norris, J., *One Hand Tied Behind Us: The Rise of the Women's Suffrage Movement* (London, 1978).

Lindert, P. H., *Key Currencies and Gold 1900–1913* (Princeton Studies in International Finance, No. 24, 1969).

Lipman, V., *A History of the Jews in Britain since 1858* (Leicester, 1990).

Lister, R., *Citizenship: Feminist Perspectives* (London, 1997).

Little, A. and Westergaard, J., 'The trend of class differentials in educational opportunity in England and Wales', *British Journal of Sociology*, 15 (1964).

Littler, C. R., *The Development of the Labour Process in Capitalist Societies* (London, 1982).

Lloyd George, D., *War Memoirs of Lloyd George* (2 vols, London, 1938).

Lloyd-Jones, R. and Lewis, M. J., *Raleigh and the British Bicycle Industry: An Economic and Business History 1870–1960* (Aldershot, 2000).

Locke, A., 'Criminal statistics', *Police Journal*, 4 (1931), pp. 188–96.

Loudon, I. and Drury, M., 'Some aspects of clinical care in general practice', in I. Loudon, C. Webster and J. Horder, eds, *General Practice under the National Health Service 1948–1997* (Oxford, 1997), pp. 92–127.

Lovell, J., *British Trade Unions, 1875–1933* (London, 1977).

Lowe, P., *Great Britain and the Origins of the Pacific War: A Study of British Policy in East Asia, 1937–41* (Oxford, 1977).

Lowe, R., *Adjusting to Democracy: The Role of the Ministry of Labour in British Politics 1916–1939* (Oxford, 1986).

Lowerson, J., *Sport and the English Middle Classes, 1870–1914* (Manchester, 1993).

Lucas, Sir C., *The Empire at War*, vols 1–4 (London, 1926).

Luckin, B., *Questions of Power: Electricity and Environment in Inter-war Britain* (Manchester, 1990).

Lugard, F., *The Dual Mandate in British Tropical Africa* (London, 1922).

Lunn, K., ed., *Hosts, Immigrants and Minorities* (Folkestone, 1980).

Lyman, R., *The First Labour Government, 1924* (London, 1957).

Lynn-Jones, S. M., 'Detente and deterrence: Anglo-German relations, 1911–1914', *International Security*, 11, no. 2 (1986).

Lyth, P. J., ed., 'Introduction', in *Air Transport* (Aldershot, 1996), pp. ix–xxi.

Macadam, E., *The New Philanthropy* (London, 1934).

McCrillis, N., *The British Conservative Party in the Age of Universal Suffrage: Popular Conservatism, 1918–1929* (Columbus, OH, 1998).

MacDonald, C. C. M., ed., *Unionist Scotland, 1800–1997* (East Linton, 1998).

MacDonald, C. C. M., *The Radical Thread: Political Change in Scotland. Paisley Politics, 1885–1924* (East Linton, 2000).

Machin, G. I. T., *Politics and the Churches in Great Britain 1869–1921* (Oxford, 1987).

McIntyre, C., *Monuments of War: How to Read a War Memorial* (London, 1990).

Macintyre, S., *Little Moscows: Communism and Working-class Militancy in Inter-war Britain* (London, 1980).

McIvor, A. J., *Organised Capital* (Cambridge, 1996).

McIvor, A. J., *A History of Work in Britain, 1880–1950* (London, 2001).

Mackenzie, J. M., *Propaganda and Empire* (Manchester, 1984).

MacKenzie, J. M., ' "In touch with the infinite": the BBC and the Empire, 1923–53', in J. M. MacKenzie, ed., *Imperialism and Popular Culture* (Manchester, 1986).

McKibbin, R., *The Evolution of the Labour Party, 1910–1924* (Oxford, 1974).

McKibbin, R., 'Class and conventional wisdom: the Conservative party and the "public" in inter-war Britain', in R. McKibbin, *The Ideologies of Class: Social Relations in Britain 1880–1950* (Oxford, 1990), pp. 259–93.

McKibbin, R., *The Ideologies of Class: Social Relations in Britain, 1880–1950* (Oxford, 1990).

McKibbin, R., 'The social psychology of unemployment in interwar Britain', in R. McKibbin, *The Ideologies of Class: Social Relations in Britain 1880–1950* (Oxford, 1990), pp. 228–58.

McKibbin, R., *Classes and Cultures: England 1918–1951* (Oxford, 1998).

Mackinlay, A. and Morris, R. J., eds, *The ILP on Clydeside, 1888–1932* (Manchester, 1991).

MacLean, I., *The Legend of Red Clydeside* (1983; 2nd edition, Edinburgh, 1991).

McLeod, H., *Class and Religion in the Late Victorian City* (London, 1974).

McLeod, H., *Religion and Society in England 1850–1914* (London, 1996).

Macleod, R. and Andrews, E. K., 'The origins of the D.S.I.R.: reflections on ideas and men, 1915–1916', *Public Administration*, 48 (1970), pp. 23–48.

MacLeod, R. and MacLeod, K., 'Government and the optical industry in Britain 1914–18', in J. M. Winter, ed., *War and Economic Development* (Cambridge, 1975).

McMahon, D., *Republicans and Imperialists: Anglo-Irish Relations in the 1930s* (London, 1984).

Maddison, A., *Dynamic Forces in Capitalist Development: A Long-run Comparative View* (Oxford, 1991).

Magri, S. and Topalov, C., 'L'habitat du salarié en France, Grande-Bretagne, Italie et aux Etats-Unis, 1910–25', in Y. Cohen and R. Baudouï, eds, *Les Chantiers de la Paix Sociale (1900–1940)* (Fontenay/St Cloud, 1995).

Maine, H., *Ancient Law: Its Connection with the Early History of Society and its Relation to Modern Ideas* (1861; Boston, 1963).

Maine, H., *Village Communities in the East and West* (London, 1895).

Maizels, A., *Industrial Growth and World Trade: An Empirical Study of Trends in Production, Consumption and Trade in Manufactures from 1899–1959* (Cambridge, 1963).

Malinowski, B., 'Practical anthropology', *Africa*, 2 (1929).

Mallier, A. T. and Rosser, M. J., *Women and the Economy: A Comparative Study of Britain and the USA* (London, 1987).

Maloney, T., *Westminster, Whitehall and the Vatican: The Role of Cardinal Hinsley 1935–43* (London, 1985).

Mandler, P., *The Fall and Rise of the Stately Home* (New Haven, Conn., 1997).

Mangan, J., *The Games Ethic and Imperialism: Aspects of the Diffusion of an Ideal* (London, 1998).

Mangan, J. A., *Athleticism in the Victorian and Edwardian Public School* (London, 2000).

Mannheim, H., *Social Aspects of Crime in England Between the Wars* (London, 1940).

Mansergh, D., *Nationalism and Independence: Selected Papers by Nicholas Mansergh* (Cork, 1997).

Mansergh, N., *The Unresolved Question: The Anglo-Irish Settlement and its Undoing, 1912–1972* (London, 1991).

Mansfield, N., 'Class conflict and village war memorials, 1914–24', *Rural History*, 6 (1995).

Marchildon, G. P., 'British investment banking and industrial decline before the Great War', *Business History*, 33 (1991).

Marder, A. J., Jacobsen, M. and Horsfield, J., *Old Friends, New Enemies: The Royal Navy and the Imperial Japanese Navy*, vol. 2, *The Pacific War, 1942–1945* (Oxford, 1990).

Marquand, D., *Ramsay MacDonald* (London, 1977).

Marrison, A., *British Business and Protection* (Oxford, 1996).

Marrus, M., *The Unwanted* (Oxford, 1985).

Martin, J., *The Development of Modern Agriculture: British Farming since 1931* (Basingstoke, 2000).

Marwick, A., *The Deluge: British Society and the First World War* (London, 1965).

Marwick, A., 'The impact of the First World War on Britain', *Journal of Contemporary History*, 3, no. 1 (1968).

Marwick, A., *War and Social Change in the Twentieth Century* (London, 1974).

Marwick, A., *Culture in Britain since 1945* (Oxford, 1991).

Marwick, A., *A History of the Modern British Isles, 1914–1999* (Oxford, 2000).

Marx, K. and Engels, F., *The Communist Manifesto* (Harmondsworth, 1967).

Mason, T., ed., *Sport in Britain: A Social History* (Cambridge, 1989).

Mason, T., 'Sport and recreation', in P. Johnson, ed., *Twentieth-century Britain: Economic, Social and Cultural Change* (London, 1994), pp. 111–26.

Massey, D., 'Regional planning 1909–1939: "The experimental era"', in P. Garside and M. Hebbert, eds, *British Regionalism 1900–2000* (London, 1989).

Massey, P., 'The expenditure of 1360 British middle-class households in 1938–1939', *Journal of the Royal Statistical Society*, 95, part 3 (1942), pp. 159–85.

Masson, U., ' "Political conditions in Wales are quite different . . .": party politics and votes for women in Wales, 1912–1915', *Women's History Review*, 9, no. 2 (2000), pp. 369–88.

Masterman, C., *From the Abyss. Of its Inhabitants. By One of Them* (London, 1901).

Masterman, C. F. G., *The Condition of England* (London, 1909).

Masterman, C. F. G., *England After the War* (London, 1922).

Matthew, H. C. G., *The Liberal Imperialists: The Ideas and Politics of a Post-Gladstonian Elite* (Oxford, 1973).

Matthew, H. C. G., McKibbin, R. and Kay, J. A., 'The franchise factor in the rise of the Labour party', *English Historical Review*, 91 (1976), pp. 723–53.

Matthews, D., '1889 and all that: new views on the new unionism', *International Review of Social History*, 36, no. 1 (1991).

Maurer, J. H., 'Churchill's naval holiday: arms control and the Anglo-German naval race, 1912–1914', *Journal of Strategic Studies*, 15, no. 1 (1992), pp. 102–27.

Mayne, A., *The Imagined Slum: Newspaper Representation in Three Cities 1870–1914* (Leicester, 1993).

Meacham, S., *Englishness and the Early Garden City Movement* (London, 1999).

Melinger, P. S., 'Trenchard and "morale bombing": the evolution of RAF doctrine before World War II', *Journal of Military History*, 60, no. 2 (1996), pp. 243–70.

Meller, H., *Patrick Geddes: Social Evolutionist and City Planner* (London, 1990).

Meller, H., *Towns, Plans and Society in Modern Britain* (Cambridge, 1997).

Melling, J., ed., *Housing, Social Policy and the State* (London, 1980).

Melling, J., 'Scottish industrialists and the changing character of class relations in the Clyde region, *c*.1880–1918', in A. Dickson, ed., *Capital and Class in Scotland* (Edinburgh, 1982).

Melling, J., *Rent Strikes: People's Struggle for Housing in West Scotland 1890–1916* (Edinburgh, 1983).

Melling, J., 'Welfare capitalism and the origins of the welfare states: British industry, workplace welfare and social reform *c*.1870–1914', *Social History*, 17 (1992), pp. 453–78.

Merriman, N., ed., *The Peopling of London* (London, 1993).

Messum, D., *British Impressions: A Collection of British Impressionist Paintings, 1880–1940* (London, 1988).

Metcalf, D., Nickell, S. and Floros, N., 'Still searching for a solution to unemployment in interwar Britain', *Journal of Political Economy*, 90 (1982), pp. 368–99.

Mews, S., 'Drink and disestablishment in the First World War', in D. Baker, ed., *The Church in Town and Country* (Oxford, 1979), pp. 444–79.

Mews, S., 'The revival of spiritual healing in the Church of England, 1920–26', in W. J. Sheils, ed., *The Church and Healing* (Oxford, 1982), pp. 299–331.

Mews, S., ed., *Modern Religious Rebels* (London, 1993).

Michie, R. C., *The City of London: Continuity and Change since 1850* (London, 1992).

Michie, R. C., *The London Stock Exchange: A History* (Oxford, 1999).

Middlemas, K., ed., *Thomas Jones: Whitehall Diary*, vol. 3, *Ireland, 1918–1925* (Oxford, 1971).

Middlemas, K. and Barnes, J., *Baldwin: A Biography* (London, 1969).

Middleton, R., 'Treasury policy on unemployment', in S. Glynn and A. Booth, eds, *The Road to Full Employment* (London, 1987), pp. 109–24.

Midgely, C., 'Ethnicity, race and empire', in J. Purvis, ed., *Women's History: Britain, 1850–1945* (London, 1995).

Miles, A., *Social Mobility in Nineteenth- and Early Twentieth-century England* (Basingstoke, 1999).

Miliband, R., *Parliamentary Socialism: A Study in the Politics of Labour* (London, 1961).

Miller, M., 'Raymond Unwin 1863–1940', in G. Cherry, ed., *Pioneers in British Planning* (London, 1981).

Miller, M., *Raymond Unwin: Garden Cities and Town Planning* (Leicester, 1992).

Millward, R. and Singleton, J., eds, *The Political Economy of Nationalisation in Britain 1920–1950* (Cambridge, 1995).

Milner, S., 'The coverage of collective pay-settling institutions in Britain, 1895–1990', *British Journal of Industrial Relations*, 33 (1995).

Milward, A. S., *The Economic Effects of the Two World Wars on Britain* (London, 1970).

Minchinton, W. E., ed., *Essays in Agrarian History* (2 vols, Newton Abbot, 1968).

Mingay, G. E., *Land and Society in England 1750–1980* (London, 1994).

Mitchell, B. R., *British Historical Statistics* (Cambridge, 1988).

Mitchell, B. R. and Deane, P., *Abstract of British Historical Statistics* (Cambridge, 1962).

Mitchell, M., 'The effects of unemployment on the social conditions of women and children in the 1930s', *History Workshop*, 19 (1985), pp. 105–27.

Moggridge, D. E., *The Return to Gold 1925: The Formulation of Economic Policy and its Critics* (Cambridge, 1969).

Moggridge, D. E., *British Monetary Policy 1924–1931: The Norman Conquest of $4.86* (Cambridge, 1972).

Mommsen, W. and Husung, H.-G., eds, *The Development of Trade Unionism in Great Britain and Germany, 1880–1914* (London, 1985).

Money, L. C., *Riches and Poverty* (London, 1908).

Moore, M. J., 'Social work and social welfare: the organisation and philanthropic resources in Britain, 1900–1914', *Journal of British Studies* (Spring 1977).

Moore, R., *Pitmen, Preachers and Politics: The Effects of Methodism in a Durham Mining Community* (Cambridge, 1974).

Moore, R. J., *The Crisis of Indian Unity, 1917–1940* (Oxford, 1974).

Moorhouse, G., *Hell's Foundations: A Town, its Myths and Gallipoli* (London, 1992).

Morgan, K. O., *Wales in British Politics 1868–1922* (Cardiff, 1970).

Morgan, K. O., *Consensus and Disunity: The Lloyd George Coalition Government 1918–1922* (Oxford, 1979).

Morgan, K. O., *Rebirth of a Nation: Wales, 1880–1980* (Oxford, 1981).

Morgan, L., *Ancient Society* (1878; Cambridge, Mass., 1964).

Moriarty, C., 'Private grief and public remembrance: British First World War memorials', in M. Evans and K. Lunn, eds, *War and Memory in the Twentieth Century* (Oxford, 1997), pp. 125–39.

Morris, J., *Religion and Urban Change: Croydon 1840–1914* (London, 1992).

Morton, D., 'Junior but sovereign allies: the transformation of the Canadian Expeditionary Force, 1914–18', *Journal of Imperial and Commonwealth History*, 8, no. 1 (1979).

Morton, J., 'The 1890 Act and its aftermath: the era of "model dwellings"', in S. Lowe and D. Hughes, eds, *A New Century of Social Housing* (Leicester, 1991).

Mowat, C., *Britain Between the Wars, 1918–1940* (London, 1955).

Mugglestone, L., *Talking Proper: The Rise of Accent as Social Symbol* (Oxford, 1995).

Murphy, J. A., 'Irish neutrality in historical perspective', in B. Girvin and G. Roberts, eds, *Ireland and the Second World War: Politics, Society and Remembrance* (Dublin, 2000).

Murray, B. K., *The People's Budget 1909/10: Lloyd George and Liberal Politics* (Oxford, 1980).

Murray, K. A. H., *Agriculture* (History of the Second World War: Civil Series, London, 1955).

Neidpath, J., *The Singapore Naval Base and the Defence of Britain's Eastern Empire, 1919–1941* (Oxford, 1981).

Neilson, K., '"Joy-rides"? British intelligence and propaganda in Russia, 1914–1917,' *Historical Journal*, 24 (1981).

Neilson, K., '"The British Empire floats on the British Navy": British naval policy, belligerent rights, and disarmament, 1902–1909', in B. J. C. McKercher, ed., *Arms Limitation and Disarmament: Restraints on War, 1899–1939* (Westport, Conn., 1992), pp. 21–41.

Nettlefold, J., *Practical Housing* (Letchworth, 1908).

Newby, H., *Country Life: A Social History of Rural England* (London, 1987).

Newby, P. and Turner, M., 'British suburban taste, 1880–1939', in R. Harris and P. J. Larkham, eds, *Changing Suburbs: Foundation, Form and Function* (London, 1999), pp. 32–55.

Newton, S., *Profits of Peace: The Political Economy of Anglo-German Appeasement* (Oxford, 1996).

Newton, S. and Porter, G., *Modernization Frustrated: The Politics of Industrial Decline in Britain since 1900* (London, 1988).

Nicholson, I. F., *The Administration of Nigeria: Men, Methods and Myths* (Oxford, 1969).

Nish, I., *Anglo-Japanese Alienation 1919–1952: Papers of the Anglo-Japanese Conference on the History of the Second World War* (Cambridge, 1987).

Nolan, A., 'Joseph Walshe and the management of Irish foreign policy, 1922–46: a study in diplomatic and administrative history' (Ph.D. dissertation, University College Cork, 1997).

Northedge, F. S., *The Troubled Giant: Britain among the Great Powers 1916–1939* (London, 1966).

Nye, A., *Philosophia* (London, 1994).

O'Connell, S., *The Car and British Society: Class, Gender and Motoring 1896–1939* (Manchester, 1998).

Offer, A., *The First World War: An Agrarian Interpretation* (Oxford, 1989).

O'Halloran, C., *Partition and the Limits of Irish Nationalism: An Ideology under Stress* (Dublin, 1987).

O'Halpin, E., *The Decline of the Union: British Government in Ireland, 1892–1920* (Dublin, 1987).

Oldfield, S., ed., *This Working Day World: Women's Lives and Culture in Britain, 1884–1945* (London, 1994).

Omissi, D. E., *Air Power and Colonial Control: The Royal Air Force, 1919–1939* (Manchester, 1990).

Oram, G., *Worthless Men: Race, Eugenics and the Death Penalty in the British Army during the First World War* (London, 1998).

Orde, A., *Great Britain and International Security 1920–1926* (London, 1978).

Orde, A., *British Policy and European Reconstruction after the First World War* (Cambridge, 1990).

Orr, W., *Deer Forests, Landlords and Crofters: The Western Highlands in Victorian and Edwardian Times* (Edinburgh, 1982).

Orwell, G., *The Road to Wigan Pier* (London, 1937).

Osborn, F. J., *Green-belt Cities: The British Contribution* (London, 1946).

O'Sullivan, C. J., 'Sentinel towers: the Irish treaty ports, 1914–1945' (Ph.D. dissertation, University College Cork, 1999).

Ó Tuathaigh, M. A. G., 'The Irish in nineteenth-century Britain: problems of integration', in C. Holmes, ed., *Migration in European History* (Cheltenham, 1996), pp. 51–75.

Overy, R. J., 'Air power and the origins of deterrence theory before 1939', *Journal of Strategic Studies*, 15, no. 1 (1992).

Packer, I., 'The land issue and the future of Scottish Liberalism in 1914', *Scottish Historical Review*, 75 (1996), pp. 52–71.

Page, R. M. and Silburn, R., eds, *British Social Welfare in the Twentieth Century* (London, 1999).

Pahl, R. E., 'Is the emperor naked? Some questions on the adequacy of sociological theory on urban and regional research', *International Journal of Urban and Regional Research*, 12 (1988).

Pakenham, F. (Lord Longford), *Peace by Ordeal* (London, 1967).

Palazzo, A., *Seeking Victory on the Western Front: The British Army and Chemical Warfare in World War One* (Lincoln, Nebr., 2000).

Palmer, R., 'The Italians: patterns of migration to London', in J. Watson, ed., *Between Two Cultures: Migrants and Minorities in Britain* (Oxford, 1977), pp. 245–56.

Panayi, P., *The Enemy in Our Midst: Germans in Britain during the First World War* (Oxford, 1991).

Panayi, P., ed., *Racial Violence in Britain in the Nineteenth and Twentieth Centuries* (revised edition, Leicester, 1996).

Pandey, G., *The Construction of Communalism in Colonial North India* (Delhi, 1990).

Parker, R. A. C., *Chamberlain and Appeasement: British Policy and the Coming of the Second World War* (Basingstoke, 1993).

Parkinson, M., *The Labour Party and the Organisation of Secondary Education, 1918–1965* (London, 1970).

Parratt, C. M., 'Little means or time: working-class women and leisure in late Victorian and Edwardian England', *International Journal of the History of Sport*, 15, no. 2 (1998).

Pearson, G., *Hooligan: A History of Respectable Fears* (London, 1983).

Peden, G., *Keynes, the Treasury and Economic Policy* (London, 1988).

Peden, G., *British Economic and Social Policy: Lloyd George to Margaret Thatcher* (2nd edition, Oxford, 1991).

Peden, G. C., *The Treasury and British Public Policy, 1906–1959* (Oxford, 2000).

Pelling, H., *Social Geography of British Elections, 1885–1910* (London, 1967).

Pelling, H., *Popular Politics and Society in Late Victorian Britain: Essays* (London, 1968).

Pelling, H., 'The working class and the welfare state', in H. Pelling, *Popular Politics and Society in Late Victorian Britain: Essays* (London, 1968).

Pelling, H., *A History of British Trade Unionism* (2nd edition, London, 1971).

Penning-Rowsell, E. C., 'Who "betrayed" whom? Power and politics in the 1920/21 agricultural crisis', *Agricultural History Review*, 45, part 2 (1997).

Perham, M., *Native Administration in Nigeria* (London, 1937).

Perham, M., *Lugard* (2 vols, London, 1956–60).

Perham, M., *The Colonial Reckoning: The End of Imperial Rule in Africa in the Light of British Experience* (2 vols, London, 1962).

Perkin, H., 'Teaching the nations how to play: sport and society in the British Empire and Commonwealth', *International Journal of the History of Sport*, 6, no. 2 (1989).

Perkin, H., *The Rise of Professional Society: England since 1880* (London, 1990).

Perren, R., *Agriculture in Depression, 1870–1940* (Cambridge, 1995).

Perry, F. W., *The Commonwealth Armies: Manpower and Organization in the Two World Wars* (Manchester, 1988).

Perry, M., *Bread and Work: The Experience of Unemployment, 1918–1939* (London, 2000).

Peters, J., 'The British government and the City–industry divide: the case of the 1914 financial crisis', *Twentieth-Century British History*, 4 (1993).

Pettman, J. J., *Worlding Women* (London, 1996).

Phelps Brown, H., *The Origins of Trade Union Power* (Oxford, 1983).

Phillips, G. D., *The Diehards* (Cambridge, Mass., 1979).

Pimlott, B., *Labour and the Left in the 1930s* (Cambridge, 1977).

Pollard, M. and Hyatt, S. B., *Sex, Gender and Health* (Cambridge, 1999).

Pollard, S., *The Genesis of Modern Management* (Cambridge, Mass., 1965).

Pollard, S., *Britain's Prime and Britain's Decline: The British Economy, 1870–1914* (London, 1989).

Pollard, S., *The Development of the British Economy 1914–1990* (1962; 4th edition, London, 1992).

Polley, M., *Sport and British Diplomacy: The Foreign Office and International Sport, 1896–2000* (London, forthcoming, 2003).

Pooley, C., ed., *Housing Strategies in Europe, 1880–1930* (Leicester, 1992).

Pooley, C. J. and Turnbull, J., 'Commuting, transport and urban form: Manchester and Glasgow in the mid-twentieth century', *Urban History*, 27 (2000), pp. 360–83.

Porter, A. (with Low, A.), *The Oxford History of the British Empire*, vol. 3, *The Nineteenth Century* (Oxford, 1999).

Porter, B., *The Lion's Share: A Short History of British Imperialism, 1850–1900* (London, 1975).

Porter, B., 'The Edwardians and their empire', in D. Read, ed., *Edwardian England* (London, 1982).

Porter, B., 'Fabians, imperialists and the international order', in B. Pimlott, ed., *Fabian Essays in Socialist Thought* (London, 1984).

Porter, B., *Plots and Paranoia: A History of Political Espionage in Britain, 1790–1988* (London, 1989).

Powell, M., 'Hospital provision before the NHS', *Social History of Medicine*, 5 (1992), pp. 483–504.

Prazmowska, A., *Britain, Poland, the Eastern Front, 1939* (Cambridge, 1987).

Pressnell, L. S., '1925: the burden of sterling', *Economic History Review*, 2nd series, 31 (1978).

Prest, A. R., *Consumers' Expenditure in the United Kingdom, 1900–1919* (Cambridge, 1954).

Pretty, D., *The Rural Revolt that Failed: Farm Workers' Trade Unions in Wales, 1889–1950* (Cardiff, 1989).

Price, R., *Labour in British Society* (London, 1986).

Priestley, J. B., *English Journey: Being a Rambling but Truthful Account of What One Man Saw* (London, 1934).

Prior, R. and Wilson, T., *Command on the Western Front: The Military Career of Sir Henry Wilson 1914–1918* (Oxford, 1992).

Prior, R. and Wilson, T., 'Paul Fussell at war', *War and History*, 1 (1994), pp. 63–80.

Prochaska, F. K., 'Philanthropy', in F. M. L. Thompson, ed., *The Cambridge Social History of Britain 1750–1950*, vol. 3, *Social Agencies and Institutions* (Cambridge, 1990).

Prochaska, F., *Philanthropy and the Hospitals of London: The King's Fund, 1897–1990* (London, 1992).

Pugh, M., 'Popular Conservatism in Britain', *Journal of British Studies*, 27 (1988), pp. 254–82.

Pugh, M., *The Making of Modern British Politics 1867–1939* (Oxford, 1982; 2nd edition, London, 1993).

Pugh, M., 'The limits of Liberalism: Liberals and women's suffrage, 1867–1914', in E. F. Biagini, ed., *Citizenship and Community: Liberals, Radicals and Collective Identities in the British Isles, 1865–1931* (Cambridge, 1996).

Pugh, M. D., 'Politicians and the women's vote, 1914–18', *History*, 59 (Oct. 1974).

Pugh, M. D., *Women and the Women's Movement in Britain* (London, 2000).

Pugh, P., *Educate, Agitate, Organize: 100 Years of Fabian Socialism* (London, 1984).

Purdue, A. W., 'Jarrow politics, 1885–1914: the challenge to Liberal hegemony', *Northern History*, 18 (1982), pp. 182–98.

Purvis, J. and Holton, S. S., eds, *Votes for Women* (London, 2000).

Pyatt, F. G., *Priority Patterns and the Demand for Household Goods* (Cambridge, 1964).

Radzinowicz, L. and Hood, R., *The Emergence of Penal Policy in Victorian and Edwardian England* (Oxford, 1990).

Rallings, C. and Thrasher, M., *British Electoral Facts 1832–1999* (Aldershot, 2000).

Ramsden, J., *The Age of Balfour and Baldwin 1902–1940* (London, 1978).

Ramsden, J., *The Appetite for Power: A History of the Conservative Party since 1830* (London, 1998).

Ravetz, A., 'Modern technology and an ancient occupation: housework in present-day society', *Technology and Culture*, 6, no. 2 (1965), pp. 256–60.

Ravetz, A., *The Place of Home: English Domestic Environments 1914–2000* (London, 1995).

Redmond, J., 'An indicator of the effective exchange rate of the pound in the nineteen-thirties', *Economic History Review*, 33 (1980), pp. 83–91.

Redmond, J., 'The sterling overvaluation of 1925: a multilateral approach', *Economic History Review* (1984).

Regan, J. M., 'The politics of reaction: the dynamics of treatyite government and policy, 1922–23', *Irish Historical Studies*, 30 (Nov. 1997), pp. 542–63.

Reid, A., 'The impact of the First World War on British workers', in R. Wall and J. M. Winter, eds, *The Upheaval of War: Family, Work and Welfare in Europe, 1914–1918* (Cambridge, 1988).

Reid, A., 'World War I and the working class in Britain', in A. Marwick, ed., *Total War and Social Change* (Basingstoke, 1988).

Reid, A., *Social Classes and Social Relations in Britain, 1850–1914* (London, 1992).

Reynolds, D., *Britannia Overrules: British Policy and World Power in the Twentieth Century* (London, 1981).

Rice, M. S., *Working-class Wives* (1939; rpt. London, 1981).

Riddell, N., *Labour in Crisis: The Second Labour Government, 1929–31* (Manchester, 1999).

Riley, J. C., *Sick, Not Dead* (Baltimore, 1997).

Rivett, G., *The Development of the London Hospital System, 1823–1982* (London, 1986).

Robb, G., *White-collar Crime in Modern England: Financial Fraud and Business Morality 1845–1929* (Cambridge, 1992).

Robbins, K., *Sir Edward Grey: A Biography of Lord Grey of Falloden* (London, 1971).

Robbins, K., *Nineteenth-century Britain* (Oxford, 1989).

Roberts, E., *A Woman's Place: An Oral History of Working-class Women 1890–1940* (Oxford, 1984).

Roberts, E., *Women's Work, 1840–1940* (London, 1988).

Roberts, M. G., *A Woman of Vision: Marion Phillips MP* (Wrexham, 2000).

Roberts, R., *The Classic Slum: Salford Life in the First Quarter of the Century* (Harmondsworth, 1973).

Roberts, R., 'The City of London as a financial centre in the era of the Depression, the Second World War and post-war official controls', in A. Gorst, L. Johnman and W. Scott Lucas, eds, *Contemporary British History 1931–61* (London, 1991).

Roberts, R. and Kynaston, D., eds, *The Bank of England: Money, Power and Influence, 1694–1994* (Oxford, 1995).

Robinson, K., *The Dilemmas of Trusteeship* (London, 1965).

Rock, W. R., *British Appeasement in the 1930s* (London, 1977).

Rooth, T., *British Protectionism and the International Economy: Overseas Commercial Policy in the 1930s* (Cambridge, 1993).

Rose, J., *The Edwardian Temperament 1895–1919* (Athens, OH, 1986).

Rosen, A., *Rise Up Women! The Militant Campaign of the Women's Social and Political Union* (London, 1974).

Roseveare, H., *The Treasury: The Evolution of a British Institution* (London, 1969).

Roshwald, A. and Stites, R., eds, *European Culture in the Great War* (Cambridge, 1999).

Ross, D. M., 'The clearing banks and the finance of British industry, 1930–1959', *Business and Economic History*, 20 (1991).

Ross, D. M., 'Commercial banking in a market-orientated financial system: Britain between the wars', *Economic History Review*, 49 (1996).

Ross, E., 'Survival networks: women's neighbourhood sharing in London before World War I', *History Workshop*, 15 (1983).

Routh, G., *Occupations and Pay in Great Britain 1906–79* (London, 1980).

Rowe, J. W. F., *Wages in Practice and in Theory* (London, 1928).

Rowlands, T., *Something Must Be Done: South Wales versus Whitehall, 1921–51* (Merthyr Tydfil, 2000).

Rubinstein, A. et al., *Just Like the Country: Memories of London Families who Settled the New Cottage Estates 1919–1939* (London, 1991).

Rubinstein, D., 'Cycling in the 1890s', *Victorian Studies*, 21, no. 1 (1977).

Rubinstein, D. and Simon, B., *The Evolution of the Comprehensive School, 1926–1966* (London, 1969).

Rubinstein, W. D., 'Wealth, elites and the class structure of modern Britain', *Past and Present*, 76 (1977).

Rubinstein, W. D., *Elites and the Wealthy in Modern British History: Essays in Social and Economic History* (Brighton, 1987).

Rumbold, A., *Watershed in India, 1914–1918* (London, 1979).

Runciman, W., *Relative Deprivation and Social Justice: A Study of Attitudes to Social Inequality* (London, 1966).

Russell, A. K., *Liberal Landslide: The General Election of 1906* (Newton Abbot, 1973).

Russell, D., 'Sport and identity: the case of Yorkshire county cricket club, 1890–1939', *Twentieth-century British History*, 7, no. 2 (1996).

Russell, D., *Football and the English: A Social History of Association Football in England, 1863–1995* (Preston, 1997).

Ryan, L., ' "Furies" and "die hards": women and Irish Republicanism in the early twentieth century', *Gender and History*, 11, no. 2 (July 1999).

Samuel, R., *East End Underworld: Chapters in the Life of Arthur Harding* (London, 1981).

Samuel, R., ed., *Patriotism: The Making and Unmaking of British Identity* (3 vols, London, 1989).

Sanderson, M., *The Universities and British Industry, 1850–1970* (London, 1972).

Sanderson, M., *Educational Opportunity and Social Change in England* (London, 1987).

Saul, S. B., *Studies in British Overseas Trade, 1870–1914* (Liverpool, 1960).

Saul, S. B., 'The export economy', *Yorkshire Bulletin of Economic and Social Research*, 17, no. 1 (1965).

Savage, M., *The Dynamics of Working-class Politics* (Cambridge, 1987).

Savage, M. and Miles, A., *The Remaking of the British Working Class, London, 1840–1940* (London, 1994).

Sayers, R. S., 'The return to gold, 1925', in S. Pollard, ed., *The Gold Standard and Employment Policies between the Wars* (London, 1970).

Sayers, R. S., *The Bank of England, 1891–1944* (Cambridge, 1976).

Scally, R. J., *The Origins of the Lloyd George Coalition: The Politics of Social Imperialism, 1900–1918* (Princeton, NJ, 1975).

Scammell, W. M., 'The working of the gold standard', *Yorkshire Bulletin of Economic and Social Research*, 17 (1965), pp. 32–45.

Scannell, P. and Cardiff, D., *A Social History of British Broadcasting* (Oxford, 1991).

Schweitzer, P., ed., *The Time of Our Lives: Memories of Leisure in the 1920s and 1930s* (London, 1986).

Scott, G., *Feminism and the Politics of Working Women: The Women's Cooperative Guild, 1880s to the Second World War* (London, 1997).

Scott, P., 'The growth of road haulage, 1921–58: an estimate', *Journal of Transport History*, 3rd series, 19 (1998), pp. 138–55.

Scott, P. and Rooth, T., 'Protectionism and the growth of overseas multinational enterprise in interwar Britain', *Journal of Industrial History*, 3, no. 2 (2000).

Scull, A. T., *The Most Solitary of Afflictions* (New Haven, Conn., 1993).

Seaborne, M. and Lowe, R., *The English School: Its Architecture and Organisation, 1870–1970* (London, 1977).

Searle, G. R., 'Critics of Edwardian society: the case of the radical right', in A. O'Day, ed., *The Edwardian Age: Conflict and Stability 1900–1914* (London, 1979), pp. 79–96.

Searle, G. R., 'The Edwardian Liberal party and business', *English Historical Review*, 118 (1983), pp. 28–60.

Searle, G. R., *The Quest for National Efficiency, 1899–1914: A Study in Politics and Political Thought* (Oxford, 1971; reissued with a new introduction, London, 1990).

Searle, G. R., *Country Before Party: Coalition and the Idea of 'National Government' in Modern Britain, 1885–1987* (Harlow, 1995).

Searle, G. R., 'National Efficiency and the "lessons" of the South African War', in D. Omissi and A. Thompson, eds, *The Impact of the South African War* (Basingstoke, 2002), pp. 194–211.

Seldon, A. and Ball, S., eds, *The Conservative Century: The Conservative Party since 1900* (Oxford, 1994).

Selleck, R. J. W., *The New Education: The English Background, 1870–1914* (London, 1968).

Selleck, R. J. W., *English Primary Education and the Progressives* (London, 1972).

Semmel, B., *Imperialism and Social Reform* (London, 1960).

Semmel, B., *Liberalism and Naval Strategy: Ideology, Interest and Sea Power during the Pax Britannica* (London, 1986), pp. 99–118.

Sen, A., *Development as Freedom* (Oxford, 1999).

Sheail, J., *Rural Conservation in Inter-war Britain* (Oxford, 1981).

Sheail, J., 'Road surfacing and the threat to inland fisheries', *Journal of Transport History*, 3rd series, 12 (1991), pp. 135–47.

Shenk, C. R., *Britain and the Sterling Area: From Devaluation to Convertibility in the 1950s* (London, 1994).

Sherington, G., *English Education, Social Change and War, 1911–1920* (Manchester, 1981).

Simey, M., *Charitable Effort in Liverpool in the Nineteenth Century* (Liverpool, 1951).

Simmons, C. and Caruana, V., 'Neighbourhood issues in the development of Manchester airport, 1934–82', *Journal of Transport History*, 3rd series, 15 (1994), pp. 117–43.

Simmons, J., *The Railway in Town and Country, 1830–1914* (Newton Abbot, 1986).

Simon, B., *Education and the Labour Movement, 1870–1920* (London, 1965).

Simon, B., *The Politics of Educational Reform, 1920–1940* (London, 1974).

Simon, E. D., *How to Abolish the Slums* (London, 1929).

Simpson, M., *Thomas Adams and the Modern Town Planning Movement, Britain, Canada and the United States, 1900–1940* (London, 1985).

Singh, K., *Race and Class: Struggles in a Colonial State, Trinidad, 1917–1945* (Mona, 1994).

Skidelsky, R., *Politicians and the Slump: The Labour Government of 1929–1931* (Basingstoke, 1967).

Smith, A. and Bull, M., *Margery Perham and British Rule in Africa* (London, 1991).

Smith, D., 'Juvenile delinquency in Britain in the First World War', *Criminal Justice History*, 11 (1990), pp. 119–45.

Smith, D., *Aneurin Bevan and the World of South Wales* (Cardiff, 1993).

Smith, D. N., *The Railway and its Passengers: A Social History* (Newton Abbot, 1988).

Smith, M., *British Air Strategy between the Wars* (Oxford, 1984).

Smith, S., *British Relations with the Malay Rulers from Decentralization to Malayan Independence, 1930–1957* (Kuala Lumpur, 1995).

Smithies, E., *The Black Economy in England since 1914* (Dublin, 1984).

Smyth, J. J., *Labour Politics in Glasgow, 1896–1936: Socialism, Suffrage and Sectarianism* (East Linton, 2001).

Solomou, S. *Themes in Macroeconomic History: The UK Economy, 1919–1939* (Cambridge, 1996).

Solomou, S. and Weale, M., 'UK national income: the implications of balanced estimates', *Economic History Review* (1996).

Southall, H., 'The origins of the depressed areas: unemployment, growth and regional economic structure in Britain before 1914', *Economic History Review*, 41 (1988), pp. 236–53.

Spackman, A., ed., *Constitutional Development of the West Indies, 1922–1968: A Selection from the Major Documents* (Barbados, 1975).

Spender, J. A., *The Life of the Right Hon. Sir Henry Campbell-Bannerman* (London, 1923).

Sponza, L., 'Italians in London', in N. Merriman, ed., *The Peopling of London* (London, 1993), pp. 129–37.

Springhall, J., *Coming of Age: Adolescence in Britain, 1869–1960* (Dublin, 1986).

Stedman Jones, G., *Languages of Class: Studies in English Working-class History 1832–1982* (London, 1983).

Steiner, Z. S., *The Foreign Office and Foreign Policy, 1898–1914* (Cambridge, 1969).

Stephens, W. B., *Education in Britain, 1750–1914* (Basingstoke, 1998).

Stevenson, J., *British Society, 1914–1945* (Harmondsworth, 1984).

Stevenson, J. and Cook, C., *The Slump* (London, 1977).

Stevenson, J. and Cook, C., *Britain and the Depression: Society and Politics, 1929–39* (Harlow, 1994).

Stewart, J., *'The Battle for Health': A Political History of the Socialist Medical Association, 1930–51* (Aldershot, 1999).

Stocking, G., ed., *Colonial Situations: Essays in the Contextualization of Ethnographic Knowledge* (Madison, Wis., 1984).

Stone, R. and Rowe, D., *The Measurement of Consumers' Expenditure* (Cambridge, 1966).

Stovel, K., Savage, M. and Bearman, P., 'Ascription into achievement: models of career systems at Lloyds bank, 1890–1970', *American Journal of Sociology*, 102 (1976).

Sturdy, S. and Cooter, R., 'Science, scientific management, and the transformation of medicine in Britain c.1870–1950', *History of Science*, 36 (1998), pp. 421–66.

Sturmey, S. G., 'Owner-farming in England and Wales, 1900–1950', in W. E. Minchinton, ed., *Essays in Agrarian History*, vol. 2 (Newton Abbot, 1968), pp. 283–306.

Sugden, J. and Bairner, A., 'Northern Ireland: sport in a divided society', in L. Allison, ed., *The Politics of Sport* (Manchester, 1986).

Sumida, J. T., *In Defence of Naval Supremacy: Finance, Technology, and British Naval Policy 1889–1914* (London, 1989).

Summerfield, P., 'Women and war in the twentieth century', in J. Purvis, ed., *Women's History: Britain, 1850–1945* (London, 1995).

Supple, B., *The History of the British Coal Industry*, vol. 4, *1913–46: The Political Economy of Decline* (Oxford, 1987).

Supple, B., 'Fear of failing: economic history and the decline of Britain', in P. Clark and C. Trebilcock, eds, *Understanding Decline* (Cambridge, 1997).

Supple, B., 'Introduction: national performance in a personal perspective', in P. Clark and C. Trebilcock, eds, *Understanding Decline* (Cambridge, 1997).

Sutcliffe, A., ed., *The Rise of Modern Urban Planning 1800–1914* (London, 1980).

Sutcliffe, A., ed., *British Town Planning: The Formative Years* (Leicester, 1981).

Sutcliffe, A., *Towards the Planned City: Germany, Britain, the United States and France 1780–1914* (Oxford, 1981).

Sutherland, G., *Ability, Merit and Measurement: Mental Testing and English Education, 1880–1940* (Oxford, 1984).

Swenarton, M., *Homes Fit for Heroes: The Politics and Architecture of Early State Housing in Britain* (London, 1981).

Swift, R. and Gilley, S., eds, *The Irish in Britain 1815–1939* (London, 1989).

Swinton, Lord (Sir Phillip Cunliffe-Lister), *I Remember* (London, 1949).

Sykes, A., *Tariff Reform in British Politics 1903–1913* (Oxford, 1979).

Sykes, A., 'The radical right and the crisis of Conservatism before the First World War', *Historical Journal*, 26 (1983), pp. 661–76.

Szreter, S., 'The importance of social intervention in Britain's mortality decline *c*.1850–1914', *Social History of Medicine*, 1 (1988), pp. 1–37.

Szreter, S., *Fertility, Class and Gender in Britain, 1860–1914* (Cambridge, 1996).

Tabili, L., *'We Ask for British Justice': Workers and Racial Difference in Late Imperial Britain* (Ithaca, NY, 1994).

Tanner, D., *Political Change and the Labour Party 1900–1918* (1987; Cambridge, 1990).

Tanner, D., 'Ideological debate in Edwardian Labour politics: radicalism, revisionism and socialism', in E. Biagini and A. Reid, eds, *Currents of Radicalism: Popular Radicalism, Organised Labour and Party Politics in Britain 1850–1914* (Cambridge, 1991), pp. 279–92.

Tanner, D., 'The Labour party and electoral politics in the coalfields 1910–47', in A. Campbell, N. Fishman and D. Howell, eds, *Miners, Unions and Politics* (Aldershot, 1996).

Tanner, D., 'Class voting and radical politics: the Liberal and Labour parties, 1910–31', in J. Lawrence and M. Taylor, eds, *Party, State and Society: Electoral Behaviour in Britain since 1820* (Aldershot, 1997).

Tanner, D., 'The development of British socialism, 1900–1918, *Parliamentary History*, 16 (1997).

Tanner, D., 'The Labour party and its membership', in D. Tanner, P. Thane and N. Tiratsoo, eds, *Labour's First Century* (Cambridge, 2000).

Tanner, D., 'The pattern of Labour politics, 1918–1939', in D. Tanner, C. Williams and D. Hopkin, eds, *The Labour Party in Wales 1900–2000* (Cardiff, 2000).

Tanner, D., Thane, P. and Tiratsoo, N., eds, *Labour's First Century* (Cambridge, 2000).

Taylor, A. J. P., *The Origins of the Second World War* (London, 1961).

Taylor, A. J. P., *English History 1914–1945* (Oxford, 1965).

Taylor, D., 'Growth and structural change in the English dairy industry, *c*.1860–1930', *Agricultural History Review*, 35, part 1 (1987).

Taylor, H., *A Claim on the Countryside* (Edinburgh, 1997).

Taylor, H., 'The politics of the rising crime statistics of England and Wales, 1914–1960', *Crime, Histoire et Sociétés/Crime, History and Societies*, 2, no. 1 (1998), pp. 5–28.

Tebbutt, M., *Making Ends Meet: Pawnbroking and Working-class Credit* (London, 1983).

Thane, P., *The Foundations of the Welfare State* (London, 1982).

Thane, P., 'The working class and state "welfare" in Britain 1880–1914', *Historical Journal*, 27 (1984), pp. 877–900.

Thane, P., 'Women, Liberalism and citizenship, 1918–1930', in E. F. Biagini, ed., *Citizenship and Community: Liberals, Radicals and Collective Identities in the British Isles, 1865–1931* (Cambridge, 1996).

Thane, P., 'Labour and welfare', in D. Tanner, P. Thane and N. Tiratsoo, eds, *Labour's First Century* (Cambridge, 2000).

Thom, D., *Nice Girls and Rude Girls: Women Workers in World War I* (London, 1998).

Thomas, W. A., *The Finance of British Industry 1918–76* (London, 1978).

Thompson, E. P., *The Making of the English Working Class* (Harmondsworth, 1968).

Thompson, F. M. L., ed., *The Rise of Suburbia* (Leicester, 1982).

Thompson, N., *Political Economy and the Labour Party: The Economics of Democratic Socialism, 1884–1995* (London, 1996).

Thompson, P., *The Edwardians: The Remaking of British Society* (London, 1992).

Thoms, D., Holden, L. and Claydon, T., eds, *The Motor Car and Popular Culture in the Twentieth Century* (Aldershot, 1998).

Thornton, A. P., *The Imperial Idea and its Enemies: A Study in British Power* (London, 1959).

Thorpe, A., *The British General Election of 1931* (Oxford, 1991).

Thorpe, A., 'The industrial meaning of "gradualism": the Labour party and industry, 1918–31', *Journal of British Studies*, 35 (1996).

Thorpe, A., *A History of the British Labour Party* (Basingstoke, 1997).

Thorpe, A. T., *The Failure of Political Extremism in Inter-war Britain* (Exeter, 1989).

Thurlow, R., *Fascism in Britain: A History, 1918–1985* (Oxford, 1987).

Tolliday, S., 'Tariffs and steel, 1916–1934: the politics of industrial decline', in J. Turner, ed., *Businessmen and Politics: Studies of Business Activity in British Politics* (London, 1984), pp. 50–75.

Tolliday, S., 'Steel and rationalization policies, 1918–1950', in B. Elbaum and W. Lazonick, eds, *The Decline of the British Economy* (Oxford, 1986), pp. 82–108.

Tolliday, S. and Zeitlin, J., eds, *The Power to Manage?* (London, 1991).

Tomlinson, B. R., *The Political Economy of the Raj, 1914–47: The Economics of Decolonisation in India* (London, 1979).

Tomlinson, B. R., 'Imperial power and foreign trade: Britain and India, 1900–1970', in P. Mathias and J. A. Davis, eds, *The Nature of Industrialization: International Trade and Economic Growth: From the Eighteenth Century to the Present Day* (Oxford, 1996), pp. 146–62.

Tomlinson, J., *Public Policy and the Economy since 1900* (Oxford, 1990).

Townshend, C., *The British Campaign in Ireland, 1919–1921* (Oxford, 1975).

Townshend, C., 'Civilization and "frightfulness": air control in the Middle East between the wars', in C. J. Wrigley, ed., *Warfare, Diplomacy and Politics: Essays in Honour of A. J. P. Taylor* (London, 1986), pp. 93–119.

Townshend, C., 'The suppression of the Easter Rising', *Bullán*, 1 (1994).

Tranter, N., *Sport, Economy and Society in Britain, 1750–1914* (Cambridge, 1998).

Travers, T., *The Killing Ground: The British Army, the Western Front and the Emergence of Modern Warfare, 1900–1918* (London, 1987).

Travers, T., 'Could the tanks of 1918 have been war-winners for the British Expeditionary Force?', *Journal of Contemporary History*, 27 (1992), pp. 389–405.

Travers, T., *How the War Was Won: Command and Technology in the British Army on the Western Front 1917–1918* (London, 1992).

Treble, J., 'Unemployment and unemployment policies in Glasgow, 1890–1905', in P. Thane, ed., *The Origins of British Social Policy* (London, 1982), pp. 147–72.

Trentmann, F., 'Wealth versus welfare: the British left between free trade and national political economy before World War I', *Historical Research*, 70 (1997), pp. 74–93.

Tressell, R., *The Ragged Trousered Philanthropists* (London, 1940).

Tuchman, B., *Practising History: Selected Essays* (New York, 1982).

Turner, F. M., *Contesting Cultural Authority: Essays in Victorian Intellectual Life* (Cambridge, 1993).

Turner, G., *British Cultural Studies: An Introduction* (2nd edition, London, 1990).

Turner, J., ed., *Businessmen and Politics: Studies of Business Activity in British Politics, 1900–1945* (London, 1984).

Turner, J., *British Politics and the Great War: Coalition and Conflict 1915–1918* (New Haven, Conn., 1992).

Tuttle, E. O., *The Crusade against Capital Punishment in Great Britain* (London, 1961).

Tweedale, G., *Magic Mineral to Killer Dust* (Oxford, 2000).

Unwin, R., *Town Planning in Practice: An Introduction to the Art of Designing Cities and Suburbs* (London, 1909).

Unwin, R., *Nothing Gained by Overcrowding: How the Garden City Type of Development May Benefit Both Owner and Occupier* (London, 1912).

Van Vleck, V. N. L., 'Delivering coal by road and rail in Britain: the efficiency of the "silly little bobtailed" coal wagons', *Journal of Economic History*, 57 (1997), pp. 139–60.

Vaughan, P., 'Secret remedies in the late nineteenth and early twentieth centuries', in M. Saks, ed., *Alternative Medicine in Britain* (Oxford, 1992), pp. 101–11.

Vaughan, W., ed., *New History of Ireland*, vol. 6, *Ireland under the Union, 2: 1870–1921* (Oxford, 1996).

Ville, S., *Transport and the Development of the European Economy 1750–1914* (Houndmills, 1990).

Waites, B., *A Class Society at War: England 1914–18* (Leamington Spa, 1987).

Walby, S., *Patriarchy at Work* (Cambridge, 1986).

Walby, S., *Theorising Patriarchy* (Oxford, 1990).

Walker, E. A., *The British Empire: Its Structure and Spirit* (London, 1943).

Walker, G., *Thomas Johnston* (Manchester, 1988).

Walkowitz, J., *City of Dreadful Delight: Narratives of Sexual Danger in Late Victorian London* (London, 1992).

Wall, R. and Winter, J. M., eds, *The Upheaval of War: Family, Work and Welfare in Europe, 1914–1918* (Cambridge, 1988).

Walton, J. K., *Fish and Chips and the British Working Class* (Leicester, 1992).

Walton, J. K., *The British Seaside: Holidays and Resorts in the Twentieth Century* (Manchester, 2000).

Walvin, J., *Black and White: The Negro and English Society 1555–1945* (London, 1973).

Walvin, J., *Leisure and Society, 1830–1950* (London, 1978).

Walvin, J., *Passage to Britain: Immigration in British History and Politics* (Harmondsworth, 1984).

Walvin, J., *The People's Game: The History of Football Revisited* (Edinburgh, 1994).

Ward, C. and Hardy, D., *Goodnight Campers! The History of the British Holiday Camp* (London, 1986).

Ward, P., *Red Flag and Union Jack: Englishness, Patriotism and the British Left, 1881–1924* (London, 1998).

Ward, S. R., ed., *The War Generation: Veterans of the First World War* (Port Washington, NY, 1975).

Ward, S. V., *Planning and Urban Change* (London, 1994).

Wark, W., *The Ultimate Enemy: British Intelligence and Nazi Germany, 1933–1939* (Ithaca, NY, 1985).

Wasserstein, B., *The British in Palestine: The Mandatory Government and the Arab–Jewish Conflict* (Oxford, 1991).

Watson, J., ed., *Between Two Cultures: Migrants and Minorities in Britain* (Oxford, 1977).

Watson, K., 'Banks and industrial finance: the experience of brewers, 1880–1913', *Economic History Review*, 49 (1996).

Webb, S., 'The necessary basis of society', *Contemporary Review*, 93 (1908), pp. 665–7.

Webster, C., 'Healthy or hungry thirties?', *History Workshop*, 13 (1982), pp. 110–29.

Webster, C., 'Labour and the NHS', in N. Rupke, ed., *Science, Politics and the Public Good* (London, 1988), pp. 184–202.

Webster, C., *The National Health Service: A Political History* (Oxford, 1988).

Weinberger, B., 'Policing juveniles: delinquency in late nineteenth- and early twentieth-century Manchester', *Criminal Justice History*, 14 (1993), pp. 43–55.

Weindling, P., 'From infectious to chronic diseases', in A. Wear, ed., *Medicine and Society* (Cambridge, 1992), pp. 303–16.

Weinroth, H., 'Left-wing opposition to naval armaments in Britain before 1914', *Journal of Contemporary History*, 6, no. 4 (1971).

Weinroth, H. S., 'British radicals and the balance of power, 1902–1914', *Historical Journal*, 16, no. 4 (1970), pp. 653–82.

Whetham, E. H., 'The mechanization of British agriculture 1910–45', *Journal of Agricultural Economics*, 21 (1970).

Whetham, E. H., 'The Agriculture Act 1920 and its repeal – the "Great Betrayal"', *Agricultural History Review*, 22 (1974).

Whetham, E. H., *The Cambridge Agrarian History of England and Wales*, vol. 8, *1914–1939* (Cambridge, 1978).

White, J., *The Worst Street in North London: Campbell Bunk, Islington, between the Wars* (London, 1986).

Whiteside, N., 'Counting the cost: sickness and disability among working people in an era of industrial recession, 1920–1939', *Economic History Review*, 40 (1987), pp. 228–46.

Whiting, R., 'The Labour party, capitalism and the National Debt, 1918–24', in P. Waller, ed., *Politics and Social Change in Modern Britain* (Oxford, 1987).

Whitson, K., 'Worker resistance and Taylorism in Britain', *International Review of Social History*, 42 (1997).

Wiener, M. J., *Reconstructing the Criminal: Culture, Law, and Policy in England, 1830–1914* (Cambridge, 1990).

Williams, C., *Democratic Rhondda: Politics and Society, 1885–1951* (Cardiff, 1996).

Williams, C., *Capitalism, Community and Conflict: The South Wales Coalfield, 1898–1947* (Cardiff, 1998).

Williams, C., 'Labour and the challenge of local government, 1919–1939', in D. Tanner, C. Williams and D. Hopkin, eds, *The Labour Party in Wales 1900–2000* (Cardiff, 2000), pp. 140–58.

Williams, D., 'London and the 1931 financial crisis', *Economic History Review*, 15 (1962/3).

Williams, D. M., ed., 'Introduction', in *The World of Shipping* (Aldershot, 1997), pp. ix–xxvi.

Williams, G., 'How amateur was my valley: professional sport and national identity in Wales, 1890–1914', *British Journal of Sports History*, 2, no. 3 (1985), pp. 248–69.

Williams, J., ' "One could literally have walked on the heads of the people congregated there": sport, the town and identity', in K. Laybourn, ed., *Social Conditions, Status and Community, 1860–c.1920* (Stroud, 1997).

Williams, J., *Cricket and England: A Cultural and Social History of the Inter-war Years* (London, 1999).

Williams, L. J., *Was Wales Industrialised? Essays in Modern Welsh History* (Llandysul, 1995).

Williams, R., *Defending the Empire: The Conservative Party and British Defence Policy 1899–1915* (New Haven, Conn., 1991).

Williams, S. C., *Religious Belief and Popular Culture in Southwark c.1880–1939* (Oxford, 1999).

Williams-Ellis, C., ed., *Britain and the Beast: A Survey by Twenty-six Authors* (Letchworth, 1937).

Williamson, H., *The Story of a Norfolk Farm* (1941; London, 1986).

Williamson, P., 'Safety first: Baldwin, the Conservative party, and the 1929 general election', *Historical Journal*, 25 (1982), pp. 385–409.

Williamson, P., 'Financiers, the gold standard and British politics, 1925–1931', in J. Turner, *Businessmen and Politics* (London, 1984).

Williamson, P., *National Crisis and National Government: British Politics, the Economy and Empire 1926–1932* (Cambridge, 1992).

Williamson, P., 'The doctrinal politics of Stanley Baldwin', in M. Bentley, ed., *Public and Private Doctrine: Essays in British History presented to Maurice Cowling* (Cambridge, 1995), pp. 181–208.

Williamson, P., *Stanley Baldwin: Conservative Leadership and National Values* (Cambridge, 1999).

Williamson, P., 'Christian Conservatives and the totalitarian challenge 1933–1940', *English Historical Review*, 115 (2000), pp. 607–42.

Wilson, J., *CB: A Life of Sir Henry Campbell-Bannerman* (London, 1973).

Wilson, T., *The Downfall of the Liberal Party, 1914–1935* (London, 1966).

Wilson, T., *The Myriad Faces of War* (Oxford, 1986).

Winch, D. N., *Economics and Policy: A Historical Study* (London, 1972).

Winkler, H., *Paths Not Taken: British Labour and International Policy in the 1920s* (Chapel Hill, NC, 1994).

Winter, J., *Socialism and the Challenge of War: Ideas and Politics in Britain, 1912–1928* (London, 1974).

Winter, J., 'Infant mortality, maternal mortality and public health in Britain in the 1930s', *Journal of European Economic History*, 8 (1979), pp. 439–62.

Winter, J., 'Unemployment, nutrition and infant mortality in Britain, 1920–1950', in J. Winter, ed., *The Working Classes in Modern British History: Essays in Honour of Henry Pelling* (Cambridge, 1983), pp. 232–56.

Winter, J. M., *The Great War and the British People* (London, 1986).

Winter, J. M., *Sites of Memory, Sites of Mourning* (Cambridge, 1995).

Winter, J. M. and Robert, J.-L., eds, *Capital Cities at War: Paris, London, Berlin 1914–1919* (Cambridge, 1997).

Winter, J. M. and Sivan, E., eds, *War and Remembrance in the Twentieth Century* (Cambridge, 1999).

Winton, H., *To Change an Army: General Sir John Burnett-Stuart and British Armoured Doctrine, 1927–1938* (London, 1988).

Wohl, R., *The Generation of 1914* (Cambridge, Mass., 1979).

Wolfe, K. M., *The Churches and the British Broadcasting Corporation 1922–1956* (London, 1984).

Wolffe, J., *Great Deaths: Grieving, Religion and Nationhood in Victorian and Edwardian Britain* (Oxford, 2000).

Wollacott, A., ' "Khaki fever" and its control: gender, class, age and sexual morality in the British homefront in the First World War', *Journal of Contemporary History*, 29, no. 2 (April 1994).

Wollacott, A., *On Her Their Lives Depend* (Berkeley, Calif., 1994).

Wood, I., *John Wheatley* (Manchester, 1990).

Wooldridge, A., *Measuring the Mind: Education and Psychology in England, 1860–1990* (Cambridge, 1994).

Wootton, G., *The Politics of Influence: British Ex-Servicemen, Cabinet Decisions and Cultural Change, 1917–1957* (London, 1963).

Wordie, J. R., ed., *Agriculture and Politics in England, 1815–1939* (Basingstoke, 2000).

Wright, A., *R. H. Tawney* (Manchester, 1987).

Wright, J. F., *Britain in the Age of Economic Management: An Economic History since 1939* (Oxford, 1979).

Wrigley, C., *David Lloyd George and the British Labour Movement: Peace and War* (Hassocks, 1976).

Wrigley, C., 'The Ministry of Munitions: an innovatory department', in K. Burk, ed., *War and the State: The Transformation of British Government, 1914–1919* (London, 1982), pp. 32–56.

Wrigley, C. J., ed., *A History of British Industrial Relations* (2 vols, Brighton, 1982, 1987).

Wrigley, C., *Lloyd George and the Challenge of Labour: The Post-war Coalition, 1918–1922* (Hemel Hempstead, 1990).

Wrigley, C., ed., *Challenges of Labour: Central and Western Europe 1917–1920* (London, 1993).

Wrigley, C., ed., *The First World War and the International Economy* (Cheltenham, 2000).

Yapp, M. E., *The Near East since the First World War* (London, 1991).

Zeitlin, J., 'From labour history to the history of industrial relations', *Economic History Review*, 40 (1987).

Index

MODERN HISTORY from BLACKWELL PUBLISHING

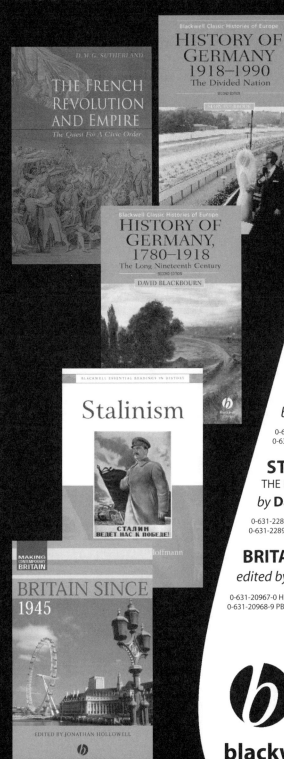

THE FRENCH REVOLUTION AND EMPIRE
THE QUEST FOR A CIVIC ORDER

by
D.M.G Sutherland

0-631-23362-8 HB
0-631-23363-6 PB NOVEMBER 2002

HISTORY OF GERMANY 1918-2000
THE DIVIDED NATION
2ND EDITION

by **Mary Fulbrook**

0-631-23207-9 HB
0-631-23208-7 PB MARCH 2002
(NOT AVAILABLE FROM BLACKWELL PUBLISHING IN NORTH AMERICA)

HISTORY OF GERMANY, 1780-1918
THE LONG NINETEENTH CENTURY
2ND EDITION

by **David Blackbourn**

0-631-23195-1 HB
0-631-23196-X PB OCTOBER 2002

STALINISM
THE ESSENTIAL READINGS

by **David Hoffmann**

0-631-22890-X HB
0-631-22891-8 PB NOVEMBER 2002

BRITAIN SINCE 1945
edited by **Jonathan Hollowell**

0-631-20967-0 HB
0-631-20968-9 PB SEPTEMBER 2002

Blackwell
Publishing

blackwellpublishing.com